INSIGHT GUIDES

WESTERN EUROPE

APA PUBLICATIONS
Part of the Langenscheidt Publishing Group

The first Insight Guide pioneered the use of creative full-colour photography in travel guides in 1970. Since then, we have expanded our range to cater for our readers' need not only for reliable information about their chosen destination but also for a real understanding of the culture and workings of that destination. Now, when the internet can supply inexhaustible (but not always reliable) facts, our books marry text and pictures to provide those much more elusive qualities: knowledge and discernment. To achieve this, they rely heavily on the authority of locally based writers and photographers.

Insight Guide: Western Europe is structured to convey an understanding of the continent and its diverse countries as well as to guide readers through its myriad attractions:

The **Best of** section at the front of the book helps you to prioritise what you want to do.

The **Features** section, indicated by a pink bar at the top of each page, provides a brief history of the region, which will help you understand the development of each country in the context of Europe as a whole. There then follows an illuminating A to Z of European cultural mores, from Architecture to Zeitgeist via Food, Kissing and Umbrellas.

The main **Places** section, indicated by a blue bar, is a complete guide to all the countries and sights worth visiting. Places of special interest are coordinated by number with the maps.

The **Travel Tips** listings section, with a yellow bar, starts with an overview of useful information applying to the whole of Western Europe, then provides tips for each individual country; how to get there and get around, and an A to Z section of essential practical information. An easy-to-find contents list for Travel Tips is printed on the back flap, which also serves as a bookmark.

The contributors

This edition of the popular *Insight Guides: Western Europe* was managed and edited by **Siân Lezard**.

It builds on the foundations of the previous edition, overseen by **Roger Williams**, who compiled the Europe from A to Z feature with **Brian Bell**, one of Insight Guides' founding editors.

The book was fully revised and updated by Nick Rider, an award-winning travel writer and Insight favourite. Nick's first memory of European travel is of eating a crêpe at a stand in Brittany when he was six years old. Since then he has explored many parts of the continent, following interests from art and battlefields to Catalan wines. He also has a Ph.D in Spanish history, and has written extensively on Spain, France, Mexico and other countries.

Previous contributors include **Nick Inman**, a freelance travel writer specialising in France (where he lives) and Spain, **George McDonald**, **Susie Boulton**, **Marc Dubin**, **Josephine Quintero**, **Derek Blyth** and **Ben Le Bas**. **Tom Le Bas** compiled and wrote the Best of Western Europe spreads.

The book was proofread by **Neil Titman** and the index was created by **Penny Phenix**.

Map Legend

▬▬ ▬ ▬	International Boundary
▬▬▬▬▬▬	Regional/Département Boundary
▬ ▬ ▬ ▬	Province Boundary
⊖	Border Crossing
▬ • ▬	National Park/Reserve
▬ ▬ ▬ ▬	Ferry Route
Ⓜ ⟨Ⓜ⟩ Ⓜ	Metro
Ⓢ	S–Bahn
Ⓤ	U–Bahn
⚑	Gondola Stand
✈ ✈	Airport: International/Regional
🚌	Bus Station
❶	Tourist Information
✉	Post Office
🏛 † ⚜	Church/Ruins
†	Monastery
☾	Mosque
✡	Synagogue
🏰 ⌂	Castle/Ruins
∴	Archaeological Site
∩	Cave
⇑	Statue/Monument
★	Place of Interest

The main places of interest in the Places section are coordinated by number with a full-colour map (eg ❶), and a symbol at the top of every right-hand page tells you where to find the map.

Contents

THE BEST OF WESTERN EUROPE: TOP ATTRACTIONS

With its unmatched cultural heritage, historic sights, great cities and endless variety of scenery, deciding where to go in Western Europe can be a real challenge. Here is our summary of the best sights to help you plan your itinerary.

△ **The Alhambra.** This apogee of Moorish architecture stands high above the city of Granada. The design and attention to detail are mesmerising, and the pools and fountains provide a delightful contrast with the arid surroundings. See page 371.

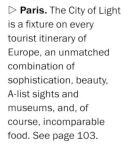

◁ **Venice.** It's hard to think of any city more distinctive, or beautiful, than Venice. The absence of cars renders this watery labyrinth wonderfully peaceful – away from the crowded main thoroughfares, at least. Venture out on the canals and admire the sumptuous grandeur from a different perspective. See page 285.

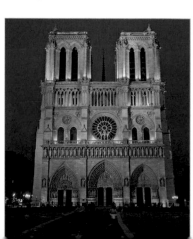

△ **Bruges.** Canals thread their way around the well-preserved medieval buildings, interspersed with bars, restaurants and chocolate shops. See page 151.

▷ **Paris.** The City of Light is a fixture on every tourist itinerary of Europe, an unmatched combination of sophistication, beauty, A-list sights and museums, and, of course, incomparable food. See page 103.

△ **Seville.** Europe's hottest city (ahead of Athens) is the heart of romantic Andalucía, the Spanish deep south. On fragrant summer evenings it can seem as if the entire population is out and about, promenading the streets or crowding into the hundreds of tapas bars. See page 370.

△ **Amsterdam.** City of canals and bicycles, Rembrandt and coffee houses, Amsterdam has long blazed a trail for an open-minded society and is still every bit as colourful and cosmopolitan as its reputation suggests. World-class museums vie with canal-boat cruises, markets and the distinctive brown cafés for your attention. See page 163.

◁ **Salzburg and the Salzkammergut.** Famous for Mozart and The Sound of Music, Salzburg and its spectacular backyard – sheer-sided mountains reflected in quiet lakes – are the very definition of picturesque. See page 253.

▷ **Berlin.** The troubled recent past of Berlin lends the metropolis a fascination all its own. Battered by bombs, brutally divided into East and West during the Cold War, then regaining its status as the German capital in the 1990s, it's nothing if not resilient. See page 183.

△ **Rhine cruise.** With its vineyard-clad slopes and romantic castles, the middle section of the Rhine between Koblenz and Mainz is a magnificent stretch of river. The best way to appreciate it, bar none, is on board a river cruise. See page 204.

▽ **Barcelona.** Gaudí's city has a great deal going for it: a wonderful climate, superb food, legendary nightlife, sandy beaches and architecture ranging from Gothic palaces to extraordinary Modernist spectaculars. See page 351.

◁ **Tuscany.** Occasionally dubbed "Chiantishire" in reference to the enduring British love affair with its timeless scenery, this land of cypresses, vineyards and beautiful towns is a place to appreciate the finer things in life. The food and wine are part of that experience. See page 298.

△ **Greek island-hopping.** From Athens's port, ferries depart for the hundreds of islands scattered across the blue waters of the Aegean. See page 323.

△ **Ancient Athens.** The power and beauty of ancient Greece can be felt despite the muddle of modern Athens, overlooked as it is on almost every street by the majesty of the Parthenon, pinnacle of Classical architecture. See page 315.

△ **Lisbon.** A wonderful city of rattling old trams, grand vistas, characterful bars, intimate neighbourhoods and handsome buildings. See page 385.

◁ **The Alps.** Extending over France, Switzerland, Austria and Italy, and perhaps most popular for skiing in the colder months, these lofty mountains offer wonderful hiking and adventure sports in summer. Many of the upper slopes can be accessed via Switzerland's superlative rail network – and the trains are always on time, too. See pages 226 and 248.

△ **Florence.** With Renaissance art, architecture and heritage in abundance, from the magnificent terracotta cupola of the Duomo to the stupendous treasures of the Uffizi, Florence is always going to be at the top of the list for culture buffs. See page 279.

△ **Provence/Côte d'Azur.** The famous sunlit landscapes and lovely old towns such as Aix and Avignon make this corner of southern France utterly entrancing. Beyond are the dazzling resorts, beaches and casinos of the Riviera. See page 129.

△ **The Costas.** Spanish beaches are hard to beat if you are looking for sun, sea and sand. The Costa Brava in the northeast has more in the way of rocky coves, while the Costa Blanca and Costa del Sol are known for their long stretches of pale sands. See pages 365 and 372.

△ **Châteaux of the Loire.** Rising above the gentle countryside of the Loire Valley are the 15th–18th-century residences of the French aristocracy, most of them stuffed full of fine art, priceless period furniture and surrounded by glorious gardens. The ultra-decadent flamboyance of palaces such as Azay-le-Rideau, Chambord and Chenonceau has to be seen to be believed. See page 118.

▽ **Rome.** Being at the centre of the Classical world and the Christian world has bequeathed the Italian capital a legacy unequalled anywhere on earth. See page 269.

THE BEST OF WESTERN EUROPE: EDITOR'S CHOICE

Our selection of the top cultural and historical sights, the best outdoor experiences, urban highlights, family attractions, eating and drinking, amazing locations, as well as some lesser-known destinations.

The Grossglockner glacier in the Austrian Alps.

ART AND CULTURE

Louvre, Paris. Housed in a former royal palace, this is one of Europe's greatest art galleries. Highlights include the *Mona Lisa* and *Venus de Milo*. See page 105.

Uffizi, Florence. The Uffizi has been used to display art since 1581, and is the world's leading repository of Renaissance works. Botticelli, da Vinci and Michelangelo feature prominently. See

The Mona Lisa, displayed in the Louvre.

page 280.

Sistine Chapel, Vatican. Renaissance art at its finest, the ceiling is alive with Michelangelo's famous frescoes and other marvellous works adorning the walls. See page 277.

Prado, Madrid. The finest collection of 12th–19th-century Spanish art, including works by Velázquez and Goya, plus notable Italian and Flemish paintings. See page 347.

Kunsthistorisches Museum, Vienna. First built to house the magnificent art collection of the Habsburg emperors, Vienna's great art museum has remarkable paintings by Dürer, Rubens, Brueghel and other artists, and stunning Greek, Roman and Egyptian antiquities. See page 243.

ANCIENT SITES

The Acropolis, Athens. A The 2,500-year-old Acropolis is the enduring symbol of the achievements of ancient Greece. See page 315.

Prehistoric cave art, Lascaux and Altamira. For really old art, head to the Dordogne region of France, or Altamira in northern Spain. See pages 122 and 361.

Colosseum, Pantheon and Forum, Rome. These remarkable remains are vivid reminders of the supreme power of Roman civilisation. See page 271.

Greek ruins, Sicily. Highlights include a superb 2,000-year-old theatre at Syracuse and Agrigento's amazing Valley of the Temples. See page 304.

Les Arènes, Nîmes. This impressive amphitheatre is one of the most complete Roman ruins in Europe. See page 127.

Aqueduct, Segovia. The Roman aqueduct is just one attraction in this lovely old Castilian town. See page 362.

Pompeii. Beneath the smouldering bulk of Vesuvius, visiting this extraordinary site is an unforgettable experience. See page 302.

The Greek Temple of Segesta in northwest Sicily.

PROVINCIAL CITIES

Avignon, France. A lively southern city bathed in luminous Provençal light. Visit the Palais des Papes and witness the street theatre. See page 128.
St-Malo, France. Small but perfectly formed, this fortified port is a delightful place to wander. Mont St-Michel is a short drive away. See page 116.
Siena, Italy. Home to one of Europe's greatest squares and the Palio festival, the medieval centre is utterly enchanting. See page 299.
San Sebastián, Spain. This Basque city has a superb setting, a marvellous sandy beach and some of the best food anywhere in Europe. See page 364.
Coimbra, Portugal. Explore the narrow streets of this ancient university town perched above the River Mondego. See page 300.

Dresden, Germany. Few war-ravaged cities have been rebuilt as successfully as Dresden. The stunning ensemble of Baroque architecture is a highlight of a visit to Germany. See page 193.
Heidelberg, Germany. Dominated by its fabulous ruined castle, this handsome city has been a centre of learning since the 14th century. See page 202.
Delft, Netherlands. Vermeer's hometown, famed for its blue-and-white pottery, is small and relaxed, and the canals are lined with lovely old buildings. See page 171.
Old Town, Ródos (Rhodes), Greece. This bustling Unesco-listed city has been in existence since the 5th century BC. Enclosed by thick walls, it is one of Europe's best-preserved ancient settlements. See page 328.

Street theatre during the Festival d'Avignon.

Carne de porco à Alentejana, a Portuguese speciality.

FOOD AND DRINK

Italy. Everyone thinks pasta and pizza, but there is more to Italian cuisine than these essential basics, with a wonderful variety of regional dishes. See page 433.
France. Fine dining for gourmets, but many people happily limit themselves to the set *menu du jour*. The cheese and, of course, wine, are superb – seek out a local market and indulge. See page 416.
Spain. Away from the well-known *tapas*, *calamares* and *paella* is a huge range of regional dishes that reward the adventurous. See page 450.
Portugal. Seafood and inventively prepared meat dishes dominate. Fresh grilled sardines with young vinho verde wine is a popular standard. See page 444.
Greece. With plenty of fish, meat dishes, *mezedes* and olive oil, eating out in Greece is a pleasure. See page 428.
The Netherlands. Bucking the trend of plain food is the *rijsttafel*, an Indonesian feast that can comprise of more than 40 separate dishes. See page 439.
Belgium. Belgian cuisine is generally of a high standard, but the country is best known for its flavoured beers and the quality of its chocolate. See page 410.
Germany. Straightforward, often hearty fare is complemented by some marvellous wines and some of the world's finest beer. See page 423.
Austria. Vienna is famous for its Wiener Schnitzel and coffee houses, with endless varieties of coffee and delectable cakes. See page 406.

12

Versailles.

GREAT BUILDINGS

Eiffel Tower, Paris. The iconic metal structure is a contender for the best-known building in Europe. See page 109.

St Peter's Basilica, Rome. Epicentre of the Catholic faith, home to the pope and an astounding array of art, the world's largest church is an amazing sight. See page 276.

Versailles. The palace of the Bourbon kings is the last word in divine-right decadence. Highlights include the Hall of Mirrors, fully 75 metres (246ft) in length. See page 111.

Reims Cathedral. This heavyweight of Gothic architecture can be seen from the surrounding wheatfields for miles around. See page 137.

Sagrada Família, Barcelona. Nothing can prepare you for the first encounter with this extraordinary building, still unfinished. Gaudí's singular genius emerges on a truly grand scale. See page 357.

Guggenheim, Bilbao. Gehry's unique "metal flower" flabbergasted the public when it opened in 1997 and is still astonishing over a decade later. See page 363.

Basilica di San Marco, Venice. St Mark's is a vivid testament to the wealth brought by centuries of Venetian trade and plunder. See page 287.

Duomo, Milan. This gigantic Gothic cathedral bristles with a total of 135 spires, and writhes with gargoyles and statues. See page 294.

Schönbrunn Palace, Vienna. Summer retreat of the Habsburgs, with 1,440 rooms set in glorious gardens. See page 245.

Reichstag, Berlin. Symbol of the new Berlin and one of the most successful examples of modern architecture in Europe. For more information, click here. See page 186.

Bilbao's Guggenheim Museum.

SPECTACULAR SETTINGS

Metéora, Greece. Perched on a series of improbably shaped rock pillars, these monasteries are a remarkable sight. See page 322.

Rocamadour, France. This ancient Christian centre seems to challenge the laws of physics as it clings to its huge cliff. See page 123.

Neuschwanstein Castle, Germany. The ultimate fairy-tale castle, high on a Bavarian hill. See pages 199.

Ronda, Spain. This classic Andalucian town is cleaved in two by the gorge El Tajo. See page 373.

Dürnstein, Austria. A romantic old town with a gorgeous setting on the Danube. See page 255.

Bellagio, Italy. This gem on Lake Como occupies one of the most emphatically picturesque locations on the continent. See page 296.

Amalfi coast, Italy. The dizzying coastline south of Naples is famed for its views and chic resorts. See page 302.

Gravity-defying Rocamadour.

THE GREAT OUTDOORS

Picos de Europa, Spain. These soaring, craggy peaks are home to bears, wolves and some of Europe's most exciting hiking. See page 361.

Corsica. Vast tracts of virtually untrammelled mountain wilderness cover much of the interior of this Mediterranean island. See page 129.

Gorges du Tarn, France. White-water rafting and hiking amid truly majestic scenery. See page 123.

Pyrenees, France/Spain. This long mountain chain, stretching from Atlantic to Mediterranean, is marked by spectacular canyons and wild forests. See pages 125 and 364.

Alps. From hiking to paragliding, ice-climbing, rock-climbing and, of course, skiing, the Alps

are a paradise for outdoor activities. See pages 134, 228.

La Camargue, France. Famed for its wild flamingos, horses and distinctive culture, this extensive wetland in the Rhône Delta is unlike anywhere else in Western Europe. See page 128.

Schwarzwald (Black Forest), Germany. Famous for hiking since the 19th century, the densely wooded hills and gorgeous valleys beside the Rhine still have plenty of remote, tranquil corners. See page 201.

Gorge of Samariá, Crete. The scenery and vegetation in this dramatically sheer sided, deep ravine resembles the Middle East or North Africa more than Europe. See page 327.

The Palio.

OFF THE BEATEN TRACK

Barging in Burgundy, France. Take to the water in this rich, beautiful region and enjoy the languid pace of rural France. See page 135.

Thuringian Forest, Germany. A favourite of Goethe, this is a hilly region whose landscapes will be familiar to readers of the brothers Grimm. See page 195.

Green Spain. With its forests, green pastures, rocky coast and Atlantic surf, northwest Spain is completely different from the rest of the country. See page 359.

Trás-os-Montes, Portugal. Life continues largely undisturbed by the modern world in this remote part of northern Portugal. See page 390.

Massif Central, France. The Massif is a large, sparsely populated upland region with some fantastic scenery and endless potential for outdoor activities. See page 121.

Aeolian Islands, Italy. A scattered archipelago off the north coast of Sicily, these islands are known for their volcanic landscapes, crystal-clear waters and rustic way of life. See page 305.

Lake Constance, Switzerland. With most visitors heading to the higher Alpine areas, the beautiful east and north of Switzerland, notably around Bodensee, can be blissfully quiet. See page 226.

CHILDREN AND FAMILIES

Disneyland Paris. Since opening in 1992, Disney's first European theme park has proved to be a great success. See page 111.

Cycling in the Netherlands. Everywhere in this extremely flat land is well suited to family cycling, with facilities to match. The Zeeland area is particularly good. See page 170.

Beaches. From Atlantic surf to the blue Aegean, there is no lack of variety to European beaches for a family holiday or day out. See page 67

Festivals. Highlights for families include the Palio in Siena, the Easter festivals in Spain and the Christmas markets of Germany. See pages 299, 372 and 194.

Cable cars in the Alps. Taking a cable car or chairlift up an Alpine peak is guaranteed to thrill. Swiss mountain railways are another exciting adventure. See page 220.

Leaning Tower of Pisa. Familiar but still amazing when seen in the flesh. Arrive early to avoid queues. See page 298.

View from Vulcano, one of the Aeolian Islands.

The villages and vineyards of Alsace.

The band at the Palio.

Restaurant at night in Ermoúpoli,
on the Greek island of Sýros.

THE HEART OF THE OLD WORLD

Europe is the heart of Western civilisation, nourishing
a rich mix of cultures and providing a fertile breeding
ground for human creativity in all its forms.

The world's second-smallest continent, after Antarctica, has a history of both violence and civilisation, and is as faithful and frac tious as any family unit. Two thousand years after being united by the *denarii* monetary system of the Pax Romana, it is now bound by another common currency, the euro, which for all its current problems makes travelling around Europe so much easier.

> "I want all of Europe to have one currency. This will make trading much easier."
> Napoleon Bonaparte

This is a book primarily about the European states that lie at the heart of the continent. It includes all the six countries that first joined together to form an economic union in 1957 – France, Germany, Italy, Belgium, the Netherlands and Luxembourg. It also covers countries that joined the European Union later, like Spain, Portugal and Austria, as well as Switzerland, which resolutely clings to its independence and its francs. It excludes the islands at the edge – Britain and Ireland – as well as the Scandinavian countries and the 10 countries of Eastern Europe that joined in 2004 and 2006. This post-Cold War drift eastwards prompted a former US defence secretary – whose grandfather was originally from Bremen in Germany – to dismiss the EU's original, key members as "Old Europe".

Students in Strasbourg, France.

Old Europe

Seen from the New World, what else could they be? This is the "Old World" of châteaux and champagne, La Scala and Monte Carlo, gondolas and gypsy violins. It is the home of democracy, Christianity, the Renaissance, royalty, Michelangelo, Mercedes-Benz, Beethoven, the Cannes Film Festival, pasta and tapas. Newer nations may complain, but even they must admit that European art is admired, its wines appreciated, its fashion copied and its languages spoken in every corner of the world.

Europeans from different nations have their own idea of themselves and their own image of Europe. To French politicians, it is a collection of well-off countries who need to get together for their own self-interest. To the inhabitants of countries ruled a few decades ago by right-wing dictatorships, like

Spain or Portugal, it represents an ideal of a progressive culture from which they once felt excluded by the accidents of their political history; similarly, for the countries of Eastern Europe, it is an entity through which they can regain the rightful place in the world that they were denied under Communism from 1945 to 1989. Romantics see Paris as its centre, bureaucrats look to Brussels, style-setters consider Barcelona and Milan the main hubs, classicists look to Athens and Rome, Catholics to the Vatican, skiers to the Alps and hedonists to the Mediterranean shores.

Traditional folk dancing in Portugal.

Wide divisions

Its countries may be physically attached, but Europe is not homogeneous, and all efforts to unite its unruly tribes have come to nothing. Charlemagne and Napoleon failed and, despite over 50 years of closer union, the sense of European identity is still weak. The fact is that most Europeans, in spite of all the handshaking and treaty signing, do not see themselves as a single entity, and voter turnout to elect members to the European Parliament can be depressingly low.

Indeed, they often don't see themselves as part of the country to which they already belong. Basques, Bretons, Catalans, Flemings, Lombards and others still dream of resurrecting independent nationhood (see page 374).

Mistrusts run deep, and stereotypes are still used in the nations' popular newspapers to stir up feeling. There are epigrams to sum up every nation, every region, every city; sayings to reinforce ideas about their stubbornness or *joie de vivre*, their cleverness or stupidity. Such cartoon characters are easy to sketch, from the hard-working Teutonic races of the north to the excitable Latins of the south, from boisterous Bavarians to arrogant French, devious Greeks and boring Belgians. "A typical Spaniard," the Viennese psychoanalyst Sigmund Freud said of the painter Salvador Dalí. "Quite mad." His statement does not bear analysis.

The north–south divide is the most noticeable, and has come to the fore yet again in recent arguments over the management of the euro and who can be held responsible for economic crises: the industrious peoples of the colder climates scorn the backward and lazy siesta-seeking peasants of sunnier parts. Typically, the strapping, healthy, fair-skinned northerner gets darker, lazier, louder and smaller towards the south. Even within countries there can be divisive stereotypes: Germany's northern Prussians look down on the beer-swilling Bavarians. The richer inhabitants of northern France and Italy consider themselves superior to the poorer, more rural "midday" lands of the south – the Midi in France, the Mezzogiorno in Italy. In Spain the industrious northerner has no time for "lazy" flamenco-playing Andalucians. Such prejudices are put aside at holiday time as northerners head for the sun. The whoops from otherwise sober Germans are said to be audible as their cars cross the Alps and slip down into Italy. Only a love of football seems to unite Europeans – football competitions are the best-run and most popular of all pan-European institutions – though the matches themselves can seem like replays of earlier hostilities.

Roman occupation

The nearest Europe came to being united was not under one country, but under one city, ancient Rome. Pax Romana stretched all around the Mediterranean and north to the River Danube, and ruled in every country in Western Europe. Perhaps Rome's most significant bequests were a written language from which the "Romance" languages of France and southern Europe subsequently evolved, and the alphabet that remained in use throughout the western part of the continent, and which is now standard in most of the world as well. And then of course there is Greek, the only language in the countries covered by this guide not to use Roman script.

Teutonic tribes shaped the languages in the north, Slavs to the east. To the west, all but pushed into the sea, are the last of the continent's Celtic-speakers, the Bretons. Trapped in pockets in between are little-used languages such as Romansch in part of Switzerland, and Basque, which shows no resemblance to other languages, spoken on the southwestern border of France and Spain.

Wider influences

The cultural and ethnic fabric of these countries of Europe has equally been shaped by many influences from outside their borders. In the early Middle Ages, Vikings came down from the north, sailing to Paris and round into the Mediterranean. In the year 711 Arab Muslim armies, driven by missionary zeal after the death of the Prophet Muhammad, swept into Spain and up through France as far as Poitiers, not far from Paris. They soon withdrew south of the Pyrenees, but remained in Spain and Portugal for another seven centuries, pro-

Catania fish market, Sicily.

Language is no respecter of borders, some of which have anyway failed to remain firm. For centuries most Europeans were probably more aware of local matters rather than any "national" – and certainly not any "pan-European" interest – and at the beginning of the 20th century modern Italy and Germany had not long been invented, Prussia had been subsumed into the German Empire, and Austria and Hungary dramatically deflated. Since then, Germany has had its borders altered twice, in 1918 and 1945, and been divided and reunited, while further east new states emerged after both World Wars and again after the collapse of Communism in the 1990s. But since the end of World War I, the heart of Europe has remained much the same.

ducing an enormously rich society and superb architecture, and having a lasting impact on both countries' culture, still visible in Spanish words and expressions of Arabic origin such as alfombra ("carpet") or ¡ojalá! ("I hope so," from the Arabic Inshallah or "If God wills"). Arabic scholars from Spain also reintroduced ancient Greek learning, lost since the fall of Rome, to Western Europe. Sicily and other parts of southern Italy were also under Muslim rule for long periods in the Middle Ages, and in the 15th century the Ottoman Turks conquered Greece, and ruled over it for 400 years.

Jewish communities existed in Western Europe from Roman times, and despite many forms of persecution in different eras – culminating in the Nazi Holocaust during World War II – spread, became established and often prospered in every country on the continent. Jewish creativity has been an inseparable part of European culture, from the exquisite synagogues of medieval Toledo to the philosopher Spinoza in 17th-century Holland and great German-speaking figures such as Mendelssohn, Marx or Freud.

More recently – and with growing momentum ever since World War II – the look of Europe has been changed again by the arrival of new migrants from virtually every part of the world, and especially areas that European

A bride arriving by donkey in Hydra, one of the Saronic Islands in Greece.

empires once colonised; North and Sub-Saharan Africa, Asia, Latin America. In cities above all, this has created a far more diverse, changing social pattern, in a way that easily surprises any visitor who still expects to find the Europe of the old, homogeneous, all-white stereotypes.

Modern-day links

A fast and integrated road system makes communications between the countries easier than ever before. Motorways, given an "E" number in addition to their national number, slip effortlessly across borders free of frontier controls since the Schengen agreement abolished them between most European Union states in the 1990s; there is often no sign where one country begins and one ends. It's the same with the railway system – reliable high-speed trains are in regular service between most major cities – while regional airports offer a proliferation of low-cost, short-haul flights connecting nearly every part of Europe, avoiding the need to pass through main city hubs.

There is no difficulty in travelling the length and breadth of this small continent, whose largest country, France, at 544,000 sq km (212,900 sq miles), is smaller than both the states of Texas and New South Wales. In spite of its size, Europe has proved to be unbeatable in its ambitions. In the past 500 years it had a good try at conquering the entire world, and residents of those former colonies and outposts return looking for their roots as names can be traced to places; Walt Disney's family was "d'Isigny" (from Isigny in Normandy).

EUROPE'S SHARED CULTURAL HERITAGE

Today, architects move around all over the world. The work of Italy's Renzo Piano or Spain's Santiago Calatrava can crop up in any part of the globe, just as Japanese or American architects will design showcase buildings in Europe. Historically, Europe's unparalleled architecture shows that ideas have always flowed freely across the continent, regardless of borders. Builders, traders, businessmen, pilgrims and mercenaries – as well as visionaries – have constantly been on the move.

The terracotta roof tiles of the Romans colour all the Mediterranean's fashionable resorts. Italians built many of Northern Europe's churches. Normans put up castles in northern Greece and southern Italy. German woodcarvers

left their marks on Spanish choir stalls. Dutch Masters followed the Hansa traders to the Baltic, and a visitor would be hard-pressed to tell the difference between 17th-century houses in Bremen and Amsterdam.

The great architectural movements of Romanesque, Gothic, Renaissance, Baroque and Neoclassicism touched all of Europe, each style taking on specific, local traits in different countries, so that an Italian Gothic church is fascinatingly different from the great cathedrals of northern France. In the 19th century, France's Art Nouveau was Germany and Austria's Jugendstil, Italy's Stile Liberty and Catalonia's *Modernisme* (see page 208).

Among the most lasting signs of Europe's colonial past are its specialist restaurants: Algerian couscous in France, Indonesian rice tables in the Netherlands and Cuban salsa bars in Spain.

The French historian Fernand Braudel (1902–85) knew how to look at a family name and point to remote European mountain valleys or city shopkeepers' alleyways as the place of its origin. This kind of non-chemical DNA can be used to excuse character or temperament. Countless millions of people scattered around the world still have a drop of "Old Europe" coursing through their veins.

Much discussion of Europe nowadays tends to divide into forecasts of disaster or triumph, black-or-white style, between those who see it as an ageing continent – mentally and physically – forever trying to cling onto its past prominence, unwilling to adapt fast enough to new conditions and with ineffectual institutions incapable of dealing with current problems, and those who still see modern Europe as a model of flexibility and cooperation between different countries and traditions, and still a great centre of creativity in all kinds of fields. Recent events suggest there's an element of truth in both views. Each European country does have its own set ways of doing things, and pan-European institutions do spend a long time in discussions that often seem to produce very little result; but the sheer variety of these countries also remains an immense resource.

Europe's incorrigibly fractious diversity – whether in the devotion of Italian chefs to strictly local ingredients, or the peculiarities of Algerian-influenced French rap songs – is also a source of endless fascination. The modern world, and Europe within it, can appear to be increasingly uniform, but the way in which new music, fashions, gadgets and attitudes are taken on board and even habits like driving styles still vary in all sorts of subtle ways from country to country. This may be what makes holding Europe together so difficult, but it's also its charm.

Multicultural Brussels.

MULTICULTURAL EUROPE

Despite the determination of Europeans to stick to their historic identities, cultural and ethnic diversity has become as much part of the identity of modern Europe as it is of New World countries. France has the largest new population, with some 19 percent of its population foreign-born or the descendants of recent migrants, while in Italy the latter make up about 10 percent of the whole.

Migrants had always come to Europe, but the big transformation began after World War II. Many migration flows followed old links between former colonies and "mother countries", as in those of North Africans and Senegalese to France, Surinamese to the Netherlands or Angolans to Portugal. Others were just drawn by European prosperity, like the millions of Turks who moved to Germany and Switzerland in the 1960s. In the early 2000s, Spain's economic boom attracted massive migration from Latin America, and in 2004 after the Eastern European countries joined the EU, huge numbers from these countries moved west looking for work.

Reporting of this new, predominantly urban, social mix often focuses on the tensions it can create, as in the rise of far-right politics, but for most Europeans it's also become an inseparable part of everyday life, its influence absorbed – and enjoyed – not just in food, through the ethnic restaurants in most cities, but in music, football, arts and on TV.

Cloister of Elne, detail,
Southwest France.

DECISIVE DATES

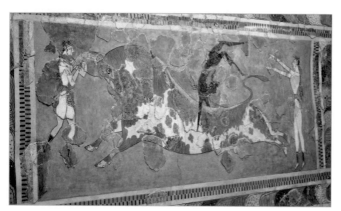

Minoan fresco, Crete.

2000–1450 BC
Minoan civilisation, centred on Knossos in Crete.

1450–100 BC
Mycenaean civilisation, based at Mycenae in the Peloponnese, southern Greece.

800–500 BC
Archaic period. Athens and Sparta emerge as major city-states.

753 BC
Rome said to have been founded by Romulus and Remus.

509 BC
Rome becomes a republic.

450–338 BC
Classical period in Greece. Parthenon built. Flowering of Greek literature and philosophy.

338–323 BC
Macedonia's Philip and Alexander the Great create unprecedented empire.

218 BC
The Carthaginians, led by Hannibal, attack Rome, unsuccessfully. Rome gradually takes over all Italy.

146 BC
Greece falls to Rome.

48 BC
Death of Pompey the Great in civil war with Julius Caesar.

Augustus, the first Roman emperor.

50 BC–AD 50
Pax Romana spreads through Europe and Mediterranean, but declines within 300 years.

AD 312
Roman Emperor Constantine adopts Christianity and establishes an eastern capital in Constantinople.

390–476
Fall of the Roman Empire. In 410 Rome itself sacked by Visigoths.

527
St Benedict founds the first monastic order, at Monte Cassino, southern Italy.

711–20
Spain conquered by Muslims.

800
In Rome, Charlemagne, the Frankish leader, is crowned Holy Roman Emperor.

11th century
Romanesque architecture evolves, characterised by simple vaulting and rounded arches. Pisa Cathedral, Italy, and the Church of the Apostles, Cologne, are good examples.

1066
French Normans (descendants of the Vikings) conquer England.

1096
First Crusade against Muslims in the Holy Land; 500,000 join up.

12th century
Gothic architecture, identified by pointed arches and external buttresses, becomes prevalent. Chartres Cathedral, France, and St Stephen's Cathedral, Vienna, are prime examples.

1150–70
First universities founded.

1283
Dante Alighieri begins writing in Florence, establishing Italian language.

1309–76
The papacy moves from Rome to Avignon.

1325–1495
The Renaissance is initiated in northern Italy, exemplified by Giotto, Michelangelo and Leonardo da Vinci.

1337–1453
Hundred Years War between France and England results in Joan of Arc's martyrdom and England losing all claims to French territory.

1346–50
Black Death sweeps the continent, killing one-third of the population.

1450
First printing press made by Johannes Gutenberg in Germany. Bible is printed five years later.

1453
Ottoman Turks capture Constantinople and Byzantine Empire falls.

1492
Last Moorish kings driven out of Spain; Jews expelled.

Chartres Cathedral.

Christopher Columbus lands in the Americas.

16th century
The Reformation in Northern Europe, as Protestant churches break away from the Catholic Church in Rome.

1503
Leonardo da Vinci paints the *Mona Lisa*.

1517
Martin Luther nails his 95 points to Wittenberg church door, challenging Church

Leonardo da Vinci.

authority and initiating the Protestant Reformation.

1519–22
Portuguese navigator Fernando Magellan circumnavigates the world.

1536
John Calvin establishes Presbyterian Church in Switzerland.

1572
Protestant Huguenots purged in St Bartholomew's Day Massacre in Paris.

1579
United Provinces established, founding the Netherlands.

17th–18th centuries
Baroque period: its opulent architecture uses gold, marble and mirrors to show off wealth and power. The Palace of Versailles and Dresden's Zwinger Palace are good examples.

1618–46
Thirty Years War: a Protestant revolt against Catholicism develops into a war involving many European powers, and devastates Germany.

Napoleon Bonaparte.

1633
The Inquisition forces Italian scientist Galileo to renounce his Copernican belief that the earth revolves around the sun.

1643–1715
Louix XIV, creator of the Palace of Versailles in France, exemplifies a phase of absolute monarchy.

18th century
Age of Enlightenment. Tolerance is urged by French writer Voltaire and others, supported by some rulers such as Austro-Hungarian empress Maria Theresa (1717–80). Mozart plays at her court.

1755
Earthquake destroys Lisbon.

1789
The French Revolution. Louis XVI and Queen Marie

Antoinette are guillotined four years later.

1796–1815
Napoleon Bonaparte of France conquers most of Western Europe. He is defeated at Waterloo in present-day Belgium.

1830
Kingdom of Belgium created.

Late 18th–19th centuries
Romanticism inspires nationalist movements, encouraging local languages (Catalan and Provençal) and regional customs.

1822
Greece declares independence.

1848
Popular revolutions take place throughout Europe.

1861
Kingdom of Italy set up after Austrians ejected from the north, Bourbon monarchs and other traditional rulers from the south.

1870–1
Franco-Prussian War; Paris besieged.

1874
First Impressionist exhibition held in Paris.

1914–18
World War I: millions die in unprecedented war of attrition. The war leads to the fall of the German and Russian monarchies, and the break-up of the Ottoman and Austro-Hungarian empires. New countries such as Yugoslavia and

Czechoslovakia appear across Eastern Europe.

1922
Mussolini's Blackshirts march on Rome, seize power and initiate the first Fascist regime.

1933
Hitler gains power in Germany.

1936–9
Spanish Civil War; Franco is victorious and becomes dictator.

1938
Hitler annexes Austria.

1939–45
World War II: Poland, Czechoslovakia, France, the Netherlands, Belgium, Yugoslavia, Albania and Greece occupied by Germans and Italians. Nazi regime launches mass extermination of Jews and other minorities. In 1943–4, Soviet advances are followed by the Western Allies' landings in Italy and Normandy, leading to the end of the war. Many German cities destroyed. Europe is divided between Western and

Marie Antoinette guillotined.

American Cemetery and Memorial, Omaha Beach, Normandy.

Soviet spheres of influence, and Germany into two separate states.

1949
Creation of NATO (North Atlantic Treaty Organization) to ensure the collective security of the US and Western Europe.

1957
Six countries – France, West Germany, Italy, Belgium, the Netherlands and Luxembourg – sign the Treaty of Rome, setting up the European Economic Community (EEC).

1961
The Berlin Wall is built, sealing off East Germany from the West.

1968
Student unrest throughout Europe. Czechoslovak "Prague Spring" crushed by USSR.

1973
Britain, Ireland and Denmark join the EEC.

1974–5
End of dictatorships in Greece, Spain and Portugal.

1978
Polish Cardinal Wojtyla becomes Pope John Paul II, first non-Italian pope for 400 years.

1981
France launches first high-speed rail link (TGV) between Paris and Lyon.

1989
Berlin Wall comes down following demonstrations across Eastern Europe.

1990
Germany is reunified.

1993
Under the Maastricht Treaty, the EEC becomes the European Union (EU).

1994
Channel Tunnel links France with Britain.

1995
Border controls between most EU countries end.

2002
The euro is adopted by all EU states apart from Denmark, Sweden and the UK.

2004
Ten new members join the EU, including eight former Communist states, to create the world's largest trading bloc, with 450 million people.

2006
Romania and Bulgaria join EU, bringing the total number of member states to 27.

2008
Global financial crisis brings several European banks to their knees.

2009–12
The crisis reveals massive debts in Greece and other Southern European countries, which eventually have to be bailed out by the rest of the Eurozone. Hopes for a new system for managing the currency are disappointed by continuing disagreements between member states.

Trading screen shows heavy selling as the financial crisis deepens.

BEGINNINGS

The Mediterranean was the great hub of early
European civilisation, and the origin of not only
the multiple traces left by Greeks and Romans,
but also of Christianity.

Europa, legend has it, was the beautiful
daughter of the king of Phoenicia, who
was carried away by the god Zeus, disguised as a bull, to the island of Crete. There
she bore him three sons, including Minos, after
whom the Minoan civilisation, Europe's earliest
"superpower", was named.

The Greek source
The Minoans flourished on Crete throughout
the Bronze Age, roughly around 3500–1450 BC.
Their great palaces, such as the famous complex
at Knossos, suggest a refined way of life. They
were succeeded by the Mycenaean civilisation
of mainland Greece, which was the source of
many of the later Greek myths.

The Archaic period of ancient Greece
(800–480 BC) saw the creation of the central
features of Classical Greek culture: the *polis*
or city-state, of which there were many, in
rivalry with each other; writing, with the Greek
alphabet; and characteristic styles of architec-

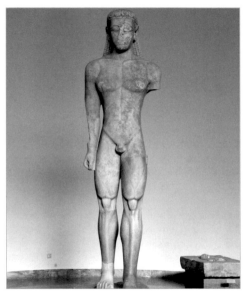

*Greek statue from the Sanctuary of Poseidon in Sounion,
c.600 BC.*

> Among the first texts written in Greek were
> the epic poems of Homer, the Iliad and the
> Odyssey, which have had a vast influence on
> all European literature.

ture and ceramics. Great traders, the Archaic
Greeks founded new cities in Sicily and across
the Mediterranean as far as southern France
and Spain. The political struggles of the Greek
polis have left us words still in use today, such
as tyrant, for a leader who unjustly seized
sole power, or oligarchy, for a tightly knit ruling group. Around 500 BC Athens, especially,
moved towards a more collective, participatory
system – even if still limited to men with wealth
– the origin of the concept of democracy.

The great threat to Greek security was the
Persian Empire, whose expansion led to the
Persian Wars of 500–478 BC, a titanic struggle
remembered for near-legendary battles like the
Athenian victory at Marathon and the heroic
defeat of the Spartans at Thermopylae. Athens
and Sparta, the two most powerful *polis*, combined forces with the other states to vanquish
the Persians.

Rise and fall
The following two centuries, the Classical
period, represent the summit of ancient
Greek culture. This was the age of the great

Athenian statesman Pericles, when Plato sat at the feet of Socrates before writing the *Republic*, on which much of Western philosophy is based. It was the period when the Parthenon was built, Sophocles wrote *Oedipus Rex* and Euripides created *Medea*. This golden age ended when Athens and Sparta fought and nearly destroyed each other in the long-drawn-out Peloponnesian War. A new, rising power, Macedonia, then gained pre-eminence over all the Greek city-states, and produced the extraordinary figure of Alexander the Great (356–323 BC). King at the age of 20, he was both a seasoned soldier and a pupil of the great philosopher Aristotle. Alexander unleashed an unprecedented campaign of conquest, crushing the Persians, seizing Egypt and carrying Greek culture as far as India.

His astonishing advances were cut short, however, when he died of disease in Babylon at the age of 32. Alexander's empire soon fell apart, but it spread Greek or "Hellenistic" cultural influences across vast areas of the ancient world, especially in the new cities – many called "Alexandria" – that he founded wherever he went.

Roman emergence

The other great European centre of early civilisation was, of course, in Italy. Every Italian knows the story of Romulus and Remus, the twins abandoned on a riverbank and brought up by a she-wolf; Romulus killed his brother, and founded Rome on the banks of the Tiber in 753 BC. Archaeologists suggest the settlement was possibly 200 years older, and was originally subordinate to the more cultivated Etruscans of modern Tuscany, but around 509 BC the Romans ousted their last Etruscan king, Tarquin the Proud, and set up a republic.

The Romans had a genius for war and organisation. Over the next two centuries Rome established its dominance over the rest of Italy, and clashed with the other power in the western Mediterranean, which was centred on Carthage in modern Tunisia. The Carthaginian Empire included cities in Spain, France, Sardinia and Sicily. In the Second Punic War (218–202 BC) Rome was nearly destroyed when the great Carthaginian general Hannibal marched up through France and famously crossed the Alps, with elephants among his army. However, Hannibal was defeated, and after that there was no stopping the Romans: within a century they had destroyed Carthage, conquered Greece and won control of the whole Mediterranean.

Beyond the Mediterranean

The Romans and Greeks dismissed the peoples away from the Mediterranean in Northern Europe as "barbarians", but modern historians rate them more highly. Most numerous were the Celts, who by around 500 BC occupied a huge area from the modern Netherlands across France to Britain and western Iberia. They were divided into many tribes with different names, although the Romans referred vaguely to the

C.1400 BC fresco from Hagia Triada, Crete.

whole area across the Netherlands and France as Gallia or Gaul, and its people as Gauls. Modern Germany to the east of the Rhine was largely occupied by other groups the Romans called the Germanic tribes; it was their restless movement that had pushed the Celts westwards.

Southern France was firmly under Roman rule by 120 BC, but Rome showed little interest in the barbarian north until 58 BC, when an ambitious new governor arrived in southern Gaul, Julius Caesar. Eager for victories to raise his prestige back in Rome, Caesar brilliantly exploited the divisions between the Gaulish tribes, and in just six years vastly extended Roman power, conquering the whole of Gaul, reaching the Atlantic and even invading Britain.

Pax Romana

Its conquests made the Roman Republic immensely rich, but it was a highly volatile society; Senate and other institutions struggled ineffectively to control successful generals, the most powerful figures in the state. Rome slid into bitter civil wars, through which by the mid-40s BC Caesar had beaten all other rivals to become dictator. However, only a few months later he was assassinated by a conspiracy of republican diehards led by Brutus, in 44 BC.

The armies of Caesar's adopted son Octavian and the dictator's leading general Mark Antony,

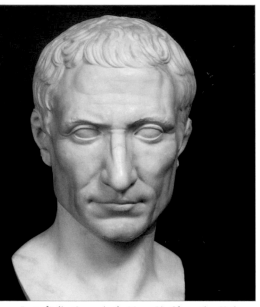

Bust of Julius Caesar in the Museo Pio-Clementino, Vatican.

however, crushed the ill-prepared conspirators. Octavian, though, also sought sole power, and by 31 BC had in turn defeated Antony and his lover, Queen Cleopatra of Egypt, and effectively made himself Rome's first emperor, with the title "Augustus" ("the great one").

Augustus' immediate successors have become bywords for decadent megalomania – Caligula declaring his horse a god, Nero burning Rome to make room for his golden palace – but they were succeeded by able rulers such as Trajan (AD 98–117) and Hadrian (AD 117–138), under whom the empire reached its greatest extent. During the 1st century AD, the whole of the Iberian peninsula and Britain were conquered; Augustus had also tried to conquer Germany, but

> *The Roman Republic was a very limited democracy – positions of power and membership of the Senate were restricted to wealthy men – but a very effective military state.*

after a defeat in AD 9 the Romans were content to keep the Germanic tribes beyond the Rhine.

For centuries the *Pax Romana* or "Roman peace" prevailed across the empire. Roman stability fostered trade and agriculture, so long as the best produce was sent to Rome. Many conquered peoples adopted Roman customs and forms of Latin. The degree of "Romanisation" varied, generally being stronger the closer to the Mediterranean, but even in northern Gaul there were important Roman cities such as *Lutetia* (Paris) or *Samarobriva* (Amiens).

An international empire, Rome unintentionally encouraged movements of peoples and ideas. There were Jewish communities in Rome and other cities. Eastern religions, such as Christianity, also spread. Roman emperors often persecuted Christians viciously, but their numbers grew, and around 312 Emperor Constantine himself converted to Christianity. Constantine also divided the unwieldy administration of the vast empire and gave it a new eastern capital in Constantinople, modern-day Istanbul.

The disintegration of the Roman Empire

Christianity did not prevent the empire's power slipping away. Mounting economic problems eroded links with outlying provinces. For years, the Romans had paid off barbarians on their borders rather than fight them, and often employed them as mercenary soldiers. Now, as these payments dried up, the Germanic tribes raided ever more aggressively into Roman territory. In 410, one of them, the Visigoths, sacked Rome itself, a date often seen as the effective end of the Western Empire. In contrast, the Eastern or Byzantine Empire, centred on Constantinople, would survive and rule over Greece and much of the eastern Mediterranean for another thousand years.

Rome's disintegration was the spur to huge movements of peoples, as the Germanic tribes exploded southwards and westwards. The Visigoths moved on from Rome to occupy Spain. Northern Italy was invaded by groups such as the

Vandals, Ostrogoths and Lombards. Most powerful of all were the Franks, who took over most of Gaul, and have bequeathed their name to France.

The empire's collapse left the Christian Church and its leader the pope, Bishop of Rome, as the one remaining solid institution in the west. Popes and bishops made great efforts to convert the pagan newcomers to Christianity, sending missionaries to every part of Europe. A major success came in 496, when the Frankish King Clovis was baptised, and over the next few centuries most of Western Europe was Christianised, including Germany

glittering civilisation in Al Andalus or Andalucia. With its capital in Córdoba, the Islamic caliphate in Spain was a great centre of learning, reviving knowledge of Greek philosophy abandoned in the west since the fall of Rome, and hosted a great era in Jewish culture. Further east, Muslims also held Sicily for 200 years.

To the north, Charles Martel's grandson Charlemagne or "Charles the Great" (768–814) created an empire that included the whole of old Gaul, western Germany and northern Italy, and advanced into the eastern Pyrenees to buttress the frontier with Muslim Andalucia.

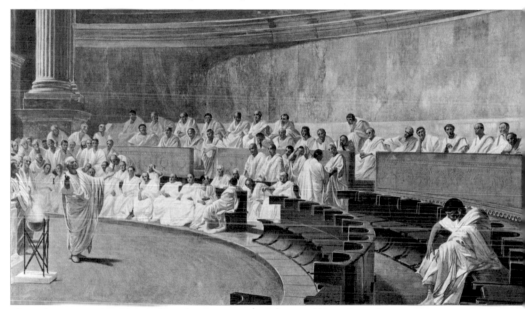

Cicero asks Rome to unite against Catiline, whose conspiracy of 63 BC attempted to overthrow the senate.

east of the Rhine. The Roman popes' claims to authority over all Christians were not accepted by the Eastern Empire, and the rift this created between Catholicism and the eastern Orthodox Churches continues to this day.

Islam and the Holy Roman Emperor

A greater challenge came in the 7th century, with the emergence of Islam. In 711 Muslim armies crossed into Spain from Morocco, and by 732 they reached as far north as Tours in France, where they were defeated by the Frankish leader, Charles Martel. They retreated south of the Pyrenees, but controlled most of Spain and Portugal for the next 500 years, creating a

The Church saw this new empire as a potential return to the stability that had been lost since the fall of Rome, and on Christmas Day 800 Charlemagne was crowned in Rome by the pope, with the new title of "Holy Roman Emperor". The Frankish Empire did not last, though, and 40 years later split into three, the western part eventually developing into France. The title of Holy Roman Emperor would pass to German kings, but, with no definition of what powers it gave, it would be a bone of contention between rulers and popes for centuries.

Europe still suffered more invasions, by the pagan Vikings from Scandinavia, attacking by sea from around 800. Initially they only raided around the coast, pillaging the wealthy monasteries, but soon raised their ambitions, sailing up rivers and seizing lands for themselves. In 911 the western Frankish king acknowledged a Viking chieftain, Rollo, as ruler of a large area of northern France, in return for his becoming a Christian. The new Duchy of Normandy – land of the Northmen – had far greater real power than its theoretical overlords the French kings. A century later Norman lords travelled to Italy as mercenaries, carving out a kingdom of their own, and in 1066 William the Conqueror, Duke of Normandy, made himself King of England.

Crusaders at Damietta, from Le Miroir Historial de Vincent de Beauvais, 15th century.

The feudal world

The society that formed during the "Dark Ages" following the fall of Rome was a mix of leftovers from the Roman world and the customs of the Franks and other Germanic peoples. Urban life had virtually disintegrated – though a little less so in Italy – and most of Europe was a world of rustic villages. The system called feudalism was one of mutual obligations. A local lord and his heirs were given authority over an area by a king to whom they swore loyalty as a vassal, while the king also had an obligation to support his vassals against third parties. Similar obligations were repeated down the social pyramid to peasants, who as serfs had to work their masters' land in return for their supposed protection.

The first kingdoms this created were inherently unstable. A ruler might supposedly have authority over a vast area – like Charlemagne – but this was only effective so long as he retained his vassals' respect. Much of Europe – most of Germany, Italy and the Netherlands – consisted of a shifting patchwork of counties and duchies with no central authority. Even where there was theoretically a king, as in France, the struggle to impose royal authority on great nobles would be a constant theme of the next few centuries.

Christendom and the Crusades

The Christian Church was the single biggest influence on European culture in this era. Missionary monastic communities had been founded in every region to spread the new religion, instructing surrounding communities in the faith and acting as centres of contemplation

ROMAN LEGACIES

Rome's most enduring legacies are its alphabet, and Latin-based languages like Italian, French or Spanish. Many of the characteristic structures that the Romans erected across their empire can also still be seen all over Europe, such as the famous aqueducts of Segovia in Spain and the Pont du Gard in France, or giant baths *(thermae)* like those at Trier in Germany.

Others traces are less obvious. In Italy, most main highways out of the capital are still more or less in line with the great roads of ancient Rome, such as the Via Aurelia towards Tuscany or the Via Appia to Brindisi. In Gaul (modern France) the

Romans built over 20,000km (12,500 miles) of roads, and the *Route Nationale 7* along the Rhone Valley is only one of many modern highways that follow a Roman road, the Via Agrippa.

Roman cities also followed a pattern. Every new Roman town had at its centre a crossing of two roads, the *decumanus* running east–west and the *cardo* north–south. Around this crossing was an open space, the forum, which served as a meeting-place and market. Some of Europe's most atmospheric squares and streets stand on these Roman crossroads, such as Plaça Sant Jaume in Barcelona or the Schildergasse in Cologne.

and learning. St Benedict had laid down the rules of monastic life in his first monasteries in Italy in the 520s.

In the depths of the "Dark Ages", the only written culture that survived was in the monasteries, and all learning and literacy was acquired in monastic schools. Monasteries also received large gifts of land from kings and aristocrats, who hoped thereby to receive "treasure" in heaven.

Religiosity and warrior feudalism could also be combined, as in the Crusades, military expeditions blessed by the Church. In the 1090s

Buying favours, from a 13th-century manuscript from the Bibliothèque Municipale, Tours, France.

Pope Urban II promised benefits in heaven to all Christians who helped the Byzantine emperor resist attacks from the Seljuk Turks. An army of knights sailed east, and seized Jerusalem in a savage siege. They established a Crusader kingdom in Palestine, which lasted nearly 100 years until Sultan Salah-ad-Din retook Jerusalem in 1187. Despite the Third Crusade, a massive campaign led by the kings of England and France, the Christians never held Jerusalem again. The last real Crusade was the Ninth, in 1271.

The Crusades were a mix of religious zeal and crude greed and self-interest, and as time went on their motives became muddier. "Military Orders" of knights such as the Templars were founded to fight these holy wars, bound by religious discipline adapted from that of monks.

The crusading impulse also found outlets within Europe. In Spain, the power of *Al Andalus* had long confined the Christians to tiny kingdoms in the northern mountains, where Asturias developed into the kingdom of Castile, and the former "Spanish March" of Charlemagne's empire grew into Catalonia. In 1031, though, the caliphate of Córdoba fell apart into feuding emirates, which gave the Christians their chance. In 1086, they took Toledo. There was a Muslim revival in the 12th century, but after 1200 the Christian kingdoms were victorious, with Portugal pushing down along the Atlantic coast, Castile seizing Córdoba and Seville in 1247–8 and the Catalan-Aragonese kings taking Valencia and the Balearic Islands. By 1300, Granada was left as the only Muslim kingdom in Western Europe.

Towns and trade

Militant religion was only one aspect of an increasingly complex society. From around 1100, there was a revival of urban life and trade. Particularly important was a unique city, Venice, founded on islands in a lagoon around 500 by Romans escaping barbarian invaders. Since it held no land, its main source of wealth was soon trade, and as an independent republic it was governed by merchants, not landowners. Venice became Europe's great gateway to the east, trading with the Byzantine Empire, the Islamic world and Asia.

Another centre of early wealth was Flanders, where Bruges, Lille and other towns grew rich on weaving and the trade in English wool. In northern Germany, port cities such as Lübeck and Hamburg expanded through trade in timber, furs and other products from the Baltic.

Kings often gave towns important privileges, seeing them as allies against disobedient lords. Cities were also centres of the Church, the seats of its bishops.

The twelfth and thirteenth centuries were the great age of medieval cathedral building, with the creation – or rebuilding, to replace earlier versions – of Gothic masterpieces like Notre-Dame in Paris (1163–1240s). The monasteries also lost their monopoly on education, which was taken up by cathedral schools in the cities. In the 12th century, these developed into Europe's first universities, in Bologna, Paris and Oxford.

Power struggles between bishops and secular lords were common, but even the most ruthless medieval baron showed some respect for the Church, feared challenging it directly, and relied on priests and monks to staff his administration.

Plague and revolt

Europe's advances seemed to halt in the 14th century. Partly this was due to particularly bitter wars, such as the Hundred Years War between England and France, which began in 1337

Joan of Arc, burnt as a heretic in Rouen in 1431.

when the English King Edward III claimed the French throne.

Most telling was a range of natural catastrophes. In the early 1300s exceptionally cold winters led to widespread famine. Then in 1347 the Black Death, bubonic plague, arrived in Europe from Asia, and within a few years wiped out from one third to one half of the continent's entire population.

The shock of the plague was felt in many ways, including a new questioning of authority. The Church was already in crisis, notoriously corrupt and with rival claimants for the pope's throne. The plague placed immense strains on a feudal system already undermined by the growth of trade. With so many fewer serfs, landowners demanded more labour from those left, but were less and less able to force them to comply. The last years of the century saw bloody peasants' revolts across Europe, which were often crushed just as bloodily.

Revival, Renaissance and discovery

But, within a few decades, European culture entered perhaps its most radically expansive era. In the cities of northern Italy, the multi-faceted phenomenon known as the Renaissance, germinating through the previous 200 years, came into full flower after 1400 – a combination of a new awareness of classical Greek and Roman thought, a new spirit of humanist enquiry, and, of course, a new approach to art and architecture. The rich wool-trading and banking city of Florence was the Renaissance's first great centre. In 1436, the dome of its cathedral (*Duomo*) was completed by Brunelleschi, and was a

---

MEDIEVAL BUILDERS

During the Middle Ages architectural styles spread rapidly across Europe, partly because different monastic orders favoured particular styles. Initially deployed only in religious buildings, they then also appeared in castles and civic buildings.

Byzantine architecture spread from Constantinople in the east, and was influential not only in Greece but also in Venice. In the 10th century, the Romanesque style – so called because its rounded arches and solid grandeur appeared to resemble ancient Roman architecture – appeared in northern Italy and spread throughout Europe over the next 200 years, with particularly beautiful examples in Normandy and Catalonia.

It was followed by the Gothic style, expressing a new airiness and grace, typified by pointed arches, vaulted ceilings, flying buttresses and lofty windows with stained glass. Northern France was its first home, with the first great Gothic church at St Denis near Paris (1137–44), rapidly followed by masterpieces such as the cathedrals at Laon (begun about 1160) and Chartres (1193–1250). As Gothic spread it took on local characteristics in every country, and its non-religious uses included the luxurious Venetian Gothic of *palazzi* such as the Ca d'Oro on Venice's Grand Canal, or northern mansions like the Maison Jacques Cœur in Bourges in France.

benchmark in Renaissance architecture. From Tuscany the Renaissance soon spread to rival Italian cities like Milan and Venice, taking on different characteristics wherever it went.

The papacy had been definitively re-established in Rome in 1417, and from around 1450, successive popes would also be great sponsors of Renaissance art and architecture, spending massively on rebuilding their capital. To fund this they called for extra contributions from all over Europe.

An event that appeared a Christian disaster, the conquest of Constantinople and Greece

Europe. In Spain, the two main Christian monarchies were unified in 1469 by the marriage of Ferdinand of Aragon and Queen Isabella of Castile. In 1492 they seized Granada, the last Muslim foothold in Spain.

Newly effective states could look beyond their borders. The Portuguese sent explorers down the coast of Africa and round to India. And in 1492 Christopher Columbus, sponsored by Ferdinand and Isabella, made his first voyage to discover America. For the first time ever, the hub of Europe's attention would shift from the Mediterranean to the Atlantic.

Portrait of Huguenot leader John Calvin.

Martin Luther, who led the Reformation.

by the Ottoman Turks in 1453, also aided the Renaissance, since many Greek scholars fled west, bringing valuable manuscripts. Renaissance ideas spread beyond Italy, and were expressed in the work of humanist writers such as the Dutch scholar Erasmus (1466–1536). In 1450 Johannes Gutenberg set up the first true printing press in Mainz in Germany, and the invention of printing would be of incalculable importance in spreading all new ideas.

The century also saw political changes. In some countries, more powerful states were finally taking shape. Although the English have ignored the fact, the Hundred Years War was a clear French victory, and France's kings emerged from it wealthy and ready to be a power in

THE WORLD BEYOND EUROPE

Before the voyages of discovery of the 1490s Europeans' knowledge of the rest of the world was extremely vague, often based on legends or second-hand stories from Arab travellers. Some popes sent monks on long journeys to make contact with China. Venice and its competitor Genoa were the great hubs for trade with the east, importing silks, spices and other luxuries, and it was accordingly a Venetian trader, Marco Polo, who was the most famous medieval traveller, describing a stay of 24 years at the court of the Mongol emperor in 1271–95. Some say he made it all up, but Polo's book was extraordinarily influential across Europe.

CONQUERORS OF THE WORLD

Despite the conflicts of religious schisms, Europe
forged ahead in science, trade, warfare and the arts,
and came to dominate the world, for good or bad.

Around 1500, Portugal and Spain began carving out the first European intercontinental empires. The Portuguese set up trading posts in Asia, and Columbus and his successors occupied Caribbean islands for Spain. By a 1494 treaty they tried to divide the entire world outside Europe between them, but this was never accepted by other European powers, who sent out explorers of their own.

Global empire

Spain became the first worldwide empire. The first discoveries were followed by far larger conquests in Mexico, in the 1520s, and Peru in the 1530s. Charles V (1516–1556), Ferdinand and Isabella's grandson, inherited not only Spain and its empire but also former territories of the dukes of Burgundy in the Netherlands and, through his other grandfather, the Habsburg lands in Germany, Austria

Ghirlandaio's Columbus, c.1520.

> Charles V has been called the first pan-
> European ruler, and supposedly said,
> "I speak Spanish to God, Italian to
> women, French to men and German
> to my horse."

and northern Italy and the title of Holy Roman Emperor. The Spanish Habsburgs thought themselves uniquely favoured by providence, as God's power on earth.

Charles V was constantly at war. In the Mediterranean he fought the Ottoman Turks. His inheritance surrounded France, and for 150 years every French ruler would see it as vital to break this Habsburg ring around them.

During Charles's reign, his armies defeated all before them.

These years saw the full flowering of the Renaissance in Italy. One of the first great non-Italian enthusiasts for the Renaissance was King François I of France (1515–47), who imported Italian artists and architects, invited Leonardo da Vinci to spend his last years in Amboise (bringing the *Mona Lisa*) and built lavish Loire châteaux in the new "French Renaissance" style. However, the Popes and other Italian states had to be wary in intriguing with the greater European powers. In 1527, Charles V's armies took the pro-French Pope Clement VII prisoner, and his undisciplined troops sacked Rome.

The Reformation

These conflicts would be subsumed within a much broader rift, the Reformation, as Protestant Christians (so called because they "protested" against Catholic dogmas) broke with the Catholic Church. Groups that rejected the Church's claims to be the sole intermediary between God and man and denounced corrupt priests had existed throughout the Middle Ages, but appeared on an all-new scale in the questioning Renaissance world. The vast sums required by the popes for Renaissance Rome intensified resentment at the Church's extrava-

Portrait of Cosimo I by Bronzino.

gance. Printing helped spread new ideas.

In 1517 Martin Luther, a German priest, posted up his "Ninety-Five Theses" in Wittenberg denouncing the Church's practice of selling absolution from sins for money. Condemned by the pope, Luther refused to back down, and towns and princes across northern Germany supported him. Lutheran ideas spread rapidly across Northern Europe. The next major Reformation figure was John Calvin, originally French, who preached a more austere Protestantism that rejected all traditional Catholic imagery as idol-worship. Calvin took refuge in the free Swiss city of Geneva in the 1540s, and his ideas took root especially in the northern Netherlands and Scotland.

The Catholic response was intransigent. In Germany an uneasy compromise allowed the various princes to decide the religion of their territories. In 1545 Pope Paul III called a special council at Trent in Italy to decide the Church's reply to these upheavals. Lasting 18 years, the Council of Trent initiated the "Counter-Reformation", reaffirming the unique authority of the popes and Catholic tradition, and calling for unorthodox ideas to be suppressed. New religious orders taught correct doctrine and implemented the militant Counter-Reformation spirit, most famously the Jesuits, founded by the Spanish former soldier St Ignatius Loyola.

Defenders of their faiths

Paranoia grew on both sides, as conflicts generated intense hatreds. In 1556 Charles V abdicated and divided his vast possessions, giving Austria and the Holy Roman Empire to his brother Ferdinand and Spain and the Netherlands to his son Philip II (1556–98). Philip's efforts to re-impose Catholic orthodoxy on the Protestant northern Netherlands led to a bloody 40-year war. He also confronted the new Protestant power of England, who aided the Dutch, culminating in the failed attempted invasion by the Spanish Armada in 1588. Philip had success in the Mediterranean, defeating the Turks at sea at Lepanto in Greece in 1571, but by 1600 constant wars had left Spain nearly bankrupt despite all its New World American wealth.

Conflict was especially bitter in France, where there was a Catholic majority but growing communities of Protestants, known as Huguenots. A massacre of Protestants in 1562 was the spark

CULT FIGURES

In the fervent atmosphere of the Reformation, all kinds of cults and sects flourished. One of the most radical was the Anabaptists, who rejected Catholic and Protestant authorities and social hierarchies, and believed that among the "elect" of true believers, all property should be held in common. They united Catholics and Protestants, who both persecuted them. In 1534 Anabaptists took over the German town of Munster and made it their "New Jerusalem", but their commune was bloodily suppressed. Spiritual descendants of the Anabaptists survive today in sects like the Amish and Mennonites, who fled to the Americas to escape persecution.

During the Counter-Reformation, Michelangelo's Last Judgement fresco in the Sistine Chapel in the Vatican was denounced for excessive nudity, the inclusion of pagan figures, and for showing Christ without a beard.

for years of vicious fighting. In 1572, some 10,000 Huguenots were killed in Paris in the "St Bartholomew's Day Massacre". Aristocratic rivalries played a part, and Spain intervened on one side and England and the Dutch on the other.

The arts after 1550

In Catholic countries, the Counter-Reformation ended the relatively free-thinking atmosphere of the early Italian Renaissance and demanded an emphatically religious approach in art, as in the "mannerist" paintings of Titian or the work of El Greco in Spain.

After 1600, this led to the extravagant Baroque style, exemplified by the sculpture and architecture of Bernini in Rome or the paintings of Rubens. Conceived to present the Church and its beliefs with maximum grandeur, Baroque was also used to exalt monarchs such as the Spanish and French kings. Protestant art would be more realist in style, as in the scenes of everyday life by Dutch Golden Age artists like Rembrandt or Vermeer.

This was also one of the greatest eras for European literature. In England, of course, it saw the immense genius of Shakespeare and Elizabethan theatre. Spain's "Golden Century" produced the first great European novel, Cervantes's *Don Quixote*, and other great plays, poetry and stories, many evoking – as in the case of *Don Quixote* – the distance between dreams and realities.

Germany's cataclysm

In France, the Wars of Religion ended after 1589 when the heir to the throne, the Huguenot Henri IV, agreed to become a Catholic to be accepted as king. In 1598 he established toleration for Protestants. The Dutch had effectively won independence by the early 1600s, and were building a their own trading empire; Dutch mariners such as Abel Tasman were the also first Europeans to explore the South Pacific.

In Germany, however, the religious divide produced one final massive explosion, the

Thirty Years War of 1618–48. Tensions had simmered for 70 years, and an attempt by the Austrian emperor to impose his authority on Protestants in Bohemia triggered a generalised war. Spain supported its kings' Catholic cousins the Austrian Habsburgs, while the Dutch, Sweden and other states joined in with the Protestants. France played a dual role, as King Louis XIII's great minister Richelieu, though a Catholic cardinal, was happy to ally himself with Protestants in pursuit of France's overriding strategic aim, of destroying Spain's power around its borders.

Botticelli's Judith, Uffizi Gallery, Florence.

Germany lost as much as 40 percent of its population, through war, disease and famine. The Peace of Westphalia in 1648 recognised the division of Germany and Austria between a largely Protestant north and Catholic south. Through this war, too, and the parallel Franco-Spanish war that continued until 1659, Spanish pre-eminence in Europe had been decisively undermined.

The Sun King

Dynastic and commercial power struggles again became the major element in political affairs. The power of kings was greatly enhanced. Grandest and most absolute monarch of them all was Louis XIV of France, which by the time he took over full powers in 1661 aged 23 had emphatically replaced Spain as the dominant power in Europe. Louis presented himself almost as the centre of the world, the "Sun King". The extravagance of his court is legendary, and he built a vast showcase for himself in the Palace of Versailles.

Louis's ambitions also required frequent wars, pushing France's frontiers eastwards. The potential scale of French dominance, though, aroused opposition, from Austria, the Netherlands and England. In the War of the Spanish Succession of 1701–14 – so called because Louis proposed his grandson the Duke

Combat devant l'Hôtel de Ville de Paris le 28 Juillet 1830, by Jean Schnetz (1787–1870).

of Anjou as heir to the vacant Spanish throne – French power was held back, and suffered major defeats. By the time Louis XIV died in 1715, France was in debt and exhausted.

New worlds

As religious warfare faded away many other changes came to the fore. One of the most fundamental was a transformation in the role of science. In 1543 a Polish priest, Nicholas Copernicus, published the first full presentation of the theory that the earth revolved around the sun. The great Italian polymath Galileo substantiated the theory, but was persecuted by the Catholic Church, which insisted that religious scripture, not observation, was

the basis of knowledge, and that the sun still revolved around the earth.

It was in northern Protestant countries and France that the "scientific revolution" really gained momentum. In the Netherlands, Van Leeuwenhoek made the first modern microscope. In England, Harvey described the circulation of the blood, and from the 1650s Isaac Newton and Robert Boyle laid down the fundamentals of physics and chemistry. In France, where René Descartes defined the scientific method in the 1630s, Pascal and Fermat made enormous advances in mathematics.

Huge economic changes were equally part of the era. The realignment of Europe to the Atlantic left the Mediterranean and its trading cities like Venice as relative backwaters. Elsewhere, cities such as Paris, London and Amsterdam grew with unheard-of speed. Worldwide commerce brought in new products: spices and porcelain from Asia, tea, chocolate. In 1683 the Ottoman Sultan unsuccessfully besieged Vienna, and this Turkish invasion is credited with introducing Europe to coffee.

Slavery and empire

Slavery was central to the production of the two most profitable new commodities, sugar and tobacco. The slave trade had begun in Spanish colonies in the 1500s, and reached a peak in the 18th century. Britain, France and the Netherlands all seized their own Caribbean colonies to plant with sugar and tobacco. The "triangular trade" developed, in which ships sailed from Europe with guns and manufactured goods with which to buy slaves in Africa, then crossed the Atlantic with them and returned home with American produce. Atlantic ports grew rich on this trade, and in Britain and France the immense profits played a major part in economic growth.

The Atlantic powers established other colonial possessions. The English founded Virginia in 1607, the French Quebec in 1608, and in the 1650s the Dutch founded Cape Town in South Africa. Within Europe, crowns and states continued their customary wars and rivalries. In Germany new states gained weight, notably Prussia in the north, with its capital in Berlin. The spread of colonial outposts, though, meant that wars were now fought on a worldwide scale. Outside Europe the Seven Years War (1756–63) was a contest for global imperial advantage between Britain and France, through which Britain seized Quebec, and laid the basis for the subsequent British Empire, though France kept its Caribbean colonies.

The Enlightenment

The empirical observation encouraged by science was also applied to human institutions, in the 18th-century movement called the Enlightenment. Human reason, it suggested, was the basis of knowledge, rather than dogma and tradition; any institution could be critically examined, including the authorities of state and Church. This raised the possibility of social progress, individual freedom, and that all men – and even women – might have equal status.

The Enlightenment's most famous centre was in France, where Diderot and D'Alembert published their great "Encyclopaedia" and Rousseau produced the most radical proposals yet for a reordering of society on rational, egalitarian lines. In Scotland, thinkers laid great emphasis on liberty, and they were not alone: one of the first applications of Enlightenment thought was in the American Declaration of Independence.

Rulers and aristocrats were fascinated too, but this placed them in a difficult position. Some kings such as Frederick the Great of Prussia (1740–86) sought to apply Enlightenment principles, rationalising administration and promoting economic development. They did so, though, as "Enlightened despots", without giving up any of their powers. Enlightenment ideas, though, inevitably spread beyond the social elites.

The great revolution

The explosion came in France. The monarchy still spent lavishly but was almost bankrupt; aristocrats and the church were exempt from most taxes, which fell on the poor and a growing middle class increasingly frustrated at their exclusion from power. In 1789 a desperate King Louis XVI called a meeting of France's parliament, the Estates-General, ignored since 1615, to discuss new taxes. The house of commoners, the "Third Estate", declared itself a National Assembly and demanded a constitution. In Paris rumours spread of royal plots against

Napoleon Bonaparte.

THE RISE OF MUSIC

One cultural phenomenon that crossed religious divisions in the 17th century was the emergence of classical music. During the Middle Ages and the Renaissance, most European music had been either choral or played on solo instruments or by small groups. A new style with more complex harmonies and early forms of orchestra with more varied instruments developed in northern Italy in the late Renaissance. Monteverdi's *L'Orfeo*, considered the first opera and premièred in Mantua in 1607, was a cornerstone of the new style.

Music crossed borders. The German composer Heinrich Schütz studied in Venice and then took the new style to Dresden in Protestant Saxony in the 1620s, thus laying the foundations of the tradition of German music that came into full flower a century later with Bach and Handel. Baroque orchestral music became fashionable throughout Europe, and rulers appointed "court composers" – like Jean-Baptiste Lully, favourite musician of Louis XIV of France – to enhance their grandeur with majestic background music. Most performances were staged in royal courts, churches or for private aristocratic audiences until well into the 18th century, but the very first public opera house opened in Venice in 1637.

The most enduring product of the French Revolution could be said to be the metric system, designed to replace older, complicated systems of measurement in 1795, and taken up across the world in the next century.

the people, and on 14 July a mob stormed the Bastille prison.

The spell of royal authority was broken. All kinds of ideas circulated freely, and the Assembly declared the Rights of Man and

Goethe in the Roman Campagna, by Johann Tischbein, 1787.

approved an extraordinary range of measures to remake France on a rational, egalitarian and patriotic model. This created enormous excitement, but unleashed pent-up fears and hatreds. The revolution's first leaders hoped for a constitutional monarchy, but the atmosphere of violence overwhelmed debates. From 1791 the royal family were virtual prisoners. The belief spread that Louis was in league with Queen Marie Antoinette's Austrian relatives to crush the revolution. In spring 1792, war broke out with Austria and Prussia, and soon Britain and other European monarchies joined the fight against the revolution.

Foreign invasion launched a new burst of patriotic fervour, and the Prussians were

driven back. It was also the spur to the proclamation of a republic in September 1792, and the rise to power of the radical Jacobins led by Robespierre. They denounced moderates as traitors, and in the "Terror" of 1793–4 thousands were executed by guillotine, including Louis XVI and his queen.

A more pragmatic government brought the Terror to an end. The French Republic was still at war with most of Europe, but its citizen armies, fired with revolutionary ardour, overwhelmed old-style mercenary armies. Everywhere French armies went they replaced centuries-old institutions with new ones on the French model. The excitement local radicals felt was tempered when they found these new "republics" were expected to be no more than puppets.

Napoleon – the ultimate ego

The republic was still unstable, and in 1799, its most successful general, Napoleon Bonaparte, seized power as dictator or "First Consul". Five years later, he made himself emperor, with all-new monarchical grandeur.

With incredible energy Napoleon reformed every institution he could find, from France's legal system (in the *Code Napoléon*) to its roads. Above all, he was a great general. His navy may have been beaten by the British, but on land he seemed invincible: in 1805–6 he defeated the Austrians and Russians at Austerlitz and the Prussians at Jena, and most of continental Europe was at his feet.

He overreached himself when he invaded Spain and Portugal, in 1808, and Russia in 1812. All Europe was united against him, and in 1814 he had to abdicate. Despite the attempt to return the next year, ending in his defeat at Waterloo, the Napoleonic epic was over.

Picking up the pieces

The victorious powers held a congress in Vienna to decide the new face of Europe. In France Louis XVIII, Louis XVI's brother, was restored as king. The old Dutch Republic was made a kingdom and united with the southern Netherlands, though these broke away in 1830 as Belgium and Luxembourg. Italy and Germany were still split into many states, and Italian affairs were dominated by Austria. Spain was left in tatters, and most of its American colonies had taken advantage of Napoleon's invasion to declare independence. Elsewhere, countries with colonies mostly followed the British example over the next decades in abolishing slavery. The European powers united later to help Greece regain independence from Turkey, in 1832. At home, though, the ministers in Vienna expected radical ideas to be kept down as much as possible.

However, the whirlwinds of the revolution and Napoleonic rule had brought too many changes to be brushed away. In France, the restored monarchy introduced only a very limited constitution. In other countries, French occupation had introduced the possibility of radical change, and also stimulated previously unseen feelings of nationalism. Romanticism, the other great current of this age, also encouraged both nationalism and ambitious ideals.

Simultaneously, the economic transformations of the 19th century were gaining pace. The Industrial Revolution had been growing since the 1780s in Britain, but after 1815, coalmines, iron foundries, textile factories and industrial towns also appeared in Belgium, northern France and Germany's Ruhr Valley. Industry brought a new working class, and urbanisation. New industries had immense effects on everyday life, and from the 1830s, railways reduced the remoteness of rural regions significantly.

Revolt and national unification

Tensions came to a boil again in 1848. In France, King Louis-Philippe was overthrown and the Second Republic proclaimed universal suffrage, at least for men. This was the trigger for revolts all over Europe, as radicals took to the streets of Vienna, Berlin and other cities to demand democratic freedoms, and seemed to have governments on the run. In Italy, revolutionaries founded provisional republics in Venice and Rome.

Back in France, however, the new electorate chose Louis Napoleon, nephew of the great Napoleon, who subsequently, as president, and in true Bonapartist style, declared himself Emperor Napoleon III. In Central Europe, the governments of Austria and Prussia, aided by Russia, held their nerve and hit back, re-establishing authority and crushing the Italian republics despite heroic resistance.

This failure of Romantic radicalism indicated to many Italian and German nationalists

that they could only achieve their aims with the support of an established state. In Italy the most romantic 19th-century freedom fighter, Giuseppe Garibaldi, still played a role with his red-shirted volunteers in overthrowing the Kingdom of Naples in 1860, but it was the Kingdom of Piedmont that did most, with French aid, to end Austrian power in the north, and it was the Piedmontese king, Victor Emmanuel II, who became the first king of a united Italy in 1861.

In Germany, liberal nationalists had never known how to deal with the problem that there

Garibaldi's Rout of Neapolitan Forces in Calatafimi, Sicily, by R. Legat.

were two powerful states, Prussia and Austria, one of which also had large non-German possessions like Hungary. This dilemma was solved when the Prussian prime minister Bismarck initiated a new Prussian-led move to German unity by the simple means of excluding Austria, with the Austro-Prussian War of 1866. In 1870, Bismarck astutely provoked Napoleon III into declaring war on Prussia, which he knew would lead other German states to accept unification under Prussian leadership.

To widespread shock, the French armies were overwhelmed, Napoleon III was taken prisoner and abdicated, and in January 1871 the German Empire was proclaimed with the Prussian king as Kaiser Wilhelm I.

> *Bismarck was renowned for his cynical sayings, such as "When you want to fool the world, tell the truth," or "Never believe anything in politics until it has been officially denied."*

A provisional Third French Republic continued resistance. Paris was besieged through the winter of 1870–1, and when its militia rejected the peace terms accepted by a new government in March 1871 they set up a revolutionary

The Berlin–Potsdam railway, 1843.

Commune, which was crushed by French troops with ferocious reprisals.

Another movement that emerged after 1880, Art Nouveau, sought to integrate industrial materials and techniques with often voluptuous natural imagery, and laid great stress on incorporating all the arts, especially architecture, and design from Metro entrances to furniture. The fluid forms of Art Nouveau glorified European cities in the early 20th century, and can be seen at their most fantastic in the work of Gaudí in Barcelona.

Europe's glory days

The Franco-Prussian War was the last major war in Western Europe for 43 years, and the Paris Commune the last burst of the French revolutionary tradition from 1789. For many Europeans, especially in the middle and upper classes, the "long peace" from 1871 to 1914 would seem like a golden age.

There was still great poverty in large parts of Europe, reflected in large-scale emigration to the Americas. For others, though, the whole 19th century appeared an age of marvels, as one invention emerged after another: railways in the 1830s were followed by photography in the 1840s, then the telegraph, electric lighting, antiseptics, motor vehicles… The middle classes could explore their countries by train, build holiday villas by the sea and even try skiing in the Swiss Alps.

This was also a great age for innovation in the arts. The Impressionists and their successors were transforming painting, and composers like Debussy were creating new patterns in music.

NEW ROMANTICISM

Romanticism swept through Europe at the beginning of the 19th century, with enormous effects in many areas of life. It was, in part, a reaction against the apparently cold rationalism of the Enlightenment, and a way of trying to make sense of the world in the light of the social dislocations brought about by the French Revolution. It was also a reaction against the ugliness of the Industrial Revolution.

In place of pure rationalism, spontaneity, subjectivity and individualism, drama and strong sensations came to the fore. One of Romanticism's precursors was Rousseau, who had idealised the "noble savage", a natural, uncorrupted human state

superior to the world of convention. Romanticism also created the figure of the romantic, celebrity artist. Lord Byron was one of its first star figures, whose 1812 poem *Childe Harold's Pilgrimage* with its lonely tragic hero caused a sensation across Europe, inspiring many other writers. Romanticism encouraged a new appreciation of history and folk tradition – including languages like Catalan – and a new fascination with nature as a source of beauty and spiritual strength, attitudes that have soaked into modern culture in countless ways. It was said of Rousseau that he was the first man ever to climb a mountain for pleasure.

Writers like Zola, Ibsen and Tolstoy forced their readers to face difficult truths.

Europe has never bossed the rest of the world as much as it did in these years. The French had taken over Algeria in the 1930s, and later seized huge swathes of Africa, in competition with their foremost imperial rivals the British. Even a small country like Belgium and the latecomers Italy and Germany joined vigorously in the "scramble" for colonies. Across the world European powers – with the increasing participation, too, of the United States – imposed their political

Before the storm

In this self-satisfied world, many did not look for causes of anxiety. Some planned for socialist revolution, and others felt threatened by it. More dangerous was the belligerent nationalism of rival states. A web of alliances linked the competing powers: Germany – which since unification had rapidly become the foremost industrial power in Europe – was allied with Austria-Hungary, while France had a pact with Russia and a growing understanding with Britain. This system ran the risk of exploding at any time.

A late 19th-century view of wealthy Europeans at leisure in Monte-Carlo.

and economic systems, even in countries like China that were too big to colonise.

At home, most countries of Western Europe had made some moves towards democratic government by 1900, extending voting rights for men (scarcely any yet gave votes to women). The middle classes were now patriotic citizens; the major threat to the system was seen as the industrial working class. Labour unions and socialist movements of different degrees of radicalism appeared in most countries. Bismarck, always original, was one of the first in Europe to introduce forms of social welfare or "state socialism", such as health insurance, to blunt the socialist appeal. The spread of state primary education meant that most Europeans could read and write.

NEW ART MOVEMENTS

French Impressionism emerged in the 1860s when, rejecting the laborious draughtsmanship and restricted subjects of "official" art and seeking to capture the true patterns of light, artists painted straight from nature, using free, loose brushwork. Scorned by the official Paris Salon, Manet, Renoir, Degas, Monet and others held their own exhibitions.

Then came the Post-Impressionists such as Cézanne, Gauguin and Van Gogh, who emphasised strong colours and powerful emotions. In France they were followed by the *Fauves* (literally the "Wild Beasts") like Matisse and Derain, whose radical experiments with colour presaged abstract art.

French soldiers in a trench at Verdun, 1916.

MODERN TIMES

Europe tore itself apart twice in the 20th century,
but from the ruins of war created an era of peace
and prosperity.

In June 1914 the assassination of an Austrian archduke by a Serbian nationalist in Bosnia sparked off the first of the two 20th-century conflagrations in which Europe unleashed unprecedented carnage on itself and on the world. World War I left over 16 million dead by November 1918, in murderous, mechanised fighting that confounded all the complacent expectations of easy victories of 1914.

The "Great War" disrupted societies in countless ways. In 1917, the Bolshevik Revolution led by Lenin had already taken one combatant, Russia, out of the war. The threat of Communism struck fear among established regimes on both sides. In late 1918 the German armies were in retreat, but it was also the government's fear of losing control to workers' revolts at home that led it to accept the armistice, and the Kaiser to abdicate.

A new map

The map of Europe was redrawn, especially in the east. The Austro-Hungarian, Turkish and Russian empires collapsed and new nations emerged in Czechoslovakia, Poland and Hungary. Germany lost Alsace-Lorraine, taken from France in 1871, and large areas in the east to Poland. A German Republic was founded in the town of Weimar and negotiated for peace, but it faced permanent challenges on right and left.

The victorious Western Allies had suggested their aim was "to make the world safe for democracy", and the Fourteen Point peace plan put forward by US President Wilson augured a new era in international relations. However, the war in the west had largely been fought in France, which demanded that Germany pay for its recovery, and the Versailles Peace Treaty of 1919 imposed crippling financial reparations.

An artist's impression of the assassination.

With all its problems, though, Germany could not pay, and the crisis this led to in 1923 was only resolved with American loans.

Revolution and reaction

Peace treaties did not end Europe's instability. The war had also intensified social conflicts, bringing galloping inflation. Many countries saw waves of strikes in 1918–20, and many socialists affiliated to the Communist International. However, in the post-war dislocation, cities were also full of young men with military training, but no prospects of work, who felt no attraction for internationalist Communism but formed a natural recruiting-ground for the extreme right. In

> At one time Mussolini wanted to stop Italians eating pasta, because he thought it made them lazy, pessimistic and unwarlike. The campaign didn't get very far.

Germany, right-wing militias had already formed in 1919.

In Italy established society gave growing support to a new movement led by Benito Mussolini, formerly a revolutionary socialist. Around 1920, in forming a uniformed militia

Hitler crossing the Czech border in 1939.

(the famous Blackshirts), Mussolini and his associates defined "Fascism", a term taken from the *Fasces* that were a symbol of authority in ancient Rome. He despised parliamentary government and unpatriotic Communism equally; instead, the Fascist ideal was an authoritarian, intensely nationalist state in which class divisions would be dissolved within the united nation.

An energetic state would bring social progress more effectively than Communism, and any dissent would be deemed antipatriotic. In 1922 Mussolini launched his "March on Rome", effectively a *coup d'état*, and King Victor Emmanuel III made him head of government.

Dictatorships took over other countries with weak parliamentary regimes. Portugal fell under military rule in 1926, and in Spain a dictatorship was installed in 1923 under General Miguel Primo de Rivera.

The Jazz Age

Political events were not Europeans' only concerns. As the 1920s went on the economy revived, helped greatly by US investment, and people had more time to assimilate other aspects of the postwar environment. World War I had brought huge changes in the position of women, filling jobs left by men. Women were rarely allowed to keep these jobs if men returned, but many changes in attitudes were permanent. Most countries gave women the vote.

The diffuse psychological legacy of the war – mixing deep sadness, and a pent-up desire for pleasure and excitement – found outlets in the hedonism of the Jazz Age, with its capitals in Paris and Berlin. Jazz music, dancing,

EXPERIMENTAL ART

Artistic experiment flourished in Europe in the 1920s and '30s, as painters, writers, architects and film-makers strove to make sense of a disjointed post-war world in which pre-1914 certainties no longer seemed to reflect personal experience, and all kinds of conventions were questioned. In Paris, the cafés of Montparnasse hummed with all kinds of new ideas, and a cosmopolitan clientele that included Picasso, Hemingway and James Joyce, who published his ground-breaking *Ulysses* in 1922. The avant-garde Surrealist movement inspired paintings by Magritte, Ernst, De Chirico, Miró and Dalí. In Germany, the Bauhaus School produced startlingly modernist architectural designs with functional lines, while the more sensuous Art Deco introduced innovative geometric forms to household objects.

Experimental plays were produced by Bertholt Brecht in Germany, Pirandello in Italy and Cocteau in France, but new styles also found a natural home in new media, especially the cinema. Films like Fritz Lang's 1927 science-fiction fantasy *Metropolis* made revolutionary use of expressionist imagery and Art Deco forms, and in 1929, the Spaniards Luis Buñuel and Salvador Dalí shocked audiences with the first two real Surrealist films, *Un Chien Andalou* and *L'Age d'Or*.

the cinema, radio, mass sports like football or motor racing were inexpensive and accessible to ever-wider circles of people.

The Crash

This brittle atmosphere was abruptly transformed by the Wall Street Crash in September 1929. Within just a few months, this stock market collapse led to a worldwide economic crisis, the Great Depression. The American boom and US loans had played a major part in Europe's recovery, especially in Germany. Without them, German unemployment

parties had been banned, the *Gestapo* police given sweeping powers and Hitler declared the *Führer* or leader of a new dictatorship.

Liberal governments seemed incapable of dealing with the misery of the Depression. Fascist regimes, inherently aggressive, were on the march. In 1935 Mussolini conquered Abyssinia (modern Ethiopia). Hitler had renounced the Versailles treaty and begun rebuilding the German army, and, in 1936 sent troops back into the Rhineland, demilitarised under Versailles. The League of Nations, formed after World War I, was incapable of imposing its will on the dictators.

General Dwight D. Eisenhower and his generals in the war-devastated Polish capital, Warsaw.

reached 30 percent by 1932.

This placed immense strain on the weak Weimar Republic. The Communist Party grew rapidly; the Communists were soon outmanoeuvred, though, by Adolf Hitler's National Socialist or Nazi Party. Founded in 1923, the Nazis had been insignificant, but support mushroomed after the Crash. They appealed to the same sentiments as the Fascists in Italy – intense patriotism, fear of Communism, a longing for authority and decisive government – but added ferocious anti-Semitism, blaming Jews and foreign interference, namely the impositions of the Versailles treaty, for Germany's woes. In January 1933 Hitler was appointed Chancellor or prime minister. Within a few months, opposition

The return to war

A "first act" of the European conflict broke out in Spain. Primo de Rivera's dictatorship had fallen in 1930, and in 1931 the monarchy had been replaced by a shaky republic. In July 1936, after the left had won the elections, a military revolt led by General Francisco Franco was the opener to a three-year civil war. Germany and Italy gave Franco massive support, while the Soviet Union aided the Republican side on a smaller scale, particularly through the "International Brigades" of leftist volunteers. Franco's victory in April 1939 inaugurated a dictatorship that would last until his death in 1975.

The British and French governments sought to avoid war by conceding what were initially

> Half of Germany's schools, a quarter of its homes and around 40 per cent of its transport infrastructure were in ruins in 1945.

presented as Germany's legitimate grievances, the policy of "Appeasement". Aggressive expansionism, though, was inherent in Nazism – as was the stigmatisation and extermination of enemies and minorities, like the Jews – and each success encouraged Hitler to make more demands. In March 1938 he proclaimed the

After the war

The second great conflict was even more destructive than the first. "Total war" hit every part of the population. The Nazis had directly exterminated around 11 million people; Jews, Roma (Gypsies), Poles, homosexuals, political dissidents and others.

At the war's end, Soviet armies occupied the whole of Eastern Europe. Tensions had already grown between Stalin and the Western Allies during the war, and by mid-1946 an "Iron Curtain", in Winston Churchill's phrase, ran between the western camp and the countries

Student protests on the Boulevard St-Germain in Paris in May 1968.

Anschluss, the union of Germany with Austria, and in November the *Kristallnacht* ("Night of Broken Glass", coordinated Nazi attacks on synagogues and Jewish businesses and homes, so called because of the number of broken windows) was the culmination of the exclusion of German (and now Austrian) Jews from normal life, the prelude to their being rounded up in concentration camps.

In September 1938 Britain and France allowed Hitler to seize the Sudetenland, German-speaking areas of Czechoslovakia, on the basis that these were his "final demands". In March the following year, however, he seized the rest of Czechoslovakia, and in September invaded Poland. Full-scale war began.

under Soviet occupation, which soon had Communist regimes. In Greece, liberated by the Western Allies, civil war broke out between Communists and monarchists.

Germany was split in two, as the zones occupied by the Western powers (USA, Britain and France) were united in West Germany in 1949, while the Soviet zone became Communist East Germany. The Western-occupied half of Berlin was an island in a Communist sea, and its isolation was set in stone in 1961 when East Germany built the Berlin Wall to seal the border within the city. Also in 1949 the NATO alliance was formed, committing the United States and most of Western Europe to mutual defence, and the Eastern Bloc formalised its corresponding Warsaw Pact in 1955. For Europeans the "Cold War" between these hostile camps, with the threat of actual war with nuclear weapons always vaguely present, would be a part of life for 45 years, and many assumed it would never end.

Putting Europe back together

When the war ended in May 1945, Europe was in ruins, physically and economically. It would largely remain so until 1947, when the United States announced the Marshall Plan, a massive programme of financial assistance to kick-start the European economy.

By the time Marshall Aid ended in 1952, Europe's revival was self-sustaining, and by the mid-1950s people talked of German and Italian "economic miracles", with rebuilt industries growing at phenomenal rates. While Spain and Portugal remained isolated, most other Western European countries also introduced significantly greater doses of democracy, and were building up the welfare states, social security, healthcare and other kinds of universal social provision that have since been hallmarks of European society.

The economic boom also began another major transformation, attracting immigrants, initially often from countries' former colonies: Indonesians to the Netherlands, North and West Africans to France, while Germany and Switzerland drew in "guestworkers" from Turkey and Yugoslavia.

For former colonial powers, some adaptations to the post-war world were traumatic. France fought unsuccessful wars from 1954–62 to hold on first to Indochina and then Algeria. One million French settlers resisted compromise with the Arab 90 percent of Algeria's population, aided by right-wing army officers. A military coup even seemed likely, until the government returned power to General de Gaulle, leader of French resistance to the Nazis in World War II. He was expected to be the settlers' friend, but even he acknowledged the inevitable and accepted Algerian independence.

Tiny "bubble cars" and Vespa motor scooters were the first motor vehicles many Europeans could afford in the 1950s. Cars very soon got much bigger.

By the mid-1960s France, like Britain, had conceded independence to most of its colonies.

Politicians were more imaginative in the first moves towards another fundamental post-war change, European integration. The impulse first came from French and German politicians who saw economic cooperation as a means of preventing their countries ever again fighting each other. The first practical step was the creation in 1952 of the European Coal and Steel Community, for the joint management of these industries in these two countries, along with Belgium, the Netherlands, Luxembourg and Italy. In 1957, the

A Croatian refugee prepares to flee her village during the civil war in the Balkans.

same countries set up the European Economic Community (EEC) or Common Market, basis of the future European Union.

Rich Europe

In the 1960s ordinary Europeans really began to feel the benefits of the new prosperity. Productivity and incomes grew steadily as post-war austerity faded, and allowed people to enjoy unheard-of leisure time and mobility. Electrical gadgets – washing machines, televisions – soon became essential parts of everyday life, and car ownership and Mediterranean holidays went from luxuries to mass phenomena.

From the 1950s, too, American pop music spread across Europe, often filtered through

Britain via groups like The Beatles, inspiring an all-new youth culture. This was only one aspect of a complex bundle of changes in attitudes, a search for new freedoms – especially sexual – and a questioning of authority and social conventions by the post-war "baby boom" generation. The spirit of the 1960s had arrived.

In some countries this took a more political form. In France, de Gaulle's great concern was to restore the "grandeur" of France after its collapse in 1940, while at home the state retained a traditionally authoritarian style. In May 1968, student protests in Paris mushroomed into

A Federalist demonstrates in Brussels in support of the Lisbon Treaty.

nationwide factory strikes demanding a raft of radical measures. A dismayed President de Gaulle was scarcely able to pacify the situation. Similar radical movements exploded in Germany and many other countries in the following months.

No government was directly overthrown by these movements – although de Gaulle, exhausted, resigned a year later – but over the next decades the "spirit of '68" seeped through society in all kinds of ways, in such things as the new feminism, the movement for gay rights and the general expansion in social freedoms. The new ethnic groups in an ever more diverse Europe – Afro-Caribbeans, South Asians, North Africans – became more assertive and more prominent.

End of the dictatorships

Winds of change also undermined other old certainties. The mid-1970s saw the collapse of Europe's last right-wing dictatorships, in Spain, Portugal and Greece, where a military regime had seized power in 1967. After Franco's death his successor, King Juan Carlos, oversaw a rapid transition to democracy. In the 1980s all three countries joined the European Union, signifying their integration in the European mainstream.

This was a preliminary to an even bigger transformation. The European Communist regimes had seemed immovable, but their economies were stagnant. The reforms initiated by Mikhail Gorbachev in the Soviet Union in 1985 left the Eastern European regimes without their main support, and in 1988–9 all collapsed and gave way to democratic reforms. In Germany, the Berlin Wall came down in November 1989 amid huge rejoicing, the prelude to the reunification of Germany's two halves a year later. Full integration of East Germany and the other Eastern European states with Western economies would bring many problems, but overall German reunification has been a major success. Other eastern countries like Poland also adopted constitutions and policies similar to Western Europe, and joined the EU in 2004–7.

New worries

By the current decade the European Union – the name that replaced the older EEC in 1993 – and its institutions had become the continent's principal political focus, but their effectiveness has been patchy. In some areas the EU and individual European countries have taken a leading role, notably on climate change, introducing a raft of measures to reduce the use of fossil fuels. In other fields, clear-cut action has often been lost in continual negotiation. Countries have tended to see the EU as a vehicle for their own national aims, and the idea of a common European interest has been slow to emerge. Those at the head of the Union have tended to see decisive actions from the top as the best way to advance their aims, most radically with the introduction of the single currency, the euro, adopted by most EU members in 2002.

In the early 2000s Europe was booming, but some still found cause for anxiety. Some argue Europeans are too fond of their past, lazy, and too attached to their social benefits

The most successful pan-European institutions are the Champions' League and Europa League football competitions, and the Ryder Cup golf team, the only team actually to compete under the EU flag.

and easygoing lifestyles – especially in the Mediterranean south – to compete with fast-rising economies like China. Booming economies also attracted fresh immigration, including that from Eastern European countries that had recently joined the EU. For some, this represented attractive multiculturalism and social diversity; for others, it threatened a loss of identity, reflected in the rise of far-right anti-immigrant groups.

These concerns have been thrown into sharp relief since the global financial crisis exploded in 2007. A general recession spread, and even in Germany, Europe's economic powerhouse, jobless numbers rose dramatically in 2008–9. This initial downturn, though, has been superseded by a specifically European crisis that has emerged since 2009. In the boom years many countries had made full use of the easy international availability of credit to embark on lavish spending programmes, and in late 2009 it became clear that several European countries – initially and above all Greece, but also others such as Spain, Italy and Portugal – had huge debts that vastly exceeded the capacities of their economies to pay.

Denied credit on international markets, first Greece and then other countries have appealed to the rest of the Eurozone for help, but have come up against the resistance of northern countries – especially Germany and its leader Chancellor Merkel – to putting their money into what is often labelled "a bottomless pit". In return for financial bailouts Greece, Spain and others have had to agree to sweeping austerity programmes, which, added to the existing recession, have had devastating social consequences: overall unemployment in Greece reached nearly 25 percent in 2012, and in Spain over 50 percent of under-25s are jobless. Crisis meeting after crisis meeting has been held since 2009, but a lasting solution has still not emerged, and fresh thinking seems thin on the ground.

Lyon was one of the first cities in France to run a share-a-bike scheme for residents.

THE EURO'S PROGRESS

Napoleon Bonaparte was one of many leaders who proposed that Europe should have a single currency. For most of the time since one, the euro, was finally put into circulation in 2002 and adopted by most EU states, it has generally been considered a great success. Since the debt crisis broke in 2009, though, opinions have been much more mixed.

One of the prime purposes of the euro, and the EU in general, is supposedly to increase economic cohesion in Europe, to reduce differences in living standards and productivity between the richer north and the south. However, it has often had the opposite effect. Integration in one currency with ultra-productive Germany meant German industry had new price advantages in southern markets, while local industries found it increasingly difficult to compete, and actually contracted. The low interest rates required by Germany for the Eurozone made available cheap credit, much of it coming from banks in northern Europe, that encouraged public bodies, companies and individuals in the south to boost their finances with unsubstantiated borrowing that crashed down after 2007. The complex management of the euro further aggravates its problems. It has many pluses, but remains a work in progress.

BEST BUILDINGS OF EUROPE

Every country in Europe has some examples of notable architecture, each with a rich story to tell. Within this vast collection of remarkable buildings, however, some stand out from all the rest.

The landscape of Western Europe is littered with castles, cathedrals, temples, mansions, palaces and other permanent, if sometimes crumbling, landmarks, which speak to 21st-century visitors of the epochs in which they were built, and of the skills and aspirations of their architects and patrons.

These emblematic structures, recognised at a glance the world over and much imitated, were often built primarily to impress. They stand on the whole in prominent sites from where they can look down on common humanity and, more importantly, be seen. They were intended as proof of political, military or religious authority, usually combined with artistic sensibilities; to instil fear, awe or obedience in the populace; or to inspire envy of the wealth, prestige and power invested in them.

In a wider sense, they were also built simply because they could be, by civilisations anxious to reassure themselves – and others – of their success and immortality. Each building is evidence of determination (sometimes to the point of folly), technological know-how, the social organisation necessary to carry out large and complex building schemes and, importantly, enough surplus prosperity to pay for the project over an extended period of time from start to finish.

The Alhambra was built in the 14th century by the Muslim rulers of Granada, and remains the most beautiful example of Islamic architecture in Spain.

Portugal's Palácio da Pena, on a rocky peak in the Serra de Sintra, is one of the finest expressions of 19th-century Romanticism. Its orange-red clock tower dominates a collection of ornate domes, faux battlements, galleries and gateways.

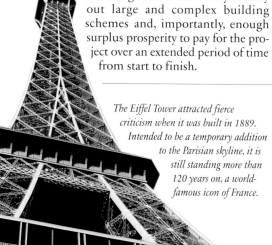

The Eiffel Tower attracted fierce criticism when it was built in 1889. Intended to be a temporary addition to the Parisian skyline, it is still standing more than 120 years on, a world-famous icon of France.

Medieval church-building reached its apogee with the daring achievements of Gothic, which included piercing the walls to make room for great areas of stained glass, as seen in this rose window in Paris's Notre-Dame Cathedral.

GLORIES TO GOD

Early churches in Europe were built on the principles of the Roman basilica; it was not until late in the first millennium AD that a distinctly Christian architecture developed into the Romanesque style, which was characterised by thick walls pierced by small windows and roofs supported on rounded arches.

The goal of church-builders, however, was always to build higher and grander buildings to the glory of God, and their experimentation led to the breakthroughs of Gothic architecture. The ingenious use of pointed arches, rib vaults and flying buttresses meant that slender spires could be built overhead and great stained-glass windows placed in the walls to flood the interior with coloured light.

During the Renaissance, in the 15th and 16th centuries, there was a return to classical ideals of harmony and symmetry, but Baroque artists rebelled against such simplicity with an emphasis placed on drama and an exuberance of ornamentation. In modern times, architects have either drawn on earlier styles or else created churches with a stark, functional aesthetic.

Neuschwanstein Castle – literally, the New Stone Castle – was begun in 1869 by Ludwig II, in honour of his favourite composer, Richard Wagner. It is dramatically sited on the top of a hill, overlooking the Hohenschwangau Valley, Bavaria.

The Emperor Vespasian commissioned Rome's immense amphitheatre, the Colosseum, in AD 72. Spectacular and bloody gladiatorial battles, as well as fights between wild animals, were staged in it for the pleasure of the 55,000 spectators.

Ágios Nikólaos Anapafsá is one of the Metéora group of monasteries on the plain of Thessaly, central Greece, built from the 14th century onwards on seemingly inaccessible sandstone towers, which are known as the "stone forest".

Lord Foster's dome on the
Reichstag, Berlin.

FEATURES FROM A–Z

A series of cultural snapshots, from Architecture
to Zeitgeist via Food, Kissing and Youth culture, to
serve as an introduction to this panoply of nations.

Anyone who travels through Europe will be
aware of the many place names associated
with war and destruction. The map is dotted with tragic names like Ypres and Auschwitz,
Waterloo and Dresden, Austerlitz and Verdun.
As you notice the countless military cemeteries, it seems fair to ask whether Europeans have
ever lived together in peace.

Yet for the past 50 years, an astonishing process of reconciliation has taken place, led by the
oldest of enemies, the French and Germans.
Political leaders have patiently built a new
Europe founded on ideas of economic cooperation and peaceful coexistence. The union has
gradually expanded to embrace 27 countries
with 23 different official languages.

Europe isn't perfect. It still doesn't have an
inspiring Constitution (all attempts so far have
failed) or an impressive capital city (Brussels has
never really risen to the challenge), and bicker-
ing between European nations has re-emerged
a little in the current economic crisis. But it has
a population who increasingly live and think
like Europeans.

You find these new Europeans scattered all
over the continent; at summer rock festivals, on
high-speed trains, or sitting on sunny café terraces overlooking restored urban squares. They
are not particularly aware of their European
identity. But it comes out in the number of
languages they speak (three is pretty common),
their tolerance and understanding of other cultures and their extended networks of friends
and family members in every European country.

To many people, therefore, Europe is much
more than a living museum, a lengthy list of
monuments to be ticked off as a dutiful obligation: it is a continent whose variety and density
of culture can always surprise and often enrich

The peaceful Place des Vosges, Paris.

the enquiring visitor. On the following pages,
we focus on some of the quirkier aspects of
Europe, from kissing customs to queuing conventions, from centres of corruption to temples
of gastronomy, from driving habits to timekeep-
ing, which may go a little way to shedding some
light on what it means to be European.

Architecture

A tourist in a new city often takes a dutiful
interest in its ancient cathedrals and palaces, but
Europe also has exciting and provocative modern public buildings to catch the imagination.

The starting point is the Bauhaus Museum in
Dessau. The Bauhaus design school, founded by
Walter Gropius, set the pace in the 1920s.

Interest was added by the Swiss architect Le Corbusier, whose designs included the modular Unité d'Habitation in Marseille, which used units proportional to the human figure. During the 1950s and 1960s, architectural heroes emerged, such as Giovanni Ponti, who designed the radical Pirelli tower block in Milan that looks down over Ulisse Stracchini's elegant white Central Station. Josep Lluis Sert, a Catalan who succeeded Gropius at the School of Design at Harvard University, designed the Maeght Gallery in St-Paul-de-Vence in the south of France and the Miró Foundation in on to design the Museum of Contemporary Art in Barcelona, where the 1992 Olympic Games brought a new wave of modern architecture. Among contributors was Norman Foster, who later designed the Millau Viaduct, the highest vehicular bridge in the world, which spans the River Tarn in southern France.

Some of the most striking new architecture in Europe is found in former dockland areas, where abandoned waterfronts were ripe for development. In Amsterdam, architects have designed astonishing new buildings in the former port area to the north of the Old

Le Corbusier's unmistakeable Chapelle Notre-Dame-du-Haut in Ronchamp, Franche-Comté.

Barcelona, near the rebuilt 1929 Pavilion of Mies van der Rohe, last director of the Bauhaus.

The economic upturn of the 1980s and the architectural ambitions of French President Mitterrand brought forth new architectural stars. Paris already had a head start with the 1977 Pompidou Centre, and it took the lead with such *Grands Projets* as I.M. Pei's Louvre pyramid and the French National Library, announced in 1988 and completed seven years later.

Museums, often drear 19th-century monoliths, were brought up to date. The American Richard Meier designed the first of his "white refrigerators" in Frankfurt to house the Museum of Crafts and Allied Arts, and went

LE CORBUSIER'S MASTERPIECE

The French town of Ronchamp in Franche-Comté is home to one of Europe's most famous post-war buildings: Le Corbusier's Chapel of Notre-Dame-du-Haut, which he designed to replace another church here that was destroyed during World War II. Unconstrained by a geometric framework, the design is dominated by curves, with walls and roof sloping at irregular angles, and windows of varying proportions placed haphazardly along the walls. Le Corbusier's unique vision was a deliberate gesture against the right angle and straight line, and was intended to reflect the forms of its hilltop setting and the natural features of the surrounding landscape.

City, including a new public library and music centre. Other major ports such as Antwerp, Hamburg and Rotterdam have been equally adventurous.

The reunification of Germany, and especially Berlin, has provided the opportunity for a whole range of spectacular new projects. In the capital, Norman Foster redesigned the Reichstag (Parliament), Daniel Libeskind built the deeply moving Jewish Museum, and British architect David Chipperfield oversaw the reconstruction of the Neues Museum, in ruins since World War II.

> At Mont St-Michel in northern France, the tide is one of the fastest in the world, covering 40km (25 miles) in six hours, and the difference in height between high and low tides can be as much as 15 metres (50ft).

Sea coast, in Germany and the Dutch Frisian Islands, is where German naturists bare themselves to the winds and billowing seas. But tidal waters can be a hazard, especially where the shore is flat and the tides encroach at a

Private beach in Baia, Bay of Naples, Italy.

Beaches

Western Europe has two different shores – sea and ocean – and their characteristics are distinct. The wide stretches of Atlantic Ocean and North Sea beaches are churned up by two tides a day, which can shift the sand. In some places at low tide, such as the giant wetlands of the Baie de la Somme or around Mont St-Michel in France, the sea disappears over the horizon, leaving vast, silent sand flats.

Some of the Atlantic's rollers, at Biarritz in France, along the Spanish Basque coast, or around Nazaré in Portugal, are perfect for surfing, while Guincho in Portugal has a reputation among windsurfers, as does Tarifa in southwestern Spain. The cooler North

pace, cutting off cliffs and causeways at a frightening pace.

In the more saline, tideless Mediterranean, beaches are often spread out between small rocky coves, where the water can be stunningly translucent. Of course, there is pollution and contamination, but to discourage it the European Union hands out annual Clean Beach awards. The Mediterranean is generally very safe, its coves often backed with dunes and umbrella pines, but rugged coasts and unexpected winds should not be underestimated. Some resorts have half a dozen beaches with a choice of amenities and perhaps attracting different users: families, nudists or members of the gay community;

or they may be colonised by one nationality. In Italy beaches at the most popular resorts, like Rimini on the Adriatic, are commonly divided up by "beach clubs" or lidos where you have to pay to rent a lounger and sun-shade and use the beach, but elsewhere around the Mediterranean arrangements are less formal and beaches more open.

The popularity of the Mediterranean's beaches prompted some resorts to import sand. The impressive 6km (4-mile) beach at Benidorm, a Spanish holiday town developed on a massive scale since the 1950s, was estab-

Busy street in Sicily.

lished with sand shipped in from Morocco, and is still regularly topped up.

City and countryside

Western Europe is one of the most densely populated and heavily urbanised areas on earth, above all in the northern countries. The whole of the central Netherlands has been described as one crowded mega-city, with old urban centres like Amsterdam, Utrecht and Rotterdam becoming amalgamated into one. The feel of cities, though, and the extent of this density still varies a lot, especially between Northern and Southern Europe. In the giant conurbations of the north, such as the cen-tral Netherlands, northern Belgium, or the

Ruhr–North Rhineland belt in Germany, the historic centres of the original towns that make them up, with their venerable buildings, are often quite loosely defined, and are surrounded by big swathes of other building from the last 200 years, from factories to residential areas made up of miles of individual houses in long rows. The suburban sprawl of different towns has a natural tendency to link up, so that it's often hard to tell when you've left one town and entered another.

Southern European towns and cities, in con-trast – which include some of the oldest in the world, such as Athens, founded at least before 1400 BC, or Cádiz, founded around 800 BC – tend to have a much more tightly defined his-toric core of narrow streets, often too narrow for modern traffic, within walking distance of a cen-tral square with the main public buildings like a cathedral and town hall. The main market would be on the same square or not far away. Housing was tightly packed together, often in apartments, and most people would live as close as possible to the centre, visit it every day, and know a great deal about everything going on in their town.

In the 20th century, industrial spread and suburbanisation also came to the major cities in the south, and housing developments of neat "English-style" single houses can be seen around places like Milan or Madrid, but it remains much less marked than in the north. Southern Europeans are more likely to live in apartments, and cities retain more of a sense of civic identity.

These differences – combined with the very different geography of each country – are also reflected in attitudes to nature and the country outside the city. In the north, especially around the big conurbations where most people live, the tendency of cities to sprawl and run into each other means they also encroach on and urbanise the countryside. There is still agricul-ture, often highly modern and "industrialised", but even small towns can have an atmosphere little different from bigger centres, and surviv-ing areas of hills or woodland are treasured and carefully conserved, as parks for urbanites.

In countries such as Italy and Spain, and in much of France, there remains a much clearer distinction between city and country. The land-scape is generally far more rugged and varied than the soft green farmlands around the Rhine, and once you get outside the cities many rural areas still feel remote. Though nowhere is entirely disconnected nowadays, villages still have a distinctly country feel, the traffic-noise level is very noticeably lower, and some people still maintain traditional customs lost in the urbanised world. It's also in the south where – in regions like the Abruzzo in Italy and the high Pyrenees between France and Spain – you can still find a real sense of European wilderness.

Driving

Linger in the outside lane of a German *auto-bahn* and your rear-view mirror will soon

Germany comes just behind Poland and Italy in the league of road deaths, all with well over 5,000 a year, closely followed by France and then Spain. But of course, the size of the country counts: Luxembourg has fewer than 50 deaths a year.

Driving habits vary markedly according to where you are. The driving style of Italians reflects their anarchic attitude towards authority in general: horns are blasted whenever traffic stops, overtaking is instinctive, and anyone foolish enough to stop immediately as a light turns red may find several drivers crashing into

Traffic is bad around the Arc de Triomphe in Paris.

reflect the flashing headlights of a Porsche or BMW bearing down on you at 240kph (150mph). Germany's love of speed usually triumphs over demands for a blanket speed limit on its *autobahn* system (though specific highways may have recommended limits). This attachment to the rights of the fast-moving is combined with a precise sense of driving discipline: slower-moving vehicles should keep to the inside lane, and return to it as soon as they have passed something, and if they stay in the fast lane and cause an accident most people would consider it the slower driver's fault. When an accident occurs at these speeds, of course, you're more likely to need a hearse than an ambulance.

his rear. On some Italian roads you may come up behind a car going very slowly, because driver and passenger are in mid-conversation; a few minutes later on the same road a teenager will shoot past you on a blind corner at terrifying speed. There are also regional differences: Naples is the one place in Italy where chaos truly reigns on the roads, and drivers don't even stop at red lights, while in the north habits are more orderly. In Spain drivers similarly take chances on bends and rarely adhere to speed limits unless they can actually see a police car, but are generally a bit more moderate than Italians. In the Netherlands, in contrast, drivers tend to be highly punctilious and drive precisely to the official speed limit or even a little below it. Swiss drivers too are awfully law-abiding.

Everywhere in Western Europe, not just in Germany, the same expectation applies on motorways and main highways: that you should stay as far to the right as possible except when overtaking, and not "lane-squat" in the middle or outside lanes as is common in Britain or North America. And, whatever the truth of driving stereotypes, the first-time visitor to Europe should bear two things in mind. One is that mixing driving and alcohol carries very severe penalties. The second is that most police forces can levy fines

Vogel" and "Frau Schmidt". They would feel very uncomfortable, they will tell you, using first names. The advantage of such formality is that it distinguishes acquaintances from friends, and when a friendship is finally cemented by the adoption of first names, it is a memorable occasion, typically celebrated with a few drinks.

Another method by which status is delineated is in the choice of second-person pronoun. All the main European languages except English have two words for "you": the familiar form (*tu* in French, Spanish or Italian, *du* in German) and the formal version (*vous*

In Northern Europe, beer is the thing to drink.

for these and other offences (speeding, using a mobile phone while driving) on the spot.

Familiarity

One of the significant differences between American and European social mores is the manner in which people address each other. Germans in particular put great emphasis on titles and can be seriously offended if they are not addressed properly. As the psychologist Carl Jung once observed: "There are no ordinary human beings, you are 'Herr Professor' or 'Herr Geheimrat', 'Herr Oberrechnungsrat' and even longer things than that."

Two colleagues can work in the same office for 20 years and still address each other as "Herr

in French, *Sie* in German, usted in Spanish). Again, the move from formal to familiar is a signal that amity has become camaraderie. In a business environment, the decision to switch is usually initiated by the person with superior status. Distinctions have been breaking down, and vary a lot from country to country. In Spain, for example, the general level of formality has diminished greatly over the last 40 years, and anyone under about 40 years old may well address anyone of roughly the same age or less with tú as soon as they've met, even in a work context, unless the occasion clearly requires some special formality. In France, on the other hand, even many young people will tend to address new acquaintances with vous, and only change to tu if they have established some kind of connection. Learning the proper practice for each place is a matter of paying attention, and finding your way. Distinctions are breaking down, particularly among young people, but they still exist.

Food

European nations take what they eat seriously, but how they do so, like so many things, varies. It has often been said that Europe can be divided between one half based on beer and butter and another on wine and olive oil. It is

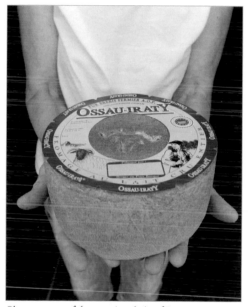

Cheeses are one of the crowning glories of France.

SAY "FROMAGE"

General de Gaulle once famously remarked that it would be impossible to unite a country capable of producing 246 different kinds of cheese. Some would say France's cheese varieties are among its greatest inventions. Classic cheeses are given *appellation d'origine* labels, as prestigious as those accorded to wine. The variety is astonishing: pungent fermented cheeses with white or yellow skin such as Camembert, Brie, Coulommiers, Pont L'Evêque; the blues of Roquefort, Fourme d'Ambert and Auvergne; the ripe and creamy Epoisses; the hard but piquant Cantal; and the goat's cheeses of Valençay or Corsica. The cheese fan has plenty to explore.

> *"What's the Italian for spaghetti?"* a young tourist was overheard asking her companion in a Naples restaurant. We are so familiar with a diverse range of European foods we forget where they come from.

in the southern, wine-and-oil countries – above all France, Italy and Spain – that what you may hear called "gastronomic culture" is most central to local life. This attitude extends into parts of the beer-drinking north where Latin languages are spoken, like northern France and Belgium. Germanic peoples like the Dutch and Germans, on the other hand, to southerners' contempt, have often had a far more utilitarian attitude to their food.

French restaurants often have a reverential air, Belgian gourmet gatherings are not for the light-hearted, while in Greece you are encouraged to visit the kitchen to see what's cooking. Chefs often have celebrity status beyond their country. In recent years French star chefs like Paul Bocuse from the foodie city of Lyon, voted "chef of the century" in 1989, have been eclipsed by Spanish cooks such as the Catalan Ferran Adrià, a pioneer of extraordinarily intricate "molecular gastronomy" who has received accolades from around the world and been invited to teach on "culinary physics" at Harvard.

The emphasis on cuisine as a central part of local culture also means that local, regional cooking styles and regional specialities are lovingly treasured. Every area in France and Southern Europe has its own cheeses, meats, wines or even styles of pasta. Local food will always be the best to try, and at its best will be made with fresh local ingredients. Not for nothing was the Slow Food Manifesto signed in Paris in 1989, three years after its forerunner, Arcigola, was founded in Italy. And it is no surprise that farmer José Bové became a hero when he went to jail for three months in 2002 for vandalising a McDonald's in the French town of Millau.

Hence any journey across the continent means a culinary journey, too. France extends from Normandy cider, cheese and tripe to the Provençal south of olives, wine and *bouillabaisse*, with goose farms, *cassoulet* and quiche on the way. Italy stretches from the boar and polenta of Piedmont in the north through the risotto lands of the Po Valley to the sunny south of pizza and mozzarella cheese. Iberia's Atlantic coast gives Portuguese, Galician and Basque cookery their flavours; the Mediterranean coast brings the Moorish influence of paella. The North Sea provides herring and smoked oily fish in the Low Countries, and you can snack on a fish sandwich in Amsterdam or dip into a bowl of *moules* in Belgium.

Away from the coast, the food of the Netherlands, Germany or Austria is much less varied and less subtle than the fare to the south and west, but excellent beers and wines can help disguise the fact. And, like Britain and other parts of the world once known for dull food, these countries have greatly refined their culinary skills in the last few years, and there's much more to modern German and Austrian cooking than dumplings and sauerkraut. A discussion of local food cannot ignore pastries, especially those from Belgium and Austria, where a coffee-house culture produces rich tortes and strudels. In Portugal the favourite tipple is tea – Portuguese merchants were the first to bring it to Europe from China.

Drag queen at Dragshowbar Lellebel, Amsterdam.

CAFE LIFE ACROSS EUROPE

Europeans enjoy spending a lot of time in cafés drinking small cups of coffee. The habit originated in Vienna, where the first coffee house was opened in 1683, by a Polish resident, Jerzy Franciszek Kulczycki. Café life reached a peak in the late 19th century when grand establishments opened in capital cities across Europe, from Lisbon to Budapest, attracting writers and artists.

The classic café offers a place to escape from the rush of the city, sit with a strong black coffee served on a silver tray and read one of the newspapers on wooden poles generously provided by the establishment.

Almost every European city has its grand cafés, like Florian in Venice, the Café de la Paix in Paris, Café Central in Vienna and Café Americain in Amsterdam. The café still forms the focus of social life in the majority of towns and villages across Europe, attracting people of all ages, from young writers and intellectuals to elderly couples. In recent years, architects have designed contemporary cafés, which appeal more to the younger generations, like Café Costes in Paris or De Jaren in Amsterdam. Whatever the style, the emphasis is still on good coffee and quiet discussion in civilised surroundings.

Gestures

In addition to the wide variety of languages spoken in Europe, there are a whole range of hand gestures which often vary greatly from country to country. Giving a thumbs-up sign will signify approval in most countries – but not in Greece, where it is a vulgar insult, equivalent to raising the middle finger elsewhere. Flick your ear with a forefinger in Italy and you could be suggesting someone is homosexual. Jerking your forearm up and slapping your other hand into the crook of the arm would be an insult in most of Europe – although their hands rather than their entire arms, but their repertoire is narrower than the Italians'.

The Italians have long been regarded as Europe's most expressive people. A wide variety of hand signals are used to convey agreement, surprise, delight, disgust, and gestures familiar to ancient Greeks can still be seen today.

Humour

Language plays a large part in forming humour. Thus, while French lends itself to puns, Spanish doesn't. Much French wit incorporates clever, sarcastic wordplay. On the other

Gestures are important.

elsewhere in the world the gesture is regarded as a sign of sexual appreciation. Make a ring with your thumb or index finger and most Europeans interpret it as meaning OK, but others see it as zero or worthless, and a Greek could be referring to a bodily orifice.

A shrug can convey different things, depending on whether it is accompanied by moving the shoulders, raising the eyebrows or pursing the mouth. Is someone resigned? Indifferent? Helpless? It's sometimes hard to tell.

In France, mouth movements are important. This is partly because nine of the 16 French vowels involve rounding the lips (compared with only five in German and two in English). The French are also great gesticulators, using

hand, there is a fine old tradition of slapstick in France, and the French have an earthy humour built around sex, though it's far from sexist. Belgians, by contrast, are conservative about sex, so there are few sex jokes in Belgium. Scatological humour is absent in France, but is strong in Spain and in Germany, where such references appear even in children's riddles. Really, there's only one thing regarded as funny throughout Europe: other Europeans.

Immigrants

Anyone imagining they will arrive in a European country and immediately start practising their phrasebook greetings on a local may be in for a surprise, for many people in the service industry are neither native-born nor native speakers. Today you will hear Gujarati in Barcelona, Turkish in Hamburg, Russian on the Riviera, and Eastern European languages everywhere. The increasing ethnic and cultural diversity of Western Europe, which began after World War II and has accelerated ever since the 1980s, is one of its foremost modern characteristics.

Migration between the main EU countries is reasonably fluid, but even within the EU, immigration causes problems: two years after joining in 2004, 1 million Poles had left home

Germany had Europe's most liberal immigration laws in terms of allowing entry to the country when Turkish *Gastarbeiters* ("guestworkers"), now numbering around 3 million, were needed by German industry in the 1960s, but was very restrictive in allowing them and their children to become German citizens, giving them only permanent resident status. This naturally tended to encourage the creation of immigrant ghettoes, with people born in Germany but denied the vote or some other rights, although a reform in 2000 made it easier for long-term migrants to become citizens.

Kissing in a bar in Greece.

to find work abroad, emptying the country of its young workforce. Most went to Britain and Ireland, since Germany, France and many other countries retained some restrictions on the movement of people from the eastern countries for the first few years after they joined the EU.

Europe's external borders are porous, letting in hundreds of thousands illegally from Africa, Asia and elsewhere. When he came to power in 2007, President Sarkozy proclaimed his intention of dealing with France's 400,000 or so illegal immigrants. But, mindful of history and the deportation of Jews, there has been support for the *sans papiers*, and a new Immigration Museum opened in Paris shortly afterwards.

Despite this, attitudes have hardened since the 1990s, when unemployment soared in the former East Germany after reunification.

Despite its current economic crises, Europe and its image of prosperity remains a magnet for millions of people in North and sub-Saharan Africa, Afghanistan, Pakistan and many other parts of the world. Greece's frontier with Turkey is one major entry point, and Africans and others regularly attempt the crossing to southern Spain, the Canary Islands, Sicily or other parts of Italy in makeshift boats, often provided by criminal people-traffickers. Many lose their way at sea and die in the attempt.

European attitudes to immigration are dependent on the current political and economic climates, and were particularly tense following the attacks of 11 September 2001, after which ultra right-wing parties gained support on a tide of racism.

However, the populations of virtually all European countries are declining, and to compete in home and world markets, cheap immigrant labour is seen by some economists as essential. Policies relating to immigration may have to change, and attitudes will need to change with them, because a whole new underclass is developing right across the continent.

Spain's Prince Felipe, King Juan Carlos, Princess Letizia and Queen Sofia attend the National Day Military Parade in Madrid.

Kissing

Latin has three words for "kiss", distinguishing between a kiss of friendship on the cheek, a kiss of affection on the mouth and a lover's kiss on the mouth. The Roman tradition lives on, for people around the Mediterranean are more spontaneously intimate than their northern cousins: they sit closer together, they touch more, they stand closer together when talking, and everyone seems to cheek-kiss enthusiastically. In France, it is common to kiss someone on the cheek each time you meet and depart, and the number of times you get pecked on each cheek varies from region to region.

> *Most European monarchs are tolerated because they have no real power, and are valued mainly for providing a sense of tradition and continuity, and a useful focus for ceremonial events.*

In Germany, men seldom kiss the cheeks of other men, and personal space is assiduously protected. Handshaking is more common, but usually only when meeting someone by appointment.

But few generalisations are reliable. The Italians are supposedly the most tactile Europeans – yet, although two men will touch frequently when talking (perhaps to deter the other person from interrupting), and even guide each other round a corner while walking, there is noticeably less touching between the sexes. Even married couples are less likely to walk along hand in hand than they are in Denmark or Austria. Could it be possible that Italian men regard hand-holding as a sign of submissiveness?

Monarchies

Hereditary kings and queens have shown remarkable endurance in an age so concerned with the spread of democracy. Spain even restored its monarchy in 1975 and, despite predictions that he would be known as "Juan Carlos the Brief", and more recent financial scandals involving the royal family, the king is still on the throne, having successfully overseen a smooth transition from dictatorship to democracy. None of Europe's other six major crowned heads – or indeed the less weighty rulers such as Prince Albert II of Monaco or Prince Alois of Liechtenstein – look set to lose their "job" in the near future.

The power of European monarchs is mostly symbolic. The Dutch permit their queen a great deal of influence in theory, but allow her almost none in practice. In 1990, the Belgian King Baudouin abdicated for two days so that he did not have to approve legislation legalising abortion. He died in 1993, childless, and his younger brother, Albert II, found himself king at the age of 59. The monarchy was still valued as an institution, however, because it seemed virtually the only glue holding together the Dutch- and French-speaking halves of a politically divided country.

European monarchies are becoming increasingly democratised as more members "marry out". In 2004 the Spanish heir Prince Felipe married a former journalist, Letizia Ortiz, and Mary Donaldson became the first Australian to join European royalty when she married Crown Prince Frederik of Denmark, and in 2010 Crown Princess Victoria of Sweden married her personal trainer, gym owner Daniel Westling.

Meanwhile, deposed monarchs are patiently standing in the wings: Henri, Comte de Paris,

Nature

Europe has some magnificent natural wonders, but these are often under threat from tourism and industrialisation. From the eagles' eyries of the snowy Alps to the lizard sunbeds of the Spanish sierras, animal habitats are under threat. Hunting is widely permitted, and migrant birds must dodge the bullets of Italians and Spaniards who will eat anything that flaps a wing. The big-game hunters are the Germans, who like wild boar and are enthusiastic chasers of wolves and bears in the newly accessible Eastern Europe.

Chamois in Furka, Switzerland.

is pretender to the French throne; Constantine would like his Greek crown back; while both Vittorio Emanuele, Prince of Naples, and Amedeo, 5th Duke of Aosta, lay claim to the Kingdom of Italy.

Monarchs have very little power in modern democracies, but they are still largely respected. The Belgian royal family can count on large crowds when they tour the country on National Day (21 July); for their part Swedes were agog when their high-living Prince Carl-Philip, third in line to the throne and one of Forbes magazine's "20 Hottest Young Royals", was attacked outside a nightclub in Cannes in August 2012, but this hasn't undermined wider regard for the monarchy.

Many countries have special animals. In France, there are the long-horned black cattle of the Camargue, from the delta of the Rhône where flamingos flock. Southern Italy has water buffalo, from which mozzarella cheese is made. Switzerland has the chamois mountain goat, Spain the Iberian lynx and the Cantabrian brown bear.

Ecological awareness has been growing for many years – Italy's first national parks date from the 1920s – and nearly all of Europe's most special landscapes and species now enjoy protection, as national parks or other kinds of reserve. Many groups also now campaign to protect wildernesses, forests and coastlines from development. Yet untold damage has already been done to Europe's natural beauty, especially in the Alps and along the Mediterranean coastline.

Punctuality

The closer you get to the Mediterranean, the slower the pace of life becomes. People even walk more slowly. Partly it's a matter of adapting to a hot climate, partly it's a reflection of the attitude that time serves people rather than the other way round. To be late for an appointment in Germany, Belgium, Austria or Switzerland would be regarded as rude, or at least inconsid-

thieves, and visitors should take precautions, especially in the cities.

Pickpocketing and bag-snatching are generally more of a risk than mugging or any kind of violent crime. The risk of having a bag snatched or pocket picked is highest where there are the largest agglomerations of tourists, and particularly in certain cities: Rome (especially around the Vatican), Barcelona (especially the Rambla and near the beach), Florence and Naples (bad for crime of all kinds) are perhaps those where you need to be most careful. Transport systems such as the Paris Metro during rush hours and

A quiet day in a small Tuscan hilltown.

erate. In Greece or Spain, by contrast, nobody is expected to show up on time. Indeed, being *very* late may even be a sign of status.

In France it is not done to discuss business at a business lunch until at least the first course has arrived; this restraint shows you know the value of friendship, not to mention food and wine, and that you are a more rounded person.

Robbery

Most of the world's 300 million tourists a year don't get robbed or mugged. Nevertheless, crowds of visitors all carrying cameras, mobile phones, jewellery, handbags and other accoutrements are a natural magnet for petty street

Roman buses can also be black spots. Street thieves may use a variety of scams: in Italy, the most traditional method is to ride around on a Vespa scooter to snatch a handbag and then speed away. Where there are street entertainers, as on the Barcelona Rambla, pickpockets will often linger around the edge of the crowds, waiting to grab things from bags when people's attention is distracted. Others work in groups: one will tell you that your jacket has some bird mess or other gunk on it and then offer to help clean it off, and then, while your guard is down, other gang members grab your bag and run off.

It's not too hard, though, to reduce the risk of such things happening to you with a few necessary precautions. One is the mere fact of being aware, irritating though it is, that these things can happen, and looking out for them. Keep an eye out particularly when wandering through crowded streets, or watching any kind of street entertainment. Keep any bag with you closed, hold it in front of you and keep a firm hand on your bag. React and walk away when anyone seems to be standing unusually close to you. When at a pavement café or restaurant, or in a bar, keep your bag close by, in view and preferably right in front of you, on the table. Never ever leave it dangling on the

a widespread belief that quality in wine is a fairly simple matter, down to the cocktail of grape varieties and the skills of the winemaker. In the main winemaking regions of Europe, by contrast, and especially in France, it has traditionally been thought that there is another vital element, terroir, the earth, or rather the specific qualities of a particular piece of earth that is used as a vineyard, and most especially of those vineyards with rare combinations of geology, aridity and location that have produced the most distinctive wines for centuries. Moreover, these vineyards

St-Emilion wine tasting, Southwest France.

back of a chair or on the floor. An amazing number of bags are stolen very easily from the backs of chairs.

A few other scams are more intricate, as when, driving on a highway, a car will suddenly go slow in front of you and try to provoke you to run into the back of them. When you stop to apologise, you can be robbed. But, these incidents are rare, which is why they are always widely reported.

Winemaking

In California or Australia, the combination of an equable climate and close scientific control can often ensure that wines from a particular estate vary little from year to year, and there's

EUROPEAN STEREOTYPES

If colonising an island, it was said in 1790, a Spaniard would first build a church, a Frenchman a fort and a Dutchman a warehouse. In 1820, Lord Byron claimed that French courage was based on vanity, German courage on phlegm, Dutch courage on obstinacy and Italian courage on anger. The modern version of the stereotype game is to define hell as a place where the Germans are the police, the Swedish are the comedians, the Italians are the defence force, the Frenchmen dig the roads, the Belgians are the pop singers, the Spanish run the railways, the Portuguese are the waiters, the Greeks run the government, and the common language is Dutch.

are at the mercy of the continent's capricious weather: one year a wine may be classed as truly great, the next year the same slopes may only produce a fairly conventional vintage. All this uncertainty adds interest.

It has also been widely said that a few years ago the great wine regions of Europe had become complacent, content to rest on their reputations, but growing global competition has led to a much more critical attitude and greatly improved wines, often produced by innovative young winemakers. French wine comes from seven main areas: Bordeaux, the

Gesturing Greeks.

most important; Burgundy in the east; the Loire Valley, in the west; the Rhône Valley from Lyon to Avignon; the Champagne area around Reims and Epernay; Alsace, along the left bank of the Rhine; and Languedoc in the south. Champagne aside, the two grandest by far are Bordeaux and Burgundy.

Italy makes prodigious amounts of wine, from the Alpine valleys down to the tip of Sicily. Among the most distinguished Italian wine regions are Chianti and Brunello di Montalcino, from Tuscany, and Barolo from Piedmont. Spain also produces many world-class wines: Rioja is still the best-known region, especially for reds, but others to explore include Ribera del Duero, Rias Baixas

in Galicia (for whites) and the Priorat in Catalonia (for uniquely rich reds).

Germany produces splendid wines, especially whites made with the Riesling grape, which can be either sweet or dry. But wherever you are, the local wine will invariably be the most interesting one to try.

Xenophobia

Jokes can, and often are, a means of voicing inadmissable opinions. Thus the French and the Dutch make fun of the Belgians. Northern Germans mock the laziness of southern Germans, who in turn deride the stupidity of northerners. Both northern and southern Germans were quick to ridicule new compatriots from the former East Germany. Copenhageners will make fun of somebody from Jutland, and Belgium's Flemings and Walloons joke about each other.

Images, like fashion, are subject to change. The idea of the Germans as aggressive and authoritarian emerged only in the middle of the 19th century; previously, Machiavelli, a shrewd observer of human nature, had described them as peace-loving and rather timid.

Europeans have known and laughed at their fellow-citizens within their countries for centuries, and indeed one feature that could be said to define a country or a cultural sphere is that its peoples know each other well enough to construct complex mutual stereotypes, even when their political structures might be shaky. In Spain, Catalans often feel detached from the rest of the country, but this doesn't mean that other Spaniards can't instantly come up with a stream of timeworn jokes about how tight-fisted Catalans are, while Catalans know all the other ones about how dumb people from Murcia in the south can be. Despite European integration, most Europeans are less familiar with their fellow–EU citizens from other countries, so their stereotypes, and the humour attached, tend to be broader and cruder: overbearing, humourless Germans, lazy, romantic Italians, and so on.

Since the movement toward European unity began, most of the time these stereotypes have fallen into the background, and indeed it could be said that one of the EU's objectives is to leave them behind completely. However, they have burst forth with new vigour since the debt crisis began in 2009. Leaving aside the dry language of meetings and official communiqués, at the popular level the option is always there to see this impasse in stereotypical terms. In Germany, much street and popular-press comment seems to see the problems of Greece (especially) and other debtor countries as essentially one of lazy stereotypical Mediterranean folk, never willing to work hard, evading taxes and giving themselves a permanent holiday on the back of Germans' hard graft and their money; in the Mediterranean countries (especially Greece) the logjam can be seen as down to Germans being rigid, uptight, intolerant, wanting to tell others

Immigration is a hot topic: in the French elections of 2012 the far-right National Front continued to gain ground, but in the 2012 Dutch elections the anti-immigrant Freedom Party lost much of the support it had won two years earlier.

own language) and desire the same clothing brands. Many European students have grown used to spending some time studying in other countries in the Union thanks to the EU's Erasmus programme.

Elder of North-African origin, Strasbourg, France.

what to do and (always a potential stereotype with Germans) having an inner jackbooted authoritarian hidden only just below the skin despite 60 years of democracy. Politicians at their most responsible try to evade these stereo-types and deal with the matter in hand; when less responsible, they fall back on them.

Youth culture

It's easy to think that in the modern world, especially for young people, any place is pretty much like everywhere else. In every city there are Starbucks and McDonald's. Kids every-where use Facebook and Twitter, see the same blockbuster movies (sometimes in the origi-nal English, sometimes dubbed into their

And yet, the idea that there is now a pretty uniform youth culture across Western Europe both is and isn't true. One example, ironically, is hip-hop music. It might seem odd that this might be the case with a kind of music that began life so deeply rooted in black urban America, but hip-hop has also proved probably the most adaptable musical style ever created. There is no country in Europe (or perhaps the world) that does not have its own hip-hop scene, with performers improvising lyr-ics in their own language and local slang. But, this doesn't mean that they all reproduce the American model the same way. They might start off with the gestures and bravado of the New York original, but Italian or Portuguese or even Swiss rappers all produce music in their own way and deal with local concerns in their lyrics, with a spontaneity that is part of hip-hop's great attraction. International music takes on local colour, in ways that uninitiated outsiders cannot immediately understand.

A similar pattern stands out in more mainstream music. Teenagers in different European countries might all listen to international megastars like Lady Gaga, but they also often have their favourite local artists singing in their own language too, especially in France, Italy and Spain. And some things don't change:

The preliminary diagnosis isn't too good. Confidence in business and political leaders plummeted as the global financial crisis hit Europe in 2009, leading to financial bailouts, bankruptcies, high unemployment and student unrest. As the crisis has developed and deepened in several of the Eurozone countries – Greece, Spain, Portugal, Italy – producing levels of unemployment reminiscent of the 1930s, Europe's leaders and its tangle of institutions have shown an often shocking inability to act decisively to deal with it. With economies in decline, old tensions returned and racism emerged in a new

Demonstrators clash with riot police in Athens.

Italian and Spanish pop still commonly has a full-on, I-adore-you romanticism that cynical northerners and English-speakers might find more than a little cheesy.

Zeitgeist

Zeitgeist, that popular word to define the spirit of the age, is hard to define. People used to say the 20th century was the American century. And the 21st, many argue, will belong to Asia. So where does that leave Europe? Will the world echo the words of writer F. Scott Fitzgerald, who exclaimed in 1921: "God damn the continent of Europe. It is of merely antiquarian interest"? Or will this millennium give the Old World a new impetus?

form, this time commonly directed against Muslims, where once it targeted Jews.

Yet it is not all gloomy. More people than ever are educated, affluent, in good health, living longer and able to enjoy a remarkable range of consumer goods and leisure pursuits. Better communications, with fast rail connections and cheap flights, have made "city breaks" a way of life for many. Anyone looking for the contemporary spirit of Europe will find it expressed in great cities like Paris, Berlin, Amsterdam and Barcelona, where exciting new architecture and progressive ideas are giving shape to the new century. In some areas, like environmental protection, social justice and urban renewal, Europe continues to lead the world.

CLASSIC RAILWAY JOURNEYS

For many travellers, trains are the easiest way to explore Europe, especially its towns and cities. Services continue across borders and some of the routes are spectacular.

Europe has the densest railway network of any continent, complemented by tram and bus connections that make public transport an easy and pleasant way to travel. And not only is rail travel safer than driving – car crashes remain the principal cause of holiday injuries and fatalities – it is kinder to the environment than cars or planes. Most countries have maintained a high level of investment in their railway networks, so levels of comfort – and speed – are high. Stations can be an aesthetic pleasure too: besides the great cathedrals of the Steam Age, modern architects such as Santiago Calatrava (Lisbon, Liège, Zürich), Norman Foster (Florence, Dresden) and Nicholas Grimshaw (Amsterdam) have added new sources of civic pride.

But the most compelling reason for choosing to travel by train is that it enhances the pleasure of travel: your holiday starts when you board. It is much easier to enjoy the landscape from a train; every passenger has stories of serendipitous meetings and good conversations, but you can just as easily take the opportunity for quiet contemplation or for reading a book; and overnight sleeping-car trains are something of an adventure, as well as a good way of saving on a hotel bill. In fact, train journeys offer the kind of experiences that travel should be all about.

The Landwasser Viaduct is a highlight on the Glacier Express route, and the train slows so that passengers can admire its curving masonry arches, which enhance the spectacular settin between Chur and Filisur.

Lisbon Oriente station was designed by Santiago Calatrava serve the Expo '98 site. One of a new generation of exciting station buildings, it adds to the legacy of great 19th- and ear 20th-century stations – the cathedrals of the steam age.

By 2020 Spain will have the longest high-speed rail network in Europe.

e Glacier Express links St Moritz and Zermatt in itzerland.

The pioneering TGV.

HIGH-SPEED EUROPE

If time is of the essence, the continent's fast-expanding network of dedicated high-speed lines and trains is the smart way to get around. Internal flights have all but disappeared from competing routes where trains beat planes on city-centre-to-city-centre timings. The French TGV – *Train à Grande Vitesse* – was the pioneer European high-speed train, in 1981, and its astonishing success encouraged most countries to follow suit. The TGV alone serves over 200 destinations throughout France (you can travel from Lille to Marseille in just 4¾ hours), and, using conventional as well as high-speed lines, Belgium, Germany, the Netherlands and Switzerland, at speeds up to 320kmh (200mph).

High-speed trains include a buffet car, and some German ICEs have a dining car with food cooked on board. Reliability is helped by having tracks clear of slower trains, and Spanish Railways is so confident about its TGV-based AVE services that passengers receive a 100 percent refund if trains are more than five minutes late. Supplements for high-speed trains are often payable if travelling on a rail pass, and reservations are required.

The Orient Express has become a byword for luxury. It faithfully recreates the travel experience of the inter-war years, especially on the popular Paris–Venice route.

The Gornergratbahn from Zermatt offers stunning views of the Matterhorn.

In the Berner Oberland, Switzerland.

The stunning setting of Almourel Castle in Portugal.

INTRODUCTION

A detailed guide to Western Europe's top
destinations, with principal sites clearly
cross-referenced by number to the maps.

*Châteauneuf-du-Pape is one of
France's most prestigious wines.*

There is something reassuringly familiar about
the continent of Europe. Its snowy mountains
and beaches, its Roman remains and cathedrals,
its vineyards and cafés are all places that have figured
in so many books and films that we feel as if we
know them. Yet there is so much architecture and art
to absorb, so many miles of countryside to explore,
such a lot of good food to try, so many fine wines to
taste, that nobody can know it all. What follows is a
full flavour of continental Europe: 10 countries that
cover the land mass from Cabo de Roca,
the westernmost point of Portugal, to
Greece, lingering en route in the hill
towns of Tuscany, or on Germany's
Romantic Road, getting caught up in
the excitement of Barcelona, Paris and Rome.

*Ancient Greek temple at
Selinunte, south coast of Sicily.*

Getting around the continent is no problem. Cities are
linked by road and rail, and airports are busy round the
clock. Theoretically the borders between most members of
the European Union were removed in 1995, and although
checkpoints remain in force, they often seem redundant,
with uniformed officers who take no notice of cars passing through.

There are few places that are not used to visitors all year
round. Spring is the time for wild flowers, which cover the
Alps and carpet the meadowlands. In summer, people flock to the playgrounds of the Mediterranean: most crowded are Rimini on the Adriatic
coast, the French Riviera and Spain's Balearic Islands and Costa del Sol,
but there are always empty beaches to seek out, on the Atlantic coast perhaps, or among Greece's myriad islands. In the autumn the vineyards of
France, Italy, Spain and Germany's Rhineland turn red, and grape-pick-
ing is often followed by harvest celebrations. In winter the Alps attract
skiers to Austria, Switzerland and France, as well as to winter sports venues in Italy and Spain. Europe has some of the world's most exciting cities, too. Gothic cathedrals and Baroque palaces overlook sleepy cobbled
squares, and galleries offer breathtaking collections of art, while startling
pieces of modern architecture, stylish shops and vibrant nightlife remind
us that Europe is about the future as well as the past.

Western Europe: Political

0 200 km
0 200 miles

N

NORTH SEA
DENMAR

ATLANTIC OCEAN

IRELAND
Irish Sea

Edinburgh
Belfast
Dublin

UNITED KINGDOM

London

Groningen

NETHERLANDS
Amsterdam
Den Haag (The Hague)
Rotterdam
Nijmegen
Duisburg
Essen
Düsseldorf
Köln (Cologne)

Hannov

Han
B

GER

English Channel

Roubaix
Bruxelles (Brussels)
BELGIUM
Liège
Amiens
LUXEM-BOURG
Luxembourg
Metz
Saarbrücken
Fra

Channel Islands
le Havre
Caen
Rouen
Reims
Mannheim

Brest
Seine
Paris
Strasbourg
St

Rennes
Orléans
Besançon
Freibur

Angers
Loire
Tours
Dijon
Basel (Basle)

Nantes
F R A N C E
Genève (Geneva)
Zürich
Bern
SWITZERL

la Rochelle
Limoges
Lyon
Milan (Milan

Bay of Biscay
Clermont-Ferrand
St-Étienne
Grenoble
Torin (Turin)

Bordeaux
Garonne
Rhône
Avignon
Genov (Genoa)
Monte Car
MONACO

A Coruña
Gijón
Santander
Donostia San Sebastián
Toulouse
Nîmes
Nice

Oviedo
Bilbao
Nice

Ourense
Vitoria-Gasteiz
Pamplona
ANDORRA
Perpignan
Marseille
Toulon

Vigo
Valladolid
Andorra la Vell
Corse (Corsica)

Porto
Douro
Salamanca
Zaragoza (Saragossa)
Lleida
Barcelona
Ajaccio

PORTUGAL
SPAIN
Ebro
Tarragona

Lisboa (Lisbon)
Madrid
Tajo (Tagus)

Évora
Badajoz
Castelló de la Plana
Islas Baleares
Menorca
Macome

Albacete
Valencia
Palma
Mallorca
Sar (Sar

Huelva
Córdoba
Alicante
Ibiza
Cagli

Faro
Jaén
Murcia
MEDITERRANEAN SEA

Sevilla
Granada
Cartagena

Cádiz
Málaga

Algeciras
Gibraltar (UK)
Ceuta (Spain)
Alger (Algiers)

Tanger (Tangier)
MOROCCO
A L G E R I A

Positive thinking at Le Touquet, northern France.

Sunflowers in the Loire Valley.

FRANCE

Europe's largest country draws more visitors than any other, attracted by its glorious variety of landscapes, wealth of monuments and museums, and perhaps above all by the superb food and wine.

The Eiffel Tower illuminating the Paris skyline.

France thinks of itself as the most essential component in Europe. Foreigners think so, too. It is the place they often think of first when they come to the continent. Its popularity is undeniable: the population of just over 63 million is far less than the number of visitors who arrive every year, making it the world's most visited country. It is Western Europe's largest country, and one of the world's richest. Its population is spread thinly through a diverse landscape covering 547,000 sq km (211,200 sq miles); even on major roads, wayside towns and villages can seem deserted. But rural France is the real France. The French are proud of their agricultural heritage, and their farmers are respected as much as the food they produce.

France is also arguably Europe's oldest nation and, give or take a few border shifts, it has existed roughly in its present form since the 15th century. The nation's boundaries are largely natural ones, with the English Channel to the north, the Atlantic to the west, the Pyrenees and the Mediterranean to the south and the Alps, the Jura mountains and the Rhine to the east. These all contrive to make the French almost insular and, as a result, its people, who are mainly Catholic by tradition but predominantly secular in practice, are sometimes not as cosmopolitan as those in other European countries that have more openly shared borders. However, in spite of its insularity, this nation has had immense cultural influence on the rest of the world.

Among the country's riches, the châteaux of the Loire stand out, buildings displaying a craftsmanship that could never be matched today. French culture encompasses all the arts, from painting to film; the annual Cannes Festival is the most important event in the cinema industry's year, an event that highlights the country's stunning Riviera. But most of all, when thoughts turn to France, they turn to Paris, a vibrant city at the hub of a conurbation of almost 12 million people, and a place whose name is synonymous with everything chic.

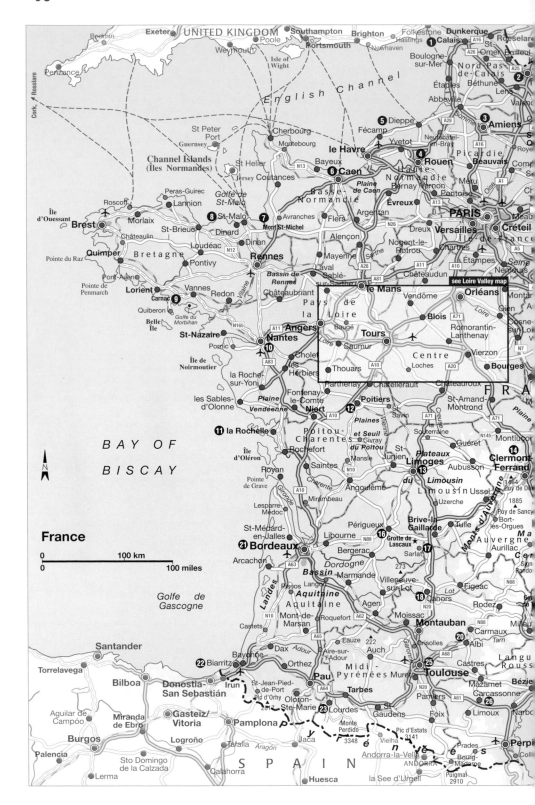

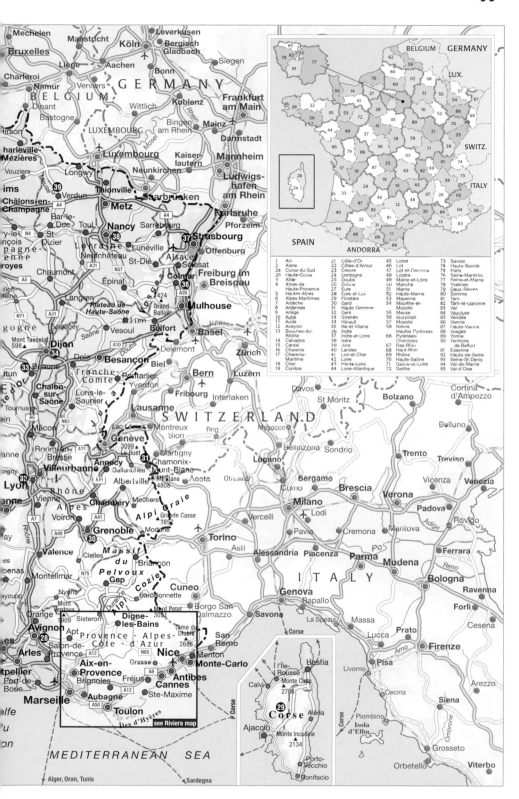

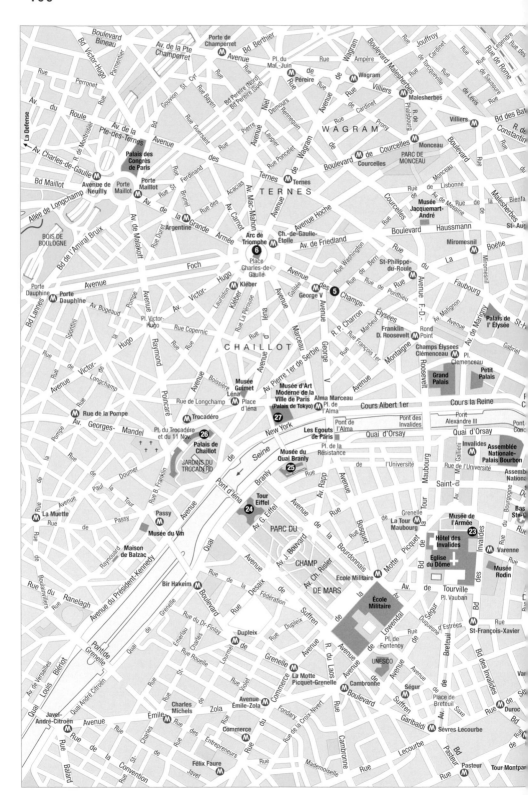

Paris

0   500 m

0   500 yds

CIMETIÈRE DE MONTMARTRE

MONTMARTRE

St-Pierre

Basilique du Sacré-Cœur **28**

Moulin Rouge

Abbesses

Blanche

Pigalle

St-Jean

Anvers

Barbès Rochechouart

Boulevard de la Chapelle

Place de Clichy

Clichy **29**

Pl. Pigalle

Boulevard de Rochechouart

Gare du Nord

Gare du Nord

St-Georges

Avenue Trudaine

Dunkerque

Château Landon

Rue Notre-Dame de Lorette

Condorcet

Maubeuge

Poissonnière

Gare de l'Est

Place du Colonel-Fabien

Colonel-Fabien

Rue St-Lazare

Poissonnière

Gare de l'Est

Trinité

Rue de Châteaudun

N.-D. de Lorette

Cadet

Folies Bergère

d'Hauteville

Château d'Eau

Jacques Bonsergent

Goncourt

Chaussée d'Antin

Le Peletier

Rue Richer

R. des Petites Écuries

Havre Caumartin

Haussmann

Richelieu Drouot

Château d'Eau

République

Palais Garnier (Opéra National de Paris) **9**

Bd Montmartre

Rd Poissonnière

Bd de Bonne Nouvelle

Uberkampf

Opéra

Bd des Italiens

Grands Boulevards

Bonne Nouvelle

St-Denis

Bd St-Martin

Pl. de la République

Bd des Capucines

4 Septembre

Bourse

Strasbourg St-Denis

Av. de la République

Place Vendôme **8**

Bibliothèque Nationale Richelieu

Sentier

Réaumur

Musées Arts et Métiers

Temple

Pyramides

R. des Petits Champs

Arts et Métiers

Turbigo

Boulevard Voltaire

Hôtel Ritz

St-Roch

JARDIN DU PALAIS ROYAL

Montorgueil

Réaumur Sebastopol

MARAIS

Filles du Calvaire

Tuileries

Étienne Marcel

Rue de Bretagne

JARDIN DES TUILERIES **2**

Comédie Française **10**

Palais Royal

St-Eustache

St-Sébastien Froissart

JARDIN DU CARROUSEL

Bourse de Commerce

Les Halles

Musée d'Art et d'Histoire du Judaïsme

Palais Royal Musée du Louvre

Forum des Halles **11**

Berger

Rambuteau

Musée de l'Histoire de France

Musée National Picasso **13**

Musée National du Louvre **1**

Louvre Rivoli

Rivoli

Centro Georges Pompidou **12**

Musée Cognacq-Jay

Pont Neuf

Les Halles

St-Merri

Musée Carnavalet

Pont du Carrousel

Châtelet

Hôtel de Ville

Chemin Vert

École Nationale Supérieure des Beaux-Arts

Institut de France

Palais de Justice

Hôtel de Ville

St-Paul

Pl. des Vosges

Germain

Quai de Conti

Cité **17**

Ste-Chapelle

Quai de l'Hôtel de Ville

Hôtel d'Aumont

Bastille

Place de la Bastille

Musée Delacroix **21**

St-Germain-des-Prés

St-André-des-Arts

Île de la Cité

Pont Marie

Opéra de Paris Bastille

St-Sulpice

Odéon

St-Michel

St-Séverin

Notre-Dame **16**

Sully-Morland

Odéon, Théâtre de l'Europe

Musée de Cluny **18**

Cluny-Sorbonne

St-Julien-le-Pauvre

Mémorial de la Déportation

Île St-Louis **15**

Palais du Luxembourg

La Sorbonne

St-Étienne-du-Mont

Cardinal Lemoine

Institut du Monde Arabe

Panthéon **19**

Université Jussieu

JARDIN DU LUXEMBOURG

N.-D.-des-Champs **20**

Place Monge

Arènes de Lutèce

JARDIN DES PLANTES

Gare d'Austerlitz

Musée Zadkine

Cimetière du Montparnasse

la Grande Mosquée de Paris

Bibliothèque Nationale de France-François Mitterrand

PARIS

Its grand architecture and reputation for high living, fine cuisine and haute couture combine to make Paris the most glamorous of all European capitals.

Paris may at first appear a really cosmopolitan city, but it maintains its quintessentially French character despite the invasion of American fast-food chains. From the *boulangeries* (bread shops) to the *bateaux-mouches* (glass-top river boats), the crêpe-makers and the *bouquinistes* (open-air book-sellers) along the Seine, Paris offers a plethora of sights, sounds and smells.

Altogether, central Paris covers an area of 105 sq km (41 sq miles) and is bounded by the parks of the **Bois de Vincennes** to the east and the **Bois de Boulogne** to the west. The city is divided into 20 districts called *arrondissements*, each with its own distinct character. *La ville de Paris*, which is the city proper (population 2.2 million), is surrounded by a belt of communities called the *banlieues* (suburbs) totalling over 12 million people.

Early settlements

The origins of Paris are found on the Ile de la Cité, the larger of the two odd-shaped islands in the middle of the Seine. Here, a Celtic tribe of fishermen called the *Parisii* founded a village in the 3rd century BC, which they named *Lutetia* – "a place surrounded by water". In 52 BC, during his Gallic War, Julius Caesar conquered the settlement. More invasions came from Germanic tribes; the strongest of

them, the Franks, made Paris their capital in the 6th century. In the 10th century Hugh Capet ascended the throne as the first of the Capetian monarchs, the first truly French royalty, and his successors made Paris a medieval centre of culture and learning.

The kings of the Renaissance era, especially François I and Henri IV, were responsible for creating much of what today constitutes the classic beauty of Paris: charming squares, the Louvre Palace with the grand Tuileries Garden and the first stone bridge

Main Attractions
Louvre
Musée d'Orsay
Champs-Elysées
Arc de Triomphe
Pompidou Centre
Notre-Dame
Eiffel Tower
Montmartre
Château de Versailles
Disneyland Paris

Café life at La Bonne Franquette.

TIP

Paris is a remarkably compact city, and it is easy to stroll from one sight to the next. When you're weary or in more of a hurry, the Metro is the best way to get around, trains run frequently and stations are in every part of the city. The RER local trains are even faster. Tickets are inexpensive (for more on Paris transport, see page 414) Traffic, on the other hand, is often atrocious, so taking a taxi can be slow and costly.

Les Invalides and beyond from the Eiffel Tower.

across the Seine, the Pont Neuf. Sun King Louis XIV moved the capital to Versailles in the late 17th century but Paris continued to prosper, with luxury trades adding to the prestige of the city. The overthrow of the *ancien régime* by the storming of the Bastille prison on 14 July 1789 at the start of the French Revolution was followed by the rise and fall of Napoleon Bonaparte, who left Paris the Arc de Triomphe and other great Neoclassical monuments.

The modern era

During the Second Empire, in the mid-19th century, Baron Haussmann oversaw the transformation of Paris from a medieval to a modern city, epitomised by the creation of the *grands boulevards*: wide avenues lined with harmonious buildings. Paris became a more vibrant and attractive place, paving the way for the Belle Epoque at the end of the century. This period of good living came to an end in 1914 when World War I broke out, and the advancing Germans shelled Paris. However, they never entered the city as they did in World War II, when Paris was occupied for more than four years.

The post-war era again changed the face of Paris, and successive presidents left their marks on the city. The **Pompidou Centre** was commissioned under President Pompidou and completed in 1977, and President Mitterrand left his mark with the **Grande Arche**, a giant rectangular office block in **La Défense** quarter to the west of the city, and the glass pyramid entranceway to the Louvre.

A city tour

The Right and Left banks of Paris grew up with distinct social traditions which still prevail today. The Right Bank has remained the mercantile centre. Here are the banks, swanky department stores, fashion houses, government offices and the *Bourse*, the Neoclassical stock exchange. The Left Bank, on the other hand, has been the domain of the intellectual community.

A tour of Paris may begin from any of its major landmarks. Those eager for an introductory panoramic view

usually head for Sacré-Cœur on the heights of Montmartre or the Eiffel Tower by the river, two classic vantage points. Others set out for the Place de l'Opéra to explore the *grands boulevards*, the ritzy shops along Rue du Faubourg St-Honoré or the beautifully colonnaded Rue de Rivoli. Beginning at the Right Bank, it may be equally tempting to take a stroll along the Champs-Elysées. You can either walk down it from the Arc de Triomphe or walk up from the Louvre, further east.

World-class museums

The **Louvre** ❶ (Wed–Mon) is the largest art museum in the world, although it was originally built as a medieval fortress to dominate the River Seine. I.M. Pei's dramatic glass pyramid in the forecourt has become the museum's modern symbol. The collection, ranging from European sculpture and painting to antiquities, decorative arts and objects, has been built up over hundreds of years, although Napoleon I made one of the greatest contributions from the spoils of his various campaigns. Spread over four vast floors, it's best to decide what you want to see and head straight for it. The *Mona Lisa* is in room 13 on the first floor of the river side of the museum.

From the Louvre to the Place de la Concorde extends the **Jardin des Tuileries** ❷, one of the best examples of a typically French formal garden where trees, plants and decorations are immaculately laid out. The small **Jeu de Paume** (Tue–Sun) has exhibitions of photography, and the **Musée de l'Orangerie** contains Monet's "Waterlilies" series, as well as Cézannes and Renoirs (Wed–Mon).

The grand glass-and-iron *Belle Epoque* railway station of Quai d'Orsay, just across the river from the Louvre, has become one of the city's great art museums, the **Musée d'Orsay** ❸ (Tue–Sun). It has a major collection of 19th-century works, particularly by

Delacroix and Ingres, as well as masterworks by the Impressionists and Post-Impressionists such as Monet, Manet, Renoir, Cézanne and Van Gogh.

The Jardin des Tuileries leads to the **Place de la Concorde** ❹, a vast square that occupies a bloody chapter in French history. In 1793 it became the site of executions, where Marie Antoinette and Louis XVI, among others, met their fate on the guillotine. Standing majestically in the middle of the traffic chaos, the central Obelisk of Luxor, dating from 1300 BC, was taken from the Temple of Rameses in Egypt and shipped as a gift to Paris in 1836.

Famous promenade

One of the world's most famous streets, the **Champs-Elysées** ❺, starts at Place de la Concorde. From here to the Rond-Point (roundabout) is a broad avenue lined with horse chestnut and plane trees. It makes an attractive promenade and has a little park if you need to rest, north of which lies the **Palais de l'Elysée**, the French president's residence. After the Rond-Point the Champs-Elysées takes on a

TIP

If you expect to be doing intensive sightseeing in the city, the Paris Museum Pass gives access to all the major museums and many other attractions (including Versailles) for 2, 4 or 6 days for a set fee, giving major savings if you visit at least 4 sights. Pass holders also avoid waiting in line at popular attractions. For details, see www.paris museumpass.com.

I.M. Pei's glass pyramid at the Louvre.

La Grande Arche at La Défense.

Inside the Louvre.

different character. It becomes an elegant and prestigious avenue of designer shops and fashionable bars and restaurants.

Walking up the Champs-Elysées gives a magnificent view of the monumental **Arc de Triomphe 6**. Built between 1806 and 1836, this impressive monument stands 50 metres (165ft) high and 45 metres (148ft) wide, and is noted for its frieze of hundreds of figures; France's Tomb of the Unknown Soldier lies beneath it. The 284 steps to the top (there is a lift) give access to a spectacular view down the Champs-Elysées and up to the business area of La Défense.

The Opéra and the Marais

Directly in front of you as you walk up Rue Royale from Place de la Concorde is the pseudo-Greek temple of **Sainte-Marie-Madeleine 7**. Napoleon wanted to dedicate this monument to the glory of his Grande Armée, but it has served as a church since 1842.

A short way southeast from here is **Place Vendôme 8**, the smartest of all squares in Paris. Shaped like an octagon, it is lined by 18th-century buildings which house some of the city's most exclusive stores, such as Cartier and Rolex and under the stone arches is the luxurious **Ritz Hôtel**. In the centre of the square towers a 44-metre (144ft) column with bas-reliefs of bronze cast from 1,200 cannons captured in 1805 from the Austrians at the Battle of Austerlitz, and modelled on Trajan's Column in Rome.

Up Rue de la Paix is the gloriously romantic **Opéra Garnier 9**, designed in 1875 by Charles Garnier and enclosed by a triangle of Haussmann's *grands boulevards*. Inside, the majestic staircase and rich marble decorations evoke visions of swirling gowns, tuxedos and top hats.

Follow the Avenue de l'Opéra back towards the river and you come to the **Palais Royal 10** (beside the Louvre), childhood home of Louis XIV and once an infamous den of libertines. A few streets to the east is the **Forum des Halles 11**, a complex of cinemas, boutiques, galleries and restaurants which is undergoing massive restoration. The city market was here until 1969, and a few remaining bistros serve traditional market fare. Across the Boulevard de Sébastopol looms the giant cultural machine of the **Pompidou Centre 12** (the Centre National d'Art et de Culture Georges Pompidou; Wed– Mon). Built between 1971 and 1977 by the architects Renzo Piano and Richard Rogers, it is still strikingly futuristic. The galleries of the Musée National d'Art Moderne have a massive collection of early modern and contemporary art.

Walk down to the river from the Pompidou from late July to August

and you can sunbathe on a beach, as each year this stretch of the Right Bank is closed to traffic and turned into "Paris-Plages" (Paris Beaches), with specially imported sand, loungers, volleyball, a swimming pool and other attractions (although you can't actually swim in the river). East of the Pompidou Centre is one of the city's most charming quarters, home to some of the finest mansions in Paris. The **Marais**, originally swampland, became a fashionable residential district in the 17th century. The **Musée National Picasso** ⓭ (Wed–Mon) in the Hôtel Salé has paintings, drawings and sculptures from the artist's prolific career; it has been closed for large-scale renovation, but is due to reopen in summer 2013. The **Musée Carnavalet** (Tue–Sun) is another excellent museum, occupying two mansions and giving a history of the city. In the same neighbourhood is the old Jewish quarter centred on the Rue des Rosiers, and the **Musée d'Art et d'Histoire du Judaïsme**, giving a history of Jews in Europe.

The 63 houses of **Place des Vosges** ⓮, the city's oldest square, on the edge of the Marais, have lovely symmetrical arcades. The writer Victor Hugo (1802–85) once lived here, and his house at No. 6 is now a museum (Tue–Sun).

Islands in the river

In the very heart of Paris, the River Seine divides to embrace two islands, the **Ile de la Cité** and **Ile St-Louis** ⓯. Traditionally a residential quarter of the Parisian gentry, the Ile St-Louis has remained a patch of tranquillity in this fast-paced city. Neighbouring Ile de la Cité is cluttered with historic landmarks, the most celebrated being the **Cathédrale Notre-Dame de Paris** ⓰ (daily). This magnificent example of Gothic architecture is simply stunning viewed from any angle. It was purportedly built on the grounds of a Gallo-Roman temple that was first replaced by a Christian basilica and a

Romanesque church. The construction of the cathedral itself began in 1163 and work was only completed in 1345.

Also on the Ile de la Cité is the **Conciergerie** (daily), the surviving part of Paris's original royal palace, which became a prison after France's kings moved across the river to the Louvre in 1358. This massive building is a truly beautiful sight at night, when its arches are illuminated. During the French Revolution, many of those sentenced to death were held here while they awaited the guillotine. Marie Antoinette was imprisoned here, and her private cell, the Chapelle des Girondins, with her crucifix and the guillotine blade, is only one of many gloomy exhibits that fascinate children.

Part of the Conciergerie houses the **Palais de Justice**, Paris's main law

The Opéra Garnier.

The Arc de Triomphe stands at the top of the Champs-Elysées.

The Pompidou Centre, or Beaubourg.

courts. In the courtyard is **Sainte-Chapelle**  (daily), the former palace chapel, built by King Louis IX – who was made a saint, as St Louis – in the mid-13th century to house holy relics. It is one of the very finest works of Gothic architecture, with stunning stained glass in kaleidoscopic colours.

The Left Bank

From the Ile de la Cité, the **Pont St-Michel** leads to the Left Bank (Rive Gauche) and straight into the **Latin Quarter**. It earned its name in the Middle Ages, when students at the Sorbonne university were required to speak Latin. East of **Boulevard St-Michel**, its main thoroughfare, the Latin Quarter is threaded with numerous narrow alleys such as **Rue de la Huchette**, a twisting lane of Greek restaurants, kebab corners, jazz spots and cinemas.

Where boulevards St-Michel and **St-Germain** meet is the **Musée de Cluny** (Wed–Mon), housing the ruins of the Roman baths, and a museum of the Middle Ages, with exhibits that include the exquisite

tapestry of *La Dame à la Licorne* (The Lady and the Unicorn). Walking down Boulevard St-Michel and turning left into Rue Soufflot, you arrive at the **Panthéon** . Built as a church to fulfil Louis XV's pious vow after he recovered from an illness, the Panthéon has, since 1791, served as a shrine to France's most outstanding citizens.

On the opposite side of Boulevard St-Michel stretches the spacious **Jardin du Luxembourg** . These gardens are popular with students whiling away time between classes, and children are thrilled by the adventures of Guignol puppets (the French equivalent of the Punch and Judy Show), which are featured in the gardens' **Théâtre des Marionnettes**.

In the evening and late into the night the Left Bank becomes even more animated, as crowds promenade along Boulevard St-Michel and Boulevard St-Germain, which leads west from the Latin Quarter into neighbouring St-Germain. The open-air terraces of its restaurants and cafés are popular spots to sit for a drink and

to soak in the ambience. Next to the pre-Gothic church of **St-Germain-des-Prés** ㉑ are two grand cafés that have been elevated to the rank of institutions: the **Café aux Deux Magots** and the **Café de Flore.**

Heading south on **Rue de Rennes** and then down **Boulevard Raspail**, you pass into the **Quartier de Montparnasse**, which replaced Montmartre as the centre of bohemian life early in the 20th century. Artists, writers, poets and revolutionaries, among them Lenin and Trotsky, flocked to live here. After World War I, American expatriate writers of the "Lost Generation", such as Hemingway, F. Scott Fitzgerald and Henry Miller, joined the locals in famous literary cafés like Le Dôme, La Rotonde, Le Sélect or the huge dining halls of La Coupole.

Montparnasse changed greatly in the 1960s, when the area was chosen for extensive urban renewal that included the huge modern Gare Montparnasse train station and the **Tour Montparnasse** ㉒, the only skyscraper in central Paris. However, it so horrified Parisians that no other similarly tall buildings have been authorised ever since. Below it, Boulevard Montparnasse has a lot more traffic than in its heyday, but its celebrated cafés retain an attractive verve.

Across the **Cimetière du Montparnasse** (where Jean Paul Sartre and Simone de Beauvoir lie together) is the entrance to the **Catacombs** (Tue–Sun), where thousands of bones are stored in an old quarry. Paris does death well, and the most popular cemetery is that of **Père Lachaise**, to the east of the city centre, which contains the tombs of Oscar Wilde, Jim Morrison and Edith Piaf among hundreds of others.

Back to the Seine

The gilded **Dôme des Invalides** faces the Right Bank from across Pont d'Alexandre III. Immediately beneath the vast cupola rests Emperor Napoleon I, whose body was transferred here from the island of St Helena in 1840. It is encased in seven separate sarcophagi, the exterior one of precious red marble. The church is surrounded by the Hôtel des Invalides, built by Louis XIV as a hospital to shelter 7,000 disabled soldiers. Today the building houses the **Musée de l'Armée** ㉓ (daily), a collection of arms, uniforms and trophies from France's military past.

Just a few steps away, at No. 77 Rue de Varenne, the former studio of sculptor Auguste Rodin (1840–1917) is now the **Musée Rodin** (closed first Mon of the month), where some of the artist's best and most famous works are on display in the house and garden.

To the west of the Invalides is the École Militaire, a military college. Its former parade ground, the Champ de Mars, leads to the **Eiffel Tower** ㉔ (daily). Named after its creator,

In summer the banks of the Seine in the heart of the city are turned into beaches.

Notre-Dame dominates the Ile de la Cité.

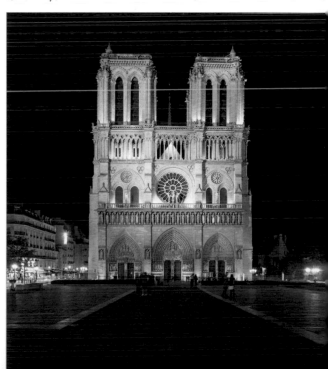

The Lady and the Unicorn tapestry at the Musée de Cluny, a wonderful museum of medieval art.

Les Deux Magots, a well established literary haunt on the Left Bank.

Gustave Eiffel, the tower was designed as a temporary installation for the 1889 Paris Exhibition. But since it proved its value as a wireless tower it remained intact, and of course it is now synonymous with Paris. The best city-gazing from the top is about an hour before sunset, and the tower is stunningly illuminated after dark.

Just below and to the east of the Eiffel Tower, beside the river, a spectacular modern building built partly on stilts houses the **Musée du Quai Branly** ㉕ (Tue–Sun), Paris's newest major museum. It presents a remarkable collection of ethnographical material and traditional arts from all around the world, with ultra-modern interactive displays, and around it there's a lovely garden.

Opposite the Eiffel Tower on the Right Bank is the **Palais de Chaillot** ㉖, dating from the International Exposition of 1937. It houses several museums. Close by, on Avenue du Président Wilson, the Palais de Tokyo contains the underrated **Musée d'Art Moderne de la Ville de Paris** ㉗ (Tue–Sun).

Bohemian quarter

Montmartre, the haunt of writers and artists early in the 20th century, is still one of the liveliest spots after dark. This was one of the birthplaces of modern art, since Monet, Renoir, Picasso and many others spent part of their careers here.

Known locally as *La Butte* (hill), it was once genuinely bohemian, and songs and comedies flowed from the dim cafés. Later, Montparnasse took over as the artistic and literary centre. At the **Place du Tertre**, however, some of Montmartre's former reputation lives on. Street artists offer tourists caricatures or Parisian townscapes. There are also plenty of bars, cafés and restaurants.

Incongruously set in Montmartre is the virginal-white **Sacré-Cœur**

LEFT BANK RENDEZ-VOUS

Paris has always been both a magnet and an inspiration for writers, aspiring and established, French and foreign, and addresses with literary associations are concentrated on the Left Bank.

The best place to start a tour with your nose in a book is the city's oldest café, **Le Procope** (13 Rue de l'Ancienne-Comédie), a favourite watering hole of Voltaire. Three other cafés with literary associations are close to each other in or near the Place St-Germain-des-Prés. Existentialist philosopher and writer Jean-Paul Sartre and his lover Simone de Beauvoir consolidated the highbrow reputation of **Les Deux Magots** (6 Place St-Germain-des-Prés) in the 1950s, and the Art Deco **Café de Flore** (172 Boulevard St-Germain), just opposite, was another favourite haunt. The other gathering place for intellectuals past and present is the Brasserie Lipp (151 Boulevard St-Germain).

A few hotels also have literary reputations. There's nothing left to see now of the "**Beat Hotel**", 9 Rue Gît-le-Cœur, where Allen Ginsberg and William Burroughs stayed in the 1950s, but in **L'Hôtel** (13 Rue des Beaux-Arts) you can reserve the room in which Oscar Wilde died in exile in 1900.

Another stop for literary types is the eccentric bookshop of **Shakespeare & Co.** just across the river from Notre-Dame at 37 Rue de la Bûcherie.

❷❽. Perched on a hill, its Byzantine cupolas are as much a part of the city skyline as the Eiffel Tower; when the lights are turned on at night, Sacré-Cœur resembles a lit wedding cake. It can be reached by walking up 250 steps or by taking a funicular railway.

At the foot of Sacré-Cœur, along **Boulevard de Clichy**, is **Pigalle**, the traditional entertainment quarter of Paris. It is symbolised by the neon-red windmill sails of the **Moulin Rouge** cabaret, home of cancan dancing since the days of Toulouse-Lautrec. Here, too, were the dimly lit cabarets where the legendary Edith Piaf, the "Sparrow of Paris", sang. **Place Pigalle** ❷❾ is a popular hotspot teeming with sex shops, peep shows and strip clubs. The **Folies-Bergère**, about 2km (1¼ miles) south on Rue Richer, is the oldest music hall in Paris and offers much the same fare as the Moulin Rouge.

Days out

The most sumptuous of all French palaces is the **Château de Versailles** (Tue–Sun; RER line C to Versailles Rive Gauche, SNCF train from Gare Montparnasse to Versailles-Chantier or Rive Droite, or bus 171). Not to be missed, it is a mere 21km (13 miles) from the capital. Once a royal hunting estate, Versailles entirely transformed on the orders of Louis XIV, the Sun King, who took 50 years to create a palace and gardens so magnificent they were copied all over Europe.

From 1682 to 1789 Versailles served as the capital of France and the palace itself housed 5,000 people. Inside, the tour takes you through the royal apartments and the stunning 70-metre (233ft) Hall of Mirrors. Outside in the park, designed by André le Nôtre, are the smaller royal residences of the **Grand Trianon** and **Petit Trianon**, as well as Marie Antoinette's make-believe village or **Hameau**.

Slightly less touristy is the other great royal palace near Paris, the **Château de Fontainebleau** (Wed–Mon; SNCF train to Fontainebleau-Avon, then bus, or Parisvision bus from Rue de Rivoli), in a forest 65 km (40 miles) south of the capital. A favourite residence of Napoleon, the palace is a mixture of styles, with formal gardens all around.

Chartres Cathedral (daily; SNCF train from Gare Montparnasse) is one of the greatest works of Gothic architecture. Around 90km (55 miles) southwest of Paris, it is especially famous for its 172 stained-glass windows from the 12th and 13th centuries, and the enigmatic labyrinth inset into the floor of the nave.

Of different appeal is **Disneyland Paris** (daily; RER line A to Marne-la-Vallée), 32km (20 miles) east of Paris. The most popular tourist attraction in Europe, the park includes all the famous Disneyland rides along with hotels and the Walt Disney Studios, where you can see and experience how movies are made, and even make your own cartoons.

Boating on the lake at Versailles.

Even at night Paris is breathtaking.

AROUND FRANCE

Every region of France has something distinctive to offer; the majestic châteaux of the Loire Valley, the medieval villages of the valley of the Dordogne river and the sun-drenched beaches of the Mediterranean coast are just some of the highlights.

France has an admirable transport network that makes for quick and efficient travel. The autoroute (motorway) system runs throughout the country and allows long-distance travellers to go round rather than through the driving nightmare that is Paris. The greatest asset of the French road network is the superlative quality of its clearly signposted secondary roads, which are often strangely empty of traffic.

The 300kph (186mph) TGV (*Train à Grande Vitesse*) makes rail travel across much of France comfortable, quick and easy, connecting Paris with the major provincial cities.

The north

Visitors coming from Britain via ferry or the Channel Tunnel might like to stretch their legs in the port towns before continuing the journey inland. **Calais ❶** is distinctly shabby, but in the **Parc St-Pierre** you'll find the famous bronze statue by August Rodin of the *Burghers of Calais* who, in 1346, offered their necks to Edward III, the English king, if he would spare the city. In **Boulogne**, the 13th-century ramparts of the picturesquely cobbled upper town (*ville haute*) make an interesting walk, with wonderful views into the Old Town and over the harbour. A little inland, **St-Omer's Basilique Notre-Dame**, begun in 1200 and

completed in the 15th century, is a triumphant union of Romanesque and Gothic styles, the jewel of Flanders's ecclesiastical architecture.

Close to the Belgian border is **Lille ❷**, the capital of French Flanders, which is distinguished by its welcoming Flemish atmosphere and richly restored civic buildings, in particular the grand 17th-century **Vieille Bourse** and Louis XIV's imposing citadel; a massive star-shaped construction that demanded the labour of 2,000 bricklayers. A little to the

Main Attractions
D-Day battlefields
Mont St-Michel
Loire châteaux
Dordogne Valley
Bordeaux vineyards
The Pyrenees
Carcassonne
Provence and the Côte d'Azur
The Alps
Champagne

Lille's Grand'Place.

TIP

The cathedrals of Amiens and several other French cities – usually including Rouen and Reims – are illuminated with remarkable coloured light shows every night during summer and (at Amiens) around Christmas. At Amiens, the lights faithfully reproduce the colours with which the medieval west facade was originally painted, an unmissable spectacle. In Chartres, the cathedral and several other historic buildings are lit up each summer, until 1am.

The white cliffs at Etretat, Normandy.

south in the old mining town of Lens is the **Louvre-Lens** (Tue–Sun), an ultra-modern art museum, opened only at the end of 2012, that will hold large-scale exhibitions and showcase items from the vast collections of the Paris Louvre not often seen in the main museum.

To the south are **Arras** and **Amiens** ❸, the former famous to the English for the tapestries through which Hamlet stabbed old Polonius, and to the French as the home town of revolutionary leader Robespierre. It is worth a visit today for its spectacular Flemish-style squares the Place des Héros and Grand Place, some of the largest squares in Northern Europe, which still host bustling markets, especially in the weeks before Christmas.

The 13th-century Gothic cathedral at **Amiens** is the tallest in France, a medieval jewel even more miraculous for having survived the bombardments of two world wars. Its great glory is the intricate stone carving of the west facade, described by critic John Ruskin as "the Bible in stone";

inside, the nave is wonderfully light, and the 16th-century wooden choir stalls are superbly carved. Back on the coast, between Boulogne and Dieppe, is the seaside resort of **Le Touquet**. Purpose-built in the early 20th century to attract the wealthy from Paris and London, it still has an air of 1920s gentility.

Normandy

Within easy reach of Paris are the house and garden of **Giverny** (Apr–Oct Tue–Sun), created by the Impressionist painter Claude Monet, who lived there until his death in 1926. Beautifully restored, it has become a popular tourist spot, particularly the Japanese garden where the water lilies, so famously painted by the artist, still bloom.

Downriver are the superb abbey ruins at **Jumièges** consecrated in 1067 to celebrate William's conquest of England. **Rouen** ❹, capital of upper Normandy, is famous as the city where Joan of Arc was burnt at the stake. The 11th- and 12th-century **cathedral** is only one of several splendid monuments in this great medieval

NORTHERN BATTLEFIELDS

The north of France, flat and defenceless, has been the poignant arena for countless invasions throughout history, and its place names sound like a litany of battlefields.

Dunkirk is famous for the providential evacuation of 140,000 French and 200,000 British troops in May 1940. From the lighthouse or the Watier locks, you can see where it happened. English historians recall glorious Crécy (1346) and Henry V's Agincourt (Azincourt in French) (1415), while the French prefer to remember even further back to Bouvines, an important victory over an Anglo-German alliance in 1214.

Other battles, whether ending in victory or defeat, soaked the fields of Flanders and Picardy, the plateau of the Ardennes and the banks of the Somme and Marne in blood. There are impressive monuments to Canadian troops at Vimy (north of Arras), to the Australians at Villers-Bretonneaux (east of Amiens) and to the Americans at Bellicourt (southwest of Le Quesnoy), while British cemeteries from World War I are found from the Somme through Flanders into Belgium. Travellers in northern France are constantly reminded of the colossal effort that went into rebuilding the towns and cities destroyed in both World Wars. Boulogne, Arras, most of Rouen and St-Malo were lovingly reconstructed from the rubble; in other cities – Le Havre, Calais, Brest – the scale of destruction was such that entirely new cities were built over the ruins.

city and port on the River Seine. Its exuberant facade was painted many times by Monet.

Dieppe ❺, on the north Normandy coast, is one of the most attractive of the traditional Channel ports. The **Boulevard du Maréchal Foch** offers a pleasant promenade following the sweep of the pebble beach. The liveliest part of town, however, is around the **Place du Puits Salé**, where you will find the renowned Café des Tribunaux. The spectacular white cliffs of **Etretat**, west of Dieppe, demonstrate why this shoreline gained the epithet of the "Alabaster Coast".

The most picturesque harbour towns of Normandy are further south on the Calvados coast, notably **Honfleur**. The **Musée Eugène Boudin** (Wed–Mon) attests to the town's popularity with painters – Boudin himself, Courbet, Monet and Dufy. **Deauville**, with its casino and nightclubs, retains much of the elegance that made it a name in the *Belle Epoque*, while its sister-town of Trouville has a more relaxed feel, and is known for its excellent seafood restaurants. Roads inland lead into the **Pays d'Auge**, an idyllic area of lush green countryside, woods, tiny villages, and half-timbered, flower-bedecked cottages so pretty they look taken from a film set. It's also the home of Normandy's most famous cheeses – Camembert, Pont l'Evêque – and its best ciders and calvados (apple brandy).

The beaches of the **D-Day landings** of 6 June 1944 – Omaha, Utah, Gold, Juno and Sword – line the Calvados coast north and west of Caen. The most important museums commemorating "Operation Overlord" are in Caen itself (**Mémorial de Caen**, daily) and Bayeux (**Musée Mémorial de la Bataille de Normandie**, daily), but there are many other smaller exhibits in towns behind the beaches. Off the beach at **Arromanches** the remnants of the former artificial Mulberry harbour peek out of the water. The huge concrete construction, comprising a breakwater and piers, was towed across the Channel and installed off Arromanches in order to land supplies for the Allied forces.

The sublime Mont St-Michel.

The Bayeux Tapestry depicts William the Conqueror's invasion of Britain, and was embroidered a year after in 1067.

The beach at St-Malo.

Caen ❻ is the capital of lower Normandy and was the favourite home of William the Conqueror, even after he conquered England in 1066. He and his wife Mathilde left two fine abbeys, *aux Hommes* and *aux Dames*, west and east of the city centre. Caen was flattened in the 1944 Battle of Normandy and largely rebuilt.

In the **Centre-Guillaume-le-Conquérant** (daily) at **Bayeux**, 28km (17 miles) northwest of Caen, hangs the highly celebrated and exquisite tapestry, stitched in 1067, depicting the events surrounding William of Normandy's conquest of England in 1066.

Bayeux escaped war damage in 1944, so its lovely historic main street is remarkably intact.

The most dramatic religious building in all France, indeed one of the wonders of the Western world, is **Mont St-Michel** ❼, in a bay at the bottom of the Cotentin peninsula. The abbey (daily), built between the 11th century and the 16th century, is an extraordinary sight when seen from a distance. It stands at the summit of an island-rock, 75 metres (250ft) above

the sea, and is reached by road along a dyke, although by 2015 this will be replaced by a bridge.

The Cotentin peninsula, jutting into the ocean north of Mont St-Michel, has Normandy's most remote-feeling green landscapes inland, and often empty sand dunes along the coast. Ferries run from charming small ports like Granville to the British Channel Islands.

Brittany

Jacques Cartier set off from the ancient port of **St-Malo** ❽ in 1534 on the voyage that led to the discovery of Canada. St-Malo's most famous mariners were corsaires, semi-pirates, and carried on virtual private wars with the English and the Dutch. As a result the Old Town – much of which was destroyed in World War II, but has been carefully restored – was ringed by defensive walls, and you can still walk all around the ramparts to get a fine view across the estuary of the River Rance towards **Dinard**, one of Brittany's most popular resorts.

But Brittany is appreciated most for the beauty of its craggy coastline.

One of the most delightful stretches is the Côte de Granit Rose or "Pink Granite Coast" extending west from the little resort of **Perros-Guirec**, so called because of the distinctive colour of its massive rocks, which often have weird shapes like giant abstract sculptures. An easy footpath allows you to stroll all the way around the coast past the rocks, and along the way – but also accessible by road – there are gorgeous sheltered inlets with excellent beaches of swimming like **Ploumanac'h** or **Trégastel**.

To the west the Breton coast ends in the Rade or Bay of **Brest**, where the modern port city – rebuilt from ruins after 1944 – is surrounded by a series of beautiful and surprisingly tranquil bays and placid fishing and holiday towns. **Douarnenez** is one of the most characterful, and a road leads past it to dramatic ocean cliffs at the **Pointe du Raz**.

The Bretons maintain their own Celtic language and customs, most notably the Pardons, religious processions by local people in their rich regional dress, and traditional music and dance. The Pays Bigouden area south of Douarnenez is one where traditions are most vigorously maintained, and has some of the best Breton music and arts festivals each summer. In the late 19th century, western Brittany was still so remote that Post-Impressionist painters, most notably Paul Gauguin, came to the lovely village of **Pont-Aven** in search of a return to nature. The charming **Musée de Pont-Aven** (daily) has work by all the artists who painted there.

Brittany's ancient origins can be seen in the extraordinary stone circles such as those at **Carnac** ❾, where 3,000 giant stones were laid out around 5,000 years ago for some form of worship. The associated dolmens and tumuli are thought to mark burial sites. Carnac is also the region's most popular beach resort, and the nearby "semi-island" of **Quiberon**, linked to the mainland by a long sandspit, is a centre for surfers and windsurfers. Just to the east, the **Golfe du Morbihan** is almost an inland sea of placid, shallow waters, dotted with tiny islands that are lovely to explore by boat.

The menhirs (standing stones) at Carnac are 1,000 years older than the Pyramids but were aligned with extraordinary precision.

The gardens at the château of Villandry are beautifully designed.

Look out for artisanal goat's cheeses from the Loire Valley.

Valley of the Kings: the Loire

Nantes ⑩, the largest city in northwest France, stands at the point where the River Loire meets the tidal estuary that takes it to the Atlantic Ocean. The celebrated valley of the Loire has been praised as the garden of France. Most of all, however, in the 16th century it was the home of kings, princes and their courtiers, who have left a splendid mosaic of châteaux.

From Paris, a tour of the Loire Valley usually begins in **Orléans** Ⓐ, an hour's drive south of the capital. The soul of Orléans, a modern city whose heart was bombed out during World War II, lives on in the cult of Joan of Arc; it was here that she successfully resisted the English army before being burnt at the stake in Rouen. The site where she stayed in 1429 has become the **Maison Jeanne d'Arc** (Tue–Sun), where scenes from her life are recreated.

The little town of **Beaugency** Ⓑ, 18km (11 miles) west of Orléans,

has an 11th-century dungeon, 12th-century abbey and bridge, and Renaissance town hall. From here, the road leads to the very heart of château country. Altogether, the Loire region has about 3,000 stately homes from various periods. The oldest, such as the castle of Loches, began life as fortified towers during the Middle Ages; more recent ones, such as the opulent palace of Cheverny, were designed for comfort rather than defence, serving as pleasure grounds for the aristocracy. The châteaux built between the late 15th and mid-16th centuries rank as the apogee of Renaissance architecture in France.

In the 1420s, the future King Charles VII of France took refuge from the English in the castle at Chinon. It was there that he was visited by a peasant girl, Jeanne la Pucelle, who demanded entry and told him that divine voices had urged her to help Charles defeat the invaders and reclaim his throne. She then proved her worth by defeating the English at Orléans and becoming, as Joan of Arc, France's national heroine. Later, as the threat of war

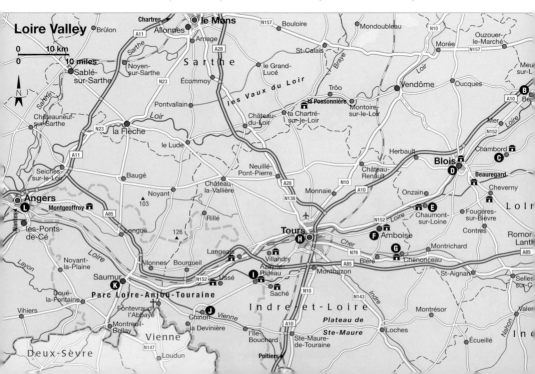

receded, the Loire Valley became more popular with French monarchs as a place for hunting and relaxation, and so it was here that they began to build their most lavish pleasure-palaces.

The first château seen when entering the Loire Valley from Orléans is **Chambord** 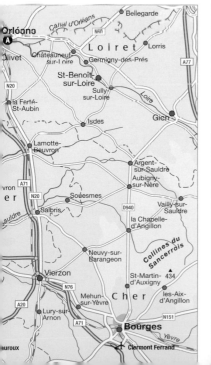 (daily), a fantasy palace that bewitched all who saw it. The building could be described as a gigantic stairway onto which a château has been grafted; this stairway, with its double turn, and supposedly designed by Leonardo da Vinci, is the structure's pivot. It soars to the roofs, and offers an unmistakable symbol of the power of the French king. Everything about Chambord is colossal, but François I, who had it built, used it only to impress his most important guests. Henri IV never came near it, and his son Louis XIII dropped in but once. Louis XIV used it as a hunting lodge, but stopped coming after Versailles was built, in 1685. A *son et lumière* show during the summer celebrates its past glories, and around it there is a magnificent park.

Blois 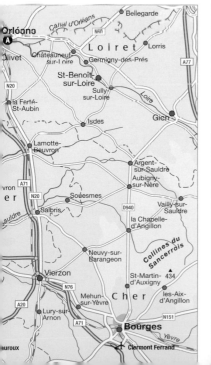 (daily) is next along the valley. In contrast to the other big Loire châteaux, Blois sits right in the middle of a charming historic town. This was the first major residential château in the Loire, its original wing built in late-Gothic style for King Louis XII in 1498 after he first began to move his court to the Loire for months at a time, preferring it to Paris. Later, François I added another wing in French Renaissance style, and then Louis XIV's brother Gaston d'Orléans built another in Baroque style, so that Blois became a display case of architectural fashions. From outside the château there is a superb panorama over the river.

The château at **Chaumont** 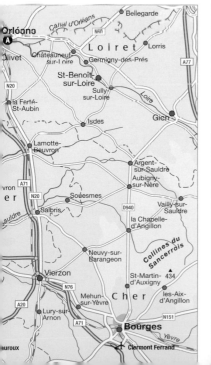 (daily) lies in a setting that the Prince de Broglie transformed into a veritable pastiche of the *Arabian Nights*. Further west is **Amboise** 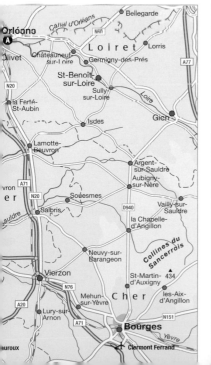, whose château (daily), once the home of Charles VIII, François I and Henri II, is considered one of the finest. Much of the palace has gone, but what is left still offers a striking contrast between the "Italianate" modifications of Charles VIII and the old medieval fortress. Renaissance master Leonardo da Vinci

The exquisite château of Azay-le-Rideau, in the Loire Valley.

This sculpture forms part of the entrance to the Louis XII wing at Blois, one of the most visited châteaux in France.

The Chapelle St-Michel at Le Puy-en-Velay.

lived in the manor house of the **Clos Lucé** (daily), beside the château, after François I gave him refuge in France in 1516. He died there in 1519, and is buried in St Hubert's Chapel. Today, the house contains varied exhibits on the work of the great genius.

There is no clash of style about **Chenonceau** ⑥ (daily), which achieves a perfect harmony in its Renaissance architecture. Anchored like a great ship in the middle of the River Cher, south of Amboise, and surrounded by broad fields, Chenonceau is a delicate jewel set in a green casket. It was the preferred home of Diane de Poitiers, the "eternally beautiful" mistress of Henri II. She was hated by his queen, Catherine de Médicis, who, after the king's sudden death in 1559, promptly seized Chenonceau for herself. Chenonceau was famous for its festivities, such as the triumphal celebration on 1 March 1560 for François II and his young wife Mary Stuart. Today, the parties are all but forgotten, but there is still magic in the great classical gallery that straddles a

bridge of five arches creating a lovely reflection in the waters of the river.

Downriver from Tours

Capital of the Touraine region, the university town of **Tours** ⑪ is a lively city. The medieval quarter, centred on **Place Plumereau**, is a showcase of Gothic architecture. About 23km (14 miles) southwest is **Azay-le-Rideau** ① (daily), a small château of exquisite proportions partly built over the River Indre. This "multi-faceted diamond… mounted on pillars, masked with flowers", as it was described by Balzac, is the quintessence of Touraine's architecture. Not far away is the **Château de Villandry** (daily) and its famous 16th-century garden.

Chinon ①, 20km (12 miles) southwest of Azay, is one of the most historic Loire towns – surrounded by vineyards that produce superb red wines – and has one of the valley's oldest castles. Most of its mighty fortifications were built in the 1150s for Henry II of Normandy and England, who made Chinon his foremost stronghold at the centre of his vast possessions in France. It was seized by the King of France after a long siege in 1205, and the castle reappeared in history in the 1420s as the refuge of King Charles VII, where he met Joan of Arc, but later it was too uncomfortable to become one of the royal pleasure châteaux. Large parts of its walls and moat remain, towering above the Old Town and giving a graphic idea of a medieval fortress.

Beyond Chinon is **Saumur** ⓚ, where the surrounding woodlands are rich in mushrooms, and the local vineyards produce prestigious light red and dry, sparkling white wines. The town is dominated by its **château** (Wed–Mon) dating from the 12th century, and the **Musée du Champignon** (Feb–Nov daily) offers guided visits to the underground galleries where mushrooms are cultivated.

At Les Ponts-de-Cé, a road leads north to **Angers** ⓛ. In the Old Town

there are fine Renaissance houses, most notably the **Logis Barrault** (housing the fine arts museum, June–Sept daily, Oct–May Tue–Sun), and the **Hôtel de Pincé** (also art museum, but closed for some time for renovation). But pride of place must go to the tapestries in the château (daily), particularly the *Tenture de l'Apocalypse*, 70 pictures from a 14th-century work.

The Atlantic coast

Travelling south of Angers down the Atlantic coast brings you to the nature reserve of **Le Marais Poitevin**. Also known as La Venise Verte – Green Venice – it consists of 15,000 hectares (37,000 acres) of lush, green countryside threaded with 1,450km (900 miles) of waterways. At Coulon, 11km (7 miles) west of Niort, boatmen await tourists for river trips on flat-bottomed boats propelled by long forked poles (*pigoulles*).

The gracious port town of **La Rochelle** ⑪ is famous for Cardinal Richelieu's ruthless siege of the Protestant population in the 17th century. Today it's a favourite port of call

for yachtsmen, and the houses of the Old Town have retained their 17th- and 18th-century charm, particularly along Rue du Palais. **Tour St-Nicolas** and **Tour de la Chaîne** face each other across the sheltered 13th-century port where a huge chain was drawn across every night to keep ships out.

Inland, the regional capital of **Poitiers** ⑫ is one of the oldest cities in France. The church of **Notre-Dame-la-Grande**, in the town centre, has a magnificent, richly sculpted Romanesque facade and 12th-century frescoes in the vault of the choir. The church of St-Hilaire-le-Grand is the oldest in Poitiers, with parts dating to the 11th century. Just outside Poitiers is **Futuroscope** (daily), a theme park on technology and the future.

Into the interior: the Massif Central and the Dordogne

France's upland heartland, the Massif Central, is relatively little visited yet holds many fine sights and dramatically rugged landscapes. Its two great cities are **Limoges** ⑬, famed for its

Inside the Saumur wine cellars.

Postcard-pretty La Roque Gageac in the Dordogne.

PAINTERS OF PREHISTORY

Sealed off in prehistoric times, the famous Grotte de Lascaux was not rediscovered until 12 September 1940 – during the search for a dog that had disappeared down a hole. Due to the preoccupations of World War II and ensuing hardships, crowds only started flocking to the site some years later. When an astute official learnt in 1963 that a green fungus was growing over the paintings, the cave was immediately closed to the public and a replica, Lascaux II, was built.

Most of the paintings, in black, yellow and red, are thought to date from the Aurignacian period, between 30,000–20,000 BC. The colour friezes use a range of techniques to obtain perspective, texture and movement. They cover the walls and roofs of the cave and represent a number of animals including bulls, cows, deer, bison and horses.

Outstanding as it is, Lascaux is just one of many decorated prehistoric caves in southwest France, mostly in the Dordogne but also in the foothills of the Pyrenees. Often the paintings are in inaccessible places and must have demanded great ingenuity and determination to execute. They also display extraordinary skill. Frequently the painters make use of the natural contours of the rock to produce particularly naturalistic effects. Exactly why prehistoric people went to such lengths to paint their pictures remains a mystery.

The Arthur 4D ride at Futuroscope in Poitiers.

The Grand Théâtre in Bordeaux.

enamel and porcelain, and **Clermont-Ferrand ⑭**, which surrounds a massive cathedral built of black lava. Rising above the city is the distinctive volcanic peak of the **Puy de Dôme** (1,464 metres/4,800ft), which is easily ascended on foot or by minibus for spectacular panoramic views. The views are even more impressive from the summit of **Puy Mary** (1,787 metres/5,863ft), reached by steps from France's highest road pass, the Pas de Peyrol, above the pretty town of **Salers**. Another high point – quite literally – of the Massif Central is the shrine of **Le Puy-en-Velay ⑮**, where the Chapelle St-Michel is built on a pinnacle of tufa rock and reached by a stone staircase.

To the south and west, the Massif Central descends into a series of beautiful valleys, with rivers flowing in parallel towards the Atlantic. The most northerly, and the best known, is

the Dordogne, which is postcard-perfect as it flows past the pretty towns of **Domme**, **La Roque Gageac** and **Beynac-et-Cazenac**. The capital of the *département* is Périgueux ⑯, with its five-domed Byzantine-Romanesque cathedral, but the one place not to miss here is **Sarlat ⑰**, a bustling, labyrinthine market town of atmospheric streets and squares.

Between Périgueux and Sarlat, the River Vézère carves what has become known as the **Vallée de l'Homme** (the Valley of Man) because of its extraordinary number of caves and rock overhangs decorated with prehistoric art. **Lascaux** is the world's most famous painted cave, but its immense popularity threatened its conservation and it has been closed to visitors. A replica nearby, **Lascaux II**, is almost as good as the real thing. Further down the valley is **Les Eyzies-de-Tayac**, renowned as the "prehistoric capital of France", and home of the **Musée National de Préhistoire** (July–Aug daily, Sept–June Wed–Mon).

In recent decades the Dordogne has been colonised by incomers,

particularly the British, drawn by the beauty of its landscapes and the promise of a bucolic lifestyle, but this influx is really nothing new, and its innate charm has long been appreciated, as witnessed by the exquisite châteaux that accumulated here over the centuries. One of the most magnificent is the **Château de Hautefort** (Apr–Sept daily), built in the 17th century.

South of the Dordogne is the Lot. The valley's highlights include the Romanesque abbey and treasury of **Conques**, the pretty perched village of **St-Cirq Lapopie**, the prehistoric cave paintings of **Pech-Merle** (Apr–Oct daily), the handsome medieval bridge over the river at **Cahors** ⑱, and an enormously deep pothole, **Gouffre de Padirac**, which is descended by stairs or lift to reveal an amazing cave system and underground river. Above all, don't miss the medieval Christian pilgrimage centre of **Rocamadour**, an extraordinary village built on the almost sheer side of a deep gorge, with an accretion of crypts, chapels and houses picturesquely clinging to the cliffs.

Far to the southeast is the River Tarn, which flows out of the wild and beautiful schist and granite uplands of the **Parc National des Cévennes** to carve the spectacular, meandering **Gorges du Tarn** ⑲ between Florac and Millau. The gorges are a magnet for the outdoors enthusiast with kayaking, canoing, hiking and a myriad of other activities on offer against beautiful vistas.

The River Tarn flows through a series of rapids and pools, a stunning location for white-water rafting, canoeing and kayaking. Further downstream the landscapes become much tamer as the river passes through the handsome redbrick town of **Albi** ⑳. Next to the massive cathedral is the old bishop's palace, which is now the superb **Musée de Toulouse-Lautrec** (Apr–Sept daily, Oct–Mar Wed–Mon), in commemoration of the artist's birthplace.

Bordeaux and its vineyards

These rivers join the much larger Garonne, on which stands the port of **Bordeaux** ㉑, self-styled – with good reason – as the "world's wine capital". It is a handsome, harmonious city of mainly 18th-century buildings epitomised by the **Place de la Bourse** on the riverbank, the **Palais Rohan** (now the city hall) and, above all, the **Grand-Théâtre** on the Place de la Comédie, at one end of the Cours du 30 Juillet. At the other end of this street is the **Monument aux Girondins**, commemorating the parliamentarians of Bordeaux who were put to death in 1793 after they clashed with Robespierre's radical Jacobins during the French Revolution. A statue of Liberty looks down from the top of a 50-metre (164ft) high column onto the **Esplanade des Quinconces**, leading from the monument to the riverbank.

While most of the city speaks of the Enlightenment and the age of commerce, there are some older monuments hidden in the tangle of streets and squares south of the Place

The extraordinary cave paintings at Lascaux are around 20,000 years old.

Rocamadour in the Dordogne.

WHERE

The Millau Viaduct, taking the A75 motorway across the valley of the River Tarn, is the world's highest road bridge. Designed by architect Norman Foster and engineer Michel Virlogeux and opened in 2004, it has become a popular tourist attraction in its own right, with a visitor's information centre on the RD 992 going towards Albi.

Sunbathing on the beach at Biarritz.

de la Bourse. Two old gateways here, the **Porte-Cailhau** and the **Grosse Cloche**, are particularly worth seeking out.

Away from the river, you emerge from the Old Town near the **Cathédrale St-André** (11th-century but much altered) and its free-standing Gothic belltower, the **Tour Pey-Berland**. Nearby is the **Musée de l'Aquitaine** (Tue–Sun), a regional museum with the focus on archaeology.

No one comes to Bordeaux just to see monuments: invariably, the city is used as a starting point for a tour of the vineyards that dominate the surrounding landscape. The Bordeaux wine region is divided into more than 30 sub-regions of greater or lesser prestige, and these in turn contain hundreds of estates, some surveyed by aristocratic châteaux. North of the city, on the **Médoc** peninsula, are the most famous wine estates, such as **Château Margaux, Château Latour, Château Lafite Rothschild** and **Château Mouton Rothschild**. The wine and tourist information office in Pauillac

is the best place to arrange visits to the various wine producers.

To the south and southeast of Bordeaux are the wine regions of **Graves** and **Sauternes** and to the east **Entre-Deux-Mers**, **Pomerol** and **St-Emilion**. At the heart of this last region, St-Emilion is an attractive town with an ancient underground church.

The *département* of which Bordeaux is capital, the Gironde, has more to it than wines. Its other attractions include the 12th–14th-century **Château de Roquetaillade** and the **Bassin d'Arcachon**, a lagoon open to the sea which is at once a holiday resort, sailing lagoon, bird reserve and oyster farm. On the coast just south of the lagoon is Europe's highest sand dune, the **Dune du Pyla.**

The French Basque Country

The extreme southwestern corner of France is the Basque Country, inhabited by a people with ancient roots and a strong sense of identity. **Bayonne**, its capital, stands at the confluence of the Nive and Adour rivers and is built around a large Gothic cathedral.

It forms a conurbation with the elegant resort of **Biarritz ㉒**, which once offered a combination of fashion and pleasure that attracted famous visitors such as Emperor Napoleon III, his wife Eugénie and Britain's Edward VII, while still Prince of Wales. The heart of the town is the **Promenades**, where steep cliffs fall to the ocean, and romantic alleys shaded by tamarisk trees lead to the **Rocher de la Vierge** (Rock of the Virgin), with beautiful views of the Basque coast. Biarritz is famous for its huge waves, and some of Europe's most important surfing competitions are held here. Nearby, **St-Jean-de-Luz** is a smaller but similar resort town.

Inland, the Basque Country has exquisitely pretty towns, most notably **Ainhoa** and **Sare**, which stands beneath the mountain of **La Rhune**, ascended by an old cog railway. Pilgrims from all over France converge on the historic town of **St-Jean-Pied-de-Port** before crossing a pass over the Pyrenees on their long way to the shrine of Santiago de Compostela in Spain.

Along the Pyrenees

Few international borders are as clearly marked as that between France and Spain, which follows the Pyrenees, a 400km (250-mile) mountain chain from the Bay of Biscay to the Mediterranean. The range is clearly visible across much of the southwest, particularly in winter when the air is clear and the peaks capped with snow. Although lower than the Alps, the Pyrenees are still a popular winter sports destination, with over 40 resorts to choose from. In summer, the mountains are busy with hikers, some of them making the trek along the GR10 footpath from coast to coast. The exceptional gradients make the Pyrenees popular also with cyclists, who come to tackle the high passes (cols) – some over 2,000 metres (6,500ft) – that provide gruelling obstacles for competitors in the Tour de France.

The mountains reach their highest elevations due south of the cities of **Pau**, **Tarbes** and **Lourdes ㉓**. The last is one of the most important Catholic shrines in the world and a sacred site

Hikers at Vignemale in the Pyrenees.

*Colourful streets in
Collioure, Pyrenees.*

which is overrun with pilgrims in search of miracle cures, as well as curious sightseers. Part of the Pyrenees is protected as a national park for its fragile flora and fauna. If your time in the mountains is short, make for the **Cirque de Gavarnie**, a stunning natural rock amphitheatre formed by glaciation; the **Pont d'Espagne**, an easily accessible beauty spot with marked walking trails; or the **Pic du Midi** (2,872 metres/9,423ft), with an observatory on top which is reached by cable car from the ski resort of La Mongie. Below it, the mountain village of **Arreau** is made up of picture-perfect balconied houses.

Moving eastwards along the range you pass through the thickly forested *département* of the Ariège. In the foothills there are a great many impressive castles associated with the Cathars, a heretic sect persecuted to extinction by the Catholic Church in alliance with the nobles of northern France in the 13th century. They made their last stand at the castle of **Montségur**, southeast of Foix, today an atmospheric ruin. The Ariège's

other major attraction is the caves at **Niaux**, with prehistoric paintings comparable to those at Lascaux, but much less well known.

French Catalonia

The French part of Catalonia (which, like the Basque Country, is a nation without a state) occupies the Mediterranean end of the Pyrenees and has its capital at **Perpignan**. It was united with the rest of Catalonia to the south until 1659, when a treaty gave it to France.

Before the mountains finally descend to sea level, they throw up the striking silhouette of the Pic du Canigou (2,784 metres/9,134ft) above the towns of **Prades** and **Villefranche-de-Conflent**. On the slopes of the Pic is the rebuilt 11th-century monastery of **St-Martin du Canigou**, reached by an uphill slog of half an hour or more, depending on your fitness. Two choice places to visit here are **Ceret**, a cherry-producing town inland, and **Collioure ㉔** on the coast – both famous for inspiring visiting artists, including Matisse and Picasso.

The Languedoc

The ancient city of **Toulouse ㉕** stands on the banks of the River Garonne, geographically and culturally midway between the Atlantic and the Mediterranean. In recent decades it has grown into France's sixth-largest metropolis on the back of its aerospace industry.

Most of the older buildings are made of the local brick, earning Toulouse the epithet of the *"Ville Rose"*, or Pink City. From the central square, the **Place du Capitole,** which contains the 18th-century town hall, all the other sights are within an easy walk. Chief among them are the massive Romanesque pilgrimage church of **St-Sernin**, its tiered tower acting as a landmark, and the fine arts museum, **Musée des Augustins** (daily), housed in a glorious 14th-century convent with a Gothic cloister.

Contemporary attractions include the **Cité de l'Espace** (Apr–Aug daily, Sept–Mar Tue–Sun), a museum dedicated to space exploration.

From Toulouse, the A61 motorway towards the Mediterranean runs beside a much older channel of communication, the Canal du Midi. Built in the 17th century and kept topped up with water by an ingenious hydraulic system, it is now used as a green artery for leisure cruising, walking and cycling. An information centre is located off the A61 motorway at Avignonet-Lauragais.

The motorway also passes alongside the magnificent walled city of **Carcassonne ㉖**, one of the undeniable glories of France. Ringed by a double set of ramparts and guarded by myriad pepperpot towers, it is a stunning example of a self-contained medieval town. What you see today is due more to imaginative reconstruction than preservation, but it still conjures up the mood of its times, especially when seen from afar.

Most of the coast of the Languedoc region, from Perpignan almost as far as the Rhône Delta, is one long beach, much of it along sandbars separated from the mainland by shallow lagoons. It is interrupted by some historic towns, such as Narbonne, once the Roman capital of the whole of southwest Gaul, and Sète, an atmospheric fishing port much visited for its exceptional seafood restaurants. There are also a number of large holiday centres, especially around Cap d'Agde, including one of Europe's largest naturist resorts. Since the sandy beaches are so open here, unlike the sheltered rocky coves of the Côte d'Azur further east or Corsica, they often experience very high winds, which make them favourites for wind- and kitesurfers, and serious sunbathers. North of Sète the A75 highway, built in the early 2000s, runs north through the Massif Central across the Millau Viaduct, a stunning example of modern engineering.

Two more great ancient cities of France's south – the Midi – stand just east of the Rhône Delta. **Montpellier,** with its thriving university, and striking contemporary architecture, is considered one of the liveliest and most artistic places to live in the south. It also has an important collection of French painting in the **Musée Fabre** (Tue–Sun).

Nearby **Nîmes ㉗** is another city that strives to be up-to-date, although its greatest assets are its Roman buildings built in the 1st century AD, especially the exceptionally well-preserved amphitheatre of **Les Arènes**, built at the end of the 1st century AD to accommodate over 16,000 spectators and which is still used today for bullfights and rock concerts. The **Maison Carrée**, a temple in a superb state of conservation, is another Roman edifice of note, but one of the greatest engineering and aesthetic achievements of Roman civilisation, however, is 20km (12 miles) north of Nîmes. The three-tiered **Pont du Gard** aqueduct (daily) is France's most visited ancient monument. It

Basque boys parading in St-Jean-de-Luz.

Street theatre at Avignon's annual arts festival.

Nuns on a pilgrimage in Lourdes in front of the Basilique de L'Immaculée Conception.

is 275 metres/yds at its longest part and almost 50 metres (164ft) high. Built of large stones that were fitted together without mortar, it once carried water flowing at 400 litres (110 gallons) per second.

Gateways to Provence

Cross the Rhône and you are in **Provence**, France's sensuous southern region, which has always attracted well-heeled foreign settlers and artists.

The lively town of **Avignon** ㉘ offers a great summer theatre festival in and around its superb **Palais des Papes** (daily). This 14th-century edifice was built at a time when the popes were in the pocket of the kings of France, and moved here rather than stay in Rome. Its silent cloisters, cavernous halls and imposing ramparts are a delight to explore. In contrast, the famous bridge (*"Sur le pont d'Avignon, l'on y danse, tous en rond"*), now only reaching halfway across the River Rhône, is a disappointing four-arch ruin. (In fact, the people didn't dance on it as the French song says, but underneath it.)

Marseille's harbour.

North of Avignon, **Orange** was a favoured resort for the Romans when it was a colony of their empire, with a population four times the size of its present-day 25,000. The Roman theatre, graced by a statue of Emperor Augustus, is regarded as the most beautiful amphitheatre of the classical era. Surrounding Orange, the area of the **Vaucluse** is richly fertile. The fascinating ruins at **Vaison-la-Romaine** provide a glimpse of the private side of Roman life in some well-preserved houses of 2,000 years ago. **Mont Ventoux** has a view over the whole of Provence down to Marseille and the Mediterranean or clear across to the Swiss Alps. One of the great attractions of this mountain region is the **Fontaine-de-Vaucluse**, where the underground River Sorgue suddenly springs into sight in a spectacular setting of grottoes.

The region's most picturesque relic of ancient Roman life is **Arles**, which, besides its fine amphitheatre and arena, has the fascinating necropolis of Les Alyscamps in a lovely setting. Arles is perhaps best known nowadays as the town where Vincent Van Gogh came to paint in the southern light in 1888, and produced many of his most famous works in the shaded cafés and heat-swirled fields. Many locations associated with him can still be recognised around the hot, sleepy little town.

South of Arles is the **Camargue**, the wild, windswept wetlands of the Rhône Delta. It's an entrancing place because of its birdlife – this is a good place to see flamingos in the wild, and many other water birds – and special way of life, which revolves around rearing bulls and horses. The principal town of the Camargue is Stes-Maries-de-la-Mer, which hosts a spectacular gypsy festival every May attracting Roma, Gitans and other gypsies from all over Europe. There's a visitor centre for this fascinating region at La Capelière, to the south of Villeneuve.

Heart of Provence

Aix-en-Provence , the most serene of university towns, with its wonderful arcade of plane trees across the Cours Mirabeau, is the intellectual heart of the region. Zola grew up in the city, along with his friend Paul Cézanne. One of the best ways to see Aix is by taking the Cézanne trail, following a free leaflet from the tourist office. **L'Atelier Paul Cézanne** (daily) preserves the artist's studio and house – his cape and beret hang where he left them.

South of Aix, **Marseille** B is France's oldest and second-largest city. Founded by Greek traders in 600 BC, the gateway to the Mediterranean, the Orient and beyond has been a bustling port for centuries. Today the **Vieux Port** has a colourful fish market and many seafood restaurants. The streets around **La Canebière**, Marseille's most famous thoroughfare, which leads from the port, are the liveliest in the city, especially in the evening.

Between Marseille and Toulon, the shore is distinguished by **Les Calanques**, steep sided fjords carved out of cliffs, best viewed by boat from **Cassis** C. This chic resort of restored houses with a popular golden beach is known for its fragrant white wines, which tantalise the palate with hints of rosemary, gorse and myrtle – the herbs that cover these hills.

Over the sea: Corsica

Across the Ligurian Sea, reached by ferry from Marseille, Toulon or Nice, is **Corsica** (La Corse) **29**, the Mediterranean's fourth-largest island. Although it has been part of France since 1769, the home of Napoleon has a distinct culture and its own language – a dialect of Italian – and often feels as much Italian as it does French. Ruggedly mountainous, it is an extraordinary bundle of landscapes within a small space, from chilly mountain summits to subtropical palm groves. Most of all, it draws holidaymakers for its unspoilt villages, lazy pace of life and beautiful beaches washed by clear waters. Around the coast there are thousands of rocky coves, ideal for relaxed swimming and sailing, and the scuba-diving is among the best in Europe.

The island's capital, **Ajaccio**, is a charming city with the **Maison Bonaparte** (Tue–Sun), Napoleon's birthplace, but more characterful are the historic towns further north, like **Corte** and **Bastia**. Some of the most beautiful beaches are on the west coast around **Porto**, from where you can climb inland up a deep rift in the mountains, the **Gorges de Spelunca**. The whole of Corsica is wonderful for hiking, and the **GR20** trail, along the whole island from north to south, is one of France's most challenging long-distance footpaths.

The Côte d'Azur

The sun-drenched Côte d'Azur meanders lazily from **Toulon** D, home to France's Mediterranean naval fleet, to the Italian border along rocky lagoons and coves. Modern **Hyères** E, east of

One of the most popular tourist sights in France is Carcassonne, a beautifully preserved medieval fortified city.

The Place d'Albertas, lined with 17th-century townhouses in Aix-en-Provence.

Toulon along the coast, is made up of a *vieille ville* and a newer area of modern villas and boulevards with date palms. This was once an ancient and medieval port, but it is now 4km (2½ miles) from the sea. Hyères was the first "climatic" resort on the Côte d'Azur, its subtropical climate encouraging sailing, scuba-diving, windsurfing and waterskiing. Within the Old Town, entered via its 13th-century gate, is the **Place Massillon**, where there is a food market every day that is especially good for Arab and Provençal specialities.

The once-tiny fishing village of **St-Tropez** ❻, made famous by Brigitte Bardot in the 1960s, is still packed with visitors in summer, and a sort of Mediterranean extension of Paris, with its very expensive restaurants permanently crowded. French painters and writers had discovered it by the late 19th century; some of the paintings from this time, showing the village in its pre-touristy state, are on display in a lovely converted chapel, the **Musée de l'Annonciade** (Wed–Mon).

The plateau town of **Fréjus** ❼, like Hyères, used to lie on the sea. Its name derives from *Forum Julii*; it was founded by Julius Caesar in 49 BC. Important Roman ruins here include the 10,000-seat arena where Picasso used to watch bullfights.

For fewer crowds, head north into the hills to the **Gorges du Verdon** ❽, France's Grand Canyon. The Verdon cuts through limestone cliffs that plunge to the torrent 600 metres (2,000ft) below. The Norman Foster-designed Musée de Préhistoire (Feb–mid-Dec Wed–Mon) at Quinson is the largest of its kind. From here stretch the Alpes de Haute Provence, a wild, barren landscape leading up into the French Alps.

Heading back towards the coast, stop if you can at **Grasse** ❾, where there have been perfume distilleries since the 16th century. The **Musée International de la Parfumerie**, in an elegant 18th-century mansion, tells the industry's history. You can also visit the commercial **Parfumerie Fragonard** (daily), opposite the **Villa-Musée Fragonard** (June–Sept

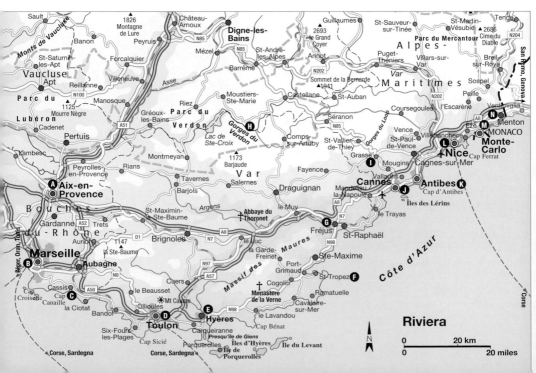

daily, Oct–May Wed–Mon), where the Grasse-born artist Jean-Honoré Fragonard lived.

The International Film Festival held each May in **Cannes**  is one of the highlights of an annual series of events that attracts a set of celebrities and a media circus. Cannes has made the most of its fashionable cachet since Lord Brougham, the Lord Chancellor of England, was stranded here in 1834 because of an outbreak of cholera in Nice, where he was headed for a winter holiday. It pleased him so much he built a house on **Mont Chevalier** and encouraged other British aristocrats to do the same. **Le Suquet** is the ancient quarter around Mont Chevalier. At dinner hour in high season, elegant couples emerge from yachts anchored in the old harbour and struggle up **Rue St-Antoine** to the fashionable restaurants for which Le Suquet is noted.

Dinner will be followed by a stroll along the **Boulevard de la Croisette** for the magnificent views of Le Suquet silhouetted against **La Napoule Bay**, with the chunky red hills of the Esterel in the background.

Antibes  and **Cap d'Antibes** face Nice and St-Jean-Cap-Ferrat across the Baie des Anges (Bay of Angels). Here the magnificent yacht harbour rests at the foot of an enormous brick citadel built in the 16th century to protect the infant town from assaults by Barbary pirates. The Château Grimaldi on a terrace overlooking the sea, originally a 12th-century building but much reconstructed in the 16th, is now home to the **Musée Picasso** (Wed–Mon). It contains a remarkable collection of works painted by Picasso during his stay here in 1946, and the ceramics that were a major part of his output while he lived in Provence.

Matisse's **Chapelle du Rosaire** (daily) at **Vence**, northeast of Grasse by the D2210, is considered his masterpiece, a finely tuned synthesis of architectural elements, the most important being stained glass and the white walls on which their coloured light falls. The artist gave it much of his time between 1948 and 1951.

Directly south of Vence, the walled town of **St-Paul-de-Vence** was discovered by artists in the 1920s, and

The Camargue is the place to go for wild watery landscapes and abundant birdlife, such as these flamingos.

The Gorges du Verdon.

St-Tropez's wealth and style make it feel a bit like Paris on the Med.

many came to live here, notably Marc Chagall. Their presence attracted actors, musicians and celebrities of different kinds, many of whom patronised **La Colombe d'Or** café, now an exclusive hotel and restaurant with a priceless collection of works originally donated by visiting artists. St-Paul itself is a perfectly formed hill village with a vista of villas and cypresses as far as the eye can see, but its popularity means that its narrow winding main street becomes jammed with visitors.

Just outside the village, the **Fondation Maeght** (daily) occupies a white concrete and rose-brick structure designed by the Catalan architect J.L. Sert. The collection includes paintings by Braque, Bonnard, Kandinsky and Chagall, and several outdoor sculpture areas with works by Giacometti, Calder, Miró, Arp and others.

Nice to Monaco

The Fernand Léger Museum at Biot.

"The English come and pass the winter here to take the cure, soothe their chronic spleens and live out their fantasies," wrote an observer of the budding Anglo-Saxon social scene in **Nice ❶**

in 1775. They can thus take credit for establishing this city as the first centre of the Riviera. The **Promenade des Anglais**, the striking waterfront roadway embellished with flower beds and palm trees, was originally built in 1822 by the English for easier access to the sea. Queen Victoria enjoyed morning constitutionals along the coastal path on several occasions; in later years, she was carried along in her famous black-and-red donkey cart.

Today, the promenade is bedecked with luxury hotels, high-rise apartment blocks and trendy cafés. A short stroll away are the narrow winding alleyways of the *vieille ville* (Old Town), where the visitor gets a salty taste of older Provençal lifestyles, heightened by aromas of garlic, wine and pungent North African spices emanating from *couscous* parlours. A diminishing number of plain but traditional restaurants around the flower market on the **Cours Saleya** specialise in *soupe de poissons* and *bourride*, a native variation of *bouillabaisse*.

North of the Old Town is the **Musée Chagall** (Wed–Mon), containing

A LEGACY OF FINE ART AND SCULPTURE

Painters have been especially fascinated by the Côte d'Azur because of its unique sunlight. The quality of the light is due largely to the Mistral, a cold, dry, strong wind that often blows in from the Rhône Valley, sweeping the sky to crystal clarity, enriching colours and deepening shadows. Earlier art of the south, such as Roman and Greek remains, also provided the inspiration for 20th-century artists.

Matisse, Picasso, Dufy and Chagall were all devoted to the region, and the products of their fidelity are displayed in museums and private collections along the Riviera.

Picasso spent 27 years on the Côte d'Azur, more than half of them at Vallauris behind Cannes, where he established a ceramics studio, the Madoura Pottery, where copies are still sold. There is also a Musée Picasso in Antibes. At the village of Biot between Nice and Cannes, the Musée Fernand Léger (Wed–Mon) houses hundreds of works by the artist, who contributed to the creation of Cubism.

Auguste Renoir spent the last 12 years of his life at Cagnes-sur-Mer, where his home, now the Musée Renoir (Wed–Mon), remains exactly as it was when he died. Nice has several important art galleries, including the Musée Chagall and the Musée Matisse. Another mecca for art-lovers is the Fondation Maeght in St-Paul-de-Vence.

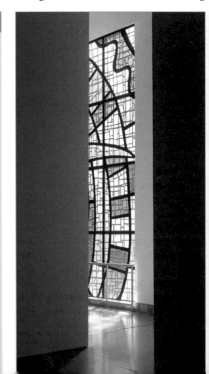

many of the artist's drawings and all his bronzes. The building was specially designed to house his masterpiece, *Messages Bibliques* – 17 monumental paintings depicting scenes from the Old Testament. There are also three stained-glass windows depicting *The Creation* and a 6-metre (20ft) mosaic of Elijah in his fiery chariot.

The remains of a Roman amphitheatre, capable of seating 4,000 spectators, and three public baths have been uncovered at **Cimiez**, atop a hill 1.6km (1 mile) northeast of the city centre. In a villa in the same district is the **Musée Matisse** (Wed–Mon), one of the finest collections in the world of paintings and other works by the artist.

East of Nice, you suddenly leave France and enter the microstate of **Monaco** . From the days of its early Genoese rulers, the principality of Monaco has survived as a political curiosity on the map of Europe. It exists under the protection of France but has remained a mini-monarchy of the Grimaldi family, with its own tax privileges, national licence plates and coat of arms. This tiny country of less than 1.5 sq km (1 sq mile) and a population of 32,000 has tried to live down its reputation as a sunny place for shady people. Today, it still dotes on the super-rich and trades on the fading glamour of its royal dynasty, now headed by Prince Albert, but also tries to attract other tourists.

If you're feeling lucky you might want to head straight for the sumptuously decorated gaming rooms of the world's most famous **Casino**, a *Belle Epoque* survivor which is open to visitors as well as to its habitual clientele of social butterflies. The western section was built in 1878 by the same architect who designed the Paris Opéra. The centre section is a tiny 529-seat Rococo-styled theatre, the home of the Monte-Carlo Opera.

Monaco's major historic monument is the **Palais des Princes** (Apr–Oct daily) a part-Moorish, part-Italian Renaissance castle on a rocky promontory jutting into the sea. Beneath the palace is the Old Town (Monaco-Ville), tinted with Provençal pink, orange and yellow hues, which surrounds a neo-Romanesque cathedral.

On the seashore stands the **Musée Océanographique** (daily), incorporating one of the finest and best-kept aquariums in Europe.

For an overview of Monaco the best place to go is the tiny village of **La Turbie**, behind the principality's yawning harbour. Here are the remains of one of the most impressive, yet least known Roman monuments, the Alpine Trophy. In 6 BC Rome commemorated the final subjugation of the warriors of the Alps region by raising an enormous stone trophy, a Doric colonnade that is still standing.

La Turbie is one of several medieval mountain villages along the giant ridge of rock above the Côte d'Azur with mesmerising views over the coast below. Consequently, they have long been favourites with visitors.

Eze, the best known because it is near the sea, is easy to reach and offers

The month of July is the best time to see fields awash with lavender in Provence.

Monaco.

Monaco's casinos attract the seriously wealthy.

a splendid panoramic overview from its 470-metre (1,550ft) elevation. It has an intriguing history of pirate assaults and Moorish massacres that can be traced back to the 1st century AD, when a colony of Phoenicians unnerved their Roman neighbours by consecrating a temple to their goddess Isis. In addition to the crowds, Eze is noted today for the crumbling ramparts of its 14th-century castle.

Close to the Italian frontier, the 17th-century town of **Menton** is probably the warmest winter resort on any French coast and offers one of the most typical townscapes in Provence. In the narrow, twisting, vaulted streets overhead balconies jut out over the alleyways until they almost bump balustrades.

To the Alps and the Rhône Valley

A scenic highway (N85) traces Napoleon's journey after he landed on French shores in 1815 following his Elba exile, and is known as the Route Napoléon. It begins at Cannes and goes through Grasse to **Grenoble** ㉚,

Menton lies close to the Italian border.

the capital of the French Alps. The best view of the city can be had from the **Fort de la Bastille**, reached by cable car. Further north and further into the mountains, Chambéry is an elegant mountain city, but less attractive than Annecy further up, which has a lovely Old Town on a mountain-ringed lake that is a favourite for boat trips.

Roads continue from Annecy or direct from Chambéry into the heart of the French Alps at **Chamonix-Mont-Blanc** ㉛, one of the world's most fashionable winter sports resorts for well over a century. It sits, as its name suggests, at the foot of the awe-inspiring giant mass of Mont Blanc, the tallest mountain in Western Europe, at 4,808 metres (15,780ft). Though most famous for skiing, Chamonix and its valley also offer a wealth of hiking and other mountain sports possibilities in summer. To the south, and reached from Chambéry, is another of the Alps' most popular winter centres in the **Val d'Isère**, an area that was developed more recently than Chamonix but is now preferred by many skiers. Just west of the valley is the **Parc National de la Vanoise**, a huge expanse of Alpine wilderness that is home to France's largest surviving population of Alpine Ibex mountain goats, and which attracts great numbers of hikers each summer. Further south again, the equally wild **Parc National des Ecrins** near Briançon is home to a recently reintroduced population of wolves.

Routes from the mountains lead down to the Rhône Valley and France's third-largest city, **Lyon** ㉜. It is often said to be the country's gastronomic capital, and where southern France begins. Standing astride the rivers Sâone and Rhone, its layout can be somewhat confusing, with the city centre on a peninsula, the *Presqu'Ile* between the two rivers. The most interesting part is **Vieux Lyon** (Old Lyon), on the west bank of the Saône, which has some fine Renaissance

houses linked by covered passages unique to Lyon, known as *traboules*. A funicular railway runs from here up the hill of **Fourvière**, where there are two Roman amphitheatres and an ostentatious 19th-century basilica, and tremendous views over the city.

For centuries, Lyon was Europe's silk capital, and its history can be seen in the **Musée Historique des Tissus** (Tue–Sun). Another excellent museum, the **Musée des Beaux-Arts** (Wed–Mon), has an exceptional collection of French and other European paintings.

South of Lyon, the Rhône Valley is lined with more and more fruit orchards and vineyards the further you head south. Near Montélimar the main river is joined by the **Ardèche**, an exquisitely beautiful river that runs through a deep limestone gorge riddled with caves and tunnels. A guided canoe trip is a great way to discover the gorge and secluded beaches along the river.

The Burgundy winelands

Beaune ㉝ has been at the heart of Burgundy's wine trade since the Middle Ages, and the auction at the Hospices de Beaune in **L'Hôtel-Dieu** (daily) – a charity hospital historically financed by wine produced on land donated by benefactors – is still the high point in the local wine calendar. Under its splendid multicoloured roof, the long ward of the hospital contains the original sickbeds. The halls off the courtyard house artworks and tapestries, crowned by a magnificently detailed painting of The *Last Judgement* by Rogier van der Weyden.

Burgundy's capital is **Dijon** ㉞. The monumental **Palais des Ducs**, where the 14th- and 15th-century dukes of Burgundy rest in grandiose tombs, is in Dijon's busy city centre. The oldest part of the palace houses the **Musée des Beaux-Arts** (Wed–Mon), one of the finest in France, with French, German and Italian statuary

and paintings from the 14th–18th centuries.

One of the world's most illustrious wine routes runs along the Côte d'Or or "Golden Slope", about 50km (30 miles) long, from Dijon through Beaune to Châlons-sur-Saône. It's very easy to navigate, as the country road is lined with villages whose names have become celebrated world-wide such as **Gevrey-Chambertin**, **Nuits-St-Georges** and **Vougeot**. Many vineyards welcome visitors, and many wine tours are available.

Burgundy, and Dijon in particular, is also the hub of France's network of canals, built to link up the rivers on the Atlantic and Mediterranean sides of the country, and one of the most enjoyable ways of seeing the winelands is on a barge cruise along these now very placid tree-lined waterways. Most popular is the Canal de Bourgogne, which runs from the River Saône at Dijon to meet the Yonne, a tributary of the Seine, near Auxerre.

Around 45km (28 miles) northwest of Dijon, the **Abbaye de Fontenay** (daily) makes for a welcome moment

The English started coming to Nice as early as the 18th century, and later, Queen Victoria liked to stroll along the Promenade des Anglais.

A typical restaurant in Lyon known as a bouchon.

TIP

Many companies offer cruises on France's canals. LeBoat (www. leboat.com) offers boats of different sizes and different routes throughout France, and the rest of Europe. Locaboat (www.loca boat.com), experts in the Burgundy canals, provide cruising itineraries in pénichettes, traditional French canal boats.

of peace in its 12th-century cloisters. Intended to be piously modest, without ornament of any kind, the bare paving stones and immaculate columns acquired, in the course of time, a look of grandeur.

West of here, set high on a hilltop, **Vézelay** ❸ is one of Burgundy's most spectacular monuments. The majestic **Basilique Sainte-Madeleine** was founded in the 9th century as an abbey, and was a major pilgrimage centre in the Middle Ages.

In the Jura mountains of Franche-Comté east of Dijon, the town of **Besançon** nestles in a sweeping curve of the River Doubs. The 16th-century **Palais Granville** was the aristocratic home of the Chancellor to Habsburg Emperor Charles V. This pleasant town also has an impressive 70-dial astronomical clock in the cathedral and a formidable 17th-century citadel built for Louis XIV's eastern defences.

Alsace and Lorraine

Saucisson for sale in Colmar.

Lorraine and Alsace have been historic bones of contention between France and Germany. Germany seized Alsace and most of Lorraine after the Franco-Prussian War in 1871, but France reclaimed them in 1918.

Belfort owes its glory to its successful resistance against the Prussians in 1870, commemorated by the monumental lion designed by Auguste Bartholdi, creator of New York's Statue of Liberty. Nearby, stop at **Ronchamp** to admire Le Corbusier's striking chapel Notre-Dame-du-Haut, a landmark of 20th-century architecture.

The point where you enter Alsace is very recognisable, since the traditional buildings have a very un-French, and decidedly Germanic look. **Colmar** ❻ has a quiet but irresistible charm, and its 16th-century houses, like something out of a German fairy tale, are the very essence of Alsatian tradition. Most cherished of its treasures is Mathias Grünewald's celebrated Issenheim altar painting in the **Musée d'Unterlinden** (May–Oct daily, Nov–Apr Wed–Mon). Above the town is the mountain ridge of the **Vosges,** a charming countryside of forests, orchards and vineyards, among

REGIONAL FOODS OF FRANCE

General de Gaulle is famously said to have asked: "How can you govern a country which has 246 varieties of cheese?" His figure is probably an underestimate, and as with cheese so with food in general: there is such a bewildering diversity of things to eat and drink that you could be tempted to forget about sightseeing altogether and spend your time in restaurants and bistros instead.

Many regions of France are proud producers of some particular speciality or other: truffles in the Dordogne; *foie gras* and garlic come from Gascony; cured ham is produced in the southwest; mustard is made in Dijon; and good fish and seafood are landed at ports almost anywhere along the coasts. And everywhere there will be a local dish to try on the menu – crêpes are a staple of Brittany; *cassoulet* is the typical meat and bean casserole of Toulouse; *bouillabaisse* the fish soup that distinguishes Marseille; and quiche the dish to order in Lorraine.

The French love not only eating, but talking about what they are eating, and an interest in food on the part of the visitor is the quickest way to the heart of the country. Show curiosity about anything on your plate or on a market stall and you will be given a lecture on the geography, climate, farming and lifestyle of the region. And, of course, there is always a wine to accompany your meal, but that is another universe in itself…

which the villages of **Riquewihr** and **Kaysersberg** are true medieval gems.

Strasbourg ③⑦ is Alsace's dignified capital and one of the seats of the European Parliament. The River Ill encircles the lovely Old Town where Goethe was a happy student in 1770. The graceful cathedral, with its intriguing asymmetrical steeple, is enormously impressive, particularly for its central porch and the stunning stained-glass rose window above.

Nancy ③⑧ is graced by a beautifully harmonious main square, the 18th-century **Place Stanislas**, its palatial pavilions flanked by magnificent gilded iron gates. In the Old Town, the renovated houses of the Grande Rue lead to the Porte de la Craffe, whose two towers and connecting bastion are impressive reminders of earlier fortifications. Along the way, the Palais Ducal contains the **Musée Lorrain** (Tue–Sun). Housed in a separate museum is the unique **Ecole de Nancy** (Wed–Sun), the epitome of French Art Nouveau.

Metz, at the confluence of the Moselle and Seille rivers, is the capital of Lorraine. It has a Gothic cathedral and what is claimed to be the oldest church in France, St-Pierre-aux-Nonnains, dating from the 4th century.

To the French, the name **Verdun ③⑨** symbolises heroic national resistance. One of the bloodiest battles of World War I was fought here in 1916; a German offensive intended to end the deadlock of trench warfare on the Western Front ended in failure, but only after nearly 600,000 men had died. There is an excellent museum, the Mémorial de Verdun (Feb–Dec daily), and other sites around the battlefield.

Champagne

Similarly of deep symbolical significance, although for difference reasons, is the city of **Reims ④⓪**. In 496 Clovis, first King of the Franks, was baptised in Reims, and thereafter each new French monarch would make his way

here to be crowned in this city's magnificent **Cathédrale Notre-Dame**, which has superb stained-glass windows ranging from the 13th-century **rose window** to 20th-century windows by Chagall. Administratively, modern Reims is only a sub-prefecture but more prestigiously it is the commercial centre for the production of a unique style of wine to which the region has given its name: **champagne.** If you can only take one souvenir home, it should surely be a bottle of the authentic stuff.

The most famous champagne houses such as Taittinger, Veuve Clicquot or Möet & Chandon are mostly in Reims itself or in Epernay a little to the south, where, in the middle of town, there is a monument to Dom Pérignon, the 17th-century monk credited with inventing champagne. Most offer tours of their opulent cellars, though it's advisable to book. Other champagne-makers and their vineyards are spread along the roads between the two main towns through the Montagne de Reims, a lovely countryside of rolling green hills.

The Hospices de Beaune, former charitable almshouses founded in 1443.

Colmar in Alsace.

EUROPE'S GREATEST ART GALLERIES

The great museums of Europe are filled with extraordinary works of art from every period of history, a breathtaking display of, and testament to, mankind's creativity and spirit.

It is almost impossible to overstate the wealth of artistic treasures awaiting the visitor to Western Europe. The great galleries of Paris, Florence, Amsterdam, Madrid and so on are as famous in their own right as the artists whose works they house.

However, while the Louvre or the Prado offer grand surroundings for the display of the greatest art, especial pleasure is offered by the intimate experience of visiting, say, El Greco's house in Toledo, where some of his greatest works are on display.

The oldest collections are of works commissioned by the Church, which was the main patron of European art from late Antiquity until the Renaissance. Later on, other collections were the creation of kings and queens, whose personal tastes and preferences shaped their choice of artists to patronise. As wealth spread through society, smaller displays of art were founded by rich merchants or bankers. The Medici, for example, amassed their wealth first as wool merchants then as bankers, and spent most of it in Florence, financing glorious new buildings and the artists to decorate them.

As one might expect, most of Europe's greatest collections have a strong national character and focus. The Rijksmuseum in Amsterdam is almost entirely filled with Dutch art of the Golden Age, while the Uffizi in Florence is a repository of Italian Renaissance art. Some, though, such as the Van Gogh Museum in Amsterdam, the Dalí Museum in Figueres and the Magritte Museum in Brussels, offer a unique insight into a single artist.

Botticelli's Birth of Venus, painted c.1480, is one of the many Renaissance masterpieces in the Uffizi gallery in Florence.

Visitors to the Museo del Prado in Madrid.

Rembrandt's Isaac and Rebecca, known as "The Jewish Bride" in the Rijksmuseum, Amsterdam. The Dutch Master won lucrative commissions to paint portraits of wealthy merchants and their wives.

In Berlin, many artists have taken to the streets. Working at night, especially in the bohemian Kreuzburg area, they adorn walls with stunning and sometimes subversive visual images.

CONTEMPORARY ART

In ateliers across Europe, young artists continue to create striking and sometimes disturbing works. You will find them working in abandoned factories in former East Berlin, cramped attic rooms in Amsterdam and low-rent workshops in the outer suburbs of Paris.

The artists regularly hold exhibitions in independent galleries and also at the big events such as the Venice Biennial and Dokumenta Kassel. Collectors can also pick up works by emerging artists or established names at big art fairs such as Art Basel or the more offbeat events devoted to new artists or affordable art.

Some contemporary art museums are located in striking buildings designed by modern architects, such as the Pompidou Centre in Paris and the Guggenheim in Bilbao. Other centres for contemporary art are located in converted industrial buildings, like Wiels in Brussels, which occupies a former brewery, and Berlin's contemporary art museum, which occupies the former Hamburger Bahnhof railway station.

Frank Gehry's Guggenheim Museum in Bilbao is one of the most striking buildings of the late 20th century.

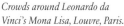

Attic red-figure vase from the National Archaeological Museum in Athens.

Crowds around Leonardo da Vinci's Mona Lisa, Louvre, Paris.

Dinant, on the River Meuse in Belgium.

BELGIUM

Although it's one of the smallest countries in Europe, Belgium offers a rich and varied culture and history, a variety of languages and, last but not least, great food.

Classic gabled houses.

I f you don't dally, you can drive across Belgium in two hours. Zooming along illuminated highways at night, rolling through deserted and drab industrial towns, you can reach the opposite border unaware that only a few miles away, off the beaten track, lie picturesque medieval villages and towns that are among the best preserved in Europe.

This small country of 30,520 sq km (11,780 sq miles) has a population of 10.7 million people. French-speaking Walloons inhabit the south and Dutch-speaking Flemings live in the north. The capital city, Brussels, lies in the centre of the country and is officially bilingual. On the eastern border, there is a small German-speaking community. In spite of sharing a common history and a small territory, Walloons and Flemings are not as neighbourly as they might be, and their rivalry has at times come perilously close to breaking up the country.

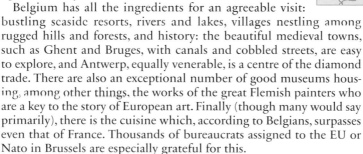

Belgium has all the ingredients for an agreeable visit: bustling seaside resorts, rivers and lakes, villages nestling among rugged hills and forests, and history: the beautiful medieval towns, such as Ghent and Bruges, with canals and cobbled streets, are easy to explore, and Antwerp, equally venerable, is a centre of the diamond trade. There are also an exceptional number of good museums housing, among other things, the works of the great Flemish painters who are a key to the story of European art. Finally (though many would say primarily), there is the cuisine which, according to Belgians, surpasses even that of France. Thousands of bureaucrats assigned to the EU or Nato in Brussels are especially grateful for this.

Belgium has its own royal family, acquired in 1831 with Leopold of Saxe-Coburg, who started the dynasty, and today headed by Albert II and his Italian-born wife Paola. Belgians are good at pageants, and some of the most colourful festivals in Europe take place here. With luck, you will arrive to find the flags flying high.

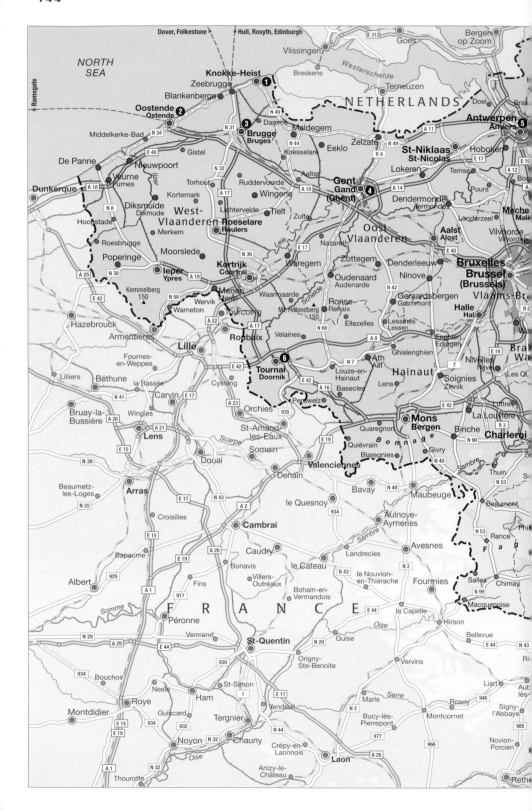

Belgium

0　　10 km
0　　10 miles

Locals and tourists enjoy a drink on the Grand'Place.

BRUSSELS

In the "capital of Europe", office blocks with tinted glass stand beside Gothic churches, and Art Nouveau masterpieces are wedged between concrete apartment blocks.

Brussels

In this city, northern and southern Belgium, represented by the Dutch-speaking Fleming and French-speaking Walloon, have been fused, more or less, into an urban hybrid, the *Bruxellois*. As befits a bilingual city, street signs are in French and Flemish. Brussels was first mentioned in 966 under the name of Bruocsella (settlement in the marshes) in a chronicle of the Holy Roman Emperor Otto I. Around 979, a fortress may have been built on an island in the River Senne. It flourished as a trading centre on the route between Bruges and Cologne, and became politically important when Duke Philip the Good of Burgundy made it his capital in the 15th century.

Some years later the Habsburg Emperor Charles V made it the capital of the Low Countries, and it was later to be dominated in turn by the Spanish, the Austrians, the French and the Dutch. The independence movement of 1830 against the Dutch finally gave the country its own identity.

The Grand'Place

The **Grand'Place ❶** is the heart of Brussels. Belgians call it the most beautiful square in the world, and many visitors agree. Here, every day except Monday and Thursday, a flower market is held, and in August in even-numbered years the square is carpeted with flowers. Seven alleys lead into the

Grand'Place and its spectacle of lavishly decorated Flemish-Baroque guild houses. Dating from the 1690s, the facades appear to have been stamped from the same mould. Each one is different, yet blends harmoniously with the others.

Dominating the square is the magnificent Gothic **Hôtel de Ville ❷** (town hall; guided tours most days) with a 15th-century spire, surmounted by a statue of St Michael (the city's patron saint). Inside, fine tapestries decorate the walls. Opposite is the

Main Attractions

Grand'Place
Hôtel de Ville
Manneken-Pis
Cathédrale des Sts-Michel-et-Gudule
Palais Royal
Musees Royaux des Beaux-Arts
Place du Grand Sablon

The Hôtel de Ville in the Grand'Place.

A label from one of the many varieties of Brussels beer.

almost equally magnificent **Maison du Roi** (Tue–Sun), which contains the Museum of the City of Brussels, where, among other exhibits, are housed the 800 or so costumes belonging to the Manneken-Pis. Behind it begins the **Ilôt Sacré**, a labyrinth of alleys and arcades filled with restaurants. Inside the many places serving good food and fine Belgian beers, the flame of an open fireplace in winter, or a cool fan in summer, provide a warm welcome to visitors.

Legendary duke

For centuries the people of Brussels have shown a particular affection for the **Manneken-Pis ③**, a fountain-statue of a little boy relieving himself. The sculpture, at the corner of **Rue de l'Etuve** and **Rue du Chêne**, incarnates the irreverent spirit and humour of the Bruxellois.

Legend claims he represents Duke Godfrey III. In 1142, when only a few months old, the baby duke was brought to the battlefield at Ransbeke and his cradle was hung from an oak to encourage the soldiers, dejected by his father's death. At the decisive moment, when his forces were about to retreat, the young duke rose in his cradle and made the gesture reproduced in the fountain. This, so legend goes, encouraged his troops to victory. However, a rival legend maintains that the statuette commemorates a little boy whose action inadvertently extinguished a time bomb intended to blow up the town hall.

Going down Rue au Beurre from the Grand'Place you come to **La Bourse**, the city's Neoclassical Stock Exchange. From the end of bustling **Petite Rue des Bouchers** in the Ilôt Sacré, it is only a stone's throw to the elegant glass-roofed shopping arcades of the **Galeries Royales St-Hubert**.

The Upper City

Uphill from the Grand'Place to the east, the white stone walls of the 13th–15th-century **Cathédrale des Sts-Michel-et-Gudule ④** (daily) rise majestically on the hillside between the Upper and Lower City. Excavations have revealed the Romanesque crypt, which can be visited. The cathedral's

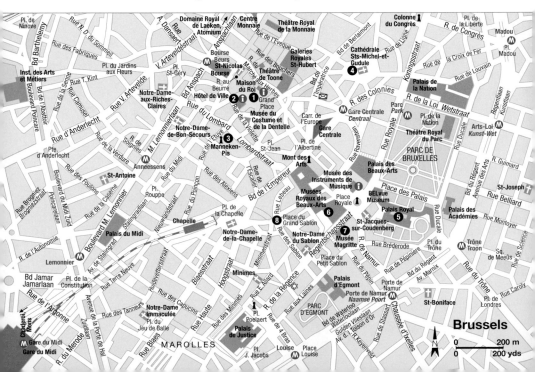

stained glass is particularly fine, and includes a remarkable depiction of *The Last Judgement* from 1528.

Going uphill onto Rue Royale, the elegant **Parc de Bruxelles** brings you to graceful **Place Royale**. Beside it is **Saint-Jacques-sur-Coudenberg**, a Neoclassical church inspired by a Roman temple. A little way downhill on Rue Montagne de la Cour is the Art Nouveau Old England department store, now home to the **Musée des Instruments de Musique** (daily). The dignified **Palais Royal ❺** was built in 1820, and is where King Albert II conducts his official business.

Fine art museums

Adjoining Place Royale are the **Musées Royaux des Beaux-Arts ❻** (Tue–Sun), Belgium's finest collection of art treasures, distributed between the **Musée d'Art Ancien** and the **Musée d'Art Moderne**. The former has a superb collection of Flemish and Dutch Masters from the 15th to the 18th centuries, including works by Rembrandt, Hals, Rubens, van Eyck and Hieronymus Bosch. The latter, with paintings and sculpture from the 19th and 20th centuries, is centred on a well of light, which illuminates the eight underground floors. Highlights are masterpieces by Belgian Surrealists such as Delvaux and Ensor, as well as works by Permeke and the Flemish Expressionists.

Almost adjacent to the Royal Museums across Rue de la Régence, though, is a true must-see for lovers of Belgium's most celebrated and most eccentric modern artist, the **Musée Magritte ❼** (Tue–Sun). Occupying a former hotel, this superb museum has many of Magritte's best paintings as well as photographs, his own home movies and many other exhibits to take you into his special world.

From here, Rue de la Régence leads to **Place du Grand Sablon ❽**, which has the High Gothic church of **Notre-Dame du Sablon**, and a number of antique shops. **Place du Petit Sablon**, a little park surrounded by 48 bronze statuettes representing traditional trades, is just across the street. Further south is the **Palais de Justice** (Law Court), occupying an area bigger than St Peter's Square in Rome.

The gigantic Atomium, a symbol of the city.

ROYAL GLASS CITY

The royal domain lies in the outlying district of Laeken, in the north of Brussels. The magnificent botanical gardens and greenhouses have earned the domain the title of "Glass City". Although the Château de Laeken is not open to the public, the grounds of the domain are crowded with curious monuments and memorials. Leopold II extended the palace and embellished the park with two oriental follies, a Chinese pavilion, with a priceless collection of oriental porcelain, and a Japanese pagoda (Tue–Sun).

But the crowning glory of the park was the creation of the Serres Royales, the Royal Greenhouses, in 1875 (open for three weeks from mid-Apr–mid-May). Attributed to Alphonse Balat and the young Victor Horta, they present an architectural treasure comprising a huge central dome, topped by an ironwork crown and flanked by a secondary chamber, cupolas, turrets and vaulted glass tunnels.

To the northwest of the park is the Atomium (daily), a gigantic model of an iron crystal with nine atoms. The monument, which has become a symbol of Brussels, was designed for the World Exhibition in 1958. After an extensive two-year refurbishment, the Atomium reopened in 2006, shinier, better equipped and with more points of interest for visitors than before. A top-sphere restaurant offers fine food and views.

AROUND BELGIUM

A country with two main languages and two clashing cultures, Belgium is far from predictable. But one thing is for sure: its people have an infectious taste for the good things in life.

Belgium's 65km (40-mile) coastline, a ribbon of golden sands washed by the North Sea, begins at **Knokke-Heist** ❶ on the Dutch border and stretches to **De Panne** next to France. The waters are safe – if cold – and more suited to family holidays than water sports, though the spectacular hybrid known as sand-yachting has plenty of aficionados along the broad beaches. The biggest and most famous of the nine main coastal resorts is **Ostend** ❷ (Oostende), with its bustling fishing and yacht harbour.

The best of the Flemish towns lie off the road from Ostend to the capital, Brussels. The route runs alongside canals, rivers and hills, past moors, heaths and lakes and through fir and pine woods. The countryside of the **Kempen**, in the north, teems with churches, and the peal of bells is a common sound in Flanders.

Medieval Bruges

Bruges ❸ (Brugge), the *grande dame* of Flemish cities, serves as a window on Belgium's history. Miniature bridges straddling its delightful canals, gabled houses and verdant lawns have helped the city retain a medieval atmosphere reminiscent of the time when it was one of Europe's greatest trade centres and known as one of the most beautiful cities in the world. Bruges declined as the reputation of its rival, Antwerp, grew. Having never extended past its

Fountain in 't Zand Square, Bruges.

13th-century fortifications, the city, with its magnificent Gothic **Stadhuis** (town hall; daily) and medieval cloth hall with an 88-metre (300ft) **belltower**, has become a kind of museum. By the town hall is the **Basiliek van het Heilig Bloed** (Basilica of the Holy Blood, daily), containing a reliquary carried in procession through the city on Ascension Day.

Bruges is also famous for its Flemish art, and some of the finest Flemish School paintings are exhibited at the **Groeningemuseum** (Tue–Sun), among them Jan van Eyck's portrait of

Main Attractions
Knokke-Heist
Ostend
Bruges
Ghent
Mechelen
Antwerp
Tournai
Liège
Bastogne
Spa

Rubens's Descent from the Cross in the Cathedral of Our Lady, Antwerp.

his wife and his *Madonna with Canon Joris van der Paele*. The **Memling in Sint-Jan/Hospitaalmuseum** (Tue–Sun) is a medieval hospice containing radiant works by the German-born Flemish Primitive artist Hans Memling. A *Madonna and Child* sculpture (1504) by Michelangelo can be seen in the **Onze-Lieve-Vrouwekerk** (daily).

Five kilometres (3 miles) north of Bruges is the village of **Damme**, where a white windmill stands prettily on a green meadow. It has one of the most beautiful old marketplaces in Flanders. To the west, towards the French border, is Ieper, better known in English by its French name Ypres, which saw horrendous fighting all through World War I, mainly involving, on the Allied side, British and Commonwealth troops (who all pronounced its name "Wipers"). After 1918 much of the medieval town was rebuilt to a remarkable extent, especially the magnificent 13th-century Gothic Lakenhalle (Cloth Hall), part of which is now the In Flanders Fields museum (Apr–mid-Nov daily, mid-Nov–Mar Tue–Sun), dedicated to the war. The Menin Gate is only the largest of several other

A boat tour is the best way to see Ghent.

war memorials around the town.

Further towards Brussels, **Ghent** (Gent) ❹ is a city of bridges and canals. The Church of Saint Nicholas, with its Gothic belfry and 52-bell carillon, dominates the old medieval centres and next to the town hall is **St-Baafskathedraal** (St Bavo's Cathedral; Mon–Sat), which houses Jan van Eyck's masterpiece *The Adoration of the Mystic Lamb*, known as the Ghent Altarpiece.

The road from Brussels to Antwerp passes **Mechelen**, a city of belfries and carillons and home of Belgium's only school for bellringers. Here, at the Church of Our Lady on the Dijle, is Rubens's masterpiece *The Miraculous Draught of Fishes*, and at St-Janskerk is his *The Adoration of the Magi*.

City of Diamonds

Antwerp (Antwerpen) ❺ is Europe's third-largest port and a centre for contemporary fashion that has become increasingly trendy in recent years. At one time, its maritime traffic surpassed even that of Venice. The home of Peter Paul Rubens (1577–1640), Antwerp has become the centre of Flemish art

---

BATTLE OF WATERLOO

The road south from Brussels leads to a location where a watershed in European history took place: Waterloo. On 18 June 1815, just south of this small town, the combined British, Dutch and Prussian forces imposed the final defeat on Napoleon Bonaparte after his escape from Elba. The defeat at Waterloo put an end to Napoleon's rule as the French emperor, and marked the end of his Hundred Days of return from exile.

From the town it is about 3km (2 miles) to the site of the battle. During the nine-hour carnage, some 47,000 soldiers were killed or wounded, 25,000 of them French. The Duke of Wellington, who led the Allied army, said the battle was "the nearest-run thing you ever saw in your life". The vast battlefield is now tranquil farmland. A prominent reminder of the battle, which changed the face of Europe, is the lofty memorial called the Butte du Lion (Lion Mound; daily). The butte rises to a height of 45 metres (147ft), and is surmounted by a 28-tonne lion. The view from the top is extensive.

Napoleon spent the night of 17 June in a farmhouse south of the battlefield at Le Caillou. The farmhouse now houses Napoleon's Last Headquarters (daily), containing mementoes of the battle and the emperor's life. Back in the town, souvenirs and T-shirts all bear the image of Napoleon, who has been immortalised by the locals.

and culture. **Onze-Lieve-Vrouwe-Kathedraal** (Cathedral of Our Lady; daily) is Belgium's most magnificent religious building. South of the city centre, the art collection at the **Koninklijk Museum voor Schone Kunsten** (Royal Museum of Fine Arts; daily) covers centuries of Flemish art. Antwerp is known as the "City of Diamonds" for its role as a major centre of the diamond industry. The **Antwerp Province Diamond Museum** at 19–23 Koningin Astridplein (Thur–Tue) offers a glimpse into the world of hot rocks and diamond cuts.

Southwest of Brussels is **Tournai** ❻, once one of the first capitals of the Frankish kingdom. It is famous for its five-towered Romanesque cathedral of **Notre-Dame** (daily). The **Musée des Beaux-Arts** (Wed–Mon), by architect Victor Horta, has modern art as well as paintings by Rogier van der Weyden and Rubens. **Mons**, east of Tournai, is another venerable Walloon city. The facade of the Hôtel de Ville on the handsome Grand-Place boasts the **Singe du Grand-Garde**, a little cast-iron monkey, which supposedly brings good luck when caressed.

Meuse and Ardennes

Straddling the River Meuse, **Liège** ❼ was the birthplace of one of Belgium's famous sons, Georges Simenon, creator of the Maigret detective series. This city of industry and craftsmen is known for Val-St-Lambert crystal and exquisitely designed jewellery. The **Musée d'Art Moderne et d'Art Contemporain** (daily) has an impressive collection of painting and sculpture from 1850 to the present, including works by Chagall, Ensor, Gauguin, Magritte and Picasso. North of Liège is **Tongeren**, the oldest town in the country, founded by the Romans in 15 BC.

Overlooking the Meuse, the capital of the Wallonia region, **Namur**, is dominated by a huge rocky peak with a 17th-century citadel. The green wooded hills of the Ardennes, where one of the great battles of World War II took place, lie east of the river. At **Bastogne**, outnumbered US forces held out against a German offensive during the winter of 1944–5 that became known as the **Battle of the Bulge**. The battle cost the lives of 19,000 American soldiers, and their sacrifice is commemorated at the **Mardasson Liberty Memorial**, on a hill outside the town.

In the northern reaches of the Ardennes, the town of **Spa** gave its name to the tradition of "taking the waters". It retains examples of architecture and installations from its 19th-century heyday as an upper-crust watering hole.

Luxembourg

In the extreme southeast of Belgium is the Province of Luxembourg, a rugged region of forests and valleys whose capital, **Arlon**, an old Roman settlement, is the site of a beautiful castle and an archaeological site. The **Musée Archéologique** (daily) contains Roman remains.

This region was once the western part of the Grand Duchy of Luxembourg, one of the EU's smallest member states. The capital, **Luxembourg City** ❽, once an important fortress, is now the seat of several EU bodies and an international banking centre, thanks to its low taxes.

Brass band concert on the Kalendenberg, Ghent.

Bike ride in Vondelpark, Amsterdam.

Windmills are synonymous with the Netherlands.

THE NETHERLANDS

Largely reclaimed from the sea, the Netherlands owes its culture to a strong maritime tradition. While it is a modern nation, the picturesque Dutch landscapes painted by the Old Masters can still be seen today.

Classic Dutch architecture.

The Netherlands is a small country. Covering some 16,000 sq miles (41,500 sq km), more than half of its area lies below sea level and almost one-fifth is covered by lakes, rivers and canals. Building and maintaining dykes, barriers and dams to guard against the threat of flooding is a full-time occupation, and few other nations are so acutely aware of the dangers of global warming. The country is flat, a lush greenness is everywhere, and the skies are sometimes filled with the silvery luminescence so distinctive in classic Dutch landscape painting. Of more than 10,000 windmills that once helped pump the land dry and featured so prominently among the favourite subjects of artists, only about 1,000 remain. They are regarded as national monuments, and many have been restored.

Most English-speakers call the country "Holland", but the Dutch know their country as *Nederland* (the Netherlands, or literally, Low Country). Strictly speaking, Holland refers only to the two western provinces of North Holland and South Holland, where the majority of the 16.5 million population lives.

The cultural and business capital, Amsterdam (pop. 755,000), is in this region, along with Rotterdam, Europe's most important port, and the governmental and administrative seat of The Hague ('s-Gravenhage, or Den Haag in Dutch), where the International Court of Justice and the International Criminal Court sit. The venerable university town of Leiden is here, as well as Delft, renowned for its blue pottery, and Edam, famous for its cheese.

The 10 provinces that make up the rest of the country are surprisingly varied. Zeeland in the south is a region of former islands that have been joined together, peninsulas, sandy coastlines and bird-filled marshes with a series of huge barriers to prevent them from flooding. The Catholic southern provinces have flamboyant architecture and wooded hills. Heath, woodlands and orchards mark the northern provinces, and the wilder landscape in Drenthe, in the northeast, is dotted with megaliths. The one thing they have in common is the warm welcome they will offer you.

Netherlands

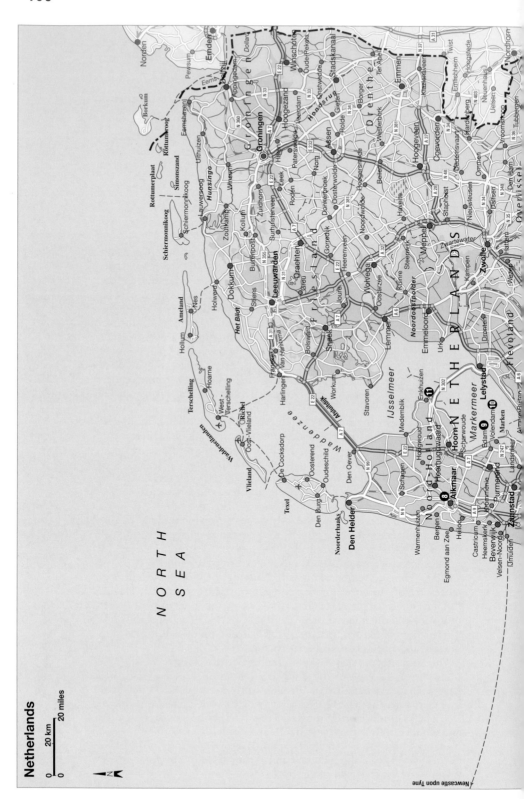

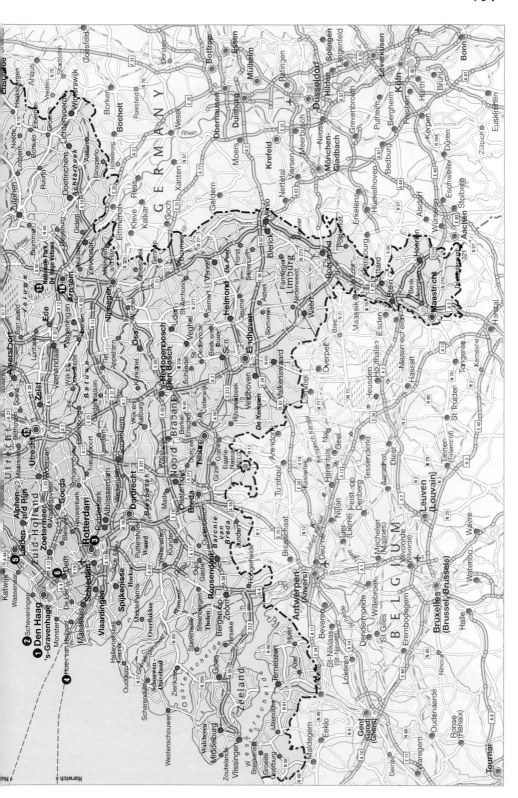

Amsterdam's gabled buildings.

AMSTERDAM

This "city of museums" lives with one foot in
its venerable past and the other on the accelerator
of the latest social and cultural trends.

The first impression of Amsterdam can be its museum-like quality. Indeed, 6,700 of its buildings are protected monuments, virtually intact from the 17th-century Golden Age, when the city rose to spectacular wealth, power and cultural heights. Amsterdam's prosperity came from opening up trade routes to the West and East Indies. Profits from these ventures funded the growth of a compact city built around a dam on the River Amstel in the 13th century. The modern Dutch character is rooted in the common-sense merchants of its earlier history, and the city's monuments tend to be private houses rather than imposing public buildings.

But there is nothing old-fashioned about Amsterdam. Here you can find a gourmet Indonesian meal, lively nightlife, a vast selection of antiques, great paintings from the Golden Age, and a healthy café society. To see all this requires only a good pair of walking shoes.

Amsterdam's canal ring

Amsterdam is built on concentric horseshoe canals. A good point to begin is the VVV Tourist Office at **Centraal Station ❶**, from where trains, trams, buses, harbour ferries and canal tour boats fan out to all points of the city. From here, the main street, **Damrak**, leads to the **Dam**, a large square that

Taking it easy by the canals.

is the city's traditional centre and the site of the stately **Koninklijk Paleis ❷** (Royal Palace; daily), built in 1665, originally as the city's town hall.

Also in the square is the **Nieuwe Kerk ❸** (New Church; daily), dating from 1400, where Dutch monarchs are crowned. It is now a cultural centre, for exhibitions and concerts.

De Wallen district

Nearby, Warmoesstraat passes close to the late Gothic **Oude Kerk ❹** (Old Church; daily), Amsterdam's oldest

Map on page 164

Main Attractions

Centraal Station
Koninklijk Paleis
Nieuwe Kerk
Oude Kerk
Amsterdams Historisch
   Museum
Begijnhof
Rijksmuseum
Van Gogh Museum
Museum Het Rembrandthuis
Anne Frankhuis

Amsterdam

N

0 | 500 m
0 | 500 yds

Java-Eiland
Javakade

IJ-Tunnel
Het IJ

Muziekgebouw aan't IJ
Piet Heinkade
Passagiers Terminal Amsterdam
De Ruijterkade

Centraal Station ➊
Centraal Station
Stationsplein
St Nicolaas Kerk
Schreierstoren

Science Centre NEMO
Oosterdok
Scheepvaarthuis
Scheepvaartmuseum (Maritime) Museum

Prins Hendrikkade

Montelbaanstoren
Oude Waal
De Waag
Nieuwmarkt
Zeedijk
Ons' Lieve Heer op Solder ➎
Oude Kerk ➍

Wertmuseum
't Kromhout
Hoogte Kadijk

OOST
OOSTERPARK
Tropenmuseum

Kattenburgergracht
Kattenburgerplein

Entrepotdok
ARTIS ZOO
Zoölogisch Museum
Aquarium
Geologisch Museum
Planetarium

St Jacob
Universiteit
Muiderpoort

Verzetsmuseum
Plantage
Hollandsche Schouwburg
HORTUS BOTANICUS
Dr Sarphatihuis

Wibautstraat

CENTRUM
Nieuwezijds Voorburgwal
Damrak
Beurs van Berlage
Nationaal Monument
Dam
Koninklijk Paleis ➋
Madame Tussaud's
Nieuwe Kerk ➌

Rokin
Allard Pierson Museum
Kalverstraat
Begijnhof ➐
Amsterdams Historisch Museum ➏
Spui

Muntplein
Muntoren
Bloemenmarkt
Reguliersgracht

Rembrandtplein
WilletHolthuysen Museum ➓
Museum Het Rembrandthuis ➒
Stadhuis
Muziektheater ➊
Waterlooplein

Joods Historisch Museum ➑
Jodenbreestraat
Visserplein

Mr Visserplein
Muiderplein

Amstelhof
Hermitage Amsterdam
Koninklijk Theater Carré

Amstel
Amsteldijk
Weesperstraat

Theatermuseum (Bartolotti) ➋
Keizersgracht
Herengracht
Singel
Noorderkerk
Anne Frankhuis ➋
Westerkerk ➊

JORDAAN
Prinsengracht
Claes Claesz Hofje
Brouwersgracht

Raadhuisstraat
Reestraat
Bijbels Museum
Metz & Co
Felix Meritis
Openbare Bibliotheek
De Kruitberg
De Appel

Goethe Instituut
Museum Van Loon
Fodor Museum

Vijzelgracht
Heineken Experience
Albert Cuypmarkt

Leidseplein
Stadsschouwburg
De Melkweg
Bellevue
De Balie
Paradiso
Casino

Vondelpark
Van Baerlestraat
Concertgebouw
Van Gogh Museum ➒
Rijksmuseum ➑
Stedelijk Museum ➓
MUSEUMPLEIN

OUD ZUID
Hobbemakade
Stadhouderskade

VONDEL PARK

Nederlands Filmmuseum
Vondelkerk

1e C. Huygensstraat
WEST
OUD WEST

Nassaukade
De Looier
Marnixstraat
Elandsgracht
Rozengracht

Stedelijk Museum Bureau Amsterdam

Frederik Hendrikplantsoen
Bilderdijkstraat

Da Costagracht
Costakade

Oostelijk Marktkanaal
Groothandelsmarkt

Wittenburgergracht
Oosterburgergracht

Kattenburgerstraat

building and the best preserved of all its churches. The 13th-century tower is still intact, and some of the stained-glass windows are 16th-century.

Incongruously, for the last few decades the church has been all but surrounded by red-fringed prostitutes' parlours and sex clubs, for this area is also Amsterdam's famous Red Light District, known in Dutch as De Wallen. This is the oldest part of the city, with some of its finest historic architecture and prettiest canals. Prostitution has long been open and legal in its narrow alleys, with semi-naked women on display behind large windows, fascinating crowds of tourists. Recently new questions have been raised about this traditional Dutch tolerance of the sex trade, increasingly associated with major crime such as people- and drug-trafficking, and new restrictions have closed many of the district's "windows" and replaced them with arts venues and fashion shops – although around half still remain. Similarly, De Wallen also has many of the "coffee shops" where cannabis is openly on sale, but from 2012, to discourage "drug tourism", non-residents are not allowed to use them.

In the same district is **Ons' Lieve Heer op Solder** ❺ (Our Lord in the Attic; daily) the finest of the city's "clandestine" churches, concealed within a 17th-century merchant's house. When Amsterdam became officially Protestant in 1578, Catholics were forced to worship in secret. The top floors of three gabled houses were linked to form two galleries with space for up to 400 worshippers.

West of centre

On the west side of the centre, **Amsterdams Historisch Museum** ❻ (Amsterdam Historical Museum; daily), in a former orphanage, chronicles the city's history with paintings, furniture and cleverly juxtaposed artefacts. Highlights include *het groei carte* ("growth map"), which traces Amsterdam's development over the centuries, and the 16th-, 17th- and

18th-century group portraits of the civic guards, in a separate gallery, the Schuttergalerij.

The adjoining **Begijnhof** ❼ (daily) is Amsterdam's finest *béguinage*, or lay nuns' dwelling, and one of the city's most spiritual enclaves. Reached through a number of inner courtyards, it comprises a series of brick and stone gabled houses built between the 14th and 17th centuries. *Het Houten Huys*, at No. 34, is the oldest house in Amsterdam, built around 1425.

Major art museums

Walk or go by tram (lines 2 and 5) from the Dam to **Museumplein** and the **Rijksmuseum** ❽ (daily), the repository of much of Holland's great art from the 17th century. For several years the museum has been undergoing a thorough renovation programme, now due to be completed in spring 2013. Until then a selection of the most outstanding works is on display under the title *The Masterpieces* in the Philips Wing, the first part to be completed. Though it's only a fraction of the 7 million items in the Rijksmuseum

The Rijksmuseum, a repository of great Dutch art.

You can visit Anne Frank's House, a poignant and chilling reminder of the fate of Jews under the Nazi occupation.

Continuing Amsterdam's long café tradition.

collection, it is still hugely impressive, with masterpieces by the great Dutch Golden Age artists such as Vermeer's *Woman Reading a Letter* and *The Milkmaid* and Rembrandt's *The Jewish Bride, Syndics of the Amsterdam Drapers' Guild* and, most prominent of all, *The Nightwatch*, among several others.

From the Rijksmuseum it is a short walk to the outstanding **Van Gogh Museum** ❾ (daily). The artist's development can be traced from the haunting grittiness of his early *Potato Eaters* to the swirling hallucinogenic brilliance of his later *Sunflowers*. A modern wing (1999) by Japanese architect Kisho Kurokawa has a striking design, incorporating a titanium roof and wall. However, the Van Gogh Museum too is due for some renovation – though not as prolonged as at the Rijksmuseum – and while it is closed, until April 2103, major works will be on show in the Amstelhof Hermitage, near Waterlooplein.

The lavishly refurbished **Stedelijk Museum** ❿ (Tue–Sun) has the best modern art collection in the Netherlands. Artists such as Chagall, Braque, Matisse and Mondrian are represented,

as are contemporary artists like Jan Dibbets, Ren Daniels and Tracey Emin.

To the west of Museumplein, **Vondelpark** is the most popular of Amsterdam's green spaces and in summer hosts lively concerts and dance events.

Returning to the city, **Leidseplein** plunges you back into buzzing Amsterdam. This square is a busy tram intersection and buzzes with street performers and bars, nightclubs and cinemas.

Along the River Amstel

A good opportunity to see behind the facades of the canal houses presents itself along **Herengracht**. At the **Willet-Holthuysen Museum** ⓫ (daily), you can see the furnishings of a luxurious 17th-century house that coal magnate Pieter Holthuysen left to his daughter Sandrina and her husband in 1858.

From here, cross the Amstel via the Blauwbrug, to the **Joods Historisch Museum** ⓬ (Jewish History Museum; daily). This is located in the Ashkenazi Synagogue complex, comprising four synagogues restored after World War II. Exhibitions trace the spread of Judaism

CAFE LIFE

The Netherlands has a long café tradition. Some claim the first bar opened its doors in Amsterdam in the 13th century when two men and a dog drifted ashore on the marshy banks at the mouth of the River Amstel. By the 17th century there were countless taverns in the city.

Traditional brown cafés (so called because walls and ceilings have turned brown from age and smoke) are identified by dark, cosy, wooden interiors. Coffee is generally brewed, not machine-made, and if you fancy a snack to go with your drink (alcohol is served too), there are usually olives or cheese. These cafés define the Dutch word *gezelligheid*, which means a state of cosiness or conviviality. This is where locals come for a few beers after work, to play cards, engage in political debates and tell tales. (Note that brown cafés are not the same as "coffee shops" – cafés where hashish and marijuana are legally sold in small quantities, now officially members-only, and so closed to non-residents.) Two of the best brown cafés are **De Tuin** (13 Tweede Tuindwarsstraat) in the Jordaan and **'t Doktertje** (4 Rozenboomsteeg) near the Begijnhof.

The more elegant and stylish grand cafés serve lunch and desserts and tend to have high ceilings, more light, reading tables and a variety of music. Call in at the **Café Americain** (28 Leidseplein) to luxuriate in Art Nouveau splendour.

in the Netherlands, culminating in the devastation of the Holocaust.

Among more than 1,000 bridges in the city, the nearby **Magere Brug** (Skinny Bridge) over the Amstel, dating from 1670, is one of the more notable, and when lit at night is one of Amsterdam's loveliest sights.

Just off Waterlooplein is the Museum Het Rembrandthuis ⓭ (**Rembrandt House Museum;** daily), where the artist lived from 1639 to 1660. The house contains 250 of his drawings and etchings.

Anne Frank's refuge

For an unmissable insight into the horror of life under the Occupation, visit the **Anne Frankhuis** ⓮ (Anne Frank House; daily) at 263 **Prinsengracht**. This is where the teenager and her family hid from the Nazis in World War II, until they were caught and Anne was sent to her death at the Bergen-Belsen concentration camp. This moving and much-visited museum also has a café.

Nearby, the **Westerkerk** ⓯ (West Church; Apr–June and Sept–Oct Mon–Fri, July–Aug Mon–Sat) dates from 1630. It is the city's finest church, and the place where Rembrandt was buried, although his grave has never been found. From the church tower, the Westertoren (186 steps), you have a superb view over the canals and the Jordaan district, one of the most characterful areas of Old Amsterdam, with attractive small shops and brown cafés.

Nightlife

On balmy nights the outdoor cafés along Rembrandtplein and Leidseplein throb with life. Jazz and folk music flourish in small clubs. The long-standing **Melkweg** (Milky Way; Lijnbaansgracht 234) is still a prime location for Latin, African, reggae and rock music, alternative club nights and fringe events; while **Paradiso** (Weteringschans 6) provides a lively venue for rock, hip-hop and world music, some by up-and-coming unknowns.

Amsterdam's celebrated concert hall, the **Concertgebouw**, to the south of Museumplein, has the reputation of

being acoustically among the world's finest, and offers a range of excellent musical performances.

Shopping and markets

Kalverstraat is the busiest shopping street, while **P.C. Hooftstraat**, near Leidseplein, is one of the most elegant. Amsterdam is a centre of the European antiques market, and **Spiegelstraat** and **Nieuwe Spiegelstraat** house more than 20 antiques shops. The city is also a leading centre for diamonds: **Coster Diamonds**, near the Rijksmuseum, offers a workshop tour and shop.

Amsterdam is justly famous for its markets. The most elaborate is the **Waterlooplein** market in the Jewish Quarter, selling clothing, jewellery and bric-a-brac. The **Albert Cuypmarkt** in the south of the city is another lively street market with a wide variety of merchandise, including fish, cheese, fruit and vegetables as well as clothes. It is an especially good place to sample a Dutch delicacy: marinated herring with chopped onion. The famous **Bloemenmarkt** on Singel is one of the best places for fresh cut flowers.

Paradiso, one of Amsterdam's many nightclubs.

AROUND THE NETHERLANDS

Outside Amsterdam – the cultural capital – the
historic cities of the Randstad give way to North
Holland's old fishing communities and the former
royal hunting forests of Gelderland.

Amsterdam

The Netherlands is an exceptional country for exploring at a leisurely pace. Its compact historic towns are ideal for strolling, and can all be reached in short train rides from Amsterdam or any other part of the country. The soft, gentle countryside is just as easy to discover by car, train or, in the Dutch way, by bike.

The Hague

Less than 100km (61 miles) from Amsterdam is **Den Haag** ❶ (The Hague), home of the royal family and seat of the Dutch Parliament. In the **Vredespaleis** (Peace Palace; guided tours Mon–Fri), a Neo-Gothic structure funded by Scottish-American millionaire philanthropist Andrew Carnegie, sit the International Court of Justice and the International Criminal Court. The Hague, with a population of 485,000, is the third-largest city of the Netherlands, often referred to as "Europe's largest and most elegant village" because of its pleasant residential character.

The historic centre was built around the **Binnenhof**, now the Dutch Parliament. This was the Inner Court of the castle of the counts of Holland. Its fairy-tale 13th-century Ridderzaal (Knights' Hall; Mon–Sat) is now only used for ceremonial purposes. Behind the Ridderzaal a gateway leads to

the classical **Mauritshuis, the royal painting collection.** One of the world's most beautiful smaller art museums, it is another of Holland's major museums that is undergoing major renovation, and will be closed until mid-2014. During this time a selection of its greatest works will be on display at the Gemeentemuseum. Though compact, the Mauritshuis collection is remarkably high in masterpieces, such as Rembrandt's *The Anatomy Lesson of Dr Tulp* and Vermeer's *View of Delft*.

Delft house.

TIP

The Netherlands is perhaps the best country in Europe for cycling – it's famously flat, and the Dutch themselves are devoted cyclists. Facilities are second to none, with a network of dedicated cycle lanes in cities and throughout the countryside. Bicycles can be rented at most main train stations, and there are also many private rental shops with good prices. See also page 437.

The historic centre of Delft.

The Mauritshuis stands beside the **Hofvijver**, a large pond that is all that remains of the castle moat. A pleasant walk around it brings you to the **Galerij Prins Willem V** (Tue–Sun). The oldest part of the royal picture galleries, it has been carefully restored exactly as it was when it was first built for Prince Willem V, a great art connoisseur, in 1774, and its works by Dutch 17th-century masters are displayed in the same way too, packed close together around the walls.

The principal role of the **Gemeente-museum Den Haag** (Stadhouderslaan 41; Tue–Sun) is as the municipal museum of modern painting and decorative arts. It has a renowned collection of works by Mondrian and impressive displays on fashion, period interiors and ceramics, and in addition it now temporarily hosts the Masterpieces from the Mauritshuis.

The seaboard

Holland's oldest bathing resort is **Scheveningen** ❷, which forms a suburb of The Hague. A modern pier

and the Belle Epoque architecture of the Kurhaus hotel dominate the promenade. All year, Scheveningen offers fresh air, a choice of sports and entertainment and a casino. At **Sea Life Scheveningen** (daily) you walk through an underwater tunnel to "experience" life on the seabed without ever getting wet.

The Netherlands' traditional role as a maritime trading nation is illustrated by **Rotterdam** ❸, whose dynamic modern skyline is worthy of a city that is one of the largest and busiest ports in the world. The city centre extends into the old harbour, around the Erasmus Bridge (1998), where a bustling dockside development of shops, cafés and housing has been created. The entire harbour can be explored by boat from a dock on the north bank of the Nieuwe Maas, just below the Erasmus Bridge. Another vantage point is the **Euromast** (daily), an observation tower 185 metres (600ft) high that is the landmark of the modern city.

The best known of Rotterdam's many museums, the **Museum Boij-mans Van Beuningen** (Tue–Sun), in **Museumpark**, just west of the city centre, houses one of the finest art collections in the Netherlands. The permanent collection includes masterpieces by Hieronymus Bosch and Pieter Brueghel the Elder; Rembrandt's tender portrait of his son Titus; and 19th- and 20th-century canvases by Monet, Van Gogh, Kandinsky, Magritte and Dalí.

Other places worth a visit are the museum of history, Museum Het Schielandshuis (Tue–Sun), and the Maritiem Museum Rotterdam (Tue–Sun), on the city's maritime history. The only surviving medieval building is the **Grote Kerk (Great Church)**, in front of which stands a statue of the humanist philosopher Erasmus (c.1466–1536). One of the most tradition-rich parts of the city is **Delfshaven** (Delft Harbour), one of the places from where the

Pilgrims started out on their journey to America in 1620.

Just 26km (16 miles) west of Rotterdam lies **Hoek van Holland** (Hook of Holland) ❹, which has ferry services to Britain.

Leiden, Delft and Haarlem

All the historic towns of central Holland have a similar look – a combination of canals and tall, gable-topped brick houses – reflecting the fact that, like central Amsterdam, they have been marked for ever by the extraordinary growth of the Dutch Golden Age in the 17th century. **Leiden** ❺ is a likeable university town, full of museums, cafés and student bookshops. The **Stedelijk Museum De Lakenhal** (daily), occupying a 17th-century canalside cloth hall, traces the history of the town and has works by 17th-century local artists. Archaeological finds from the Netherlands, Greece, Rome and Egypt are displayed in the **Rijksmuseum van Oudheden** (Tue–Sun, daily in school holidays). The centrepiece is the mysterious floodlit Temple of Taffeh, from the 1st century

AD, and presented to the Dutch people by the Egyptian government.

Picturesque **Delft** ❻, midway between The Hague and Rotterdam, has changed little over the centuries. In the Middle Ages it was a centre of weaving and brewing, but an explosion of the national arsenal in 1645 destroyed much of the medieval town. The distinctive blue-and-white pottery for which the town is famous was developed from Chinese originals introduced by traders in the 17th century. Tours of local factories are available, where you can also buy reasonably priced Delftware.

Lovers of classical Dutch painting should make a trip to **Haarlem** ❼, the capital of North Holland province. Here, in the **Frans Hals Museum** (daily) you can study the incisive group portraits that Hals painted of the Dutch at a time when the nation had attained the pinnacle of its economic and political power. He shows faces with a marvellous complexity of character; each is a bundle of motives, a worldly person possessed of few illusions. Artists from Hals's period are

The Erasmus Bridge on Rotterdam's dynamic modern skyline.

Holland is famous for its wheels of cheese.

The distinctive blue-and-white pottery for which Delft is known.

A canal ride in Utrecht.

also represented, and there are temporary exhibitions.

North Holland

North of Haarlem is **Alkmaar** ❽, a pleasant old town with tree-lined canals and a traditional cheese market, held every Friday morning in summer. The town of **Edam** ❾, 22km (14 miles) northeast of Amsterdam, was once an important whaling town but is now famous for its round cheeses, which are produced by farms on the fertile Beemster and Purmer polders (dyke-enclosed, low-lying land). Edam cheeses can be bought in the 16th-century Waag (weigh house) on Waagplein.

The Zuiderzee used to be an inlet of the North Sea, but a dyke built in 1932 transformed it into a freshwater lake, the **Ijsselmeer**. **Volendam** ❿, on the western shore, was a Catholic village, and nearby **Marken**, a one-time island now connected to the mainland by a causeway, was its Protestant counterpart. Residents of both have distinctive costumes, now worn largely (if at all) for the benefit of visitors drawn here by the Old World character of the two towns.

The Zuiderzee's history is vividly presented at the **Zuiderzeemuseum** (daily) in **Enkhuizen** ⓫. Traditional fishing boats and pleasure craft are displayed in a waterfront Dutch Renaissance building, while the outdoor museum is reached by boat. Its focus is a reconstruction of old fishing communities, made up of around 130 buildings rescued from the towns around the Zuiderzee, some of them shipped intact across the Ijsselmeer.

Tulipmania

In the early 17th century, newly acquired bulbs from Turkey produced a "tulipmania" which swept the country. The tradition of bulb production and flower-growing has flourished ever since. You can enjoy this floral world by touring the flower regions west of Amsterdam in the blooming time – the 28-hectare (70-acre) **Keukenhof garden** (late Mar–late May), outside Lisse, is one of the most spectacular.

Alternatively, you can go (early in the morning) to the flower auction held daily in **Aalsmeer** ⓬, 10km (6 miles) south of Amsterdam. From the public balcony, you watch the carts of flowers being brought in and the buyers sitting below. A huge clock-like bidding wheel starts with a price higher than expected and then swirls around slowly to a lower bid.

Utrecht

Utrecht ⓭ is one of the oldest cities in the Netherlands, founded by the Romans in AD 47. The **Oudegracht**, its oldest canal, was dug in the 11th century to allow for sudden changes in the level of the Rhine. It is lined with brick quays and cavernous cellars that now house restaurants and bars. It is known as Holland's city of churches, and the **Domtoren** (cathedral tower) is one of the architectural marvels of the Gothic age. Built between 1321 and 1383, it rises to an ethereal octagonal lantern 112 metres

(376ft) high. All that remains of the **Domkerk** (daily), begun in 1254, are the choir and transepts; the nave came crashing down in a freak hurricane in 1674. The skyline of Utrecht was once a mass of spires, but many were also toppled by the hurricane. The Centraal Museum (Tue–Sun) has some fine pre-1850 art and an impressive collection of modern works.

The Veluwe and around

Bounded in the north by the former Zuiderzee coastline, the Veluwe is dominated by wild heather, pines, heathland and sand dunes. The main attraction is the **Nationale Park De Hoge Veluwe** ⓮ (daily). Once royal hunting territory, it still has mile upon mile of forests rich in wildlife. At the centre of the park is the exceptional **Kröller-Müller Museum** (Tue–Sun), a stunning glass-walled structure housing a magnificent collection of 278 of Vincent Van Gogh's paintings, as well as works by other modern masters such as Mondrian, Manet, Matisse, Braque and Picasso. A fabulous sculpture park in the grounds has

pieces by Rodin, Moore, Paolozzi and Hepworth, among others.

Just outside the town of **Apeldoorn** ⓯, north of the Veluwe, is the **Paleis Het Loo** (Tue–Sun), largest and most impressive of the Dutch royal palaces. It was built by William III, Stadtholder of the Netherlands and King of England and Scotland, in 1692 as a hunting lodge, and generations of the House of Orange used it as a summer palace. The interior and Baroque gardens, now restored to their former opulence, constitute a museum tracing the history of the House of Orange-Nassau.

In the southern part of the Veluwe, **Arnhem** ⓰, on the Neder Rijn (Lower Rhine), will always be associated with the Allied paratroopers who landed here in September 1944 in a gallant but doomed attempt to secure the city's strategic road bridge across the Rhine and thereby shorten the war (dramatised in the 1977 film *A Bridge Too Far*).

At the beautifully kept **Airborne Cemetery**, in Oosterbeek, 8km (5 miles) west of Arnhem, lie the remains of 1,748 British and Polish troops.

The Gothic Domtoren in Utrecht.

Regensburg's waterfront, Germany.

Frauernkirche in Dresden, Germany.

Flower-decked facades in Rothenburg.

GERMANY

The cities of Germany are strong in culture, but
it's the picturesque villages and countryside
that perhaps linger longer in the memory.

Schloss Sanssouci in Potsdam.

Germany is the financial and industrial powerhouse of Europe. But behind the skyscrapers and beyond the industrial ribbon of the Ruhr, castles and countryside remain romantic and alluring. The land the country occupies is made up of peoples of greatly differing origins and characters. Aside from the slowly fading yet still "germanc" gap between east and west, at the two extremes are the Prussians of the north, sombre and upright even if they have given up their spiked helmets and monocles, and the jolly Bavarians of the south, who are typically represented in *leder-hosen* and chamois hats, swilling foaming tankards of beer. In between is the Swabian who lives in a neat cottage and keeps his carefully washed Mercedes in a garage, the Ruhr District miner (if he still has a job) who keeps pigeons in the colliery loft, and the Lower Saxony cattle farmer who warms his damp days with glasses of schnapps.

Urban areas in the east have been substantially rebuilt, refurbished and generally prettified since the Iron Curtain and the Berlin Wall came down in 1989, just as many of those in the west also had to be substantially rebuilt after World War II. Germany's eastern cultural centres – Potsdam, Dresden and Weimar – are bustling centres of tourism once more, as are the largely unspoilt Baltic coast resorts.

The transport network is excellent. The major cities have airports, but it is just as practical and often quicker to travel by rail; the inter-city trains generally run hourly, while the expanding network of high-speed ICE trains has reduced travel times dramatically. For a country that produces some of the world's most prestigious and expensive cars, it is not surprising that the roads are good. If the *autobahn* pace becomes a bit nerve-racking (much of the motorway network has no speed limit), take the secondary roads, leading from one picturesque village to another. You may find a small country festival, for Germans are good at organising their fun, not just at the explosive springtime Cologne Carnival or the Munich October Beer Festival, but at any time of year.

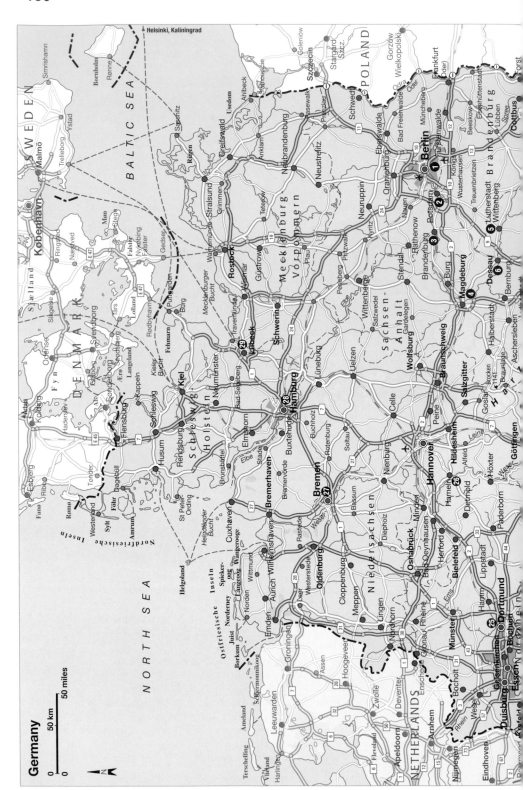

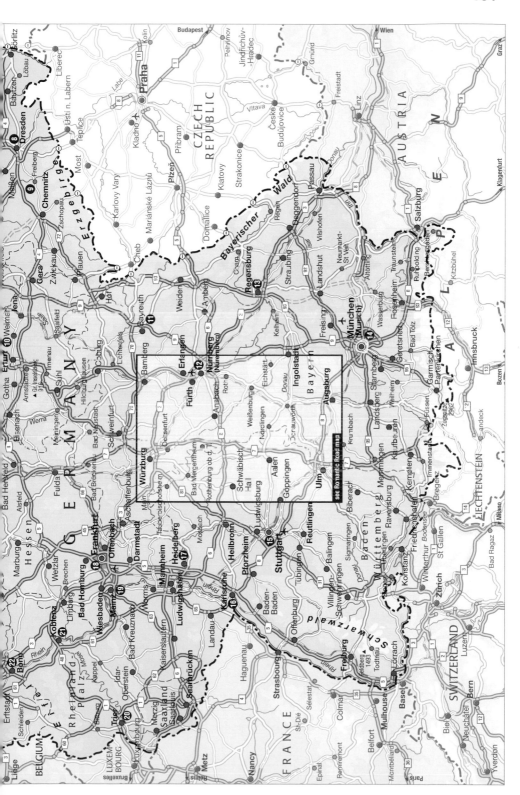

BERLIN

Over two decades since the Wall became history, Berlin has fully settled into its regained role as one of Europe's most adventurous and vibrant capitals.

N o other city in Europe underwent such massive physical transformations in the 20th century as Berlin. Given a new shine around 1900, as the capital of the German Empire, the city was devastated in World War II, and then divided into two for nearly 45 years, a victim and a symbol of the Cold War. West Berlin was a capitalist outpost, with a sometimes tacky prosperity and wild nightlife; east of the Berlin Wall that ran across the middle of the city, the austere standards of the Communist bloc prevailed. Economic growth in both sectors attracted large immigrant communities: mostly Turks in the west, mostly Vietnamese in East Berlin.

Since the Wall came down in 1989 and Berlin was again declared capital of a united Germany an enormous amount has been spent on rejuvenating and unifying the city once again. Grand old museums in the former eastern sector have been lavishly renovated – making this one of the most museum-rich cities in Europe – and formerly run-down districts in the east have become newly fashionable, their old-style architecture and prices (still often lower than those further west) attracting artists, students and people working in the creative industries. Most of the Wall has been deliberately swept off the map. Making Berlin one

integrated city, though, has been complicated, and plenty of traces of its disjointed personality remain, which all adds to its fascination.

One of the most striking things about modern Berlin is that it still has two – or even three – centres. In the east, on **Alexanderplatz**, the Fernsehturm (TV tower; daily), the city's tallest structure and once the emblem of the "capital of the GDR", marks the historical centre of Berlin – Berlin-Mitte – and the former hub of East Berlin. To the west, the blue

The Berlin Sculpture.

Mercedes Star affixed to the Europa-Center marks the location of the **Kurfürstendamm**, the bustling heart of the western part of the city. And, in between, is the shiny modern architecture of the new shopping and entertainment centre around **Potsdamer Platz**, rebuilt from top to bottom since 1989.

The Ku'damm

Known locally as the Ku'damm, **Kurfürstendamm**, which means "The Electors' Road", used to be just a broad track leading out to the country, a bridle path for the bluebloods who rode out towards the forest at Grunewald to go hunting. Only with Germany's rapid industrial expansion after 1871 did the street begin to take shape. Inspired by the Champs-Elysées in Paris, Bismarck decided that he wanted such a boulevard for the new capital of the Reich. Building work proceeded in "Wilhelmine" style: generous, ornate and florid, truly representative of the age.

By the 1920s, Kurfürstendamm had become the place where everything considered bohemian was on offer. The street was all but wiped from the map in World War II but, during the post-war years, it became a symbol of the prosperity of West Berlin and again acquired a dazzling nightlife. On the night following the collapse of the Wall, it was to Ku'damm that most East Berliners flocked.

At the eastern end of Ku'damm is **Breitscheidplatz**, with the ruins of the neo-Gothic **Kaiser-Wilhelm-Gedächtniskirche** ❶ (Kaiser Wilhelm Memorial Church; daily) and its blue-glazed modern incarnation, raised in the 1960s amid the bomb-blasted ruins. A popular meeting place in summer is the **Weltkugelbrunnen** (1984), a vaguely globe-shaped fountain next to the **Europa-Center** ❷ shopping complex, with a huge range of shops, restaurants, bars and a noted cabaret theatre, the Stachelschweine. A lift goes up 20 storeys to a viewing platform. On nearby **Wittenbergplatz** is the stylish Kaufhaus des Westens (Department Store of the West), known as the **KaDeWe**, the only one

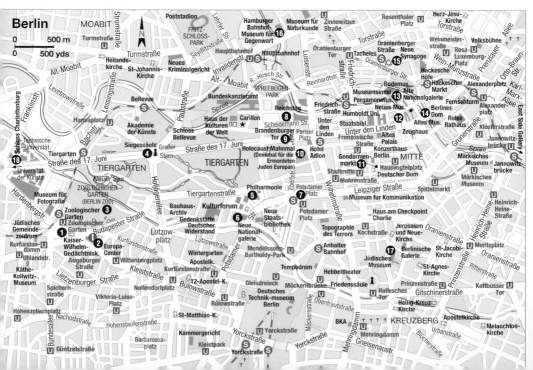

of the city's great department stores to survive World War II bombing.

Close by (Ku'damm 18–22) is the Neues Kranzler Eck mall (2000), a Helmut Jahn high-rise, with offices, stores and a wide plaza housing an aviary. The new complex incorporated older 1950s buildings, including the Café Kranzler, one of West Berlin's most famous cafés in the Cold War era of the 1960s and 1970s. It's now reduced to a smaller space, in the second-floor rotonda, but still has some of its 1950s decor. Behind the Zoologischer Garten station, on Jebensstrasse, the **Museum für Fotografie** (Museum of Photography; Tue–Sun) holds the Helmut Newton Collection, the legacy of the renowned photographer who died in 2004, and hosts excellent temporary shows.

In the side streets, called **Off-Ku'damm**, are some of the better restaurants, cafés and pubs; the city has more than 8,000 places to eat and drink. Close by, on Lehniner Platz, stands the avant-garde **Schaubühne**, a theatre built in the expressive style of the 1920s.

Tiergarten and the Culture Forum

In the middle of the city is the 212-hectare (525-acre) **Tiergarten**, a wonderful park where many Berliners spend time at weekends. The **Zoo Berlin ❸** (daily) is in its westernmost corner. One of the largest in the world, it is home to around 14,000 animals. In the centre of the Tiergarten, the 67-metre (223ft) **Siegessäule** or Victory Column ❹ was built in 1873 to commemorate the Prussian victory over the Danes in 1864. From here there is a grand view down to the Brandenburg Gate.

Just south of the Tiergarten, the **Kulturforum** is dominated by the Philharmonie ❺ concert hall, home of the Berlin Philharmonic. Designed in geometric, modern style in the 1960s to replace an older hall destroyed in 1944, the Great Hall is famous for its superb acoustics, and the building also contains the **Kammermusiksaal** for chamber-music recitals. There are also several major museums in the Kulturforum (all Tue–Sun), among them the **Musikinstrumentenmuseum,** with more

TIP

In a city with such a complex and changing history as Berlin, tours with guides who really know its obscure corners are particularly useful. **New Berlin Tours** (www. newberlintours.com) offer a very popular free walking tour and others on particular subjects such as the Alternative scene or "Red Berlin". **Insider Tours** (www. insidertour.com) include Jewish Berlin, the Third Reich and the Cold War among their themes.

The Brandenburg Gate was built as a symbol of peace; it now stands as an enduring testament to the reunification of East and West Berlin.

than 2,500 musical instruments; the **Neue Nationalgalerie**  (New National Gallery), Mies van der Rohe's minimalist glass-and-steel structure, which displays the work of Kokoschka, Dix, Picasso, Léger, Magritte and many other modern artists; and above all the **Gemäldegalerie** (Painting Gallery), one of the world's finest collections of European art from the Middle Ages to the 18th century, which showcases masterpieces by Dürer, Cranach, Brueghel, Vermeer, Caravaggio and Rembrandt.

The Kulturforum stands just west of **Potsdamer Platz** ❼. Under the Weimar Republic this was one of the great hubs of Berlin, the busiest traffic junction in Europe and the location of the most opulent hotels and department stores. The division of 1945, however, cut straight across the giant square, and its conversion into a desolate wasteland was confirmed when the Wall was laid across it in 1961. It was here that important guests such as US presidents were brought to see the Wall, from a special viewing platform. Consequently, after reunification Potsdamerplatz

Children at the Memorial to the Murdered Jews of Europe.

became the foremost centre of projects to rebuild and reunite Berlin, Europe's largest and most prestigious development site. Now unrecognisable from its 1989 emptiness, the square is ringed by sleek, ultra-modern giant buildings by famous contemporary architects, such as the Daimler-Benz complex by Renzo Piano and Richard Rodgers. The **Panoramapunkt** (daily) on the 24th floor of the Kolhoff Tower building is a viewing platform from where you can marvel at the scale of reconstruction in the new Berlin.

On the eastern edge of the Tiergarten is the **Reichstag** ❽, built in the late 19th century in Neo-Baroque style, which is once more home to Germany's national parliament, the Bundestag. Damaged by the infamous Reichstag Fire in 1933, the building was a primary target of Soviet troops as they advanced into Berlin in 1945. By the battle's end the interior was completely gutted, although the massive outer walls still stood. During the years of division it was only partially restored. Then, after reunification,

THE BERLIN WALL

For a quarter-century (1963–89), the Berlin Wall was the city's grimly defining feature. Today, virtually nothing of it is still standing. Visitors who want to see what little remains can visit important stretches along Niederkirchnerstrasse, between Potsdamer Platz and Checkpoint Charlie; along Spree-side Mühlenstrasse, at the East Side Gallery, in the Friedrichshain district; and along Bernauer Strasse, in Mitte. None of these gives the complete picture of the Wall, with its death-strip, watchtowers and surprising depth, but they do afford a small insight into what it was like. Elsewhere, there are some odd bits and pieces here and there, and a line of double cobblestones running through the city, in some places supplemented by memorial plaques, shows where the once formidable barrier stood.

it was comprehensively rebuilt to a design by British architect Norman Foster, with an entirely new structure inside the original walls. Its most striking feature is the spectacular glass dome, with a spiral ramp from where visitors can watch parliamentary proceedings, leading up to a roof garden with great views across Berlin (daily; advance booking required).

Former East Berlin

Since its inauguration in 1791, the **Brandenburger Tor** ❾ (Brandenburg Gate), between the Tiergarten and central Berlin's grand boulevard, Unter den Linden, has been a symbol of the fate first of Prussia, then of Germany. Napoleon marched through it on his way to Russia, and sent back to Paris the gate's crowning ensemble, the Quadriga (the goddess Victory on her horse-drawn chariot). In 1814, the Quadriga was brought back in triumph by Marshal Blücher. Kings and emperors paraded here; the revolutionaries of 1918 streamed through it to proclaim the republic; and it was where the Nazis staged their victory parades. After 1945 it stood on the line between East and West Berlin.

After the Wall came down, the Gate became a symbol of the hopes of a united Germany, and is again the favoured setting for public events. New York architect Peter Eisenman's striking Holocaust memorial, a vast "field of stelae" titled the **Denkmal für die Ermordeten Juden Europas** (Memorial to the Murdered Jews of Europe) ❿ lies to the south of the gate.

Beyond the Gate you enter former East Berlin. Immediately on the other side is **Pariser Platz**, another square that has been thoroughly rebuilt with emphatically modern structures such as the DZ Bank, by US architect Frank Gehry. The **Hotel Adlon**, one of the city's most historic hotels, was also rebuilt. The most Prussian of Berlin's streets, **Unter den Linden**, lined with *linden* (lime) trees, leads east from

here towards the heart of Old Berlin, **Berlin-Mitte**.

Curiously, East Berlin contained much of the city's grandest architecture. The imposing Neoclassical structures of Karl Friedrich Schinkel (1781–1841) around Unter den Linden testify that Berlin was once among the most beautiful of European cities. Some maintain that the **Schauspielhaus** theatre on the **Gendarmenmarkt** ⓫ is Schinkel's finest building, and the square is aesthetically perfect. Others say the **Neue Wache** (New Guard House) on Unter den Linden is Schinkel's best. Since 1993 this building has been the **Central Memorial of the German Federal Republic for the Victims of War and Tyranny**, and contains an enlarged version of the bronze *Pietà*, from 1937, by Käthe Kollwitz.

On the left (going east) are the monumental buildings of the **Staatsbibliothek** (State Library) and the **Humboldt University**. Opposite the university, in the old Opern Platz, now **Bebelplatz**, the Nazis burnt 20,000 books in 1933. The square,

Colourful remnants of the Berlin Wall

planned by Frederick the Great, is graced with splendid structures. There is the Baroque **Zeughaus** ⓬, the old arsenal, now the **Deutsches Historisches Museum** (daily), covering German history from earliest times; the **Staatsoper** (Opera House) directed by Daniel Barenboim, the **Alte Bibliothek** (Old Library) and **St Hedwig's Cathedral**, modelled on the Roman Pantheon, combine to create a harmonious architectural masterpiece.

Museum Island

Museumsinsel ⓭ (Museum Island) is one of the world's finest museum complexes, with collections that include everything from ancient artefacts to early 20th-century art. Before 1989 its five museums were neglected; some had not been restored since World War II. This is another part of Berlin that has received massive attention since reunification, and visitors benefit from long-drawn-out renovation programmes that are only now coming to fruition, and in some cases will not be entirely finished until 2015. It requires a day, at least, to visit all the museums (all open Tue–Sun).

The **Altes Museum** (Old Museum) is another of Schinkel's masterpieces. Its Neoclassical rooms house superb Greek, Roman and Etruscan antiquities, in a new display unveiled in 2011. The **Pergamon Museum** contains one of Berlin's most remarkable treasures, a section of the Pergamon Altar (180–159 BC), controversially taken from the ancient Hellenic city in Turkey after excavations in 1878. The museum also has large Islamic collections. The **Bode-Museum,** with late Roman and Byzantine art, is in a splendidly restored building next to the River Spree, but one of the island's jewels is the Neues Museum (New Museum, though it first opened in 1855). This had been virtually a ruin since 1945, until another comprehensive reconstruction project was begun, incorporating the remains of the original building, under British architect David Chipperfield. It now provides a stunning setting for its celebrated Egyptian and ancient artefacts, especially a famous bust of the Egyptian queen Nefertiti.

Charlottenburg Palace, built in the 18th century.

Lastly, the **Alte Nationalgalerie** (Old National Gallery) was the first building on Museum Island to be renovated (1998–2001). Its impressive collection of 19th–20th century paintings is particularly strong in German artists like Caspar David Friedrich or Max Liebermann, but also includes French artists such as Manet.

Just south of Museum Island is **Berliner Dom** ⑭ (Berlin Cathedral), built in 1894 as "the chief church of Protestantism".

New Berlin

Around Mitte are the once shabby districts of former East Berlin that became centres of alternative culture in the 1990s, and are now being gentrified. The neighbourhood around **Hackescher Markt** and north into **Prenzlauer Berg** is now one of the liveliest in the city, with a thriving art scene and cafés, restaurants and clothes shops. On Oranienburger Strasse, the **Neue Synagoge** ⑮ was the grandest Jewish temple in Europe when it was built in 1866. Almost destroyed by Nazi attacks and World War II bombing, it was extensively renovated in the 1990s and now again houses a functioning synagogue and the **Centrum Judaicum** (Jewish Centre; Sun–Fri) museum. To the northwest on Invalidenstrasse is the most cutting-edge of Berlin's post-reunification museum schemes, the **Hamburger Bahnhof-Museum für Gegenwart** ⑯ (Museum for the Present; Tue–Sun), the former Hamburg railway station, transformed into a dynamic space for the showing of contemporary art by figures such as Joseph Beuys, Andy Warhol and Anselm Kiefer, as well as spectacular temporary exhibitions.

Kreuzberg, south of Mitte, is known as a rough-and-ready district that has also been a centre of the immigrant – mainly Turkish – communities, the punk and radical music scene, and gay Berlin. As in other old districts, this bohemian atmosphere had led it to become more gentrified and upmarket in recent years. Within it is one of the great must-sees of modern Berlin, the stunning **Jüdisches Museum** ⑰ (Jewish Museum; daily). In an extraordinary jagged-walled building by architect Daniel Libeskind, the museum presents 2,000 years of Jewish history in highly imaginative displays, with immensely powerful memorials to the Holocaust. A tunnel leads to a lovely green space, the Garden of Exile.

Charlottenburg

West of the city centre is the impressive Baroque **Schloss Charlottenburg** ⑱ (Charlottenburg Palace; daily). Built in 1695 as a country house for Sophie Charlotte, grandmother of Frederick the Great, it was extended in the 18th century. Across from the beautiful palace grounds are the **Bröhan Museum** (Tue–Sun), a lovely collection dedicated to Art Nouveau, Art Deco and other early 20th-century decorative arts, and the Berggruen Museum, a modern art gallery currently closed for restoration.

Berlin Cathedral, said to be the Protestant answer to St Peter's in Rome.

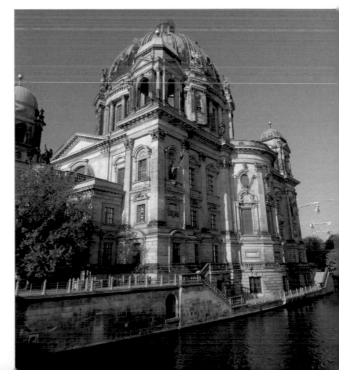

The castle at Heidelberg
dominates the town.

AROUND GERMANY

From the sparkling vineyards of the Rhine to the fairy-tale castles of the Romantic Road, Europe's leading industrial nation has a rich variety of historic sites.

Leipzig.

Berlin

T he renowned modernity of its cities and infrastructure contrasts with the venerable charm and fairy-tale architecture of its country towns, or the dense remoteness of its hill forests. Germany's landscapes run from glittering lakes and snow-capped Alpine peaks in the south to spectacular river gorges and even long sandy beaches, on the Baltic Coast.

Around Berlin

Germany offers all the qualities of a classic tourist destination – cosmopolitan cities, ever-changing landscapes and a wealth of cultural attractions. Its rich and turbulent history is ever-present. Visitors to **Berlin ❶** (see page 183) should also take in **Potsdam ❷** and **Sanssouci** (Tue–Sun), the grand palace that Frederick the Great designed in 1744. Here he patronised the arts and entertained his famous guests, such as the French philosopher Voltaire.

Today tourists flock to Sanssouci, which has 12 gloriously decorated Rococo rooms and a 290-hectare (717-acre) park. Beside the main alley the gold of the **Chinese Tea House** reflects the sunlight. At the end of the long path is the Neues Palais (New Palace), the residence of Frederick the Great's household and guests towards the end of his reign. Within the park there is also a Sicilian Garden, with subtropical plants; the Renaissance-style

Orangery; and the **Picture Gallery**, with paintings by Caravaggio, Rubens and Van Dyck. **Cecilienhof Palace** (Tue–Sun), venue for the 1945 Potsdam Conference, is nearby.

Through the Harz

The journey from Berlin through the modern state of Saxony-Anhalt to Leipzig is a series of contrasts. Until 1990 this area was part of East Germany, the GDR, and many of its small towns and villages still have a sleepier, more old-fashioned feel

Main Attractions

Potsdam
Leipzig
Dresden
Nuremberg
Romantic Road
Augsburg
Neuschwanstein Castle
Munich
Heidelberg
Köln
Hamburg

Decorative plaster-work in the Church of St Nicholas in Leipzig.

Bauhaus Building in Dessau.

than those further west. In the Harz Mountains, the picture-book landscape is one of half-timbered houses and fine Romanesque buildings. **Brandenburg ❸**, straddling the River Havel, flourished in the 14th and 15th centuries as a centre for the cloth trade, but its importance declined with the rise of Berlin. Today, the town is dominated by the steel industry, but some gems remain, such as the cathedral, transformed into a Gothic basilica in the 14th century.

Magdeburg ❹, on the River Elbe, is the capital of Saxony-Anhalt and the biggest inland port in eastern Germany. The city suffered extensive damage during World War II, but many Romanesque buildings survive, including the **Unser Lieben Frauen Kloster** (Monastery of Our Lady; 1064–1160), which now serves, among other cultural roles, as a concert hall.

Approaching **Lutherstadt Wittenberg ❺** from the west, the first impression is of the **Schlosskirche**, whose dome looks like a well-fitting crown. It was on the door of this church, on 31 October 1517, that Martin Luther posted his 95 Theses against the Catholic practice of selling indulgences or forgiveness from sins, which within a remarkably short time led to the Reformation.

Dessau and Leipzig

Dessau ❻, on the main route between Berlin and Leipzig, was home to the ground-breaking Bauhaus School, one of the birthplaces of modern functionalist architecture, from 1925 until it moved to Berlin in 1932. In 1977 the town reopened the **Bauhaus-Dessau Building** as a museum (daily). It is on the Unesco World Heritage list. There are several other surviving examples of Bauhaus architecture around the town, including the old labour exchange on August-Bel-Platz designed by Walter Gropius, the Bauhaus housing estate with the Cooperative Building in the Törten district, and the Meisterhäuser in Ebertallee.

Dessau's heyday was the era of Prince Leopold Friedrich Franz von Anhalt-Dessau (1740–1817), who surrounded himself with artists, poets and architects and established

a country park at **Schloss Wörlitz** (Apr–Nov Tue–Sun). Over 800 varieties of trees grow among winding paths, canals and lakes. The art collection includes works by Rubens and Canaletto, while the grounds are dotted with imitation buildings, such as an Italian farmstead, a Greek temple, a Gothic folly and a palm house.

With the founding of its university in 1409, **Leipzig** ❼, already an important trading centre, also became a cultural enclave, subsequently attracting such influential students as Leibnitz, Nietzsche and Goethe, who named Leipzig "Little Paris". The division of Germany hit the city hard, but today the streets are fast returning to their former elegance. The exquisite interior of the **Nikoleikirche** (Church of St Nicholas), begun in the 12th century, is testament to the city's former wealth. The **Thomaskirche** (Church of St Thomas), home of the Thomanerchor choir, was begun around 1212 and assumed its late Gothic form in the 15th century. The world-famous choir was founded at the same time, at first consisting of only 12 boys who sang at Mass, but soon going on to sing at all major Church and state ceremonies. Celebrating its 800th anniversary in 2012, the choir has maintained its tradition unbroken through the centuries, even under Nazi and Communist rule. Leipzig in the 18th century was above all the city of Johann Sebastian Bach (1685–1750), who became choir-master and organist at St Thomas's in 1723 and remained there for the rest of his life, writing his major cantatas for this choir. More can be learnt about his life in the **Bach-Museum** (Tue–Sun), where the Bach Archive is kept. The Bach Festival is held annually in spring or early summer (www.bach-leipzig.de for dates).

The palaces of Dresden

Dresden ❽ will for ever be associated with the devastating bombing raid of 14 February 1945, when almost the entire city centre was destroyed. A great deal of rebuilding has been done since then, however, to restore the city's epithet of "most beautiful city in Germany". A key symbol of the city's rebirth was the reconsecration in 2005, after 13 years of rebuilding, of the **Frauenkirche** (Church of Our Lady), a Baroque masterpiece dating from 1743.

Six buildings comprise the Dresden State Art Collections. They include the stunning **Dresden Royal Palace**, including the **Grünes Gewölbe** (Green Vault; Wed–Mon), with jewellery, precious stones and paintings belonging to the Saxon princes who built the palace. The **Zwinger Palace**, a masterpiece of German Baroque (1710–32), was based on the Orangery at Versailles, but the complex of pavilions, galleries and gardens grew to take up a vast area. It contains the **Gemäldegalerie Alte Meister** (Old Masters' Gallery; Tue–Sun), holding 2,000 works of art, including the *Sistine Madonna* by Raphael and Rembrandt's *Self-Portrait with Saskia*, plus works by Titian, Ribera and Murillo.

The **Albertinum** was first built in the 1880s, to house part of the royal art

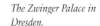

WHERE

To get a feel for the city of Dresden, take a trip on one of the historic paddle steamers, some dating back to the 1870s, that ply the River Elbe (www.saechsische-dampfschiffahrt.de).

The Zwinger Palace in Dresden.

Thuringian Forest.

collection. Blown apart in 1945, it was, like much else in royal Dresden, painstakingly rebuilt by the East German regime, but then devastated again by the Elbe floods in 2002. This was taken as an opportunity for comprehensive refurbishment, concluded in 2010. It houses two fine museums (both open Tue–Sun). The Galerie Neuer Meister (New Masters Gallery) has a superb collection of painting from German Romantics like Caspar David Friedrich through the Impressionists and Expressionists to emphatically modern figures like Gerhard Richter; the Skulpturensammlung (Sculpture Collection) has sculpture from the same periods. The **Jägerhof** (Tue–Sun) houses a fascinating Museum of Saxon Folk Art and a near-unique collection on the history of puppet theatres. Nearby is the former **Garrison Church**, once the only multi-denominational church in Europe, since it contained a Catholic chapel attached to the main Lutheran church. Finally, in the environs of Dresden is the **Schloss Pillnitz** (Pillnitz Palace; May–Oct daily), the opulent summer residence of Augustus the Strong (1670–1733). With its sweeping pagoda-like roofs, it is an important example of the Chinoiserie style so fashionable at the time. A large collection of camellias imported from Japan in 1770 provides a riot of blossom in spring. The palace also houses a Museum of Decorative Arts.

The mountain range bordering the Czech Republic southwest of Dresden is the Erzgebirge (Ore Mountains), where minerals such as lead, tin, silver and iron ore have been extracted since the 12th century. The silver-mining town of **Freiberg** ❾ was the richest town in Saxony until the 15th century, and some of the town's old buildings, such as the 15th-century town hall and cathedral, still display its former wealth.

Weimar and around

Further west is **Weimar** ❿, the natural starting point for any journey across the Thuringian Forest. From the mid-18th century Weimar was one of the great hubs of German cultural life. The poet, playwright, polymath and virtual

founder of modern German literature Johann Wolfgang von Goethe (1749–1832) lived here from 1775, when he became privy councillor of the duchy of Saxony-Weimar-Eisenach, and later he served as education minister and director of the Weimar Theatre, where he came into contact with the philosopher, playwright and poet Friedrich Schiller (1759–1805), with whom he shared a close friendship.

The ensemble of 16 historic monuments known as Classical Weimar are now a Unesco World Heritage site. Among them are the Goethe-Nationalmuseum (Tue–Sun) which includes the house where he lived for 50 years, with his 6,500-volume library, and his garden and **Gartenhaus** (summer house; daily), and also the Schiller-Museum (Tue–Sun), which again includes the writer's residence. The Stadtschloss (Castle; Tue–Sun) contains a very fine art collection originally amassed by Weimar's dukes, with paintings by Lucas Cranach the Elder, Tintoretto and Caspar David Friedrich, among others. For more details on all Weimar's attractions, visit www.klassik-stiftung.de).

West of Weimar, ancient **Arnstadt** was the home from 1620 of the Bach family. Johann Sebastian Bach was the organist from 1703–7 in the church that today bears his name. To the south, undulating, thickly forested hills, narrow river valleys and rounded mountain tops combine to form the unique quality of the **Thuringian Forest**. Goethe enjoyed the natural surroundings of this region, and today's hikers will be in good company if they follow the **Rennsteig** – a famous 168km (105-mile) ridge path that crosses the area. The route also passes the Grosser Inselsberg (916 metres/3,000ft), only the fourth-highest mountain in the region but the one offering the best views.

Into Bavaria

As you pass beyond the Thuringian Mountains you also cross from the former eastern zone into what was West Germany. This border is fading into history, but at some points marks of the "Green Belt" – where the East Germans cut a swathe through the forest, for security reasons – can still be seen. The town of **Bayreuth** ⓫ is forever associated with another composer – Richard Wagner, who built an opera house here in 1876. Every year it is the setting for the Bayreuth Festival, from late July to late August, devoted to Wagner's operas.

The city of **Nürnberg** (Nuremberg) ⓬ was devastated during World War II but has been faithfully restored, so that much of its old charm remains. In the 12th–16th centuries it was regarded as the unofficial capital of the Holy Roman Empire. The River Pegnitz divided the **Old City** into the Sebalderstadt in the north and the Lorenzerstadt in the south, both surrounded by a sturdy 13th-century defensive wall with 46 fortified towers.

The oldest parts of the enormous **Kaiserburg** (Imperial Castle; daily), built on sandstone crags high above

Goethe and Schiller still dominate the cultural landscape of Weimar.

Würzburg's Residenz, a splendid Baroque palace and Unesco World Heritage site.

the Old City, date from the 11th and 12th centuries. Between the 15th and 17th centuries, the city attracted artists and scientists such as Albrecht Dürer, Adam Krafft and Veit Stoss. The **Albrecht Dürer Haus** (Tue–Sun), near the castle, is now a museum dedicated to the artist who once lived there. The **Hauptmarkt** (main market) is the site of Nuremberg's famous annual **Christmas Market** (Christkindlesmarkt); while at the Kornmarkt the **Germanisches Nationalmuseum** (Tue–Sun) has a huge collection of artefacts related to German arts and culture, some dating back to prehistory. The city's biggest museum, though, is the **Verkehrsmuseum Nürnberg** (Transport Museum) on Lessingstrasse, which houses two separate collections (both Tue–Sun), the DB Museum, the official historical collection of German Railways, and the Museum für Kommunikation (Communications Museum) on postal history.

A darker but still hard-to-escape chapter in Nuremberg's history was written by the Nazis, who held rallies here between 1933 and 1938.

Würzburg, a must-see in Bavaria.

The Romantic Road to Rothenburg

The Romantische Strasse (Romantic Road), the name given to the route from **Würzburg** Ⓐ to Füssen near the Austrian border, leads visitors through many of Bavaria's greatest attractions. Following massive Allied bombing of Würzburg in March 1945, a painstaking rebuilding programme restored every major structure in the city. Start your tour at the **Residenz** (daily), built in 1720–44 by Balthasar Neumann as the palace of the prince-bishops who ruled the town. Ranked as one of the finest Baroque palaces in Europe, it is a Unesco World Heritage site. The impressive stairwell is crowned by a single concave vault 30 metres (100ft) long by 18 metres (59ft) wide; even more famous is the **ceiling fresco** by Giambattista Tiepolo, who was summoned to Würzburg in 1750 to create the largest painting in the world in which he depicted the gods of Olympus and allegories of the four continents known at the time. Leave time to stroll in the **Hofgarten** behind the Residenz, with its fine

wrought-iron gates and beautiful Baroque figures.

From the Residenz follow Hofstrasse to Kiliansplatz and the Romanesque **cathedral**, rebuilt after its destruction in 1945. The **Schönborn Chapel**, one of Balthasar Neumann's most important works, contains a shrine to the prince-bishops from the Schönborn family. Cross the River Main by the Alte Mainbrücke (Old Main Bridge) and follow the steep path up to the **Festung Marienberg** (Marienburg Fortress; mid-Mar–Oct Tue–Sun). Begun in the 13th century, the massive rectangular fortress encloses a courtyard and 13th century keep as well as the Renaissance fountain and the Church of St Mary. After 1631, when the city was taken by Gustavus Adolphus of Sweden during the Thirty Years War, the fortress was extended and began to take the form seen today, with its Baroque facades and the Fürstengarten (Princes' Garden).

One of the main attractions of the fortress is the **Mainfränkisches Museum** (Main-Franconia Museum; Tue–Sun), whose exhibits include a remarkable

collection of statuary by the woodcarver and sculptor Tilman Riemenschneider (1460–1531), who came to Würzburg from the Harz Mountains in 1483.

The Romantic Road continues through **Tauberbischofsheim** Ⓑ (Home of the Bishop), where St Boniface founded a convent in 725, and **Lauda-Königshofen** Ⓒ, which for centuries has been a wine-producing centre. Riemenschneider's greatest achievement can be admired in **Creglingen** Ⓓ at the **Herrgottskirche** (Church of Our Lord), where his carved altarpiece is dedicated to the Virgin.

One of the best-preserved medieval towns in Germany is **Rothenburg ob der Tauber** Ⓔ, whose special status from 1274 as a free imperial city provided the basis for its prosperity. Its streets converge like the spokes of a wheel from the city walls to the central market place and the **Rathaus** (town hall) with a Renaissance archway and Baroque arcades. Its 55-metre (180ft) Gothic tower affords the best view of the town's maze of red-tiled roofs. The medieval churches are rich in ecclesiastical art, the pride of the town being

Marienberg Fortress, Würzburg.

the Heilig-Blut Altar (Altar of the Holy Blood) in the **St-Jakobs-Kirche** (Church of St James), commissioned from Riemenschneider in 1501–5. The **Plönlein** area in the centre is the prettiest part of Rothenburg.

Continuing south to Neuschwanstein

The Romanesque cloisters of the Stiftskirche (Collegiate Church) in **Feuchtwangen ⒡** serve as a stage for excellent open-air theatre in summer. **Dinkelsbühl ⒢**, a little further south, can only be entered through one of its four main gates. Here, each July, the **Kinderzeche** play and a colourful parade commemorate the time in the Thirty Years War when the town was besieged by the Swedes. From the tower of St George's Church in **Nördlingen ⒣** there is a panoramic view of the 99 villages of the **Rieskrater**, a crater formed 15 million years ago when a meteorite struck the earth's surface at a speed of around 70,000km (40,000 miles) per hour, creating a wall-like formation of rock and earth about 13km

(8 miles) in diameter. The modern **Rieskratermuseum** (Tue–Sun) has a multimedia show explaining the geological history. Continue on through **Harburg ⒤**, with one of Germany's oldest castles, and **Donauwörth ⒥**, home of the Käthe Kruse dolls, made here since 1910. The Käthe-Kruse Puppen-Museum (Doll Museum; Apr–Oct Tue–Sun pm, Nov–Mar Wed, Sat–Sun pm) is worth a detour for doll-lovers.

The medieval trading city of **Augsburg ⒦** grew into a commercial centre, noted for its goldsmiths and silversmiths, and an episcopal seat at the crossroads of the important routes linking Italy and the centre of Habsburg power in the Holy Roman Empire. By about 1500 it was among the largest cities in the German-speaking world. The immensely wealthy Fugger banking family, bankers to the Emperor Charles V, was responsible for the extraordinary social housing settlement of the **Fuggerei** (1516), where poor Catholic senior citizens could live for a peppercorn rent; the same applies today.

Medieval Rothenburg.

The town has a wealth of artistic treasures, including the Renaissance **Rathaus** (**City Hall**), with onion-domed towers and magnificent **Goldener Saal** (**Golden Hall**; daily). The Romanesque-Gothic Cathedral (Dom) is the home of precious works of art, including the oldest stained-glass windows in Germany, dating from around 1130.

Neuschwanstein Castle (daily) near **Füssen ⓛ** was built by the "Mad King" of Bavaria, Ludwig II in 1869–86 as a realisation of his Wagnerian romantic fantasies, and was a total anachronism even then. Its sole *raison d'être* was as a glorified stage set. In the **Sängersaal**, the "Minstrels' Hall" that forms the centrepiece of the fairy-tale castle, Ludwig staged performances of scenes from *Tannhäuser* and other Wagner operas.

Regensburg to Munich

The 2,000-year-old city of **Regensburg ⓭**, at the northernmost point of the River Danube, was largely undamaged during World War II. There is a fine view from the **Steinerne Brücke** (Stone Bridge), a masterpiece of medieval engineering some 310 metres (1,017ft) in length. The river is lined by stately mansions, over whose roofs tower the Gothic spires of St Peter's Cathedral. To the north, the landscape of the dense Bavarian Forest extends as far as the Czech border, and is a great place to get away from it all.

Duke Heinrich der Löwe (Henry the Lion) of Bavaria performed a historic function 800 years ago when he put a new bridge across the River Isar to transport salt from the mines in Bad Reichenhall to Augsburg. **Munich ⓮** (München), the town that grew up around the bridge, took its name from the occupants of a nearby monastery and was originally called Mönchen (Little Monk). Its symbol is still a child-like monk, the *Münchner Kindl* (Munich Child). It was not until the 19th century that the city, in the reigns of Ludwig I and Ludwig II, acquired a reputation as a centre for the arts and sciences, due to these monarch's hugely ambitious and flamboyant architectural projects.

Munich's true centre begins near the **Hauptbahnhof** (main railway station) at busy **Karlsplatz**. Through

Neuschwanstein Castle belongs in a fairy tale.

Frauenkirche in Munich is one of the largest and most impressive hall churches in southern Germany.

The Hofbräuhaus in Munich.

the imposing gate, the 14th-century **Karlstor**, you reach a pedestrian zone, passing the Renaissance **Michaels-kirche** (St Michael's Church) where Ludwig II is buried. The **Frauenkirche** (Church of Our Lady), one of the largest hall churches in southern Germany, is a late Gothic edifice of red brick, with two distinctive onion-domed towers. Central **Marienplatz** throbs with life throughout the year. In winter the Christmas Market takes over, the stalls clustering around the statue of Munich's patron, the Virgin Mary. One side of the square is taken up by the Neo-Gothic **Neues Rathaus** or **New Town Hall** (1867–1908), with a world-famous **Glockenspiel** in its tower. The mechanical figures perform three times a day in summer (11am, noon and 5pm) and at 11am and noon in winter. South of the square is bustling **Viktualienmarkt**, where you can buy sausages, herbs, fruit, wines and home-brewed beer. Most visitors find their way (east of the Rathaus) to the famous **Hofbräuhaus,** the former beer halls of the court brewery, for true Bavarian atmosphere, beer and food.

The historic rooms of the **Residenz** (Royal Palace; daily) are worth a tour. They include the **Antiquarium**, an impressive Renaissance hall now used for state receptions, the ornate **Schatzkammer** (Treasury) and the Rococo **Cuvilliés Theatre**, which is still in use. To the east, beyond the **Isartor**, another of the old city gates, lies the **Deutsches-Museum** (daily), focusing on science and technology.

The **Königsplatz,** northwest of the centre, is perhaps the most impressive square in Munich, built on a huge scale in monumental Neoclassical style. Here you will find the **Antikensammlung** (Museum of Classical Art; Tue–Sun), with renowned Greek vases and Roman and Etruscan statues, and the **Glyptothek** (Tue–Sun), devoted to Greek and Roman sculpture. The square is also the hub of Munich's Kunstareal or "Art District". Not far away, the **Alte Pinakothek** (Old Picture Gallery; Tue–Sun) houses one of the greatest of all collections of art by European Old Masters from the 14th to the 18th centuries, originally drawn from the Bavarian royal collection. Its

THE CITY IN LOVE WITH BEER

By five o'clock on a hot summer's afternoon, you can find most of Munich's population sitting out under the chestnut trees in one of the city's beer gardens, hoisting a mass (a litre mug) of beer, polishing off a *hendl* (roast chicken) and lingering into the night, when lights in the trees light up the area like a stage set.

Class barriers are unknown here. At the same table, a group of rowdy teens may be seated between middle-aged men in *tracht* (national costume) and elegantly coiffed ladies. Self-service is the rule, and standing in line is part of the experience. Not that you have to buy all your food: many families come with picnic baskets and even checked tablecloths, just picking up beer to complete the meal.

The summit of Munich's beer culture, and its biggest beer garden, is of course Oktoberfest, the 16–18-day festival of drinking and eating – which actually begins in late September – that each year attracts millions, including hordes of young Antipodeans and North Americans, to the huge permanent site of Theresienwiese on the west side of the city. Oktoberfest statistics are staggering: each year 7 million litres (12.3 million pints)) of beer, half a million chickens and 70,000 pigs' knuckles are consumed, and there are plenty of entertainments too, in scores of tents and fairground rides, with Bavarian oom-pah music as accompaniment.

many masterpieces include Dürer's astonishing 1500 Self-Portrait and major works by Raphael, Rembrandt, Poussin and Rubens. The adjacent Neue Pinakothek (New Picture Gallery; Wed–Mon) has mainly 19th-century art, with standout paintings by Monet and Van Gogh. Nearby there is now a third museum, the Pinakothek der Modern (Gallery of the Modern; Tue–Sun), a stunningly sleek building housing four separate collections covering contemporary art, graphic art, design and architecture.

Oktoberfest and Nymphenberg

The open space of Theresienwiese, just west of the centre, is the site of the world-famous 14-day **Oktoberfest**, which has been held in the city since 1810 and draws more than 6 million visitors every year. The ultra-modern headquarters and **museum** of the BMW motor company (Tue–Sun), shaped like a car cylinder, lie to the north of the ring road around the city.

Also outside the city centre is **Schloss Nymphenburg** (daily), the huge and opulent summer residence of the Bavarian princes and kings, amid a gorgeous park with both French-style and English-style gardens and the **Amalienburg** hunting lodge, a masterpiece of Rococo decoration. The palace's central pavilion, completed in 1675, has spectacular ceiling frescoes by Johann Baptist Zimmermann. The southern pavilion contains the famous **Schönheitsgalerie** (Gallery of Beauty), with paintings of women commissioned for the delectation of King Ludwig I, including his mistress the dancer Lola Montez, as well as, in the former stables, samples of the work of the former royal Nymphenburg porcelain factory.

Stuttgart and the Black Forest

West of Bavaria, in the historic territory of Württemberg, the whole length of road from the ancient university town of **Freiburg** to **Stuttgart** winds along narrow river valleys of outstanding natural beauty. Tourists have been coming to the **Schwarzwald** (Black Forest) since the 18th century, attracted by the contrast between the Rhine Plain and the mountains rising some 1,200 metres (4,000ft) above it. There are lovely quiet roads for drivers to explore, and the forested slopes above the picture-postcard valleys are great for walking. Grouse and pheasant, buzzards and hawks, deer, foxes and badgers populate more remote areas. Among the many famous beauty spots are Germany's most celebrated waterfalls at Triberg, the Feldberg, the Black Forest's highest peak, which towers above Freiburg, the lakes of Schluchsee and Titisee in the southern forest and medieval Calw and its surrounding villages near Stuttgart.

Stuttgart ⓫, surrounded by forested hills and speckled with parks, has one of the highest per capita incomes of any city in Germany, due in part to its manufacture of Mercedes cars. Opulence was displayed differently by the rich and powerful in earlier

The BMW Museum in Munich.

Ornate decorations adorn many of the buildings in Heidelberg.

times, as evidenced by the striking central ensemble of the 16th-century Altes Schloss (Old Palace; Tue–Sun) and 18th-century Neues Schloss (**New Palace**; open only for specially arranged tours) on Schillerplatz. Well worth a visit outside the city centre are the **Daimler-Benz Museum** (Tue–Sun) in the district of Untertürkheim, and the **Porsche Museum** (open Tue–Sun) in Stuttgart-Zuffenhausen.

Down the Neckar valley to Heidelberg

Although the spa tradition of **Baden-Baden** goes back to Roman times, it was not revived until 1838, when Jacques Bénazet opened his luxurious **Casino** in the Kurhaus, making the town newly fashionable among the wealthy of Europe. The existence of **Karlsruhe** ⑯, further north, is entirely due to Schloss Karlsruhe, the palace that Margrave Karl Wilhelm of Baden-Durlach built around 1715. Most of its attractions are found around the palace, which houses the **Badisches Landesmuseum** (Baden State Museum; Tue–Sun), with a

A view of Heidelberg from the castle.

varied display on the region's history and arts. Nearby are the Staatliche Kunsthalle (State Art Gallery; Tue–Sun), a large collection particularly strong on German Old Masters, the Impressionists and contemporary art, and the lovely Botanischer Garten (Botanical Garden; Tue–Sun). The Museum beim Markt (Museum in the Market Square; Tue–Sun), in the town centre, is an attractive small museum of 20th-century decorative arts, and the Museum in der Majolika (Tue–Sun) displays one of Karlsruhe's traditional products, majolica pottery.

Heidelberg ⑰ lies on the edge of the Odenwald Forest, where the Neckar reaches the Rhine Plain, and is regarded as the epitome of German Romanticism. High above the picturesque lanes, the ruins of the **castle** (daily; guided tours) rise majestically. To the left of the massive gate tower, the simple **Gothic House** is the oldest part of the complex. In the cellar is the famous **Heidelberg Tun**, one of the largest wine vats in the world. The most interesting part of the castle is the Otto-Heinrich Wing, which houses

the **Deutsches Apothekenmuseum** (German Apothecary Museum; daily), a collection of furniture, books, medical instruments and medicine bottles. Beneath the castle, the six arches of the **Alte Brücke** (Old Bridge) span the river. Its 13th-century gate is topped by Baroque spires and leads to **Philosophenweg** or "Philosopher's Way", a hillside promenade around the **Heiligenberg** (Holy mountain). In the Old City, near the Kornmarkt, you will find two of Heidelberg's most famous student taverns, and the mighty, late Gothic **Heiliggeistkirche** (Church of the Holy Ghost).

Frankfurt

Germany's financial centre is **Frankfurt ⑱** on the River Main, which has developed into a pulsating metropolis thanks to its location at the intersection of road, rail and air traffic routes. The skyscrapers housing international banks and financial corporations create a dramatic skyline that epitomises the power of this bustling city.

Reflected in the glass of soaring modern buildings is the Gothic tower of Frankfurt's cathedral, and apple-wine pubs stand at cobblestone-street level in **Sachsenhausen**. An impressive collection is on show at the **Museum für Moderne Kunst** (Museum of Modern Art; Tue–Sun); and nine museums line the south bank of the Main, in a district known as the **Museumsufer**. The **Städel Museum** (Tue–Sun) displays paintings from the 14th century to the present, while the **Liebighaus** (Tue–Sun) exhibits sculptures from antiquity to the Baroque period. The **Deutsches Filmmuseum** (Tue–Sun) documents the German film industry, and also screens films. Others include the **Deutsches Architekturmuseum** (German Architecture Museum; Tue–Sun), the **Museum für Angewandte Kunst** (Museum of Applied Arts; Tue–Sun) and the **Museum der Weltkulturen** (Ethnological Museum; Tue–Sun).

In the city centre, the Römer or **town hall** (daily) is a collection of three Neo-Gothic buildings and includes the church where the Holy Roman Emperors were crowned. The nearby **Goethehaus** (Grosser

The colossal Roman Porta Nigra in Trier.

TIP

Cruises down the Rhine to see the beauties of the river were among Europe's first regular tourist excursions in the 19th century, and are just as popular today. Many routes are available, including the complete cruise from Zurich into Holland, but the most famous section is the Rhine Gorge either side of Koblenz, with beauty spots celebrated in German folklore such as the Lorelei Rock, home of the Rhine maidens. One-day river trips operate from Mainz and Koblenz; see www. kdrhine.com.

Cyclists on the bridge near Cologne's cathedral.

Hirschgraben 23–25; daily) is the house where Goethe, Germany's greatest man of letters, was born in 1749.

The Rhine and Moselle

The Main slices through Frankfurt on its way to join the Rhine. Not far from their confluence lies the ancient city of **Mainz** ⓳, founded in 38 BC. In AD 747 St Boniface made it the seat of an archbishopric, and the centre of Germanic Christendom. Johannes Gutenberg (c.1397–1468), the inventor of printing, is Mainz's most famous son. Two of his 42-page Latin Bibles can be seen in the **Gutenberg-Museum** (Tue–Sun), along with old printing apparatus and a replica of the master's workshop.

Almost due west, in the heart of the Moselle Valley, is **Trier** ⓴, the oldest city in Germany, founded in 16 BC by the Roman Emperor Augustus. Dominated by the well-preserved **Porta Nigra**, the huge Roman gate, the city is a treasure chest of ruins and relics, and many residents dabble in archaeology. It is said that, to store potatoes safe from the winter frost, the people

simply dig down to the Roman mosaics. The **Rheinisches Landesmuseum** (Rhineland Museum; Tue–Sun) has a wealth of Roman treasures, including mosaics, sculpture, glass and coins. The fortress-like, Romanesque Trierer Dom (**St Peter's Cathedral**) is one of Germany's oldest churches.

At **Koblenz** ㉑, the Mosel (or Moselle), perhaps Germany's loveliest river, joins the Rhine. Where the two great rivers meet stands an impressive monument known as the Deutsches Eck (German Corner). On the opposite side of the river, high on the edge of a ridge, stands **Ehrenbreitstein** (daily; guided tours), a 13th-century fortress that once controlled this key area and changed hands several times between the French and Germans. Above the Pfaffendorfer Brücke (Pfaffendorf Bridge), with the Moselle on the left and the Rhine on the right, is the famous **Wine Village**, built in 1925 as a replica of a wine-producing village, complete with authentic vineyards and typical half-timbered houses from the most celebrated German wine-growing regions.

Germany's industrial heartland

With the fall of the Berlin Wall, the city of **Bonn** ㉒ gave the role of German capital back to Berlin. Before it was chosen as the seat of the Federal Government in 1949, the major claim to fame of this sleepy city was as the birthplace of Ludwig van Beethoven (1770–1827). But, thanks to its **Museum Mile**, Bonn still has a lot to offer, including the **Kunst und Ausstellungshalle** (Art and Exhibition Hall), the **Kunstmuseum** (Museum of Art) and the **Alexander Koenig Museum** (Zoological Museum; all museums open Tue–Sun). Exhibits at the **Beethoven-Haus** (Tue–Sun) include the piano made specially for the composer in Vienna.

Köln ㉓ (**Cologne**) is a lively city, famous for its twin-spired cathedral

(dom) and exuberant carnival celebrations and religious processions. The spirit of Cologne is embodied in its mighty **cathedral** and the **Severinsbrücke** (Severin Bridge) named after a 4th-century bishop of Cologne, a unique construction crossing the Rhine, supported by only one off-centre pillar. The cathedral contains what are said to be the remains of the Wise Men of the East, the paintings of Stephan Lochner (c.1445) and a feeling of immense space that has an awesome effect on the visitor. Begun in 1248, its twin spires, each 157 metres (515ft) high, were not built until 1842–80.

The city also has some excellent museums. The **Römisch-Germanisches Museum** (Romano-Germanic Museum; Tue–Sun) contains priceless treasures and offers an insight into the city's Roman past. It was built around the world-famous **Dionysus Mosaic**, which was discovered during construction work on an air-raid shelter. The 2nd-century masterpiece covers an area of 70 sq metres (84 sq yds) and consists of more than 1 million

ceramic and glass components. Next door is a museum complex that includes the Museum-Ludwig (Tue–Sun), with gleaming white spaces that house a fabulous collection of contemporary art and superb temporary exhibits. Cologne's most unmissable museum, though, may be the Schokolade Museum (Chocolate Museum; Tue–Sun), beside the river near the Severinsbrücke, which comprises a comprehensive display on everything to do with chocolate, with of course plenty of tasting opportunities in the café.

If you have time, take a detour to **Aachen**, one of Germany's oldest cities and the favourite residence of Charlemagne, who is buried in the **Cathedral** there, before visiting **Düsseldorf** ㉔, 40km (25 miles) north of Köln. Düsseldorf's trademarks, the **Schlossturm** (Castle Tower) and the **Lambertuskirche** (Church of St Lambert), with its characteristic slightly crooked spire, stand directly by the Rhine. Take a stroll along the Uferpromenade, the pedestrianised space between the

WHERE

The idyllic Moselle Valley is the best known of Germany's wine-producing areas. Winningen, Zell, Bernkastel-Kues and Piesport are typically picturesque towns and villages along the river's route.

In the Dortmund Brewery Museum you will learn all you ever wanted to know about brewing beer.

river and the bustling Old Town – a square mile packed with pubs and restaurants. The **Kunstsammlung Nordrhein-Westfalen** (State Art Collection; Tue–Sun) on Grabbeplatz has 20th-century works by artists ranging from Picasso to Lichtenstein, and a comprehensive collection of works by Klee.

The towns to the north in the Ruhr district – Duisburg, Essen – have been the industrial heartland of Germany since the mid-19th century. Nowadays many of its old installations are no longer productive and are being turned into tourist attractions, notably the vast Zollverein mining complex in Essen, with imposing Bauhaus architecture, which is open for tours (daily), and houses a visitor information centre for the whole Ruhr area. **Dortmund ㉕**, on the eastern edge of the Ruhr, is at the top of the German brewing league. Indeed, more brewing goes on here than in any other city in Europe, including its rival to the south, Munich. All is explained in the **Brauerei-Museum** (Brewery Museum; Tue–Sun).

On the trail of the Brothers Grimm

Further east, the picturesque Weser Valley picks up the trail of the **Märchenstrasse or "Fairy-Tale Road"**, which leads from **Hanau**, birthplace of Jacob and Wilhelm Grimm, to Bremen. Riverside meadows, spruced-up towns, castle ruins and Renaissance palaces make it seem as if time has stood still here. In **Hameln ㉖** (Hamelin), the **Rattenfängerhaus** recalls the story of "The *Pied Piper of Hamelin*", and every Sunday in summer a play depicting the legend is performed in front of the **Hochzeitshaus** (Wedding House), dating from 1617.

The old Hanseatic town of **Bremen ㉗** is the oldest German maritime city, although its modern deep-sea port of **Bremerhaven**, 57km (35 miles) further north, was founded in the 19th century. "*The Bremen Town Musicians*", a dog, a donkey, a cat and a cockerel, from the story by the Brothers Grimm, stand near the Rathaus (town hall). The cavernous cellar beneath this building is famous for its Gothic vaults. In Bremerhaven,

Lübeck's town hall and marketplace.

the Zoo am Meer (daily) is a striking modern zoo making the most of its coastal location that particularly focuses on aquatic birds and animals, which can be observed through huge glass screens.

Maritime Hamburg

Hamburg ❷❽ is Germany's second-largest city (population 1.8 million), and a major port, although it is 110km (66 miles) from the sea. Ships reach it by sailing up the River Elbe, and one of the most attractive areas is the **Speicherstadt**, the old warehouse district, which can be explored on a narrow-boat cruise.

Hamburg's red-light district, the **Reeperbahn,** may be one of Europe's raunchiest, but the area is well policed. A more salubrious side of town can be seen by strolling from the railway station into the centre. To the north of the station is the Kunsthalle (Art Gallery; Tue–Sun), with paintings and sculpture from the 13th–20th centuries. On the other side of the station is one of the world's best *Jugendstil* (Art Nouveau) collections, in the

Museum für Kunst und Gewerbe (Arts and Crafts Museum; Tue–Sun). Surprisingly, Hamburg's most popular visitor attraction is **Miniatur Wunderland** (daily), a vast model-railway complex in an old harbour warehouse.

Lübeck ❷❾, on the Baltic Sea, was a commercial metropolis of the Holy Roman Empire for 250 years, and by 1356 was the most powerful of the Hanseatic towns that controlled Baltic trade. It is now a prime port for ferries to Scandinavia. The **Holstentor** (Holsten Gate), one of the few remaining sections of the city wall, leads to the Old Town, and Lübeck's five Gothic brick churches with their combined Seven Towers, a trademark image of the city. **Travemünde** in Lübeck Bay has been Lübeck's beach outlet since the 19th century. Since unification, other Baltic coast towns lying further east such as Heiligendamm near Rostock or Stralsund have regained their traditional status as some of Germany's most popular summer beach resorts, attracting crowds from all over the country.

Lübeck's Holsten Gate.

DESIGN ICONS OF EUROPE

Across Europe, over the course of the 20th century, industrialism, ingenuity and a drive towards aesthetic appeal came together to create classic designs.

In the early days of industrialisation objects were made in the only way they could be, with form dictated by function. But improved processes of production and increased competition encouraged manufacturers to engage artists to give products a deliberate style. And so was born the notion of design.

It could be said that we live in an age of design, and that Europe in the 20th century was the crucible in which many of the ideas we now take for granted were born. But it wasn't always like that.

For a long time, design was the humblest of the arts, a marriage between jobbing creativity and the mundane commercial world in which the object was to get consumers to part with their money for desirable products. Then, with the emergence of pop culture, design came into its own, and gradually the concept spread that you do not have to look in an art gallery for artefacts to admire: they are there, too, on the breakfast table or parked in the street outside.

Design is very much an evolutionary force, with the weak, unpopular idea passing quickly out of sight and the strong becoming so familiar to us that it is hard to imagine a world without it. The objects on these two pages have all, by general agreement of the critics, attained the status of design classic through longevity, functionality and good looks.

The Italian Vespa motor-scooter was created by a former aircraft designer in 1946. Beloved by European youth for its streamlined sense of freedom, it has passed effortlessly from contemporary cool, when it was first launched, to being toda retro chic.

Adult wristwatches were sombre and serious affairs until Swatch came along in the 1980s with thin plastic watches co in colourful and fun designs, often sold at affordable prices.

Gerrit Rietveld's red-and-blue chair (Netherlands, 1917). Its simplicity made it suitable for mass production.

...d signs can be stylish as well as functional.

A lithographed poster by Czech artist Alphonse Mucha (1897) illustrates late 19th-century fusion between what had been hitherto the preserve of high art, and the needs of commerce.

ART NOUVEAU

At the end of the 19th century a "new style" spread across Europe, partly as a reaction to the academic, rule-bound art that preceded it, partly as a response to the new materials and techniques available, partly as a reaction against the potential anonymity of industrial products, and partly because modern communications allowed the rapid international diffusion of its ideas.

Usually known as Art Nouveau, after a trend-setting shop of that name which opened in Paris in 1895, the style developed simultaneously in different countries under a variety of names: Jungendstil in Germany, Secession in Austria, Modernisme in Catalonia.

Each of these has its distinguishing features, but all Art Nouveau shares the same delight in ornament, drawing inspiration particularly from organic forms, as seen in its emblematic sensuous curves.

After 1900 the influence of Art Nouveau waned, but it has never really gone out of fashion. The objects it created – genuine or reproduction – have always been in demand, and the style has served as an inspiration for many subsequent schools of art and design.

This clay and bronze Liberty vase demonstrates Art Nouveau's ability to push technique beyond its previous limits.

Few cars have won such affection as the Volkswagen Beetle, originally conceived as a "people's car" in 1930s Germany. It saw massive sales in the post-war years, and although it went out of production in 2003, the New Beetle has replaced it as a design icon.

Lake Lucerne in the heart of the Swiss Alps.

SWITZERLAND

Landlocked at the heart of Europe, the country has attractive cities and an interesting history, but its most treasured possession is its breathtaking Alpine landscape.

Switzerland is famous for dairy farming.

The identification letters on Swiss cars, CH, stand for Confoederatio Helvetica, in Latin, for this is one country where it's still convenient to use the old international tongue rather than have to choose between any of its four official languages. The Helvetii were a Celtic tribe who occupied most of the Swiss plateau before they were crushed by Julius Caesar. The source of the word Switzerland comes from Schwyz, one of three cantons that formed the original union at Rütli in 1291. Today there are 26 member-cantons in the confederation, which all have a strong sense of Swiss identity, even though they are divided between those that speak French, German, Italian and Romansh, a Latin-based language still spoken in the country's easternmost corner.

Switzerland is a small country, about the same size as the Netherlands but with half the population. About 21 percent of its 7.7 million inhabitants are foreigners. It is renowned for its banking, neutrality, watches and outstanding scenery, and works hard to maintain its independence: all able-bodied male citizens spend time in military training each year. The only remnants of the *Reisege*, mercenaries who fought in Europe's wars for four centuries, are the Swiss Guard of the Vatican.

Eastern Switzerland and the lowlands are at their best in spring. Summer visitors head for the lakes. Autumn can be enjoyed in the vineyards of the Valais or the Vaud, or in the south-facing, Italian-speaking Ticino, where even in October the days seem longer and certainly warmer than in much of the rest of Switzerland. Finally, winter provides endless possibilities throughout the Alpine region, for skiing, or simply enjoying the beautiful snow scenes.

The climate can range from subtropical warmth to Alpine cold. This results in an equal variety of vegetation; from fertile plains in the lowlands to mountain pastures and vineyards.

In contrast to tourists of the past, who were compelled to explore the Swiss Alps on foot, on the backs of mules, or in coaches, today's travellers have an astonishingly comprehensive and, in Swiss style, unerringly efficient public transport system at their disposal.

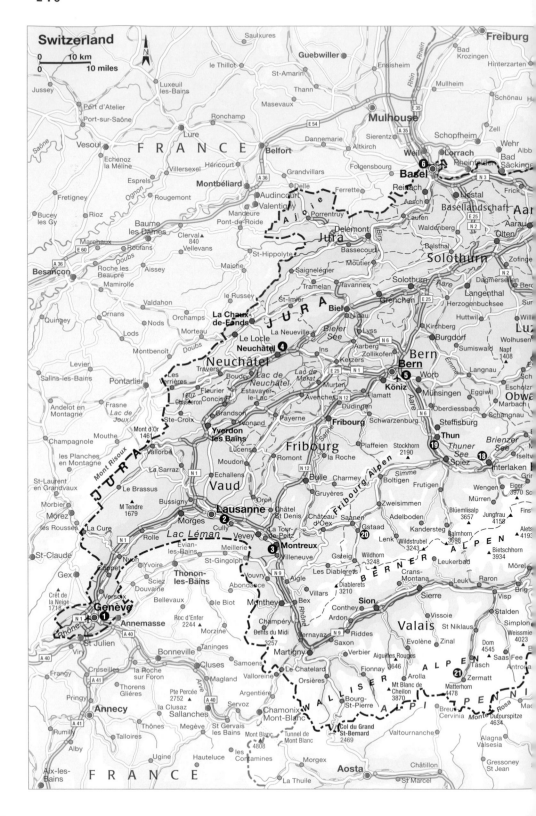

Switzerland

0 10 km
0 10 miles

FRANCE

Freiburg
Bad Krozingen
Hinterzarten
Schönau
Albb
Wehr
Bad Säckingen
Frick

Guebwiller
St-Amarin
Ensisheim
Mullheim
Schopfheim
Zell

Saulxures
le Thillot
Thann
Masevaux
Dannemarie
Sierentz
Altkirch
Weil
Lorrach
Rheinfelden
Basel
Reinach
Aesch
Laufen
Waldenberg

Luxeuil
les-Bains
Jussey
Ronchamp
Belfort
Grandvillars
Delle
Ferrette
Delemont
Waldenberg
Liestal
Basellandschaft
Aarau
Olten
Zofingen

Vesoul
Echenoz
la Méline
Port d'Atelier
Villersexel
Héricourt
Montbéliard
Audincourt
Valentigny
Porrentruy
Bassecourt
Moutier
Solothurn
Dagmersellen

Port-sur-Saône
Espreis
Fretigney
Rougemont
Mandeure
Pont-de-Roide
St-Hippolyte
Saignelégier
Tavannes
Solothurn
Langenthal
Herzogenbuchsee

Bucey
les Gy
Rioz
Baume
les Dames
Clerval
840
Vellevans
Maiche
Tramelan
St-Imier
Biel
Grenchen
N 25
Huttwil

Marchaux
Mamirolle
Roulans
Roche les
Beaupré
Aissey
Orchamps
le Russey
JURA
Niau
Aarberg
Kirchberg
Burgdorf
Sumiswald
Napf
1408
Wolhuse

Besançon
Quingey
Ornans
Nods
Morteau
La Chaux-
de-Fonds
La Neuveville
Bieler
See
Lyss
Zollikofen
Langnau
Eschol

Valdahon
Lods
Montbenoît
Doubs
Le Locle
Neuchâtel
Ins
Kerzers
Bern
Bern
Worb
Eggiwil
Obw
Marbach

Levier
Salins-les-Bains
Pontarlier
Travers
Les
Verrières
Boudry
Lac de
Neuchâtel
Murten
Klamatt
Köniz
Münsingen
Oberdiessbach
Schangnau

Andelot en
Montagne
Frasne
Lac de
Joux
1602
Chasseron
Fleurier
Concise
Estavayer-
le-Lac
Avenches
Düdingen
Schwarzenburg
Steffisburg

Champagnole
Mouthe
Mont d'Or
1461
Ste-Croix
Grandson
Yvonand
Payerne
Fribourg
Plaffeien
Thun
Thuner
See
Brienzer
See
Iselt

St-Laurent
en Grandvaux
les Planches
en Montagne
Vallorbe
Yverdon
les-Bains
Lucens
Romont
la Roche
Stockhorn
2190
Spiez
Interlaken

Morbier
Mórez
les Rousses
La Cure
La Sarraz
M Tendre
1679
Echallens
Moudon
Bulle
Charmey
Gruyères
Simme
Boltigen
Frutigen
Wengen
Eiger
3970
Grin

St-Claude
Gex
Crêt de
la Neige
1718
Le Brassus
Bussigny
Morges
Rolle
Lausanne
Châtel
St Denis
Château-
d'Oex
Saanen
Zweisimmen
Adelboden
Kandersteg
Balmhorn
Blüemlisalp
3657
Jungfrau
4158
Mürren
Fins
Alets
4193

Coppet
Nyon
Yvoire
Sciez
Douvaine
Bellevaux
Lac Léman
Cully
Vevey
La Tour-
de-Peilz
Montreux
Villeneuve
Gstaad
Lenk
Wildstrubel
3243
Wildhorn
3248
Bietschhorn
3934

St-Julien
Versoix
Genève
Annemasse
Thonon-
les-Bains
Evian-
les-Bains
Meillerie
St-Gingolph
Aigle
Les Diablerets
Diablerets
3210
Crans-
Montana
Leukerbad
Leuk
Raron
Mörel

Frangy
Viry
Bonneville
Taninges
Abondance
Vouvry
Villars
Bex
Monthey
Champéry
Conthey
Ardon
Sion
Sierre
Vissoie
St Niklaus
Stalden
Simplon
Weissmie
4023

Cruseilles
la Roche
sur Foron
Thorens
Glières
Roc d'Enfer
2244
Morzine
Dents du Midi
3257
Vernayaz
Riddes
Saxon
Evolène
Zinal
Dom
4545
Saas Fee
Antrona

Annecy
Pringy
Rumilly
Alby
Cluses
Magland
Samoens
Valloreine
Le Chatelard
Orsières
Martigny
Verbier
Aiguilles Rouges
3646
Fionnay
Arolla
Matterhorn
4478
Zermatt
21
PENNI

Aix-les-
Bains
Talloires
Ugine
Megève
Sallanches
St Gervais
les Bains
Argentiére
Servoz
Chamonix
Mont-Blanc
Pte Percée
2752
la Clusaz
Mont Blanc
4808
Tunnel de
Mont Blanc
Mt Blanc de
Cheilon
3870
Bourg-
St-Pierre
Col du Grand
St-Bernard
2469
Breu
Cervinia
Monte
Rosa
4634
Dufourspitze
Alagna
Valsesia

Frangy
les
Contamines
Morgex
La Thuile
Aosta
Châtillon
St Marcel
Valtournanche
Gressoney
St Jean

FRANCE

Villages nestle between Alpine peaks in Switzerland.

AROUND SWITZERLAND

Despite its small size, Switzerland has an
extraordinary variety of landscapes and traditions
and some of the most culturally rich cities in Europe.

L andlocked in the middle of
Europe amid its lakes and
mountains, with a unique linguistic mix, Switzerland has cultivated a determined, often almost
eccentric individuality. Its insistence
on neutrality has kept it apart from
all Europe's great conflicts of the
last 200 years – and the resulting
devastation – and its policy of not
signing international treaties meant
that it did not even join the United
Nations until 2002. At the same time,
its special status in standing aside
from other nations' conflicts has also
made it a preferred location for the
headquarters of many international
organisations, including many that
are part of the UN. This is one of
the things, along with the proverbial
Swiss thoroughness and business
sense, that has also helped make the
country rich.

Undamaged by war, Switzerland
conjures up an image of precision,
wealth, neatness and good health.
Its landscapes are stunning, from the
high Alps to the lush green lower valleys with their picture-book lakes and
villages, and their beauty and invigoratingly fresh air have made this one of
Europe's foremost tourist destinations
ever since people first began to travel
for pleasure in the 18th century.

*Tourists and skiers onboard a Gornergrat Bahn
train, with the peak of the Matterhorn visible in
the background*

International Geneva

Geneva ❶ (Genève) is at the westernmost tip of Lake Geneva (Lac Léman)
which feeds the River Rhône, and is
surrounded by France on three sides.
It has a panorama of water, mountains, parks and flower beds, and the
elegant villas lining the lakeshore and
coloured sails on the water create a
delightful setting for Switzerland's
most cosmopolitan city.

Many of its well-known sights are
found right where the Rhône leaves
Geneva. The **Water Fountain** (Jet

Main Attractions

Lake Geneva
Neuchâtel
Basel
Zürich
Luzern
Bodensee
The Engadine
Ticino
Bernese Oberland
Zermatt

Reformation Monument in the Parc des Bastions, Geneva.

d'Eau) in the harbour sends a dazzling plume of white foam 145 metres (476ft) into the air. The first bridge to span the Rhône is the **Pont du Mont-Blanc**. From here and from **Quai du Mont-Blanc**, on the right bank, one can enjoy (on clear days) an unobstructed view of **Mont Blanc far to the south**, the highest peak in Europe at 4,808 metres (15,780ft).

The **Jardin Anglais** (English Garden) and Flower Clock, decorated with over 6,300 plants, are nearby on the left bank, while a little further on is **Ile Rousseau**, a place for literary pilgrims. Philosopher Jean-Jacques Rousseau (1712–78) was born in the city, and the island, reached by a footbridge from the **Pont des Bergues**, was renamed when a statue of him was erected in 1834.

Behind the Jardin Anglais, crossing the main shopping street of Rue de Rhône are numerous steep, narrow lanes leading to the **Old Town** (*vieille ville*), with its picturesque streets and squares. Don't miss the **Place du Bourg-de-Four** and the **Cathédrale St-Pierre**. Geneva was the birthplace

of Swiss watchmaking; the **Patek Philippe Museum** (Tue–Sat) displays timepieces and music boxes dating back to the 16th century.

Next to the cathedral is the **Musée International de la Réforme** (International Museum of the Reformation; Tue–Sun), which explores the roots and development of the Protestant break with the Catholic Church, while on the far side of the Old Town in the Parc des Bastions, the **Reformation Wall** commemorates some key figures of Protestantism. As the city of John Calvin (1509–64), Geneva figured prominently in the history of the Protestant Reformation. Fleeing from persecution in France, he inspired the city to take up the cause in 1536, and made it the "Protestant Rome", promulgating his doctrine of predestination and rigidly austere morality, which included the banning of theatres, dancing and jewellery.

Calvin's influence was not entirely negative, for it could be argued that it was he who made Geneva such an international city. Protestant refugees flocked in from England, France and

THE BEST PUBLIC TRANSPORT SYSTEM

The country's special landscape, with acute ascents and massive mountain barriers dividing the main valleys, might be expected to make getting around difficult, but visitors to Switzerland benefit from the world's best public transport system. Many of the most scenic places can be reached only by mountain railway or cable car, so it makes sense to buy one of the Swiss Travel System passes and enjoy the landscape without driving.

Narrow-gauge mountain railways are an essential part of the Swiss Alps. Most famous are the Rhaetian Railway (www.rhb.ch) in Graubünden, running from Chur to Klosters, Davos, St Moritz and into Italy – a line so beautiful it has been declared a Unesco World Heritage site – and the Matterhorn-Gotthard line (www.matterhorngotthardbahn.ch) from Disentis, where it connects with the Rhaetian, to Zermatt. The two companies provide the hugely popular Glacier Express (www.glacierexpress.ch), all the way from St Moritz and Davos to Zermatt.

Mountain trains and cable cars take skiers and sightseers up the **Kleines Matterhorn**, **Jungfrau**, **Corvatsch** and hundreds of other peaks. Among the best known is Europe's highest railway, to Jungfraujoch, and the Alps' longest aerial cableway. The world's highest underground funicular railway, the Metro-Alpin, at a height of 3,456 metres (11,339ft) up in **Saas Fee** in the Valais, makes year-round skiing possible.

Italy, and Calvin also founded an academy that evolved into the university. And since there were no recreational activities, the people of Geneva had no choice but to work and accumulate wealth.

Geneva's next major figure, Rousseau, was the wellspring of many of the ideas that led to the French Revolution of 1789, combining the excitement of the French Enlightenment with a certain, rather Swiss, dogmatism. Rousseau's theory of the equality of man caused the whole Western world to rethink the notion of aristocratic government, and his ideas on nature also helped spark the Romantic movement in literature and the arts. The French philosopher Voltaire was also a Genevan by adoption, and Romantic writers such as Byron and Shelley were drawn to the area too.

Geneva is important today because of its role as the headquarters for many international organisations. The **Palace of Nations** was built between 1929 and 1936 for the League of Nations, the predecessor to the UN, and is now its European headquarters.

Several other UN subsidiary organisations, including the International Labour Organization (ILO) and the World Health Organization (WHO), are based in Geneva, as is, most famous of all, the Red Cross.

Around Lake Geneva

The Swiss side of Lake Geneva is known as the **Vaud Riviera**, and the name is appropriate. Mountains protect the area from north and east winds, giving it a mild climate with 2,000 hours of sunshine a year. The lakeside towns and villages are lined with well-tended flower beds and trees. Behind them, neat vineyards grow on terraces that date from the 11th century; the Lavaux Vineyard Terraces are a World Heritage site. A ferry service – extensive in summer – links the towns around the lake, including Evian, Thonon and Yvoire on the French side.

A string of pretty towns and villages lines the lakeshore between Geneva and the eastern end of the lake at Montreux. **Coppet**, with its picturesque main street and small

Geneva's clock tower is one of the city's best-known sights.

The SS Savoie sets off from Geneva.

The Palace of Nations in Geneva is the European headquarters of the United Nations.

Vineyards overlooking Lake Geneva.

Château de Coppet (Apr–Oct daily, pm only) is the first of these. The Château is celebrated as the home of the author Mme de Staël (1766–1817). Expelled from Paris by Napoleon for her liberal ideas, she returned to her family home at Coppet, entertaining the literary figures of the day, including Byron, at her salons. Further along, and clinging to a steep hillside, **Nyon** was founded by the Romans and is today an attractive town with a lakeside castle, winding streets and tree-lined lakeside promenade. The **Château de Prangins**, 2km (1¼ miles) east of Nyon, is a beautiful 18th-century building housing the **Musée Suisse** (Swiss National Museum; Tue–Sun) for the French-speaking part of the country, detailing Switzerland's recent history. In the grounds, the castle's pretty kitchen garden has been faithfully recreated.

Lausanne ❷, the "second city" of French Switzerland and capital of Vaud Canton, enjoys a sheltered, sunny spot on the southern slopes of steep terraces and gorges. The old quarter, **La Cité**, is the location of the medieval **cathedral**, which has the most impressive exterior in Switzerland. The International Olympic Committee is based in the city, and the **Olympic Museum** stands by the lake at **Quai d'Ouchy**. However, it is undergoing large-scale modernisation, and is not due to reopen until late 2013. In summer, this lakeside area attracts a cosmopolitan crowd for boating and other water sports.

The region of **Montreux-Vevey** lies along the lakeside near the southeastern end of Lake Geneva. While on a visit there, the mother of Tsar Alexander II wrote: "I am in the most beautiful country in the world." The tsars are long gone, and **Montreux ❸** now seeks to attract a different kind of international clientele. Only 72km (45 miles) from Geneva Airport, the city has a huge conference and exhibition centre to host international festivals such as the Montreux Jazz and Classical Music festivals. The pre-World War I glitter may have faded, but the beautiful setting remains. The lush green hills still slope down to the lake, with mountain peaks in the background. Flowers bloom easily in the unusually mild climate.

The literary set of the 18th and 19th centuries could not stay away. Rousseau set his 1761 novel, *La Nouvelle Héloïse*, in **Clarens**, now part of Montreux. Voltaire arrived, followed shortly by Byron, who put Montreux on the itinerary of British tourists for the next 150 years. Dickens, Tolstoy, Hans Christian Andersen and Dostoevsky are some of the other literati who came. The best-known resident of **Vevey**, just west of Montreux, was Charlie Chaplin, who is buried here. His statue stands in the main square.

Just 1.6km (1 mile) east of Montreux is the **Château de Zermatt** (daily). Built by a Duke of Savoy in the 9th or 10th century, and expanded in the 13th century, it has large dungeons into which critics and plotters were tossed.

Gruyères and the Jura

The Montreux-Vevey area provides a starting point for several excursions, such as one to the cheese-making town of **Gruyères**, home of the most famous of Swiss cheeses, Gruyère.
The Gruyères district is idyllic. In addition to the famous cheese, it produces country ham, cream, strawberries and chocolate. Both cheese museum (a model dairy farm next to the railway station demonstrates the cheesemaking process, and samples are provided) and chocolate factories can be visited by the Swiss Chocolate Train from Montreux, using Belle Epoque Pullman and panoramic cars.

The medieval town of Gruyères has only one main thoroughfare: a wide cobblestone area from which cars have been banned and which is lined with traditional buildings. This street, which leads up the hill to a **castle**, is liberally planted with flowers.

The northernmost part of French-speaking Switzerland is covered by the **Jura** Mountains, running northwest of Lake Geneva towards Basel. They also extend into France, and though relatively low by Alpine standards are still ruggedly beautiful, with wonderful locations for hiking. The **Haut Jura Neuchâtelois**, one of the most impressive parts of the range, can be reached from **Neuchâtel ❹**, at the eastern end of the largest lake of the same name. Founded in the 11th century, under the counts of Neuchâtel, the city expanded on land reclaimed from the lake, and won fame as a centre of Swiss watchmaking. There are also some fine museums here, in particular the **Musée d'Art et d'Histoire** (Museum of Art and History; Tue–Sun), which among many other exhibits has a large collection of historic clocks and watches.

Into German Switzerland

The linguistic border between French- and German-speaking Switzerland runs just east of Lake Neuchâtel. **Bern ❺** is the national capital of the Swiss Federation and also known as the town of bears, translated as *Bearn* in the local dialect. There are automated metal bears on the *glockenspiel* of the city's famous **Zeitglockenturm**

The Musée des Beaux-Arts in Lausanne.

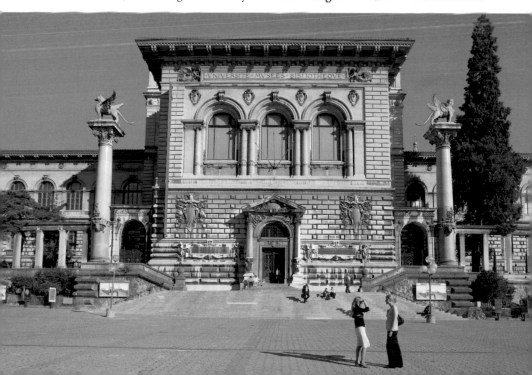

Gruyères Castle, dating from the 11th century.

(Clock Tower) and bears in the zoo. The Old City is located on a peninsula, a sharp bend in the **River Aare**, with bridges heading off to the "mainland" in three directions. After a disastrous fire in 1405, the town was rebuilt with local sandstone, and the result is so impressive it is a World Heritage site. Gothic sandstone buildings, with elaborate bay windows, overhanging gables and red geraniums in window boxes, are ubiquitous, as are squares with flower-decked fountains. There are more arcades than in any other city in Europe. The neoclassical **Bundeshaus** (Parliament Building) and a number of banking houses face each other on the same square. Notable among Bern's many museums is the **Zentrum Paul Klee** (Paul Klee Centre; Tue–Sun), in a striking building designed by Renzo Piano, which houses the world's largest collection of the painter's work.

Switzerland's second-biggest economic centre after Zürich is **Basel ❻**, one of the largest ports on the Rhine. It is home to the **Zolli** (Basel Zoo; daily), Switzerland's largest zoo, and

plays a leading role in the international arts and antiques trade.

Nearly all the sights of the city are in **Grossbasel**, the **Old Town**, which rises steeply from the Rhine's right bank. Among the striking Gothic buildings are the impressive **Rathaus** (**Town Hall**) and the 12th-century cathedral. Basel has no fewer than 35 museums, catering for every taste. A cast of Rodin's *Les Bourgeois de Calais* welcomes visitors to the most prestigious, the **Kunstmuseum** (Fine Arts Museum; Tue–Sun), which has a very fine collection of works by 16th-century painters such as Holbein and Grünewald combined with an outstanding selection of 19th- and 20th-century art by figures such as Gauguin, Van Gogh, Picasso, Chagall, Klee, Max Ernst, Kandinsky and Basel native Arnold Böcklin.

To the north of the Old Town, The **Dreiländereck** (Three Country Corner) is something of a novelty. By walking around a marker, you are able to pass in seconds through Switzerland, France and Germany – all without having to show a passport.

Zürich

Tucked in between high hills at the north end of Lake Zürich is the country's largest city, **Zürich ❼**, one of the world's key financial centres. The region here is not yet part of the Alps, but the **Mittelland** (Midland), a wide strip that cuts across Switzerland from northeast to southwest. The River Limmat divides the **Altstadt** (Old Town) between the **Hauptbahnhof** (main train station) on the west side and **Limmatquai**, a riverside promenade, on the east. **Bahnhofstrasse**, one of Europe's most elegant shopping streets, runs south from the Hauptbahnhof parallel to the river. Price tags, if there are any, suggest a city of millionaires.

Zurich has some architectural gems, notably the Romanesque-Gothic **Grossmünster church** with twin towers, cut down to size

somewhat after an 18th-century fire. At the nearby **Kunsthaus** (Museum of Art; Tue–Sun) on **Heimplatz** you can race through an impressive range of mostly 19th- and 20th-century art in one of Switzerland's largest galleries. The labyrinthine **Schweizerisches Landesmuseum** (Swiss National Museum; Tue–Sun) has Roman relics, medieval artefacts, heraldic shields and rooms furnished in the styles of the 15th to 18th centuries. On the west bank of the Limmat is the Rococo **Zur Meisen Guildhall** (Zunfthaus zur Meisen; Tue–Sun), a jewel-box of a building, alongside the slim Gothic grandeur of the **Fraumünster**, and **St Peter's** church, with the largest church clockface in Europe.

Lucerne

Its French and English name, Lucerne, leaves the visitor totally unprepared for the very German character of **Luzern ⑧**. The covered **Kapellbrücke** (Chapel Bridge), built in 1333 and reconstructed after a fire in 1993, is the city's best-known landmark. It has a distinctive red-tile roof and its interior is lined with gable paintings glorifying the martyrs and heroes of the region. A few hundred yards further downstream a second medieval bridge with a small chapel crosses the **River Reuss**, which drains **Vierwaldstätter See** (Lake Lucerne). The wooden **Spreuerbrücke** (Spreuer Bridge) also has a gabled roof. The gable ends are decorated with Caspar Meglinger's paintings of the *Totentanz* ("Dance of Death").

For visitors coming from the north, Lucerne is a gateway to the Alps, and its medieval ambience enhanced by its breathtaking surroundings. The large lake, criss-crossed by majestic paddle steamers, is flanked on either side by the two giants of mounts **Rigi** and **Pilatus**. The crystal-blue waters meeting the mountain faces are the perfect setting for a romantic evening dinner cruise. Boat cruises stop at various points, from where cable cars stretch up to the surrounding peaks. You can walk up from the village of **Vitznau** to the peak of Rigi in about four hours, or take the cog-wheel train. The Alpine panorama is splendid,

The symbol of Bern. Legend says that Duke Bechtold of Zähringen hunted down a bear in the area shortly after establishing the town in 1191.

Every September in Heidiland farmers lead their cows, all beautifully garlanded, down the valley and into the village, where they are welcomed.

A TRIO OF LANGUAGES

Travelling through Switzerland reveals that the linguistic and cultural background of each region, whether predominantly German, French or Italian, influences everything, especially food, architecture and lifestyle.

About two-thirds of the Swiss are German-speaking. They speak *Schwyzerdütsch*, a specifically Swiss dialect that is used at all social levels. Other German-speakers can have difficulty in understanding it and its regional variations, and often find Swiss German oddly archaic. French has worked its way into Swiss-German, too, so that people say *merci vielmals* for "thank you very much". Menus may use a mix of German, French and *Schwyzerdütsch*. The languages in the French and Italian areas of the country are more similar to those spoken in France and Italy, although Swiss-French pronunciation tends to be a bit more emphatic than standard French, so can be easier to understand for foreigners.

Language divisions do not always follow the borders of the cantons. Basel, Zürich and St Gallen in the north, and Bern and Luzern are all fully German-speaking, but the Fribourg Canton, east of Montreux, has French- and German-speaking areas. The Italian Swiss are primarily concentrated in Ticino, but also extend into Graubünden or the Grisons, where different Alpine valleys have often maintained linguistic differences, and Romansch, the fourth official language, can be heard.

stretching 300km (nearly 200 miles) in every direction. The cog-wheel railway (closed Dec–Apr) on Pilatus, with a 1 in 2 gradient, is one of the world's steepest. Yodelling, flag-throwing and alphorn concerts are kept alive for tourists.

Lucerne is also known as the place where Richard Wagner wrote three of his major works, *Die Meistersinger, Siegfried* and *Götterdämmerung*. He lived in Luzern between 1866 and 1872, in a mansion on the Tribschen peninsula that is now the **Richard Wagner Museum** (mid-Mar–Nov Tue–Sun). This was where Wagner lived with Cosima von Bülow, the daughter of Franz Liszt, having begun their affair when she was still married to the conductor Hans von Bülow.

Each summer Lucerne is host to the **Lucerne Festival**, a celebration of classical music. A popular feature of the festivals are outdoor serenades at the **Löwenplatz**. The acoustics of the water and rock, and the soft illumination of the colossal lion carved from a cliff, provide an enchanting nocturnal experience.

The town of **Schwyz** ❾, on the east side of Lake Lucerne, gave its name to the country. Switzerland's most important document – the Swiss Charter of 1291 – is housed here in the **Bundesbriefmuseum** (Museum of the Swiss Charters of Confederation; Tue–Sun). Close to the centre, the wonderfully preserved 17th-century manor house, the **Ital Reding-Hofstatt** (Tue–Sun) – a classic of Swiss traditional architecture with its chalet-style roofs – houses exhibits that tell the story of the rich families who supplied foreign courts with the town's most famous export – mercenary soldiers – in the 17th and 18th centuries.

Bodensee

Eastern Switzerland receives relatively few visitors, but the area around the broad expanse of **Bodensee** (Lake Constance) ❿, on the border with Bavaria, has vine-covered slopes, orchards, meadows and historic towns and villages. The city of **St Gallen** ⓫ is easy to reach from Zürich. It originally developed from a monastery precinct, now dominated by the Baroque **cathedral** (daily). The city also contains a series of exceptionally fine Baroque facades, particularly the **Zum Greif** house (Gallusstrasse 22) and the **Haus zum Pelikan** (Schmiedgasse 15).

In a quiet corner on the Swiss-Austrian border, next to the cantons of St Gallen and Grisons, lies **Liechtenstein** ⓬. This independent *Fürstentum* (principality), left over from the Holy Roman Empire and occupying only 162 sq km (62 sq miles) between the Rhine and the Vorarlberg mountains, offers fabulous scenery.

Into the Alps: Graubünden

Switzerland's easternmost canton, Graubünden or, in French and English, Grisons, is also the most mixed: within it some areas speak German, Italian, and the oldest language of the mountains, Romansch.

A Zürich tram, with the towers of the Grossmünster in the background.

Chur ⑬, the capital, is the oldest town in Switzerland, having been settled by the Celts 5,000 years ago. The old part of town is exceptionally beautiful when snow lies on the mighty roofs of the Gothic **town hall**, the **Bishop's Palace** and the Romanesque **cathedral**, which contains a magnificent late Gothic carved high altar.

Southwest of Chur the true high Alps begin in the Silvretta and Albula ranges, with famous glaciers and a string of peaks well over 3,000 metres (9,850ft) high, separating the town from the **Engadine**, the upper valley of the River Inn, which flows northeast into Austria. The towns in or above the valley became the first winter sports resorts anywhere in the world in the 1860s, and have never lost their cachet

Anyone crossing the passes to the Engadine has to take one of the routes through the narrow gap around Chur, via **Lenzerheide** and **Tiefencastel** south to St Moritz or from **Landquart** through the Saars tunnel to **Klosters**, a small but discreetly luxurious ski resort that is the favourite skiing spot

of the British royal family. A few kilometres along the same valley is the much larger but still opulent **Davos** ⑭. Wealthy sufferers from tuberculosis were already sent to Davos in the 18th century, due to its famously clean mountain air, and hotels and sanatoria grew up to cater for them. It was thus well placed to join the boom in winter sports when they became fashionable in the 1880s, and more recently, Davos has diversified its activities again and acquired new fame by hosting the annual World Economic Forum, where the world's most powerful gather to compare notes. For skiers, its prime attraction is the **Parsenn** mountain located between Davos and Klosters, which offers 200km (125 miles) of ski slopes

St Moritz ⑮ is, however, where the whole history of winter tourism began in 1864, when Johannes Badrutt, owner of the Kulm Hotel, invited some English summer guests to spend the winter here. Within a few years ice-skating and curling competitions were held, and skiing, demonstrated by visiting Scandinavians, was taken

Lucerne and its covered bridge.

The Rococo library in St Gallen abbey.

up by fashionable guests. With many upscale hotels and chic nightlife, St Moritz remains one of the Alps' most lavishly equipped resorts.

To escape the bustle and crowds of the town and lake, take the route up the north side of the valley to **Maloja**, which leads across wooded, sheltered slopes through an idyllic landscape with wonderful views of Lake Silvaplana below, and continue past the foot of the **Corvatsch**, considered by many the best mountain for skiing in the world.

Italian Switzerland: Ticino

Apart from part of Graubünden, Italian Switzerland consists of just one canton, **Ticino**. It is still possible here to find wonderfully quiet valleys filled with sunshine and sub-Alpine vegetation, although they may be just a few kilometres from motorways and railways. Predominantly mountainous, the region has two great lakes at the foot of the Alps bordering Italy, **Lago Maggiore** and **Lago di Lugano**.

The town of Lugano  has a modern banking quarter, but the developers spared a few arcaded alleyways; the **Cathedral of San Lorenzo**, a Lombard Renaissance masterpiece on the steep slope between the railway station and the lower part of town, has also survived. The **Museo Cantonale d'Arte** (Tue–Sun) in the Villa Malpensata has a good collection of works by Swiss artists.

Locarno ⑰ and the small villages on the banks of Lago Maggiore enjoy the mildest climate in the Ticino. This has encouraged tourism to the extent that traffic around the lake can sometimes be unbearable. The 14th-century **Castello Visconteo** (Apr–Oct Tue–Sun) now houses the **Museo Archeologico** (Archaeological Museum; Apr–Oct Tue–Sun), which has Bronze Age and Roman artefacts. **Ascona** is one of the most ancient settlements on the lake, and the houses here along the promenade are now colourful cafés and restaurants overlooking the small harbour. Boat services on the lake call at 36 piers, most of them in Italy. The most notable Swiss port of call is the island of Brissago, for its villa and botanic garden.

SWISS WINTER WONDERLAND

As the original home of winter sports, Switzerland's ski-slopes have never lost their appeal. The most famous Swiss mountain towns – St Moritz, Klosters, Davos, Gstaad – also created the image of a classic ski resort: luxurious, with glamorous bars for "après-ski" socialising, and patronised by royalty and the kind of celebrities once known as "the international jet set". Many are now a little elderly but still rich enough to afford the very high prices, but recently towns like St Moritz have discovered a fresh clientele in the all-new super-rich from Russia.

This kind of clientele often spends more time mingling and shopping than skiing, but these resorts still have excellent, though unavoidably expensive, facilities. There are, however, many less costly options. Bernese Oberland villages such as Grundelwald have a more relaxed atmosphere and less astronomic prices, and many skiers prefer other, lesser-known areas such as Laax, in the Glarner Alps west of Chur, or smaller valleys in the Valais like the Val d'Anniviers south of Sierre, with enjoyable resort villages like Vissoie and Zinal. Their slopes are often now used for snowboarding, snow-kiting, sledging and other options, as well as classic skiing. The official website www.myswitzerland.com lists some 355 winter-sports centres across the country.

The Bernese Oberland and the Valais

Ticino is connected to central Switzerland via the **San Gottardo** (St Gotthard) pass, one of the historic routes over the Alps. There are some 51 peaks over 4,000 metres (13,000ft) high in the mountain chains formed by the Bernese Oberland (Alps) and their continuation in neighbouring Valais, and this is another of the great Alpine sports regions. If the Engadine was where Alpine skiing began, the Bernese Oberland was one of the first centres of mountaineering, especially around the **Jungfrau**, 4,158 metres (13,640ft) high and first climbed in 1811, and neighbouring **Eiger**, lower at 3,970 metres (13,000ft) but with a more dangerous reputation. The town of **Interlaken ⑩** grew up in their shadow, and is full of splendid hotel buildings from its glory days in the 19th century. Above it, villages such as Grindelwald, Mürren and Wengen are popular ski centres. The area is also a favourite for hiking in summer, as well as for adventure sports like canyoning or paragliding. **Thun ⑲**, considered the gateway to the Oberland, is dominated by its castle, perched on a steep hill. The 12th-century keep, with its four corner towers, is reminiscent of a Norman castle.

The route to Montreux passes through the mountain resort of **Gstaad ⑳**, another spot where high society from all over the world meets up in the winter months. To the south is the Valais, a mainly French-speaking canton that is another major Alpine sports region. In the last few decades **Crans Montana** near Sierre has risen in fashionable status, drawing in many celebrity names, but the older skiing and mountaineering mecca of **Zermatt ㉑** has the great plus of lying at the foot of the majestic Matterhorn, 4,478 metres (14,690ft) high. The finest easily reached view of the famous mountain is from Gornergrat, summit of a cog-wheel railway from Zermatt and the highest open-air station in Europe, at 3,092 metres (10,145ft). In the east of the Valais, the road from Sierre leads to the Simplon Pass and rail tunnel through to Italy.

View over Lake Thun to the Bernese Oberland.

Stunning Tyrolean scenery.

AUSTRIA

Combining Alpine scenery with the musical genius
of Mozart and Strauss, the country is hard to beat
when it comes to romance.

"Waterfall hat" in the National Park.

The opening words of Austria's national anthem are "Land of mountains…", and that is exactly what this 84,000 sq km (32,000 sq mile) country is. For centuries these uplands were a bugbear, making life hard for the farmer. The American writer John Gunther remarked in the 1930s that "the chief crop of provincial Austria is the scenery". That scenery is now the country's highest earner, and the year-round tourist industry accounts for the largest slice of the national economy.

Nestled among the wild Alpine scenery are hundreds of mountain lakes and idyllic watercourses that are especially attractive in summer. The gentle charms of the Salzkammergut and the Carinthian Lake District are emphasised by the majestic backdrop of mountains. To the east, the foothills of the Alps gradually peter out in the Vienna woods, reaching right up to the suburbs of the capital. Vienna was for 600 years the centre of one of Europe's superpowers, the Austro-Hungarian Empire, and this has endowed it with a grandeur far beyond the norm for the capital of a small country. It is a beautiful city today, and it houses a wealth of treasures. Salzburg, on the north side of the Alps and for many perpetually associated with the film *The Sound of Music*, is equally romantic, and has become almost a theme park for its most esteemed inhabitant, Wolfgang Amadeus Mozart.

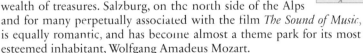

Every period of European cultural development is reflected in Austria. Romanesque, Gothic, Renaissance and Baroque buildings are scattered across the land. Statues, frescoes, ceiling and wall paintings document more than 1,000 years of often turbulent history.

Austrians are known for their politeness and hospitality, and attachment to tradition. Older people here, especially, can be observed exchanging a variety of traditional courtesies – men greeting women with a short, clipped bow of the head, a respectful use of titles with anyone who possibly merits one – that hark back to the days of the Habsburg Empire. This all adds to the sensation experienced by many visitors, that this is very much part of the Old World.

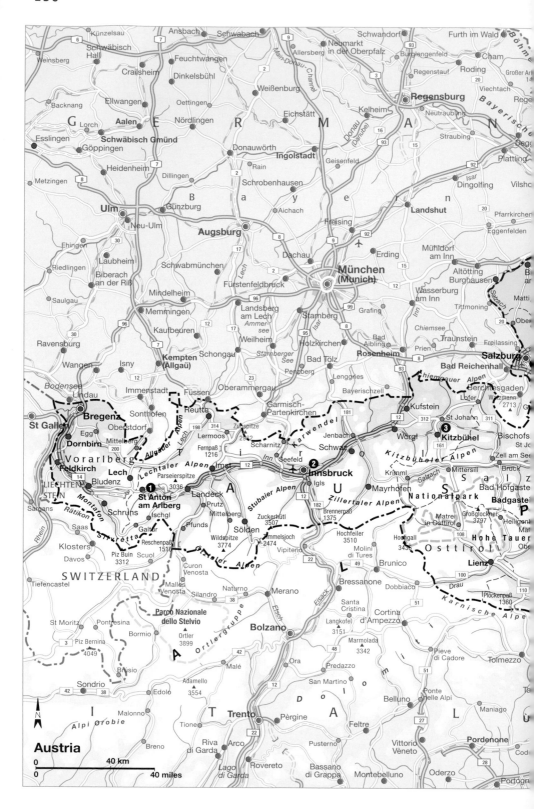

Austria

0   40 km

0   40 miles

Vienna

0   500 m
0   500 yds

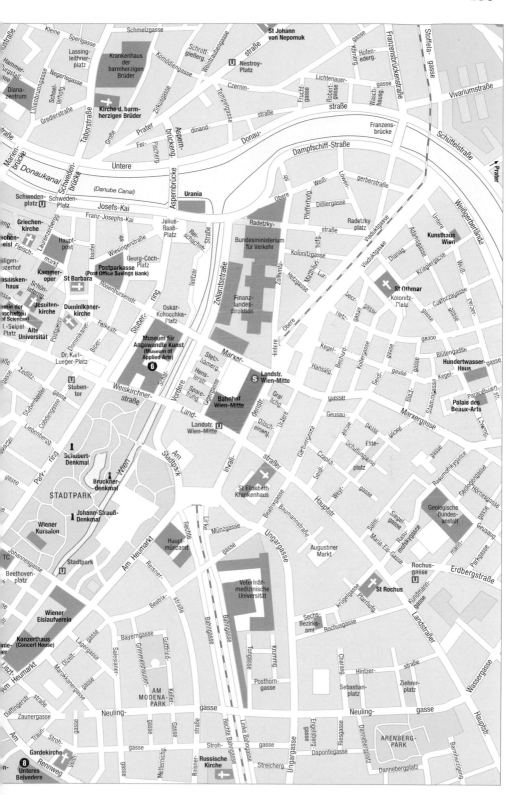

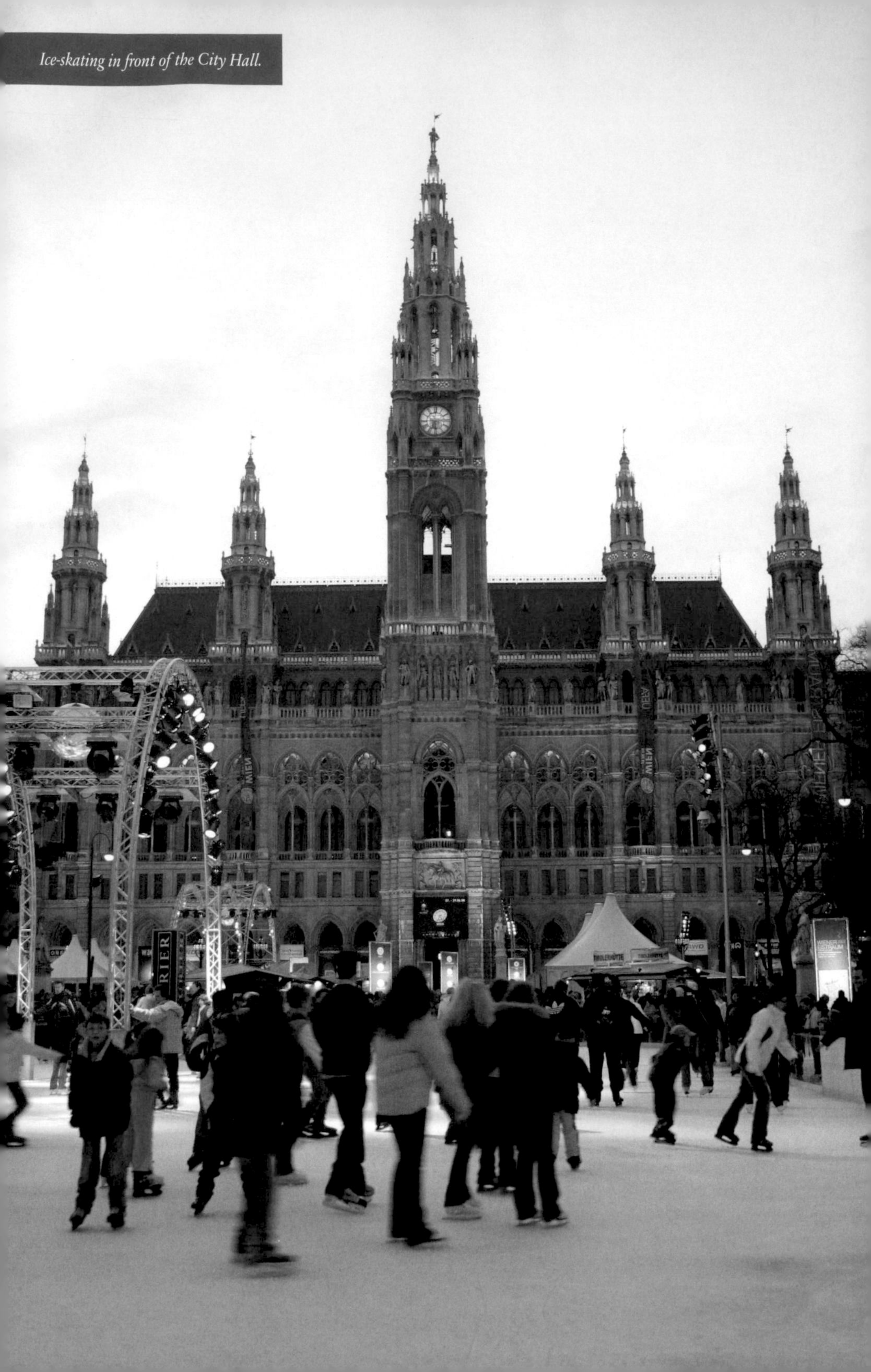

Ice-skating in front of the City Hall.

VIENNA

The capital of the former Habsburg Empire gave the world the waltz, high-stepping horses and psychoanalysis, and has been home to some of the world's great composers.

Vienna is an easy city to get to know, not because nobody ever gets lost in its maze of streets and passages (they do), but because the Viennese themselves have a reputation for being courteous and helpful. There is a diversity of people here that, like most things about Vienna, can be traced directly to the far-flung Habsburg Empire.

First settled by Celts around 500 BC, and later a Roman frontier town called Vindobona, Vienna became the main seat of the Habsburg dynasty in 1278. From 1443 the Habsburgs effectively held in perpetuity the title of Holy Roman Emperor, and up until their collapse in 1918 extended their rule over a huge area of Central and Eastern Europe, from Austria through Hungary to much of Poland. Vienna was built to be the centre of a vast multinational empire, and so has a scale and grandeur far in excess of the requirements of the capital of what is now a middling-sized country.

Imperial Vienna was also a bulwark between East and West, applauded by Europe when it repelled the Turks in the Siege of 1683. Their imperial status made the Habsburgs the most prestigious of all German dynasties by far, and Vienna was the foremost cultural centre of the Germanic world, especially in the 18th century. All manner of ideas flourished among its cultural palaces and cafés. Art and music, theatre and science

Vienna's Imperial Palace.

found the ideal climate in which to grow. Vienna was home to the greatest composers, from Haydn, Mozart and Beethoven to Schoenberg, and equally great architects, from the historicist Von Ferstel to Otto Wagner, founder in 1890s of the Vienna Secession movement, the local variant of Art Nouveau.

Even in the last years of the empire, from the 1860s to 1914, Vienna experienced a new, brief golden age, acquiring the Ringstrasse and many of its grandest buildings, and witnessing Freud founding psychoanalysis, Klimt

Main Attractions
Hofburg
Burgkapelle
Spanische Hofreitschule
Kunsthistorisches Museum
The Ring
Staatsoper
Stephansdom
Belvedere
Schönbrunn

and the Secession artists breaking new ground in visual art and Mahler producing glorious music. Its population included Czechs, Poles and many other nationalities.

When these other nationalities seized independence in 1918, grand Vienna was left only with the empire's German-speaking rump, like a star actor reduced to playing provincial theatres. The Nazi takeover confirmed its decline; Jews – such as Freud and Mahler – had been particularly central to Viennese cultural life, and they left in droves. More recently Vienna has regained status as a meeting point for international organisations, but the sense of past glories lost is inescapable. It is the only European capital whose population, 1.7 million, is less than it was a century ago.

Habsburg legacy

The Habsburgs were great builders. At the heart of the Old Town they erected the immense **Hofburg** (Imperial Palace) ❶, a town within the city, which was "always being built but never finished". Construction began about 1220, but it was enlarged and renovated right into the 20th century, and today its sprawling buildings contain a variety of museums. The **Neue Burg** (Wed–Mon) wing was completed just 10 years before the collapse of the Habsburg Empire; it now houses collections of musical instruments, armour and weapons, the **Ephesus Museum**, with antiquities from the Greek city of Ephesus in Turkey, and the **Museum für Volkerkunde** (Museum of Ethnology).

The oldest part of the Hofburg is the **Schweizerhof** (Swiss Court), begun in the 13th century. Around it are the Imperial Apartments, spreading over several wings including the 16th-century Renaisssance Amalienburg. Nearby too are the Gothic Burgkapelle (Court Chapel), home of the Vienna Boys' Choir, and the Stallburg or Imperial Stables, built in the 1550s as a princely residence but since used as an art gallery and stables, and now a museum on Lippizaner horses. Between the apartments are lovely courts and gardens.

Notable collections in the Hofburg include the **Imperial Silver Collection** (daily) and the **Schatzkammer** or **Imperial Treasury** (Wed–Mon). This contains the bejewelled crown of the Holy Roman Empire, founded in 800 by Charlemagne. Most important of all is the **Albertina** (daily), in a separate wing on the east side of the palace, one of the world's greatest collections of graphic arts and engravings, including superlative drawings by Dürer and Michelangelo. The Albertina also hosts fine exhibitions of contemporary art.

The all-white Baroque confection of the **Spanische Hofreitschule** (Spanish Riding School; www.srs.at) dates from the 18th century, when it was commissioned by Emperor Karl VI. The name comes from the Spanish horses imported to breed with native Karst horses and subsequently other thoroughbreds; the famous Lipizzaner horses were first raised in Lipizza, Slovenia. It is a unique experience to watch the white stallions perform their delicate dressage steps to the music of classical dances.

The Café Central, famous for its history as well as its coffee and cakes.

Major museums

The final extension of the Hofburg that produced the Neue Burg also included the creation of two vast museums, separated from the main palace by the Ringstrasse. The **Naturhistorisches Museum** (Natural History Museum; Wed–Mon) ❷ is one of the largest museums of its kind in the world, benefiting from imperial collections of dinosaur skeletons, gemstones and other scientific artefacts initiated over 250 years ago. Opposite in an identical Renaissance-style building is the **Kunsthistorisches Museum** (Museum of Fine Arts; Tue–Sun) ❸. This is another of the great art collections – based, again, on the imperial collection – with a vast array of paintings that includes masterpieces by Rembrandt, Vermeer, Van Eyck, Rubens, Titian, Bruegel and Velázquez, as well as sculpture, decorative art and Greek, Roman, oriental and Egyptian antiquities.

The magnificent Ring

Vienna has hundreds of palaces, large and small, but the biggest building spree the city has ever seen was the Ringstrasse, better known just as **the Ring**. This wide avenue, 57 metres (187ft) across, follows the line of the city's medieval fortifications, which stood until Emperor Franz Joseph ordered them razed to allow Vienna to expand in 1857. Architectural competitions were launched, and the city received a brand-new face. The first major building to be completed, in 1869, was the **Staatsoper** ❹, Vienna's world-renowned Opera House. Designed in a romantic Neo-Renaissance style, it was lovingly restored to its former grandeur after damage in World War II.

The architect Heinrich von Ferstel set the tone of the Ring with the **Votivkirche** (Votive Church), to the northwest, built in gratitude for the failure of an assassination attempt against Franz Joseph in 1853. The church is Neo-Gothic in every detail, and later buildings nearby followed the style.

Von Ferstel's other major Ring building is the **university**, near the church, built in a more Italian Renaissance style. The soaring architecture continues with the **Neues Rathaus** (City

Tickets for Spanish Riding School performances can be obtained from the visitor centre in Michaelerplatz (Tue–Sun), or at the box office in Josefsplatz (Tue–Sat), when the horses' morning exercise takes place.

The Secession Building.

VIENNA'S MUSICAL HERITAGE

Vienna loves music, and musicians of every kind thrive in Vienna. In the **Burgkapelle** in the Hofburg, members of the Vienna Boys' Choir and the Vienna State Opera form the Court Music Orchestra (Hofmusikkapelle), and sing Mass at 9.15am on Sundays from mid-September to June (book through www.wsk.at).

Waltzes by Johann Strauss and Franz Lehár are especially popular in Carnival season, when elegant balls continue until dawn. Then there are the great composers like Haydn, Schubert, Mozart, Mahler, Bruckner and Schoenberg. Traces of them can be found in many streets throughout Vienna.

Among the houses which have been turned into small museums or memorials are: the house where Haydn wrote his *Creation* (Haydngasse 19; Tue–Sun); the apartment where Mozart spent the happiest years of his life (Figaro House, Domgasse 5; daily); the places where Schubert was born (Nussdorferstrasse 54; Tue–Sun) and died (Kettenbrückengasse 6; Fri–Sun). Beethoven had more than 25 different addresses. In 1800, he moved to Heiligenstadt in the district of Döbling. It was here at Probusgasse 6, today the **Beethoven Museum** (Tue–Sun), that he wrote his *Heiligenstädt Testament*, a moving document in which he revealed his feelings about his growing deafness.

Hall) in imitation Gothic, and the **parliament building** in Hellenistic style. The **Burgtheater ❺**, opposite the City Hall, was built in the shape of a Greek lyre; the convex arch of the central tract is particularly impressive. Beyond the parliament building, the Ring passes through the Hofburg before reaching, just before the Danube, the **Museum für Angewandte Kunst** or **MAK ❻** (Museum of Applied Arts; Tue–Sun). This is a fabulous repository of porcelain, textiles, glass and other decorative arts from around the world, with especially fine Austrian furniture, glass and other designs from Baroque to Art Nouveau. Nor is it simply a historical collection, for the MAK also presents the best contemporary design.

The Old City

Within the Ring is the **Innere Stadt** or Old Vienna. Its heart is the **Stephansplatz**, Vienna's most famous square and the city's bustling centre. The south tower of the **Stephansdom ❼** (St Stephen's Cathedral; daily, guided tours available) gives a fabulous overview from the top of 343 steps. As an alternative, an elevator ascends the unfinished north tower as far as *Pummerin* (Boomer), a copy of the giant bell that was destroyed in World War II. The original *Pummerin* was cast in 1711 from cannons captured from the Turks. St Stephen's (Steffl to the Viennese) was the site of many Habsburg royal marriages.

Around the asymmetrical Steffl is the smart shopping centre of Vienna, the pedestrian zone including the **Graben** and **Kärntnerstrasse**. The area behind St Stephen's best retains the air of the past, though it is not actually the oldest quarter. In the web of narrow lanes a jumble of building styles from the 16th and 17th centuries are well preserved. In **Bäckerstrasse** and **Schönlaterngasse**, in particular, there are many bars and restaurants often thronged with people until the early hours of the morning.

Around the Belvedere

On the east side of the Ring lies the **Stadtpark**, laid out in 1862 and the most extensive patch of green in central Vienna. Its trees are reflected in the ponds and River Wien, which is flanked by a string of pavilions and a promenade.

The **Belvedere ❽** (daily), a palace of sumptuous proportions, was built between 1714 and 1723 for Prince Eugene of Savoy, the Empire's greatest general. In fact, it is really two palaces, the Upper and Lower Belvedere, joined by terraced gardens. As well as their exuberant Baroque decor they contain museums (all daily). The **Upper Belvedere** is the grandest section, with the **Palace Chapel**, and houses the **Österreichische Galerie** (Austrian Gallery), another of Vienna's great art collections, with stunning exhibits from the Middle Ages and the Baroque, but also major modern work by artists like Kokoschka, Klee and, above all, Gustav Klimt. The Lower Belvedere with its extraordinarily lush Baroque reception rooms, and the Orangery are now venues for temporary exhibitions, while

Johann Strauss plays on in the Stadtpark.

the Palace Stables house medieval art and the Augarten workshops are an all-white space for contemporary art shows.

Just west of the Belvedere entrance is the Karlsplatz, and the splendid Baroque **Karlskirche** ❾ (St Charles Church). The finest ecclesiastical Baroque building in the city, from 1713–37, its unique design includes a magnificent green cupola, twin triumphal pillars with spiral reliefs, and exterior belfries.

Tucked in between the Karlskirche and the Hofburg, at Friedrichstrasse 12, is the Art Nouveau **Secessionsgabäude** ❿ (Secession Building; Tue–Sun). It was designed by Joseph Maria Olbrich as a demonstration of the Secession movement's ideas and a showcase for artists such as Schiele, Kokoschka and Klimt, whose *Beethoven Frieze* (1902) covers three walls of a basement room.

Beyond the centre

A map of Vienna shows that it is laid out in concentric circles, with the Old City enclosed by the Ring and the Donaukanal (Danube Canal). On the other side of the Ring is the **Vorstadt**, the part of the city that grew up outside the fortifications. It is surrounded by another ring road, the Gürtel, outside of which come the suburbs, little villages such as Grinzing, Nussdorf and Severing, and their wine taverns, called *heurigen*.

The woods and meadows between the Danube and its canal east of the city centre enclose the **Prater** (daily), once a playground of emperors but a public park since 1766. Its landmark is the *Riesenrad* (daily), a giant Ferris wheel that arcs to a high point of nearly 65 metres (213ft). The park also offers a Planetarium, miniature railway, an old-fashioned amusement park that has recently gained some adrenalin-pumping rides, bicycle-hire shops and a swimming pool, and the lovely 4.5km (3-mile) **Hauptallee** (main avenue) is a favourite of joggers and cyclists.

On the east side of the city lies **Schönbrunn** (daily), the imperial summer residence. Perhaps the most beautiful of all the Habsburgs' palaces, it was originally commissioned in the 1690s as a grand hunting lodge by Emperor Leopold I, but was greatly extended in the 1740s under Empress Maria Theresa, who made it her favourite residence and employed Nikolaus Pacassi to create the fabulous palace and gardens we see today.

Schönbrunn contains 1,200 rooms, around 45 of which are open to the public, including the main Imperial Apartments. There are the private rooms used by Emperor Franz Joseph – who was born in the palace and died here in 1916 – and others used by Maria Theresa, including the Breakfast Room and jewel-like Vieux-Lacque Room. In the grounds are the Baroque Zoo, the English Botanic Garden, and the Gloriette with its views over the whole complex.

Beyond Schönbrunn the city fades into the **Wienerwald**, the Vienna Woods, forested hills that have been a favourite place for Viennese for centuries, and famously celebrated in a Strauss waltz.

The Upper Belvedere houses some wonderful works of Austrian art.

The Baroque splendour of Karlskirche.

Off-piste skiing from Valuga peak in St Anton, Austria.

AROUND AUSTRIA

With two-thirds of the country taken up by the Alps, Austria is the place for winter skiers and summer hikers. The charming towns of Salzburg and Innsbruck make good centres to stay.

Austria is a land of valleys and peaks, high roads and mountain passes, ski slopes and Alpine meadows that fall away eastwards to the Hungarian Plains. The spectacular scenery, friendly people, good food and well-developed resorts have earned it a deservedly high reputation around the world. Where farmers once eked out a living during the short summers, there are well-established hotels and restaurants. A network of lifts and cable cars lace the mountainsides, taking visitors, winter and summer, to the high playgrounds.

The Arlberg

In the very west of the country, **Arlberg** mountain region, straddling the border of the Tyrol and Vorarlberg provinces, is considered the cradle of Alpine skiing in Austria. Hannes Schneider gave the first ski lessons to tourists in 1907 in **St Anton am Arlberg ❶**, a village that has grown into a first-class ski resort.

While the **Tyrol** is the most famous of Austria's ski regions, good skiing is by no means limited to that province. The heart of the Vorarlberg is the **Montafon Valley**, gateway to the Silvretta High Alpine Road, with the 3,312-metre (10,863ft) **Piz Buin** towering in the background. The Montafon has been the site of many Austrian ski

championships, and villages such as Schruns have a special charm.

Innsbruck

The capital of the Tyrol, **Innsbruck ❷** owes its long history to its position at the foot of the Brenner Pass south to Italy. Of the historic Alpine passes, this is the easiest to cross and so was already an important military and trade link in Roman times, when a bridge was first built across the River Inn (the town's name simply means "Bridge over the Inn").

Main Attractions

Innsbruck
Kitzbühel
Grossglockner
Graz
Salzburg
Wachau
Stift Melk

Melk Abbey is an Austrian Benedictine abbey and one of the world's most famous monastic sites

Cows graze the green pastures in summer.

Klagenfurt's Dragon Fountain has become the emblem of the city, now that the legendary creature no longer terrifies the local population.

It enjoyed a golden age as one of the residences of the House of Habsburg in the 15th and 16th centuries, and reached its prime in the reign of Emperor Maximilian I (1493–1519), one of the dynasty's greatest monarchs, who spent long periods here. Trade and manufacturing flourished, as well as architecture, and many of the city's landmarks hail from this period.

Innsbruck's **Altstadt** or Old Town constitutes a precious assembly of medieval architecture. It is bordered by the **River Inn** and the streets of **Marktgraben**, **Burggraben** and **Herrengasse**. Almost every street offers a view of high mountain peaks nearby. The narrow lanes have been pedestrianised, allowing visitors to stroll without hindrance past the pergolas, oriel windows, painted facades and stucco ornaments. Another way of viewing these architectural treasures is by hiring one of the horse-drawn carriages that wait on Rennweg, in front of the **Tiroler Landestheater** (Tyrolean Provincial Theatre).

Herzog-Friedrich-Strasse leads into the heart of the Old Town to the **Goldenes Dachl or Golden Roof**, the most striking part of the **Neuer Hof** (New Palace), a magnificent late Gothic mansion built as a royal residence in the early 15th century. In 1500, Maximilian I had an extraordinary balcony added in commemoration of his betrothal to Bianca Maria Sforza, daughter of the Duke of Milan. The decorative balcony, adorned with elaborate reliefs and over 2,600 gilded copper shingles, served as a box for spectators watching tournaments and plays in the square below, and is Innsbruck's best-known landmark.

Herzog-Friedrich-Strasse is known for a string of medieval houses among which **Trautsonhaus**, built during the transition from Gothic to the Renaissance, and **Katzunghaus**, with unique balcony reliefs from 1530, stand out. Another landmark is the 56-metre (180ft) **Stadtturm** (City Tower), built in 1360 as a watchtower against fire. From its gallery there is a magnificent view of the

SKIING IN AUSTRIA

The Swiss may have invented the Alpine winter resort at St Moritz, but Austrians followed them soon afterwards, and were among the very first to adapt the original Scandinavian skiing style to suit their own steep slopes, as well as founding a system of teaching. Today, Austria boasts some of the world's finest winter sports facilities. Ischgl, south of St Anton in the Vorarlberg, has become one of the hippest resorts in the Alps in recent years, with a high-speed nightlife that attracts a celebrity crowd and the "Top of the Mountain" pop concerts each spring to mark the end of the ski season. Star names that have performed there include Beyoncé, Elton John, Rihanna and even Bob Dylan.

In the Tyrol, Innsbruck is not only a major winter sports centre itself, but is surrounded by smaller, often more enjoyable ski resorts, such as Igls and Mutters in the south or Seefeld to the northwest, which is particularly popular for cross-country skiing. The Kitzbühel area offers perhaps the greatest range of possibilities, with over 168km (105 miles) of slopes to choose from, covering every range of difficulty from beginner's slopes to the most adventurous. Nearby St Johann has a more laidback atmosphere than Kitzbühel itself.

town and the mountains. Sights one can see include the **Ottoburg**, a residential tower built in 1495, and the **Burgriesenhaus** in **Hofgasse**, which Duke Siegmund built in 1490 for his court favourite, Niklas Haidl, a 2.4-metre (7ft 10ins) giant.

In the opposite direction through Pfarrgasse is **Domplatz**, at the rear of the Golden Roof, with the **Domkirche zu Jakob** (Parish Cathedral of St James) a splendid example of Baroque architecture with twin towers. A copy of *Mariahilf* (Our Lady of Succour) by Lukas Cranach the Elder adorns the high altar.

Nowhere else in Austria conveys such a vivid impression of the 16th-century as the eastern part of the Old Town. The 15th-century **Hofburg** (Imperial Palace; daily) was rebuilt from 1754 to 1773 in late Rococo style. One highlight of the guided tours is the Riesensaal (Giant's Hall), with Rococo stucco work. The **Hofkirche** (Imperial Church) houses the **Mausoleum of Maximilian I**, although he was actually buried in Wiener Neustadt near Vienna. Twenty-eight of his forebears and contemporaries – all cast as larger-than-life bronze statues – stand guard around the grave.

To the east of the Hofkirche, in an old Franciscan monastery, is the **Tiroler Volkskunst-Museum** (Tyrol Folk Art Musuem; daily), which contains rustic interiors, traditional costumes and art illustrating the creativity of the Tyrolean people.

Outside the Old Town

Leading south from Herzog-Friedrich-Strasse is Innsbruck's principal thoroughfare, **Maria Theresien Strasse**, where the **Anna Säule** (St Anne's Column) commemorates 26 July 1703, St Anne's Day, when Bavarian troops forced the inhabitants out of Innsbruck. Leopoldstrasse, a continuation of the street, leads both to **Stiftskirche Wilten** (Wilten Abbey Church), founded in 1138 by the Premonstratensians, and to the **Basilika Wilten** (Wilten Basilica), built in 1755 on the foundations of a previous building. The present abbey church was completed in 1670 and is one of the loveliest early Baroque churches in Austria, while the Basilica is an outstanding example of exuberant Rococo.

The residence of Archduke Ferdinand II, who governed the Tyrol in the late 16th century, **Schloss Ambras** (Ambras Castle), lies on the southeast edge of the city. Today it is a museum housing a collection of rare 16th-century art and armour, royal portraits and Ferdinand's "Chamber of Art and Curiosities", a unique collection of oddities including portraits of people with strange disabilities, mechanical toys, oriental armour and other things amassed by the archduke.

Innsbruck has hosted the Winter Olympics twice, in 1964 and 1976, the Winter Paralympics in 1984 and 1988, and many international winter sports competitions. An imposing legacy of these events is the stadium on the **Bergiselschanze**, a hill south

Cathedral of St James and mountain backdrop, near Innsbruck.

of the city, seating 28,000 spectators and with a modern Olympic-standard ski jump designed by architect Zaha Hadid, with a tower that provides great views. Another reminder of the Olympics is the bobsleigh run at **Igls**, a popular resort a short distance further south from Innsbruck. You can experience flying down the run with a professional driver from December to March. Southwards, roads run up to the Brenner Pass and Italy.

The Eastern Tyrol

The reputation of **Kitzbühel ❸** as a chic winter sports centre dates from the triple Olympic victory in 1956 of local boy Toni Sailer – the "Kitz Comet". The famous **Hahnenkamm** mountain to the west of the resort – with famously steep slopes that host one of the annual Alpine Ski World Cup events – and the **Kitzbüheler Horn** to the east, ensure that the Kitzbühel skiing area attracts top enthusiasts from all over the world. Kitzbühel is also an all-year sports destination, as in summer it hosts the **Austrian Open** tennis

tournament in July, while the relatively tame Kitzbühel Alps afford an extensive range of mountain walks; for those who prefer it rockier and more challenging, there are the vast limestone peaks of the **Wilder Kaiser**. The best starting point for a mountain walk is **St Johann**, the resort town in the valley to the north between the Kitzbüheler Horn and the Wilder Kaiser.

The East Tyrol and the provinces of Salzburg and Kärnten (Carinthia) converge at the **Grossglockner**, the highest point in Austria at 3,797 metres (12,460ft). At its foot glistens the **Pasterze Glacier**. The best view of both mountain and glacier is from **Franz-Josef-Höhe**, a spur at the end of one branch of **Grossglockner High Alpine Road**, an extraordinary road, open from May to October only, that is one of the great Alpine highways, beginning at **Bruck** and ending at the mountaineering town of **Heiligenblut** in Carinthia.

Carinthia

A faster scenic route linking north and south is the **Tauern-autobahn** (**A10**), the motorway that travels from Salzburg via two large tunnels to the Carinthian capital, **Klagenfurt ❹**. This is a region of lakes and rivers, majestic mountains, gently rolling meadows and secluded valleys. Legend tells of a winged dragon that once struck terror into the hearts of local inhabitants. The Dragon Fountain statue, the emblem of Klagenfurt, is in the middle of the Neuer Platz, where most of the lovely houses date from the 17th century.

The town has a number of important historical buildings; **Zur Goldene Gans** (The Golden Goose), listed in records of 1489, was planned as an imperial residence; the **Landhaus** (Palace of the Estates, now the Carinthian State Assembly), dating from the 16th century, displays 665 coats of arms, while the **Palais Porcia** (now a hotel) and town hall also date from the 16th century. There are also

Decorative balcony of the Golden Roof, one of Innsbruck's finest medieval buildings.

no fewer than 22 castles within a radius of a few miles. At **Magdalensberg** north of the city is the site of the largest archaeological excavations in Austria: a Celtic-Roman town, with an open-air museum (May–mid-Oct daily).

Wörthersee (Lake Wörther), beside Klagenfurt, is a gorgeous Alpine lake popular for summer bathing, sailing, and beach volleyball and other sports. In spite of its depth of 85 metres (275ft) in places, the water temperature can reach 28°C (83°F). Numerous resorts adorn the lakeshore, including **Krumpendorf**, **Pörtschach**, **Velden** and **Maria Wörth**. A further attraction beside the lake is **Minimundus** (Apr–Oct daily), a miniature world on a grand scale, with more than 140 replicas of famous buildings, a miniature railway and a harbour with model ships. Carinthia has over 1,200 lakes, providing excellent beaches, sports facilities and amenities in idyllic surroundings to suit all tastes.

North of Klagenfurt is the pilgrimage town of **Gurk** ❺. Its 12th-century cathedral is the finest example of Romanesque architecture in Austria, built between 1140 and 1200, although the two huge towers were added much later, in the 17th century. Inside, the medieval interior is virtually unchanged, decorated with 13th-century frescoes and with a crypt with 100 columns sheltering the shrine of St Hemma, who founded the abbey of Gurk in 1043.

Villach ❻, a chic and historic town, lies at the centre of the Carinthian Lake District. The Romans built a bridge over the Drava here during the 1st century AD. The Renaissance physician Paracelsus spent his youth here and described the healing powers of the springs, and even today the warm waters offer relaxation and healing to guests from all over the world.

Styria

Further east is **Graz** ❼, the capital of the province of Steiermark or Styria, the second-largest Austrian city, with a population of 250,000, and the hometown of Arnold Schwarzenegger. This distinction aside, the Italian influence on the city's architecture is unmistakable, notably the **Rathaus** (Town

A street musician gets a young audience.

Hall), the late Gothic Franciscan Church (1520) and the magnificent Renaissance-style **Landhaus**, now the state assembly. On the south side of the Landhaus is the **Landeszeughaus** (Styrian Armoury; Apr–Oct Wed–Mon; Nov–Mar with guided tour by reservation), the largest intact 17th-century armoury in the world, with suits of armour, two-handed swords, shields, muskets, guns and rifles all on view. Other architectural jewels include the 15th-century Gothic **Dom** (Cathedral), the **Burg** or Castle complex built for Emperor Frederick III in the 1440s and now the Styrian state government offices, and Renaissance and Baroque mansions including the spectacular **Gemaltes Haus** (Painted House) in Herrengasse, with a facade covered in frescoes from the 1740s.

Modern Graz is also a lively cultural centre, with many museums, all of which have a common website (www. museum-joanneum.at). Standing out among them are the **Neue Galerie** (New Gallery; Tue–Sun) in the centre, with an impressive art collection

from the 19th century to the present day, and the city's outstanding modern landmark, the **Kunsthaus Graz** (Graz Art House; Tue–Sun), beside the River Mur. Appearing to some like a giant spaceship that has somehow landed in Old Graz, this was built for the city's spell as European Capital of Culture in 2003, and is an exceptional multipurpose space for contemporary art of all kinds. At night the outer skin forms a giant screen of changing colours, and though some residents still have reservations, others are proud that Graz has something so at variance with the typical Old World feel of Austrian towns.

One can return to the past by climbing the **Schlossberg**, the massive crag 470 metres (1,550ft) high in the middle of the city, which can be ascended by funicular, a glass lift or on foot. Once topped by a castle demolished by Napoleon, it is now a park, crowned by the **Uhrturm** (Clock Tower), which has become a city landmark and is visible for miles around. Amid lovely gardens on the west side of Graz is **Schloss**

Altausee, a beautiful setting for a popular Styrian ski resort.

Eggenberg (Eggenberg Castle; Apr–Dec Wed–Sun), built for the family of the same name, which has also been beautifully restored and houses three museums, the **Alte Galerie** (Old Gallery) with art from the Middle Ages to the Baroque era, an Archaeology Museum and the "Coin Cabinet", a huge historic coin collection. Just as interesting is the palace itself, designed in the 1620s for Hans Ulrich von Eggenberg, a polymath specially interested in astronomy, with an intricate layout reflecting Renaissance ideas of the cosmos.

Austrians regard Styria as the "Green Province" of Austria. Its scenery includes Alpine landscapes – perpetual ice and deeply cut ravines – as well as extensive forests which slowly give way to rolling ranges of hills.

Eisenerz ❽ lies in a wild, romantic basin at the mouth of the Krumpental and Trofeng valleys. The centre of an ore-mining region, it also has a well-developed infrastructure for tourists: campsites, climbing school, fitness circuit, footpaths and a lake for swimming. The **Erzberg** (1,465 metres/4,806ft) rises high above the valley floor and is still in use as an opencast iron ore mine.

Salzburg

Many towns in Austria are blessed with splendid churches, squares and ornamental fountains, but none benefit from such an atmosphere and setting as **Salzburg ❾**. The birthplace of Wolfgang Amadeus Mozart (1756–91), this is one of the most visited towns in Austria, especially during the annual **Mozart Week** festival at the end of January. The annual summer **Salzburg Festival** (www.salzburgerfestspiele.at) also bears Mozart's indelible stamp. His birthplace, the **Mozarts Geburtshaus** (daily), in the lovely old street of **Getreidegasse**, is now a museum, with many mementoes of his life, including his violin, and his later home, the **Mozart-Wohnhaus** in Makartplatz, can also be visited.

The **Mönchsberg** and the **Burgberg** – the two mountains within the city boundaries – still stand sentinel over the narrow alleys of the **Old**

Salzburg, seen from Mönchsberg.

Town, with their tall, narrow merchants' houses, arcaded courtyards, Baroque-domed churches, palaces and spacious squares of the prince-bishops' quarter. The entire Old Town is a World Heritage site, but among its most distinguished buildings are the Baroque **Salzburger Dom** (Cathedral), built by Italian architects in the 1620s, and the **Alte Residenz**, the former Bishops' Palace, which now houses the **Residenzgalerie** (Tue–Sun), a gallery with many works by 16th- and 17th-century masters. Clinging to the side of Mönchsberg, and dominating the Old Town, is the majestic **Hohensalzburg** fortress (daily). Archbishop Gebhard began its construction in 1077, and the castle was continuously expanded until the 17th century. It includes staterooms, a torture chamber and an observation tower.

Salzburg is a city of palaces, and there are even more outside the Old Town, such as **Hellbrunn** (daily), a Baroque villa built amid exquisite gardens around 1615 for one of the Prince-Archbishops of Salzburg purely for day trips, so that it does not

The Old Cathedral in Linz main square.

have any bedrooms, or, just north of the Old Town, **Mirabell** (daily), built for another prince-archbishop as a home for his mistress and their 15 children, with more fabulous gardens with delightful fountains. Apart from Mozart, Salzburg's other great claim to modern fame is as the location of the *Sound of Music*, which continues to draw crowds despite the film being over 40 years old. Among the favourite locations from the film are the Mirabell fountains, the Residenz, the Leopoldskron palace and the Nonnberg Abbey.

The Salzkammergut

East of Salzburg is another of Austria's regions of extraordinary natural beauty, with a series of glacial lakes ringed by mountains and charming villages of traditional architecture. More of a summer than a winter destination, the lake country is equally popular for hiking, cycling, swimming in the lakes or just relaxing in the famously invigorating air. The spa town of **Bad Ischl** is the area's most historic centre, since the Habsburg emperors came here for their health from the 1800s onwards, and its **Kaiservilla** (Imperial Villa) was the favourite home of Emperor Franz Joseph. This is the only imperial estate still owned by the Habsburg family, and is only partially open (Apr–Oct daily, Dec Sat–Sun, Jan–Mar Wed only).

The **Traunsee** is one of the busiest lakes, with a well-developed resort at **Gmunden**. Most beautiful of all, though, is the village of **Hallstatt** on the **Hallstättersee**, 12km (7 miles) south of Bad Ischl. The lake is surrounded on all sides by dramatic mountain scenery, and its clear, deep waters make it ideal for swimming and scuba-diving. With time visitors can also explore more remote lakes, such as the **Toplitzsee** east of Hallstatt, in a dramatic cleft accessible only on foot.

The Wachau

Apricot blossoms, the waves of the Danube, castles, fish and wine are all

aspects of this charming river region, the **Wachau**. The Danube flows through **Linz** ⑩, which is a modern industrial port city, but pretty in spite of that, especially around the **Hauptplatz** (**main square**). A white marble Trinity Column stands in the centre, and among the buildings surrounding the square are the **Ignatiuskirche** (Old Cathedral) with its twin spires. Entirely different is the **Lentos Kunstmuseum** (Lentos Art Museum; Tue–Sun), an adventurous glass-walled modern art museum opened in 2003. The **Brucknerhaus** is the location of the annual festival dedicated to Anton Bruckner (1824–96), who was born nearby.

The Danube meanders across the north of Austria, past woods and fields, and in the shadow of churches and abbeys. The spectacular Benedictine **Stift Melk** ⑪ (Melk Abbey; daily, Nov–Mar guided tours only), its side facade 340 metres (1,115ft) long, is poised in all its Baroque splendour on a promontory above the river. One of the summits of Austrian religious Baroque,

the abbey is vast, and still contains a monastic community.

Overlooking the Danube, in a gorgeous setting, **Dürnstein** ⑫ is probably the region's most visited village: in the 1190s, Richard the Lionheart, King of England, was taken prisoner by the Duke of Austria on his return from crusading and languished in the dungeons of Dürnstein Castle. According to legend, Blondel, his faithful minstrel, found him by singing Richard's favourite song beneath the castle walls. Soon afterwards, on payment of a huge ransom by the English, Richard was released.

A few kilometres downstream is **Krems an der Donau** ⑬, nestling among terraced vineyards on the bank of the Danube. Every visitor to the Wachau should taste the region's wines and, in particular, its apricot brandy. The valley is filled with apricot trees, whose springtime blossom turns the countryside into a spectacle of great beauty. The river continues past the **Vienna Woods**, where the Vienna High Road affords a magnificent view of the capital.

TIP

Cruises on the Danube are some of the most popular ways of seeing eastern Austria. A wide range of routes are available: from day or evening cruises just around the Danube Canal in Vienna, to longer cruises around the city, and longer all-day trips such as from Vienna to Durnstein and back, or through the Wachau as far as Melk, a particularly lovely route in spring. DDSG (www.ddsg-blue-danube.at) offers a full range of routes, including theme tours, from April to October.

Sunset reflected in the gleaming glass of the Brucknerhaus, where the Bruckner Festival is held each September.

EUROPE'S BEST FESTIVALS

Noisy, colourful, passionate affairs, festivals across Europe nowadays often show few signs of their religious roots and many are well worth seeking out.

From earthy fun to highbrow culture, Europe has a busy programme of recurring (usually annual) festivals. Several are internationally renowned and are worth going out of the way to see.

Broadly, festivals divide into two kinds, the traditional and the contemporary. Traditional festivities are often at least partly religious in form, although even these may have pagan roots and usually derive from the customs of country life, such as giving thanks for fertility, and the changing of the seasons. Many traditional festivals may be religious in origin – like San Fermín in Pamplona in Spain in July, with its famous bullrunning – but are now really occasions for raucous celebration. More recently created festivals celebrate some particular performing art: opera, classical music, rock, pop, jazz, theatre, dance, film – or a mixture of all of these and more. Usually entrance to the main events in these kind of festivals is by ticket only, but there are likely to be other things going on in the streets for free.

Both kinds of festival happen in the summer when the weather is warm enough for things to happen outdoors, and several take place in stunning locations, against the backdrop of some ancient building or in the grounds of a château. To get the best out of Europe's festivals you need to plan ahead. The most popular events tend to get booked up well in advance, and the same goes for accommodation. By the same token, festival time is not the best time for sightseeing. Monuments and museums may be closed, and the crowds can make a city difficult to negotiate your way around.

Effigies are burnt in an enormous conflagration at Las Fallas in Valencia, a hugely popular – and fairly dangerous – festival in mid-March that welcomes spring and commemorates San José, patron saint of carpenters.

The Oktoberfest in Munich has been running since 1819. Huge amounts of beer are drunk and vast quantities of meat and sausages consumed over a period of 16 days in autumn.

Mark Ronson at the Montreux Festival in Switzerland, an annual lakeside event that draws top-line performers and large crowds.

The Palio, held in the Campo in Siena, is one of the wildest and most exciting horse races in the world.

CARNIVAL EXTRAVAGANZAS

Many countries across Western Europe, especially those with a significant Catholic population – including Spain, Portugal, Italy, Germany and Belgium – celebrate Carnival. This takes place on the days leading up to Shrove Tuesday (Mardi Gras), the start of the Christian fast of Lent, which usually falls sometime between early February and early March. The most famous European Carnival is in Venice. Other major ones include Cologne in Germany, Binche in Belgium and Cádiz in Spain.

Carnival developed as a time for ordinary people to buck authority before knuckling under for the fast. It involves dressing up, street parades, music and generally licentious behaviour. The word "carnival" is often used for events at other times of year that have nothing to do with the traditional festival, except for sharing the same spirit of an anything-goes street party.

...ese are the Gilles of Binche, who celebrate Mardi Gras ...rove Tuesday) in their traditional masks and costumes.

The statue of the Virgin Mary is carried in procession in Fátima, Portugal, where she is believed to have appeared to three shepherd children in 1917.

Penitents (Nazarenos) in procession during Semana Santa (Holy Week) in Málaga, Spain.

Teatro Massimo in Palermo, Sicily.

Patriotic Naples street.

ITALY

Italian art and architecture draw the visitors, as do the stunning landscapes, pretty villages and the country's reputation for some of Europe's best food and wine.

Pizza and beer in Lipari.

The Italian boot, which dips its toes into the middle of the Mediterranean, has the Apennine hills running up it and is divided between the more businesslike north and the Mezzogiorno, the poorer, agricultural south. It is said that a man's assets in the north are his shares and property. In the south a man's only asset is his honour: thus even a poor man can be rich. The two halves are divided by Rome, which is on roughly the same latitude as New York.

Every town has its Duomo (Cathedral) and each region has its own architectural style, from Byzantine Ravenna and elegant, Renaissance Tuscany to the lavish Baroque of Lecce. Every town has at least one piazza or main square: in the south they are frequented by men smoking and playing cards; in the north, the men are still there, but so are women and tourists. In Italy, the past is always present: a housing development rises above a crumbling Roman wall; ultra-modern museums display pre-Roman artefacts; old people in mountain villages preserve centuries-old customs, while the young embrace the latest styles of Armani and Versace.

There are few idle pastimes more rewarding than observing Italians going about their lives. They are past masters at showing off, at preserving *la bella figura*, an untranslatable term that means "looking right". Both their public and social life is intricate and intriguing. Governments lurch from one crisis to another and scandals regularly invade public lives.

This is the country that inspires imagination in the dull, passion in the cold-hearted, rebellion in the conventional. Whether you spend your time under a beach umbrella on the Riviera, shopping in Milan or diligently examining churches and museums, you cannot be unchanged by the country. Whether you are struck by the beauty of a church facade rising from a perfectly proportioned piazza, the aroma of freshly carved *prosciutto*, or the sight of a stylish passer-by spied over the foam of your cappuccino, there is the same superb sensation: nowhere else on earth does just living seem so extraordinary.

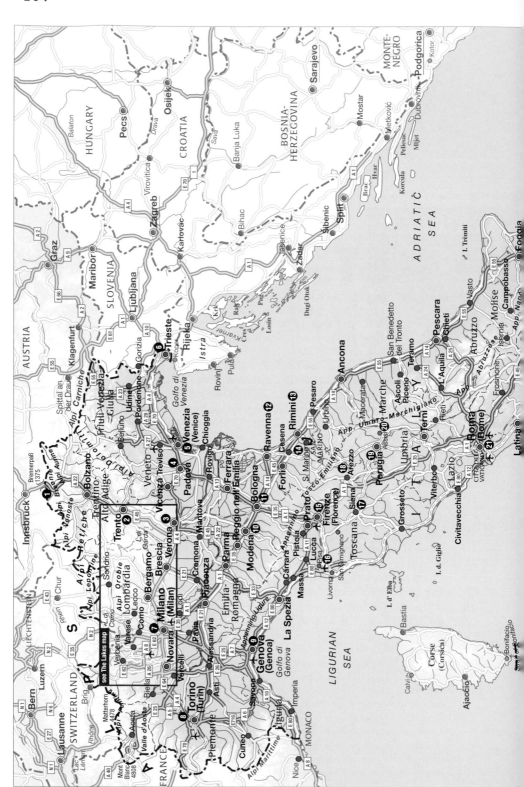

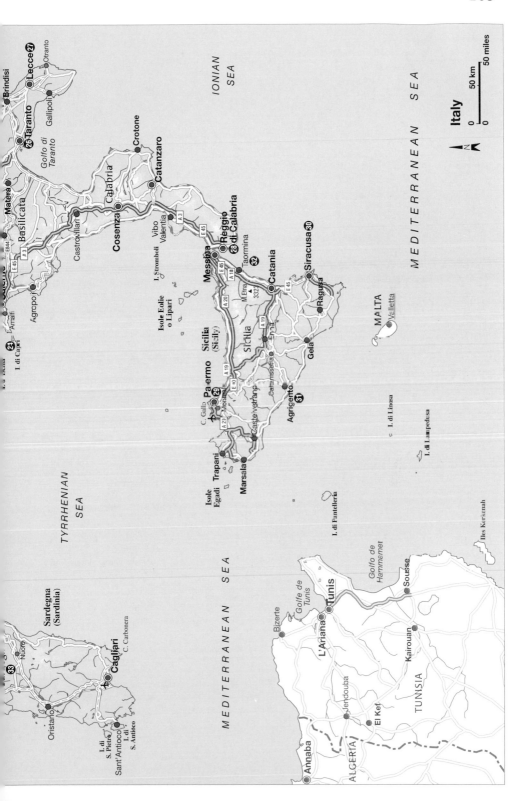

Italy

0   50 km
0   50 miles

MEDITERRANEAN SEA

IONIAN SEA

TYRRHENIAN SEA

Brindisi
Lecce 27
Otranto
Taranto 26
Gallipoli
Golfo di Taranto
Matera
Basilicata
Crotone
Calabria
Catanzaro
Castrovillari
Cosenza
Agropoli
Amalfi
I. di Capri 21
Vibo Valentia
I. Stromboli
A 3
Reggio di Calabria 29
Messina
E 45
A 18
Taormina 32
Isole Eolie o Lipari
Catania
M. Etna 3323
Sicilia (Sicily)
A 20
A 19
Siracusa 30
Ragusa
Enna
A 19
Gela
Palermo 20
C. Gallo
Monreale
E 90
A 29
Castelvetrano
Agrigento 31
Caltanissetta
Trapani
Isole Egadi
Marsala
MALTA
Valletta
I. di Linosa
I. di Pantelleria
I. di Lampedusa
Iles Kerkenah

Golfe de Tunis
Golfo de Hammamet
Bizerte
L'Ariana
Tunis
Sousse
Kairouan
Jendouba
El Kef
TUNISIA
Annaba
ALGERIA

MEDITERRANEAN SEA

Sardegna (Sardinia)
Nuoro
Oristano
Cagliari 33
C. Carbonera
I. di S. Pietro
Sant'Antioco
I. di S. Antioco

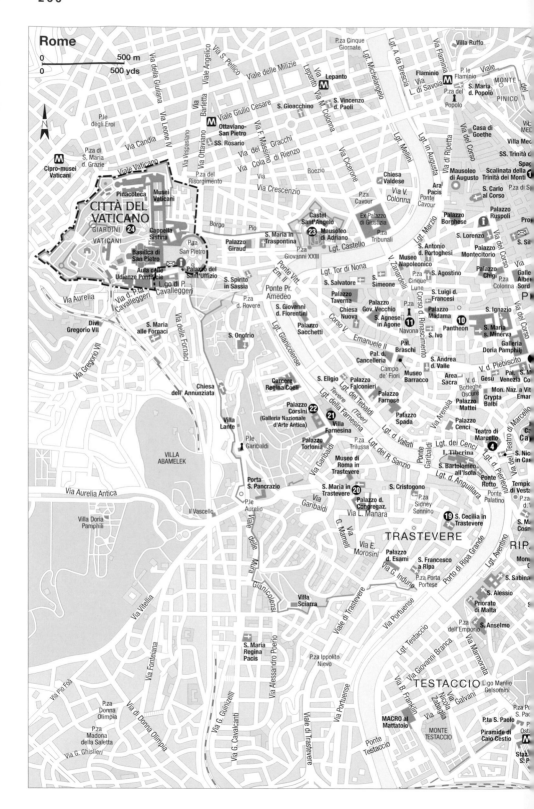

Rome

0   500 m
0   500 yds

CITTÀ DEL VATICANO

GIARDINI VATICANI

TRASTEVERE

TESTACCIO

The Trevi Fountain.

ROME

The 21st century is not invisible in Rome, but this glorious city mostly invites you to follow in the footsteps of emperors and saints, discovering the monuments and churches that mark Rome as the one-time capital of Christendom and the ancient world.

Rome, the "Eternal City", has so many different aspects – the ancient city, the papal capital, fashionable modern Rome – intertwined with each other, that visitors looking for one continually come up against the others. However, to begin at the beginning, a good introduction to Rome is to go first to the **Palatino ❶** (Palatine Hill; daily; combined ticket with the Forum and Colosseum). It was here, the story goes, that Romulus and Remus were brought up by a wolf in a cave, before Romulus went on to found Rome in 753 BC. Archaeologists have discovered traces of Iron Age huts that actually date back even earlier, to the 10th century BC.

Much later, the Palatine with its view of the city below became the preferred residence of Rome's emperors. Byron's description of the romantic pastoral ruins still rings true: "*Cypress and ivy, weed and wallflower grown/ Matted and mass'd together, hillocks heap'd/ On what were chambers, arch crush'd, column strown/ In fragments, choked up vaults, and frescos steep'd/ In subterranean damps...*" You can wander around the romantic ruins of imperial dwellings, see the frescoes in the Domus Augustana (**House of Augustus**) and view relics from the Palatine villas in the Museo Palatino (**Palatine Museum**; daily). Excavations

are ongoing at the Palatine, which sadly means that several of its buildings are periodically closed.

Heart of ancient Rome

Below the Palatine lies the **Foro Romano**, the **Roman Forum ❷** (daily), ancient Rome's commercial and political centre. In the fading light, and with some imagination, the columns and ghostly white blocks of weather-beaten marble take on flesh and life. And if there are pieces missing, the blame should be placed

Main Attractions

Foro Romano
Musei Capitolini
Colosseum
Pantheon
Piazza Navona
Fontana di Trevi
Galleria Borghese
Trastevere
Vatican City

The Temple of Saturn.

TIP

An excellent information source is the Rome Call Centre, www.060608.it, tel: 060608, with English-speaking operators. You can call daily from 9am–9pm to reserve tickets for museums, shows and events, book hotels or find out information on local transport. Tickets can be paid for by credit card and picked up at the venue.

on later Romans, grand or obscure, who for over 1,000 years used it as a stone quarry. The star attraction is the **Arco di Settimio Severo** (Arch of Septimius Severus), built in 203 after the emperor had conquered the Parthians and made Mesopotamia a new province of Rome.

To the west of the main Forum are the **Fori Imperiali** (Imperial Fora, added by five successive emperors. The **Museo dei Fori Imperiali** (Museum of the Imperial Fora; Tue–Sun) occupies the best preserved of the five, **Trajan's Forum and Markets** (Mercati di Traiano), dominated by the soaring **Trajan's Column**. The market buildings are astonishing, and just as astonishingly well preserved is an ancient multi-storey shopping mall that now forms a superb backdrop to the museum's illuminating displays on every side of ancient Rome.

The Capitoline and Piazza Venezia

Fragments of a colossal statue of Emperor Constantine in the Capitoline Museums.

Overlooking the Forum on its western side, the **Capitolino** ❸ (Capitoline Hill) was also a centre of power in the ancient city, but its most prominent feature today is the magnificent Piazza del Campidoglio, created in the 1530s by Michelangelo. The two palazzi either side of it – Palazzo Nuovo and Palazzo dei Conservatori – house the **Musei Capitolini** (Capitoline Museums; Tue–Sun). The collection comprises priceless treasures from ancient Rome, along with artworks by Italian 16th- and 17th-century masters such as Veronese, Titian, Caravaggio and Tintoretto. The equestrian state of Marcus Aurelius on the piazza is a replica; the original is given pride of place in the museum's new glass-roofed hall.

On the western side of the hill, the ruined **Teatro di Marcello** (Theatre of Marcellus) ❹, looking almost like a small Colosseum, was built as a classical theatre in the reign of Augustus.

Ancient and modern Rome and all the main streets of the modern city meet at **Piazza Venezia** ❺, with on one side the **Palazzo Venezia**. The central balcony of this Renaissance palace, built in 1455 for a Venetian Cardinal, is famous as the place from

HOW ROME LOOKED IN HADRIAN'S DAY

Rome was famously founded on seven hills – the Palatine, Capitoline, Aventine, Caelian, Quirinal, Viminal and Esquiline – although the oldest settlement was on the Palatine, and the early citadel was on the Capitoline. The dip between these two hills was used for markets, public business and social contacts, and so grew into the first Forum. As well as ever larger markets, this would contain the Curia or Senate House, the Rostra where public announcements were made – and from where Mark Antony supposedly asked fellow Romans to lend him their ears – and many temples and other public buildings.

Wealthy Romans lived with their slaves in large houses of several patios, called a *domus*, on the central hills, but the Roman poor occupied blocks of small apartments and shops called *insulae*. On the Esquiline there was a notorious criminal slum called the *Suburra* (a status some streets around Stazione Termini still maintain). Public baths were an important part of Roman life, open to rich and poor. Rome's famous aqueducts were built up over centuries to supply them and the city in general with water, but providing all kinds of services for a city the size of Rome – under Hadrian it had perhaps a million people – was not something its rulers attempted. All around the ancient city were vast heaps of fetid refuse, where its waste was simply dumped each night.

where Mussolini addressed adoring crowds in the 1930s. Today it houses a **museum** (Tue–Sun), with a varied collection that includes medieval and early Renaissance paintings, Bernini sculptures, tapestries and armour. However, visually the square is unavoidably dominated by the bombastically vast white wedding cake of the **Vittoriano**, a giant "Roman-style" monument erected in the 1880s to the first King of a united Italy, Vittorio Emanuele II. Visible from all over the city, it has been the butt of jokes ever since it was built.

The Colosseum and Baths of Caracalla

South of the Palatine are some of the most famous relics of ancient Rome. At the foot of the hill one can still see the line of the track of the **Circo Massimo** (Circus Maximus), where chariot races were held. Nearby is the most awesome monument to Roman ambition (and bloodlust), the **Colosseum** ❻ (Colosseo; daily), built in AD 72–80, and which in its heyday had room for up to 55,000

spectators to watch gladiatorial combats and other bloody entertainments. Every kind of animal from across the empire was brought to be fought and killed here, along with criminals, Christians and other unfortunates. To create space to build it, the Emperor Vespasian drained the lake of the **Domus Aurea** ❼ or Golden House, a palace built for the tyrannical Emperor Nero after the great fire of Rome in AD 64, which Nero was accused of having started in order to clear the way for his own megalomaniac plans. The Domus Aurea was near-legendary as the most extravagant of all Roman palaces, but after Nero's fall in 68 most of it was rapidly destroyed. It was forgotten until the 15th century, when a young man fell down a hole and discovered it, and artists such as Raphael and Michelangelo climbed down too, to be stunned by its elegant frescoes. Modern conservation has been complex, and the house is often closed, but it's worth checking whether it's currently open.

From the Colosseum a broad street leads to the **Piazza di San Giovanni**

Piazza Venezia is dominated by Palazzo di Venezia, Rome's first Renaissance palace, built in 1455.

The Colosseum is even more impressive at night.

The Trevi Fountain.

The Pantheon.

in Laterano **8**, overlooked by the magnificent **Basilica di San Giovanni in Laterano**. In few other places is Rome's extraordinary accumulation of history so palpable: this is actually the oldest Christian basilica in Rome, founded by Constantine in 313, but rebuilt many times. Borromini created the marble-clad Baroque interior in the 1640s, while the grand facade dates from the 1730s. Across the street, the pope's private chapel in the former Lateran Palace is reached via the **Scala Santa**, a staircase said to be made of steps that were trodden by Jesus before his trial by Pontius Pilate, and so are ascended by pilgrims on their knees.

From the piazza, Via Amba Aradam leads southwest towards the **Terme di Caracalla 9** (Baths of Caracalla; Tue–Sun and Mon am). Many baths had been built by previous emperors, but Antoninus Caracalla was determined to relegate them all to history when construction began in AD 212 on the largest baths Rome had ever seen. Holding up to 1,500 bathers at a time, the baths functioned until the Goths invaded two centuries later and destroyed the aqueducts that supplied them with water.

The poet Shelley composed his *Prometheus Unbound* (1820) on a visit to the ruins of the baths, and their cultural associations are evoked each summer when operas and ballet are staged here.

Southwest of the baths, the **Testaccio** district was once Rome's dockside. Vast amounts of oil and wine were landed here in clay pots or *amphorae*, which were then discarded in a giant heap that became the base of **Monte Testaccio**. Modern Testaccio was a working-class quarter around Rome's main slaughterhouse (Mattatoio), but recently has become trendy for restaurants and nightlife, and **MACRO Testaccio** (Tue–Sun), in the old slaughterhouse, is the city's leading contemporary art centre. On the district's eastern side is the tranquil **Protestant Cemetery**, where both Keats and Shelley are buried.

The heart of papal Rome

After the empire's fall, the core of Rome shifted northwest of the Capitoline to the bend in the River Tiber that juts west towards the Vatican, and this, the **Centro Storico** or historic centre, has remained its heart. This is Rome's most charming district, and the best for exploring in no particular direction. Away from the broad **Corso Vittorio Emanuele II**, created in the 1880s to speed up traffic, the Centro is a maze of intertwining alleys and squares, with streets like Via dei Carbonari, full of antique shops, or Via del Governo Vecchio off Piazza Navona, with tiny individual shops and cupboard-sized wine bars. **Campo de' Fiori** is one of Rome's most popular squares, with an exuberant food market by day and buzzing restaurants and cafés at night. Among these atmospheric streets there is also plenty of magnificent architecture, such as the Renaissance **Palazzo Farnese** south of the Campo.

In the southwest corner of the Centro is the former Jewish **Ghetto**. Jews had lived in Rome since ancient times, but were confined to this area by papal order from 1555 to 1870. Much of the community survived persecution in World War II, and the district retains some of its Jewish character. Jews have a place of honour in Roman traditional cookery, and the Ghetto is the place to sample Roman-Jewish specialities such as fried artichokes.

There are also, naturally, relics of ancient Rome. The **Pantheon** ⑩ (daily) was first built as a temple in 27 BC, rebuilt by Hadrian in the 2nd century, and converted into a church in the year 609. The best preserved of all Rome's ancient buildings, astonishingly unchanged, its most extraordinary feature is its massive dome, which has a single hole at the centre of the coffered ceiling, providing the only light. The gracious 16-columned portico, too, has been a model for all Neoclassical architecture. In 1520 the artist Raphael, on his own wishes, was buried inside the Pantheon, and he has been followed by many other distinguished figures.

The great hub of the Centro Storico is the **Piazza Navona** ⑪, one of Rome's most popular squares with locals and tourists, with pavement restaurants, cafés and *gelaterie* that are great for people-watching and soaking up the atmosphere. The Piazza's oval shape reflects the fact that it follows the shape of an ancient stadium for chariot races, but it was given its definitive appearance in the mid-17th century, when Bernini added the superb **Fontana dei Quattro Fiumi** (Fountain of the Four Rivers) to the two earlier fountains by Giacomo della Porta, the **Fontana del Moro** (of the Moor) at the south end and **Fontana del Nettuno** (Neptune) at the north. On the west side is the equally magnificent church of **Sant'Agnese in Agone**, by Bernini's great rival Borromini.

Tridente and Villa Borghese

Modern Rome's central thoroughfare of Via del Corso, from Piazza del Popolo to Piazza Venezia, forms the boundary of the Centro Storico. Just to the east, the extravagant Baroque **Fontana di Trevi** ⑫ (Trevi Fountain) is a popular rendezvous, where tourists come to have their picture taken and toss coins into the water, which, so the superstition goes, ensures their return to the Eternal City. Designed by Nicola Salvi and completed in 1762, the central figure is Neptune, flanked by two Tritons holding sea creatures.

To the north is the area known as the Tridente, because of the three streets that run out like prongs of a fork from Piazza del Popolo; Via del Babuino, Via del Corso and Via Ripetta. They and the little streets between them are Rome's fashionable shopping area par excellence, and Via Condotti, especially, is lined with the outlets of designer labels. The ancients are still present, though, for by the river near Via Ripetta is the Ara Pacis (Tue–Sun), an intact 1st-century altar temple celebrating

The only light in the Pantheon comes from a large hole in the centre of the dome (the oculus), which means the building has been open to the elements for 2,000 years.

Boating on the lake of the Villa Borghese.

The Castel Sant'Angelo, the setting for the last act of Puccini's Tosca.

the achievements of Augustus that is now displayed in a beautiful modern museum space, and the less well-maintained Mausoleo di Augusto, the emperor's tomb.

On the east side of the Tridente is another of Rome's perennially popular meeting places, the **Spanish Steps** ⑬ leading up from the **Piazza di Spagna** to the twin-towered church of **Trinità dei Monte**. The steps take their name from the Spanish embassy, which once stood here. Everyone gathers here to watch the world go by, as they have done for centuries. The **Keats-Shelley House** (Mon–Sat) is the place where the poet John Keats died in 1827; Henry James stayed at the Hotel Inghilterra; Goethe lived nearby at No. 18 Via del Corso, where there is a museum devoted to his travels in Italy.

Behind Trinità dei Monti is the **Villa Borghese**, so called because it was once the estate of the aristocratic Borghese family, but is now Rome's favourite park. Its gardens provide a wonderful respite from the heat and hassle of the city; here you'll find an artificial lake, fountains and follies, a zoo and museums and galleries. The cultural highlight is the **Galleria Borghese** ⑭ (Tue–Sun; reservations obligatory; www.galleriaborghese.it) within the Baroque Villa Borghese, built in 1613–15 for the extravagant Cardinal Scipione Borghese. His exquisite art collection features works by Raphael, Titian, Caravaggio and Bernini, supplemented by later works including Canova's famous marble sculpture of Napoleon's sister, Pauline, the wife of a later Borghese prince, as a topless, reclining Venus.

The Quirinale

Sant' Andrea al Quirinale ⑮, on Via del Quirinale, is often considered the finest architectural work by the Baroque genius Bernini. Its interior decoration is supreme justification for the high esteem in which he is held: every inch is covered with gilt and marble, and carved cherubs ascend the walls as if in a cloud of smoke.

Bernini, along with his rival Borromini and Carlo Maderno, all

played a part in the design of the **Palazzo Barberini** in the 1620s, and Bernini's sculpture also features inside in the **Galleria Nazionale d'Arte Antica** 🅰 (National Gallery of Historic Art; Tue–Sun), a priceless collection of medieval, Renaissance and Baroque art.

Northeast of the Palazzo, the church of **Santa Maria della Vittoria** 🅱 is home to one of Bernini's supreme creations, the *Ecstasy of St Theresa*. This depiction of the 17th-century Spanish mystic evokes for many visitors a sense of sensual ecstasy rather than the physical pain that might seem more appropriate.

The tomb of Bernini lies in **Santa Maria Maggiore** 🅲 to the south. The basis of this huge basilica was built in the 5th century; the marble floor and belltower are medieval; the interior with its gilded ceiling is unmistakably a product of the Renaissance; while the twin domes and imposing facades are pure Baroque. Inside the church there are stunning mosaics from the 5th century in the nave and on the triumphal arch, and medieval mosaics in the loggia and apse.

A few streets to the east is one of the great hubs of modern Rome, the **Stazione Termini**, the huge main train station and axis of the Metro lines. The Esquilino area around the station is one of Rome's busiest, with a great many hotels.

Across the Tiber

Trastevere, from *trans Tiberim* ("over the Tiber"), was a working-class, bohemian neighbourhood, which has developed into a trendy and colourful tourist quarter, with atmospheric restaurants and bars. It is also popular for the Porta Portese flea market that bursts into life every Sunday morning. There are also two churches of note: **Santa Cecilia in Trastevere** 🅳 is dedicated to the patron saint of music, who was martyred here in AD 230, and has a fresco of *The Last Judgement* by Pietro Cavallini (*c.*1290).

Santa Maria in Trastevere 🅴 is one of the oldest churches in Rome, and its foundation is credited to Pope Callixtus I in the 3rd century. Inside are spectacular 13th century mosaics.

The Spanish Steps are a popular meeting place.

Harry's Bar on Via Veneto.

BAROQUE SPLENDOUR IN ROME

The Baroque movement was born in Rome, spurred by a desire, rooted in the Counter-Reformation reaction against Protestantism, to glorify the Catholic Church and present its beliefs in the most visceral and dramatic way possible. The popes decided that their capital had to be a city of unchallengeable grandeur, "for the greater glory of God and the Church".

One of the first great architects of Roman Baroque was Carlo Maderno (1556–1629), who in 1612 added its august facade to St Peter's, left unfinished by Michelangelo. His work was surpassed by that of Gian Lorenzo Bernini (1598–1680), who was equally brilliant as an architect and a sculptor. Curving forms and stunning light effects are a Bernini trademark, as in Sant'Andrea al Quirinale, but his most famous constructions are the great colonnade embracing St Peter's Square, and the giant *Baldacchino* or canopy above the main altar inside. His sculptures such as Apollo and Daphne in the Galleria Borghese, or the fountains of Piazza Navona, have an unrivalled sensuous vitality.

Bernini's rival as an architect was Francesco Borromini (1599–1667), whose eccentric designs were far more adventurous. Many hinge on a complex interplay of concave and convex surfaces, as in the undulating facades of San Carlo alle Quattro Fontane, Sant'Ivo, and Sant'Agnese in Piazza Navona (1652–5).

Detail of the School of Athens frescoes by Raphael in the Vatican Museums.

A little way north is the Renaissance **Villa Farnesina** ㉑ (Mon–Sat am), built around 1510 for Agostino Chigi, "the pope's banker", who commissioned Raphael and his pupils to decorate the interior with frescoes, many of which survive.

Across the road, the late Baroque **Palazzo Corsini** houses another part of the **Galleria Nazionale d'Arte Antica** ㉒ (Tue–Sun), with works by Rubens, Van Dyck, Caravaggio, Tintoretto, Poussin and Guido Reni.

Castel Sant'Angelo and the Vatican

Dominating the Tiber to the north are the mighty brick walls of **Castel Sant'Angelo** ㉓ (Tue–Sun), linked to the city by the ancient Ponte Sant'Angelo. The castle started life as a mausoleum for Emperor Hadrian in AD 139, and was later adapted as a fortress, a prison and a hideout for popes (a secret passageway links it to the Vatican). Over 50 rooms chart its remarkably chequered history, from dark prison cells to lavish Renaissance papal apartments. If time is short, seek

An overview of St Peter's Square.

out the trompe-l'œil frescoes by Perin del Vaga and Tibaldi in the 16th-century papal apartments that play little tricks with the eye, and admire the views from the terrace, scene of the last act of Puccini's *Tosca*.

From Castel Sant' Angelo, Via della Conciliazione leads to the **Città del Vaticano** ㉔ (Vatican City). **Piazza San Pietro** (St Peter's Square) is packed when the pope appears on the balcony to address and bless the vast crowds. When the square was completed by Bernini in 1656, the effect he intended for his grand colonnades, which sweep into an embrace of the **Basilica of St Peter** was quite different from what is experienced today. His idea was to surprise the pilgrim visitor with a sudden view of the basilica, but when Via della Conciliazione was built in the 1930s it provided a new, monumental approach to St Peter's.

Around Rome

Not far from the city are more attractions that complete any visit to Rome. Some 31km (19 miles) east, the hill town of Tivoli has been an escape for Romans for over 2,000 years. The Villa Adriana (Hadrian's Villa; daily), built for Emperor Hadrian around AD 117, is mostly a ruin, but its pools and gardens still give a vivid impression of a Roman luxury retreat. Nearby, the Villa d'Este (Tue–Sun) and its famous gardens have a similar feel but are much later (and so more intact), having been created for the d'Este family in the 1550s. About the same distance to the southwest of Rome is the ancient port of Ostia Antica with streets, temples, mosaics and baths among the site's impressive remains.

Southeast of Rome, the small towns in the Alban Hills known as the **Castelli Romani** ("Roman Castles") such as **Frascati**, **Grottaferrata** or the papal summer residence of **Castel Gandolfo** all have a distinctive charm, and are known for their wines and food.

The Vatican

The Vatican is an anomaly, a sovereign city within a city. A place of pilgrimage for devout Catholics, it is on every visitor's itinerary.

Rome and the Vatican have lived for more than one and a half millennia in symbiosis, not always perfect, not always happy, but always mutually rewarding. Rome is where the Church gained its martyrs, where Emperor Constantine made Christianity the predominant religion by the time of his death in AD 337. In return, the Vatican eventually gave Rome another empire, a spiritual and a political one, at times almost as powerful as the worldly one lost to the barbarians.

Vatican is the name given to a hill on the right bank of the Tiber. There Emperor Nero completed the circus that Gaius (Caligula) had built and adorned with an obelisk brought from Egypt (the one which now rises in the middle of St Peter's Square). Early Christians were tortured here, and Emperor Constantine gave the land to the church where, over the grave of St Peter, who had been

Nuns posing in St Peter's Square.

martyred in Nero's persecutions of AD 64, a place of worship was built that developed into the vast complex seen today. St Peter's Basilica is the largest in Christendom, and more than one billion Catholics are governed from this walled-in hill known as the Vatican City.

There is plenty to see and do, beginning perhaps with the purchase of some Vatican stamps and the posting of a card from the Vatican post office, or a climb up the 244 stairs to the top of St Peter's dome. As you enter St Peter's, on the right, Michelangelo's *Pietà* enthrals today as much as it did in 1499 when the artist finished it at the age of 25. Since being vandalised in 1972, the marble sculpture has been enclosed by glass. Further up the nave is the bronze statue of St Peter, its toe worn away by the countless kisses of pious pilgrims. A highly ornate Baroque canopy by Bernini dominates the nave above the Papal Altar.

The **Vatican Museums** (Mon–Sat, last Sun of the month 9am–1.45pm) comprise eight museums, five galleries and the Borgia Apartments, with tours culminating in the star attractions: the Stanze di Raffaello (Raphael Rooms) and Michelangelo's **Cappella Sistina** (Sistine Chapel). The walls of this famous chapel are covered in frescoes by Botticelli (*Temptations of Christ*, with the devil disguised in a monk's habit, and *Punishment of the Rebels*), Ghirlandaio (*Calling of St Peter and St Andrew*) and Perugino (*The Delivery of the Keys*); the celebrated ceiling was painted by Michelangelo between 1508 and 1512, and he added the awe-inspiring Last Judgement above the altar in 1535–41.

Michelangelo worked alone on the ceiling from a specially designed scaffold, and the controversial restoration work of the 1980s has allowed a new generation of visitors to appreciate the skill and passion that went into the work. The only subject matter that is not from the Old Testament is the classical Sibyls, and they only get a nose in because of the highly suspect story that they prophesied the birth of Christ.

"All the world hastened to behold this marvel and was overwhelmed, speechless with astonishment," the art historian Vasari wrote of Michelangelo's handiwork. The validity of his judgement may help sustain you as the queue to enter the chapel makes its way slowly forward.

The extraodinary facade of the Duomo in Florence.

FLORENCE

One of the world's great artistic centres, packed
with aesthetic masterpieces, this Tuscan city
is the essential destination for students of
Renaissance art and architecture.

Florence and the Renaissance are almost synonymous. No city in Italy has produced such an avalanche of genius: Leonardo da Vinci, Michelangelo, Dante, Brunelleschi, Donatello, Machiavelli, Botticelli, Raphael, Fra Angelico, Fra Filippo Lippi, Ghirlandaio, Giotto, Ghiberti, Uccello. No city has so reshaped modern thought and art, nor gathered within its walls such a treasure of local art and architecture. Florentines ushered in the Renaissance and took the arts to heights not even the Greeks had attained.

Magnificent cupola

The beautiful black and white **Duomo ❶** (Cathedral; daily) lies at the heart of Florence. Its dome (Mon–Sat), a free-hanging cupola designed by Filippo Brunelleschi, has astonished architects and builders for centuries. Florentines refer to it as *Il Cupolone*, the dome of domes; it was added in 1420–36 after the rest of the cathedral had been under construction, with many interruptions, for over a century. In its radical departure from earlier styles, the dome is one of the foundation stones of Renaissance architecture, and has been immensely influential. A seemingly endless stairway leads to the lantern gallery where Brunelleschi's

building secret is revealed: there are two mutually supporting domes, one shell inside the other. Giotto's freestanding **Campanile** (Belltower) entails another long climb (414 steps), but rewards you with intimate views of the cathedral dome and roofline. Close by, the octagonal Romanesque **Battistero ❷** (Baptistery; daily) is one of the oldest buildings in Florence, constructed between 1060 and 1128, and is celebrated for its bronze doors by Ghiberti, added in 1452, and wonderful ceiling mosaics.

Main Attractions
Duomo
Battistero
Piazza della Signoria
Uffizi
Bargello
Ponte Vecchio
Accademia

A copy of Michelangelo's David in the Piazza della Signoria.

To see other cathedral treasures, visit the **Museo dell'Opera del Duomo ❸** (Mon–Sun) on the east side of Piazza del Duomo. This cathedral museum is full of outstanding sculptures, from Donatello's haggard *Mary Magdalene*, carved in wood in the 1460s, to Michelangelo's unfinished *Pietà*, begun around 1545.

Florentine sights

Michelangelo Buonarroti (1475–1564) was the man who perhaps best symbolised both the greatness and the parochialism of this city. He was, like many Florentines of his time, thrifty and endowed with a dose of insolence. A firm republican, Michelangelo mourned the public burning in 1498 of the Florentine Dominican friar Girolamo Savonarola, who ruled Florence from 1494 to 1497. Savonarola denounced the sins of the pope and corruption in the Church and, during the Lent Carnival of 1497, organised the "Bonfire of the Vanities", a massive conflagration of books and works of art deemed indecent or frivolous.

On the orders of the pope, he was arrested, tortured, hanged and burnt. On the **Piazza della Signoria ❹** a plaque on the spot pays tribute to this rabble-rousing orator.

After midnight, it is said, when the city is asleep, a ghostly spectacle appears in this piazza. "The Great White Man", Ammanati's imposing Neptune, climbs from his fountain, walks across the piazza and talks to his friends. Florentines believe he is really the river god Arno, famous for spurning the love of women.

Florentines have believed for centuries that spirits are imprisoned in their marble statues. They believe that the spirits begin to move and talk as soon as the **Uffizi ❺** (Tue–Sun), one of the world's greatest art galleries with a stunning collection of Rennaissance works, closes down at night. The galleries were built in the 1560s as offices (*uffizi*) attached to the **Palazzo Vecchio** or town hall. The collection is arranged chronologically, so you can trace the development of Florentine art from 13th-century formal Gothic

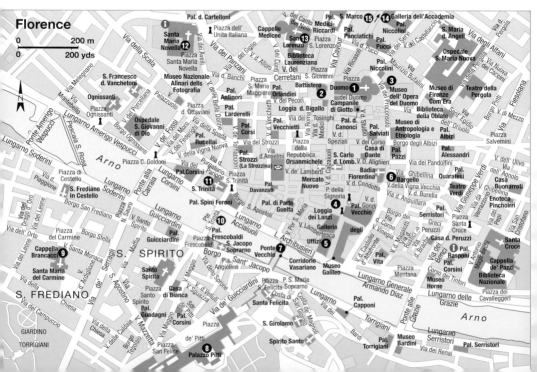

to the Mannerist period of the 16th century. The Palazzo Vecchio (daily) itself, built in the early 14th century, is still Florence's town hall today, its crenellated roof and clock tower an unchanging symbol of the city. Its grandest chamber, the **Salone dei Cinquecento** (Hall of the 500), was the meeting room of the 500-member Grand Council that governed the Florentine Republic, and was transformed in 1560s for the first Medici Grand Duke, Cosimo, with giant frescoes glorifying Florentine military victories. In the process, fragments of older unfinished frescoes by Leonardo and Michelangelo were swept away. Duke Cosimo also commissioned the **Vasari Corridor**, a secret passage linking the Palazzo Vecchio with the Uffizi and the duke's residence in the Palazzo Pitti, allowing him to move between the various palaces without being seen by his subjects below.

From here it is a short step to the **Bargello** ❻ (Tue–Sat and some Sun and Mon), an outstanding sculpture museum where you can see works by Donatello, Michelangelo, Cellini and Giambologna.

From the Uffizi you can walk across the **Ponte Vecchio** ❼, the historic bridge across the River Arno, which dates in its present form from 1345. Some of Italy's finest silver jewellery is made and sold in kiosks lining the bridge and there is always a throng jostling to see it. In boutiques in the Old City, a tradition of leather goods and textiles still flourishes.

Home of the Medicis

On the other side of the bridge is the enormous and forbidding-looking **Palazzo Pitti** ❽, begun for a Florentine banker, Luca Pitti, in the 1460s and residence of the Medici Grand Dukes of Tuscany and their successors from the middle of the 16th century to the abolition of the Duchy in 1860. It now houses a number of museums containing art treasures. If you visit only one, make it the **Galleria Palatina** (Palatine Gallery; Tue–Sun), where you can admire masterpieces by Raphael, Titian and Rubens. Behind the palace,

TIP

Queues for the Uffizi and the Pitti can be dauntingly long, so it's best to reserve tickets in advance. Do so through Firenze Musei, www.firenzemusei.it, or www.uffizi.com. You can also book tickets in person for both at the information office in Palazzo Pitti.

ROME'S FIRST FAMILY - THE MEDICI

Florence's wealth began its impressive growth in the 13th century through trading in fine wool, not just with the rest of Italy but also with France and Spain. On the back of trade Florentine merchants also began to engage in banking, and by the 1250s the gold coins of Florence, *florins*, were already being used as a reliable currency across Europe. Like many Italian towns Florence was an oligarchical republic, governed by a small group of merchant families who often bickered viciously with each other. Around the beginning of the 15th century, one family, the Medici, began to stand out from all others. Through astute marriages and business ventures they became the centre of a web of mutual obligation, and the Medici Bank, founded in 1397, was the most advanced financial institution in Europe, lending to several popes. Cosimo "the Elder" (1389–1464) was the first Medici to dominate Florence. The dynasty's grandeur reached its peak under his grandson Lorenzo "the Magnificent" (1449–92), one of the great patrons of the Renaissance, who commissioned works by Leonardo, Botticelli and Michelangelo.

The Medici were also great intriguers in Italy's complicated politics, but at times this could get beyond them, as in 1494, when Piero de Medici allied himself with Charles VIII, who had just invaded Italy, and provoked the anti-Medici revolt led by the radical priest Savonarola. This forced the family to flee Florence, though they returned in 1512, and in 1569 their power formally became hereditary when another Cosimo was made Grand Duke of Tuscany.

The Medicis produced four popes: Leo X (1513–21), Clement VII (1523–34), Pius IV (1559–65) and Leo XI (1605, pope only for four weeks). In 1533 Clement VII's niece Catherine de Medici married the future King Henri II of France, becoming notorious for her intrigues in the tumult of the French Wars of Religion and rivalling Elizabeth I of England as the most powerful woman in Europe. A younger cousin, Marie de Medici, married Henri IV of France in 1600 and was the mother of Louis XIII, acting as regent when he was still a child after Henri was assassinated. However, in Tuscany the Medici male line came to an end with the death of Duke Gian Gastone who died without an heir in 1737, when the Grand Duchy passed to the Austrian Lorraine family.

the **Giardino di Boboli** (Boboli Gardens; daily), is one of the finest Renaissance gardens, and the model for many later Italian gardens. On the same side of the Arno the church of Santa Maria del Carmine **houses the Brancacci Chapel** ❾ (Mon, Wed–Sun) that contains Masaccio's restored fresco cycle of *The Life of St Peter* and *The Expulsion from Paradise*, one of the great works of the early Renaissance.

Back by the River Arno, the **Ponte Santa Trinità** ❿ had a miraculous rebirth after retreating Nazis blew the bridge up in 1944. After World War II the city launched a frenetic search for the missing head of "Spring", a vital member of the Four Seasons quartet guarding each end of the bridge. It was found at the bottom of the River Arno and, in a noisy procession, taken back to the bridge.

The bridge is named after the nearby church of **Santa Trinità** ⓫, famous for its frescoes by Ghirlandaio, depicting the life of St Francis against a recognisably Florentine background. The church

of **Santa Maria Novella** ⓬ to the north is home to Masaccio's celebrated *Trinity* and in its **museum** (Mon–Thur, Sat and Sun) is Paolo Uccello's *Universal Deluge*, a painting that itself fell victim to heavy flooding in 1966, but was not damaged beyond recognition.

To the east, the church of **San Lorenzo** ⓭ (daily) was the Medici family church and contains the tombs of various members of the illustrious dynasty within both the Old Sacristy by Brunelleschi and the New Sacristy by Michelangelo. Affordable and colourful market stalls fill the streets around the church. Find time for a visit to the northeast of this area, where one of the most famous works of world art, Michelangelo's sculpture *David*, is on display in the **Accademia** ⓮ (Tue–Sun). Worth considering, if your patience is challenged by the length of the queue, is a visit instead to the nearby convent of **San Marco** ⓯ (daily), where the heavenly paintings and frescoes of Fra Angelico are on view.

View of Florence from the Piazzale Michelangelo.

A gondolier navigates the narrow canals of Venice.

VENICE

For a millennium the Republic of Venice repelled
unwelcome invaders. Now the city built on water
embraces a tidal wave of tourists – on its own terms.

n the early morning, when the mist
still lingers over the lagoon, and
the palaces seem to float on water,
you may be forgiven for thinking that
Venice is only an illusion. Nothing in
Venice is ever quite what it seems.
The placid lagoon is gnawing at the
foundations, having already gobbled
up all but 30 of the 490 islands that
existed 1,000 years ago. Yesterday's
Venetians defended their city for 986
years with bluff, bluster, cunning and
masterly diplomacy – and then let
it fall without a blow. The city itself,
once the bazaar of the world and the
centre of cosmopolitan life, today
has a fast-declining population and
an infrastructure threatened by the
20 million tourists that descend here
annually, as well as by the high tides
which occasionally flood its streets
and squares.

The republic soared to power
in 1203 with an act of treachery as
wicked as it proved expedient. In
exchange for allowing the Crusaders
to use his port, Enrico Dandolo, the
blind doge – Venice's chief magistrate,
elected by the 41 powerful men who
made up the republic's Great Council
– persuaded the flotilla of 500 ships
to ransack Constantinople, capital
of Byzantium, the Eastern Roman
Empire. It had become the richest
city in the world, and its power and
seafaring influence had long been a

Piazza San Marco.

thorn in the side of Venice.

In 1204, the pious Crusaders sacked
Constantinople, murdering the
city's inhabitants. As booty, Venice
was awarded the legendary "quarter and a half of a quarter" of the
Eastern Roman Empire. The priceless
monuments and relics looted from
Constantinople, and now in St Mark's
Basilica, include the Quadriga from
the emperor's box at the Hippodrome
and the Madonna Nicopeia, a sacred
icon. Venice became the greatest
repository of Byzantine art.

Main Attractions

Basilica di San Marco
Palazzo Ducale
Grand Canal
Guggenheim Venice
Galleria dell'Accademia
Rialto
Scuola Grande di San Rocco

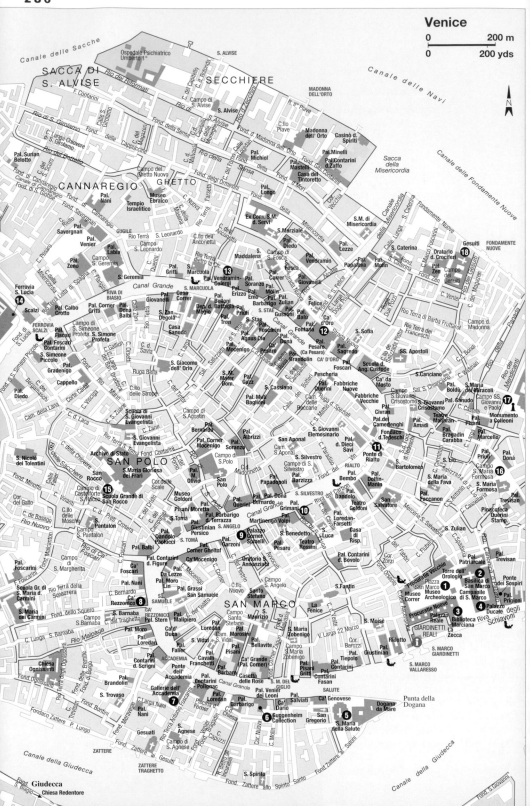

Piazza San Marco

Heart of the Venetian Republic, **Piazza San Marco ❶** (St Mark's Square) is still the city's great showpiece and home to some of its finest monuments. The square teems with tourists and pigeons, while café orchestras play on, determined to see the Grand Old Lady dance to her grave. When Napoleon first set eyes on the gossiping multitudes and lavish decor, he called it "the finest drawing room in Europe". Byron, Dickens, Proust and Wagner all sat at the famous Caffè Florian, which still serves the best (and most expensive) coffee on the piazza; Thomas Mann brooded here and wrote *Death in Venice*; and Ernest Hemingway drank six bottles of wine a night here while he wrote some of his best prose.

Despite the queues, be sure to visit the **Basilica di San Marco ❷** (St Mark's Basilica; daily) to see the gold-backed mosaics, carved galleries, jewel-encrusted altar screen (Pala d'Oro) and the original four bronze horses that used to adorn the facade (the ones outside are replicas). A striking feature of the square is the soaring **Campanile**

or belltower, a replica of the original tower that collapsed in 1902. Inside, a lift (daily) ascends 100 metres (330ft) for a sweeping panorama of the city. The piazza's other tower is the **Torre dell'Orologio** (Clock Tower; pre-booked guided tours only, www.visit muve.it), designed in 1496.

Adjoining the piazza and extending to the waterfront is the **Piazzetta San Marco**. On the right as you face the lagoon stands the 16th-century **Biblioteca Marciana ❸** (daily). Palladio, Italy's greatest 16th-century architect, considered this structure, with its finely sculpted arcades and detailed figures, one of the most beautiful buildings ever constructed. It houses Venice's historic library, with many fine manuscripts and early books. Adjoining it in the Procuratorie Nuove building facing the main square is the **Museo Correr** (daily), an interesting collection of works by Venetian Renaissance artists and exhibits on Venetian history displayed in sumptuous, recently restored rooms that formed the residence of the Habsburg royal family when they visited Venice while it was under Austrian rule, from 1815 to 1866.

TIP

Several of Venice's major attractions (the Palazzo Ducale, Museo Correr, Ca' Rezzonico) are administered by the same foundation (www.visitmuve. it). The best way to see the Palazzo Ducale without the queues and the crowds is to book a place on the Secret Itineraries (Itinerari Segreti) tour, a fascinating behind-the-scenes visit which also gives you (unguided) access to the rest of the palace. Tours take place daily in English at 9.55am, 10.45am and 11.35am, and bookings can be made through the website or at the museum information desk. Book well ahead.

The Palazzo Ducale, once the residence of the doges.

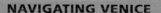

NAVIGATING VENICE

The city is small enough to be covered on foot, but a good map is essential for exploring the maze of alleys and squares. For longer or faster trips, use the vaporetto (water-bus). Information on the 24 routes is available from the ACTV office near the train station (tel: 041-2424, www.actv.it). Tickets can be bought online or at the tourist office (www.veniceconnected. com). Single tickets cost around €7 and are valid for 60 minutes, but tourist travel cards, valid for from 1 to 7 days, are more economical. The ACTV is introducing an electronic ticketing system, the imob, with which you can recharge a card once an amount of credit has been used.

The more private alternative to vaporetti are water-taxis, which take up to four people and, like regular taxis, display meters. There are water-taxi "ranks" at many points in the city. Charges are high, and often complicated; contact Consorzio Motoscafi Venezia, tel: 041-522-2303, www. motoscafivenezia.it, and Venice Link, tel: 041-240-1715, www.venicelink.com.

The most famous Venetian transport, though, is of course the gondola. To hire one during the day costs from around €80 for 40 minutes, with extra charges for any time over that, and at night (after 8pm) the basic charge will be €100. If he (or she) sings it will also cost extra, although it's common to haggle with gondoliers. A maximum of six people are accepted. Very much cheaper are the traghetto gondolas, which cross the Grand Canal where there are no bridges.

The island of San Giorgio Maggiore, with Palladio's church of the same name at its heart.

A view of the Grand Canal from the Accademia Bridge.

Overlooking the lagoon stands the sumptuous, oriental-looking **Palazzo Ducale ❹** (Doge's Palace; daily), residence of Venice's doges, seat of government and home to the law courts and prisons. Behind the palace is the **Bridge of Sighs** (Ponte dei Sospiri), where prisoners from the palace who crossed to the dungeons drew their last breath of free air.

Two columns bearing St Theodorus and the Lion of Venice dominate the lagoon end of the square. From the wharf where pleasure boats set out for trips around the lagoon, merchant ships used to ride at anchor. *Vaporetti* and speedboat taxis stop here, with the remaining gondolas from the flotilla that was once 10,000 strong.

Along the Grand Canal

The **Grand Canal** (Canal Grande) is the Champs-Elysées of Venice; along its winding 3.5km (2-mile) route stand 200 palaces and seven churches. At times this unique waterway is as congested as an urban road. Polished mahogany speedboats jostle for space with the *vaporetti*. Dodging in and out between them are the freight barges, the postman's barge, the milkman, the debt collector, the gondolas and the traghetti that ferry pedestrians across the canal.

Venice was one of Europe's largest ports until the 16th century, after Columbus discovered America and the Portuguese navigator Vasco da Gama found a new sea route to Asia around the Cape of Good Hope. These discoveries ruined the overland spice traffic that had filled Venetian treasuries with revenue far greater than the income of the papacy or the empires of the time.

One of the great symbols of Venice, the majestic domed church of **Santa Maria della Salute ❺**, presides over the Grand Canal entrance at the San Marco end, from the south bank. In gratitude for the deliverance of Venice from the plague, the city's fathers built the church in the 17th century. On the same side of the canal, the **Guggenheim Venice ❻** (Wed–Mon) is housed in the squat Palazzo Venier dei Leoni, once the home of millionaire art collector Peggy Guggenheim. She knew most great 20th-century artists personally, and her collection – kept here, separate from the other Guggenheim museums in New York, Bilbao or Berlin – is exceptional. Classical Venetian art – Bellini, Giorgione, Titian, Tintoretto – is housed further along in the **Galleria dell'Accademia ❼** (Mon–Sun). The poet Robert Browning (1812–89), a great admirer of Venetian painting, died in the **Ca' Rezzonico ❽**, which is now the museum of 18th-century Venice (Mon–Wed). Nearby, **Campo Santa Margherita** is one of Venice's main tourist-magnets, ringed by hotels and restaurants.

Beyond the bend in the canal, on the opposite side, the **Palazzo Corner Spinelli ❾** is a fine example of the early flowering of the Renaissance spirit in Venice; **Palazzo Grimani ❿**, a little further along, represents a final Renaissance flourish from the master Sanmicheli. Up ahead is one of the city's most famous sights, the **Ponte di Rialto** (Rialto Bridge) ⓫, built in the late 16th century. In its day the area around the bridge was the Wall Street of Europe. The Rialto

is lined with tightly packed little shops selling jewellery, leather goods, carnival masks and other souvenirs.

The Grand Canal's most famous palace, the Gothic **Ca' d'Oro ⑫** (Golden Palace; daily), stands at the first landing stage beyond the Rialto. The pink, lace-like facade was once covered in gold, hence the name. Further up is the **Palazzo Vendramin-Calergi ⑬**, designed by Mauro Coducci – yet another superb Renaissance creation – now houses the city's casino. This is the last major building before the railway station, **Ferroviaria Santa Lucia ⑭**.

Venetian quarters

North of the Grand Canal, between the station and the Palazzo Vendramin Calergi, is **Cannaregio,** home to the **Ghetto**. Venice is the origin of the English word Ghetto, since Jews were first confined to this area in the 16th century. Cannaregio is one of the best areas for tranquil strolling along its canals, and getting an idea of modern Venetian life away from the crowds.

The area of **San Polo** that lies within the large bend of the Grand Canal is home to the **Scuola Grande di San Rocco ⑮** (daily), visited for its works of art by Tintoretto (1518–94). They include *The Crucifixion*, which inspired Henry James to exclaim: "Surely no single picture in the world contains more human life, there is everything in it including the most exquisite beauty."

The eastern section of the city, **Castello**, has charm of its own, and a good place to begin a visit is the **Campo Santa Maria Formosa ⑯**, a congenial market square. The elegant church is worth visiting to admire Palma il Vecchio's *St Barbara and Saints*.

Further north is another fine square, **Campo Santi Giovanni e Paolo ⑰**, enlivened by an imposing statue the of the mercenary Bartolomeo Colleoni, and the great Gothic church of **Santi Giovanni e Paolo**, commonly called San Zanipolo and known as Venice's Pantheon as it contains the tombs of 25 doges. In the Baroque church of the **Gesuiti ⑱** near the Fondamente Nuove, the prize work of art is Titian's *Martyrdom of St Lawrence*.

The islands

The Fondamente Nuove is the ferry departure point for the northern islands. Across the water lies **San Michele**, the lagoon's cemetery island. Further north is **Murano**, the island of the glass blowers, which produces the world-famous Murano glass. The **Museo Vetrario** (Thur–Tue) houses a fine collection of antique pieces.

The Laguna Nord ferries carry on from here to the lively island of **Burano**, traditionally known for lace making and fishing, and with narrow streets lined with brightly painted houses. From here it's a short ferry hop to **Torcello**, an evocative and remote little island, where the Byzantine Cathedral is the sole evidence of its former glory. In the opposite direction, to the south, boats also run to the Lido, Venice's beach island. It's no longer the elite resort Thomas Mann portrayed in *Death in Venice*, but its sands and sea air provide a welcome break in a hot summer.

EAT

Bacari are a special Venetian institution, small, snug traditional wine bars with a choice of Venetian wines and delicious *cicheti* snacks, the local equivalent of tapas. It's traditional to stand at the bar and visit several in an evening, but one of the most atmospheric is the Antico Dolo on Ruga Vecchia in San Polo, near San Giacomo dell'Orio, which also has a restaurant if you want a full meal.

The Rialto Bridge.

Driving through Ragusa Ibla in Sicily.

AROUND ITALY

On a tour of Italy, the northern lakes and the
rolling Tuscan landscape will soothe the spirits,
while the Bay of Naples and the sun-drenched
island of Sicily promise excitement.

talians are very proud of being the
source of many of Europe's greatest
cultural traditions – ancient Rome
itself, the Renaissance, opera – and
virtually every town has its historic
buildings and artistic highlights. Italy
also offers a remarkable range of landscapes, from Alpine peaks and the
wild empty crags of the Abruzzo to
the flat, misty plains of the Po Valley
or brilliantly white sand beaches.

Alpine regions

Travellers arriving from Austria
through the **Brenner Pass** ❶ may
not immediately notice much difference. The Alpine landscape of
wooden chalets and onion-domed
churches appears more Austrian than
Italian, and most of the people in this
region, the **Alto Adige** or the South
Tyrol, speak German and maintain
distinctly Germanic traditions and
hearty mountain cuisine. It became
Italian, essentially, because Italy was
one of the victors in World War I.
Today it is officially bilingual and
enjoys administrative autonomy, and
both languages mix in the vibrant
regional capital of **Bolzano** (or
Bolzen, in German).

To the east Italian dialects become
more prevalent in the **Dolomites**, the
most spectacular range in the Italian
Alps. The valley of **Val Gardena**, with
popular winter resorts such as **Ortisei**

On the roof of Milan Cathedral.

or **Selva**, leads up and up to the
Sella Pass, at 2,244 metres (7,360ft),
to meet the dramatic switchback
Great Dolomite Road to the chic and
world-famous ski resort of **Cortina
d'Ampezzo**. The Dolomites are as
renowned for summer hiking as for
winter sports, especially the ranges
south of Cortina, with a wonderful
range of high-mountain paths including *vie ferrate*, precarious paths of iron
cables and ladders that were built into
mountainsides by the Italian army
during World War I.

Main Attractions

The Dolomites
Milan
Italian Lakes
Pisa
Siena
Pompeii
Capri
Amalfi
Sicily
Sardinia

South of Bolzano, the Brenner Highway runs down past castles and fortifications medieval **Trento ②**, famous for the "Council of Trent" held here over 19 years, from 1545 to 1563, which launched the Catholic Counter-Reformation. It has a Romanesque **Duomo** (Cathedral; daily) and the **Castello del Buon Consiglio** (Castle of Good Counsel; Tue–Sun), a 13th-century castle with remarkable medieval frescoes depicting the Cycle of the Months, which also houses touring exhibitions.

The Veneto and Trieste

As you leave the mountains and enter the green plains of the Veneto, roads converge on **Verona ③**, where, according to Shakespeare, Romeo and Juliet lived and loved. Their story is of course a beautiful fiction (though local families called something like Montague and Capulet did exist), but Verona delights in its romantic connections, and thousands visit **Casa di Giulietta** (Juliet's House; Mon pm, Tue–Sun) at Via Cappello 23, a real medieval townhouse, with balcony, of the kind Juliet could have inhabited. Modern Verona is also one of the most prosperous towns in Italy, with plenty of other attractions. In the centre of town, beside the animated main square the **Piazza Brà**, is the **Roman Arena**, built in the 1st century AD but wonderfully well preserved. Each summer it provides an unforgettable setting for an enormously popular opera season. The narrow streets north of the Arena, in a bend of the River Adige, are delightful for strolling and window-shopping.

A short distance to the east is **Vicenza**, a city associated above all with one architect, Andrea Palladio (1508–1580), who from the 1540s was given extraordinary freedom by its merchant-rulers to redesign their town, reviving the proportions of Roman builders and so effectively creating the Neoclassical style in architecture, emulated across Europe for the next 300 or more years. Palladio's masterpieces begin on the main square, **Piazza dei Signori**, with the exquisite **Basilica** – not a church but a seat of government and justice, the original Roman meaning of the

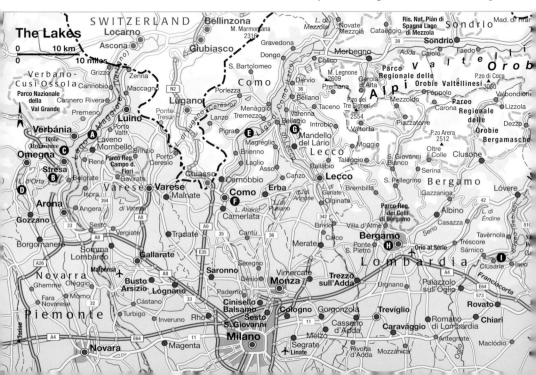

word – with two-storey loggia, and continue with the *palazzi* on **Corso Palladio**, the main street, which leads to his last great construction, the **Teatro Olimpo**, the oldest intact indoor theatre in the world. Palladio was also famed for the country **villas** he built for noble families, imitated in many English stately homes. Many can be seen in the countryside to the east towards Treviso, or along the Brenta Canal south of Venice.

A mainland "partner" to Venice for centuries, the lovely city of **Padua** ❹ (Padova) also looms large in Shakespeare, as, among other scenes, the setting for Katherine's challenge to the male order in Shakespeare's The *Taming of the Shrew*. An important city since ancient times, with Italy's second-oldest university (established in 1222), it is also the resting place of St Anthony of Padua, a Franciscan preacher whose remains draw pilgrims to the immense **Basilica di Sant'Antonio** (daily). In the town centre on the **Piazza delle Erbe**, the 12th–13th-century town hall, **Palazzo della Ragione** (Tue–Sun) has the largest medieval hall in Europe. Padua's greatest treasures, though, are Giotto's beautifully preserved frescoes from 1305 in the **Scrovegni Chapel** (daily; reservations compulsory; www.cappelladegliscrovegni.it).

From Padua it is a short hop to **Venice** ❺ (Venezia; see page 285), and the Adriatic coast. In northern Italy's easternmost corner, **Trieste** ❻ has been subjected to many ownership disputes, and was the last major city to be incorporated into the country, after World War I. None of this bothered Irish writer James Joyce when he arrived in the city in 1905, when it was part of the Austrian Empire. He thought his stay would be a short one, but Trieste became his home for 10 years. Among Trieste's attractions today are its curious Italian-central European architectural mix, and its many Old World cafés.

Milan, Piedmont and Liguria

A web of highways and rail lines speeds into **Milan** ❼ (Milano), Italy's second-biggest city after Rome, which,

TIP

Verona's open-air opera season in the fantastic setting of the Roman Arena runs from early July to mid-September. Each year it features some of the leading figures in the opera world, and in 2013 will celebrate its centenary, with Plácido Domingo as artistic director. Tickets can be booked up to a year in advance through www.arena.it.

The western shore of Lake Garda.

perhaps understandably, regards itself as the country's true capital. Not only is it the centre of industry and finance, but it has forged ahead to become the country's most dynamic and influential city in everything but pure politics. Milan is also the hub of Italian fashion, and very conscious of its stylish status.

The city's most famous landmark is, nevertheless, the gargantuan **Duomo** (Cathedral; daily), one of the largest of all Gothic cathedrals, with a soaring facade of multiple spires and an interior of giant columns. Outside, on the north side of the main square, **Piazza del Duomo**, is a cathedral of another kind, the **Galleria Vittorio Emanuele**, Italy's most beautiful 19th-century shopping arcades. On the south side of the square, the **Museo del Novecento** (Museum of the 20th Century; Mon pm, Tue–Sun), opened in 2010, exhibits a superb collection of modern art, highlighting the role of Italian artists such as Modigliani, Di Chirico or Boccioni but also featuring works by Picasso, Matisse, Mondrian and many others.

North of the Galleria Vittorio are **La Scala**, sumptuous centre of the world of opera, and the **Pinacoteca di Brera** (Tue–Sun), another august art collection housed in a 16th-century palace, with art from the 15th to the 19th centuries including Raphael's *Marriage of the Virgin* and Caravaggio's *Supper at Emmaus*. Milan's most famous artistic possession by far, though, is in the west of the city in the **Cenacolo Vinciano** (Tue–Sun; reservations essential, from www.vivaticket.it, tel: 02-9280 0360, or ticket agencies). This former monk's refectory attached to the church of **Santa Maria delle Grazie** contains Leonardo da Vinci's *Last Supper*; the restoration of the mural in the 1990s has attracted huge criticism, but it still has an awe-inspiring power.

On the east side of the centre, in contrast, is the heart of fashionable Milan. **Via Montenapoleone** and the streets around it are home to an enticing range of designer shops, large and small.

Turin ❽ (Torino) was capital of the Piedmontese kingdom under which Italy was united in 1860, and

Sunbathing in Rimini on the northeast coast.

SKI IN THE DOLOMITES

Dubbed the world's loveliest winter playground, the Dolomites do not disappoint. Even the kitsch après-ski is the perfect relaxation after days spent among the stark peaks and spires of the mountains. The resorts, with a few celebrity-studded exceptions such as Cortina d'Ampezzo or Madonna di Campidoglio, are stylish rather than snooty; cosy rather than blasé. The Dolomiti Superski (www.dolomitisuperski.com) centred on Cortina is the world's biggest skiing region, offering 1,220km (760 miles) of pistes around 16 different centres, with the 26km (16-mile) Sella Ronda circuit the jewel in the crown. Resorts en route include Ortisei, Selva and ritzy Alta Badia above Val Gardena. The Dolomite resorts also offer superb food, from hearty Tyrolean feasts in Alpine inns to Michelin-starred fare in the restaurants of the Alta Badia.

so was for a time the whole country's first capital. It still likes to challenge larger Milan as the capital of Italian industry, and to keep up with it as one of Italy's most stylish cities. The centre of fashionable strolling and shopping in Turin is **Via Roma**, the long main street that runs up to the disproportionately large **Piazza Castello** and former **Palazzo Reale** (Royal Palace; Tue–Sun). Next to the palace, the Renaissance **Duomo** (Cathedral) safeguards one of Italy's most famous relics, the much-contested Holy Shroud. Modern Turin is also inseparable from car making (especially Fiats), and near the company's former Modernist factory – now an arts centre – at Lingotto south of Turin (as featured in *The Italian Job*), the **Museo Nazionale dell'Automobile** is one of the world's biggest motor museums.

The lush Piedmontese countryside around Turin is famous for fine food and drink. **Alba** is the capital of truffles, while **Barolo** is noted for red wines and **Asti** is Italy's foremost producer of sparkling wines. In the northwest, the **Valle d'Aosta** is another of Italy's prime Alpine winter sports regions, with attractive resorts like **Courmayeur** beneath Mont Blanc.

A line of mountains separates Piedmont from the Mediterranean and **Liguria**, centred on the ancient maritime republic of **Genoa** ❾ (Genova), Italy's busiest port. Sandwiched between mountains and the sea, Old Genoa has a unique layout, with a web of long but narrow streets, and a distinctively tangy, maritime atmosphere. The 12th-century Romanesque **Duomo** (Cathedral) was built with horizontal white and dark bands in the exterior, and Moorish-influenced columns inside. The once run-down **Porto Antico** (Old Harbour) has been extensively renovated since the 1990s, and has a futuristic **Acquario** (Aquarium; daily) by Genoa-born architect Renzo Piano.

Either side of Genoa along the coast is the **Italian Riviera**, with towns that have been fashionable summer resorts since the 19th century. To the west, **San Remo** retains an air of sophistication, while **Bordighera** is more charming. East of Genoa the coast is steeper and the villages prettier and less traditionally developed: gorgeous but exclusive **Portofino** and the idyllic cliff-hanging villages called the **Cinque Terre** are well known.

The Lakes

Across the foothills of the Alps above Milan are the Italian Lakes, made up of five major lakes. The most westerly is **Lago Maggiore** ❹ (Lake Maggiore), with the *grande dame* resort of **Stresa** ❸ on its western shore. From here it's a quick ferry hop to the **Borromean Islands** ❹ (Apr–Oct daily) and a short drive or cable-car ride from Stresa Lido to the top of **Monte Mottarone,** for a wonderful panorama of the lakes and Alps.

On the far side of Monte Mottarone lies little **Lago di Orta** ❹ (Lake Orta), the setting of the perfectly preserved

Bologna is famous for its ancient university and its cuisine.

medieval village of **Orta San Giulio**, with mesmerising views across the lake to **Isola San Giulio**.

The most visually stunning of the lakes is **Lago di Como ⓔ**, almost 50km (30 miles) long and up to 5km (3 miles) wide. The Alps enclose the lake to the north and skiers enjoy unparalleled views as they whoosh down the glaciers. Ferries are the best way of seeing the lake. From the town of **Como ⓕ** you can take a slow, scenic cruise north to **Bellagio ⓖ**, "pearl of the lake", which enjoys sublime views of the Alps from its setting on a peninsula that separates the Y-shaped lake's two arms. Grand old villas and luxuriant gardens line the lakeshores of Como, the most celebrated among them **Villa Carlotta** at Tremezzo (Apr–Oct daily), across the water from Bellagio.

Southeast of Lake Como is **Bergamo ⓗ**, which has one of Italy's most enchanting medieval centres, reached from its lower town by funicular. **Piazza Vecchia** is flanked by magnificent medieval and Renaissance monuments, and **Piazza Duomo** is overlooked by the jewel-like **Colleoni Chapel** (daily). In the lower town, the **Accademia Carrara** (Tue–Sun) has a rich collection of Venetian masterpieces.

East of Bergamo is **Lago d'Iseo ⓘ** (Lake Iseo), where Monte Isola in the centre of the lake dominates the view. **Brescia ⓙ**, southeast of the lake, contains the **Santa Giulia Museo della Città** (Tue–Sun), one of the best archaeological and historical museums in Italy. It incorporates the 8th-century Basilica of San Salvatore, the Romanesque oratory of Santa Maria in Solario and other historic buildings.

Largest of the lakes, and the most popular, is **Lago di Garda ⓚ**. Windsurfing and sailing draw in water-sports enthusiasts, and beaches in the southern section of the lake are popular with families. A reminder of one aspect of Italy's history is found in **Gardone Riviera ⓛ**, on the western shore. Gabriele d'Annunzio, the flamboyant poet, pilot, patriot and early Fascist, was given a home here by Mussolini. His eccentric residence, **Il Vittoriale** (Tue–Sun), is a shrine to his imperialistic dreams. Neighbouring **Salò ⓜ** is synonymous with the notorious wartime Republic of Salò, where Mussolini made his last stand. On a peninsula jutting into the lake at its southern end, the ancient town of **Sirmione ⓝ** is a near-impossibly picturesque medieval village.

The Po Valley and Emilia-Romagna

The great plain of the Po Valley runs right across northern Italy, cut by irrigation channels and shivering with ghostly poplar trees. This fertile region between Milan in the west and Rovigo in the east is Italy's larder as well as its fruit and vegetable garden. Emilia-Romagna on the south side of the valley, especially, is famed as having the finest cuisine in the country, and each town in the region has its own delicious specialities.

San Marino, Europe's smallest republic.

Italy's longest highway, the Autostrada del Sole ("Motorway of the Sun), begins at Milan and runs for 1,200km (780 miles) right down the length of the peninsula to Reggio di Calabria. As it leaves the Po Valley it skirts **Modena** ⑩. A more ancient road, the Via Emilia, was built by the Romans, and still runs through the centre of Modena with the city's most illustrious sight, the Romanesque **Duomo** (**Cathedral**), sitting grandly beside it. The **Palazzo dei Musei** contains several galleries, including the **Galleria Estense** (Tue–Sun) and the **Biblioteca Estense** (Mon–Sat), the library of the d'Este dukes of Modena. Modena's great culinary speciality is balsamic vinegar, aceto di Modena, the quality of which is zealously regulated.

Parma and **Reggio Emilia**, west of Modena, are the homes of dry-cured Parma ham and *parmigiano* (parmesan cheese) respectively. Further along the Via Emilia, the historic city of **Bologna** ⑪ is a prosperous place with a finely preserved historic centre and a well-deserved reputation for gastronomy. The city is centred around the grand **Piazza Maggiore** and **Piazza del Nettuno**, near which is the **Mercato di Mezzo**, one of the finest of all Italy's food markets, with eye-popping stalls loaded with gourmet delights. To the east are the two **Torri Pendenti** (Leaning Towers), built by two aristocratic families in the 13th century who competed to build the tallest tower in the city. One is now only 48 metres (157ft) high, having been shortened for safety reasons in the 14th century, but still leaning distinctly; the other tower stands 97 metres (318ft) tall, and has 500 steps up for a rooftop view. Bologna's university is the oldest in Europe, founded in 1088, and was attended by the great poet Petrarch (1304–74). Its official centre is the 16th-century **Palazzo Poggi**. Beyond the university, the **Pinacoteca Nazionale** (Tue–Sun) is a gallery mainly devoted to the Bolognese School, notably Carraci and Guido Reni.

The Adriatic

The main highway reaches the coast near **Ravenna** ⑫, which stands out from all other Italian cities for its churches with dazzling Byzantine mosaics. The city acquired these treasures in the 6th and 7th centuries, when under the Emperor Justinian (527–565) the Eastern Roman Empire regained control of part of Italy and made Ravenna the capital of its Italian territories. The finest mosaics are in the 6th-century **Basilica of San Vitale** (daily) and the 5th-century **Mausoleum of Galla Placidia** (daily).

Stretching south are the sandy beaches of the *Riviera Romagnola*, Italy's most popular beach holiday area. **Rimini** ⑬ is its principal resort. Millions come here each year to lie on the beach in rather expensive "beach clubs", eat in the hundreds of restaurants and mingle in its nightclubs. It also has a cultural attraction: the **Tempio Malatestiano** (daily) Renaissance church, which was commissioned around 1450 by Sigismondo Malatesta. Rimini's ruler

EAT

An excellent place to sample Bologna's celebrated cooking is Buca del Petronio, Via de' Musei 4, tel: 051-224 589, in an old palazzo a short walk from Piazza Maggiore, with an outside terrace. The atmosphere is relaxed, and the tortelloni with ricotta and other classic dishes, excellent.

The Leaning Tower of Pisa still leaning, but still standing.

Siena's Gothic Cathedral has a colourful facade.

View of Siena's Piazza del Campo from the Torre del Mangia.

and a *condottiere* (mercenary), Malatesta was condemned by the pope and the church was never finished, but it is now the city's cathedral.

Half an hour's drive inland from Rimini lies Europe's oldest and smallest republic – **San Marino** ⑭. It has just 29,000 inhabitants and is dramatically set on the rocky slopes of Monte Titano. To the southwest of San Marino stands the hilltop fortress of San Leo, a conspicuous sight that attracts thousands of visitors.

Tuscany

Tuscany presents the quintessential Italian landscape: medieval hilltop towns, silvery olive groves, neat vineyards carpeting gently rolling hills, and old farms and villas watched over by cypress trees. The beauty of the landscape, the intensity of the light and the natural harmony were the

inspiration of Renaissance artists and architects in its capital, **Florence** ⑮ (see page 279).

One of the main gateways to Tuscany is **Pisa** ⑯, west of Florence and famous for its Leaning Tower (Torre Pendente) in the **Campo dei Miracoli** (Field of Miracles). Pisa is also renowned as one of Italy's great cities of art. It was one of the most powerful Italian maritime republics in the early Middle Ages, aiding the Normans in their conquest of Sicily, but it was defeated by its great rival Genoa in 1284, and eclipsed by its neighbour Florence in the following century. The Campo dei Miracoli is a theatrical architectural ensemble built during the city's golden age, and apart from the tower – now safe from falling since long-drawn-out rescue work was completed in 2001 – is home to the **Baptistery** and **Duomo** (Cathedral). It is the Islamic influence on the architecture of these buildings that makes them so distinctive, a legacy of the Pisan merchants who established important trading links with North Africa and Moorish Spain.

South of Florence, **Siena** ⑰ is a perfect medieval town of narrow lanes and alleys. The fan-shaped Piazza del Campo is one of the finest squares in Italy, a great place to enjoy a drink at one of the many pavement cafés or, if you're here on 2 July or 16 August, to watch the fantastic scene of horses and their riders charging around the square in one of the wildest horse races in the world, the Palio. A colourful procession of pages, knights, flag-wavers and men-at-arms, all in 15th-century costumes, opens the spectacle. Riding bareback, the participants risk life and limb.

The square slopes down to the graceful Gothic **Palazzo Pubblico** (**town hall**), with a crenellated facade and fluttering banners. This is now home to the **Museo Civico** (daily), housing outstanding early Renaissance art, including two great frescoes by Simone Martini and Ambrogio Lorenzetti's *Allegories of Good and Bad Government*. The strenuous climb up 500 steps to the top of the slender **Torre del Mangia** (Belltower; daily) is worth it for the panorama of the city.

The facade of Siena's Gothic **Duomo** (Cathedral; daily) is a festival of green, pink and white marble, while the interior is decorated with black-and-white geometric patterns. A crypt (daily; guided tours only) below the Duomo is decorated with stunning Sienese School frescoes. Other fine examples of Sienese art can be found in the **Pinacoteca Nazionale** (daily), in the Palazzo Buonsignori on Via San Pietro, south of the Campo.

The best introduction to the Tuscan hill country is a tour of **Chianti**. The SR222 (Via Chiantigiana) from Siena leads north through the region amid rolling hillsides of vineyards of the famous estates that produce this classic Italian wine. A little to the west is **San Gimignano**, perhaps the archetypal Tuscan hill town, a "medieval Manhattan" bristling with extraordinary tall towers built by competing aristocratic families in the early Middle Ages. South of Siena is yet more gorgeous countryside with exceptionally beautiful hill villages known for fine wines and foods, especially **Montalcino** and **Montepulciano**.

Tuscan landscape south of Siena.

View of Naples from the castle.

East of Siena, **Arezzo** ⓲ offers worthy relief from the rigours of the highway. The chief attraction lies in Piero della Francesca's remarkable fresco cycle depicting *The Legend of the True Cross* in the **Basilica di San Francesco** (daily).

Fresco of St Francis in the Basilica of San Francesco, Arezzo.

Umbria

To the east of Tuscany is the province of Umbria and its handsome capital,

Perugia ⓳. The city reflects the bellicose side of a region where the martial and the mystical are inextricably intertwined. Perugia's churches were never completed by the same generation that created them, since the citizens were too busy with wars, feuds, pillage and murder.

If you have only enough time for one museum, make it the **Galleria Nazionale dell'Umbria** (Tue–Sun), which displays works by many of Umbria and Tuscany's most noted painters; Fra Angelico and Piero della Francesca are both well represented. This barbed hilltop fortress town is also where Raphael studied under the great artist Pietro Perugino.

The tradition of fresco painting was established by the Florentine Giotto at **Assisi** ⓴. This beautiful medieval town, with its famous frescoed basilica, is worth staying in for its unique atmosphere.

Naples and Campania

Some 240km (150 miles) south of **Rome** ㉑ (Roma; see page 269), the Bay of Naples reveals rich historic and

ST FRANCIS OF ASSISI

The picture-postcard town of Assisi in Umbria, flower-decked and wood-smoke-scented, draws tremendous crowds, who come to experience something of the spiritualism of the Franciscan order, founded by the town's most famous son, Francis of Assisi.

Born Giovanni Bernadone in 1181, Francis embraced asceticism at an early age, and by 1219 had a brotherhood of 5,000 monks. The main tenets of the original Franciscan order were poverty, chastity and obedience; in particular, Francis repudiated the decadence of the Catholic Church, posing a challenge to the worldliness of the papacy. On his return from preaching in the Holy Land, Francis is said to have received the marks of the stigmata, and was canonised in 1228, two years after his death.

Construction of the two-tiered Basilica di San Francesco (Basilica of St Francis; daily) began in the mid-13th century. The Basilica Inferiore (Lower Basilica; often closed) was built around the saint's crypt and commemorates Francis's modest life with frescoes by Simone Martini and Cimabue. The Basilica Superiore (Upper Basilica), contains Giotto's famous fresco cycle of *The Life of St Francis*. It has been faithfully restored after damage caused by the 1997 earthquake, although it will never be quite what it was.

scenic attractions. Founded by Greek colonists who named it "Neapolis" (the New City), **Naples** ㉒ (Napoli) was captured by the Romans in 326 BC, and enriched with temples, gymnasiums, arenas and all the luxuries of a major Roman city. Later it became a Byzantine dukedom, and the capital of a kingdom that became one of the territories of the Spanish crown. Often under foreign rulers, it was a place where laws were never taken too seriously.

Naples's teeming streets, unemployment and widespread crime, and the increasing prevalence of the Camorra (the region's own home-grown mafia) have not exactly given the city a positive image. Actual criminality aside, the traffic alone is insane. Nevertheless, Naples is still a city of stubborn vitality and theatricality, and continues to exert a fascination.

A good place to begin a tour is the **Castel Nuovo** (New Castle; Mon–Sat), where a stupendous Triumphal Arch stands in commemoration of Alfonso I's 15th-century defeat of the French.

From outside the castle, Via San Carlo leads to Italy's largest opera house, the **Teatro San Carlo**. The Gothic **Duomo** (Cathedral) of Naples is sandwiched between apartment blocks in the north of the historic centre.

In the cathedral's Chapel of San Gennaro is a treasured relic: a phial containing the blood of San Gennaro, martyred in AD 305. The blood must liquefy three times a year – on the first Saturday in May, on 19 September and on 16 December – if Naples is to escape disaster, and these ceremonies are highlights of the Neapolitan ecclesiastical year.

Among Naples's many other churches is the 16th-century **Gesù Nuovo**, perhaps the most harmonious example of Neapolitan Baroque, and **San Pietro a Maiella**, with a ceiling painted by Mattia Preti between 1656 and 1661.

Naples' great cultural highlight, though, is the **Museo Archeologico Nazionale**. Often known just as the Naples Museum (Wed–Mon), it is one of Italy's greatest museums of Roman and Greek antiquities, housing the

The local wine is usually the best.

Exploring the remains of Pompeii.

Shiny and speedy, the favourite form of transport for young people in Naples, ideal for nipping in and out of traffic.

The interior of Monreale Cathedral, Sicily.

most spectacular finds from Pompeii and Herculaneum, wonderful mosaics and fine Greek sculpture. Two other excellent museums are the **Museo di Capodimonte** (Mon–Sat), in the Palazzo di Capodimonte once owned by Naples's 18th-century kings, with delightful porcelain along with paintings by Titian and Caravaggio; and the **Certosa di San Martino** (Thur–Tue), a beautifully restored Carthusian monastery on the hill above the city, with spectacular views over Naples and its bay.

Looming over the Bay of Naples is the giant volcano of **Vesuvius**, which last erupted in 1944, with the remnants still scattered in a vast heap around the crater. The most famous explosion, however, occurred in AD 79, when the flourishing cities of **Pompeii ㉓** and **Herculaneum** (both daily) were buried under a deep covering of ashes and brimstone. The last moments of Pompeii's inhabitants and their daily life, preserved in volcanic ash, have come to light

as archaeologists have excavated the remains: a rich man, his fingers still clutching the keys to the treasure chests his slaves carried behind him; wine in jugs on tables, bread baking in the oven; a dog in its death throes; graffiti proclaiming love, obscenities and political baiting. The details and richness of the ancient lives caught in that fateful event make Pompeii one of the world's most impressive ancient monuments.

Some parts of the site are notoriously badly maintained, and the size of its tour groups can be dismaying, but a visit to lesser-known Herculaneum is one way of dealing with the problem. Although the town was smaller than Pompeii, there is still plenty to see, such as the well-preserved mosaics which decorate the **Casa dell'Atrio Mosaico** (House of the Atrium Mosaic) and the **Casa dei Cervi** (House of the Stags).

Around the eastern side of the Bay of Naples are more of Italy's most famous landscapes. The island of **Capri ㉔** is easily reached by fast hydrofoil from Naples or Sorrento. Tiberius chose the island as his retirement home in AD 27, and while he may or may not have organised orgies on the island, the story has not diminished Capri's appeal. The ruins of his luxurious imperial villa, **Villa Jovis** (daily), have spectacular sea views. But the most popular island excursion is the **Grotta Azzurra** (Blue Grotto; tickets for boat trip available from Marina Grande). The sun shining through the water in this cave creates a strange blue light, which has made it the most visited attraction in the region after Pompeii.

On the mainland lies **Sorrento, the** largest resort of the "Amalfi Coast" and the start of the extraordinary, twisting **coast road**, which winds round the rocky peninsula sometimes halfway up an almost sheer cliff. Travellers are rewarded by unforgettable views over the dazzlingly blue sea. The road dips into pretty villages that

have become fashionable beach hide-aways, such as **Positano** and **Amalfi** itself, before reaching the beautiful cliff-top village of **Ravello**.

Apulia and Calabria

Due east of Naples, the jutting peninsula of Puglia (Apulia) forms the heel of Italy's boot. **Bari** ㉕, originally a Greek colony, is its main commercial centre, but there is a wonderful absence of modernity in the warren of narrow streets and dazzling white houses in the ancient half of the city. Two sights are the fine Romanesque **Basilica di San Nicola**, built to house the bones of St Nicholas, brought back from Asia Minor in 1087 by local sailors; and the **Pinacoteca Provinciale** (Tue–Sun), devoted to local art. Picturesque **Alberobello**, 50km (30 miles) southeast of Bari, is a major tourist attraction, consisting almost entirely of Puglia's distinctive *trulli* single-storey, whitewashed shepherds' huts with conical slate roofs.

The coastal road continues to **Brindisi**, where a column marks the end of the Via Appia, the greatest of the ancient roads that lead to Rome. Today, as in ancient times, this is the main ferry port between Italy and Greece.

Taranto ㉖, on the instep of Italy's boot, and founded by Spartans in 706 BC, was once the largest Greek city in Italy. Its **MARTA** archaeological museum (daily) displays superb sculpture and Greek and Roman ceramics. In a region of restrained Romanesque architecture, the sumptuous buildings of **Lecce** ㉗ to the east come as something of a pleasant surprise. The

Wall mosaic in the House of Neptune and Amphitrite, Herculaneum, near Pompeii.

The clear waters of Capo San Marco in Sardinia.

WHERE

You can either climb Mount Etna or circle it on the Circumetnea private railway. This slow single-track train runs Monday to Saturday from Catania to Riposto, affording spectacular views of the volcano. For information go to www.circumetnea.it.

The Greek temples in Sicily's Valley of the Temples are extraordinarily well preserved.

flamboyant style of its 17th-century churches and palazzi became known as "Lecce Baroque".

And so to the toe of the boot, and **Reggio di Calabria ㉘**, from where ferries between the mainland and Sicily arrive and depart. The first Greek settlers made the sea journey from Sicily in the 8th century BC; the most celebrated evidence of this early contact only came to light in 1972, when fishermen discovered two colossal Greek statues thought to have gone down with a ship. They are, deservedly, the chief exhibits in the **Museo Nazionale della Magna Graecia** (Tue–Sun).

Sicily and Sardinia

The fertile island of **Sicily** (Sicilia) has always been at the confluence of the Mediterranean world, It is best seen by road, although the ever-smouldering Mount Etna provides the most dramatic single vantage point. Around the central town of **Enna**, the countryside is one rolling plain of golden cornstalks.

Palermo ㉙, Sicily's capital, is a turbulent place, known for both its Mafia connections and some wonderful architecture. The **Palazzo dei Normanni**, originally a Norman palace, is now the seat of the Sicilian Parliament, and contains the exquisite **Capella Palatina** (**Palatine Chapel**; Mon–Fri). Within easy reach of Palermo is the glorious **Cathedral of Monreale** (daily), which has some of the finest medieval mosaics in Europe. East of Palermo on the north coast is the pretty seaside town of **Cefalù**, with a surprisingly impressive 12th-century cathedral.

Siracusa ㉚ (Syracuse) was one of the most important Greek colonies, and in its sprawling **Parco Archeologica della Neapolis** (daily) is a great **Greek Theatre** (Teatro Greco) that holds up to 15,000 spectators. High-quality classical performances are staged here each summer (details from tourist office). Even more spectacular is the **Valle dei Templi** (Valley of the Temples) at **Agrigento ㉛**; the Temple of Concord is arguably the best-preserved Doric temple in the world.

Further up the coast, clinging to the cliffs, is pretty **Taormina** ㉜. This chic resort also has a **Teatro Greco** (daily), dramatically positioned above the village, that is also still in use for music and drama.

Off Sicily's northeastern tip, the volcanic **Aeolian Islands** (Isole Eolie) include **Stromboli**, which spews lava into the night, and are where the Greeks believed the god Aeolus imprisoned the winds. The pace of life here is slow even in summer when tourists descend in their droves to "get away from it all". The wild and rugged island of **Sardegna** ㉝ (Sardinia) has been a world of its own virtually throughout its history. It would be hard to find a concentration of such enticing white beaches anywhere else in the Mediterranean, and while the coves of the northeast on the Costa Smeralda ("Emerald Coast") are associated with the international elite, elsewhere around the island, such as north and south of the old Catalan town of Alghero, it's easy to find swathes of beach to yourself. The interior is striking too, with wild

In summer you'll see lemons growing wild in the countryside

gorges and valleys carved into it. The most distinctive of Sardinia's cultural attractions are the *nuraghi*, Bronze Age stone towers. Their exact function is still unclear; they may have been dwellings, fortifications and sanctuaries, but nevertheless, these megaliths offer a tantalising glimpse of Sardinia's early civilisation. Sardinia's food and wine, though relatively little-known, are among Italy's best.

Boats moored off the coast of Capri.

The Temple of Apollo in Corinth, Greece.

Beach taverna in Agni, Corfu.

GREECE

A heady mix of sun, sea and ancient sites bathed
in brilliant Aegean light, Greece has been
enchanting travellers to its mainland and
myriad islands for centuries.

Shrine in Ássos, Kefalloniá.

Modern Greece, which emerged in the 19th century from 400 years of Ottoman rule, covers scattered, rocky peninsulas and islands in the eastern Mediterranean, with a language evolved directly from the ancient Greek of the philosophers and playwrights. There are several fertile plains, in central mainland Thessaly and also on the Peloponnese, the southwestern part of the country beyond the Corinth Canal. But in general the country's rugged profile makes life hard. To the north, this 132,000-sq km (51,000-sq mile) Balkan nation is bordered by Albania, former Yugoslav Macedonia, Bulgaria and, for a short distance, its former master, Turkey.

Modern towns and regions echo the familiar names of kingdoms and city-states that vied for supremacy two, three and more millennia ago: Corinth, Sparta, Mycenae, Knossos, Athens. Here too is Delphi with its oracle, the Athenian Acropolis, the shrine and games venue at Olympia, and Mount Olympus, still haunted by the ancient gods and uniquely important in Western culture.

Modern Greece, as anyone who follows the news knows, has become mired in immense problems. The recklessness of its own politicians and governing class, who took full advantage of the easy credit on offer prior to the 2007 global crisis to embark on a wild spending spree centred around the 2004 Athens Olympic Games – but ending only in vast debts – has combined with the inflexibility of the financial structures of the EU to produce a situation in which unemployment hit 25 percent. In 2012 more than 10,000 people protested in Athens against the austerity measures, as the government steers its way through the worst recession of any country in modern history. This necessarily affects social life and has resulted in the deterioration of some services.

Greeks, however, are great survivors, and while many protest about their situation, the crisis is characterised by people helping each other rather an atmosphere of tension or violence. It is still easy to fall in love with Greece – its beauty is self-evident. Travellers return time after time, for the mirror-smooth Aegean Sea shimmering in the still of the morning, for the *kafenía* with their marble-topped tables and wicker-bottomed chairs offering respite from blistering afternoon heat, and for the silvery olive groves where cicadas trill until dark. It is a land for connoisseurs and explorers, with an ancient inheritance that remains relevant to this day.

Greece

0   50 km
0   50 miles

N

ITALY

Brindisi

Lecce

Durrës

Tiranë

MACEDONIA

Elbasan

Ohridsko
Izero

Bitola

Nidže

Mavrovoúni
1179

Langa

Prespansko
Izero

Flórina

Édessa

①

Thessal

Berat

Vlorë

ALBANIA

Vérmon
Óros

Vegoritidas

Véria

Hałki

Kastoriá

Aliákmonas

Kateríni

Kassá

Grámmos
2637

Kozáni

Óros
Olympos
2917

③

Olympos

Voïa Pindos

Grevená

Elasóna

Thermekós
Kólpos

Tymfi
2204

Zagóri

Metéora

⑦

Kalambáka

Piniós

1978

Karoússades

Sarandë

Lárisa

Kassiopi

Ioánnina

⑤

Tríkala

GREECE

Paleokastritsa

Kérkyra

Pillo Óros

Kérkyra
⑫ (Corfu)

Kérkyra

Igoumenítsa

Nótia Pindos

Kardítsa

Vólos

④

Arghyradhes

Párga

Árta

Fársala

Paxí
(Paxos)
Andípaxi

Árta

Tehnití Limni
Kremastón

Tymfristós
2315

Lamía

Sk

Préveza

Karpenísi

Ág. Konstandín

Levkáda

I
o
n
i
a
n

Levkáda
(Lévkas)

Meganísi

Agrínio

⑥

Delphi

Livadiá

I
s
l
a
n
d
s

 Itháki

Astakós

Náypaktos

Ámfissa

Palovoúna
1748

Thiva

IONIAN

Mesolóngi

Korinthlakós Kólpos

At
(Ath

Argóstoli

⑬

Pátra

Pir

SEA

Kefalloniá
(Cephallonia)

Varda

Salan

Kyllíni

Córinthos
(Corinth)

⑮

Kórinthos

⑯

⑩

Zákynthos

2224

Mycénae

⑭

Zákynthos
(Zante)

Kerí

Pýrgos

Olympia

⑳

Pelopónnisos
(Peloponnese)

Árgos

⑰

Návplio

Trípoli

⑱

Kyparissía

Leonidion

Spétses

Messiní

Kalamáta

⑲

Spárti
Mystrás

Taýgetos

Methóni

Koróni

Gýthio

Monemvas

Gherolímenas

Lakonikós
Kólpos

Neápoli

Kýthira

Andík

[Inset map]

MACEDONIA

BULGARIA

TURKEY

ALBANIA

Dhráma

Xánthi

Rodhópi

Flóina

Pela

Kilkís

Serres

Évros

Kastoría

Imathía

Thessaloníki

Kavála

Kozáni

Piería

Halkidhikí

Ágio
Óros

Grevená

Ioánnina

Larisa

Trikala

Kérkyra

Thes-

Etolía

Magnisía

Lésvos

Préveza

Arta

Karditsa

Évia

Lefkáda

Ioánia Fthiótida

GREECE

TURKEY

Akarnanía

Fokídha

Évia

Kefalloniá

Viotia

Híos

Zákynthos

Ilía

Ahaía

Korinthía

Atikí
Pireás

Sámos

Arkadía

Argolída

Kykládes

Messinía

Lakónia

Dodekánisa

Haniá

Réthymno

Iráklio

Lasíthi

K
Kiss
Pale

The Parthenon crowns the Acropolis.

ATHENS

The power and beauty of the ancient Athenian Empire breathe through this muddle of a modern city, overlooked by the pinnacle of classical architecture: the Parthenon.

T he English novelist John Fowles described Athens as a mass of dice scattered across the Attic Plain. It certainly isn't the prettiest European capital: looking down from Mount Pentéli you'll appreciate the full extent of its architectural sprawl. Combine this visual chaos with hooting traffic, the *néfos* (air pollution) that envelops the centre and the agitation, nervous tension and uncertainty created by the debt crisis, and you might be tempted to head straight for the islands.

But, a certain resentment of Germany aside, Greeks do not take their problems out on foreign visitors in any way, and for the visitor Athens's attractions still emerge with a little patience: catch the Parthenon when the crowds are thinnest, visit one of the richly endowed museums, patronise an *ouzerí* until the small hours as locals do, and engage with Athenians – many of whom speak excellent English – to get their own, human view of their present situation, and this chaotic city will grow on you.

Acropolis

The **Acropolis ❶** (daily; ticket valid for surrounding archaeological sites) rises over 60 metres (200ft) above the city. Viewed from the streets below, the "upper city" makes all else in Athens fade into insignificance. The best

times to visit are early morning in summer or early afternoon in winter.

On top is the **Parthenon** (Virgin's Chamber). Fifteen years under construction, this temple to the goddess Athena was the crowning glory of the giant public works programme launched by Athens's great statesman Pericles during the 440s BC. The spectacle it presented then is hardly matched by the familiar ruin we know today.

There was colour everywhere, so much so that some observers found it quite offensive. "We are gilding

Main Attractions
Acropolis
Acropolis Museum
Byzantine and Christian Museum
Benáki Museum
National Archaeological Museum
Pláka
Poseidon Temple, Cape Soúnion

The Peplos Kore in the New Acropolis Museum.

The Erechtheion, the site where Poseidon left his trident marks and where Athena's olive tree sprouted.

and adorning our city like a wanton woman," was how Plutarch reported these complaints, "decking her with costly statues and offerings and 1,000-talent temples." But when you catch a glimpse of the temple's tawny marble columns you'll forgive Pericles his extravagance. In fact the columns incline slightly inwards and not a single structural line is straight, testament to the mathematical genius of its architect, Iktinos.

Conservation and reconstruction work has made the Parthenon the most attractive it has been in centuries, although some of the recent work may not be sustained due to the crisis. Hundreds of blocks of masonry were remounted to replace rusting, 1920s-vintage iron clamps with non-corrosive titanium, and restorers collected about 1,600 chunks of its marble scattered over the hilltop.

Beyond the Propylaia or "stepped entry" looms the **Erechtheion**, an elegant temple completed in 396 BC. The Caryatids – noble maidens in the service of the goddess Athena – now supporting the porch are copies,

but five originals are displayed in the Acropolis Museum. On what was once the citadel's southern bastion is the small, square temple of **Athena Nike**, completed in 421 BC and reconstructed since 2000. According to legend, from this spot Theseus' father, King Aegeus, threw himself to his death on seeing a black-sailed ship approaching. Theseus had promised to hoist a white sail on his return if he succeeded in killing the Minotaur in Crete, but forgot to change the colour.

The sculptures and reliefs that Lord Elgin failed to loot can be viewed in the **Acropolis Museum ❷** (Tue–Sun) opened in 2009 in a huge building overlooking the Acropolis. For an idea of the ancients' notions of beauty, take a close look at the *korai* (statues of women) also displayed there: you can still discern traces of make-up and earrings, and the patterns of close-fitting dresses.

Below the Acropolis

On the south approach to the Acropolis is the **Theatre of Dionysos**

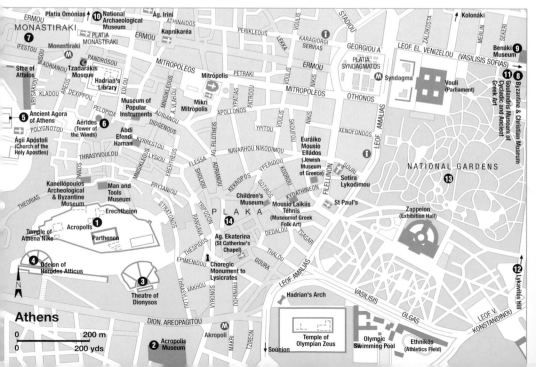

③ (entrance on Leofóros Dionysíou Areopagítou; daily). The theatre's origins date back to the 6th century BC, when it was a simple structure of wooden stands. Later on, an amphitheatre was dug out of the hillside. The marble seating tiers date from 320 BC, but the stage area hosted the plays of Aeschylus, Sophocles, Euripides and Aristophanes at the Festival of Dionysia during the 5th century BC. The theatre fell into disuse after the fall of Rome in the 5th century AD.

Just west, up Dionysíou Areopagítou, the smaller **Odeion of Herodes Atticus ④** was built in the 2nd century AD by a prominent Athenian. Here, from its steep, semicircular rows of seats, you can have a summertime taste of the atmosphere of the ancient Greek theatre.

On the other side of the Acropolis, extending northeastwards, lies the sprawling site of the **Ancient Agora ⑤** (daily), a marketplace and centre of public life. Its focal point is the **Stoa of Attalos**, an impressive two-aisled colonnade 122 metres (400ft) long, now housing a small museum. Further east stands the **Tower of the Winds** (Aérides) **⑥**, built in the 1st century BC as a water-driven clock, compass and weathervane; it predates the surrounding **Roman Agora** that was built 200 years later by philhellene Roman Emperor Hadrian.

Modern Athens

Athens's heart lies within an almost equilateral triangle defined by Platía Omónias (Omónia Square) in the north, Monastiráki in the south and Platía Syndágmatos (Sýndagma Square), or Constitution Square. Cars are restricted to a handful of main arteries. Ermoú, once a traffic clogged mess, is now pedestrianised, and has the exquisite Byzantine church of Kapnikaréa about halfway along.

Sýndagma is ringed by hotels and a few cafés and, presiding over it, Greece's Parliament, which has made the square the main focus of protests during the crisis. Less than a mile northeast lies **Omónia**, with its noisy (and thus cheaper) businessmen's hotels, swirling traffic and jobless immigrants.

TIP

Buy a daily travel card, which is valid for all transport modes: tram, bus and metro. Currently €4, you'll get your money back after just four rides. Even better value is a one-week card for €14.

Exhibits in the New Acropolis Museum.

THE ELGIN MARBLES

During the 18th and early 19th centuries, Greece attracted Grand Tourists intent on mega-souvenir-hunting in the form of archaeological pillaging. None has acquired more notoriety than Lord Elgin, who while ambassador to the Ottomans in the early 1800s secured permission from the Sultan to excavate on the Parthenon and study stones with inscriptions. He interpreted this as a licence to remove most of the pediment friezes with their rich bas-reliefs, as well as one of the six Caryatids, which were all sold to the British Museum. Elgin's actions were controversial even then – Lord Byron deplored them in his poetry – and in recent decades have sparked a major dispute between Greece and the UK. The Greeks, who studiously use the term "Parthenon friezes" and regard Elgin as a vandal, have long demanded their return. The top floor of the new Acropolis Museum is pointedly designed for their eventual accommodation, with a mock-up of the pediment orientated exactly like the original structure, visible just uphill through glass windows.

Defenders of British retention point out that Elgin's behaviour was normal for the time and probably saved the friezes from local lime kilns, and returning them would set a precedent that could strip many museums of their treasures. So despite a vociferous lobby in Britain advocating restitution, these treasures are unlikely to come back to Athens soon.

Eating out in Pláka.

Tzisdarákis Mosque in Monastiráki Square.

Linking these two squares are the parallel streets of Stadíou and Panepistimíou, with shopping arcades between them, the Attica department store and cinemas. Heading uphill from Panepistimíou, the streets get smarter as they blend with **Kolonáki**, the trendiest area for well-heeled Athenians. Contrastingly downmarket is **Monastiráki** ❼ to the west, with shops selling everything from tools, beads and religious paraphernalia to gaudy tourist tat. The famous **Flea Market** occupies Platía Avyssinías, where weekend mornings see browsers of genuine (and expensive) antiques and furniture.

Top museums

Athens is well endowed with museums. The revamped **Byzantine and Christian Museum** ❽ (Tue–Sun) houses a brilliant array of icons, frescoes and other religious art, while the **Benáki Museum** ❾ (Wed–Sun) is an eclectic collection of Greek treasures from all periods, including jewellery, costumes and contemporary art.

The **National Archaeological Museum** ❿ (daily) is a fantastic storehouse of ancient Greek art. Among the treasures here are the so-called Agamemnon's mask, found by the famous German archaeologist Heinrich Schliemann at Mycenae; a lifelike equestrian statue of Emperor Augustus; the bronze of Poseidon poised to throw his (now vanished) trident; the Antikythera mechanism, a geared astronomical computer a millennium ahead of its time; plus Minoan frescoes from Akrotíri.

The highlight of the **Goulandrís Museum of Cycladic Art** ⓫ (Wed–Sun) is a unique collection of slim, stylised Cycladic figurines in marble, originally painted but now white. Dating from 3200–2000 BC, they fascinated such artists as Picasso, Modigliani and Henry Moore. The museum also hosts temporary exhibitions with distinctly un-archaeological themes.

CUTS AND CLOSURES

The cuts in public spending have had a knock-on effect at cultural institutions. From April to September most monuments and public museums used to operate "summer hours", staying open until 6pm or 8pm; since 2011, except for a few major sites – including the Acropolis and Acropolis Museum – most stay on winter hours all year, closing at 4pm or 5pm.

Other restrictions are less predictable: due to staff cuts many sites may be closed on other days as well as their usual closing day (usually Monday) and in museums, entire rooms may be closed off at different times. Finding out about closures in advance is difficult (official published information and websites are often inaccurate); it's best to check with tourist offices or the site itself. The useful expat site livingin greece.gr does its best to keep up.

Other local attractions

A saving grace of Athens is the variety of easy ways out of the urban din. Take the funicular railway up **Lykavitós Hill** ⓬ for spectacular views from the top of Ploutárhou Street, near Platía Kolonáki. In mythology, Lykavitós Hill resulted from a fit of pique on the part of the goddess Athena, who hurled a large rock at the daughters of King Kekrops, and missed; the missile, on landing, became the ridge.

A jungly haven for birds and cats, criss-crossed by irrigation rivulets, the **National Gardens** ⓭ are a stone's throw from the Byzantine and Benáki museums. Not particularly green, but certainly an oasis, is **Pláka** ⓮, the 19th-century quarter clustered at the foot of the Acropolis. In amongst protected domestic architecture and part-pedestrianised streets are several minor museums, Byzantine churches, a Turkish bath and a mosque. Pláka ends and more raucous Monastiráki begins at **Hadrian's Library** (and another mosque, the Tzisdarákis, now home to a ceramics museum).

The one "must" excursion out of Athens is to **Cape Soúnion**. On this sea-lashed promontory towers the **Temple of Poseidon** (Tue–Sun), probably Greece's most evocative ancient temple and, with 16 out of 34 columns remaining, one of the best preserved. On the column nearest the entrance, Romantic poet Lord Byron scratched his name in 1810; because of subsequent imitation, the temple precincts are now off-limits. In clear conditions, especially near sunset, you can see the Cyclades to the southeast and the Peloponnese to the west.

Mosaic in the Byzantine and Christian Museum.

A view of modern Athens.

Skiáthos street scene.

AROUND GREECE

Greece's ancient monuments reflect an expansive culture that, at its height, stretched from Iberia to India. The islands also offer paradise – and beaches galore.

Greece's second-largest city is **Thessaloníki** ❶ once better known as Salonica. Founded in 315 BC by the Macedonian King Kassander, the town later rose to prominence thanks to its position on the Via Egnatia between Rome and Byzantium. A dozen Byzantine churches survive, many clear adaptations of colonnaded Roman basilicas, in turn descended from Greek temples. The **Museum of Byzantine Culture** (daily) features superb wall paintings rescued from early Christian tombs. Macedonian, Hellenistic and Roman finds from the region grace the **Archaeological Museum** (daily), including many gold, silver and ivory treasures from the Vergina tombs of the Macedonian dynasty.

The furthest east of the three peninsulas extending east of Thessaloníki into the Aegean Sea is **Mount Áthos** ❷, one of the Balkans' most stunning monastic realms. There are 20 surviving monasteries; the first, founded by St Athanasios in AD 963 and the most spectacular, is **Símonos Pétra**, with vertiginous drops on three sides. Women are still banned from the peninsula, with only a limited number of non-Orthodox male pilgrims admitted.

South from Thessaloníki, where Macedonia blends into Thessaly, **Mount Olympus** (Ólympos) ❸,

Skiáthos smile.

home of the ancient gods, rises to 2,917 metres (9,750ft), the highest point in Greece. From here, Zeus let fly with his thunderbolts; this close to the sea, the weather is still fickle, and climbers or trekkers should take care.

Thessaly and Epirus

Further south, mostly modern **Vólos** ❹ is the major port of Thessaly, but not without charm and a lively nightlife; it's the major gateway to the Sporádes. Directly above rises **Mount Pílio**, with exquisite traditional

Main Attractions

Metéora
Delphi
Kérkyra
Mycenae
Mystrás
Olympia
Knossos
Rodos Old Town
Monastery of St John, Patmos
Mastic villages, Híos

The ruins of the Temple of Apollo at Delphi date from the 4th century BC.

villages, secluded beaches and dense forests in which the mythical centaurs were said to dwell.

Just beyond the Meteóra loom the **Píndos Mountains**, the spine of mainland Greece, separating Thessaly from **Epirus**, the country's remotest region, though the Vía Egnatía expressway now eases its isolation. Both this and the old highway cross the mountains to the scenic upland around the lakeside city of **Ioánnina** ❺, with a citadel, mosques and inhabited islet with frescoed monasteries. Immediately north lies **Zagóri**, the most scenic stretch of the Píndos, fissured by the deep **Víkos Gorge** and speckled with 47 villages built from the same grey limestone as the mountains.

Delphi: the world's navel

Metéora, built on sandstone.

Nestled in a natural amphitheatre on the southern slope of **Mount** **Parnassós**, the terraced sanctuary of **Delphi** ❻ was for centuries the site of antiquity's most revered oracle. The ancient Greeks believed that here, where Zeus' two released eagles met, was the "navel of the earth".

The site closest to the road is the **Castalian Spring**; across the road is the **Gymnasium** area, with its mysterious round **Tholos**. The main **Sanctuary of Apollo** (daily) has ruins spanning all eras from Classical Greek to Roman, and there's also a rich museum. The meandering **Sacred Way** ascends among temples, statue bases, stoas and treasuries. Only the Doric **Athenian Treasury** is intact, though it was rebuilt in 1904–6 with the marble of the original structure dating from 490 BC.

The present **Temple of Apollo** was the third built on the site, during the 4th century BC. The god Apollo, son of Zeus and Leto, was associated with music, art, philosophy, law, medicine and archery – though prophecy was his main function here. The small **theatre** just above, dedicated to Dionysos, seats 5,000 people, has

THE METEORA

At the western edge of the Thessalian Plain, on molar-like rock pinnacles, eroded from prehistoric seabed, perch the **Metéora monasteries** ❼, worthy rivals to the Áthos group, but able to be visited (variable hours) by all. As on Mount Áthos, religious hermits appeared here in the 10th century, but only in 1344 was the first proper monastery built, and by the 1500s 24 religious communities had colonised the monoliths. From this zenith, decline set in, and only six foundations survive today. Historically the only way up was by winched rope-basket, until stairs were built in the early 1900s. **Megálou Meteórou** – the highest and largest – took nearly three centuries to complete, but **Ágios Nikólaos Anapafsá** and **Roussánou** have better frescoes from the 16th-century heyday.

marvellous acoustics and a wonderful view. Near the top of the sanctuary, the **stadium**, 178 metres (600ft) long, hosted the Pythian Games in honour of Apollo, and its tiers of Roman seats accommodated up to 7,000 spectators.

The Sporádes and Saronic Gulf Islands

Scattered across the three Greek seas – the Aegean, Mediterranean and Ionian – are more than 1,400 islands, though fewer than 100 are permanently inhabited. A popular destination east of Vólos are the strikingly green Sporádes, the closest being **Skiáthos** ⑧, which has more than 60 good beaches. Nightlife is lively, especially in the busy main Skiáthos Town. With a scooter or a car, you can explore more tranquil bays and remote monasteries. **Skópelos** ⑨, next island out and now famous as the film location for *Mamma Mia!* is prettier, better wooded and boasts one of Greece's handsomest port towns. **Alónissos** is for nature-lovers and hikers, while **Skýros**, accessed from eastern Évia,

has a spectacular *hóra* (capitol) and a lively carnival.

Southwest of Athens lie the islands of the **Saronic Gulf**. Closest is **Aegina** (Égina) ⑩, a 45-minute hydrofoil ride from Piraeus. Its most interesting monument, on a pine-tufted hilltop, is the well-preserved Doric **temple** of the nymph **Aphaea**, The elegant port-town, facing vivid sunsets, was briefly the first capital of modern Greece.

Mountainous **Hydra** (Ýdra) ⑪, about 90 minutes out of Piraeus, has just one exquisite town. It is virtually car-free, and mules still haul most of the cargo. The slopes above are forested, with several monasteries to which you can climb; the few beaches must be reached on foot or by boat.

The Ionian Islands

The islands in the Ionian Sea off Greece's west coast are often rainy and thus green, unlike the Aegean's arid outcrops. Best known is **Corfu** (Kérkyra) ⑫, just off the mainland but closer to Italy than Athens. The Venetian-influenced capital of **Kérkyra** is a gem, comparing well to

TIP

The three domestic airways (Olympic, Aegean, Athens Airlines) are largely web-based, and tickets bought from walk-in agents are heavily surcharged. Get online early enough, however, and fares from Athens to the islands can be the same as or less than a ferry cabin berth.

Dining alfresco in Skiáthos Town.

Kefallonian honey makes a great gift.

Dubrovnik further up the Adriatic. Although its beach resorts are often overcrowded, Corfu is big enough to preserve quiet spots, especially in the inland villages on the slopes of Mount Pandokrátor, and the exclusive resorts of the northeast coast. If it all gets too much, escape to the tiny, olive-cloaked satellite islet of **Paxí**.

Kefalloniá ⓭, of late inextricably linked to Captain Corelli and his mandolin, is the largest and most mountainous Ionian island, culminating in fir-covered, 1,628-metre (5,340ft) **Mount Énos**. But Kefalloniá's main business – especially after a 1954 earthquake destroyed its rich architectural heritage – is beaches and the traffic in and out of its little ports. The peninsula beyond westerly Lixoúri, the coast around southeastern Skála, and the photogenic bay of **Mýrtos** on the west coast near **Ássos** and its castle are all sandy, while the northerly port **Fiskárdo** survived the earthquake unscathed.

Old Perithia, on the slopes of Mount Pantokrator, Corfu.

Directly east stretches **Ithaca** (Itháki) island, Odysseus' legendary homeland: it is quieter, with few beaches but three fine harbour villages sympathetically rebuilt after the quake.

Zákynthos ⓮ offers more green mountains and plains, stunning beaches and both good and awful tourist developments. Villages in the mountainous west largely escaped earthquake damage; not so the busy main town. Laganás Bay in the south is a loud and boisterous party resort full of bars catering to young crowds from across Europe, yet just a sandy cove east at unspoilt **Gérakas** on the Vassilikós peninsula, sea turtles lay their eggs.

The Peloponnese

The little isthmus joining the **Peloponnese** (Pelopónnisos) to the mainland is cleft by the deep, narrow **Corinth Canal**; blink and you'll miss it. **Ancient Corinth** ⓯, just beyond its modern namesake, prospered from trans-isthmian haulage in pre-canal days. The Hellenistic city was razed in 146 BC by the Romans but re-founded a century later. What remains is the most complete Roman imperial town in Greece (daily).

The new motorway towards Kalamáta forges southwest from here, while the old highway enters the Argolid Plain at modern **Mykínes**, behind which stands the ancient fortified palace complex of **Mycenae** ⑯ (daily). Heinrich Schliemann excavated here on 1874–6, relying on little other than intuition and the accuracy of Homer's epics. Greek archaeologists had already revealed the citadel's imposing **Lion Gate**, but Schliemann's tomb finds, now in the National Archaeological Museum of Athens (see page 318), amply corroborated Mycenae's Homeric epithet "rich in gold".

Near modern Árgos, further into the Argolid, stands **ancient Árgos** ⑰, among the oldest Greek settlements; notable are the huge, steeply raked classical **theatre** (Tue–Sun), and the Frankish castle atop Lárissa hill, the ancient acropolis. The upmarket resort of **Návplio** ⑱ is overawed by **Akronávplia** just overhead, plus the sprawling, 18th-century **Palamídi**, comprising three self-contained Venetian fortresses. Almost 900 steps lead up from the Old Town to the summit and sweeping views.

The best route southwest takes in **Spárti**, successor to ancient Sparta, and the Byzantine strongholds of **Mystrás** ⑲, with exquisite ruined palaces and frescoed monasteries. Atmospheric, walled **Monemvasiá**, a mini-Gibraltar southeast of Spárti, was the port of Mystrás and later an important Venetian stronghold. A drive west over the mountains from Spárti leads to **Kalamáta**, of little intrinsic interest but the gateway to **Messinía** with its balmy climate, fine beaches, more Venetian castles at **Koróni** and **Methóni** and (unsurprisingly) a huge expat population.

Proceeding north along the coast brings you to **ancient Olympia** ⑳ (daily). For almost two millennia, the religious sanctuary here hosted that most prestigious of pan-Hellenic athletic competitions, the Olympic Games. The most salient

The port of Fiskárdo on Kefalloniá is a beautiful spot to stay, although expensive in high season.

Antísamos beach in Kefalloniá.

EAT

Because of the Orthodox tradition of avoiding meat or fish during fasts, traditional cooking includes quite a variety of vegetarian dishes, especially on Crete. One Cretan speciality is *Ladera*, artichokes and broad beans cooked in olive oil.

monuments are the **Palaestra**, the Archaic **Hera Temple**, the enormous **Zeus Temple**, and the **stadium** with its vaulted entrance.

The Cycládes

Adorning the central Aegean, the 24 inhabited **Cycládes** are the original island-hopping archipelago; in summer, inter-island boats (and flights from Athens) make connections easy. On **Sýros** ㉑, the elegant, Unesco-listed town of Ermoúpoli is capital of the group; **Mýkonos** ㉒, just across a strait and veteran of around half a century of concentrated tourism, offers the quintessential Cycladic profile of marshmallow windmills and churches, plus sybaritic beaches. **Páros** ㉓ is a marginally calmer place for beginners, with a bit of everything in a more expansive landscape. Just east lies **Náxos** ㉔, largest of the Cycládes, with high ridges, fertile farmland, great (if sometimes windy) beaches and labyrinthine Naxos Town, with Venetian fortifications and mansions. Beyond, the last of the Cycládes before Crete and the

Oia Town on Santoríni.

Dodecanese, **Amorgós** ㉕ is long, narrow and steep-sided, with a cult following for its excellent walking on cobbled trails and 11th-century monastery of Hozoviótissa, clinging limpet-like to a sheer cliff.

A separate ferry line threads through the westerly islands; **Sífnos** ㉖, with its multiple villages and white monasteries and culinary tradition, is the busiest. Boats continue to **Síkinos** and **Folégandros**, once (like Amorgós) used to exile political dissidents but now celebrated for their unspoilt architecture and way of life. Transport converges on **Santoríni** (Thíra) ㉗, most famous (and visited) of the group aside from Mýkonos. About 3,500 years ago this volcano-island erupted cataclysmically, leaving only a submerged caldera and high, banded cliffs of a remnant isle behind. It is considered to be the inspiration for Atlantis, the utopia-city lost beneath the waves; myth perhaps meets fact at **Akrotíri** on Santoríni's south cape, a Minoan town that was preserved Pompeii-like under volcanic ash.

Crete

Crete (Kríti) **28**, Greece's largest island, could probably just survive as an independent country (certainly proud Cretans think so). It has a vibrant folk culture, a strong regional cuisine, atmospheric Ottoman-Venetian harbour towns on the north coast, and sheltered beach resorts, mostly on the south shore. Crete also produces – as the British writer Saki (H.H. Munro) noted wryly – "more history than can be consumed locally", from the Minoan culture of the 2nd millennium BC to one of the fiercest battles of World War II. Start at the reconstructed Minoan palace complex of **Knossos** **29** (daily) outside the capital Iráklio (Heraklion), a monument as much to the personal whims of excavator Sir Arthur Evans (including an unlikely colour scheme) as to this vanished people. To appreciate it fully, try to visit Iráklio's outstanding **Archaeological Museum**, although currently several rooms may be closed.

Iráklio, except for its medieval centre, is not the most alluring of Cretan towns; for those head instead west to Réthymno **30** and Haniá **31** , each with postcard-perfect old harbour districts lined with Venetian buildings, fortifications and graceful Ottoman mosques. East of Haniá is Crete's biggest resort, the full-on party town of Mália, location for a British TV reality show titled Sex on the Beach. Further east again, Ágios Nikólaos is also well established on the tourist trail, but prettier, with an old harbour, and much more tranquil.

Inland, the countryside is dotted with monasteries – the most celebrated being **Arkádi** near Réthymno – and hundreds of little frescoed Byzantine and post-Byzantine churches. Nature-lovers will find beaches in all sizes and consistencies – the busiest resorts on the south coast, still much lower-key than those on the north, are **Plakiás**, **Agía Galíni** and **Paleóchora**   and challenging hiking in the **Lefká Óri** (White Mountains) above Haniá. You can traverse the 18km (11-mile) **Gorge of Samariá** – the longest and deepest in Europe, and also thought to be one of the continent's most scenic – for just a taste of a day in the

Iráklio's Archaeological Museum has the most magnificent collection of Minoan art; here is the Phaistos Disc, dating from the 2nd millennium BC.

The Palace of Knossos, Crete.

A fisherman untangles his nets in the sun.

The barren caldera at Níssyros.

life of a Cretan shepherd or World War II resistance fighter. The hike is strenuous, and if you are attempting it independently be sure to pick up information from the tourist office in Haniá and bring enough water and provisions for the day.

The Dodecanese

In the southeast Aegean off the Turkish coast lie the **Dodecanese**, although this group has, in fact, 17 inhabited islands, not 12 as the name implies. **Rhodes** (Ródos) ❷ is the largest, most populated and most crowded, because of its Unesco-listed walled city, vast beaches, and acropolis-castle at **Líndos**. Rhodes is a palimpsest legacy of ancient Greeks, crusading Knights of St John, Ottoman overlords and Italian colonialists. Although the **fortified Old Town** contains a clutch of worthwhile museums, the showcase Street of the Knights and a few prominent mosques whose minarets pierce the skyline, more rewarding are random wanderings along pebble-paved lanes, past medieval houses and under flying buttresses. South of the town, Faliráki is as notorious as Mália on Crete as a place for kids to drink and go wild, but elsewhere around Rhodes you can find much emptier beaches.

Smaller, but still impressive, islands lie a day trip (or longer) away: **Hálki** and **Sými** with their stage-set port towns built from sponge-diving wealth, and **Kárpathos** with its natural grandeur and tenaciously retained traditional life.

On the second-largest Dodecanese, **Kós** ❸, a 1933 earthquake devastated most of **Kós Town** but allowed Italian archaeologists to excavate the ancient city. Thus, much of the town centre is an archaeological park, with the **Roman Agora** (the eastern excavation) lapping up to the 18th-century **Loggia Mosque**, the millennial **Plane Tree of Hippocrates** and the **Nerantziás** castle.

In the western excavation stand the *cardo* (main colonnaded street) and some excellent mosaics. The most sheltered beaches line the coast facing southeast towards the volcano-island of **Níssyros**, a popular day-trip destination with its photogenic villages.

Northwest from Kós are smaller islands that are governed from rambunctious **Kálymnos**, all with prominent castles and distinctive vernacular architecture. **Astypálea**, close to Amorgós, seems more like a Cycladic island, as does **Pátmos** ㉞, at the fringes of the group, with its volcanic scenery and fine beaches. But Pátmos is best known for its sumptuous *hóra* (Old Town) clustered around the massive walls of the monastery of **St John the Theologian** (daily), one of the most revered sites in the Orthodox world.

Northeast Aegean Islands

Beyond Pátmos, **Sámos** ㉟ boasts two high mountains, hill villages amidst wine terraces, emerald waters and a superb **Archaeological Museum** (Tue–Sun) showcasing items from the Archaic Sanctuary of Hera. **Híos** ㊱ exhibits outstanding domestic architecture in its fortified mastic villages, designed by the Genoese to protect the precious resin extracted from the mastic bush. More preserved medieval villages face the west coast, culminating in **Vólissos** with

its castle overlooking fabulous beaches.

Lésvos ㊲ is a major olive-producing centre, but also draws visitors with its thermal springs, and resorts like **Mólyvos**, **Plomári** and **Skála Eressoú**, the last a mecca for lesbians due to Sappho having been born there. The capital Mytilíni's **Archaeological Museum** (Tue–Sun) houses superb Roman mosaics. Languorous **Límnos** ㊳ has the best beaches in the group, exceptional food and wine, and a Byzantine-Genoese castle dominating the port-capital, **Mýrina**.

Samothráki ㊴ to the northeast has an ominous, legend-cloaked mountain to climb, and the mysterious **Sanctuary of the Kabiri** (daily) at its base. **Thássos** ㊵, which, like Samothráki, is most reliably accessed from the north mainland, offers beaches and characterful hill villages, although not much pine forest since a series of devastating fires.

Island-hopping is easy to do in the Dodecanese.

The resort of Mólyvos, on Lésvos.

WILDLIFE OF EUROPE

The animals and plants of Western Europe are surprisingly varied, and some regions extremely wild – despite the best efforts of generations of inhabitants to tame the continent – and support an impressive natural diversity.

Centuries of development have cut vast swathes through the natural habitats of Western Europe, but the area still retains a remarkably wide range of wildlife. Remote mountainous or infertile corners hold rich pockets of virtually pristine biodiversity, but agricultural and even urban areas can turn up real surprises.

The best parts of the Mediterranean Sea and the wilder Atlantic coasts still harbour whales, dolphins and sharks. Inland, the desiccated regions of Spain, Italy and Greece are a few degrees short of being deserts, and have fauna to match: trumpeter finches, sandgrouse, scorpions and a variety of vultures. Centuries of grazing and browsing have created the *maquis* and *garrigue* scrublands of the Mediterranean, which teem with insects, orchids and reptiles.

There are still deep, dark forests in Western Europe. None could be called truly natural, but some corners remain undisturbed enough for brown bears to subsist in small numbers.

Where farming is of low intensity, ancient hedgerows, pastures and meadows exist alongside woodland, wetlands and open waters to provide a microcosm of the natural habitats that were once present across the continent. Though the larger fauna have long gone, such places can provide engrossing interest for the visiting naturalist.

And to cap it all, Europe's mountains are vast regions with a great many endemic species – plants and insects in particular – that have developed in geographical isolation.

A spectacle reminiscent of Africa's Rift Valley: at least 10,000 greater flamingos breed on the salt pans of the Camargue in France.

Sea turtles were quite common in the eastern Mediterranean, but are decreasing as tourists take over the beaches where they lay their eggs.

Eurasian griffon vultures are numerous in the Cévennes in France, where there has been a very successful reintroduction programme.

Although on the increase in mountain areas, the wolf's nocturnal habits and huge territories mean it is rarely seen. It is prone to taking livestock, which inevitably leads to conflicts with farmers.

RESERVED FOR NATURE

Western Europe is now peppered with national parks, nature reserves and other protected areas, although the conservation of its natural heritage only became widespread in the last 40 years. While each country has its own laws, powerful EU legislation now spotlights the most significant habitats and species, and huge areas of member states are being designated.

Doñana National Park in southern Spain is among the natural showpieces of Europe. Its 40 pardel lynx comprise almost a fifth of the remaining population of the world's most endangered feline. An estimated 8 million birds breed, migrate through or winter on the site annually.

Few mountain parks can better the magnificent Pyrenees National Park for spectacular vistas, populated by bearded vultures and dozens of rare plants.

Abruzzo National Park in Italy's Apennines was a refuge for Western Europe's persecuted wolves. With protection, their fortunes have reversed, and there are even a very few wolves in France.

Of Western Europe's many orchid species, Lady's Slipper is one of the most distinctive. It is generally rare in the lowlands but more common in mountain woodlands.

...e of the truly dramatic plants around the Mediterranean is ...s monstrous Arum, over 1 metre (3ft) tall, with a livid ...rple flower and a terrible smell of rotting meat.

There are many chameleon species in Africa and Asia, but just one has a toehold in Europe. It inhabits sand dunes and trees along the southern Iberian coast, and has also been introduced to a few other sites elsewhere in the Mediterranean.

RICARD

Liqueur

Kas

HORCHATA DE CHUFA

cha

Anisette
BENDOR

AMADEUS
MOZART

SKOL

International
LAGER

Mirador on Mallorca's west coast.

Hillside village in Valencia.

SPAIN

A relaxed atmosphere, plenty of sun, and towns
with a medieval flavour all help give Spain its
inimitable down-to-earth appeal.

*Flamenco comes from
southern Spain.*

Continental Spain covers about four-fifths of the Iberian peninsula, Europe's south-west corner on the sunny side of the Pyrenees. The other fifth belongs to Portugal, and a few square miles at its extreme tip is Gibraltar, which belongs, somewhat contentiously, to the United Kingdom. Spain is divided into 50 provinces, grouped into 17 semi-autonomous regions, one of which is the Balearic Islands in the Mediterranean, and another the Canary Islands in the Atlantic (not featured in this book). Some of the regions, especially the Basque Country and Catalonia, have very distinct identities and use their own languages.

With an area of 505,000 sq km (195,000 sq miles), the country is Europe's second-largest after France.

From the wet Atlantic coast in the north, which has often been compared to Ireland, to the desert of Almería province in the southeast corner, Spain is a country of great contrasts. It is the most mountainous country in Europe after Switzerland, and much of its landscape is breathtakingly vast. It is a land of illusion: in the clear, bright air the windmills on the horizon seem close enough to touch, and nearly every journey is longer than it appears on the map. It has thousands of romantic castles and a number of splendid cities where old town quarters seem locked in the 16th century.

At the heart of the central plateau, or *meseta,* which covers 40 percent of the country, is Madrid. Established as the capital in the 16th century, it is as far inland as you can get. Its great rival, Barcelona, Spain's second city, is the largest metropolis on the Mediterranean. Other cities that should be on any itinerary are Valencia, Seville, Granada, Córdoba, Salamanca, Bilbao and the pilgrimage shrine of Santiago de Compostela. But for most visitors, cities and scenery come second to Spain's greatest natural asset: the beaches along its famous coastlines, especially the Balearics, the Costa del Sol, Costa Blanca and Costa Brava.

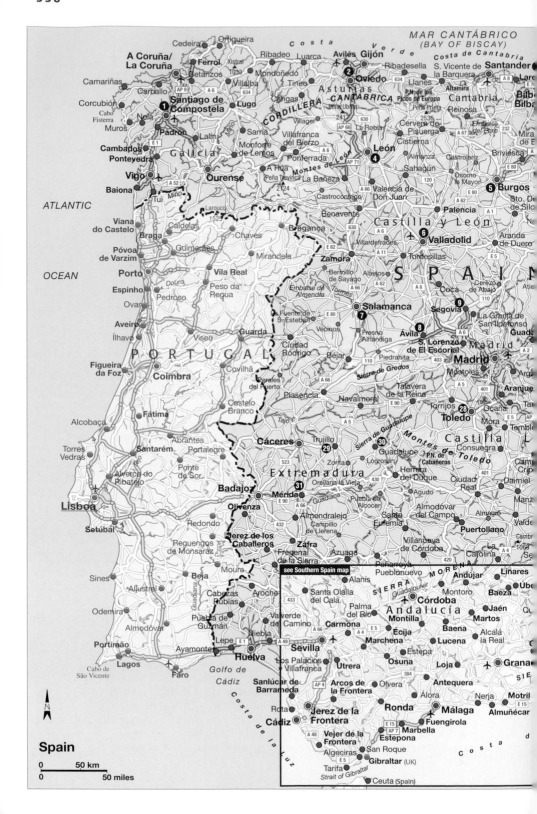

Spain

0   50 km

0   50 miles

Madrid

0   200 m
0   200 yds

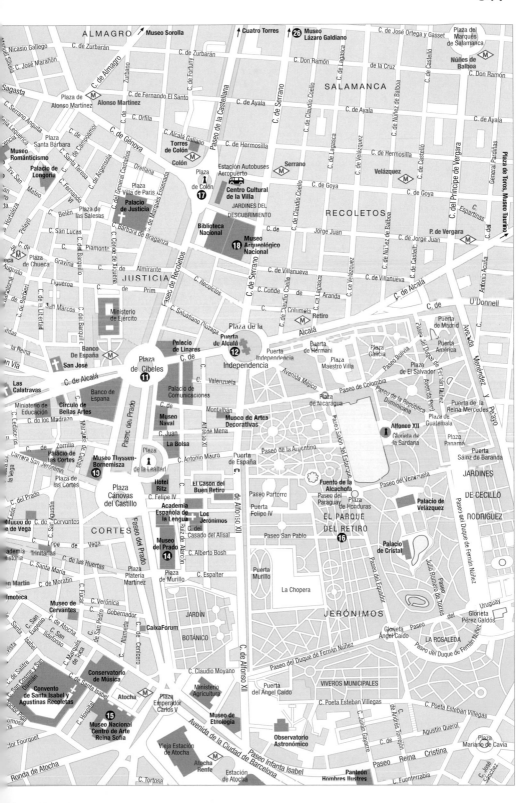

ALMAGRO   ↗ Museo Sorolla   ↑ Cuatro Torres   26 Museo Lázaro Galdiano   C. de José Ortega y Gasset   Plaza del Marqués de Salamanca

C. Nicasio Gallego   C. de Zurbarán   C. de Zurbarán   C. Don Ramón   de la Cruz   M Núñes de Balboa

C. José Marañón   Zurbano   C. de Almagro   C. de Fortuny   C. Don Ramón,   C. de Castelló   C. Don Ramón

Sagasta   Plaza de Alonso Martínez M Alonso Martínez   C. de Fernando El Santo   SALAMANCA

C. Serrano Anguita   C. de Orfila   C. Alcalá Galiano   C. de Ayala   C. de Ayala

Plaza Santa Bárbara   C. de Génova   C. de Hermosilla   C. de Ayala

Museo Romántismo   C. de Campoamor   Torres de Colón   C. de Lagasca   Velázquez M

Palacio de Longoria   Colón   C. de Goya   C. de Goya

Estación Autobuses Aeropuerto   Serrano M

Plaza de Colón 17   Centro Cultural de la Villa   RECOLETOS

Palacio de Justicia   JARDINES DEL DESCUBRIMIENTO   P. de Vergara

Biblioteca Nacional   C. de Jorge Juan

JUSTICIA   18 Museo Arqueológico Nacional   C. de Villanueva   C. de Villanueva   U'Donnell

Ministerio de Ejército   Retiro   C. de Alcalá

Plaza de la Alcalá   Puerta de Madrid

Banco De España M   Palacio de Linares   Puerta de Alcalá 12   Puerta Independencia   Puerta de Hernani   Plaza Galicia   Puerta América

San José   Plaza de Cibeles 11   Independencia   Plaza Maestro Villa   Plaza de El Salvador

Las Calatravas   C. de Alcalá   Banco de España   Palacio de Comunicaciones   Valenzuela   Avenida Méjico   Paseo de Colombia

Ministerio de Educación   Círculo de Bellas Artes   Museo Naval   Museo de Artes Decorativas   Plaza de Nicaragua   Alfonso XII   Puerta de la Reina Mercedes

Palacio de las Cortes   La Bolsa   Paseo de la Argentina   Glorieta de la Sardana   Plaza Panamá

13 Museo Thyssen-Bornemisza   Puerta de España   Puerta Sáinz de Baranda

Plaza Cánovas del Castillo   Hotel Ritz   El Casón del Buen Retiro   Paseo Partcrrc   JARDINES DE CECILIO RODRIGUEZ

CORTES   Academia Española de la Lengua   Los Jerónimos   Puerta Felipe IV   EL PARQUE DEL RETIRO 16   Palacio de Velázquez

Museo del Prado 14   Casado del Alisal   C. Alberto Bosch   Palacio de Cristal

Plaza Platería Martínez   Plaza de Murillo   C. Espalter   Puerta Murillo

Museo de Cervantes   La Chopera

CaixaForum   JARDIN BOTÁNICO   JERÓNIMOS   LA ROSALEDA

Conservatorio de Música   Glorieta Ángel Caído   Glorieta Pérez Galdós

Convento de Santa Isabel y Agustinas Recoletas   Atocha M   Plaza Emperador Carlos V   Ministerio Agricultura   VIVEROS MUNICIPALES

15 Museo Nacional Centro de Arte Reina Sofía   Museo de Etnología   C. Poeta Esteban Villegas   Plaza Mariano de Cavia

Vieja Estación de Atocha   Observatorio Astronómico   Paseo Infanta Isabel

Ronda de Atocha   Atocha Renfe   Estación de Atocha   Pantéon Hombres Ilustres   Reina Cristina

MADRID

Europe's loftiest capital has some splendid monuments from its regal past, enticing shopping streets and a lively population who like to stay out late.

Madrid is the geographical centre of mainland Spain. At 655 metres (2,150ft) above sea level, it is the highest capital in Europe, with a population of 3.3 million. Situated on Spain's central plateau and surrounded by mountains, it has not only been climatically sheltered from maritime influences, but culturally and socially insulated as well.

In the 10th century the future capital of Spain was a Moorish fortress named Majerit, which, a century later, was captured by Alfonso VI, King of Castile. In 1561, during Spain's Golden Age of empire, Philip II moved his residence here from nearby Toledo. He never explained the reasons why – other cities were then much more important – but, except for the brief period between 1601 and 1607 when Philip III moved to Valladolid, it has remained the capital ever since. In 1808, the French invaded Spain and installed Joseph Bonaparte, Napoleon's brother, on the Spanish throne. The city rose in rebellion. In his paintings *Dos de Mayo, 1808* and *Tres de Mayo, 1808*, in the Prado Museum, Goya chronicles the gruesome street battles and reprisals that cost more than 1,000 lives. The resulting Peninsular War, known in Spain as the War of Independence, brought British troops under the command of the Duke of Wellington to Spain's side

and the conflict dragged on until 1814, when the French were finally defeated.

The city was again besieged in November 1936, three months after General Franco's Nationalist uprising against the Republican government. Intense fighting took place in the southern suburbs and all around the western edge of Madrid, especially in the university. Nationalist artillerymen took their sights from the recently built hotels on the avenue of the Gran Vía, and the central post office sustained 155 direct hits, but the

Main Attractions

Puerta del Sol
Plaza Mayor
Palacio Real
Museo Thyssen-Bornemisza
Museo del Prado
Centro de Arte Reina Sofía
Parque del Retiro
El Escorial

Cervantes memorial, Plaza de España.

city did not succumb until 28 March 1939. Franco remained in power until his death in 1975, when the monarchy was restored under King Juan Carlos.

Heart of the city

Most of Madrid's sightseeing attractions are intimately linked with its history as a royal residence and the centre of a vanished empire. The oldest part of the city is the area between the Palacio Real (Royal Palace) and the Paseo del Prado. It embraces the Plaza Mayor, the Puerta del Sol and the districts of La Latina and Lavapiés. The chaotic arrangement of narrow streets and small irregular squares has changed little since the 17th century.

The centre of this area, of Madrid, and in a sense of the whole of Spain, is the **Puerta del Sol** ❶, the site of a city gate that disappeared in the 16th century. Today it is Madrid's Times Square, where Metro and bus lines, as well as major roads, converge. On New Year's Eve, revellers gather here to tick off the final seconds of the old year and usher in the new with the tradition of *las uvas*, the grapes. The idea is to swallow one with each stroke of the midnight clock. The occupation of the square on 15 March 2011 by young *indignados* ("the angry") protesting at austerity measures imposed due to the economic crisis helped inspire the worldwide Occupy movement.

In its younger days the **Plaza Mayor** ❷, a square just to the west surrounded by 17th-century townhouses, saw tournaments and bullfights, political gatherings, book burnings, and an occasional hanging or *auto da fé*. With the passing of time it has become the scene of coin and stamp fairs on a Sunday morning, theatrical productions in summer, and fiesta celebrations. In the centre of the square stands a statue of Philip III.

Not far south of the Plaza Mayor is the gloomy 17th-century former cathedral of **San Isidro** ❸, where the bones of Madrid's patron saint lie. Keep going in the same direction and you come to the site of the **Rastro,** Madrid's animated Sunday flea market. If you're hoping to find a bargain, arrive before 11am, and watch out for pickpockets.

Plaza Mayor in spring.

In the midst of central Madrid there are also two enclosed convents of nuns, still functioning, their interiors – which can be visited – almost entirely unchanged since they were first established in the 17th century. Heading north from the Plaza Mayor across Calle Mayor and Calle del Arenal you come to the **Monasterio de las Descalzas Reales** ❹ (Tue–Sun), a royal convent where many Habsburg princesses and aristocrats became nuns, with an impressive collection of art treasures. Nearby, the **Real Monasterio de la Encarnación** ❺ (Tue–Sun) was founded by the wife of Philip II, and has a renowned reliquary.

Across the Plaza del Oriente is the **Palacio Real** ❻ (daily). Built between 1738 and 1764 after the earlier Baroque palace of Philip II had burnt down, it was designed by Italian architects in the ornate Neoclassical style then fashionable in Italy and France. The palace is quite conventional to look at from the outside, but inside it is overwhelming. Sumptuous and elegant, this is one of the most splendid palaces in Europe; it has more than 2,000 rooms, but only some are open to the public. The highlights are the immense great staircase and Hall of Columns with ceiling frescoes by Tiepolo, the lavish apartments of Charles III such as Sala Gasparini, the throne room and the dining room. King Juan Carlos and Queen Sofía do not live here, but frequently use the palace for receptions and gala banquets. The inner courtyard has statues of the Roman emperors Trajan, Hadrian, Theodosius and Honorius, who were all born in Spain.

On the south side of the palace is the **Catedral de Nuestra Señora de la Almudena** ❼, Madrid's cathedral, consecrated by Pope John Paul II in 1995, 110 years after it was begun.

From the Plaza de España to Cibeles

The focal point of the west end of Madrid is the **Plaza de España** ❽, where larger-than-life statues of Don Quixote and his faithful servant Sancho Panza ride into the sunset. Looming up above the square is the

Dining hours in Madrid – as in most of Spain – are particular: lunch is normally around 2pm, dinner from 8.30–9pm, and in the summer heat, or at weekends, hours can be even later. Do not expect any decent Spanish restaurant to serve full meals much before 12.30 at lunchtime, or 8pm in the evening. Tapas bars of course are open through the day, as are bland chain restaurants. After dinner, people think nothing of going out for a drink at around 11pm or midnight.

Metro sign in the busy Puerta del Sol, the heart of the city.

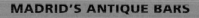

MADRID'S ANTIQUE BARS

Madrid has a prodigious variety of bars to choose from, and while the trend is towards contemporary and cutting-edge design, of perennial popularity are the city's old-fashioned *tabernas* (taverns), dating from the 19th or early 20th centuries. Before the days of television, *tabernas* provided homes from home for *madrileños* to congregate and discuss politics, intellectual matters, football or whatever was going on around them.

Around 100 original *tabernas* survive, mostly in the old part of the city. Some have beautiful tilework outside and dim, atmospheric interiors with old chairs and tables and shining zinc countertops. Classic examples include **Taberna de Antonio Sánchez** (Calle del Mesón de Paredes 13), **Angel Sierra** (Plaza de Chueca), **La Dolores** (Plaza de Jesús), **Casa Labra** (Calle Tetuán 12) and **El Abuelo** (Calle Victoria 12). Most *tabernas* serve food – tapas at least – as well as wines and other drinks, but a few have become renowned restaurants in their own right, notably **El Botín** (Calle de los Cuchilleros 17, off the Plaza Mayor) and **La Bola** (Calle Bola 5), both of which specialise in Madrid's traditional warming winter stew, *cocido madrileño*.

Recently, new *tabernas* have been created in the spirit of the real thing, and you may be hard put to tell the difference between the authentically old and the modern re-creation.

TIP

The most traditional way to get bullfight tickets is just to go to the taquillas (ticket windows) at the Plaza de las Ventas, but they can now be bought online, through www.lasventas.com (Spanish-only) or through agencies such as www.ticketstoros.com, which sells tickets for bullrings throughout Spain.

The Palacio Real.

Edificio España, a prestige project built under the Franco regime in the 1950s, combining a skyscraper with neo-Baroque Spanish Golden Age decoration. A short walk from here is the **Parque del Oeste**, in which stands the 4th-century BC **Templo de Debod ⑨** (Tue–Sun), a gift to Spain from the Egyptian government. Further into the park, the *Rosaleda* or rose garden is gorgeous when in full bloom in spring, while a **Teleférico** or cable car (daily) runs from the park across the River Manzanares to Madrid's largest open space in the former royal hunting estate of the **Casa de Campo**, with great views en route.

The Plaza de España marks one end of Madrid's principal street, the **Gran Vía ⑩**, which has some magnificent buildings along it in an intriguing mix of 20th-century styles, particularly near its junction with the Calle de Alcalá. This in turn leads to the city's emblematic traffic hub, the **Plaza de Cibeles ⑪**, at the top of the Paseo del Prado, with a fountain with a statue of the goddess Cybele in a chariot drawn by lions. Dominating

the plaza is the extraordinary white mass of the **Palacio de Cibeles**, which since 2011 contains Madrid's city hall. Still better known to locals as the Palacio de Comunicaciones or just correos (the post office), it was built in 1904–18 as the central post office, on a scale and in a hotch-potch of styles – Neo-Gothic, Neo-Baroque, Austrian Art Nouveau – that symbolised the ambitions of Spain's governing elite during one of their boom times. The equally grand main hall inside now contains an imaginative cultural centre, **CentroCentro** (Tue–Sun), and visitors can also examine the opulent stained glass and soaring columns and go up to the highest tower for a panoramic view.

A short way up the continuation of the Calle de Alcalá is another of Madrid's landmarks, the **Puerta de Alcalá ⑫**, an 18th-century monumental gateway. To the north, the grid-pattern streets make up the wealthy neighbourhood of **Salamanca**, which contains Madrid's most fashionable shopping area, especially around Calle Serrano. On its eastern edge is

the **Plaza de las Ventas**, the Hispanic world's most prestigious bullring.

Art treasures

Madrid's greatest attractions for visitors are its three major museums of art, all within a short stroll of each other. Heading down the Paseo del Prado from Plaza de Cibeles, you soon come to the first great art gallery, the **Museo Thyssen-Bornemisza** ⑬ (Tue–Sun) in the Palacio Villahermosa. The collection, amassed by the German Baron Thyssen-Bornemisza, gives a remarkable overview of Western art, from the Renaissance and German 16th-century portraits through Italian Mannerists – Caravaggio's awe-inspiring *Saint Catherine of Alexandria* – to Goya, early American painters and 20th-century Expressionists and pop art.

Across Plaza Cánovas del Castillo is the world's greatest art museums, the **Museo del Prado** ⑭ (Tue–Sun), with holdings of more than 6,000 paintings and sculptures, including a very high proportion of masterpieces. The core of the museum is the Spanish royal collection, amassed from the 15th century

by monarchs such as Charles V and Philip IV who were enthusiastic collectors and employed the greatest artists of their day – Titian, Rubens, Velázquez and others. If time allows for only a brief visit, it should include Francisco de Goya (1746–1828). His work is represented in its full range and shines at its brilliant best on its home turf, with superb images of a unique vigour and intensity. A first visit should also include the works of Spain's other celebrated artists, Diego Velázquez (1599–1660) and El Greco (1541–1614),

The new wing of the Prado, designed by Rafael Moneo, has been described as "quietly heroic".

Painted fresco ceiling at El Escorial.

although El Greco is seen to better advantage in his adopted hometown of Toledo (see page 369). Among the unmissable works of Velázquez are *Las Meninas* (The Maids of Honour), *Las Handeras* (The Spinners) and *Los Borrachos* (The Drunkards).

The Prado has still not entirely finished an expansion programme, the biggest change in its history, consisting of the addition of an all-new modern wing by architect Rafael Moneo (dubbed by locals El Cubo de Moneo, Moneo's Cube) and the incorporation of the Gothic former church of the **Jerónimos**, alongside the Cube, and of the **Casón del Buen Retiro**, a much-restored pavilion of the former Retiro palace. The Cube and the Jerónimos are used as additional space for temporary exhibitions and for showing more of the museum's non-Spanish paintings (Titian, Veronese, Rubens), while the Casón has given room to expand for the Prado's illustrious art library. It is also planned for the museum to restore and take over the **Salón de Reinos**, the finest surviving part of the Retiro palace and the original location of Velázquez's grand equestrian portraits of the Habsburg royal family, but due to the financial crisis this is unlikely to be completed for some time.

To get to the last of the trio of art galleries, continue down the Paseo del Prado. The **Centro de Arte Reina Sofía** ⑮ (Wed–Mon) is a showcase of modern art. It houses Picasso's *Guernica*, a depiction of the obliteration of a Basque town by Nazi war planes during Spain's civil war. Once the city hospital, the building has been dramatically renovated to house works by 20th-century Spanish masters Dalí and Miró, as well as Picasso. It also has a lively programme of contemporary exhibitions.

For a delightful respite from sightseeing and the summer heat, Madrid's main park, **El Retiro** ⑯, is conveniently located a few streets behind the Prado. The park began life in the 1630s as the gardens of the Palacio del Buen Retiro, a giant palace-complex built for King Philip IV that was mostly destroyed in the Napoleonic Wars. Open to all since 1868, the gardens

El Retiro, Madrid's main park.

have many shady areas to explore, including, at the centre, the grand **Estanque** or boating lake, and three pavilions that host attractive free art exhibits, the **Casa de Vacas**, **Palacio de Velázquez** and the glass-walled **Palacio de Cristal**.

Paseo de la Castellana

Modern Madrid could be said to start at the **Plaza de Colón** ⑰, north of Plaza de Cibeles. Here the Paseo de Recoletos, a continuation of Paseo del Prado, turns in the Paseo de la Castellana, the immense multi-lane main artery that runs north right up through the newer areas and its main business centres of Madrid to culminate in the stunning **Cuatro Torres**, four skyscrapers completed in 2007–9, which can be viewed from Chamartín railway station.

Some of Madrid's most interesting museums are off the southern sections of the Paseo de la Castellana. Behind the Plaza de Colón is Spain's national antiquities museum, the **Museo Arqueológico Nacional** ⑱ (Tue–Sun), which recently underwent a major renovation. Its prize exhibits include the Iberian statue of the *Dama de Elche* (*Lady of Elche*).

Madrid's quaintest museum is the **Museo Lázaro Galdiano** (Wed–Mon), up Calle de Serrano from the Archaeology Museum. An eclectic private collection displayed in the owners' mansion includes paintings, furniture, enamels, ivories, armour and jewellery.

Just across Paseo de la Castellana from here is the **Museo Sorolla** (Tue–Sun), former home and studio of Spain's best-known Impressionist painter, Joaquín Sorolla. A pleasant villa almost engulfed by modern apartment blocks, it is a good spot to escape from the noise and rush of the city and savour Sorolla's romantic, sun-drenched images.

Days out

Two of Madrid's most popular sights require a day trip from the city, one to the south, one to the north. The royal summer retreat, the **Real Palacio de Aranjuez** (Tue–Sun; guided tours only), made famous by Rodríguez's Guitar Concerto, is 45km (27 miles) south of the capital. Stuffed with portraits and porcelain, the palace's real attraction lies in its setting in 300 hectares (740 acres) of gardens.

San Lorenzo de El Escorial (Tue–Sun) often known simply as El Escorial, 50km (30 miles) northwest of Madrid, is the monstrously grandiose fantasy of Philip II, built between 1563 and 1584. Part palace, part monastery, part church and part pantheon, the king had it built in honour of San Lorenzo, on whose feast day (10 August) in 1557 the Spanish won an important victory over the French at St-Quentin. The Museum of Art houses a very fine collection of Flemish, Italian and Spanish paintings, and the king's library is magnificent. In a country that has always built its cathedrals and monuments in an overwhelming style, El Escorial remains in a class of its own.

TIP

Real Madrid's home stadium – Estadio Santiago Bernabeu – can be visited by guided tour (daily, but not after five hours before a match; bookings through www.realmadrid.com). The tour includes the pitch, presidential box, dressing rooms and trophy room.

The Infanta Margarita in Velázquez's Las Meninas.

Inside the Sagrada Família.

BARCELONA

Almost half the population of the region of Catalonia lives in Barcelona, Spain's second city and one of the most vivacious and stimulating places in Europe.

Spain's principal Mediterranean port is a lively, cosmopolitan city. Although now somewhat smaller than Madrid, it has a distinctive commercial and cultural energy as the capital of Catalonia, an autonomous community of Spain and in effect a country – in most things except official statehood   with a very strong sense of identity. Among other things Catalonia has its own traditions in architecture, and Barcelona is known for its own brand of Art Nouveau, *Modernisme*, and in particular, the strikingly original architectural creations of Antoni Gaudí (1852–1926).

The heart of Barcelona is **Plaça de Catalunya ❶** a broad space that forms the boundary between the medieval city and the 19th-century grid of the **Eixample** (Extension). Seven thoroughfares converge on the square, which hides beneath it major Metro and overground railway stations and the main tourist office. Surrounded by banks and big stores, the square is also a centre of political demonstrations. The large monument in the southwest corner commemorates Francesc Macià, president of the first modern autonomous government of Catalonia within the Spanish Republic of 1931.

The Rambla

The Plaça de Catalunya connects the elegant Rambla de Catalunya with

La Rambla ❷, Barcelona's most famous avenue, which heads 1.2km (¾ mile) down to the port. The *rambla*, a long pedestrian avenue with traffic confined to either side, is perhaps Catalonia's finest architectural invention, and many Catalan towns have one. Barcelona's Rambla began life as a seasonal riverbed alongside a medieval city wall, and developed into the famous promenade more or less by happy accident. It has five parts. The Rambla de Canaletes at the top is named after a drinking fountain,

Main Attractions
La Rambla
Gran Teatre del Liceu
Catedral and Barri Gòtic
Museu Picasso
Casa Batlló
Casa Milà
Sagrada Família
Museu Nacional d'Art de
  Catalunya
Fundació Joan Miró

View from Parc Güell.

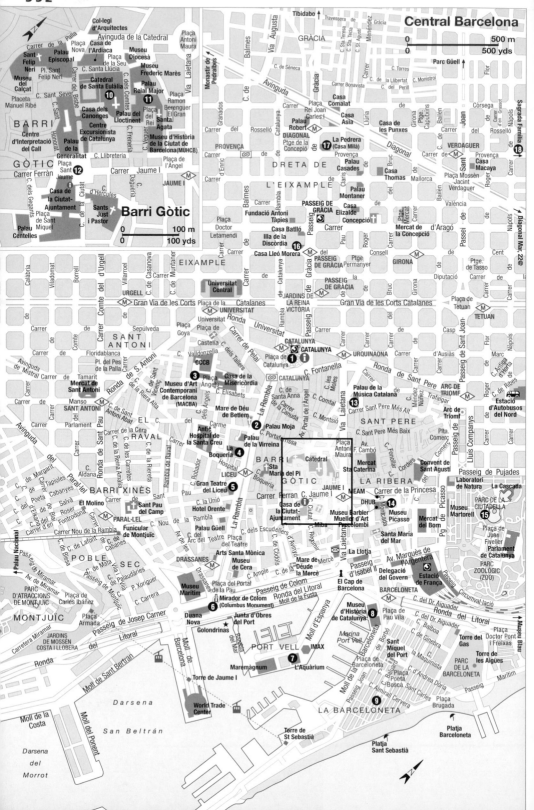

Col·legi d'Arquitectes
Avinguda de la Catedral
Casa de l'Ardiaca
Plaça Nova
Museu Diocesà
Sant Felip Neri
Palau Episcopal
Pl. Sant Felip Neri
Museu Frederic Marès
Museu del Calçat
Placeta Manuel Ribé
Catedral de Santa Eulàlia
Palau Reial Major
Santa Agata
Casa dels Canonges
Palau del Lloctinent
Centre Excursionista de Catalunya
Palau del Rei
Museu d'Història de la Ciutat de Barcelona (MUHCB)
Palau de la Generalitat
Casa de la Ciutat-Ajuntament
Sants Just i Pastor
Palau Centelles
Casa de Sant Miquel

Barri Gòtic

0   100 m
0   100 yds

Central Barcelona

0   500 m
0   500 yds

GRÀCIA
Parc Güell
Sagrada Família
Casa Comalat
Casa Asia
Casa de les Punxes
VERDAGUER
Casa Macaya
La Pedrera (Casa Milà)
Casa Casades
Casa Thomas
Palau Montaner
Casa Elizalde
Fundació Antoni Tàpies
Casa Batlló
Illa de la Discòrdia
Casa Lleó Morera
Mercat de la Concepció
PASSEIG DE GRÀCIA
GIRONA
DRETA DE L'EIXAMPLE
EIXAMPLE
Universitat Central
URGELL
SANT ANTONI
Gran Via de les Corts Catalanes
UNIVERSITAT
Universitat Central
CATALUNYA
Palau de la Música Catalana
SANT PERE
ARC DE TRIOMF
Arc de Triomf
Estació d'Autobusos del Nord
Mercat de Sant Antoni
Museu d'Art Contemporani de Barcelona (MACBA)
CCCB
Casa de la Misericòrdia
Mare de Déu de Betlem
Antic Hospital de la Santa Creu
Palau Moja
Palau de la Virreina
La Boqueria
EL RAVAL
BARRI GÒTIC
Catedral
Sta Caterina
LA RIBERA
Convent de Sant Agustí
Laboratori de Natura
La Cascada
Gran Teatre del Liceu
LICEU
Sta Maria del Pi
JAUME I
MEAM
DHUB
Museu Picasso
Santa Maria del Mar
Mercat del Born
Museu Martorell
PARC DE LA CIUTADELLA
Sant Pau del Camp
BARRI XINÈS
PARAL·LEL
El Molino
Hotel Orient
Casa de la Ciutat-Ajuntament
Miba
Museu Barbier-Mueller d'Art Precolombí
Plaça de Joan Fiveller Parlament de Catalunya
Funicular de Montjuïc
Palau Güell
POBLE SEC
Arts Santa Mònica
Museu de Cera
La Llotja
Delegació del Govern
PARC ZOOLÒGIC (ZOO)
MONTJUÏC
Museu Marítim
Plaça del Portal de la Pau
Mare de Déu de la Mercè
El Cap de Barcelona
Estació de França
Drassanes
Duana Nova
Golondrinas
Mirador de Colom (Columbus Monument)
Junta d'Obres del Port
Museu d'Història de Catalunya
BARCELONETA
Torre del Gas
Torre de les Aigües
World Trade Center
Torre de Jaume I
PORT VELL
IMAX
Maremàgnum
L'Aquàrium
Marina Port Vell
Sant Miquel del Port
PARC DE LA BARCELONETA
Museu Blau
LA BARCELONETA
Platja Barceloneta
Torre de St Sebastià
Platja Sant Sebastià

where Barcelona FC football supporters celebrate victories. Next comes the Rambla dels Estudis, also known as the Rambla dels Ocells (Rambla of the Birds). Canaries, parakeets and other exotic birds, as well as chinchillas, iguanas and terrapins, are on sale here, despite calls for the stalls' closure.

To the right of the Rambla, looking down towards the port, is the **Raval** district, once a byword for poverty and social agitation, and leading to the once-notorious red-light district the Barri Xinès. Since the 1980s major renovation has gone on in the Raval, with new streets and cultural institutions, making much of it trendy rather than down-at-heel. Standing out among the new structures is the emphatically modern white and glass **MACBA** ❸ (Wed–Mon) contemporary art museum, by American architect Richard Meier. Its changing exhibitions of cutting-edge art and installations sometimes seem secondary in attraction to the building itself.

From the Rambla dels Estudis the twitter of birds gives way to the kaleidoscope of a line of flower-stalls in the Rambla de Sant Josep or Rambla de les Flors (Rambla of Flowers), overlooked by the imposing **Palau de la Virreina** (1778). Built for the Viceroy of Peru, it now contains a bookshop and exhibition spaces.

Just beyond is **La Boqueria** ❹, or the Mercat de Sant Josep, Barcelona's justly celebrated main food market. Built in the 1870s, this emporium of iron and stained glass contains all the best food of the season Catalonia has to offer, from mushrooms and truffles to bright fruits, neat piles of vegetables and shimmering fish. Shop before 10am for the best bargains, and try the bars, such as La Garduña, at the market's edge. Outside the market, coloured pavings by Joan Miró in the middle of the Rambla mark the Plaça Boqueria, once just outside the city gates.

The **Gran Teatre del Liceu** ❺ on Rambla dels Caputxins is one of Europe's great opera houses, which

rose from the ashes of a devastating fire in 1994. Opposite is the Cafè de l'Òpera, a delightful 19th-century café.

Below the Liceu, Carrer Nou de la Rambla leads to **Palau Güell** (Tue–Sun), gloomiest of Gaudí's buildings, bristling with dark metalwork. Ten years before it was built, in 1878, Gaudí designed the lamp-posts in **Plaça Reial**, opposite Carrer Nou. With classical, arcaded facades, restaurants, palm trees and a central fountain, this is one of the liveliest squares in the city, though also one where visitors need to be most wary of pickpockets.

The Rambla Santa Mònica is the last wide stretch of promenade before the sea. At weekends craft stalls give this traditionally low-life end of the Rambla an innocent air. The Rambla terminates in front of the 50-metre (160ft) **Colom** ❻, the Columbus Monument (daily), built in 1888. A lift takes visitors to the top for a grand view over the port. Barcelona's seafaring activities can be appreciated with a visit to the **Museu Marítim** (daily), housed in the impressive 13th-century Reials Drassanes (Royal Shipyards).

The Rambla is busy night and day.

At the end of his first American voyage, Columbus is said to have came ashore on the steps in front of his statue, where the *Golondrinas* (pleasure boats) now give trips round the harbour and to the Olympic port. The quay to the right is the Moll de Barcelona, site of the World Trade Centre and the terminal for cruise liners.

After this brief interruption, the Rambla continues in some way as the **Rambla del Mar**, a walkway out over the harbour to the **Moll d'Espanya** quay. Barcelona's inner harbour or **Port Vell** (Old Port) was spectacularly transformed in the 1990s, from a grimy and disused industrial harbour to a smart marina and leisure area, its quays lined with restaurant and café terraces. In the centre on the Moll d'Espanya are the **Maremàgnum** mall, a striking complex whose mirror-walls contain shops, restaurants and nightclubs, shops, an IMAX cinema and the **Aquàrium ❼** (daily), where visitors walk through glass tunnels to see creatures of the deep. The only remaining industrial building on the north side of the port is the warehouse designed by Modernist architect Elies Rogent and now turned into the Palau de Mar, where the **Museu d'Història de Catalunya ❽** (Tue–Sun) tells the story of the region.

Behind it is the fishermen's quarter of **La Barceloneta ❾**, a night-time haunt of good small bars and fish restaurants, extended by the port's renovation with the restaurant terraces beside the Palau de Mar. Barceloneta is the start of the city's 6km (4-mile) beach, which leads past Nova Icària, the former Olympic Village, to the **Port Olìmpic**, a marina entirely created for the 1992 Olympic Games and dominated by twin towers and a huge steel fish, Peix, designed by Frank Gehry for the Games. This stretch is lined with restaurants, bars and clubs that are hugely popular with the young crowds that converge on Barcelona as a prime party city.

The Barri Gòtic

The Barri Gòtic or Gothic Quarter is the oldest part of Barcelona, begun by the Romans and one of the most intact medieval districts in Europe, with

CATALAN WAYS

Visitors to Barcelona who know a little Spanish are often still surprised to find that signs are in another language, Catalan. Many other things – architecture, art, folklore, cuisine – also give Catalonia a very individual flavour.

The language is different because it has a different source. The seeds of Catalonia were in the frontier territories of Charlemagne's Frankish Empire, while Castilian-speaking Spain grew out of communities that took refuge from the Moors in the Cantabrian mountains far to the west. Catalans were good businessmen but poor state-builders: Barcelona merchants traded across the medieval Mediterranean, but politically were part of a complex amalgam called the "Crown of Aragon". When the Spanish kingdoms were united under one crown, the Habsburg monarchs naturally preferred the centralised power of Castile to this mass of local rights. Even so, Catalonia's institutions were only abolished, by force, and Castilian Spanish imposed as the language of public affairs in 1715.

Differences grew in the 19th century, when Catalonia embarked on the Industrial Revolution, while much of Spain ignored it, and simultaneously experienced its Renaixença or renaissance of Catalan language and culture. This multi-faceted outburst of energy culminated in the brief re-establishment of an autonomous Catalan government, the Generalitat, under the 1931 Republic. Conservative Spanish nationalists, though, have always regarded Catalanism with special venom, and the Franco dictatorship set out determinedly to suppress the language and other Catalan symbols. It was under Franco that Barcelona Football Club took on its special status as an outlet for Catalan identity.

Since Catalan autonomy was regained with democracy in 1980, many problems seem to have been resolved. Catalan is again the primary language in much of public life, although this has also created difficulties, especially in Barcelona, with the many people who primarily speak Spanish. Tensions have reached a new high, too, with the current financial crisis. The Spanish conservatives who rule in Madrid get few votes in Catalonia, and many Catalans feel their policies treat Catalonia virtually as a colony. Around 50 percent of Catalans now favour outright independence, though how to achieve it is an open question.

thick-walled buildings, narrow lanes and heavy doorways. The **Catedral de Santa Eulàlia** ❿ is built near the high point of Mons Taber, selected by the Romans for their settlement. To the right of the main entrance is the Romanesque Capella de Santa Llúcia, dating from 1268. The cloisters are not to be missed; this shady quadrangle surrounds a garden of ferns, tropical plants and a family of geese, which has lorded it here for centuries.

Behind the cathedral and cloisters is a wonderful network of stone alleys and courtyards. Carrer dels Comtes, on the left, leads to the **Museu Frederic Marès** (Tue–Sun), an eccentric museum assembled by a private collector, with eclectic items from religious art and sculpture to fans and cigar labels. Beyond it, the various sections of the **Palau Reial Major** ⓫, the royal palace of the medieval Count-Kings (since they were Counts of Barcelona, but Kings of Aragon) surround the loveliest of the city's Gothic squares, the **Plaça del Rei**. This was not one palace but a hotch-potch of buildings, assembled from the 12th to the 15th centuries. They are now part of the **Museu d'Història de la Ciutat** (Tue–Sun), entered through the Palau Clariana Padellàs just beyond the square. Visitors can walk up the steps to the 36-metre (120ft) **Saló de Tinell**, built in 1370 and a superbly proportioned space where Ferdinand and Isabella greeted Columbus on his return from America. Beside the hall is the 14th-century royal chapel of **Santa Agata**, with a fine altarpiece from 1464 by Jaume Huguet, and you can also climb up the tall, angular 15th-century **watchtower** of King Martí I that soars above the square. Another great attraction of the museum is the opportunity to descend into the basement to wander through a remarkable cluster of Roman streets and walls that have been excavated beneath the medieval city.

Between the Cathedral and Plaça del Rei is **Plaça Sant Jaume** ⓬, the city's political hub, with the **Palau de la Generalitat**, the seat of Catalonia's government, on one side and the **Casa de la Ciutat**, home of the city council, on the other. The Palau de la Generalitat opens up on the day of Catalonia's patron saint St George, 23 April, when its Gothic patios are decorated with roses. Behind the Generalitat building was the medieval **Jewish Quarter** or Call, which occupied the streets between Carrer del Call and Carrer Banys Nous. A Hebrew inscription on the wall of No. 1 Carrer Marlet dates from 692. The Jews were forced from the city in 1424.

La Ribera and the Picasso Museum

East of the Via Laietana, cut through the Old City in the 1900s, are two more of Barcelona's most atmospheric districts, **Sant Pere** and **La Ribera**. In the former, furthest from the port, is the **Palau de la Música Catalana** ⓭, an extraordinary *Modernist* concert hall designed by Lluís Domènech i Montaner (1850–1923) in 1908, a riot of decoration in brick, stained glass and vibrant mosaics, both inside and

The Palau de la Música Catalana.

EAT

Some of the best places to find good tapas in Barcelona are on Carrer Montcada, right by the Museu Picasso. Bar del Pla on the corner with Carrer Princesa has excellent classics (patatas bravas, mussels and more), and the Euskal Etxea at the bottom of the street has delicious, more varied Basque-style tapas.

View of Barcelona, with the green thoroughfare of the Rambla on the left.

out. Towards the harbour, La Ribera was the commercial heart of Barcelona when it was one of the great trading cities of the medieval Mediterranean. Its noblest street is the fascinating Carrer Montcada, a narrow walkway lined with 13th–16th-century merchant palaces. Palau Berenguer d'Aguilar, built in the 15th century by Marc Safont, is one of the finest, and with the adjoining Palau Castellet and Palau Meca is now home to the **Museu Picasso** ⑭ (Tue–Sun), with around 3,000 of Picasso's works, including some ceramics. Some of the most remarkable are from his early years when he was a student in the city, and show what a competent and precocious draughtsman he was. Pride of place goes to *Las Meninas*, 58 paintings based on Velázquez's originals in the Prado in Madrid.

Carrer Montcada leads into Passeig de Born, and **Santa María del Mar**, the summit of Catalan Gothic and the finest church in the city, built in one harmonious hit, between 1329 and 1384. Beneath it, Passeig del Born and the tiny streets around it are one of modern Barcelona's hippest nightlife

zones, and also hosts art spaces and individual shops.

Beyond La Ribera lies the 34-hectare (85-acre) **Parc de la Ciutadella** ⑮. The Catalan Parliament sits here in the former arsenal. The city **zoo** (daily) covers the south side of the park, and beside it is a fountain with the *Dama del Paraigues*, a captivating sculpture of a young woman beneath an umbrella.

The Modernist city

In the 1850s permission was given for Barcelona to knock down its medieval city walls and expand north, into the **Eixample** or Extension. It did so following a set plan by the great urban planner Ildefons Cerdà, with a grid of long, straight streets of blocks with clipped-off corners. This all-new district provided a platform for the city's newly enriched industrialists to show off, and for the development of the distinctive Catalan form of Art Nouveau, *Modernisme*. The best examples stand within *the Quadrat d'Or*, the Golden Square, centred on the fashionable **Passeig de Gràcia**, which leads up from Plaça de Catalunya. **Casa Lleó Morera** ⑯ at No. 35 is by Domènech i Montaner, perhaps the purest of the Modernist practitioners, and from here you can obtain a ticket to visit the main Modernist sites.

The Casa Morera is one of three buildings in the so-called *Mançana de la Discòrdia* (Block of Discord), because each is by a very different *Modernist* architect. No. 41 is **Casa Amatller**, a beautiful, eclectic building by Josep Puig i Cadafalch (1867–1967), beside the more radical work of its neighbour, **Casa Batlló** (daily), by Antoni Gaudí (1852–1926), a glazed and undulating facade typical of the movement's greatest exponent.

Further up Passeig de Gràcia is Gaudí's best-known non-religious work, **Casa Milà** ⑰, known as La Pedrera (the Stone Quarry): an eight-storey apartment block devoid of straight lines and topped with sinister

chimneys nicknamed *espantabruixes*, "witch scarers". It's now a cultural centre (daily), and visitors can also explore the building.

After he finished La Pedrera, Gaudí devoted himself exclusively to his most famous work, the **Sagrada Família** ⑱ (daily), reached along Carrer de Provença. He finished only the crypt and the Nativity facade with three doorways to Faith, Hope and Charity. Work continues to complete the ambitious project, which should eventually be twice the height of Barcelona's old cathedral. Gaudí spent his last 10 years living, unpaid, in a hut on the site, abandoning the house he had lived in at **Park Güell**. This stunning park and pleasure garden, originally designed as a residential estate, is 15 minutes' walk from Lesseps Metro station on the outskirts of the Collserola hills.

Pedralbes

Count Eusebi Güell, Gaudí's industrialist patron, had a country estate at Pedralbes, and, after his death, his manor house was turned into a palace for visiting royalty. **The Palau Reial de Pedralbes** houses the **Museu de Ceràmica** (Tue–Sun), an excellent collection of pottery and kitchenware going back to the 8th century. Just to the north in the charming former village of Pedralbes is the exquisite **Museu Monestir de Pedralbes** (Tue–Sun), one of the jewels of the city. Founded in 1326 by Queen Elisenda, wife of Jaume II of Aragón, this imposing monastery with magnificent three-storey Gothic cloister is remarkably intact, and, away from view, still houses a small community of nuns.

Montjuïc and Tibidabo

Montjuïc, the hill overlooking the port, has been the city's playground since it was laid out for the International Exhibition of 1929. One of the projects for the 1929 Exhibition was the **Poble Espanyol** (daily), a "village" comprising buildings that display the architectural differences of various regions of Spain. It's a touristy but popular place to visit, with many bars and restaurants.

Montjuïc also has the austere **Palau Nacional**, which houses the **MNAC** or **Museu Nacional d'Art de Catalunya** (National Museum of Catalan Art; Tue–Sun). Among its many highlights are some of the greatest of all Romanesque murals, saved from churches in the Pyrenees, medieval art – some from the Thyssen collection – and superb *Modernist* paintings and decorative art. Alternatively, located in a stylish white building, is the **Fundació Joan Miró** (Tue–Sat and Sun am), built by the painter's friend Josep Lluís Sert in 1975.

The city's other hilltop playground is **Tibidabo**, the giant mountain at the back of the city, which also offers great views, and has an always popular funfair at the top where the height adds an extra thrill to the rides. The last word in heights, however, must go to Norman Foster's nearby tower, the **Torre de Collserola**, a vertiginous needle with a glass viewing panel 115 metres (337ft) above the ground.

The view from Torre de Collserola.

*A human tower in Tarragona,
a Catalan tradition.*

AROUND SPAIN

Most visitors head for Spain's beaches, but inland the country has a rich heritage to explore, including Roman and Moorish monuments, historic towns and cities and wild nature reserves.

Madrid

Spain is the most mountainous country in Europe after Switzerland. Not only does it have the giant, famous high ranges such as the Pyrenees or the Cantabrian Mountains, but also countless lesser-known but still awe-inspiring mountain systems such as the Sierra Morena or Catalonia's Serra del Cadí, and you can even ski in winter as far south as the Sierra Nevada outside Granada. These many mountains have often isolated different parts of the Iberian peninsula from each other, and given Spain a fascinating variety of landscapes, climates and cultures.

Galicia

The northwest of the country, which juts out into the Atlantic beneath the Bay of Biscay, is "Green Spain", where Atlantic winds are driven onto the mountainous coast and rainfall averages up to 250cm (100in) a year. This area was the least touched by the Moorish occupation, and among its mountains, valleys and sheltered harbours there are some of the most ancient and characterful towns in Iberia.

Immediately north of Portugal, Galicia has its own language – Galego – and a rich Celtic heritage, having been largely unconquered not only by the Arabs but also, earlier, by the Romans. **Santiago de Compostela** ❶ has been drawing pilgrims to the

region since the apparent discovery of the tomb of the apostle St James (Santiago), subsequently patron saint of Spain, around AD 812. The city's present cathedral, begun in 1075, is the end goal of pilgrims on the *Camino de Santiago* (Way of St James), a network of paths that run from all over Europe to converge on the north Spanish coast. Remarkably, its ornate 18th-century Baroque facade conceals the more subtly beautiful 12th-century Romanesque one, left intact behind it. They face onto Praza do

Main Attractions

Santiago de Compostela
Picos de Europa
Salamanca
Girona and the Costa Brava
Valencia
Toledo
Seville
Córdoba
Granada and the Alhambra
Costa del Sol

Santiago de Compostela.

Obradoiro, where the grand **Hostal de los Reyes Católicos**, begun in 1501 by order of Ferdinand and Isabella as an inn and hospital for pilgrims, is now an elegant Parador hotel.

Pilgrims from England and other northern countries sometimes reached Santiago by sailing to **La Coruña** (A Coruña, in Galician), Galicia's principal city and port in the northwest corner of the country, where white buildings with characteristic enclosed glass balconies *(miradores)* line the seafront. The city's showpiece is the Torre de Hércules, a Roman lighthouse.

Southwest of La Coruña, the coast of Spain intrudes into the wild Atlantic as the headland of Cabo Fisterra, "Land's End", which in medieval times was thought to be literally the limit of the world. The most attractive stretch of Galicia's coast is the **Rias Baixas**, a series of deep inlets between green hills with sheltered harbours stretching roughly from Padrón to Baiona. **Pontevedra** and **Vigo**, home to the largest fishing fleet in Europe, are the main cities, but the prettiest spots include **Combarro**,

with its numerous *horreos* (stone granaries on stilts), **Cambados** and the island of **A Toxa**, joined to the mainland by a bridge. There are plenty of gorgeous sandy beaches with invigoratingly cool Atlantic water, and anywhere on this coast you will eat fish and seafood without equal accompanied by the local dry white wines. Galicia's foremost wine-growing area is the steep-sided valley of the **Ribeira Sacra**, running east from **Ourense**.

Asturias and Cantabria

The **Cordillera Cantábrica** is a high range of mountains that cuts the Atlantic regions of Asturias and Cantabria off from inland Spain. With a long maritime history, a centre of 19th-century industry and coal-mining, but with huge areas of lush green mountains and remote valleys, Asturias is a region with a character as pungent as one of its specialities, the powerful Cabrales goat's cheese. The coastal drive along the northern coast, the **Costa Verde**, winds over cliffs and through valleys, arriving at picturesque fishing ports such as **Luarca**. Asturias

Picos de Europa.

is a land of cider, and the apple brew is poured from fizzy heights in the cider bars around the region, often accompanied by Cabrales cheese or local sausages. Inland, the capital, **Oviedo ❷**, is a treasure house of pre-Romanesque architecture. Part royal palace, part church, **Santa Maria del Naranco** dates from the time of Ramiro I in the 9th century; adjacent is the delightful **San Miguel de Lillo**, and **San Julián de los Prados**, in Oviedo's suburbs, should also not be missed.

The first King of Asturias was Pelayo, who according to tradition began the "Reconquest" of Spain from the Muslim Arabs in 722 by defeating them at **Covadonga**, in what is now the **Parque Nacional de los Picos de Europa**, one of Spain's most spectacular mountain regions. Only a short way from the ocean, the Picos are full of wonderful locations for hiking and climbing, such as the **Garganta del Cares** path 11km (7miles) through a gorge from north to south – the only way actually through the mountains, since all roads run around them. The main entry points to the Picos are **Cangas de Onís** near Covadonga in the northwest, and **Potes** in the southeast. From Potes a road leads to **Fuente Dé**, where a cable car climbs 900 metres (2,950ft) to the wild plateau above, giving heavenly views.

The Cantabrian coast has a variety of relaxed beach resorts, such as **Comillas**, which has a house designed by Gaudí. There are sandy beaches at **Laredo** and around **Santander ❸**, the principal city and port, sitting serenely between the green hills and blue sea. **Santillana del Mar** is a stunningly preserved historic town, packed with medieval and 16th-century mansions. Nearby at **Altamira** is the "Sistine Chapel" of prehistoric cave art, dating from 18,000 BC or earlier. The bison, deer, boar and horses painted on the ceilings in ochres, manganese oxide, charcoal and iron carbonate are the largest known group of prehistoric polychrome figures in the world.

Because of its fragile state visitors are no longer allowed into the cave itself, but an informative **museum** (Tue–Sun) leads to the **Neocueva**, a remarkably faithful modern replica.

Castilla y León

In the 11th century, the Christian Spaniards came down out of the mountains of Asturias onto the depopulated *meseta or central plateau*, where winters are cold and summers baking hot. The land was still contested for centuries, and so became dotted with castles (castillos), the origin of the name Castilla, or Castile. The first two major cities in this new land were León and Burgos, both on the main route from the Pyrenees to Santiago de Compostela, and both given Gothic cathedrals.

León ❹, has a particularly fine **cathedral**, with 1,800 sq metres (20,000 sq ft) of wonderful stained-glass windows, yet its construction is fragile and no one is sure quite how it still manages to stay up. Even more impressive is the **Basilica de San Isidoro**, with its adjoining **Panteón**

TIP

A novel way of seeing the north of Spain is to take the luxury Transcantábrico train from San Sebastián to Santiago de Compostela. See www.transcantabrico. com for full information.

Plaza Mayor in Salamanca.

Real, where some 20 monarchs are entombed, and which has delightful ceiling frescoes of the seasons.

Burgos ❺ was the city of the semi-legendary warrior of the early Reconquest, Rodrigo Díaz de Vivar (1043–99), known as El Cid, whose tomb lies in the cathedral. But the great treasures of this town are in the **Real Monasterio de las Huelgas** (Tue–Sun), founded in 1187 by Alfonso VIII and decorated with Moorish patterns, as are the clothes, still in fine repair, worn by the medieval monarchs and their families. Southeast of Burgos is the **Monasterio de Santo Domingo de Silos** (daily), famous for its cloisters and chanting Benedictine monks.

Much of the rest of Old Castile, between Madrid and the Cantabrian Mountains, is bleak and apparently remote, but several great cities punctuate the plains. **Valladolid ❻**, a rambling town with elaborate churches, has the **Museo Nacional de Escultura** (Tue–Sat and Sun am), housed in a sumptuously carved 15th-century college, which offers a crash course in the history of Spanish sculpture. More celebrated as one of the great cultural centres of Spain is **Salamanca ❼**. Its university was the first in Spain, founded in 1218. Central Salamanca is stunning, its streets dominated by 15th- and 16th-century colleges, churches and aristocratic palaces such as the **Casa de las Conchas** (House of the Shells) from c.1500. The main square or **Plaza Mayor** is one of the largest and most gracious city squares in Spain, with Baroque facades in the magnificently opulent style of the architect brothers Churriguera, whose work inspired a new adjective, *Churrigueresque*.

Ávila ❽, 113km (70 miles) northwest of Madrid, is the highest city on the peninsula, and its centre is still sealed within perfectly preserved medieval walls 10 metres (33ft) high, with 88 round towers and nine fortified entrances. The city is most famous as the city of the mystic Saint Teresa of Ávila, and its streets still retain a feel of austere religiosity. Across the south of Ávila province runs the long ridge of the **Sierra de Gredos**, rising up to a height of 2,590 metres (8,500ft). The sierras are home to mountain goats, eagles and many other birds, and memorable hiking routes run up from villages where time appears to stand still.

Closer to Madrid is **Segovia ❾**, whose charms are evident at first sight. It fills up with *madrileños* every weekend who come to admire the beautifully designed 1st-century AD Roman **aqueduct**, originally built to transport water from the River Frío 18 km (11 miles) away and still in use as a backup water system for the city until the 1970s. The fairy-tale **Alcázar** (palace) and the city's *mesones* or traditional restaurants, where roast lamb and suckling pig for which the province is famous are served, are other big attractions. The *Alcázar* (daily) is a child's dream of a castle, and there are great views of it from the riverbank below.

Segovia's Roman aqueduct at dusk.

The Rioja winelands

To the east of Burgos lies **Rioja**, Spain's best-known wine country, which extends into the Basque Country and Navarra as well as the Rioja region as such. Wine-making in the upper Ebro Valley dates back to 873, but its modern prestige began in the late 19th century, when more sophisticated techniques were introduced from France. **Laguardia**, **Haro** and **Logroño ⑩** are the main centres, but there are some 350 wine houses spread around the region, which has become a major destination for wine tourism. Some of the modern wineries are spectacular, such as **Bodegas Ysios** near **Laguardia**, designed by Santiago Calatrava with an undulating roof, or the **Marqués de Riscal** bodega and luxury hotel built of sinuous metal by Frank Gehry, in **Elciego**. Haro holds the bacchanalian Batalla del Vino on 29 June, when everyone is drenched with wine.

The Basque Country and Navarra

In the eastern corner of Spain's green coast, straddling the border with France, is the Basque Country, home of a singular people with ancient roots who speak a language (Euskera) of uncertain origin. The official capital of the Spanish Basque Country is **Vitoria ⑪** (Gasteiz in Basque), built on a high point. The *miradores* on the old houses around its main square, **Plaza de la Virgen Blanca**, are typical of the northern coast. The main city and port of the Basque Country is **Bilbao ⑫** (Bilbo), an old industrial city squeezed into the narrow valley of the Nervión, which has reinvented itself around the **Guggenheim Bilbao** (Tue–Sun), a shining "metallic flower" of a museum designed by the Canadian-American architect Frank Gehry. Radically modern, reflecting the river in its metal shell, it hosts changing exhibitions, though most people come to see the building itself. Nearby, the Old City of Bilbao around the narrow **Siete Calles** (Seven Streets) and the gracious arcaded **Plaza Nueva** has also been very effectively spruced up, and is a delightful place for strolling and sampling delicious tapas in its many characterful bars.

Gehry's Guggenheim Museum, Bilbao, has attracted many visitors to the city.

A cove in Begur on the Costa Brava.

The splendid Dalí Museum in Figueres.

Basque food is one of the wonders of Spain, and there are many places along the coast where the seafood is fresh and delicious. **San Sebastián** ⓭ (Donostia) is queen of the resorts, with a curving beach, great restaurants and an old quarter that is great for bar-hopping. Along the coast between the two cities are charming towns like **Zarautz** and **Mundaka**, with a strong maritime flavour and some of Europe's best surfing beaches.

Heading eastwards takes you to Navarra in the foothills of the Pyrenees. Northern Navarra is strongly Basque in character, southern Navarra is not, which has caused problems, although lately the two communities get along pretty well. The two meet at **Pamplona** ⓮ (Iruña), former capital of the kingdom of Navarre, famous above all for its wild, week-long festival of San Fermín, publicised beyond Spain by Ernest Hemingway in *The Sun Also Rises* (1926), which begins each 6 July and features daily *encierros*, when bulls are run through the streets to the bullring, challenged by reckless crowds. There are often

serious accidents among the daredevil participants.

The **Monasterio de Leyre** (daily), southeast of Pamplona, was Navarre's 11th-century spiritual centre and pantheon for its kings. It is a beautiful Romanesque building with a fine vaulted crypt, consecrated in 1057. Recently restored by the Benedictines, whose chants can be heard, it now includes a hotel.

Aragón

Landlocked Aragón is one of the most austerely beautiful of Spain's regions, with arid rocky plains and hills in the south and Alpine-scale mountains in the north. The monastery of **San Juan de la Peña** (daily) is perhaps its most extraordinary sight, built in the 11th century and wedged between enormous boulders under a sheer rock cliff. Inside are the tombs of early Aragonese kings. Just to the north is **Jaca** ⓯, which is a centre for both summer hiking and winter sports. It is also a natural base for exploring the High Pyrenees, leading to dramatic mountain valleys with abundant

wildlife and charming old stone villages. The most spectacular scenery of all is in the Parque Nacional de Ordesa, a national park with peaks over 3,500 metres (11,500ft) high.

Aragón's capital and only substantial city is **Zaragoza** ⑯, a Roman town (its name derives from Caesaraugusta), which was knocked about in the Napoleonic Wars. It has two cathedrals: **Nuestra Señora del Pilar** has 11 distinctive domes and a cupola painted by Goya, a native of Aragón. More impressive is the **Aljafería**, built in the 11th century by the ruling Moorish king.

Catalonia

Seafaring Catalonia united with Spanish-speaking Aragón in the 12th century, but Catalans have never lost their language and independent character (see page 354). Also a part of Catalan territory, by accident of medieval history, is the **Val d'Aran**, the one part of Spain clearly on the north side of the Pyrenees. Accordingly the valley has its own language, a variant of the Provençal once spoken in the region to the north. The lovely valley around the town of **Vielha** ⑰ is a popular ski centre, notably at **Baqueira-Beret**, a haunt of the royal family. Catalan is the official language of **Andorra** ⑱, the anomalous 468-sq km (180-sq mile) principality (see page 374). The upper reaches of the principality are beautiful in summer and hugely popular for skiing in winter, consequently the roads leading to the capital, Andorra la Vella, can be hell during peak seasons. In Catalonia-proper, **La Seu d'Urgell**, on the other hand, is a sleepy old mountain town with a 12th-century cathedral, a 13th-century cloister and an excellent collection of Romanesque art in its Museu Diocesà (Episcopal Museum; daily).

Catalonia's Pyrenean valleys are notable for their stunning Romanesque churches with tall belltowers, such as **Sant Climent de Taüll** in the Boí Valley, just south of the **Parc Nacional de Aigüestortes**, with its idyllic mountain lakes. The churches' finest frescoes, among the greatest works of early medieval art, were removed for their preservation and are now in the **MNAC** museum in Barcelona (see page 357), and in the churches themselves are modern copies. Another masterpiece of Romanesque carving can be seen on the facade of the former monastery of Santa Maria in **Ripoll** ⑲, founded in 888 by Guifré el Pilós, first Count of Barcelona, and often called "the cradle of Catalonia". At the nearby monastery of **Sant Joan de les Abadesses**, where Guifré's daughter was abbess, there is more fine carving, and an exquisite Romanesque calvary.

The Costa Brava and Dalí

Brava means wild or rugged, and the Catalan coast from the French border to **Blanes** certainly twists and turns for some 90km (60 miles) around coves and over cliffs in one of the most celebrated shores of the Mediterranean. This was where the Greeks and Romans first arrived on the Iberian peninsula, and the Greeks made a trading base at **Empúries** (mid-Feb–Oct

WHERE

Spain has the most extensive calendar of traditional celebrations – *fiestas* – in Europe, and the most famous like San Fermín in Pamplona or the April Feria in Seville are only the tip of the iceberg. Nearly every town has its own *Fiesta Mayor* or main fiesta, usually in late spring or summer. Regional tourist offices have details.

Girona's Gothic cathedral was begun in 1312. Girona is a charming, small city, full of historical interest and contemporary buzz.

daily, Nov–mid-Feb Tue–Sun) in the Bahia de Roses (Bay of Roses). The well-excavated site includes the remains of the Greek harbour wall, and gives a vivid impression of a small ancient town. On the north side of the bay are Cap de Creus and the isolated, picture-perfect town of **Cadaqués** . This is the St-Tropez of the coast, with galleries and boutiques in steep cobbled streets. The painter Salvador Dalí lived at **Port-Lligat**, just to the north, and the **Casa-Museu Salvador Dalí** (mid-Feb–Dec Tue–Sun, July–Sept daily; reservation necessary, www. salvador-dali.org), consists of the two fishermen's houses he famously made his home. It is a strangely enchanting place. A Dalí route takes in the castle he bought inland at Puból, and the town of **Figueres**, where the **Teatre-Museu Dalí** (Oct–May Tue–Sun, June–Sept daily) is one of the most popular museums in Spain.

Around the coast there are intimate coves with gloriously clear waters and beach villages with a tranquil, unhurried feel, as at **Aiguablava**, **Tamariu** or **Calella de Palafrugell**. Elsewhere the sandy beaches are bigger and the resorts busier, as at **Roses**, **Platja d'Aro**, **Tossa de Mar** and especially brash **Lloret de Mar**, a long-running spot for rowdy nightlife.

The main city behind the Costa Brava is **Girona** ㉑, some 20km (12 miles) inland, and for many an ideal combination of the style of Barcelona without the big-city hassle. It is attractively sited beside the River Onyar, where bridges lead to a rambla and steep cobbled streets heading for a Gothic **cathedral** with the widest nave in Christendom. An archaeological walk follows the Old Town walls, which were breached in a heroic siege in the Napoleonic Wars. In the Old Town, the former Jewish quarter or **Call** has been extensively excavated, and the **Museu d'Història dels Jueus** (Jewish History Museum; daily) has illuminating exhibits and incorporates the preserved buildings.

Southern Catalonia and the Costa Daurada

South of Barcelona (see page 351), **Sitges** ㉒, just 45 minutes away by

Tossa de Mar looks romantic at night.

train, is an eternally stylish resort, popular for Sunday lunch and equally popular with gays, who also dominate the outrageous pre-Lent carnival. Inland are the hills of the **Penedès**, Catalonia's most prominent wine region, with its twin centres of **Vilafranca del Penedès** and **Sant Sadurní d'Anoia**, the home of cava, Catalan sparkling wine. Many wineries and all the main cava houses welcome visitors. To the northeast, and also an easy day trip by train from Barcelona, is the extraordinary mountain-top monastery of **Montserrat** (daily). A cable car runs to the top from the train station. The "spiritual heart" of Catalonia for Catholics, it contains the 12th-century statue of the "Black Virgin", La Moreneta, one of Catalonia's patron saints.

South of Sitges are the beaches of the Costa Daurada. **Tarragona** ㉓, today a Unesco World Heritage site, was in Roman times the most important city in northeast Spain, and its Roman monuments are well preserved, especially the **Amfiteatre** (Amphiteatre; Tue–Sun) overlooking the sea beneath the Balcó de Europa at the end of the Rambla. Also visitable are the massive **Roman walls** and remains of the Forum, Roman Circus and other monuments. Two museums, the Museu d'Història (History Museum; Tue–Sun) and Museu Nacional Arqueològic (National Archaeology Museum; Tue–Sun) have finds from the sites, while in the countryside around the city are yet more Roman relics, including a grand arch dedicated to Augustus and a dramatic 1st-century AD aqueduct.

Tarragona's Gothic **cathedral** stands on the site of a Roman temple and Arab mosque. In the rolling hills inland is the "Cistercian Triangle" of three magnificent medieval Gothic monasteries, at **Poblet** (daily), **Santes Crcus** (Tue–Sun) and **Vallbona** (Tue–Sun), each containing royal tombs.

Near the big resort of Salou, south of Tarragona, is **Port Aventura**, one

Santiago Calatrava's L'Hemisferic in the City of Arts and Sciences, Valencia. Although 14 years old now, the complex is strikingly, beautifully modern.

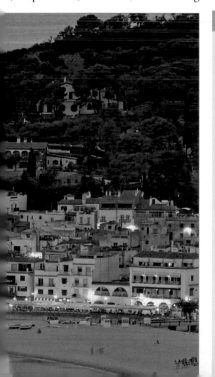

THE BALEARICS

Spain's Mediterranean archipelago consists of four main islands: Mallorca, Menorca, Ibiza and Formentera. At their closest point the Balearics are only 85km (53 miles) offshore and are easily reached by domestic flight or ferry from Barcelona, Valencia, Denia or Alicante. Their local language is a dialect of Catalan.

The Balearics are best known for their high-rise holiday resorts and extravagant nightlife, but the islands have much more to offer than beaches, raves and clubs.

Mallorca is the largest and most varied of the islands, with mountains reaching over 1,445 metres (4,740ft) and a dramatic series of caves near its east coast. Palma, the capital, has a Gothic cathedral and many other historic buildings. The tiny offshore island of Cabrera is a national park.

Menorca, furthest from the mainland, is littered with prehistoric megalithic monuments and has a famous June festival in which horses prance in crowded streets. Ibiza (properly called Eivissa) also has surprises if you eschew the bars and beaches. The eponymous main town has a pristine old quarter and in its countryside are pretty, brightly whitewashed villages to explore. Formentera, smallest of the main islands, can be reached from Ibiza, has ravishing beaches and, being mainly flat, is best explored by bicycle.

of the biggest theme parks in Europe (mid-Dec–Oct daily, Nov–mid-Dec weekends and holidays). The Costa Daurada ends at the rice-growing delta of the Ebro (Ebre), Spain's largest river, which fans out into the sea to create an important habitat for flamingos and other birdlife. There is an information centre in **Deltebre**.

Valencia and Alicante

Valencia ❷ lies in the most fertile farmlands of Spain. The country's third-largest city is known for its oranges, paella and the sensational conflagration that ends the city's Las Fallas fiesta on 19 March. Ceramics are also a speciality, and there is some lovely tilework to be seen in the city, as well as at the **Museo Nacional de Cerámica** (Mon–Sat). One of the city's most handsome buildings, the 15th-century **Lonja**, is now a concert and exhibition venue, and Valencia's hugely ambitious recent renovation schemes produced the **Ciutat de les Arts i Ciències** (City of Arts and Sciences), a spectacular all-new park at the mouth of the Turia river with curvaceous buildings that

One of the Casas Colgadas (Hanging Houses) in Cuenca.

are almost science-fiction in style, including a planetarium, an IMAX cinema, an interactive science museum, an opera house, beautiful park areas and other attractions.

South of Valencia is the **Costa Blanca**, one of the most popular holiday areas of Europe, especially with the British. Many of its attractive old towns, such as **Dènia**, **Altea** or **Xàbia** (Javea in Spanish) have every kind of tourist service and large resident foreign populations, but it was **Benidorm**, with a fine sandy beach and acres of high-rise hotels, that first gave the area its package-holiday reputation. **Alicante** ❷ (Alacant) is the Costa Blanca's main city, with a port and airport, and a fine, palm-lined esplanade.

Near Alicante is the extraordinary plantation at **Elche** (Elx) of a quarter of a million palms, said to have been planted by the Phoenicians. A 5th-century BC stone bust of a priestess found here, La Dame de Elche, is one of Spain's great treasures, now in Madrid. Away from the coast, much of the Valencian region is mountainous. One of the most picturesque upland

THE QUIXOTE TRAIL

A tour of central La Mancha is an opportunity for fans of *Don Quixote* to trace key points in Miguel Cervantes's novel – the world's first bestseller, published in 1615 and fully titled The Ingenious Gentleman Don Quixote of La Mancha.

El Toboso, on the N-301 between Albacete and Ocaña, was the village of Dulcinea, Don Quixote's fantasised true love for whom he was so quick to risk all. The Casa de Dulcinea (Tue–Sun), thought to be the house of the woman on whom Cervantes modelled his damsel, has been restored to its 16th-century appearance. Puerto Lápiz, 20km (12 miles) southeast of Consuegra, matches Cervantes's description of the inn where Don Quixote was sworn in as a knight errant.

The line of windmills nearby at Campo de Criptana look as if they might be the ones Quixote mistook for giants, their flailing sails "attacking" the deluded knight tilting at them. The Cueva de Montesinos near San Pedro Lake in the Lagunas de Ruidera Valley is the cave where our hero was treated to elegiac visions of other bewitched knights and of his beloved Dulcinea, and the town of Argamasilla de Albais a firm candidate for the place where it began: *"En un lugar de La Mancha…"* – In some place in La Mancha…

areas is **El Maestrazgo** (Maestrat) in the north, where crags and flat-topped summits form a backdrop to stout medieval towns such as **Morella 26**.

Toledo and Castilla-La Mancha

The saffron that colours Valencia's paellas comes from the inland region of **La Mancha**. On the edge of the plains – the stamping ground of Don Quixote – is **Cuenca 27**, one of Spain's most dramatically sited towns. Here, the Casas Colgadas (Hanging Houses) teeter on the edge of a cliff over the River Huéscar. One contains the **Museo de Arte Abstracto** (Tue–Sun), with works by several major Spanish contemporary artists.

Far across the plains is **Toledo 28** – at different times a Roman, Muslim and Christian city and still the main seat of the Catholic Church in Spain – situated on a bend in the River Tajo (Tagus) 70km (45 miles) south of Madrid. The city has many claims to fame: damascene metalwork, El Greco and a fabulous Old Town that is a Unesco World Heritage site. The city's **cathedral** is deeply impressive, with superbly rich carving in stone and wood, and extravagant Baroque painting. The city's other worshippers are also represented: 9th-century mosques can be discovered, and there are two exquisite 12th-century **synagogues**, one of which contains a Sephardic museum. It is uncertain whether the **Casa-Museo de El Greco** (daily) in the former Jewish Quarter was actually the artist's home, but it is an atmospheric 16th-century house of the kind he may well have lived in, and contains several major paintings such as the Vista de Toledo (View of Toledo). The city is dominated by the **Alcázar** (**Thur–Tue**), a mainly 16th-century fortress but one that dates back to the time of El Cid. It was the object of a protracted siege in the 1936–9 Civil War and today contains an Army Museum.

Extremadura

West of Madrid is **Extremadura**, one of the least visited parts of Spain, but which provided many adventurers for the New World. Francisco

The Roman theatre in Mérida is still used for drama festivals.

Pizarro, conqueror of Peru, was born in **Trujillo** ㉙, where his statue adorns the Plaza Mayor. His brother Hernando built the **Palacio del Marqués de la Conquista** opposite the statue. The facade has a bust of Francisco Pizarro and his wife, Inés Yupanqui, sister of the Inca emperor Atahualpa.

Many Catholics make their way to the **Real Monasterio de Guadalupe** ㉚ (daily) to see the deeply revered Virgin de Guadalupe.

Southwest of Guadalupe is **Mérida** ㉛, capital of Lusitania, the western Iberian province of the Roman Empire. The remains of Roman Mérida are scattered all over the town: for example, the impressive theatre, which is still used for summer drama festivals, and the **Museo Nacional de Arte Romano** (Tue–Sun), designed in 1988 by Rafael Moneo, which has the largest collection of Roman artefacts outside Italy.

Sultry Andalucía: Seville and Córdoba

Named Al Andalus by its Arab conquerors, Andalucía, spreading across the south of Spain, is the source of many classic images of the country: flamenco, flashing-eyed dancers, olive-clad hills, whitewashed hilltop villages. Under Muslim rule in the Middle Ages, it had one of the most highly developed civilisations in Europe, and the traces of Al Andalus are visible in every part of the region. Today, too, its coasts form Europe's most thriving tourist area.

Seville Ⓐ (Sevilla), capital of Andalucía and the country's fourth-largest city, is the dazzling setting of Bizet's *Carmen*, Rossini's barber and the adventures of Don Juan. The city's two finest buildings face each other across Plaza del Triunfo in the central Santa Cruz district. On the north side is the **cathedral** (daily), Europe's largest, where Christopher Columbus has a highly figurative tomb. The magnificent adjoining Moorish tower, **La Giralda**, was built in the last years of Muslim rule in the 12th century, and has fine views from the top. The cathedral has such an unusual shape – effectively square – because it was built on the site of and incorporated parts of

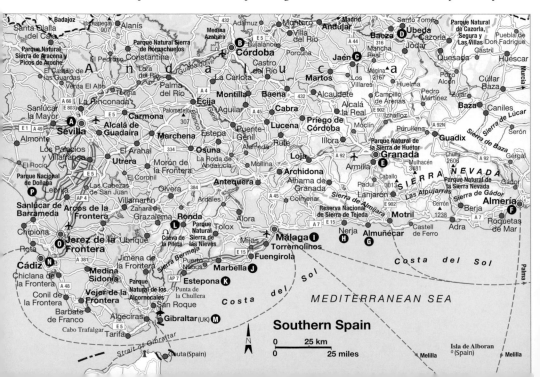

Southern Spain

0   25 km

0   25 miles

MEDITERRANEAN SEA

the earlier great mosque: Muslim worshippers had washed their hands and feet in the fountain of the **Patio de los Naranjos**, the cloisters of the orange orchard.

On the south side of the square is the **Real Alcázar**, the Royal Palace (daily). Although most of it was built for Christian kings after they conquered Seville in 1248, this is to all intents a Moorish palace, since the Castilian rulers clearly appreciated the luxuries of Moorish Andalucía and for centuries favoured the *Mudéjar* (Hispano-Moorish) style in their southern palaces. They employed Muslim craftsmen, whose work can be seen in the main patios and beautiful Ambassadors' Hall, both fantasies in filigree. After Columbus's discovery of America, Seville was for a time the busiest port in Europe. The dockyards were to the south, in El Arenal district, where the fine 18th-century bullring can be found.

Córdoba ⓑ, smaller and less flamboyant than Seville, was the capital of the Andalus Caliphate, and its Great Mosque, the **Mezquita** (daily), dating from Abd al-Rahman in the 8th century, is one of the greatest works of Islamic architecture. Take a walk in the Jewish Quarter beside the mosque for an idea of how the medieval city must have been; the area includes the remains of a 14th-century synagogue.

One of the pueblos blancos (white villages) in the hills near Ronda.

Jaén to Granada

On the eastern side of Andalucía is Jaén province, an undulating expanse of 150 million olive trees. Its capital, **Jaén** ⓒ, perched above the western plain, has a massive cathedral, fine Arab baths and hilltop Moorish castle. The towns of **Úbeda** ⓓ and **Baeza**, on adjacent hilltops, are superb compilations of Renaissance buildings, and both Unesco World Heritage sites.

The jewel of Moorish Spain is the **Alhambra** (daily; reservation advised, for more information, see www.alhambra degranada.org) in **Granada** ⓔ, the final stronghold of the last Moorish kingdom in Spain, only conquered in 1492, and the home of Spain's great

The exquisitely carved Court of the Lions in the Alhambra, Granada.

modern poet and playwright Federico García Lorca (1898–1936). No amount of description can prepare the visitor for the Alhambra's exquisite architecture, the epitome of Islamic imagination and artistry. The royal residence is highlighted by the **Patio de los Arrayanes** (Patio of the Myrtles) and **Patio de los Leones** (Patio of the Lions). The **Alcazaba** (castle), at the western end of Alhambra Hill, is a 9th-century citadel, with grand views over the city. The adjoining **Generalife**, dating from 1250, was the summer palace of the Emirs: cool and green and full of restful pools and murmuring fountains. In summer, festivals of music and dance are held in the grounds. The conquerors of Granada, Ferdinand and Isabella, share a mausoleum in the Royal Chapel attached to the cathedral below the Alhambra.

Andalucía's Costas

The coastlines of Andalucía, now labelled as various different costas, stretch from **Almería** Ⓕ in the east, a province that has the only real deserts in Western Europe, past the mouth of the Mediterranean to Cádiz in the west. Although famous for their big and ultra-developed resorts, they also have great variety, and even some relatively unfrequented beaches.

The strip south of Granada around **Salobreña** and **Almuñécar** Ⓖ has a microclimate suitable for the cultivation of exotic fruits, and hence is known as the Costa Tropical. To the west, the Costa del Sol starts at the attractive town of **Nerja** Ⓗ, standing on cliffs above sandy coves. A series of caves was discovered here in 1957, and summer concerts are held in the largest one.

Málaga Ⓘ is the capital of the Costa del Sol, a bustling city visited by cruise liners. This was the port of Granada, and its Moorish castle, the 11th-century **Alcazaba** (Tue–Sun), was built inside an extensive Roman fort beside an amphitheatre. Phoenician, Roman and Moorish artefacts are displayed in the **Museo Arqueológico** inside. Picasso was born here, and the **Museo Picasso** (Tue–Sun), in the Palacio de Buenavista in Calle San Agustín, shows some of his works. Some of his early sketches are in the **Museo de**

Wealth on view at Puerto Banús.

Bellas Artes (Tue–Sun), which also has paintings by Murillo and Zubarán, and by the train station in Calle Alemania is the **CAC Málaga** (Tue–Sun), a dynamic contemporary arts centre in a former wholesale market.

The most overgrown resorts on the Costa del Sol are between Málaga and Marbella, such as **Torremolinos** and **Fuengirola**, names associated with cheap, loud, no-frills holidays throughout Europe. High-rise buildings pack the water's edge all the way to **Marbella ❶**. and its flashy marina of **Puerto Banús**, which has a far more upscale image as the playground of celebrities, bullfighters, sheikhs and Russian billionaires. **Estepona ❶**, most westerly of the Costa's swollen fishing villages, is surrounded by small villas, but has avoided too many high-rises.

The villa developments have been spreading inland for years, but have not managed to change the character of **Ronda ❶**, one of the most dramatic of all Andalucian towns, perched atop a precipitous gorge and with the oldest permanently functioning bullring in Spain. To the west are the *pueblos blancos* or "white villages", atmospheric, once-fortified hamlets of whitewashed houses built clustered together high on rocky hilltops for their own protection in Moorish times. **Grazalema**, **Ubrique**, **Gaucín** and **Arcos de la Frontera** are only some of the best known. From each village there are hypnotic views over the wild landscape below.

Gibraltar and the Costa de la Luz

Gibraltar ❶, Britain's enclave in Spain, can be freely entered. With pubs and policemen, its 7 sq km (3 sq miles) are a strange place warp. The rock upon which it sits looks out across the narrow strait, and joins the Mediterranean to the Atlantic. Industrial **Algeciras** next door is the boarding point for ferries to Morocco and the Spanish North African enclaves of Ceuta and Melilla.

West of Gibraltar the tidal Atlantic washes the **Costa de la Luz**. The wind and waves make the whole coast, particularly around **Tarifa**, a superb spot for wind- and kitesurfing. **Cádiz ❶** is the oldest city in Western Europe, first established by Phoenician traders around 1100 BC. As well as for its port and long history it is known for its seafood and flamenco artists. Its grand **cathedral** contains the tomb of the composer Manuel de Falla, and the Oratorio de la Santa Cueva has paintings by Goya.

Inland from Cádiz is the rolling landscape of the sherry triangle, centred on **Jerez de la Frontera ❶**.

Sanlúcar de Barrameda, north of Cádiz, produces its own light, dry sherry, *manzanilla*. It looks across the mouth of the Guadalquivir to the dunes and marshlands of the **Parque Nacional de Doñana ❶**, one of the country's principal nature reserves. The imperial eagle and Spanish lynx are among its rarer inhabitants. Organised tours start from **El Acebuche** (book ahead at www.donanavisitas.es).

TIP

The meeting-point of the Mediterranean and Atlantic is a unique point in the world's oceans, with a rich mix of nutrients that each year attracts hundreds of dolphins and whales. Whale- and dolphin-watching trips operate from Tarifa: for information, see www.firmm.org.

Graceful architecture in the centre of Palma de Mallorca.

MICROSTATES

Dotted around Europe and squeezed between their larger neighbours are a handful of tiny countries, each with its own idiosyncratic national identity.

We tend to think of Europe in terms of its most conspicuous political chunks: the major nation states that coalesced behind established borders in the 19th century. There are, however, a few much smaller entities that usually slip under the radar. These are the microstates, diminutive areas of sovereign territory inhabited by correspondingly small populations that are counted in their thousands rather than millions.

The microstates – Andorra, Liechtenstein, Luxembourg, Malta, Monaco, San Marino and the Vatican – are in almost all aspects fully functioning countries, with their own constitutions, passports, currencies and symbols of national identity. They are recognised by international organisations such as the EU and UN, even if their prestige and influence are small. But it would be a mistake to think of them as existing independently of their gigantic neighbours, on whom they inevitably depend for an inflow of revenue, services like electricity and the kind of resources only size can bring, such as defence against any possible external threats.

Some people dismiss the microstates as quaint anachronisms in the modern world; anomalies that only survive by economic specialisation, such as offering duty-free shopping, gambling or the opportunity to evade taxes, or by peddling themselves as mini-geopolitical theme parks for tourists. For others, the microstates represent a bastion against globalisation: proof that diversity and idiosyncrasy can exist despite the trend towards international homogenisation. What is true is that each microstate is a unique oddity in how it came to be and how it functions today; and each is a curiosity worth visiting in its own right.

The 12th-century Vaduz Castle dominates the capital of Liechtenstein, a tiny constitutional monarchy with 36,000 inhabitants.

The cross of the Knights of St John carved on the wall of Valletta Cathedral. The order ruled the independent island state of Malta from 1530 to 1789.

The Grand Duchy of Luxembourg is a polyglot state, bordered by France, Germany and Belgium. It has an economy that larger countries can only dream of, and has found a modern role as home to several European institutions, including the European Commission.

The flag of the Principality of Andorra. Sandwiched between Spain and France in the Pyrenees, it has a population of just 86,500, but the highest life expectancy in the world.

The Vatican in Rome is the smallest independent state in the world, with just 830 official citizens, half of whom do not live there. It is an absolute monarchy under the auspices of the pope.

WOULD-BE NATIONS

Several Western European countries have regions within them that aspire to nationhood in their own right, and there is often an uneasy tug of war between capital and province. These would-be countries-within-a-country base their claim for greater or full autonomy on a shared language and culture that is not the same as that of the existing nation state of which they form a part.

In Spain, the Catalans and the Basques enjoy considerable degrees of autonomy, but central questions of the control of finances have not been resolved, and resentments have revived and taken on new energy in the financial crisis since 2009. France also has Catalans and Basques, although they are far less vociferous than the Corsicans who rail against control of their island emanating from Paris.

One controversial vision for the European Union is that it should allow such regions to enjoy statehood under the umbrella of a federalised EU that provides internationalised services, such as foreign policy and defence, but this is one that none of the major European states is ever likely to allow.

elota is the traditional game of the Basques, a people of ncient and mysterious origin whose land is divided between bain and France.

The Republic of San Marino, surrounded by Italian territory, has a strong ceremonial tradition.

Farmer in Tras os Montes, Portugal.

Surfers on Guincho beach, near Cascais, Portugal.

The village of Estremoz in the Alentejo region of Portugal.

PORTUGAL

Europe's most westerly country is best known for
the beach resorts of the Algarve, but its rugged
interior, pretty villages and ancient cities are
also worth exploring.

Azulejo, or painted tile.

Tucked in the corner of the continent, nobody passes through Portugal because, really, there is nowhere else to go. It is a land on the edge, "where land ends and sea begins" as the 16th-century epic poet Luís Vaz de Camões put it. At the western periphery of Europe, the country appears suspended between a culture of traditional living – fishing and farming – and the technology that has made the world smaller, more integrated, more complex. However, it attracts a great many tourists, who come for the unspoilt landscape and lifestyle, as well as delightful villages, family-geared beach resorts, and the proud historic towns and cities.

Although in many ways Portugal has a Mediterranean feel, its light is more limpid and its shores are washed clean by the Atlantic tides. The cosmopolitan nature of the country is evident everywhere: nearly 2 million returned from former colonies when they were granted independence in the mid-1970s. Many headed for the countryside rather than towns, and Lisbon, the capital, has a comparatively small population of 1 million – out of a total population for the country of well over 10 million.

This is a country that is easy to explore, thanks to an ever-improving network of motorways and secondary roads. Covering some 92,100 sq km (35,550 sq miles), its land borders Spain, to which it was briefly attached in the 16th century: their languages, as well as the overall character of the people, are surprisingly different. Portugal benefits from Spain's gift of three important rivers. In the north are the Minho and the Douro, while Lisbon lies on the Tagus (Tejo), south of which is the Alentejo and the popular Algarve coast. The cities have a distinct flavour, and the people savour their differences. "Coimbra sings, Braga plays, Lisbon shows off and Porto works," is one way the Portuguese people sum them up.

Portugal is one of the southern European countries that has been hardest hit by the financial and debt crisis since 2009 (though less so than Greece). There is considerable economic hardship, and many young Portuguese are once again looking to emigration for a future, but this situation does not create any particular problems for foreign visitors, nor has it caused the kind of closures of monuments and attractions seen in Greece.

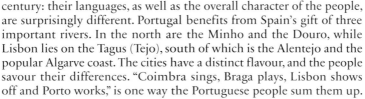

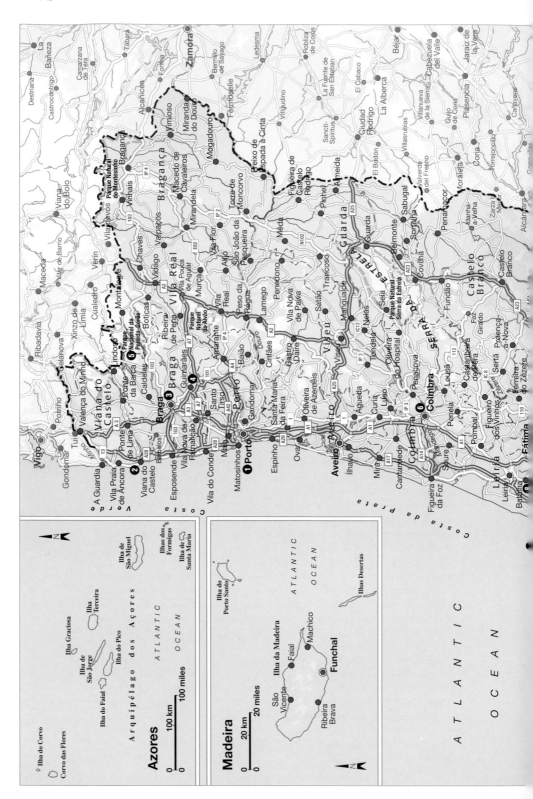

Azores

Arquipélago dos Açores

ATLANTIC OCEAN

Ilha do Corvo
Corvo das Flores

Ilha de Faial
Ilha de São Jorge
Ilha Graciosa
Ilha do Pico
Ilha Terceira
Ilha de São Miguel
Ilhas dos Formigas
Ilha de Santa Maria

0   100 km
0   100 miles

Madeira

ATLANTIC OCEAN

Ilha do Porto Santo
Ilha da Madeira
São Vicente
Faial
Machico
Funchal
Ribeira Brava
Ilhas Desertas

0   20 km
0   20 miles

ATLANTIC OCEAN

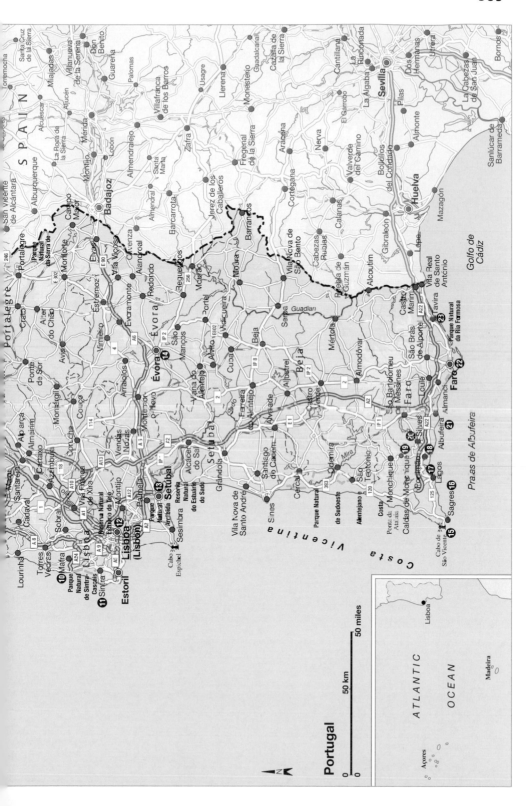

Portugal

LISBON

With a population of just 1 million inhabitants, Lisbon feels more like a large town than a major city; nevertheless, it is a vibrant and cosmopolitan capital.

Lisbon

Lisbon is one of Europe's smallest capitals, but bristles with the evidence of Portugal's former empire, that stretched from Brazil to Macao. The city is set on the right bank of the River Tagus (Tejo), facing south, and spread over seven hills, which have a number of *miradouros* – terraces and viewing points looking down over the city's rooftops. One such is the **Castelo de São Jorge ❶** (daily). Originally Roman, this castle was where the Moorish governor had his residence until 1147, when the city was taken by the Christians and it became the Portuguese royal palace, embellished by Dinis I (1279–1325) and Manuel I (1495–1521). When the palace moved down to the river, it became a fortress, then a barracks. Ten towers and sturdy walls remain, surrounded by a moat, and there is an audiovisual show of the city's history.

The area around the castle, the **Alfama**, is the oldest part of the city, where lanes and tram lines meander up and down hill and some of the alleys are so narrow two people can barely pass. One such is Rua de São Pedro, where fisherwomen sell the daily catch or eat fresh fish in tiny front rooms. The **Sé ❷** (cathedral) is a solid structure fronted by two towers and a fine rose window. Inside is the font where St Anthony of Padua, the city's unofficial patron saint, was christened in 1195. The relics of St Vincent, the city's

The Castelo de São Jorge.

official patron saint, are displayed in the treasury. Opposite is **Sant Antonio de Sé**, a small church built over the room where St Anthony was born.

Historic heart

The royal residence was transferred from the castle to the waterfront at what is now the **Praça do Comércio ❸**, still known to locals as Terreiro do Paço (Palace Square). The palace was just one of the casualties of the 1755 earthquake that reduced most of Lisbon to rubble. The massive rebuilding programme was

Main Attractions

Castelo de São Jorge
Sé (Cathedral)
Praça do Comercio
Museo do Design e do Moda
Fundação Calouste Gulbenkian
Museu Nacional do Azulejo
Mosteiro dos Jerónimos

The Santa Justa Elevator was designed by Gustave Eiffel of Paris fame.

undertaken by the Marquês de Pombal, the autocratic prime minister who didn't bother to wait for the rubble to be cleared away, but just rebuilt the new city on top. The Neoclassical pink arcades of this square are typical "Pombaline Lisbon". In 1908, in the northwest corner, King Carlos I and his heir Luís Felipe were assassinated in an open carriage.

Two years later a republic was declared from the balcony of the 19th-century **Municipio** (town hall) in nearby Praça do Municipio. At its centre is a twisted column with a banded sphere, a symbol of the city and of Portuguese knowledge and power and a typical device of the Manueline or Portuguese Gothic style from the country's "golden age" under King Manuel I (1495–1521). A central archway on the north side of Praça do Comércio leads to the **Baixa**, the downtown shopping district. Its Rua do Ouro and Rua da Plata, Gold and Silver streets, hark back to the times when precious metals arrived from the New World.

Up on the west side of the Baixa is the **Bairro Alto**, reached via steep lanes by the Santa Justa lift, a whimsical iron structure designed by Gustave Eiffel.

The 18th-century earthquake demolished the monastery of **Carmo** ❹ and left its church roofless; today it is an archaeological museum (Mon–Sat). The quake also brought down the facade of the pretty little church of **São Roque**.

The Bairro Alto is full of restaurants and nightspots, and *fado*, the famous Portuguese song, can be heard here. The city's Italianate opera house, **Teatro de São Carlos**, built in 1792, is also here, as is the smart shopping district, **Chaido**. An evening out may well start at the **Solar do Instituto do Vinho do Porto** ❺, the Port Wine Institute in Rua São Pedro de Alcântara, a bar with a club-like atmosphere where a large selection of port is available to try. The *miradoura* opposite has a grand view across the Baixa to the castle. The Gloria funicular leads back down to Praça de Restauradores and the neo-Manueline Rossio station, where suburban trains run to Benfica and Sintra. **Rossio** was once the city's main square, and where bullfights, carnivals and *autos da fé* took place. Today, entertainment is confined to the **Teatro Nacional** (National Theatre) ❻, built in 1840. The two large

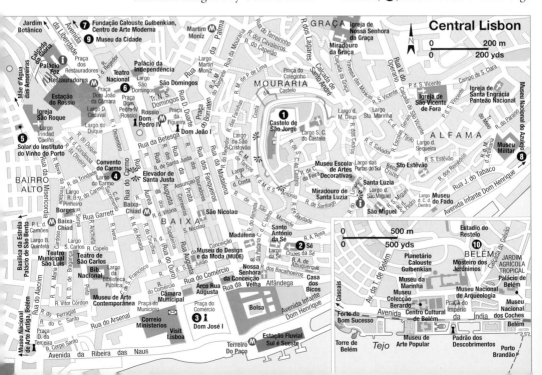

fountains in the square were brought from Paris in 1890.

Beyond Restauradores is Avenida da Liberdade, the city's grand avenue. At the top, in a square named after him, is a statue of the Marquês de Pombal, looking down on all he created.

Other attractions

Lisbon's other great benefactor was Calouste Gulbenkian, the Armenian oil magnate. His gift to the city is the **Fundação Calouste Gulbenkian ❼** (Tue–Sun) the city's principal culture centre, with a large general art collection and a Museum of Modern Art. It is above the Pombal statue beside Parque Eduardo VII, which has two fine botanical houses.

To the east of the city, beyond the Alfama, is the **Museo Nacional do Azulejo ❽** (National Museum of Tiles; Tue–Sun). Housed in the splendid Madre de Deus church, this is a museum dedicated to Portugal's principal native art: highly coloured glazed tiles. The **Museu da Cidade ❾**, the City Museum (Tue–Sun), is in the 18th-century Palacio Pimenta at Campo Grande.

Although **Belém ❿** is 5km (3 miles) west of the centre, no visit to the city should exclude it. This is the Lisbon of the navigators, the visionaries and the soldiers of fortune. On the flat land beside the river is the **Torre de Belém**, the city's enduring landmark. Built in 1521 to defend the harbour called Restello that used to be here, this was the navigators' point of departure.

In 1497, at the start of his epic voyage to India, Vasco da Gama prayed in a small chapel beside the Restello, built by Prince Henry the Navigator. The chapel was levelled shortly afterwards, and in its place arose the spectacular **Mostciro dos Jerónimos** (Tue–Sun) and its church of **Santa María**. It is a perfect symbol of the extravagant Age of Discovery, the epitome of the Manueline style.

Beyond Belém the river widens as it enters the ocean. On the same bank are the smart resorts of **Cascais** and **Estoril**, 30 to 45 minutes from Cais do Sodré station on Lisbon's waterfront. This is the former "Coast of Kings", where several deposed European monarchs spent their years of exile.

The Monument to the Discoveries by the River Tagus in Belém

DESIGN SHOWCASE

One of the world's top museums for 20th-century design, Lisbon's **MUDE** or **Museo do Design e do Moda** (Design and Fashion Museum; Tue–Sun) opened after a comprehensive transformation of its home in the heart of Baixa, in what was formerly a bank. What this contemporary white space now has on permanent display includes Portuguese businessman Francisco Capelo's fashion collection, which comprises some 1,200 couture pieces, including the famous Jean Desses gown worn by Renee Zellweger to the Oscars. Other top designers represented include Philippe Starck, Charles Eames, Arne Jacobsen and Tom Dixon. The centre also hosts temporary shows. Visit www.mude.pt for information on forthcoming programmes.

AROUND PORTUGAL

On the edge of Europe, this is the land of sad songs called *fados*, and the place from which two great navigators, Vasco da Gama and Ferdinand Magellan, set sail to discover new worlds.

Main Attractions

Vila Nova de Gaia, Porto
Peneda-Gerês National Park
Coimbra
Tomar
Sintra
Évora
Portimão
Silves
Faro
Tavira

ortugal is a compact country, making it easy to get to know. Essentially, it has three main regions: the green, cool north, traditionally the area least visited by foreigners – except for Porto itself and its wine cellars, but with many other fascinating historic towns; the centre, with Lisbon, spectacular Atlantic beaches and great cultural highlights such as Coimbra and Sintra; and the hot, brown south, with the beach towns of the Algarve.

Porto

Portugal takes its name from its second city, **Porto ❶** (Oporto), which has become synonymous with its fortified wine. Majestically sited on rocky cliffs overlooking the River Douro, it was originally two cities each side of the river's mouth: Portus on the right bank, Cale on the left. And, when Alfonso Henriques united the country in the 12th century, he called his new kingdom Portucalia. Porto is a stern and sober city of granite church towers and narrow streets, and its Baroque treasures must be hunted out. The **Igreja de São Francisco** (Church of San Francisco) in Praça do Infante Dom Henrique should be seen for its Baroque splendour, while the **Salon de Arabe** in the Palacio da Bolsa is a remarkably opulent Neo-Moorish

reception hall. Up the hill from the stock exchange, wines can be tasted at the **Solar do Vinho do Porto** or at any of the 60 or so port-wine lodges in **Vila Nova de Gaia** on the south side of the Dom Luís I Bridge. The **Cais de Ribera** on the riverbank is the liveliest part of the city, where small shops and restaurants are built into the old city wall.

Nighttimes are quiet, and young people tend to head for the Foz de Douro suburb; an older set to the coastal resort of Espinho, where

Boats along the Douro River, Porto.

The Convento do Cristo in Tomar was built as part of a defensive system against the Moorish invaders.

The Church of Bom Jesús do Monte is a place of pilgrimage.

there is a casino and nightclub. When festivities are on the calendar, however, the town livens up. At the **Alameda das Fontainhas**, a square overlooking the Dom Luís I Bridge, people sing and dance round bonfires, drink *vinho verde*, the refreshing, slightly sparkling local wine, and feast on roast kid and sardines.

The Green Coast

The verdant wine lands of the Douro and Minho rivers colour the whole coast, giving it its name, the **Costa Verde**. The main resort town north of Porto is **Viana do Castelo ❷**, where the splendid Basilica of Santa Luzia looks over the sweep of sandy beaches.

Minho's capital, **Braga ❸**, is the former seat of powerful bishops. Its Baroque **Sé** (cathedral) was built in the 12th century by Henri of Burgundy and his wife Dona Teresa, whose tombs you can find in one of the richly decorated chapels. A famous church in the vicinity is the **Bom Jesús do Monte** (5km/3 miles from Braga), an important place of pilgrimage.

Just to the south is **Guimarães ❹**, the first capital of Portugal, with a 10th-century castle (Tue–Sun) and the Church of Our Lady of the Olive Tree, which has a Romanesque cloister and an interesting museum. The massive granite Paço do Duques (daily), the Palace of the Dukes of Bragança, can also be visited.

In the far northwest is the remote **Trás-os-Montes**, where life was so harsh in post-war years that many people emigrated to what were then the Portuguese colonies in Africa; in the current crisis, emigration is more often an option for well-educated young college graduates. The attractions here include Miranda do Douro and Rio de Onor, two quiet villages where life is a million miles from the 21st century. On its edges is the 70,000-hectare (173,000-acre) **Peneda-Gerês National Park ❺**, which is crossed by several rivers, has a series of lakes and is superb for water sports.

Coimbra to Nazaré

South of Oporto, perched on a hill overlooking the River Mondego, is the university town of **Coimbra ❻**. The tangle of narrow streets at the heart of the Old Town leads to the Pátio das Escolas, reached through the 17th-century Porta Férrea. Behind the statue of João III, who gave his palace to the university, is a magnificent view of the river below, and one of the most beautiful libraries in the world, with magnificent ceiling frescoes. Luís de Camões (1524–80), Portugal's greatest poet, was a student here. University students have something of a monopoly on the local *fado*, which is more serious and intellectual than the *fado* sung in Lisbon, and to show their approval the people in the audience are not supposed to clap but merely to clear their throats.

Map on page 382

One of the country's greatest traditions is the pilgrimage at **Fátima** ❼, between Coimbra and Lisbon. On 13 May 1917 three shepherd girls had a vision of the Virgin Mary, who appeared in a glow of light over an oak tree. She asked them to pray for the peace of the world and promised to return on the 13th day of each month until October. Those are the days that have been celebrated ever since, when thousands come to the basilica beside a colonnaded square, which has accommodated up to 1 million people during visits by the pope.

Tomar, east of Fátima, is a delightful town with a castle, the former Portuguese headquarters of the Knights Templar, and the splendid Convento do Cristo, a Unesco World Heritage site (daily). **Batalha** ❽, 20km (12 miles) west of Fátima, has a beautiful Gothic abbey, Santa Maria da Vitória. The ornate façade hides a simple, elegant interior, while the cloister is built in Portugal's elaborate Manueline Gothic style, named after the monarch who benefited most from the riches brought by the

early discoveries. Its typical flourishes include nautical fantasy and, the symbol of Portuguese knowledge and power, the armillary sphere. Most striking of all are the **Capelas Imperfeitas**, the Unfinished Chapels, which suffered when the royal coffers ran low.

At **Alcobaça**, just to the south, is the Mosteiro de Santa Maria de Alcobaça (Monastery of Alcobaça), Portugal's largest church and Cistercian abbey, and another World Heritage site. Fine medieval stone carvings tell the tale of Pedro I, who exhumed his mistress who was assassinated by his father, crowned her queen and ordered his nobles kiss her hand. On the coast is **Nazaré** ❾, a timeless fishing village where fishermen wear stocking caps, and the colourful boats are hauled up the beach by oxen. Thanks to a deep underwater cleft some of the biggest waves in the world have been recorded on the beach at Nazaré, which has made the area a surfing mecca. However, the currents here are also very powerful, so all bathers need to take great care. On the road to Lisbon, stop off at Óbidos, a picturesque gem

The flamboyant Royal Palace at Sintra.

WHERE

Portugal has its own distinctive style of bullfighting. The main performers are horsemen (and women) who taunt the bull and stick small spikes in its back, and groups of eight men who run in front of it and try to wrestle it to the ground. In contrast to Spain, the bull is not killed in the ring. Lisbon's Campo Pequeno is Portugal's main bullring, and there are also often fights in the Algarve.

Praia da Rocha is famed for its strange rock formations.

of a town perched on a hill, with narrow cobbled streets lined with whitewashed, bougainvillea-draped houses.

Around Lisbon

Near Lisbon is **the Palácio Nacional de Mafra** ❿ (Palace: Wed–Mon; Church: daily), which started life as a Capuchin monastery and was expanded into something more palatial by João V in the 18th century after gold started to arrive from Brazil. A craft school was established, and among the teachers was the sculptor Joaquim Machado de Castro. The building dwarfs the town of Mafra itself; the limestone facade is 220 metres (720ft) long, and behind it is a church, which shows off Portugal's wonderful marble. But the high spot of the building is its beautiful Baroque library of 35,000 books, including the first editions of Camões's *Os Lusíadas* and the earliest edition of Homer in Greek.

Mafra is a good place to visit from Lisbon, but **Sintra** ⓫, 25km (15 miles) northwest of the city, is a must, captivating everyone who sees

it. The **Royal Palace** (daily), used by Portugal's monarchs for 600 years, was built by King João I at the end of the 14th century, and extended by Manuel I in the 16th century. It has Portugal's finest *azulejos* (tiles), which cover its Arab and Swan halls and the chapel. Beautifully situated, the palace is floodlit at night and there is often a *son et lumière* performance in summer.

Another royal residence (daily) is at **Queluz**, an 18th-century small-scale Versailles 14km (9 miles) west of Lisbon. Among the interior's gilt and glass is a magnificent throne room, now used for concerts. A ferry ride across the Tagus from **Lisbon** ⓬ (Lisboa; see page 385) is the industrial heartland of **Setúbal** ⓭, which is worth negotiating for the **Igreja de Jesus** (Church of Jesus). This was an early work of Bioitaca, the architect of the Jerónimos Monastery, with Manueline details such as gorgeous entwined columns in the interior. There are some good primitive paintings in the museum, which is worth a visit.

Alentejo is the "land beyond the Tejo"; in other words, south of the

River Tagus. This is the flattest part of the country, one-third of it covered by parched plains of oak woods and olive groves. Its main town is **Évora** ⑭, an ancient city which had its time of brilliance as a favoured residence of the kings of the Burgundy and Avis dynasty; its sites, from a Roman Temple of Diana to the cathedral and university, are worth a day trip.

The Algarve

The south-facing 150km (95-mile) southern coastal strip of Portugal is very different from the rest of the country. Its architecture is Moorish, its vegetation is almost subtropical and the sea temperature in winter rarely falls below 15°C (59°F). In the 1970s it took off as a tourist destination, served by the airport at Faro. Time-share villas and apartments and second homes began surrounding the towns and springing up as isolated "property resorts". But there are still characterful villages and undeveloped beaches to go with the infrastructure of golf courses, casinos, water sports and other tourist necessities.

Algarve is from the Arabic *al gharb*, meaning "the west". Its western extremity is **Cabo de São Vicente** ⑮ described as *o fim do mundo*, "the end of the world". It is a wild corner, where the wind has bent almond trees double. Europe's second-most powerful lighthouse, which can be visited, can be seen 96km (56 miles) away. The red earth rises in cliffs of impressive height, reaching 150 metres (500ft) at **Tôrre de Asp**.

Five km (3 miles) east of Cape St Vincent at the lobster-fishing port of **Sagres** ⑯, Henry the Navigator (Infante Dom Henrique, 1394–1460) established a school of navigation, where Vasco da Gama, Christopher Columbus and many other explorers acquired their skills. It was housed in the Forteleza, the huge, severe-looking fortress, rebuilt in the 17th century, and the 39-metre (130ft)

Traditional pottery in Alentejo.

An olive grove in the Alentejo countryside.

compass rose Henry used to make his calculations is laid out in stone. Henry's interest in Sagres helped open up an area cut off from the rest of the country: the **Caldeirão** and **Monchique** mountain ranges stretching behind it had seen to that, while in the east the River Guadiana provided a border with Spain.

In the whirl of adventure in the 15th century, as riches were brought back from the east, the port of **Lagos** ❿ was filled with caravels, and it was here that the first slave market was established in Europe. The town has a good natural harbour, which the Romans used, and in Moorish times it was a trade centre with Africa. An especially delightful church is the **Igreja de Santo António**. Its rich gilt Baroque interior has earned it the name of the "Golden Chapel" and reflects the wealth this town once had. Near the town are a number of grottoes that can be explored by boat.

Portimão to Albufeira

Off to the beach at Ilha de Tavira.

From Silves, the River Arade slips down to the sea at **Praia da Rocha**,

the longest-established resort on the coast. The wide sandy beach is backed by a cliff-top promenade lined with villas and hotels. The resort was initiated at the beginning of the 20th century by the wealthy people of **Portimão** ⓲, an attractive old fishing port 3km (2 miles) up the estuary which has become the busiest town on this western stretch of the coast. *Carinhas*, horse-drawn coaches, take tourists between the two places.

Portimão is a good shopping centre, and the tuna and sardine catches can be sampled in its many restaurants, such as the Lanterna, where smoked swordfish and fish soup are specialities and its fish soup is claimed to be the best on the coast. *Caldeirada*, a fish chowder, is often on local menus, as is *cataplana*, a dish of clams and meat. This part of the Algarve is the biggest remaining game-fishing centre in Europe, and fishing cruisers can be hired in Portimão. The reefs where the sharks hunt are 20km (12 miles) offshore, about two hours out. Blue and copper sharks lie in wait, as does the tasty *mako* – the sharp-nosed mackerel shark. **Ferragudo** on the eastern side of the River Arade, with a fort overlooking the estuary, is a centre of windsurfing and surfboarding.

Caldas de Monchique ⓳, a spa town in the hills behind the coast, makes a change from the cosmopolitan resorts. The water is supposed to have healing properties, but people also come to buy bottles of *Medronho*, a spirit distilled from the strawberry tree, *Arbutus uneda*, which blossoms all around the spa. In the town of **Monchique** the Franciscan convent has good views over the coast.

In between is **Silves** ⓴, which as *Chelib* was the region's Moorish capital. Then it was on a navigable part of the Arade. Chelib was a centre for arts and learning, and at its height it had a population of 30,000. It fell to Sancho I of Portugal in 1189 after a six-week siege, and from then on the monarchs took the title of "King of Portugal and the Algarve". Silves has a 13th-century cathedral with part of a mosque behind the altar, and its huge castle, with solid square towers, is one of the best Moorish buildings in Portugal. The earthquake of 1755 reduced most of the town to rubble, and today the population has settled at 20,000. The **Cross of Portugal** is a 16th-century stone lacework cross on the Silves–Messines road just outside the town. Beside the main Estrada Nacional 125, 5km (3 miles) east of Lagos near **Porches**, a town famous for its decorated pottery, is an artisans' village where local wines can be tasted.

The morning fish market is one of the attractions of **Albufeira ㉑**, a small port with steep narrow streets and a tumble of whitewashed houses, topped with Moorish cupolas. It has been overwhelmed, though, by the biggest resort on the Algarve coast, and is now turned over entirely to tourism, with lines of fish restaurants, and souvenir shops spilling out onto the main street. The beach is crowded in summer, but there are quieter beaches, such as **São Rafael** and **Olhos d'Água**, nearby.

Regional capital

Albufeira is 36km (22 miles) west of **Faro ㉒**, the finest town on the coast and the regional capital. The 1755 earthquake put paid to earlier buildings, but many fine Baroque flourishes remain. The Old Town is inside what remains of its old walls and is approached through the 18th-century entrance, the Arco da Vila. Built on the site of a mosque, the Sé (cathedral) has a fine interior with a Renaissance misericordia and a lacquered organ. Among other notable churches are São Francisco, with a gilded interior, São Pedro, with good *azulejos*, and the curious Igreja do Carmo, with a chapel decorated with human bones. The Museu de Arqueologia (Archaeological

Museum; Tue–Sun) in a 16th-century convent has a good Roman collection, some of which comes from the ruins of Milreu in **Estói** 11km (7 miles) to the north. In the harbour there is now a large yacht basin. With a boat it's possible to explore the islands and sandbars just off the coast that make up the **Parque Natural da Ria Formosa**, and from Faro spits continue towards the Spanish border.

The prettiest resort on the coast is the surprisingly untouched fishing village of **Tavira ㉓**, 32km (20 miles) east of Faro. The River Asseca on which it stands, crossed by a seven-arch Roman bridge, has long silted up. Sparkling white with a castle, several churches, Moorish cupolas and lovely little gardens, it is the epitome of an Algarve town.

The country east of Tavira is little visited. The drive up to the hilltop castle at **Castro Marim** beside the Guadiana gives a feeling of remoteness, and the salt marshes to the south are busy breeding grounds for storks and noisy black-winged stilts.

A quiet but colourful street in Evora.

Café in Brussels.

INSIGHT GUIDES TRAVEL TIPS WESTERN EUROPE

Overview

Austria

Belgium

France

Germany

Greece

Italy

The Netherlands

Portugal

Spain

Switzerland

OVERVIEW

USEFUL TIPS ON TRAVELLING IN WESTERN EUROPE

ACCOMMODATION

Reservations

Unless you really wish to improvise your itinerary as you travel around, it is always advisable to reserve accommodation in advance in all European countries, at any time of year. Booking is especially recommended during peak seasons (June–Aug, particularly around the coasts, Dec–Feb in winter sports areas), and if you aim to visit particular cities it's a good idea to check whether there are any major festivals coinciding with your planned trip. To stay locally during some of the most famous festivals, such as San Fermín in Pamplona in Spain in July or the Palio in Siena in Italy in July and August, accommodation needs to be booked months ahead.

Nowadays the easiest way to book accommodation is on the internet through one of the major online travel services, which frequently offer discounted deals if you combine a room booking with a flight, car rental and other services. Alternatively, for greater simplicity many tour companies offer all-inclusive European packages combining various destinations, although this will naturally mean you have much less control over your choice of accommodation. If you are prepared to surf the internet, most hotels and bed-and-breakfasts now have their own websites, and there are many private and specialist booking services. As a starting point, the national, regional and often local tourist offices in each country also have accommodation listings on their websites, and will advise if you have a problem.

If you do travel without reservations, local tourist offices in airports and major train stations generally have room-finder services (often for a small fee), but again, at peak times you may find the choice is limited and this can be a risky strategy.

Types of accommodation

There is naturally a wide variety of accommodation in all these countries, but places to stay often fall into certain types. Some are represented by international associations or chains. Classic luxury hotels are found especially in the major cities and most traditional resort areas: **Relais & Chateaux** (www.relaischateaux. com) and **Orient Express** (www. orient-express.com) are two groups with sumptuous member hotels throughout Europe.

Over the last few years there has been a boom in most countries in small, charming or "boutique"-style hotels, on a smaller scale and with more individual character and service. Also, bed-and-breakfast accommodation in small guesthouses, private homes and farmhouses is well established in some countries – such as France – and growing in others, and often provides the best-value and most attractive rooms. Individual countries have their own B&B organisations, with online booking services.

In beach areas, there is naturally a big range of hotels with pools and other facilities. In cities and towns there are always at least a few business hotels, often run by one of several major chains: the French-based Accor Group (www.accorhotels. com) is the largest, with hotels throughout Europe under different names at varying prices and comfort levels (Sofitel, Mercure, Novotel, Ibis, All Seasons and others). Primarily aimed at business travellers, these hotels do not offer special charm, but can be a convenient option, since they have reliable modern facilities, high availability and good rates, especially for families. Some budget chains, such as Accor's Formule 1, have ultra-low prices for their functional – if soulless – rooms.

CLIMATE AND WHEN TO GO

It is difficult to generalise about the weather, but using the Alps as a rough dividing line helps. North of the Alps you can count on cold, damp winters. Summers are warm but can be rainy. The maritime climate in the west has moderate temperatures all year round. In parts of northwestern Spain, for example, the winter/summer variation might be no more than 10–18°C (18–32°F). Rainfall is fairly even, but can be heavy in spring or autumn, and a bit less in summer. The climate becomes more continental further to the east, with increasing summer warmth. Temperatures fall well below freezing in midwinter in parts of Germany and Austria.

South of the Alps, it tends to be a different story. The Mediterranean region has dry, hot summers and mild, rainy winters – although rainy days are interspersed with days of brilliant sunshine. Alpine and other highland regions are, of course,

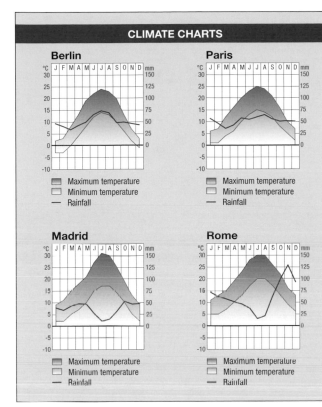

CLIMATE CHARTS

Berlin

°C J F M A M J J A S O N D mm
30 — 150
25 — 125
20 — 100
15 — 75
10 — 50
5 — 25
0 — 0
-5
-10

▩ Maximum temperature
▢ Minimum temperature
— Rainfall

Paris

°C J F M A M J J A S O N D mm
30 — 150
25 — 125
20 — 100
15 — 75
10 — 50
5 — 25
0 — 0
-5
-10

▩ Maximum temperature
▢ Minimum temperature
— Rainfall

Madrid

°C J F M A M J J A S O N D mm
30 — 150
25 — 125
20 — 100
15 — 75
10 — 50
5 — 25
0 — 0
-5
-10

▩ Maximum temperature
▢ Minimum temperature
— Rainfall

Rome

°C J F M A M J J A S O N D mm
30 — 150
25 — 125
20 — 100
15 — 75
10 — 50
5 — 25
0 — 0
-5
-10

▩ Maximum temperature
▢ Minimum temperature
— Rainfall

cooler throughout the year, and winters are commonly cold, with snow and temperatures regularly below freezing, in all mountain areas, even in Greece. Central Spain also has noticeably cooler winters than other Mediterranean areas.

Southern Spain and mainland Greece are usually the hottest places in Europe in the warmer months, between May and September, which is when most people visit Europe. In all the southern Mediterranean regions, the heat in July and August can be fierce, and cities are largely left to the tourists, as locals head for the beach; hence May–June and September are the best times to visit Mediterranean cities, for the optimum combination of warm but not uncomfortable sunshine and cultural life.

What to wear

Throughout Europe, travellers' dress can be pretty informal, except if you make an occasional evening out at the opera, a smart restaurant or some of the more glamorous casinos (such as in Monte Carlo). Men and women should dress respectfully when visiting churches or cathedrals,

especially in Italy, where anyone wearing shorts, short skirts, bare-backed dresses and anything that looks like beachwear may be refused entry.

CRIME AND SAFETY

The main problem for tourists is petty crime – pickpocketing, bag-snatching, theft from cars – and you should always have insurance to cover minor thefts. The risk of such thefts can always be greatly reduced with some sensible precautions:

1. Don't keep all money, credit cards or travellers' cheques in one wallet or purse; disperse them so one theft won't leave you totally penniless.
2. Hold bags close and keep them fastened. Never leave them unattended, and when sitting at a restaurant or café table, especially outdoors, never leave a bag hanging on the back of a chair or on the floor where you cannot see it. Keep it within reach and in sight at all times.
3. Make use of the hotel safe.
4. When walking, especially at night, be aware of anyone walking unusually

close to you.
5. Avoid using ATMs/cash machines at night or in areas with few people around.
6. Always lock your car and never leave luggage, cameras or other valuables inside, even in the boot. This applies particularly in major cities.
7. Have some form of identification in your wallet or purse, because sometimes the thief will drop stolen items (minus the money, of course) where someone might recover them. Immediately notify the local police station and (if your passport was included) your nearest consulate or embassy of any theft, and see if any of your property turns up.

If you are the victim of a crime (or lose any item) and wish to claim against your insurance, it is essential to make a report at the nearest police station and get documentation to support your claim. Refer to the Travel Tips for each individual country for emergency numbers.

CUSTOMS

All the countries featured in this book except Switzerland are members of the European Union (EU), and have a common customs regime. The exact limits sometimes vary slightly in different countries, but in general travellers not resident in the EU can import the following items duty free: up to 200 cigarettes, 100 small cigars (cigarillos), 50 cigars or 250g of tobacco; 1 litre of spirits of more than 22 percent alcohol, or 2 litres of sparkling wine or other beverage of under 22 percent alcohol, and 4 litres of still wine and 16 litres of beer; and other goods up to a value of €430 for travellers by air and sea and €300 for land travellers, provided they are not intended for sale. EU residents can carry unlimited amounts between EU states provided they are for personal use, though customs officials may question whether this is really the case if you have very large amounts of any item.

Switzerland maintains its own customs system. Allowances for foreign visitors are similar to those in the EU, but are more strictly enforced. For details look under "Swiss Customs" on the official website www. ch.ch.

If you are in doubt about what you can bring back, check with your local customs office in your home country.

AUSTRIA BELGIUM FRANCE GERMANY GREECE ITALY NETHERLANDS PORTUGAL SPAIN SWITZERLAND

EMBASSIES AND CONSULATES

Foreign embassies and consulates are usually located in the national capitals, but many governments have additional consulates in other cities and tourist regions. In extreme cases, if you lose your passport, and/or are without money or transport, they can arrange for your return home, though if you do not have suitable insurance you will subsequently be charged for this service.

Embassies and consulates are listed on the websites of your home country's foreign ministry, and in local phone directories. For main embassies, refer to the A–Z section of the relevant country in this guide.

HEALTH, INSURANCE AND MEDICAL CARE

Emergencies

Hospitals throughout Europe have emergency or casualty departments (the names for which vary), where in a medical emergency you will be treated free of charge. Otherwise, if you have a less urgent medical problem and require a doctor or dentist who speaks English or another language, lists will be available from your national consulate or, in many places, local tourist offices. Many hotels also have this information, so this is the first and most convenient place to ask. In most of the countries listed in this guide, pharmacies operate a local rota system for Sunday and night duty.

The phone number 112 has been introduced across the EU (and Switzerland) as a single number for all emergency services (police, fire, ambulance, coastguards and others), but many countries also still have their own emergency numbers for different services, which are listed under each country in this book. In an emergency you can call 112 or the local number.

Food and drink

Generally speaking, drinking and eating in Northern European countries is entirely safe. More caution may be advisable in Mediterranean countries, and in parts of Italy, Greece, Spain and Portugal, for example, it's advisable to drink bottled rather than tap water.

Electricity

Electricity systems throughout Europe run on 220–240 volts, but many modern 110v appliances from North America have built-in transformers, so an external one is not needed. All the countries in this guide use the same two-round-pin plugs (with minor local variations), so visitors from North America or the UK and Ireland will need the corresponding adaptors.

Travel insurance and medical treatment

Visitors from outside the European Union or Switzerland should always have a comprehensive travel insurance policy. This should cover you for all possible medical expenses, including repatriation to your home country if necessary, personal accidents, theft, loss or damage to any of your property and baggage and compensation in case of cancellations or delays. With private travel insurance, if you require medical treatment, you can make use of the state health services in each country on a paying basis, or private clinics. If you do have any medical treatment be sure to obtain statements of the treatment and receipts for any money paid, so that you can make an insurance claim.

EU nationals can make use of the health services in any other EU country so long as they have a European Health Insurance Card (EHIC). This has some limitations (it does not cover repatriation, for example) so it's good to have a travel insurance policy as well.

Vaccinations

No vaccinations are normally required within Europe. North of the Alps is almost always free from diseases requiring vaccination, and while Southern Europe has had instances of cholera, typhoid and hepatitis they are very rare. If you want vaccinations against any of these, you need to arrange them with your doctor several weeks before departure.

MONEY

Changing money

All but one of the countries featured in this guide uses the European common currency, the euro (€). Throughout Europe, foreign currency can be exchanged at banks, exchange agencies and (in many countries) post offices during normal working hours. Outside these hours, and sometimes round the clock, there are also bureaux de change (exchange offices) open at major train stations, airports, seaports and some frontier crossings. Money can be changed in larger hotels, but you will always get better rates at a bank or exchange office.

Switzerland is the only non-euro country in this guide, and uses the Swiss Franc (SFr, or CHF or SF). Its usual value is around SFr 1.20 = €1.

Credit cards, ATMs and travellers' cheques

Credit and debit cards are now the easiest way of obtaining money while travelling. Major cards (MasterCard and Visa) are accepted in nearly all hotels and businesses, and are essential for large transactions such as renting a car. ATMs (cash machines) with instructions in different languages are also available at nearly all bank branches that dispense euros and (in Switzerland) Swiss francs. Always check before travelling on the charges levied by your bank or credit card company for cash withdrawals abroad, which can be high; an international currency card, which you load up with a set amount from your home bank account, can be a good way of reducing charges.

Most European credit and debit cards work on a chip-and-pin system; you slot the card into a machine and enter your PIN security number to authorise payment. If your card does not operate in this way you must asked for it to be swiped in the older style.

Travellers' cheques are now so uncommon that they can be difficult

Lost Property

If your passport is lost or stolen, report this to the police and to your nearest consulate as soon as possible. The consulate will issue you with a new passport or emergency travel papers for travelling home. Make sure you have your document number or, better still, a photocopy of it (kept in a separate place) and extra passport photos, as this will speed up the process. If you lose other items, many European cities have central lost property offices, often run by the police.

Shopping

European sizes

The clothing chart is a general guide when shopping in Europe, but there will often be local variations,

Clothing chart

Women's clothing

Europe	US	UK
34	6	8
36	8	10
38	10	12
40	12	14
42	14	16
44	16	18

Women's shoes

Europe	US	UK
36	4½	3
37	5½	4
38	6½	5
39	7½	6
40	8½	7
41	9½	8
42	10½	9

Men's Suits

Europe	US	UK
44	34	34
46	36	36
48	38	38
50	40	40
52	42	42
54	44	44
56	46	46

Men's Shirts

Europe	US	UK
36	14	14
37	14½	14½
38	15	15
39	15½	15½
40	16	16
41	16½	16½
42	17	17

Men's Shoes

Europe	US	UK
39	6½	6
40	7½	7
41	8½	8
42	9½	9
43	10½	10
44	11½	11

to exchange. In many countries they can only be exchanged at larger, city bank branches, which can be inconvenient. You will very rarely be able to use travellers' cheques to pay directly for purchases, as you can in the USA, so never count on this means of payment in Europe.

Customs

You may enter or leave the countries mentioned in this book with amounts in any currency equivalent in value to up to €10,000 in cash without declaring it (or SFr10,000, equivalent to about €8,250, in Switzerland). Any larger amounts must be declared on entry. There are not usually any restrictions on movements of cash between EU countries.

Tipping

Tipping habits vary between European countries, but certain patterns commonly apply. Generalised tipping for all services at rates of around 15–20 percent, in the US style, is rare in Europe. In many countries a service charge is already applied to all restaurant bills (sometimes by law), so an additional tip is often not expected, and only given as a recognition of particularly good service. In this case, you need only leave a small amount, not a full 10 percent tip. If there is no service charge, a tip of about 10–12 percent is usually acceptable. In most countries it is not usual to leave tips in bars.

Taxi drivers often expect tips of about 10 percent, but this again varies a lot. For more details, see the sections on individual countries.

Prices and returns

In the majority of European countries, fixed prices are normal. You should bargain only at stalls in flea markets and bazaars.

Under EU law consumers have an automatic right to exchange or ask for a refund for any item if it becomes defective during two years after the date of purchase if you can demonstrate this was due to a fault in the product.

VAT and tax-free shopping

Value Added Tax (VAT) or sales tax is included in the advertised prices of most goods in all EU countries. The level of tax varies between countries. Many larger shops and stores in Europe display the "tax-free" sign, which means that travellers from non-European Union countries can receive a refund of the Value Added Tax or sales tax levied on the more substantial purchases they intend to take home. By filling out a form available at the place of purchase, you can receive a refund, amounting to as much as 25 percent of the purchase price, either upon leaving the country or by mail at your home address: see www.global-blue.com.

In tax-free shopping at airports and aboard ships, when leaving the country or in transit, the tax is excluded from the purchase price, eliminating the need for refunds. This does not apply when travelling between EU countries.

TELECOMMUNICATIONS

Internet and Wifi

Most European hotels and even many guesthouses and B&Bs now have internet and Wifi connections, in bedrooms or in public areas. A declining number of hotels still charge extra for using Wifi. There are also public Wifi areas in many cities, in museums, rail stations and sometimes public squares. For those who travel without a laptop or smart phone, internet cafés are quite easy to find in most European cities, though harder to find in France and Italy.

Mobile/cellphones

Mobile (cell) phones from outside Europe will work here so long as they have a tri- or quad-band facility, which is now standard in most phones. Check before travelling on your home service provider's charges for using a phone abroad, which can be high. Buying "bundles" of foreign calls in advance is one way of keeping costs down, and if you expect to make a lot of calls in one country it may be worth your while buying a cheap pay-as-you-go phone in Europe. A choice of phone shops can be found in any European city.

If you have a smart phone, take care to turn off automatic data roaming or its equivalent before travelling, and only connect to the

Take home some clogs.

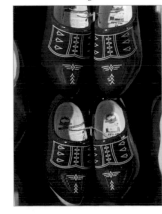

AUSTRIA
BELGIUM
FRANCE
GERMANY
GREECE
ITALY
NETHERLANDS
PORTUGAL
SPAIN
SWITZERLAND

Rules of the Road

1. Drive on the right, pass on the left (passing on the right is strictly forbidden).
2. The wearing of safety belts by the driver and the front-seat passenger is compulsory, as is the use of crash helmets by both the driver and the passenger on a motorcycle.
3. Children under 12 years must sit in the back of a car and wear seat belts.

4. As a rough guide, speed limits in built-up areas are 50–60kph (31–37mph) or as posted. On motorways they are generally 100–130kph (62–80mph) and 80–100kph (49–62mph) on dual carriageways (divided highways), with the exception of Germany, where there is no maximum speed limit on some *autobahnen* (motorways) and disciplined driving is therefore essential.

internet when you wish to, to avoid unseen charges.

Phone boxes

Public phone boxes and booths can be found at airports, railway stations and on the street, although because of the ubiquity of mobile (cell) phones they are much scarcer than they were a few years ago. Many countries offer prepaid phone cards to use in public phones, which are more convenient than paying with coins. Cards can be bought from post offices, tobacco shops, newsstands and some other outlets. Wherever you go, making phone calls from hotels will be expensive.

TIME ZONES

Most of Western Europe uses CET (Central European Time) during the winter months and Central European Summer Time (CEST) in summer (between 1:00 UTC on the last Sunday of March, and 1:00 UTC on the last Sunday of October). UTC is Coordinated Universal Time, the international time standard that is roughly the same as GMT (Greenwich Mean Time). CET is one hour ahead of UTC (+1), CEST is two hours ahead of UTC (+2). Greece uses EET (Eastern European Time) and EEST, (UTC +2 and UTC +3 respectively), while Portugal uses WET (Western European Time) and WEST (UTC +0 and UTC +1 respectively; the same as GMT and BST).

TOURIST INFORMATION

All the countries listed in this guide have extensive tourist information services. The national tourist bodies all have websites that provide an ample range of information, and

below them there are regional, city and local offices, which also have their own websites. Cities and many towns also have helpful tourist offices that will be the best place to go to for city and area maps, guides to local activities and a great variety of other material. Useful addresses and websites are listed under individual countries later in this guide.

TRANSPORT

Getting There

By air

Most visitors travel to Europe by air, through one of the continent's major international gateway airports, such as London, Paris, Amsterdam, Frankfurt, Rome or Madrid. From these air hubs it's possible to travel on to smaller airports in virtually every part of the continent, with the main carrier airlines or with one of the many low-cost European operators, such as Ryanair, EasyJet or German Wings, which have transformed the price and availability of air travel within Europe over the last 20 years. Note that low-cost flights can usually be bought only through each airline's own website, not from travel agents, major airlines or as part of a tour.

The major international airport in most European countries is near the capital city. Exceptions to this rule are Germany, where the main gateway is Frankfurt, and Switzerland, where travellers generally fly to Zürich or Geneva.

By rail

Continental Europe can be reached from the Far East by the Trans-Siberian Railway via Moscow, with onward connections to Berlin, Paris and other cities. Trains and buses link

Istanbul and the continent, travelling via Bulgaria, Romania and Hungary.

By sea

Passenger ferry services depart from Dover and various other British ports to destinations in the Netherlands, Spain and different harbours all along the north French coast, from Dunkerque in the east to Roscoff in Brittany. In the Mediterranean, there are regular ferry services from North African ports such as Tangier, Algiers and Tunis to Spain, France and Italy.

Cunard's *Queen Mary 2* is the only passenger ship still operating a regular transatlantic schedule, making 7- and 8-day crossings from the USA to Britain, France and other destinations.

Getting Around

By air

Europe has a dense network of airways interlinking all the countries in the continent, and the competition provided by low-cost airlines means that prices can be very low. Low-cost operators offer a basic, no-frills service, with no extras such as food (and often hold luggage) included, and tickets are normally available only through the companies' own websites, so you have to book them yourself, not through an agent. But they're relatively reliable, and the attraction is all in the cost. For specific information, refer to sections on individual countries.

By rail

Trains provide one of the most attractive ways of moving about Europe – allowing you to see the countryside en route – and are often the most convenient too. Modern, very comfortable high-speed trains – under different names in each country, such as TGV in France, ICE in Germany or AVE in Spain – link many cities and are competitive with flights in price and (since you don't have to waste time with airport check-ins) travel times. Other cities are linked by slower but still comfortable trains, and most countries have extensive regional and local rail

Travelling with Pets

An EU pet passport is needed if you live within the EU and wish to take your pet (dog or cat) between EU countries. Pets entering the EU from non-EU countries need a Third Country Official Veterinary Certificate.

Weights and Measures

Western Europe uses the metric system. Useful conversion rates include:

Metric to imperial
1 gram (g) = 0.04 ounces (oz)
1 kilogram (kg) = 2.2 pounds (lb)
1 litre (l) = 1.76 UK pints (pt)
1 litre (l) = 2.11 US pints (pt)
10 centimetres (cm) = 4 inches (in)
1 metre (m) = 3.28 feet (ft)

1 kilometre (km) = 0.62 miles
8 kilometres = 5 miles
Imperial to metric
1 ounce (oz) = 28 grams (g)
1 pound (lb) = 454 grams (g)
1 US pint (pt) = 0.47 litres (l)
1 UK pint (pt) = 0.55 litres (l)
1 inch (in) = 2.54 centimetres (cm)
1 foot (ft) = 30 centimetres (cm)
1 mile = 1.6 kilometres (km)

networks with trains that stop at small stations. On many long-distance and international routes overnight sleeper services are also available.

A wide range of rail passes is available providing unlimited travel in one or more countries for a set period of time, from 15 days to 3 months, which must be bought outside the countries covered by the pass. Eurail passes are the main types available to non-European residents, while the similar pass for EU residents is called InterRail. Rail passes will save money if you make a lot of train trips, but if you only make a few main journeys it will be cheaper to buy individual tickets, especially since in some countries pass holders pay supplements to use some of the most attractive trains (such as high-speed lines).

Rail Europe (www.raileurope. com) is the global information and bookings portal for railways throughout Western Europe (including the Eurostar between London, Paris and Brussels), with full information on mainline services, timetables, and all rail passes. Through it you can also book mainline tickets and rail passes. Information on regional and local services is normally available only from each country's rail company. Another invaluable source of information on all aspects of travelling by train in Europe (including rail passes) is the **Man in Seat 61** site, www.seat61.com.

By road

Buses: Eurolines (www.eurolines. com) is a consortium of European coach companies that operate routes all around the continent, connecting all major cities, and Megabus (www. megabus.com) offers very cheap bus services between Paris, Amsterdam, Brussels and many destinations in Britain. Buses provide the cheapest form of long-distance transport in Europe, but journey times are often very long, so flying or taking the train are generally more attractive.
Cars: To get the best prices for car rentals across Europe it is always

advisable to book online, either through the websites of any of the major international rental chains or one of the specialist car-rental websites such as www.autoeurope.com, which allow you to compare prices. It's always worth checking around, as most companies have occasional special offers. Lower rates can also be obtained if you book a rental car together with a flight and/ or hotels through any of the major web travel services.

There is a choice of rental agencies in most European cities, located especially at airports and main train stations. To rent a car drivers must normally be over 21 and have a valid driving license and a credit card. International Driving Permits are not usually necessary. Insurance conditions may vary between companies, so check when renting.

Motoring Advice

All vehicle insurance policies issued in the EU automatically include basic third-party insurance cover in all EU countries, but if you take a car around Europe (for example from the UK) it is advisable to take out comprehensive European cover as well. In several countries (notably France, Spain and Italy) it is a legal requirement to carry in all cars a yellow reflective waistcoat and a red warning triangle for use in case of accidents or breakdowns. If you ever have to pull over by the roadside, you must put on the yellow jacket, and place the triangle at least 30 metres (98ft) behind the car. When renting, check that this equipment has been supplied with the car.

Driving while under the influence of alcohol carries stiff penalties in Europe, and motorists with a blood-alcohol content of 0.8 percent or more are considered intoxicated. In some countries, *any* use of alcohol before or while driving is illegal and punishable by a fine.

Motorways

An extensive network of fast main highways (autoroutes in France,

autobahnen in Germany, autopistas and autovías in Spain, and so on) links the whole of Western Europe. Main motorways have rest stops open 24 hours a day and except during peak-season traffic jams generally allow you to travel very fast, but are dull to drive. In most countries, with the important exceptions of Germany, Belgium and the Netherlands, tolls have to be paid to use most motorways. In Spain and France some have tolls and some are free.
Taxis: Taxis are abundant in the larger cities and can be hailed in the streets, booked by telephone or obtained at taxi ranks, usually found at railway stations, airports and in main city squares. Fares differ from place to place, but in general are significantly lower (and taxis scarcer) in small towns. All official taxis are equipped with meters – avoid any that aren't. Supplements are generally charged for luggage, and for trips outside the city limits (to airports, for example). A tip of 10 percent or rounding up the fare is customary.

VISAS AND PASSPORTS

All the countries featured in this guide, including Switzerland, are part of the EU's Schengen Agreement, with open borders between them and shared entry procedures. Visitors from the USA, Canada, Australia, New Zealand, Japan, Brazil and some other countries need only a valid passport for stays anywhere in the Schengen area for up to 90 days. Citizens of Russia, China and many other countries must obtain a Schengen visa valid for their stay before they travel. This will be valid for the whole Schengen Area, not just the country in which you first arrive. For more information, see www. theschengenoffice.com.

Schengen visas are not valid for travel to the UK and Ireland, for which citizens of these countries must apply for a separate visa.

Greek passport control post.

AUSTRIA

ESSENTIAL TRAVEL TIPS

FACT FILE

Area: 83,883 sq km (32,371 sq miles)
Capital: Vienna
Population: 8.4 million
Language: German
Highest mountain: Grossglockner 3,798 metres (12,460ft)
Religion: Roman Catholic (68.5 percent), Protestant (4.7 percent), none (17.1 percent), plus Muslims, Jews, Hindus, Sikhs and Buddhists.
Time zone: CET/CEST, see page 402.
Currency: the euro (€)
International dialling code: 43

TRANSPORT

Getting to Austria

By air

Vienna's Swechat Airport or **Vienna International** (www.viennaairport.com) has long-haul flights (from Singapore, China, Japan, Thailand, South Korea, Russia and the USA) and flights from every part of Europe, with **Austrian Airlines** (www.austrian.com), British Airways, Air France and many other operators. Of the low-cost airlines, **easyJet** (www.easyjet.com) flies to Vienna, Salzburg and Innsbruck from the UK, **Ryanair** (www.ryanair.com) flies to Salzburg, Graz, Linz and Klagenfurt, also from the UK, and **Air Berlin** (www.airberlin.com) and **German Wings** (www.germanwings.com) fly from Vienna and Salzburg to destinations all over Germany and most other European countries.

Schwechat Airport is 15km (9 miles) east of the city. Information desks are located in the arrivals hall. The quickest connection to the city (16 mins) is by the CAT (City Airport Train), which runs half-hourly to and from the City Air Terminal at Wien Mitte station from 6.05am–11.35pm (from Vienna 5.38am–11.03pm). A cheaper but slower (24 minutes) connection is provided by S-Bahn (Schnellbahn or suburban railway) every 30 minutes from the airport to Wien Mitte from 4.54am–12.18am (from Vienna 4.31am–11.46pm).

The Vienna Airport Line express bus links the airport with Vienna's two main railway stations every 20 minutes between 6am–8pm, and every 30 minutes between 8pm–midnight, and to the U-Bahn (underground) Schwedenplatz/Morzinplatz station in the city centre every 30 minutes between 6.20am–12.20am. Airport Service Wien is a private shuttle service that takes you to your exact address (tel: 676-351 6420; www.airportservice.at). **Vienna Airport information:** tel: 01-7007-22233.

At Austria's smaller airports, such as Salzburg, there are local bus and taxi services.

By rail

There are two main stations in Vienna: the Westbahnhof serves Germany, France, Belgium, Switzerland and the Netherlands, while the Südbahnhof serves Slovenia, Slovakia, Italy, Hungary and the Czech Republic. Fast "Railjet" trains run to Vienna from Munich and overnight sleeper trains from Cologne, where they connect with trains from Paris, Brussels, Amsterdam and other destinations. Journey time from Paris is about 16 hours, with a stop in Germany; the Cologne–Vienna sleeper takes about 13 hours. For information and bookings see www.raileurope.com.

By road

Vienna is about 1,300km (800 miles) from the northern French coast at Calais. Driving to Vienna from Paris, for example, can take just under 13 hours, with scarcely any stops and taking full advantage of Germany's fast toll-free motorways. Entering Austria from Italy in winter can be slow, particularly via the less busy Alpine passes, which may be closed completely at night. You can put your car on the train for part of the journey, as Austrian Railways (www.oebb.at) operates car-trains between Vienna and Feldkirch, Linz, Villach, and (during the ski season) Innsbruck.

Eurolines (www.eurolines.com) international buses provide services from several starting points around Europe, particularly in Germany, to Vienna and other Austrian cities, at very low fares.

Getting around Austria

By rail

Given the reliable services operated by öBB (Österreichische Bundesbahnen, the Austrian State Railway; www.oebb.at) and a small number of private companies, rail is the preferred method of travel within Austria. The network is comprehensive, leaving only remote villages to be served by bus. The fast Railjet and InterCity trains link the main centres. The Greater Vienna area is served by an extensive S-bahn (suburban rail) network, with trains running at 15- or 30-minute intervals.

Eurail passes are valid on most trains in Austria, but supplements have to be paid on most international routes.

By road

Bus: Places without a rail service can be reached with Postbus or Bundesbuses, operated by the post office and federal railways. For more bus information, call 0810-222 333 within Austria; www.postbus.at.
Motoring advice: (See also page 403.) Drivers in Austria must have a red breakdown triangle and yellow reflective jacket waistcoat in the car, whether it is their own or rented. If you use motorways or main highways, you must display a toll sticker on your windscreen, available from Austrian Automobile Clubs, post offices, border posts and gas stations. Your car rental company should also supply one. They can be valid for 10 days (€8), two months or one year.

Parking is often free in town centres, but time-limited, in which case a parking disc must be obtained and set (available from tobacco shops). Elsewhere, on-street parking is controlled by vouchers or meters.

The alcohol limit is 0.5 percent, meaning that you are at risk after a single drink. The police must be called to the scene of all car accidents in which anyone is injured. ÖAMTC (Austrian Automobile Club; www.ocamtc.at) and ARBO (Austrian Drivers' Association; www.arboe.at) provide breakdown services along main roads.
ARBÖ breakdown service: tel: 123.
ÖAMTC breakdown service: tel: 120.

Getting around Vienna

A car is superfluous in Vienna, and may even be a liability, as parking

Cruising on the Danube

From April to mid-October boats operate regular cruises along the Danube, as well as on all larger lakes in Austria.
DD Blue Danube (Handelskai 265, A-1020 Vienna; tel: 01 588 80; www.ddsg-blue-danube.at) operates one of the most comprehensive schedules: daily one-way and round-trip cruises of Vienna and the World Heritage-listed Wachau Valley; cruises from Vienna to Dürnstein, and Donau-Auen National Park; and longer trips to Bratislava and Budapest (both daily May–Sept). More reduced timetables operate in winter.

is limited and the city has excellent urban and regional transport systems. The **Vienna Card**, which provides unlimited travel by underground, bus and tram over a three-day period for €19.90 and discounts on entry to 210 city attractions, is available from the Vienna Tourist Information Offices at the airport and in Albertinaplatz, and in advance online (www.wien.info). Children under 16 travel free with an adult with a card. For full current information on local transport see the local transport authority site (in English), www.wienerlinien.at.
Bicycles: The Ringstrasse makes a perfect circular route for sightseeing, and the Wienerwald on the city outskirts has 230km (144 miles) of cycle paths. Rent bicycles from main-line railway stations or from Pedal Power (www.pedalpower.at), which organises guided tours (advance booking required).
Trains (Schnellbahn/S-Bahn): Rapid transit suburban trains depart from the Sudbahnhof, Wien Nord and Wien Mitte stations for outlying districts.
Buses: Tickets are bought from a conductor or a machine. The main city-centre routes are 1a (from Schottentor to Stephansplatz), 2a (from Burgring to Graben) and 3a (from Schottenring to Schwarzenbergplatz).
Trams (Strassenbahn): These cover some 35 routes, and on most, the driver serves as the conductor. If you have a ticket, enter by the door marked *Entwerter* and have it stamped; otherwise board at the front and buy your ticket from the vending machine.
Underground (U-Bahn): Five lines cover the main parts of the city. Purchase tickets from vending machines or ticket offices. Most services operate daily 5am–midnight, and the U-Bahn operates all night on Fridays and Saturdays. Elsewhere, night buses operate. A single ticket for a journey by tram, bus and underground costs €2. Travel passes are available for 24 hours (€6.70), 48 hours (€11.70) and 72 hours (€14.50). Children under six travel free.

AUSTRIA A–Z

Accommodation

The Austrian Tourist Office (www.austria.info) and Vienna Tourist Board (www.wien.info) provide extensive lists

of hotels, *Pensionen* (guesthouses), Alpine chalets, *kinderhotels* (specialist hotels for families) and other accommodation on their websites, with booking services. Alternatives to hotels include staying on a farm or wine estate (Ferien im Bauernhof; www.farmholidays.com has farm accommodation throughout Austria), renting an apartment, dossing down in a mountain hut or using campsites and youth hostels.

Arts and activities

In the capital, the Vienna Tourist Board has event listings at offices and online (www.wien.info), and the Vienna Card provides discounts on 210 attractions, theatres, concerts, restaurants and *Heurigen* (wine taverns).

Classical music, opera and theatre are major attractions in Vienna. The two main opera venues are the **Staatsoper** (tel: 01-514-44 7880; www.staatsoper.at) and the **Volksoper** (tel: 01-514-44 3670; www.volksoper.at). The Vienna Philharmonic Orchestra performs at the **Musikverein** (tel: 01-505 8190; www.musikverein.at). At **Schönbrunn Palace** (www.schoenbrunn.at), the Palace Orchestra performs Mozart and Strauss concerts. Tickets sell out early.

Jazz, gospel, world, pop and classical music can be heard at the **Konzerthaus** (tel: 01-242 002; www.konzerthaus.at).

The Vienna Boys' Choir (Wiener Sängerknaben) sings every Sunday at 9.15am (Jan–June and Sept–Dec) in the Hofburg's Burgkapelle (Court Chapel). Tickets must be booked in advance, through www.wsk.at or www.hofburgkapelle.at, or tel: 01-533-9927.

Salzburg also has an extensive cultural programme, focused naturally on Mozart but also including more contemporary arts. The Salzburg Festival from July–Oct is the highlight, but there are also a Whitsun Festival of classical music (May) and jazz festivals (Oct–Nov). For information see www.salzburg.info.

Budgeting for your trip

Accommodation:
Meals: Allow €18–25 per person for a standard meal with a glass of wine.
Sightseeing: Museum entrance fees vary, with concessions for holders of the Vienna Card, schoolchildren (passport required) and students (ISIC card required). Allow €30 for a short *fiaker* (horse-drawn carriage) tour, €8 for a visit to the cinema, and €5–10

for entrance to a club.

Transport: From the airport, the CAT airport train to the city centre costs €12 single. A single ticket on the S-bahn is €4. Children under 15 travel free on Sundays, public holidays and during Viennese school holidays (ID essential). Taxi meters start at around €2, then add €1 per kilometre. Car rental (with advance booking from abroad) is from €25–30 per day.

Children

With numerous attractions, and many hotels offering special rates for family rooms, travelling in Austria with children is remarkably hassle-free. In Vienna, children under 6 years of age travel free on all public transport, and those under 15 travel for free on Sundays and public holidays. There are reduced fares on other public transport, and for admission to museums.

Climate

Spring is Vienna's most pleasant season, with chestnut trees in bloom for the city's music festival. In July and August the Viennese leave the city relatively free for visitors, and in autumn, the Wienerwald is in splendid colour for the Heuriger wine gardens (Mar–Oct), and the opera and theatre season kicks off. Winter is, of course, the great sports season in the Tirol and the Alps, with snow normally from December to March. Austrians dress up for the theatre, concerts and opera, but a dark suit or cocktail dress is nearly always appropriate.

Disabled travellers

Vienna and Austria in general have become much more welcoming to travellers with disabilities, with improved access to public transport, sights and hotels. Free assistance for disabled travellers is provided at Vienna Airport and all the airport taxi-transfer services have adapted vehicles (www.viennaairport.com). The CAT Airport Train is accessible, and the U-Bahn has lifts and restrooms to accommodate wheelchairs at many stations. However, older trams and buses are less accessible due to their steps. Outside Vienna, Austrian Railways' trains, and most stations, are also accessible. For more information see the "Accessible" page on www.wien.info.

Eating out

Remember that Vienna was once the centre of the old Habsburg Empire, so Bohemian dumplings, Hungarian goulash, Polish stuffed cabbage and Serbian *schaschlik* all feature. Three Austrian staples are the *Wienerschnitzel* (thinly sliced veal sautéed in a coating of egg and seasoned breadcrumbs), the *Backhendl* (roast chicken prepared in the same way) and dumplings (*knödel*). Try the *Apfelstrudel*, a flaky pastry filled with apples, raisins and cinnamon, and the *Sachertorte*, one of the world's most famous chocolate cakes. Viennese sausage stands are popular, the most famous being Hoher Markt on Marc Aurel Strasse.

Wine in Austria is almost always white, the best known being the Gumpoldskirchner. Of the reds, the Vöslauer and the Kalterersee are recommended. The local Gösser beer is a fine alternative to the imported Pilsner Urquell. Try the Hungarian Barack (apricot) and Serbian Slivovitz (plum) brandies. The Viennese

Festivals

January: Mozart Week music festival in Salzburg.
March/April: Vienna Osterklang (Sounds of Easter) music festival.
May: Gauderfest beer festival in Zell im Zillertal.
May/June: Wiener Festwochen (Vienna Festival Weeks) featuring music, dance, drama and film.
June/July: Innsbruck Tanzsommer festival of dance. Lower Austrian Danube festival of all the arts, various locations.
July–August: Bregenz Festival of music and opera with performances on a floating stage on Lake Constance. Innsbruck Festival

of Ancient Music in Schloss Ambras. Jazz Fest Wien. Mörbisch Lakeside Festival of operetta on the Neusiedlersee. Salzburg International Festival of opera, music and drama (continues into October).
August/September: Spittal an der Drau drama festival in the courtyard of Schloss Porcia.
September/October: Haydn Festival in Schloss Esterhazy in Eisenstadt; Linz International Bruckner festival; Vienna Viennale film festival. In October, Zell am Ziller Alpabtrieb celebrations to mark the return of cattle from the Alpine pastures.

Kaffeehaus dates back to the 17th century, and the varieties of coffee are virtually endless.

Embassies and consulates

Australia: Mattiellistrasse 2–4, 1040 Vienna, tel: 0800-29 18 47; www. austria.embassy.gov.au.
Canada: Laurenzerberg 2, 3rd floor, 1010 Vienna, tel: 01-531-383 000; www.canadainternational.gc.ca/austria-autriche.
South Africa: Sandgasse 33, 1190 Vienna, tel: 01-320-6493; www.dirco. gov.za/vienna.
UK: Jauresgasse 12, 1030 Vienna, tel: 01-716 130; www.britishembassy. at.
US: US Citizen Services Section, Parkring 12a, A-1010 Vienna; tel: 01-31339-7535; www.usembassy.at.

Gay and lesbian travellers

Vienna has plenty of gay-friendly bars and other establishments, and in June stages an annual gay festival, Wien Andersrum ("Vienna the Other Way Round"), which ends with a Rainbow Parade along the Ringstrasse. The Life Ball in May was founded as an AIDS awareness event. A Vienna Queer Guide is available on the city's tourism website: www. vienna.info. Smaller-scale gay scenes exist in Linz, Innsbruck, Salzburg and Graz. In the countryside, while overt hostility is unlikely, attitudes are much more conservative. The age of consent for gay men is 18.

Health and medical care

Austria is generally a very safe country with excellent medical services. Citizens of non-EU countries should ensure they have a travel and health insurance policy (see page 400). EU citizens can use the Austrian state health services with an EHIC card. The

German for hospital is *krankenhaus*, and for an emergency room/casualty department is *notaufnahme*. In case of a serious emergency, call an ambulance on tel: 144.

Visit a pharmacy *(apotheke)* for minor health problems. Chemists operate a rota system for night and Sunday duty, and display the address of the nearest shop on duty. Alternatively, call 1550 to find an on-duty pharmacist.

Nightlife

Vienna has more than 6,000 bars, nightclubs and cabarets. The area around Ruprechtsplatz, Seitenstettengasse and Rabensteig forms the previously hot Bermudadreieck (Bermuda Triangle). Apart from the excellent First Floor bar (Seitenstettengasse 5), this area is now passé, and much of the action has moved on to the Naschmarkt and Bäckerstrasse districts, and the railway arches along the Hernalser Gürtel. The tacky nightclubs around Karntnerstrasse cater largely to the tourist trade. Flex is one of Vienna's best-known clubs (www.flex.at), while along the Gürtel the scene revolves around chic bars, such as Chelsea (www.chelsea.co.at) and Q[kju:] (www.kju-bar.at). Consult the listings magazine *Falter* (www.falter.at, mostly in German only) for the latest information.

Opening hours

Banks: Monday to Friday 8am–3pm (sometimes until 5.30pm on Thursday). Most branches close 12.30–1.30pm.
Museums: Most open at 9am or 10am and close at 5pm or 6pm; there may be late opening on one day a week. Many are closed Monday.
Shops: Monday to Friday 9am–6pm. Small shops close at lunchtime while major department stores are open 8am–6pm, and in some cases 8pm. Most shops close on Saturday afternoon (though some remain open until 5pm) and all day Sunday. Shops in railway stations are open daily 7am–10.30pm.
Pharmacies: Monday to Friday 8am–noon and 2–6pm, Saturday

Tipping

Tipping is traditionally expected in restaurants, in taxis, at hairdressers and at service stations. Usually 5–10 percent is adequate.

Austria is famous for its cakes and pastries.

8am–noon.

Postal services

Post offices are generally open 8am–noon and 2–6pm. A few open on Saturday from 8–10am. In Vienna, the Central Post Office (Fleischmarkt 19) and the post offices at the Südbahnhof railway station are open 8am–10pm daily, while the Westbahnhof rail station post office is open Mon–Fri 8am–10pm, Sat, Sun 8am–8pm. Letterboxes and post office signs are yellow. Stamps can also be bought at tobacconists *(tabaktrafik)*.

Public holidays

Banks, museums, official services and many restaurants are closed on public holidays.
January: 1 New Year's Day, 6 Epiphany; **March/April**: variable Easter Monday; **May**: 1 Labour Day; **May/June**: variable Ascension Day, Whit Monday, Corpus Christi; **August**: 15 Assumption Day; **October**: 26 National Holiday; **November**: 1 All Saints' Day; **December**: 8 Immaculate Conception, 25 Christmas Day, 26 St Stephen's Day.

Shopping

Austria has an abundance of high-quality, valuable and handmade articles, including glassware, jewellery, china ware and winter-sports gear.

In Vienna, the most elegant and expensive shops, as well as art galleries and antique shops, are in the inner city area along Kohlmarkt, Graben and Karntner Strasse. Mariahilferstrasse and the university district also provide good shopping opportunities. Almost every city district has an open-air market, the most famous of these being the Naschmarkt, held along the Wienzeile near Kettenbrückengasse and open

daily. Other traditional markets include: **All Saints' Market** (Allerheiligen-markt) in front of gates 1–3 of the Central Cemetery (early November). **Christmas Market** (Christkindlmarkt) in front of the City Hall in Rathausplatz (December). **Lenten Market** (Fastenmarkt), 17 Kalvarienberggasse (February – March).

Telecommunications

Telephone calls can be made from post offices and telephone kiosks; phone cards for use in public phones can be bought from post offices. On using mobile/cellphones, see page 401. Directory enquiries: 118 899. The international code for Austria is 43, and the area code for Vienna 01. When calling from outside the country, omit the initial 0.

Tourist information

Austrian National Tourist Office, (in Austria) 00-800 400 200 00; www.austria.info.
Vienna Tourist Board, main information centre, Albertinaplatz 1 (behind Vienna State Opera), tel: 01-24555; www.wien.info. The nine federal provinces all have their own tourist boards and websites, links to which can be found on www.austria.info.

Tourist offices abroad

All can be contacted through www.austria.info.
Australia: tel: 02-9299 3621
Canada: tel: 416-967 3381
Ireland: tel: 189-093 0118
UK: tel: 0845 101 1819
US: tel: 212-944 6880

What to read

Insight Guide: Austria is a companion volume to this book. The *Salzburg Smart Guide* packs information into an easily portable format

AUSTRIA | BELGIUM | FRANCE | GERMANY | GREECE | ITALY | NETHERLANDS | PORTUGAL | SPAIN | SWITZERLAND

BELGIUM

ESSENTIAL TRAVEL TIPS

FACT FILE

Area: 30,520 sq km (11,780 sq miles)
Capital: Brussels
Population: 11 million
Languages: Flemish (Dutch), French and German
Highest point: Signal de Botrange 694 metres (2,277ft)
Religion: Roman Catholic (±50 percent), plus Protestant, Muslim, Hindu, Sikh, Buddhist and others.
Time zone: CET/CEST, see page 402.
Currency: the euro (€)
International dialling code: 32

TRANSPORT

Getting to Belgium

By air

The main gateway to Belgium is Brussels Airport (tel: 0900-70000 from inside Belgium, 02-753 7753 from outside; www.brusselsairport.be) at Zaventem, 11km (7 miles) from the city centre. Among the many airlines that fly to Brussels are: **Aer Lingus** (www.aerlingus.com), **Air Canada** (www.aircanada.com), **British Airways** (www.britishairways.com), **Brussels Airlines** (www.brusselsairlines.com), **Delta** (www.delta.com), **US Airways** (www.usairways.com) and **United Airlines** (www.united.com). From the airport train station, beneath the main terminal, four trains each hour run to all the three main Brussels rail stations (daily 6.30am–10.30pm; single fare from €7.60), and there

are also direct trains to other parts of Belgium, and bus services.

Of the low-cost airlines, **easyJet** (www.easyJet.com) has flights to Brussels from Liverpool, Berlin, Geneva and several French cities, and **Flybe** (www.flybe.com) flies there from Scotland and Northern Ireland. **Ryanair** (www.ryanair.com) has flights from airports throughout Europe, including the UK, Ireland, Spain and Italy, to the smaller Belgian airport of Charleroi, also labelled "Brussels-South" (www.charleroi-airport.com). Charleroi is 46km (29 miles) south of Brussels: a shuttle bus leaves Charleroi Airport every 30 min daily, 4am–8.30pm, for Brussels-Midi train station in the city centre (single fare €13), and there are also direct buses to Antwerp, Luxembourg and Lille and to Charleroi train station, on the main Belgian rail network.

By rail

Brussels is a major hub of the European rail network, with Eurostar trains from London via the Channel Tunnel and Lille, and high-speed Thalys or ICE trains from Paris, Amsterdam, Cologne and other cities. International trains arrive at the largest city station, Brussels South (also called Brussels Midi or Brussels Zuid). It is connected by rail to the two other main city stations, Brussels-Central and Brussels-North, and to suburban stations. Bookings for long-distance and international trains can be made through Belgian Railways or www.raileurope.com.

By road

Buses: Bus services to Brussels with often ultra-low fares are operated by Eurolines (www.eurolines.com) and Megabus (www.megabus.com), from several points in the UK as

well as Amsterdam, Paris and other European cities.

Cars: Brussels is the hub of as many European motorways as it is rail lines. Driving time to the city using major roads with no stops from Paris is about 3hrs 15min, from Amsterdam about 2hrs 30min, from Berlin 7hrs 20min. Motorways in Belgium are toll-free and, since the country is mostly flat, traffic moves very fast.

By sea

Passenger and car ferries operate regularly between the UK and the Belgian ports of Ostend and Zeebrugge. P&O Ferries (tel: UK 0871-664 2121; www.poferries.com) sail between Hull and Zeebrugge, and Transeuropa Ferries (tel: UK 01843-595 522; www.transeuropaferries.com) go between Ramsgate and Ostend.

Getting around Belgium

Belgium is small enough and the transport infrastructure good enough to make getting around the country pretty straightforward. The train is generally the best way to go by public transport, with the bus service being useful for short distances and for places not served by train. Excellent motorways and other fast roads criss-cross the country.

By rail

Belgium has extremely good trains that cover practically the whole country, operated by Belgian Railways (SNCB/NMBS; tel: 02-528 2828; www.belgianrail.be). From the three main Brussels stations there are frequent services to all the main cities (Bruges, Antwerp, Liège) and even to small destinations. As well as the standard European rail passes,

AUSTRIA

BELGIUM

FRANCE

GERMANY

GREECE

ITALY

NETHERLANDS

PORTUGAL

SPAIN

SWITZERLAND

Belgian Railways also offers its own useful discount passes, such as one giving 10 trips of any duration within Belgium of €76, and several other combinations and youth tickets. Full details are on the SNCB website. As well as by phone and online, train information is also available by mobile phone on SMS number 2828.

By road

Distances are relatively short, and motorways serve most of the country with the exception of the hilly regions of the Ardennes. All roads are toll-free. **Motoring advice:** Drivers must have a red warning triangle and yellow reflective waistcoat in their car. Parking is restricted in Brussels and other major cities, usually with a "Blue Zone" system; in these areas, parked vehicles must display a blue badge with a type of clock, which you can buy from petrol stations, tobacco shops and automobile clubs. When you park, you should set the clock at your arrival time, and will then be allowed 2–3 hours parking time, indicated on signs nearby. In Brussels and some other cities there are also pay-and-display parking zones and large pay car parks. The blood alcohol limit for drivers is 0.5 percent.

Be aware that in the northern part of the country, road signs appear in Flemish – in the southern part, in French. Several towns and villages have two names, one in each of the official languages, but road signs only show place names in the language of that particular region. In case of accident, call the emergency numbers 100 or 112.
Brussels Transport Tickets: Tickets and cards must be inserted into machines on Metro station platforms, or on board trams and buses, which automatically authorise the journey and cancel the fare. Single- and multiple-journey cards permit unlimited transfers within a one-hour period, provided the card is inserted after each vehicle change.

Getting around Brussels

The excellent public transport network of Metro, trams and buses, operated by STIB (tel: 070-232 000; www.stib.be), is easy to use and tightly integrated. Tickets of different kinds can be bought in Metro stations, newsagents and several other shops, and at tourist offices and STIB information offices. A range of combinations is available: single tickets cost from €2, 5- or 10-journey cards €7.50–13, but you can also get cards valid for 1–3 days or the Brussels Card, which gives you

unlimited access to public transport, reduced admission to many museums and discounts in some restaurants, bars and other venues. Cards can be valid for one, two or three days and cost €24–40.
Bicycles: Brussels is striving to become a cycle-friendly city, and cycle routes are increasing. Like Paris and other cities, Brussels has a public-access cycle scheme, allowing subscribers to rent a bike for an hour or more from bike stations around the city; for details see www.villo.be. Subscribing is easy online, and very cheap. For bike tours and rentals contact ProVelo, tel: 02-502 7355 (English spoken); www.provelo.org.
Buses and trams: Buses can be reduced to near-immobility in rush hours, but for short distances, the tram is usually the fastest way to travel.
Cars: Travelling by car in the city is not recommended. Trams and buses always have traffic priority, as, usually, do vehicles coming from the right, unless the road is posted with orange diamond signs.
Metro: The fast and modern Metro consists of four main lines, connecting the eastern and western parts of the city. The underground network is supplemented by two "premetro" lines, which run partly underground.
Trains: The suburban above-ground train service is also good, but is not so useful for tourists within the city limits.

BELGIUM A–Z

Accommodation

Because of its role as a centre of European institutions and business Brussels has a large number of functional business-oriented hotels, but there are also many more individual and relaxed options at different prices. Boutique-style hotels have appeared in Brussels and most other cities, and in cities and the countryside there is a wide choice of attractive guesthouses, bed-and-breakfasts and hotels in historic buildings. Extensive listings of all types of accommodation can be found on http://visitBrussels.be (for the capital) and on the separate websites for Flanders and Wallonia.

Arts and activities

In Brussels, world-class institutions like the **Théâtre Royal de la Monnaie**

(tel: 070-23 3939; www.lamonnaie.be) for opera and dance, and the **Palais des Beaux-Arts** or **BOZAR** (tel: 02-507 8200; www.bozar.be), which contains exhibition halls, cinemas and concert halls, are complemented by a large range of local museums, galleries and performance venues. Highlights include the **Musée Horta** (www.hortamuseum.be) for Brussels's Art Nouveau heritage, and the **Centre Belge de la Bande Dessinée** (www.comicscenter.net), which caters to the city's obsession with comic-strip art.

The much-praised **Royal Ballet of Flanders** (tel: 03-234 3438; www.balletvlaanderen.be) is based at the **Theater 't Eilandje** in Antwerp, and presents an adventurous range of classical and contemporary dance.

Budgeting for your trip

Prices of comparable hotels vary considerably, and those of restaurants, clubs and museums to a lesser extent, from place to place around Belgium. Brussels and Antwerp tend to be the most expensive among the major cities, followed by Bruges, Ghent and Liège.
Accommodation: The starting rate for a double room is €50; for a decent mid-range hotel in most cities, expect to pay €100–200; above €300 is starting to get into de luxe territory.
Meals: Dining costs are €10–25 for a 2–3-course meal at a decent local restaurant, €25–60 at a fine restaurant, and €100 and beyond for Michelin-level cuisine. A glass of beer can cost as little as €2 and a glass of house wine €4.
Transport: A taxi from Brussels Airport to the centre of Brussels costs about €35. The Brussels Card, valid for 1, 2 or 3 days, and the similar Bruges City Card (www.bruggecitycard.be) give unlimited use of local transport and discounts on all the main attractions in each city, and so can be a handy way of cutting costs.

Children

In Brussels travel is free for children under 6 on all public transport, provided there are no more than four children per each paying adult. Children aged 6–11 can also effectively travel for free, provided they have a "J-Card", available from the usual ticket outlets for a refundable deposit of €5. Similar concessions are also provided in other cities. There are reduced ticket prices for children under 12 on Belgian Railways, which also offers

"B-Excursions", combining train tickets with reduced-price admission to various attractions around the country. Many hotels offer special family rates and packages.

There are many places of interest for children in Belgium. The coast, the Kempen district and the Ardennes are especially rich in theme parks and other attractions. The country's only regular zoo is the superb Antwerp Zoo, Koningin Astridplein 26 (www.zooantwerpen.be). In Brussels, a fascinating attraction is Mini-Europe, Bruparck (www.minieurope.com), with miniature replicas of buildings from across the continent. Bruges scores high with the dolphins and other marine creatures at the Boudewijn Seapark (www.dolfinarium.be).

Climate

Belgium's climate is temperate and much influenced by its proximity to the sea, becoming noticeably colder the further inland you go towards the German border. The best weather is between April and October, and July and August can be quite hot, but rain is probable even then. Snowfalls are common in the Ardennes in winter, though temperatures rarely fall below freezing for long.

Disabled travellers

Like the rest of Europe Belgium has made major efforts to improve accessibility for all disabled people in recent years. In Brussels the airport trains are fully accessible and the local transport authority has a programme to improve access to all Metro stations, and provide assistance where this has not yet been done. Belgian Railways is also providing access to all its trains and stations, and free assistance is provided on request. Adapted taxis are available in Brussels from Taxis Verts, tel: 02-349-4949. Many hotels and guesthouses now have adapted rooms, and are listed on tourist authority websites.

Eating out

Belgium has plenty of regional cuisine and specialities, from the *jambon d'Ardenne* (smoked Ardennes ham) and *salade liégoise* (Liège bacon salad) of the French-speaking areas, to the *waterzooï op Gentse wijze* (a fish or chicken stew from Ghent) and *paling in 't groen* (eel in a green sauce) of Flanders, and the *moules/mosselen* (mussels) and *steak-frites* (steak with French fries) that are popular everywhere. Vegetarian food is becoming ever more popular, both by way of dedicated restaurants and vegetarian options on menus. Belgium's famous beers are just as good an accompaniment to a meal as wine, and Belgians like to linger over lunch and dinner in a restaurant.

Embassies and consulates

Australia: Rue Guimard 6–8, 1040 Brussels, tel: 02-286 0500; www.belgium.embassy.gov.au
Canada: Avenue de Tervuren 2, 1040 Brussels, tel: 02-741 0611; www.canadainternational.gc.ca/belgium-belgique
Ireland: Chaussée d'Etterbeek, 1040 Brussels, tel: 02-282 3400; www.embassyofireland.be
South Africa: Rue Montoyer 17–19, 1000 Brussels, tel: 02-285 4400; www.southafrica.be
UK: Avenue des Nerviens 9–31, 1040 Brussels, tel: 02-287 6211; http://ukinbelgium.fco.gov.uk
US: Boulevard du Régent 25–27, 1000 Brussels, tel: 02-811 4300 ; http://belgium.usembassy.gov

Gay and lesbian travellers

Brussels has a vibrant gay scene, focused just off the Grand' Place, and which has a dedicated page on the VisitBrussels website. In Flanders, Antwerp has become one of Europe's gay centres, with a huge range of venues and services and a big range of gay-centred events; for information see www.gay-antwerp com.

Health and medical care

Citizens of non-EU countries should ensure they have a travel and health insurance policy (see page 400). EU citizens can use Belgian state health services with an EHIC card. A hospital in Flanders is a *ziekenhuis* (or AZ), and an emergency department is indicated with a sign for *Spoedgevallen*; in Brussels and the French-speaking south the equivalents are *Hôpital* and *Urgences*. In case of a serious emergency, call an ambulance on tel: 100.

Pharmacies close on Saturday afternoon and all day Sunday, but some pharmacies in each area stay open according to a rota, which will be displayed with details of the nearest on duty in all pharmacy windows. Alternatively, you can also find duty pharmacies by calling tel: 0900-1500, on www.servicedegarde.be or in local newspapers, where the current rotas will be listed.

Language

Three official languages are spoken in Belgium: Flemish, a variation of Dutch, in the north (*Vlaanderen* or Flanders); French in the south (*Wallonie* or Wallonia); and German in the east, by a small minority. In Brussels, the majority of people speak French, but the city is officially bilingual. Relations between the two linguistic communities are often tense, and each language disappears remarkably quickly when you cross from one linguistic area to the other. Nowadays each area has separate institutions in many areas of life, such as travel services.

One consequence of Belgium's linguistic complexities for foreign

All Emergency Services: 112; it can be faster to call individual services directly.
Ambulances and medical emergencies and Fire Service: 100
Police: 101
Doctor (Brussels): 24 hours, 02-479 1818
Dentist (Brussels): 02-426 1026

Festivals

March/April: Carnival, Binche, Sunday to Shrove/Pancake Tuesday (the day before Ash Wednesday). Belgium's most colourful pre-Lenten Carnival culminates in the parade of the fabulously costumed Gilles de Binche.
April/May: Heilig-Bloedprocessie (Procession of the Holy Blood), Bruges, Ascension Day (fifth Thursday after Easter). The bishop of Bruges leads a costumed procession bearing the Relic of the Holy Blood from the basilica in the Burg through the city streets.
July: Ommegang, Brussels, first Tuesday and Thursday in July. A spectacular costumed pageant in the Grand'Place re-enacts the "Joyful Entry" of Habsburg emperor Charles V into Brussels.
Gentse Feesten (Ghent Festivities). Ten days of street parties, music and cultural performances in July.

visitors is that to avoid tensions the two communities often speak to each other in English rather than either of their own languages (especially in Flanders, where people commonly prefer to use English more than French). Consequently the level of English is very high and it is widely used, and websites and other information literature are automatically produced in English as well as Dutch or French.

Nightlife

The city of Brussels publishes *Bru XXL*, a free bimonthly guide to entertainment in the city. Information about scheduled events in Brussels and around Belgium is contained in the weekly English-language magazine *The Bulletin*.

Brussels and Antwerp are Belgium's nightlife hotspots, followed by Ghent and Liège. Dining out and lingering in bars is more typical of Brussels life than nightclubbing, but in the last few years some more trendy venues have appeared such as The Wood (Avenue de Flore 4; www.thewood.be). For a guide to upcoming events throughout Belgium, see www.noctis.com.

Opening hours

Shops usually open Mon–Sat 9am–6pm, although some of them close on Monday. There are a few late-night shops in the city centre, and the neighbourhood corner store may stay open until 9pm. It's best to ask around as to the best after-hours shops and chemists. Banks are open 9am–4pm or 5pm. On Friday, some larger stores and supermarkets stay open until around 9pm.

Postal services

Post offices normally open Mon–Fri 9am–6pm, Sat 9am–noon. Smaller branches may close for lunch

Tipping

Service charges are included in most prices in Belgium (in restaurants, bars, hairdressers and many other businesses) so there's no automatic expectation of a tip, even in taxis. It is quite common though to leave a little extra for particularly good service. Toilet attendants, however, will make your visit a misery if you pass their saucer without leaving a few coins.

noon–2pm, close by 4 or 5pm and on Saturdays. Letterboxes are red and marked Post/Poste. In Brussels the main post office by Brussels-Midi (or Brussels South) train station, on Avenue Fonsny, is open Mon–Sat 7am–11pm, Sun 11am–10pm. Stamps can also be bought at newsstands and in many small shops.

Public holidays

On these holidays banks and most offices will be closed, and museums may be closed or operate Sunday hours. Some holidays are not observed throughout the country. **January**: 1 New Year's Day; **March/ April**: variable Easter Monday; **May**: 1 Labour Day; **May/June**: variable Ascension Day, Whit Monday; **July**: 11 Flemish Community Holiday, 21 Independence Day; **August**: 15 Assumption Day; **September**: 27 Walloon Community Holiday; **November**: 1 All Saints' Day, 11 Armistice Day, 15 King's Feast; **December**: 6 St Nicholas's Day, 25 Christmas Day.

Shopping

Belgium is noted for hand-beaten copperware from Dinant; crystal from Val Saint Lambert of Liège; diamonds from Antwerp; handmade lace from Bruges, Brussels, Binche and Mechelen; tapestries from Mechelen, Sint-Niklaas, Brussels and Ghent, and sporting guns from Herstal, for which Liège is world-famous. Credit cards are accepted everywhere, and many shops offer tourists special terms exclusive of VAT on certain goods.

Brussels

There are numerous areas in Brussels where you can shop to your heart's content. In the Lower City go to Place de Brouckère, Place de la Monnaie, along Boulevard Anspach (predominately fashion and books), and Rue Neuve, including the City 2 shopping complex.

Rue du Beurre is good for food and gift shops. Rue du Midi is another well-known shopping beat, where there are quite a few art-supply shops and music stores. One of the best places for window-shopping is the glass-roofed arcades of the famous Galeries Royales Saint-Hubert, which opened in 1847. Rue Antoine Dansaert is the place to find ultra-fashionable and expensive boutiques.

Fancy shops with internationally recognised designer names are concentrated in the Upper City.

Streets to look out for include Avenue Louise, Chaussée d'Ixelles, Boulevard de Waterloo and Avenue de la Toison d'Or. The most chic arcades are also located here. You'll find Galerie Espace Louise and Galerie Louise at Place Louise; Galeries de la Toison d'Or and the Galerie d'Ixelles are at Porte de Namur. Department stores generally open Mon–Sat 9am–6pm and stay open until 8pm on Friday.

The city has many markets: **Antique market**: Grand Sablon, Sat 9am–6pm, Sun 9am–2pm. **Flea market**: Place du Jeu de Balle, daily 7am–2pm. **Flower market**: Grand'Place, Mar–Oct Tue–Wed and Fri–Sun 8am–6pm. **Food and textile market**: Place Bara (South station), Sun 5am–1pm.

Telecommunications

Most public phones are operated by phone cards, which are available from post offices, newsstands and newsagents. On using mobile/cell phones, see page 401.

For local directory enquiries in English, tel: 1405. The international code for Belgium is 32, and the area code for Brussels 02, for Antwerp 03. When calling from outside the country, omit the initial 0.

Tourist information

Because of the federalised structure of Belgium, the country's three sections – Brussels, Flanders and French-speaking Wallonia – each now have separate tourist information services, although abroad Brussels shares its promotion with Wallonia. **OPT** (Brussels and Wallonia Tourist Board), Rue Saint-Bernard 30, 1060 Brussels, tel: 070-221 021; www.opt.be.

Toerisme Vlaanderen (Flanders Tourist Board), Rue du Marché aux Herbes 61, 1000 Brussels, tel: 02-504 0390; www.visitflanders.co.uk. **Visit Brussels**, main information centres, Rue Royale 2, in the City Hall, Grand' Place, and at Brussels-Midi train station, tel: 02-513 8940, www.visitbrussels.be.

Tourist offices abroad

UK: Brussels & Wallonia Tourism, tel: 020-7537 1132; www.belgiumtheplaceto.be; Flanders Tourism, tel: 020-7307 7738; www.visitflanders.co.uk.

US and Canada: Brussels & Wallonia Tourism, tel: 212-758 8130; www.visitbelgium.com; Flanders Tourism, tel: 212-584 2336, www.visitflanders.us.

FRANCE

ESSENTIAL TRAVEL TIPS

FACT FILE

Area: 547,030 sq km (210,026 sq miles)
Capital: Paris
Population: Around 65.3 million
Language: French. Minority languages (Breton, Alsatian, Basque, Occitan, Catalan and Corsican) are still spoken in several parts of France, but first-time visitors are unlikely to encounter them.
Highest mountain: Mont Blanc 4,808 metres (15,775ft)
Religion: Roman Catholic (51 percent), with large Muslim (6.3 percent) and other minorities.
Time zone: CET/CEST, see page 402.
Currency: the euro (€)
International Dialling Code: 33

TRANSPORT

Getting to France

By air

Paris-Charles de Gaulle Airport (CDG; tel: 3950; www.aeroportsdeparis.fr), also known as Roissy, is France's pre-eminent air hub and the entry point for most visitors from outside Europe. It has flights from every part of the world, with **Air France** (www.airfrance.com) and also **British Airways** (www.britishairways.com), **Air Canada** (www.aircanada.com), **American Airlines** (www.aa.com), **Delta Airlines** (www.delta.com), **Emirates** (www.emirates.com), **Cathay Pacific** (www.cathaypacific.com), **Qantas** (www.qantas.com)

and many other major carriers. For transport to the city from the airport *see below* **Getting into Paris**.

Air France, British Airways and some other major carriers also have direct flights to other major French cities such as Lyon or Nice, but the principal providers of flights to France's many regional airports from other parts of Europe are the low-cost airlines. **Ryanair** (www.ryanair.com) flies to over 25 airports all around France from the UK, Ireland, Germany and other European countries; **easyJet** (www.easyjet.com) flies between both Paris airports (Charles de Gaulle and Orly) and destinations in the UK, southern France, Spain, Italy and Eastern Europe; **Flybe** (www.flybe.com) flies to French regional airports from every part of the UK and Ireland. By using these airlines travellers can bypass the congestion of Paris.

By rail

International rail services from around Europe converge on Paris, and connect with the French high-speed rail (TGV) network. Eurostar trains (tel: UK 0843-218 6186; www.eurostar.com) run to Paris from London via the Channel Tunnel; Thalys trains run from Belgium, Holland and Germany; TGV Lyria trains run from Switzerland; Artesia trains from Italy, and nightly Elipsos sleeper trains (which are not yet TGV speed) from Spain. Some Eurostar trains also stop at the special station for Disneyland Paris theme park. Information on all trains is on www.raileurope.com, which also handles bookings.

Travellers who do not wish to visit Paris itself can also change trains in other hubs of the TGV network, such as Lille or Lyon, for destinations

in other parts of France. Changing trains there will be much quicker than in Paris.

By road

Motorways from throughout Europe run into France and converge, like everything in France, on Paris. To drive to Paris from Brussels will take about 3hrs 15min, from London via ferry or the Channel Tunnel takes about 6–7 hours, from Berlin a minimum of about 10 hours, from Rome around 14 hours, not allowing for any stops. Vehicles travelling from the UK through the Channel Tunnel must board a shuttle train (Le Shuttle) actually to go through the Tunnel, which takes around 35min. There are four trains an hour each way during the day, and at least one an hour at night; for information and bookings see www.eurotunnel.com.

Driving from Southern Europe (Italy or Spain) will generally be slower than routes in the north because of the more mountainous terrain. For more on roads in France *see below* **Getting around France**.

Buses provide one of the cheapest but also the slowest means of getting to Paris and other parts of France from elsewhere in Europe. Eurolines (www.eurolines.com) is a consortium of European coach companies operating routes from around the continent to many places in France. Since buses stop frequently, journey times are long. Megabus (www.megabus.com) now offers even cheaper bus services to Paris from Amsterdam, Brussels and many places in the UK.

By sea

Several ferry routes operate from the UK, the Republic of Ireland and the Channel Islands to ports in northern

France. Dover–Calais and Dover–Dunkerque are the shortest and busiest routes, mainly served by P&O Ferries (www.poferries.com) and DFDS Seaways (www.dfdsseaways.co.uk). Ferry prices are keenly competitive with the Channel Tunnel and often cheaper, but ferries are slightly slower, and can be affected by bad weather. Several routes in the western Channel (Portsmouth to Caen, Cherbourg and St-Malo, Poole to Cherbourg, Plymouth to Roscoff and Cork to Roscoff) are offered by Brittany Ferries (www.brittanyferries.com), and Irish Ferries (www.irishferries.com) sails regularly between Rosslare in Ireland, Cherbourg and Roscoff. Western Channel routes are longer and more expensive, but depending on where you intend to go in France can save a lot of time by avoiding the busier areas of central France.

In the Mediterranean there are regular ferries from North Africa. SNCM (www.sncm.fr) sails between Marseille and Algeria and Tunis, and Grande Navi Veloci (www2.gnv.it) to Sète from Tangier and Nador in Morocco.

Getting around France

By air

Because of the high quality and fast speeds of French railways domestic flights are used less than in some other countries, but there is an extensive range of flights available, mostly with Air France or its subsidiary Air Régional (www.regional.com). Ryanair and easyJet also now operate several routes within France. In Paris some flights operate from Charles de Gaulle but most domestic flights operate from the city's second airport, Paris-Orly (ORY; tel: 3950; www.aeroportsdeparis.fr), in southern Paris. RER suburban trains and direct buses connect between the two airports.

Apart from Orly, other domestic flight hubs are Lyon and Toulouse. One part of France for which internal flights can naturally be useful is Corsica, where the four airports (Ajaccio, Bastia, Calvi and Figari) have frequent flights from Paris CDG and Orly, Lyon and many other parts of France with Air Régional, easyJet and other airlines.

By rail

France's national railway, the **SNCF**, is famously fast, comfortable and efficient, and generally makes taking the train the best way to get around the country for anyone without a car,

The ferry from Nice to Corsica.

especially since you can see so much on the way. There are three main types of SNCF train within France, with some variations in each group. Luxury **TGV** high-speed trains are the stars of the system, travelling between cities and towns at speeds up to 300kph (186mph), so that total journey times can be shorter than those for flights. Trains are extremely comfortable, with high-standard restaurant cars and, in some, play areas for young children. **Intercité** trains are slower but still comfortable long-distance trains that operate in areas that still have no TGV service, and stop more frequently. Some are overnight sleeper services, including some motorail services in which you can put your car on the train, as on the Calais–Avignon route. Lastly, **TER** trains are regional services on the SNCF's great many branch lines through small towns, stopping at every station and allowing you to reach sometimes very remote spots. In some cases where rail services are no longer economical SNCF buses now run on the same TER routes.

Tickets, information and other services

Seats on TGV and Intercité trains must be booked in advance, but bookings can be made up until 5 minutes before you travel. You can book and buy tickets from machines or ticket windows at any SNCF station (not just the one from which you will travel), but you will find better prices and choice of seats if you book ahead online, through www.raileurope.com or the SNCF's own site (in English) www.voyages-sncf.com, which also have full TGV and Intercité timetable information. For each route there are several price options, depending on when you travel; look out for Prem fares (advance fares), which give substantial savings. A wide range of Eurail or France-specific rail passes is also available from RailEurope (see

page 403), but note that unless you travel by train a lot it may be cheaper to buy separate tickets.

Information on local TER trains is not provided on the RailEurope or Voyages-SNCF sites but only on the separate www.ter-sncf.com (in French only). From the map of France there are links to the TER pages for each region, with detailed maps of all lines and available stations. It is not usual or necessary to book TER tickets much in advance.

With (almost) all tickets, on all trains in France, you must remember to date-stamp (*composter*) your ticket before you board the train, by inserting it into one of the orange machines by station platforms. You can be fined if you do not do this. The only tickets that do not have to be *composté* are e-ticket printouts for online bookings.

By road

Most motorways (*autoroutes*) in France are toll roads. Tolls can be paid in cash, by credit card or (for regular users) prepaid subscription cards, and the website www.autoroutes.fr (in English) usefully allows you to calculate potential tolls for any particular route. To drive across France from north to south, using motorways as much as possible, should cost about €70–75 in tolls. There are also, though, many main highways that are toll-free: all those around Paris, Lille and some other major cities, all those in Brittany and most in Alsace.

The benefit of using the *autoroutes* is only speed. Away from the motorways driving in France can be hugely enjoyable, because of the low traffic densities, but can also get slow when you come upon some farm traffic. Country and coast roads become much more congested during French holiday seasons, especially during August.

AUSTRIA BELGIUM FRANCE GERMANY GREECE ITALY NETHERLANDS PORTUGAL SPAIN SWITZERLAND

Motoring advice: Drivers must have a red warning triangle, a yellow reflective waistcoat and spare headlamp bulbs in their car, and should always drive with dipped headlights in poor weather or reduced visibility. In France, it is now also a legal requirement to carry your own breathalyser kit in the car.

Parking in Paris is very restricted, and if you do drive into the city it's advisable to leave your car in a hotel car park or one of the large pay car parks. In nearly all French towns, as well as pay car parks there are restricted parking areas marked in blue (zones bleues) where you must pay to park at a machine and display the ticket on the car. Charges are rarely high and there is often no charge during lunch (noon–2am).

In country districts you need to be wary of the priorité à droite rule, which means that if there are no special markings on the road you have to give way to vehicles entering from the right, even if you are on a larger road. Speeding and other fines can be levied on the spot. Also, be warned traffic lights are not always visible until the last moment.

An invaluable source of information on current traffic conditions in France, including blocked roads, is the official Bison Futé service (www.bison-fute-equipement.gouv.fr), in English and French.

By sea

Car and passenger ferries run frequently from Marseille, Toulon and Nice to different ports in Corsica (Ajaccio, Calvi, Ile Rousse and Bastia, operated by Corsica Ferries (www.corsicaferries.fr), SNCM (www.sncm.fr) and La Méridionale (www.lameridionale.fr). There are also direct ferries with the same companies to Sardinia, and between this Italian island and Corsica. Though Corsica ferries are frequent, they still need to be booked well ahead for the July-August holiday season, when they are in great demand.

Getting into Paris

By air

From Paris-Charles de Gaulle Airport

Paris-CDG is 23km (15 miles) northeast of Paris via the A1 autoroute. The quickest and most reliable way to get to central Paris is by the RER suburban train, Line B. Trains run every 15 minutes from 5am to 11.45pm to Metro Gare du Nord

Paris Metro sign.

or Châtelet-Les Halles. The average journey time is 50 minutes and a single ticket will cost €9.25.

Several buses are also provided to other parts of Paris: Air France buses run to Charles-de-Gaulle-Etoile (the Arc de Triomphe) and Gare Montparnasse (every 30 minutes, 5.45am–11pm; fare about €15), and the Roissybus run to Rue Scribe, near Place de l'Opéra, stopping at all the main rail stations (every 15–30 minutes, 6am–11pm) and taking about 45 minutes. Fares are similar to those for the train.

Taxis into Paris from CDG can take from 30 minutes to well over an hour, depending on the traffic. The fare should be around €50, with higher rates after 5pm and on Sundays, and supplements for luggage.

From Orly Airport

Orly is 14km (9 miles) south of central Paris, and has two terminals. To get a train into Paris take the shuttle bus from either terminal to Pont de Rungis station on RER line C, for east-central Paris, or the Orlyval shuttle train to Antony station on RER line B, for the heart of the city. Shuttles run 6am–11pm daily and fares are around €11.

Air France buses run to Les Invalides and Gare Montparnasse, daily 6am–11pm, and Orlybus to Montparnasse, 6am–11.30pm. A taxi from Orly to central Paris should take around 40 minutes (much longer in rush hours) and cost about €40.

RER line B can also be used to transfer between the two airports, and they are also connected by Air France buses (every 15 minutes daily 6am–11.30pm, fare €20). There are also shuttle services from both airports to Disneyland Paris.

By rail

Train travellers arriving in Paris do so at one of seven main stations in a ring around the centre: from Britain on Eurostar, Belgium, Holland, north Germany and northeast France at the **Gare du Nord**; from central and southern Germany, Lorraine and Alsace at the **Gare de l'Est**; from Burgundy, the Rhône Valley, Switzerland, the Mediterranean coast, Italy and eastern Spain at the **Gare de Lyon** or nearby **Gare de Bercy**; from most of Spain and southwest France at the **Gare d'Austerlitz**; from Brittany and western France at the **Gare Montparnasse**; and from Normandy at the **Gare St-Lazare**. Allow an hour if you have to change between stations. Note, most stations do not have lifts, so if you have luggage you will have to factor in time for carrying cases up and down steps.

Getting around Paris

Paris is one of the most densely populated urban centres in the world, divided into 20 arrondissements (districts). Its main attractions are all within a tight area, now limited by the Boulevard Périphérique ring road, except for a few suburban excursions like Disneyland Paris and Versailles. There is little point in driving within central Paris, and because of the traffic even taxis move slowly. The city is ideal for strolling and many places are within walking distance of each other, and for longer journeys an excellent public transport system provides the best way to get around.

Public transport

Parisian public transport forms an integrated system, operated by the RATP transport authority. Extensive information on tickets, routes and so on is provided in English on www.ratp.fr, and there is a special information line on tel: 3246. Free Metro and other maps are also available from all stations.

Bicycles: Paris is the home of the public bike scheme (Velib'), with which you can rent cycles cheaply from many points around the city and return them at another. Traffic may make this intimidating during the week, but it's more attractive at weekends. For full information see www.velib.paris.fr.

Buses: There is a comprehensive bus network, with most routes operating daily 6am–midnight, and Noctilien night buses through the night. Route details are posted up at bus stops. Parisian buses travel slowly but can be a good and cheap way to sightsee. Many are now wheelchair-accessible. In Paris, as on city buses everywhere in France, you board the bus at the front, and get off at the middle or rear doors. **Metro**: The **Paris Metro** (underground railway) is quick, efficient and generally the most convenient way to get around the city. There are 14 lines that operate daily 5.30am–1am (Sat until 2.20am). Lines are identified by number, a colour and the names of the last station in each direction. Supplementing the Metro is the **RER**, five suburban rail lines, identified as A–E, which run out from the centre to destinations such as the airports, Disneyland Paris and Versailles. In the centre of Paris, RER lines have fewer stops than the Metro, so are faster.

Tickets and passes

The RATP has common tickets for all systems. The same T-Tickets are valid for Metro, buses and RER trains within the city, and can be bought at Metro and RER stations, airports, tourist offices and tobacco shops (*tabacs*). Metro/RER stations have ticket machines and staffed booths. Buying a single ticket (€1.70) every time you travel wastes time and money, so it's better to buy a *carnet* of 10 tickets (€12.70). There are lower fares for children aged 4–9, and free travel for those under 4.

Another option specially for tourists is the *Paris Visite* card, which is valid for from 1 to 5 consecutive days on the Metro, bus and rail lines in Paris and the Ile de France, in zones 1–3 or 1–6. Prices for adults vary from about €10–55. Card holders also get discounted entry to many museums and attractions, and again there are reduced rates for children. Cards can be bought from Metro and SNCF stations, airports and tourist offices.

FRANCE A–Z

Accommodation

France has a very wide choice of accommodation, much of which is listed on the excellent national, regional and *départementale* tourist websites. Every town of any size has at least one small hotel, traditionally family-run. Many small hotels are represented by the Logis de France association (www.logis-de-france.fr).

France also has many chain hotels oriented to business travellers, which

Festivals

Every part of France hosts some kind of cultural festival and fête, especially during the summer, when they take the place of regular theatre and music programmes. Extensive information can be found through the national Franceguide and local tourist websites, and (in French) on www.culture.fr. Among the highlights are the **Nantes Carnaval** in April (www.nantes.fr), the **Festival d'Avignon** in the city in July, France's most prestigious multi-arts festival (www.festival-avignon.com), and the **Festival Interceltique** in Lorient in August (www.festival-interceltique.

may not offer great charm but do have reliable modern facilities and good-value rates. Many are in different brands of the huge Accor group (www.accorhotels.com), which cater for all tastes and budgets, from luxury (Sofitel) through mid-range (Mercure, Novotel, Ibis) to cheap and no frills (HotelF1). Some have particularly good facilities for families, especially Novotels.

Top of the range, meanwhile, are the luxury hotels, including some of the most sumptuous in the world, which may be in a château or other historic monument. See for instance www.relaisetchateaux.com or, www.bienvenueauchateau.com.

Bed-and-breakfasts with fewer than 5 bedrooms, called *chambres-d'hôtes* in French, are very popular in France and often the most enjoyable and characterful places to stay, in the countryside and, increasingly, in towns. Since generous breakfasts are included they are also often better value than comparable hotels. *Chambres-d'hôtes* can be found through tourist office websites or through two main organisations, Gîtes de France (www.gitesdefrance.com), which mainly lists rural locations, or Clévacances (www.clevacances.com), which has addresses in towns. Both represent hundreds of members throughout France, and also list self-catering houses and apartments for holiday rentals. For B&Bs in Paris, try www.goodmorningparis.fr.

France is extremely well equipped with campsites – you can find information about them at www.campingfrance.com.

Arts and activities

There is a huge variety of live entertainment in France, much of

com), for Breton and Celtic music and culture.

The primary national holiday **Bastille Day** (14 July) is naturally celebrated with parties and fireworks throughout the country, but one event not to be missed if you're in France at the time is the **Fête de la Musique** on 21 June, when leading musicians give free concerts in squares and other special venues, and also anyone who can play an instrument throughout France is encouraged to perform too in the streets, to charming acclaim from their neighbours.

it concentrated in Paris and other cities, but even in small towns you can often find attractive exhibitions or outdoor concerts. In the summer, many cities (and even small towns) present a programme of events, including music and drama festivals featuring street theatre and other outdoor performances that are often free. Village *fêtes* take place throughout the summer, and offer a window into true French provincial life, with varied activities from *pétanque* competitions to dances (*bals*) and communal food.

In Paris, the theatre and opera companies of the Comédie Française and Opéra National de Paris are most famous for their classical productions, but there is a good choice of theatre, concerts, opera and ballet for all tastes. Look out for the adventurous concerts and performances at the Pompidou Centre, the classical music seasons at the Musée d'Orsay, and the many music recitals in churches.

Summer is dominated by a range of festivals around France, while conventional theatre and opera seasons generally run from September to June, so that many city theatres and music venues are closed in July and August.

Son et lumière displays are highlights of some sites, notably Versailles, Amiens Cathedral, Chartres and Mont St-Michel. Performances normally begin at dusk.

Guides to events can be found on national and local tourist office websites, and for more information and reservations contact local tourist offices. In Paris the weekly listings magazine Pariscope (www.spectacles.premiere.fr) is the first-choice guide to what's on in the city, from cinemas and exhibitions to nightclubs.

Budgeting for your trip

Paris and some other cities are generally more expensive to survive in than rural France, and what you spend will vary according to how lavishly you live, but as a rough guide across France you'll need to allow for the following:

Accommodation: Double room per night (including breakfast) in an average hotel: €60–120, depending on the season. Hotel prices around the coasts go up significantly in July–August, and in winter resorts in December–February.

Meals: Modest à la carte or *menu du jour* lunch will cost €13–20 per person; a three-course à la carte dinner with wine, around €30–50 per person.

Sightseeing: Admission charges: €10–20 per person per day, and miscellaneous (drinks, snacks, tips, etc.): €20 per person per day.

Paris has a range of all-in-one discount cards help reduce costs for visitors seeing several of its sights. Most popular is the Paris-Visite travel card, but there is also the Paris Museum Pass (www.parismuseumpass.com), valid for 2, 4 or 6 days, which gives you access to over 60 museums and monuments in Paris and area (including Versailles) for around €40–70, a major saving if you visit all the main museums. Pass holders can also bypass queues. The Paris Pass (www.parispass.com) is a more expensive package that includes Paris-Visite and Museum Pass cards.

Children

France is a great place for a family holiday, although you might have to adjust your itinerary to include more child-centred attractions. Disneyland Paris is the country's number-one family attraction, and the Eiffel Tower will also be a highlight of any child's stay. Elsewhere in the country there are other theme parks, and you'll never be far from a wildlife attraction or activity centre – you only have to ask at the local tourist office.

A variety of discounts make life easier for families travelling in France. There is free admission to all national monuments and museums for EU residents aged under 25 and for everyone under 18, and most private venues have lower prices for children under 12. Under-12s also travel for half the adult fare on most transport, and children under 4 (or 6, in some cities) travel for free. Many hotels and

chambres-d'hôtes have well-sized family rooms or connecting rooms, and the hotels of the Novotel chain have particularly good family offers. Many restaurants have a reduced-size children's menu (menu enfants) for under €10.

Climate

The French climate is varied and seasonal. In the north there is a moist, Atlantic climate, and springtime is often suggested as the best time to see the capital. However, be prepared for showers. In the autumn, mornings can be quite sharp, but by midday the skies are usually clear and bright.

In the southeast, summers are dry and temperatures frequently rise to over 30°C (86°F). However, watch out for heavy thunder and hailstorms. Winters are mild (the temperature rarely falling below 10°C/50°F on the Mediterranean coast) and often wet; spring is even wetter.

Many areas of France have quite distinct microclimates, and the weather can change rapidly. The south coast has its own particular *bête noire*, the fierce wind known as the Mistral, which blows from the northwest, mainly in winter and spring, leaving clear blue skies in its wake.

Disabled travellers

Facilities, services and access for travellers with special needs and mobility problems in France have improved greatly over the last 20 years. There are well-indicated disabled parking spaces in all public car parks and many streets, which holders of the European-standard blue parking badge can use for free. On trains, the SNCF (French Railways) operates the Accès Plus scheme, through which wheelchair-users and others with disabilities can reserve spaces and free assistance on and off trains, by calling tel: 0890-640 650. More information on the scheme can be found on the English pages of www.sncf.com (under Services), but complete details are in French only on www.accessibilité.sncf.com. All taxis are required by law to carry wheelchair-users for no extra charge, but adapted taxis (taxis aménagés) are available from many companies.

Many hotels and *chambres-d'hôtes* (B&Bs) have adapted rooms, which are indicated on booking agency websites. Access ramps and other facilities are also provided at most public museums,

but architecture still makes visiting some historic buildings difficult. A blue label, "*Tourisme & Handicap*", is used in France to indicate facilities and venues of all kinds that have full access. A very useful introduction is provided on the national tourist service's FranceGuide websites, under "Special Needs Travellers", and every city and local French tourism information website has dedicated sections on disabled facilities.

Eating out

Eating out is one of the quintessential pleasures of a stay in France, and in the summer it's never hard to find a shady outdoor terrace for lunch. While the range of choices to eat is huge, there are certain characteristics that are worth being aware of. One is timing: in rural and small-town France people keep regular mealtimes, and anywhere called a restaurant or bistro will expect to take orders for lunch around 12.30–1pm, and for dinner at 8.30–9pm (later at weekends). Once you have sat down you can stay as long as you like, but if you arrive much earlier or later you may well be disappointed. The traditional alternative to the restaurant is the *brasserie*, which is open for breakfast and between mealtimes, has a more varied menu and may serve snacks during the afternoon, but these are scarce in rural France. In Paris, especially, and other major cities and resort areas mealtimes are more flexible.

Crêperies serve Breton pancakes, either thin with varied sweet toppings (*crêpes*) or slightly thicker savoury ones (*galettes*) made of buckwheat flour, and are a great standby for anyone with children. *Salons de thé* serve light lunches as well as tea.

Most French restaurants offer a choice of fixed-price (prix-fixe) set menus, with a few choices for each of two or three courses, and sometimes including wine and coffee. At lunch many also offer a *plat du jour*, a single main dish. Choosing from the set menu is the most usual and most economical way of ordering in restaurants. If you order dishes separately from the much larger *carte* offered by most restaurants, your meal will be much more expensive.

Gay and lesbian travellers

France claims to be the first country in the world to legislate against discrimination on the basis of sexual preference, and is generally an easygoing, gay-friendly place, although you might feel more at ease in one of the great cities or Mediterranean resorts than in a small village where life is more traditional. Paris in particular prides itself on its innumerable gay and lesbian bars, clubs, cabarets and shops. Le Marais is renowned as the centre of the city's gay life. Two good sites to go for information are www.paris-gay.com and www.tetu.com.

Health and medical care

Citizens of non-EU countries should ensure they have a travel and health insurance policy (see page 400). EU citizens can use the French state health services with an EHIC card, but note that under the French system you will usually have to pay for treatment, and then reclaim most of the cost later following the procedures indicated in the booklet that came with your EHIC card. At a hospital (*hôpital*), the emergency room/casualty department is indicated by *urgences*. In case of a serious emergency, call an ambulance on tel: 15.

Pharmacies (designated by a green cross) are open Mon–Sat 9am–noon and 2–7pm. Sunday and evening rotas are posted in all pharmacy windows. The duty pharmacy is officially on call at night – you will find a bell (*sonnette de nuit*) by his door. Doctors also have night and weekend rotas. They, and pharmacies, are listed in local papers under *Pharmaciens de Garde* and *Médecins de Garde*.

In Paris, the Pharmacie Dhéry, 84 Avenue des Champs-Elysées, tel: 01-45 62 02 41, is open 24 hours (Metro: George V). Two private hospitals serve the Anglo-American community: American Hospital of Paris, 63 Bld Victor-Hugo, tel: 01-46 41 25 25; www.american-hospital.org; and the Hertford British Hospital, 3 Rue Barbès, Levallois-Perret, tel: 01-46 39 22 00; www.british-hospital.org.

Nightlife

Inevitably, the best French nightlife is

Emergency Numbers

All emergency services: 112; it can be faster to call individual services directly
Ambulance: 15
Fire brigade: 18
Police: 17

Embassies and Consulates

Paris
Australia: 4 Rue Jean Rey, 75724 Paris, tel: 01-40 59 33 00; www.france.embassy.gov.au.
Canada: 35 Avenue Montaigne, 75008 Paris, tel: 01-44 43 29 00; www.canadainternational.gc.ca/france.
Ireland: 12 Avenue Foch, 75116 Paris, tel: 01-44 17 67 00; www.

confined to the big cities, and if you are demanding you might not want to stray out of Paris. But provincial cities have their share of nightspots, and there is usually something going on in coastal resorts during the summer. Wherever you are, it is worth asking around, as almost every town and village stages an annual *fête* which usually includes a disco or a performance by a live group, sometimes outdoors. If you're lucky and the weather's good, you might get a night out on a balmy summer's evening for free.

Paris
The action starts in Paris as soon as the sun goes down. Bars and clubs are all over the city, but particularly in the central areas around the Marais, Bastille, Montmartre, Pigalle and the Latin Quarter. Check the listings magazine *Pariscope* to find out more or log on to www.lemonsound.com and www.novaplanet.com. For national information try www.cityvox.com, www.citegay.fr or www.flyersweb.com.

Opening hours

Hours of business vary across the country, but as a rule, shops open 8 or 9am to 7pm. In small towns and quieter city districts many shops close for lunch, typically between midday and 2pm, although some shops including small supermarkets may close 1pm to 3.30 or 4pm. Large stores and out-of-town hypermarkets and chain stores do not close for lunch, and may stay open later in the evening, although each operates its own policy. In many towns all the shops are closed on Monday. Boulangeries (bakers) and *patisseries* are traditionally the only shops open on Sundays, but you may now also find some small convenience stores that are open, and in central Paris a much wider variety will be.

Markets generally start work early, around 8am or earlier, and in

provincial France will often by closing up by noon–1pm. City bank branches are normally open Monday–Friday 9am–5pm, and sometimes on Saturday mornings, but small-town and suburban branches often close for lunch, from 12.30–2pm.

Postal services

Provincial post offices – *Bureaux de Poste* – are generally open Mon–Fri 9am–noon and 2–5pm, Sat 9am–noon (opening hours are posted outside); in Paris and other large cities they are generally open continuously 8am–6.30pm. The main post office in Paris is open almost 24 hours every day, at 52 Rue du Louvre, 75001 Paris.

Stamps may be purchased in post offices, cafés, tobacco shops (*tabacs*) and newsstands. Post boxes are yellow, but at large post offices there are separate boxes for domestic and foreign mail.

Public holidays

January: 1 New Year's Day; **March/April**: variable Easter Sun/Mon; **May**: 1 Labour Day, 8 VE Day; **May/June**: variable Ascension Day, Whit Sun/Mon; **July**: 14 Bastille Day; **August**: 15 Assumption Day; **November**: 1 All Saints' Day, 11 Armistice Day; **December**: 25 Christmas Day.

Shopping

In many ways France is a shopper's paradise, with many small, local shops clinging on to loyal customers in small towns. The personal service you get in such places is an attraction in itself.

The best places to hunt for bargains are local markets. Most towns hold one on an advertised day each week. Although the emphasis is on food and drink, there are usually other items for sale too.

Almost everywhere you go in France there are local craftspeople

embassyofireland.fr.
South Africa: 59 Quai d'Orsay, 75343 Paris, tel: 01-53 59 23 23; www.afriquesud.net.
UK: 16 Rue d'Anjou, 75008 Paris, tel: 01-44 51 31 00; http://ukinfrance.fco.gov.uk.
US: 2 Avenue Gabriel, 75008 Paris, tel: 01-43 12 22 22; http://france.usembassy.gov.

who open their studios to the public and sell their products direct.

At the other end of the scale are the great hypermarkets to be found on the outskirts of every French city and large town. They stay open later than smaller shops and don't close at midday.

Paris

Elegant department stores such as Galeries Lafayette and Au Printemps are on the Right Bank, as are the expensive shops of the Champs-Elysées. For younger (and cheaper) fashions try the Left Bank, particularly around St-Michel and St-Germain boulevards.

The flea market (Marché aux Puces) opens Sat, Sun and Mon (Metro: Porte de Clignancourt). For flowers and plants: Ile de la Cité (Quai de la Corse), Mon–Sat 8am–7.30pm (Metro: Cité). Other street markets are at Rue Mouffetard and Rue Poncelet (Metros: Censier-Daubenton and Ternes respectively), daily 9am–1pm and 4–7pm except Mon and Sun morning.

Telecommunications

All phone numbers have 10 digits. Paris and Ile-de-France numbers begin with 01; the rest of France is divided into four zones (northwest 02, northeast 03, southeast and Corsica 04, southwest 05). When calling from outside the country, omit the initial 0. Freephone numbers begin 0800; 0836 numbers are charged at premium rates; 06 numbers are mobile phones. France Télécom directory enquiries is tel: 118 712.

Most French phone boxes do not accept coins but only a phone card (*télécarte*). They can be bought from newsstands, *tabacs* and post offices.

On using mobile/cellphones, see page 401. If you wish to buy a phone to use in France, all the major local networks like Bouygues and Orange France have phone shops throughout the country, and offer low-cost pay-as-you-go deals.

Tourist information

France's tourist information and help services are exceptionally comprehensive and well organised, and mirror the structure of French administration. The national tourist service's FranceGuide (www.franceguide.com) leads automatically to separate websites for whichever country you access it from, and provides ample information on all aspects of France, including accommodation. It also has links to the next level down, the regions, each of which has its own tourist board (CRT) and website, and to the *département* (CDT) and city websites. The further you go down, the more detail you will find, and *départements* in particular produce an enormous variety of material on facilities and activities, and excellent free maps.

Paris

The Paris city tourism bureau's website, www.paris.info, provides comprehensive information and an accommodation-finding service. The main tourist information office is at the bottom of the Champs-Elysées at 25 Rue des Pyramides (Metro: Pyramides),and is open daily May–Oct

Tipping

The practice of adding 12–15 percent service charge to bills is common in restaurants, hotels and cafés all over France, so there is no obligation to leave anything additional, although most people either round up the change or leave around €1 extra, depending on the size of the bill, especially if the service has been notably good. Tip room service in hotels; taxi drivers usually get 10–15 percent.

9am–7pm, Nov–Apr 10am–7pm. There are other permanent offices at the Gare de l'Est, Gare du Nord, Gare du Nord, Boulevard Rochechouart (Metro: Anvers) and Porte de Versailles, and in summer additional information points are open on the Champs-Elysées and at Notre-Dame, the Hôtel de Ville and Place de la Bastille.

The Paris-Ile-de-France regional tourism authority (www.new-paris-ile-de-france.com) has information desks at the airports (all terminals), Versailles, and Disneyland Paris.

French tourist offices abroad

All can be contacted through the relevant page on www.franceguide.com.
Canada: tel: 514-288 2026
UK: tel: 0906-824 4123
US: tel: 514-288 1904
Monaco: Direction du Tourisme et des Congrès de la Principauté de Monaco, tel: 377-92 16 61 16;
www.visitmonaco.com
UK: tel: 020-7491 4264
US: tel: 800-753 9696 or 212-286 3330

Local lavender for sale in the Saleya market, Nice.

GERMANY

ESSENTIAL TRAVEL TIPS

FACT FILE

Capital: Berlin
Population: 82 million
Languages: German, plus small minorities speaking Frisian, Danish and Sorbian. There is also a wide range of regional dialects.
Highest mountain: Zugspitze 2,962 metres (9,718ft)
Religion: About one-third Protestant, one-third Roman Catholic, one-third other religions or agnostic/atheist.
Time zone: EET/EEST, see page 402
Currency: the euro (€)
International dialling code: 49

TRANSPORT

Getting to Germany

By air

Germany's busiest airports are not in the capital Berlin but in Frankfurt and, after that, Munich and Düsseldorf. Frankfurt Airport (tel: 01805-372 4636; www.frankfurt-airport.com) has long-haul flights from every part of the world and ongoing connections to the rest of Germany and Europe. Munich has slightly fewer long-haul flights but almost as many European and German routes. The principal other German airports with international services are Düsseldorf, Berlin, Hamburg, Cologne-Bonn, Stuttgart, Hanover-Langenhagen and Nuremberg, but there are other regional airports around the country.

The relative shortage of flights to Berlin is due to the small size of its

two old airports, Tegel in the former West Berlin, up to now used by most main carriers such as Lufthansa and British Airways, and Schönefeld in the former East, used by most low-cost airlines. An entirely new expanded airport, Berlin-Brandenburg, is being built next to Schönefeld, due to open in October 2013. Once this is open all flights will be concentrated there, and Berlin can be expected to have more long-haul flights.

Germany's traditional national carrier **Lufthansa** (www.lufthansa. com) has flights serving every part of the world and many domestic destinations, with Frankfurt as its main hub. **Air Berlin** (www.airberlin. com) is Germany's second-largest airline, based at Berlin-Tegel and with partly low-cost services to every part of Germany and European and long-haul destinations. **German Wings** (www.germanwings.com) is a true low-cost airline, operating especially within Germany and to the UK, Eastern Europe, Spain, Italy and Greece. Non-German low-cost airlines such as **Ryanair** (www.ryanair.com) and **easyJet** (www.easyjet.com) also fly to German airports from many parts of Europe and operate some domestic German routes.

From the airports

Reliable local rail lines and/or shuttle buses link all German airports with the nearest city centres. In most cities, taxis from airports to city centres will cost around €16–30.
Berlin Schönefeld: There are S-Bahn and mainline train services to the centre of Berlin, and express bus services to the U-Bahn station closest to the airport.
Berlin Tegel: Express buses connect the airport with the city centre.

Frankfurt Airport: Frequent trains travel to the main transport interchange in the city centre (the Hauptwache) in about 15 minutes, from about 4.30am–1.30am daily, depending on the route. There are also direct trains from the airport station to many other cities around Germany, so you do not have to go into Frankfurt itself.
Munich: S-Bahn trains and express bus services run from the airport to the city centre.

By rail

International Thalys and ICE high-speed trains from Paris, Amsterdam or Brussels (where they connect with Eurostar from London) converge on Cologne, the main hub of German railways. Journey time between London and Cologne can be as low as 5 hours. From Cologne there are connections to every part of Germany, and trains go on via Berlin to Poland and Russia. In southern Germany, there are very frequent services to Austria and Switzerland, and from Munich via Innsbruck to Italy. For full information and bookings see www. raileurope.com.

By road

Germany's famously fast motorway (autobahn) network extends throughout the country and makes driving times very fast. To drive from Paris to Cologne (without stops) can take around 5–6 hours, depending on the traffic, and then from Cologne to Berlin another 5 hours or less. Driving from Munich to Rome can take about 9–10 hours. However, it is important to make sure that you factor in enough stops to drive safely.

Eurolines buses (www.eurolines. com) provide the cheapest public transport to some 25 main destinations in Germany, from many different European countries.

By sea

In the Baltic Sea several regular ferry lines run between the German ports of Kiel, Lübeck and Rostock and Norway, Sweden, Finland, Russia, Latvia and Lithuania, operated particularly by Scandlines (www.scandlines.com), DFDS Seaways (www.dfdsseaways.com) and Finn Lines (www.finnlines.com).

Getting around Germany

By air

Because of Germany's size people make considerable use of domestic flights, and there are regional airports throughout the country. Low-cost operators such as German Wings, Ryanair and easyJet have led the way in opening up regional airports to internal services.

By bicycle

In general, Germany is a very bicycle-friendly country, but still not perfect. Many country areas have separate bicycle paths and special routes marked out for scenic bicycle tours. Cycling along the banks of lakes, rivers and canals is a good way to travel, as it allows you to enjoy pleasant scenery without any overly strenuous contours.

In towns, travelling by bike is naturally much more attractive in small, university cities than in the major centres. However, local authorities encourage bike use and German Railways operates its equivalent of Paris-style public-

Velotaxis nip around Berlin.

A welcoming hostelry in Oberwesel, the Rhineland.

access bike schemes in Berlin, Frankfurt, Munich and several other cities, Call-a-Bike (tel: 07000-522 5522; www.callabike-interaktiv.de). The website is in German but under "Infos+Details" there is a flyer in English. With this you first have to register, with a credit card, and then when you want to use a bike you call a special number from a mobile phone. You will then be sent a code number with which to unlock a bike from one of the stands in each city, and can then leave it wherever you wish and send a message when you have finished with it.

By bus

Buses are a primary means of transport in cities and connect the smaller villages in the countryside that have no rail service. Information on regional buses is provided at railway stations and tourist information centres. Bahnbusse (owned by German Railways) link towns with smaller villages in the country, generally departing from railway stations. In remote parts of the country this is usually the only form of public transport, and the Europabusse are a cheap way of travelling between cities.

By rail

Germany railways (Deutsche Bahn or DB; tel: 01805-996 633; www.bahn.com) operates thousands of passenger trains daily over a huge domestic network, as well as many international services. The star services are the **ICE** (InterCity Express) and ICE Sprinter high-speed trains, which now reach most large cities, and lines are still being extended. Intercity (IC) and international Eurocity (EC) trains are slightly slower, but still modern and comfortable. ICE and IC trains do not operate at night, when City Night Line trains operate on long-

distance routes, with sleeper cabins, couchettes and ordinary seating cars. All these trains should be booked in advance, through Rail Europe (www.raileurope.com) or directly through Deutsche Bahn.

The DB also runs regional trains throughout Germany, which make frequent stops and details of which are on its website. It is possible to take your own bicycle on many trains for a small extra charge.

By road

Germany is renowned for its 13,000km (8,100 miles) of motorways, the *autobahnen*, which are marked with an "A" on blue signs; regional roads are marked with a "B" on yellow signs. They are toll-free and, in most cases, have no upper speed limit, so drivers are expected to drive in a very disciplined manner. Commercial vehicles are required to stay in the inside lane, and other vehicles should only enter the outside lane to overtake, and turn in again immediately afterwards. It is not obligatory for drivers to carry a warning triangle and yellow waistcoat in their cars, but it is recommended. In areas with severe winter weather it is obligatory to exchange tyres for special winter tyres during the winter months.

The ADAC motoring organisation (www.adac.de) provides roadside assistance.

City transport

Every city has an extensive network of public transport. Cities with a population of over 100,000 have efficient and frequent bus systems. You can buy bus tickets from the driver or at machines on the bus or at the bus stop. In large cities like Berlin, Hamburg, Cologne, Munich, Frankfurt and Stuttgart, bus lines are integrated with the underground (U-Bahn), trams and overground trains (S-Bahn), and

Cruising Germany's Waterways

Germany has a huge system of inland waterways linking Europe's largest rivers – the Rhine, the Elbe, the Danube and others – and they are still major economic highways. For cruising, the most popular routes are on the central Rhine around Koblenz and on the Danube from Nuremberg into Austria, but there are also cruises on the Elbe from Berlin to Dresden and Prague. Viking River Cruises (www.vikingrivercruises.co.uk) offers a good range of trips.

the same tickets are used for all four means of transport.

Trams (Strassenbahn) run on rails through most cities, at speeds that make them good for sightseeing. Look out for yellow signs with a green "H" at bus and tram stops: they list the schedules.

Urban Rail: There are also underground railway networks (**U-Bahn**) in Berlin, Hamburg, Munich and Nuremberg, their stations usually identified by a sign with a white "U" on a blue background. Every station has route maps on the wall. Many more cities have overground light rail or **S-Bahn** lines, which are often as fast as the U-Bahn. Among them are Berlin, Dresden, Hamburg, Munich and Stuttgart, and in Cologne and Frankfurt the S-Bahn is shared with several other surrounding cities.

Getting around Berlin

By public transport

Berlin's public transport system (BVG; tel: 030 19 110; www.bvg.de) operates underground lines (U-Bahn), fast local and suburban trains (S-Bahn), day and night buses, tramlines in the eastern part of the city, and boat connections crossing the River Havel between Wannsee and Kladow. Tickets are bought at counters or ticket machines at all stations or (some tickets only) on board trams and buses, and are the same for all systems as Berlin is divided into three simple fare zones, A (the centre), B and C. You can buy single tickets (€2.40), one-day tickets or a range of other combinations, or a Berlin Welcome Card is available that gives unlimited travel for 2, 3 or 5 days together with discounts on museum admissions, a range of tours, trips and other attractions, for around €18–36.

By road

Driving in Berlin is generally better avoided, as parking space is very limited. Park-and-ride car parks can be found at suburban U-Bahn and S-Bahn stations.

The cheap Call-a-Bike system operates in Berlin, and holders of the Berlin Welcome Card can transport a bike on the U-Bahn or S-Bahn for free.

GERMANY A–Z

Accommodation

Travellers should have no problem finding accommodation in most places. In the peak season (June–Aug) it is advisable to book in advance in popular places such as the Bavarian Mountains or the Black Forest. Some listings for major hotel groups can be found on the national tourism website www.germany.travel.

A range of modern business hotels, often part of German or international chains, can be found in all cities and towns, but there are many more options. Many castles and historic buildings have been turned into spectacular luxury hotels, several of which are represented by Relais & Chateaux (www.relaischateaux.com). A choice of both castle hotels and sleek modern design hotels in Bavaria can be seen on www.bavaria.by. At a different point on the scale, the traditional family-run gasthaus or guesthouse is a German institution, found in many small towns and country areas, and staying in them is a great way to discover the countryside and sample hearty local breakfasts. Local tourist offices are the best way to find them, as they still do not have central booking agencies.

Farm stays and bed-and-breakfasts are also increasingly popular throughout Germany; listings can be found on www.germanplaces.com (which also has information on apartment rentals), or www.bed-and-breakfast.de. Well-equipped campsites are also plentiful; for listings and information see www.eurocampings.eu.

Arts and activities

Because of Germany's diversity, with several major cities, the arts too are less focused in the capital than in a country like France. Classical music is naturally a highlight of the cultural scene: Berlin has the most august of the German orchestras in the **Berlin Philharmonic** (www.berlinerphilharmoniker.de), which performs regular seasons at the Kulturforum, but others such as the Munich-based **Bavarian Radio Symphony Orchestra** (www.br.de) or the **Leipzig Gewandhaus** orchestra (www.gewandhaus.de) all play to a similar standard, and there are over 50 symphony and chamber orchestras around Germany and a huge number of choirs, standing out among which is the **Thomanerchor** or "Bach Choir" of Leipzig (www.leipzigonline.de/thomanerchor). Opera and other performance arts are similarly flourishing, and regular seasons are complemented by festivals throughout the country (see page 422).

Information on cultural programmes is available from all tourist offices, and most cities and larger towns publish a "What's On" type booklet that is also distributed in hotels. Berlin and Munich have English-language magazines with detailed listings of what's on when and where. In Berlin, the best way to get a feel for what is going on is to take a look in either of the city's German-language listings magazines, *Tip* (www.tip-berlin.de) or *Zitty* (www.zitty.de), but a lot of information is also on the city website www.visitberlin.de.

Budgeting for your trip

Accommodation: A double room in hotels can cost from €100 or less to €500, depending on the

Eat, drink and be merry.

standard, but in a *gasthof* (pension) or *fremdenzimmer* (B&B) will cost about €50–75. Hotel rates may double during trade fairs.

Meals: A decent two-course meal ordered from the set menu could cost as little as €12, while a gourmet meal with wine at a sophisticated restaurant will cost upwards of €60.

Sightseeing: Entry to museums and similar establishments averages around €8. Most museums grant free admission or reduced prices on certain days, and there are reductions for children and students.

Children

You only need to observe the generous provision in cities of playgrounds and other facilities to realise that children are well catered for in Germany. Children under 15 travel free on German railways provided their names are registered on an adult's ticket (if aged under 6, not even this is required), and on most city and local transport there are reduced fares for children under 14 and free travel for under-6s. Children from countries where trams are a novelty may enjoy riding round town aboard a Strassenbahn. With an abundance of lakes and rivers, and mountains with chairlifts, cable cars and, at the Brocken (the highest peak in the Harz Mountains), a steam railway, there's usually plenty to do in the German countryside, to say nothing of the North Sea and Baltic Sea coasts and islands.

Admission is free to most museums and many other attractions in Germany for all under-18s, and there are reduced charges at other venues. Among the museums most successful with younger children are the ones with plenty of interactive exhibits like Munich's Deutsches Museum or those with huge model railways like Nuremberg's Transport Museum. The Chocolate Museum in Cologne is also a sure winner. Many museums have special programmes for children, though some German is usually required. The single most popular visitor attraction in Hamburg is Miniatur Wunderland, a vast model-railway exhibit.

There are also several world-class zoos in Germany, among them Hellabrunn in Munich, Hagenbeck in Hamberg and Berlin's Zoo Berlin, along with "safari parks" in many country areas. The Zoo am Meer in Bremerhaven focuses on sea creatures and animals from the Arctic.

Climate

Germany has a continental climate tempered by Atlantic influences. This gives warm rather than extremely hot summers, and cool rather than icy winters. The northwest tends to have cooler summers and milder winters than the rest of the country. Rainfall occurs throughout the year, increasing somewhat in the summer months, particularly in the south.

The Alps are the wettest region and also experience the most snowfall, with ski slopes generally functioning between mid-December and March. Snowfall in other upland areas is less predictable. Winds are strongest on the North Sea coast, while the warm, dry wind known as the Föhn blowing north from the Alps can create exceptionally clear conditions.

The best time to come to Germany is from May to September, though city visits can be made at any time. Popular tourist areas like the Rhine Gorge can get very crowded at the height of summer.

Disabled travellers

Access facilities and other services for disabled people and anyone with mobility problems are generally of a high standard. Accessible venues in Germany are called *Barrierefrei* (barrier-free), and a dedicated association lists them across the country, although their website (www.barrierefreie-reiseziele.de) is

Festivals

Music festivals

These are held in nearly every city – from small chamber music events to the internationally acclaimed Bayreuther Festspiele.

Bayreuth: The Bayreuth opera festival (July/August) was founded by Richard Wagner and has been devoted to his operas ever since. Bayreuth's theatre is famous for its acoustics and unpadded wooden seats, which grow harder in the course of a five-hour work like *Parsifal* (www.bayreuther-festspiele.de).

Berlin/Dresden: Berlin's Staatsoper (www.staatsoper-berlin. de) and Dresden's Semper Oper (www.semperoper.de) both hold festivals in spring,

Brandenburg: Brandenburgische Sommerkonzerte take place every weekend in a village church or castle within the state of Brandenburg, round Berlin (www.brandenburgische-sommerkonzerte.de).

Munich: Some of the world's top soloists perform at the Münchner Opernfestspiele in July (www. muenchner-opern-festspiele.de).

Rheinsberg: The Kammeroper Schloss Rheinsberg (in July and August) is well known as a springboard for young talent (www. kammeroper-schloss-rheinsberg.de).

Schleswig-Holstein: The sprawling festival of Schleswig-Holstein, scattered through several towns in Germany's northernmost state, presents a wide range of orchestras, soloists and chamber groups (www. shmf.de).

Schwetzingen: Another beautiful festival is held every spring in the Rococo palace of Schwetzingen, summer residence of the Electors of Mannheim, where audiences stroll in the Baroque formal gardens during the intermission (www.mozart gesellschaft-schwetzingen.de).

Würzburg: The Mozart Festival with its torchlit concerts in the formal gardens of the Residenz is a magnificent occasion (www. mozartfest-wuerzburg.de).

Other festivals

Berlin stages the International Film Festival in February; the biennial MaerzMusic festival in March; the German Theatertreffen in May (the latest productions from the German-speaking world); the Berliner Festwochen (Sept–Oct), with a wide range of concerts and performing arts; and the JazzFest in November, to which famous international artists are invited (www.visitberlin.de).

Hamburg: The Reeperbahn Festival showcases edgy new bands (Sept).

Munich: The Munich Biennale is devoted to new music theatre, but the most famous festival of all is the Oktoberfest, which attracts over 7 million visitors every year. A massive jamboree, it actually takes place mainly in September, ending early October, and is a thronging fête with processions, folk music, rides, circus, bands and much (beer) drinking. The opening ceremony, with horse-drawn carriages leading a gigantic procession to the beat of brass bands, takes place on the first Saturday. A week later the brass bands hold a concert. Book rooms well in advance. For information see www.oktoberfest.de.

AUSTRIA

BELGIUM

FRANCE

GERMANY

GREECE

ITALY

NETHERLANDS

PORTUGAL

SPAIN

SWITZERLAND

currently in German only. German railways provides extensive facilities for disabled travellers (listed under "Services-Barrier-Free Travel" on www.bahn.com) including a 24-hour phone hotline on tel: 0180-599 6633. In cities most buses and an increasing number of U-Bahn and S-Bahn stations are accessible to wheelchairs, and taxis are required to take chairs for no extra charge.

Many hotels now have accessible rooms, although older hotels and small *gasthausen* cannot always be redesigned to admit wheelchairs. For more information and links look under "Themes-Barrier-Free Travel" on www.germany.travel.

Eating out

Traditional German cuisine is unfussy, prepared from a limited range of good ingredients, with an emphasis on nourishing soups and quantities of meat, potatoes, dumplings and various kinds of cabbage. It is satisfying, if unsubtle. More recently, *Neue deutsche Küche* – new German cooking – has extended the range, lightened the preparation and reduced quantities. In addition, foreign cuisines have been enthusiastically adopted, making eating out in Germany an enjoyable, varied and often inexpensive experience.

To accompany the meal, there is, of course, beer, Germany being one of the world's great brewing nations. The country's numerous breweries turn out distinctive products, often with a strongly regional character. But this is also a wine country, producing mainly white wines, but with a number of palatable reds, as well as Sekt, the local equivalent of champagne. By and large, Germany follows the North European pattern of mealtimes, except that, as many Germans start work early, breakfast may be available in hotels, restaurants and bakers from about 7am onwards. Otherwise, lunch is taken in the middle of the day (around 12–1pm) and dinner from about 6–7pm. Vegetarian food is increasingly available, but still takes a distant second place to meat dishes. Ethnic restaurants are often a good source of vegetarian food. A tip is always welcome, but since service is

Emergency Numbers

Ambulance, fire service and all emergencies: 112
Police: 110

Embassies

Australia: Wallstrasse 76–79, 10179 Berlin, tel: 030-880 0880; www.germany.embassy.gov.au.
Canada: Leipziger Platz 17, 10117 Berlin, tel: 030-2031 2470; www.canadainternational.gc.ca/germany.
Ireland: Jagerstrasse 51, 10117 Berlin, tel: 030-220 720; www.embassyofireland.de.
South Africa: Tiergartenstrasse 18, 10785 Berlin; tel: 030-220 730; www.suedafrika.org.
UK: Wilhemstrasse 70, 10117 Berlin, tel: 030-204 570; http://ukingermany.fco.gov.uk.
US: Pariser Platz 2 (Consular Service Clayallee 170), 10117 Berlin, tel: 030-83050; http://germany.usembassy.gov.

included in the bill, a modest amount is acceptable.

Gay and lesbian travellers

Germany is one of the more gay-friendly countries, though there are striking contrasts between acceptable behaviour in big cities and rural areas, which can be very conservative. At the other end of the spectrum, Berlin has a claim to rival Amsterdam as the gay capital of Europe, with a visible history going book to the Weimar era as depicted in the novels of Christopher Isherwood. The "scene" is vibrant, with numerous welcoming cafés, bars and clubs, and high-profile events like the Gay-Lesbian City-Festival in late June. For information in English see www.gay-berlin.net and www.maneo.de.

Health and medical care

Germany has excellent medical services. Citizens of non-EU countries should ensure they have a travel and health insurance policy (see page 400). EU citizens can use German health services with an EHIC card. The German for hospital is *krankenhaus*, and for an emergency room/casualty department will be *unfallstation* or *notaufnahme*. In case of a serious emergency, call an ambulance on tel: 112. There are free emergency telephones outside larger post offices and many other locations.

Pharmacies *(apotheken)* are open 8am–6.30pm, and in their windows have list of the pharmacies in the area open during the night and at weekends on a duty-rota basis.

Nightlife

The larger the city, the more choices you have for entertainment at night. Although in many areas early-closing laws hamper night owls, anyone who wants an evening on the town should not have any problem in cities like Munich, Hamburg, Cologne or Frankfurt. There are numerous concert halls and theatres, and also variety shows, cabaret and late-night revues.

Many cities have English-language magazines/information sheets highlighting what's on and where, such as Munich's, *Munich Found* (www.munichfound.com).

In Berlin closing restrictions are minimal and the city is pretty much open 24 hours a day, so going from a drink at a bar or two to plunging into the thick of city nightlife is relatively effortless.

Hotspots are in Charlottenburg around Savigny-Platz, Wilmersdorf (south of Ku'damm), Schöneberg (near Winterfeldtplatz) and Goltzstrasse. Kreuzberg has two main meeting points: around Bergmannstrasse and Marheinekeplatz or in Oranienstrasse near Mariannenplatz. The social scene in Prenzlauer Berg around Kollwitzplatz is more relaxed and diverse – you'll find students, artists, tourists and locals all having fun. As well as the main German listings magazines (see above, Arts and Activities) a good guide to Berlin life in English is *Exberliner* magazine (www.exberliner.com).

Opening hours

Traditionally, shop opening hours have been strictly regulated across

An inviting offer.

Germany, and virtually no shops except bakeries, petrol stations, railway station and airport shops and some tourist souvenir shops were allowed to open on Sundays. From Monday to Saturday, most shops open from about 9.30am–6pm, and some small local shops open earlier, and close for lunch. No shops were traditionally allowed to stay open after 8pm. However, since 2006 the different German states (*Lander*) have been allowed to introduce their own rules on shopping hours. The near-complete ban on Sunday opening still applies in Bavaria, but most other states have brought in rather looser regulations, so that more shops now open on Sundays and in the evenings. Even so, outside the cities you will still find very few shops open on Sundays except for the traditional exceptions, and even bakeries will only be open in the morning.

Banks are usually open Monday to Friday 8.30am–12.30am and 1.30–4pm, with longer hours on Thursday evenings, and some branches at major rail stations and airports are open until 11pm and on Saturdays. Business hours are usually Monday to Friday 8am–5.30pm, and government offices open to the public 8am–noon.

Postal services

Post offices are generally open Mon–Fri 8am–6pm and Sat 8am–noon. Station and airport post offices in larger cities open until late on weekday evenings, and some are open 24 hours a day. Post boxes are yellow.

Public holidays

January: 1 New Year's Day; **March/April**: variable Good Friday, Easter Mon; **May**: 1 Labour Day; **May/June**: variable Ascension Day, Whit Mon;

June: 17 National Holiday; **August**: 15 Assumption Day; **October**: 3 Unification Day; **November**: 1 All Saints' Day, 11 Armistice Day; **December**: 25 Christmas Day, 26 St Stephen's Day.

In some Catholic regions (southern Germany), the following are also public holidays: **January**: 6 Epiphany; **June**: variable Corpus Christi. In Protestant regions (mostly northern, eastern and middle Germany), Repentance Day, which usually falls on the last Wednesday in **November**, is also celebrated.

Shopping

Germany, being a popular tourist destination, offers lots of souvenirs. The shop to look out for is the *Andenkenladen*, which has anything from valuable souvenirs to all sorts of knick-knacks. Antiques enthusiasts will find many elegant, well-stocked shops, and numerous flea markets. If you can't afford to take home a Porsche or a Mercedes, or some other example of Germany's engineering skills, look for locally made products like beer (and beer steins) and wine; porcelain from Meissen; handmade Christmas decorations from the Erzgebirge; and cuckoo clocks from the Black Forest.

Among the country's top shopping streets are Kurfürstendamm ("Ku'damm") and Friedrichstrasse in Berlin, Maximilianstrasse in Munich, Königsallee ("Kö") in Düsseldorf, and the shopping arcades near Jungfernstieg and Neuer Wall in Hamburg. In practically every town you will find a *Fussgängerzone* (pedestrian zone) with all kinds of shops – including big department stores and small specialised shops. Cigarettes and tobacco may be bought in newspaper shops, which also stock postcards.

Telecommunications

Area codes for some of the main German cities are: Berlin, 030; Bremen, 0421; Cologne, 0221; Dresden, 0351; Frankfurt, 069; Hamburg, 040; Leipzig, 0341; Munich, 089; Nurmberg, 0911. The international code for Germany is 49. Numbers beginning with 0800 are free of charge. For national telephone information, tel: 11833; international telephone information, tel: 11834; national directory enquiries (in English), tel: 11837.

Most public telephones require phone cards, which are sold at post offices, newspaper stands and some other shops. On using mobile/cell phones, see page 401. If you wish to buy a phone to use in Germany, the major UK networks like T-Mobile or Vodafone all have low-cost pay-as-you-go deals.

Tipping

Generally, service charges and taxes are included in hotel and restaurant bills. However, satisfied customers usually leave an additional tip or at least the small change. It is also customary to tip taxi drivers and hairdressers 10 percent, and cloakroom attendants a few coins.

Tourist information

Tourist information offices, marked with an "i", can be found in most towns. The national tourist office website, in multiple languages, is www.germany.travel, and the private www.germanplaces.com is also very useful. Many cities and the 16 German states also have their own tourism services, links to which are on the main national site.

Germany no longer maintains separate tourist offices abroad, so all enquiries should be made via the main website.

Berlin

The Berlin tourist service Visit Berlin provides all kinds of information in English (tel: 030-2500 2333; www.visitberlin.de). Its main information centre is at the Hauptbahnhof (main railway station) in Europaplatz, but there are other offices at the Brandenburg Gate; at Neues Kranzler Eck Passage, Kurfürstendamm 21; and at the airports.

Some souvenirs tend to emphasise national stereotypes.

GREECE

ESSENTIAL TRAVEL TIPS

FACT FILE

Area: 131,950 sq km (50,950 sq miles), including around 25,050 sq km (9,670 sq miles) of islands.
Capital: Athens
Population: About 11 million, 10 percent foreign-born. Greater Athens and Piraeús have a population of 4 million. Thessaloníki, the second-largest city, 1 million, and the most populated island is Crete, with just over half a million inhabitants.
Language: Modern Greek
Religion: Predominantly Greek Orthodox Christianity, with small minorities of Muslims, Catholics, Protestant sects and Jews.
Time zone: EET/EEST, see page 402.
Currency: the euro (€)
International dialling code: 30

TRANSPORT

Getting to Greece

By air

Almost 50 international airlines, large and small, serve Athens from around Europe and many other parts of the world. Elefthérios Venizélos International Airport (tel: 0210-353 0000; www.athensairport-2001. gr) is at Spáta, around 33km (20 miles) east of central Athens. An expressway called the Attikí Odós links Athens Airport with Elefsína via the northern suburbs, and taxis to the city cost a flat rate of €35 during the day and €50 at night. The Metro runs half-hourly from the airport to the town centre (€8 for one person, discounts for two or more), while express buses prefixed "X" serve a variety of points around Athens every quarter of an hour (€5). All services run around the clock (less frequently 11pm–5am).

As well as being served by the Greek national airline **Olympic** (www. olympicair.com) and major carriers like British Airways or Lufthansa, as a popular holiday destination Greece also has many low-cost flights, many of which go to other airports apart from Athens. **EasyJet** (www.easyjet. com) flies from the UK, Germany, Italy and other European countries to Athens and direct to Corfu, Haniá (Chania) and Iráklio (Heraklion) on Crete, Mykonos, Zanthe, Kefalonia and Rhodes, **Ryanair** (www.ryanair. com) flies to Thessaloníki, Volós, Corfu, Crete and Rhodes and **German Wings** (www.germanwings.com) flies from Germany to Athens and many of the Greek islands.

By rail

Though Greece is obviously not directly connected to Western Europe it is possible to travel there by train. Getting there all the way overland by the most traditional route (Paris–Munich–Vienna–Budapest–Bucharest–Thessaloníki) is no longer possible since rail connections between Greece and Bulgaria were suspended in 2011 due to Greek government cuts, but you can take a train down through Italy to Bari and then a ferry to Pátras in Greece, from where trains run to Athens. The journey from Paris can take only 48 hours. For information, bookings and an explanation of the routes see www. raileurope.com and www.seat61.com.

By road

Greece is accessible by a number of major European arteries. Roads out of Albania and former Yugoslav Macedonia are pretty bad; the main E75 trunk route through Bulgaria has been improving due to EU money, but still has its dangerous patches.

By sea

Several ferry routes run year-round between Italy and Greece. Brindisi or Bari to Igoumenitsa (near Corfu, 6–7hrs), Corfu itself or Pátras (16hrs) are the most popular routes, but longer, more cruise-style ferries are also available to both Greek ports from Ancona (16hrs to Igoumenitsa, 22–24hrs to Pátras) and Venice (25hrs to Igoumenitsa or Corfu, 36hrs to Pátras). Some of the main operators are **Anek Lines** (www.anek. gr), **Superfast** (www.superfast.com) oand **Grimaldi Lines** (www.grimaldi-lines.com).

Getting around Greece

With so much of its territory as islands, inevitably travelling around Greece inevitably involves extensive use of seagoing transport and flying. Bus services on the mainland (and largest islands) are adequate, though the rail network (mainland only) is rudimentary. Many visitors imitate the car-mad Greeks by renting their own vehicle.

By air

Domestic air services, mostly operating out of Athens, are provided by several internal carriers. **Olympic Airlines** (www.olympicair.com) has the most extensive network, but you'll generally have better service from **Aegean Air** (www.aegeanair.com) or **Athens Airways** (www.athensairways.

com). Crete-based **Sky Express** (www. skyexpress.gr) offers expensive links between Iráklio and a number of island and mainland destinations. Routes and flight frequencies vary radically between summer and winter.

By rail

Greek train travel is generally slow, if relatively cheap and often scenic. Many schedules have been reduced, and all international trains to Macedonia or Bulgaria suspended, as part of the national austerity programme. The main route north from Athens (Lárissa station) reaches Thessaloníki, where it now ends. Another line operates from Athens (Peloponnese station) to the Peloponnese via Corinth. All trains are run by **Hellenic Railways/OSE** (tel: 1110; www.ose.gr).

By road

Buses: A syndicate of bus companies, known as **KTEL** (Tel: 14505), offers relatively cheap and generally punctual service between all major towns (though increasingly rarely to depopulated villages). Additional bus services along major routes are provided by OSE, the state railway. Larger towns will often have different bus stations for different destinations – for example, Iráklio on Crete has three, Thessaloníki still has two (one for Halkidikí, one for everywhere else), and Athens also has two: Terminal A at Kifissoú 100 and Terminal B at 260 Liossíon 260.

Cars: Driving licences from outside the European Union are not officially recognized in Greece, so travellers from elsewhere wishing to drive should obtain an International Driving Permit (IDP). This rule is often waived by rental companies, but it's still advisable to have one. Vehicles must carry a first-aid kit, warning triangle and a fire extinguisher. Front seatbelt use is mandatory, or risk a €175 fine. Greece has the highest accident rate in EU Europe after Portugal, so drive defensively; speeding, aberrant overtaking and ignoring stop signs are common local driving habits.

Tolls are charged on the two main motorway,: Athens–Thessaloníki and Athens–Pátras. Petrol stations off the main highways generally close by 8pm, but automated pumps operated by banknotes or credit cards are becoming common.

The Automobile and Touring Club of Greece (**ELPA**; www.elpa.gr) has an emergency road service (tel: 10400). Other organisations, used by car-rental firms, include Express

Service (tel: 1154) and Hellas Service (tel: 1057).

Car rental is easily arranged, either on the spot or in advance through the usual websites. All the major international chains are present, but you will often get a better deal through smaller, equally reputable local chains. Even in high season you shouldn't pay more than €200 per week inclusive.

By sea

Seagoing transport schedules are famously erratic, a feature that has worsened with the economic crisis, and best obtained online from each company's website.

Ferries: Two websites that try to give an overview of all Greek ferries are www.gtp.gr, updated regularly, and www.greekferries.gr. Major tourist information offices and the *Athens News* supply weekly schedules, which should not, however, be trusted implicitly. The most authoritative information source on each port's sailings is the Port Police *(limenarhío)*, which has offices at Piraeús and near the harbours of all fair-sized islands. They post complete timetables and are the final arbiters of whether a ship will sail or not in stormy weather conditions.

Hydrofoils: nicknamed *delfínia* or "dolphins", connect Piraeús with most of the nearby islands such as Ýdra, and many of the Dodecanese between Kós and Sámos. In Piraeús the embarkation booths are on Aktí Miaoúli. Hydrofoils tend not to sail in conditions above Force 6.

Catamarans: Also called *tahyplóa* (high-speed boats), catamarans are newer, purpose-built craft which would have seen off slower conventional ferries were it not for their very high running costs (though fares are often little more). Unlike hydrofoils, they carry cars and are permitted to sail in weather conditions of up to Force 7. The bad news: often there are no cabins (if they finish their journeys before midnight), food service is abysmal and there are no exterior decks. The aeroplane-style seating salons are ruthlessly air-conditioned and subject to an unavoidable barrage of Greek TV on overhead monitors.

Getting around Athens

A Metro system, a tramway, a fleet of buses and taxis do the lion's share of getting locals and visitors around what is, by Mediterranean standards, a huge city. Suburban rail systems

and (for the stout-hearted) driving yourself are more esoteric choices. The centre, however, is compact enough that you'll often choose to walk to and between attractions.

All city public transport is coordinated by OASA (tel: 210-8200-999; www.oasa.gr). The same tickets are valid for the Metro, trams, buses and suburban rail lines and can be purchased with cash only from counters and automatic machines (coins only) at Metro stations or tram platforms, the yellow and blue booths by some major bus stops or from many newsstands. With single tickets (currently €1.70) you must validate the ticket in the machines at the entry to platforms or on buses before boarding, after which your ticket will be valid for 90 minutes travel. If you are caught with no ticket or an expired one by plainclothes inspectors, you get an on-the-spot fine of 60 times the standard fare. The best strategy is to buy a daily (€4) or weekly (€14) pass allowing you to use all means of transport during that time.

Much of Athens's public transport system is very modern, having been built or renovated for the 2004 Olympics. However, because of Greece's financial cuts and austerity programme, services are under severe pressure, and schedules can be reduced at short notice.

By bus

The most useful suburban services for tourists are the orange-and-white KTEL Attikís buses going from 14 Mavromatéon Street, Pédio toú Áreos Park, to Rafina or Lávrio (alternative ferry ports for the Cycládes) and Soúnio (for the famous Poseidon temple there).

Trolley buses running on overhead pantographs have also been upgraded and their routes can be easier to fathom; number 1 links the centre of the city with the main railway station, number 15 calls at the taverna-rich central district of Petrálona, numbers 5 and 9 pass the Archaeological Museum, and number 7 does a triangular circuit of the central districts.

By car

Drive at your peril in Athens during rush hours. The traffic flow is intense and unpredictable and parking space very scarce, so most visitors prefer not to try.

By Metro and tram

The Athens Metro (www.ametro.gr) has three intersecting lines operating from just after 5am until just after midnight. Line 1 (green-coded) is the older ISAP (electric train line) running mostly above ground between Kifissía and Piraeús (for ferries and hydrofoils). Lines 2 (red) and 3 (blue) were inaugurated in 2000. The three city-centre interchange stations are Monastiráki, Omónia and Sýntagma.

There is also a suburban rail service from the airport to Nerantziótissa on line 1, and on to OSE's Lárissa station; of more interest to most visitors is the tramway, with separate lines from Sýntagma to the beach suburbs of Néo Fáliron and Glyfáda, as well as a link line between the last two.

The tram is circuitous and slowish (though it runs until late), but the Metro is sleek, modern and with adverts kept to a minimum. The most central stations display archaeological artefacts and even entire sections of street or water mains uncovered during the excavation of the tunnels.

By taxi

If a taxi flashes its headlights it wants your custom. If you decide to take it, ensure that the meter is switched on and registering 1, rather than 2 which is the rate from midnight–5am. Don't be worried if you find yourself joined, en route, by a cross-section of Athenian society going roughly your way. It is perfectly legal for drivers to pick up as many as four passengers, and charge them all individually for the distance they cover, plus the current minimum fare. Tariff rules are posted on dashboard cards in all taxis. There is a surcharge from airports, seaports, railway stations and bus terminals; passengers will also be charged a small fee for luggage.

The alternative is to call a radio taxi. You pay more, but this is worth it if you need a car at a busy time or if you're luggage-laden. Íkaros, tel: 210-51 52 800; www.athens-taxi.gr, is one

established firm. Otherwise your hotel will arrange a pick-up for you.

GREECE A–Z

Accommodation

Lodging in Greece includes standard Mediterranean beach hotels, high-standard urban hotels, some worthwhile restored boutique accommodation in the provinces, standard Mediterranean self-catering villas, and that old warhorse of the more touristed islands, *enikiazómena domátia* (rented rooms). Hotels run the gamut from de luxe to the all-but-extinct D-class (five stars down to one in the new categorisation). Best prices are typically found through major travel websites if not the hotels' own pages. Island and coastal hotels, with some local variations, tend to be open from April to October, or perhaps a bit into November on southerly Crete. By contrast, mainland hotels and inns can be busy in winter if near a ski resort and charge high-season prices because of heating costs. Villa rentals are best booked through specialist agencies and websites. Proprietors of rented rooms still often meet arriving ferries armed with glossy photos of their offerings, and they are the budget set's mainstay given the almost complete absence of youth hostels as understood elsewhere in Europe. In less commercial provincial locales, a rented room or hotel room can be found for under €80 even in peak season, but in big-name resorts like Zagóri, Pílio, Rhodes or Santoríni the sky is literally the limit.

Arts and activities

The weekly (Friday) English-language paper *Athens News* has selected

events listings for Athens and to a limited extent Thessaloníki, as does the daily English edition of *Kathimeriní* (www.ekathimerini.com). If you can puzzle out the Greek script, the main listings magazine for Athens is *Athinórama* (every Thursday).

Athens and Epidaúros Festival

This runs, with slight annual variations, from late May to late August/early September, featuring ballet, opera, jazz and modern music, and modern and classical plays from world-class artists. The main Athens venues are the Iródio (Herod Atticus Odeion), Pireós Avenue 260, and the Mégaro Mousikís; the Epidaúros amphitheatre is used during July and August. Top performances are popular, so book tickets online (www.greekfestival.gr/en), or as soon as you arrive in Greece. Information and tickets can be obtained from the main festival box office in the arcade at Panepistimíou 39 (tel: 210-32 72 000), or, for events at the Iródio only, its own box office on the day of performance. Bring cushions and binoculars for the cheap seats – they're hard marble and quite far from the stage.

Budgeting for your trip

Entrance into the euro in 2002 meant that prices rose across Greece, but this has to some extent been knocked sideways by the massive financial crisis since 2009. What you'll find is now hard to predict:

Accommodation: Some hotels and other businesses struggle to maintain their pre-2009 prices, while elsewhere you may find what are – by international standards – amazingly cheap offers. Nevertheless, overall, travelling as one of a couple, you should allow a minimum of €30 each for accommodation (€40–50 in Athens or Thessaloníki). To keep costs

Menu signs in Greek and English

down, look for hotel deals online, which, again, can be very low-priced.
Meals: Count on €14–25 for a meal with modest intake of beer or cheap wine.
Sightseeing: It usually costs €4–12 each for site admission, and €30–36 for the cheapest small rental car – before petrol costs.

Children

Children are adored in Greece, so expect your own kids to be the centre of attention. Children, especially boys, are treated very indulgently, though at the same time are not allowed to determine adults' schedules – they are very early on inculcated into the stay-up-late routine, including being taken to taverna meals. Resort hotels are slowly introducing dedicated kids' activities.

Children aged under 6 travel for free on Athens public transport, and under-10s travel for half the adult fare on most buses and ferries. There are also reduced prices at museums and archaeological sites.

Climate

The Greece of tourist posters is a perennially warm and sunny place – and it is, by European standards. But this picture does not reflect the considerable climatic variety. The north and inland regions have a modified continental climate, so winters are quite cold and summers extremely hot. In Ioánnina, Trípoli and Kastoriá, for example, snow and freezing temperatures are not uncommon in winter. In mountainous regions, winters are even more severe, with ski centres operating above elevations of 2,000 metres (6,500ft).

The southern islands, the coastal Peloponnese and the Attic peninsula conform more to the traditional Mediterranean image: a long, warm season of rainless, sunny days extending roughly from late May to

mid-October. But here too the winters can be cool and rainy.

In general, spring (late April–June) and autumn (September–October) are the best times to visit. During these periods, you will find mild to warm temperatures, sunny days and fewer tourists. Throughout July and August, Greece is at its hottest and stickiest, and most crowded.

Disabled travellers

Despite nudging from the EU, Greece has some way to go before becoming fully compliant with regulations on facilities for disabled people.

Athens, with lifts in the Metro, "kneeling" buses on many routes, recorded announcements of upcoming stops on the Metro plus some buses, and ramps at kerbside, is furthest ahead. Elsewhere, amenities are poor.

Few hotels in the provinces are disabled-friendly, though things are improving, with some preparing a few rooms with wide doors and safety handles in the bath – ask when booking. Otherwise, the best way to find accessible facilities in Greece is through international disabled travel websites.

Eating out

Eating out in Greece is a social affair, although the ritual of families and friends patronising tavernas twice a week is less observed now owing to hard economic times. A meal with bulk wine or local beer will cost at least €13 per person: €16–20 is a more typical figure. If you order fish or bottled wine, then it's €25 minimum, and more realistically €35. Check bills carefully – variance from the cited menu price is far from unknown.

Cuisine has improved in recent decades, with the dousing of everything in superfluous quantities of oil somewhat reined in. *Estiatòria* or *magería* specialise in the more elaborate, home-style casserole

dishes known as *magireftá*; *psistariés* are grillhouses featuring only meat platters plus a few salads and *mezédes* (starters); while tavernas try (with varying degrees of success) to do all these things. *Psárotavernas* specialise in fish, with some exceptions as expensive as anywhere in the Mediterranean.

Booking at all but the most upmarket eateries is not required. Greeks eat late by Northern European standards: 1.30–4pm for lunch, 9pm–midnight (later at weekends) for dinner. Sunday night and part of Monday are the typical days of closure outside the more tourist areas.

Kalamári-and-chips or *moussakás* may be the resort stereotypes, but the best-value main dishes include *frikasé* (any meat stew with celery), *spetzofáï* (sausage and pepper hotpot), *papoutsákia* (aubergine "shoes" stuffed with ground meat) and *kounélli stifádo* (stewed rabbit). Vegetarians – and the impecunious – will do better assembling a meal from various *mezédes*, and a whole class of eatery – the *ouzerí* – specialises in this.

Gay and lesbian travellers

Overt gay behaviour is not a feature of Greek society. The age of consent is 17, and bisexual activity fairly common among younger men, but few couples (male or female) are openly gay. Mýkonos is famous as a gay mecca, and Skála Eressoú on Lésvos (birthplace of poetess Sappho) is essentially a lesbian resort. Elsewhere in Greece single-sex couples are liable to be regarded as odd, but are usually as welcome as any other tourists. If discreet, you will attract no attention asking for a double room and will find most people tolerant.

Health and medical care

Citizens of non-EU countries must ensure they have a travel and health insurance policy before travelling in Greece (see page 400). EU nationals are entitled to free basic healthcare at state clinics or hospitals with an EHIC card, but must pay for medication and

Festivals

Carnival/Apokriátika – three weeks up to the seventh weekend before Easter. Pátras with its elaborate floats and gay participation is the liveliest, but the very pagan "goat dance" on Skýros and the *boúles* revels at Náoussa in Macedonia are also well attended. **Easter weekend** (variable April/May) – sombre, moving procession of the *Epitáfios* or Christ's funeral bier in all major towns Good Friday evening, with brass band accompaniment; each parish competes for the most elaborate floral bier. Saturday midnight sees (and hears) the Anástasi or Resurrection church service, with deafening fireworks and the best

chanting into the small hours. **Firewalking by** anastenarídes **cult members** – at Agía Eléni (near Sérres) and Langadás (near Thessaloníki) on 21 May. This observance, which commemorates the rescue of precious icons from a medieval church fire, was brought to northern Greece by refugees from what is now Bulgarian Thrace (where identical rites still occur). **Dormition of the Virgin** (15 August) – major festivals on Kárpathos, Agiássos and Tínos, where the icon is carried over the unwell kneeling on the street. But almost every island and mainland county has a bash of some sort; the second-most important festival after Easter.

Telecommunications

All telephone numbers within Greece, whether fixed or mobile, have 10 digits. Land lines start with 2, mobiles with 6. The prefix for Athens and Piraeús numbers is now 210, for Thessaloníki 2310. The code for Greece is 30.

For local or intercity calls, purchase an OTE (Greek Telecoms) telephone card from a kiosk and use (invariably noisy) street-corner phone booths. The best way to make international calls is with a laptop with Skype or similar software. With the growing prevalence of Wifi zones, this is generally feasible from your hotel. Avoid making any calls from hotels – charges are typically quadruple the basic local phone rates.

On using mobile/cellphones, see page 401. The amounts charged foreign mobile users by Greek networks have been particularly high. If you're going to stay for more than a week, it makes sense to buy a local pay-as-you-go phone for €20 or less.

specialist tests. Also, public hospitals vary widely in reputation, and the recent austerity cuts have caused many new problems including the closure of some services, so it's best also to have travel insurance, allowing you to use private healthcare. In Athens and major resorts your hotel should be able to suggest a reputable private doctor, and consulates keep lists of English-speaking doctors.

In Athens, the **Evangelismós Hospital**, Ypsilándou 45, Kolonáki, tel: 210-72 01 000, is a good general hospital, next to a Metro station of the same name.

Chemists/pharmacies are open during normal morning shop hours, but some stay open day and night. Duty rotas are displayed on chemists' windows, or tel: 1434 for information (in Greek). Most pharmacists speak English.

Opening hours

Banks are open Mon–Thur 8.30am–2.30pm, closing at 2pm on Friday. In heavily visited areas like Rhodes, however, you may find banks open additional late-afternoon hours and on Saturday mornings.

Business hours vary. The main thing to remember is that businesses generally open at 8.30am and close for the rest of the day on Monday, Wednesday and Saturday at 2.30pm. On Tuesday, Thursday and Friday most businesses close at 2pm and reopen in the afternoon from 5.30–9pm. An increasing number of business and shops, especially in Athens, are working continual shifts of 9am–6pm or even later.

Supermarkets are typically open Mon–Fri 8.30am–9am, closing Saturday at 8pm. Some branches of the Carrefour Marinópoulos chain open on Sundays.

Postal services

Most local post offices are open weekdays from 7.30am–2pm. The main post office in central Athens on Sýntagma Square is open Mon–Fri 7.30am–8pm, Sat 7.30am–2pm and Sun 9am–1pm. There are also long-hours post offices in Thessaloníki, Ioánnina and Rhodes.

Public holidays

January: 1 New Year's Day, 6 Epiphany; **February/March**: variable Orthodox Shrove Monday; **March**: 25 Independence Day; **March/April**: variable Orthodox Good Friday/Easter Mon; **May**: 1 Labour Day; **May/June**: variable Orthodox Whit Mon; **August**: 15 Assumption Day; **October**: 28 Ochi Day; **December**: 25 Christmas Day, 26 St Stephen's Day.

Shopping

Handcrafted jewellery and durable-but-crude leather goods are favourite purchases. Worry beads, Greek coffee pots *(bríkia)*, colourful tin retsina-measuring cups and olive-oil soap will remind you of your visit. Foodstuffs (but bear in mind baggage/customs regulations at your destination) are also popular: pickled capers, honey, pistachio nuts, olives and olive oil, pickled wild bulbs, ouzo or dried figs make ideal souvenirs or gifts.

Tipping

Restaurant prices notionally include "service", but an extra 5–10 percent depending on the size of the party is expected as coins on the table. Round up the charge on the taxi meter. Around Christmas and Easter, all taxis (and a few restaurants) add a *filodórima* (holiday gratuity) to the bill. At the end of your stay a few large euro coins for your hotel chambermaid are much appreciated.

Tourist information

The Greek National Tourism Organisation (www.visitgreece.gr) has information desks in Athens at: D. Arepagitou 18–20 (tel: 210-33 10 392; daily, Sat–Sun closes 4pm); and Athens's tourist authority (www.breathtakingathens.com) has "Info Points" at the Airport and Amalias Avenue (both open daily) and at Piraeús harbour (closed Sun). Local authorities also maintain tourist offices in all the islands and resort areas, which all supply free maps and other information.

Tourist offices abroad

All can be contacted through www.visitgreece.gr.
Australia: tel: 02-9241 1663
UK: tel: 020-7495 4300
US: tel: 212-421 5777

ITALY

ESSENTIAL TRAVEL TIPS

FACT FILE

Area: 301,245 sq km (116,280 sq miles)
Capital: Rome
Population: 60.8 million
Language: Italian
Highest mountain: Gran Paradiso 4,061 metres (13,323ft); Mont Blanc on French/Italian border 4,810 metres (15,781ft).
Religion: Roman Catholic
Time zone: CET/CEST, see page 402.
Currency: the euro (€)
International dialling code: 39

TRANSPORT

Getting to Italy

By air

Italy has two hub airports for intercontinental flights: Rome's Leonardo da Vinci (better-known as Fiumicino; tel: 06-65951; www.adr. it), and Milan-Malpensa (tel: 02-232 323; www.milanomalpensa1.eu). As well as the national airline, **Alitalia** (www.alitalia.com), many major airlines fly direct to Italy, and some North American and European airlines fly to more convenient provincial cities such as Venice as well as the main hubs.

In addition, low-cost airlines now fly from other parts of Europe to most of Italy's smaller airports, making previously isolated areas (especially Sardinia and Sicily) much more accessible. Some of these airports act as regional hubs: Pisa is the main airport for Tuscany, and Naples is the busiest airport in the south. **Ryanair** (www.ryanair.com) flies to and between around 20 Italian destinations from all over Europe, and **easyJet** (www. easyjet.com), **Jet2** (www.jet2.com) and **German Wings** (www.germanwings. com) also have many Italian services. At major cities Ryanair generally uses secondary airports (Ciampino for Rome, Linate or Bergamo for Milan, Treviso for Venice) rather than the main airports.

From the airports

Fiumicino is 35km (22 miles) southwest of Rome. Depending on your Rome destination, the most convenient way into the city is on the *Leonardo Express* train direct to the central station, Stazione Termini. It runs daily from around 6am–11.30pm, and takes about 30 minutes; a single ticket is €14. There are also slightly slower, cheaper trains that stop at suburban stations. A taxi from the airport should cost around €45–50, with higher rates at night and on Sundays. Ryanair and most other low-cost airlines fly to Rome's second airport, Ciampino, which is closer to the city, only 12km (7½ miles) southeast. Shuttle buses run from there to Ciampino Città suburban rail station, from where frequent trains run to Termini in Rome, for a cost of about €10. There are also direct buses. A taxi will cost about €30.

Malpensa is 40km (25 miles) from central Milan. The Malpensa Express train runs every 30 minutes to Cadorna station in the city (where it connects with the Metro) with some stops en route from about 6.30am–10pm, and costs about €10. There are also 24hr bus services. Full timetables of airport trains can be found on the Italian Railways (Trenitalia) website (www. trenitalia.com).

At smaller airports there are generally bus services for transfers to the nearest town. They're often timed to coincide with flights but are sometimes infrequent, so it's often worth hiring a car.

By rail

Travelling to Italy by rail is naturally slower than flying but can be a very attractive way to get there. Nightly Thello sleeper trains run from Paris to Milan and Venice, or via Florence to Rome, and in Milan connect with the Italian high-speed rail network. There are also spectacular routes across the Alps to Milan from Zurich, and from Munich via Innsbruck to Verona and Venice.

For information and bookings Rail Europe, www.raileurope.com, and for more orientation see www.seat61.com.
Breakdown services: The **Automobile Club d'Italia** (ACI; www. aci.it) has offices at all main frontier posts, offering information, maps and emergency breakdown services. Throughout Italy, 24 hours a day, call tel: 803 116 for breakdown services (English-speaking service available).

By road

Buses: Eurolines (www.eurolines.com) international buses run to several Italian cities from many parts of Europe. Since Italian rail fares are not high bus fares are ultra-low to compete, but journeys take far longer.
Cars: Italy is naturally fully connected to the European motorway network, but driving into the country is complicated by its geography, ringed as it is in the north by different Alpine ranges. Several of the main

routes run through tunnels (the Mont Blanc Tunnel, the Great St Bernhard between the Swiss Valais and the Val d'Aosta) or narrow corridors (European highway E74 along the coast east of Monaco, the busiest route) can be congested in summer. Others run over Alpine passes (the Brenner, from Austria, is one of the most famous) and are often slow going, and may even be closed in severe weather in winter. Tunnels and passes are well organised to minimise congestion, but it can't always be avoided. The smaller Alpine passes are spectacular, so it's best to build this into your trip.

By sea

Car and passenger ferries link Venice with Greece, Slovenia, Croatia and Albania; Genoa, Livorno and Civitavecchia with Barcelona, Tunis and Morocco; and Venice, Ancona, Brindisi and Bari with Greece. The companies are the same ones that provide ferries to the Italian Islands.

Getting around Italy

By air

Alitalia continues to serve the whole country, but is increasingly challenged by independent operators with much lower fares such as **Meridiana** (www. meridiana.it), **Blu-express** (www. blu-express.com) and **Ryanair**, which operates many routes within Italy. Every area has its airport, and there are several on each of the main islands. Though the efficiency and accessible fares of the railway system generally makes trains the most attractive means of travel for visitors to Italy, flights can be useful for long distances, and of course for getting to Sardinia or Sicily.

By rail

The cheapest, fastest and most convenient way to travel is by train; most rail lines are operated by **Trenitalia** (www.trenitalia.com). There are several types of train: the figureheads of the network are the *Frecciarossa* luxury high-speed trains between major cities; next down are the only slightly slower *Frecciargento* trains, and then the *Frecciablanca* and *InterCity* trains, which stop rather more frequently. All are air-conditioned and very comfortable. Supplements (*supplementi*) are charged for these trains, and it is obligatory to reserve a seat, although this can be done up to a few minutes before the train departs. On long-distance routes, overnight sleeper

trains are also available.

More local trains may be called *Regionale*, *Diretto*, *Interregionale* or, rather inappropriately, *Espresso*. They are much slower, since they generally stop at a great many stations. No reservations are necessary.

Tickets for nearly all Trenitalia trains can be bought online through www.trenitalia.com (in English) and at stations, which have self-service ticket machines that accept cash and credit cards. Discounts are offered if you book your ticket more than a week or two weeks in advance, and there are also occasional special fare offers, shown on the website. If you book online you will be emailed a booking code; when you get on the train, show this to the ticket collector, who will issue your ticket. If you have a conventional paper ticket from a counter or a machine you must validate it by stamping it in one of the yellow machines on station platforms just before you board the train; otherwise you can be fined. Mainline trains can also be booked through Rail Europe, but a booking fee will be added. Because of the generally low level of Italian rail fares, and the discounts available, rail passes are of limited benefit in Italy. For more on trains in Italy see www.seat61.com.

Some local lines are operated by regional companies, notably Ferrovie Emilia Romagna (FER, www. fer-online.it) around Bologna; Ferrovie Nord Milano (www.ferrovienord. it) from Milan; SAD (www.sad.it) in the Dolomites; and Ferrovie della Sardegna (www.ferroviesardegna.it) in Sardinia, which in summer runs Trenino Verde sightseeing trains on a spectacular line through the centre of the island (which also has Trenitalia lines). In the south and Sicily, buses can be a better option because some areas are poorly served by rail. Exceptions to this are the fascinating Circumetnea line around Etna and the Naples Circumvesuviana, which is the best way of seeing Pompeii, Herculaneum and other classical sites.

By road

Buses are an important supplement to the rail system, particularly in mountainous areas. Each Italian province has its own regional bus company. This can lead to confusion since, particularly in Sicily, connections are not always coordinated. SITA (www.sitabus. it) is a large company that runs long-distance services and regional services in several parts of Italy.

Cars: Italian motorways (*autostrade*) are generally fast and uncongested, except in midsummer and on key holidays, such as Easter. Virtually all are toll roads; an *autostrade* website (in English, www.autostrade.it/en) allows you to check current tolls for any journey. Tolls can be paid in cash or by credit card, and you can also buy a Viacard at various outlets, prepaid with autostrada credits for different amounts.

Motoring advice: Drivers must have a red warning triangle and yellow reflective jacket, and seatbelts must be worn at all times. Dipped headlights must be turned on during the day in poor visibility, and in tunnels. In mountain areas in winter, it is often compulsory to fit snow chains; check on current conditions with the nearest tourist office.

Having a car in Italy is excellent for exploring the countryside, but generally of little use in cities, due to the often impenetrable traffic. For outsiders, city driving is especially to be avoided in Rome and Naples. In many Italian towns the old centre (*Centro Storico*) is closed to all drivers except residents. A sign with a red circle on white and *traffico limitato* indicates when this is so. If you are staying at a hotel in the historic centre of any town, ask the hotel beforehand what to do with your car. Parking space in general is also at a premium in Italian towns, so again, it is best to leave your car in a hotel car park. Hiring a car at short notice can also be relatively expensive in Italy, so book ahead online.

By sea

Frequent car and passenger ferries run between mainland ports and Italy's islands. For Sardinia, there are ferries from Genoa, Livorno, Civitavecchia, Naples and Palermo to various ports on the island. For Sicily the fastest route is Caronte Lines' (tel: 800 627 414; www.carontetourist.it) 20-minute shuttle between Villa San Giovanni, near Reggio di Calabria, and Messina, but there also ferries from Genoa, Livorno, Civitavecchia, Naples and Salerno. Two of the main ferry operators are **Grimaldi Lines** (tel: 081-496-444; www.grimaldi-lines.com) and **Grande Navi Veloci** (tel: 010-209-4591; www2.gnv.it).

Ustica Lines (tel: 0923-873-813; www.usticalines.it) also operates boat connections to the Aeolian Islands, Pantelleria and other small islands around Sicily, and frequent fast hydrofoils and car ferries run from Naples to Capri, Ischia and other

Tram in Piazza Porta Maggiore.

islands in the bay of Naples.

Getting around Rome

Rome's city buses and Metro are run by the transport authority ATAC. The great hub of the transport system is Stazione Termini, where all long-distance and most local trains arrive (information tel: 89201). ATAC information and route maps are available from the kiosk in front of Termini, and main Metro stations and tourist offices.

The same ATAC tickets are valid for Metro, bus or tramlines, and can be bought from Metro stations, tobacco shops, newsstands, some bars and tourist offices. Single tickets cost only €1.50, and you can also get passes valid for 1, 3 or 7 days for €6–24. Single tickets must be bought before you travel and time-stamped in special machines when you enter the Metro or board a bus, and passes must be stamped the first time you use them. A Roma Pass is also available which gives unlimited travel on local transport, admission to several museums and archaeological sites and other concessions for 3 days, for €30.

Bicycles: Rome has a 35km (22-mile) rarely used network of cycle paths. To encourage cyclists the city has introduced a bike-sharing scheme based on the Paris model, www. bikesharingroma.it, whereby you leave a deposit at a tourist office, and pick up a swipecard to unlock a bike. For bike rental try **Top Bike** at Via dei Quattro Canti 40, tel: 06-488 2893; www.topbikerental.com.

Buses: Unlike the Metro, city bus routes cover every part of the city and run 5.30am–midnight, after which time there are night services. Among the most useful routes are the 40 and 64, which connect Termini with Piazza Venezia, the Centro Storico and the Vatican, and there are also small electric buses which cope with the narrow alleys of the historic centre: line 116 passes through or close to Piazza Navona, Campo de' Fiori and St Peter's.

Metro: Rome has two underground lines (*metropolitana* or Metro), line A and line B, which operate daily 5.30am–11.30pm and pass most of Rome's popular tourist sights and intersect at Termini. A third line, C, is under construction and being opened in phases, and will eventually link the Colosseum to Largo Argentina. There are also extensive suburban rail lines.

Taxis: You can order a taxi by calling Radiotaxi, tel: 06-3570; www.3570.it.

ITALY A–Z

Accommodation

Italy has a wonderful variety of accommodation in all categories, from its luxurious villa hotels and palatial apartments to small family-run hotels and rural B&Bs. The Italian hotel scene has been very traditional, and its world-famous grand hotels in Venice, Rome and around the northern Lakes still retain their sumptuous appeal. However, it has been enlivened in recent years by new additions such ultra-stylish and equally luxurious boutique hotels, especially in Milan and Turin and, lower down the price range, "eco-hotels" in restored historic buildings, often in spectacular settings in remote villages. In addition, in every Italian city there is a choice of functional business hotels that have less charm but very good prices. The Italian tourist office, however, does not have a central accommodation-search service, so when looking for rooms it's best to look at the websites of individual cities and regions, or hotel associations.

The bed-and-breakfast idea has also taken off in Italy, notably in its historic cities, and B&Bs now provide some of the most characterful and best-value accommodation. A good place to look for rooms is www.bbitalia. it, but there are many local sites such as www.b-b.rm.it for Rome. An offshoot of the B&B idea is *agroturismo*: B&B rooms or self-catering cottages in the countryside, which can run from rustic farmhouse rooms to luxury stays on wine estates. There are now thousands of *agroturismo* possibilities, which offer a real experience of the Italian countryside and (especially) its special foods. Regional tourist offices all list *agroturismo* locations in their areas, or look on www.agroturismo.it.

Most Italian hotels still operate on a very seasonal basis, and have very different rates in low and high seasons. Also, Italians generally only go to beaches in summer, so many hotels in seaside areas such as the Adriatic coast or Sardinia may close completely between November and March–April.

Arts and activities

The Italian national tourism website www.italia.it and city and regional tourist office websites give extensive information on major events, exhibitions and festivals around Italy, and all local tourist offices provide free guides to cultural events and programmes in their area. The range is naturally huge: regular arts seasons generally run from September or October to around May, and in summer the attention shifts to a range of festivals. Be aware that for Italy's most celebrated arts venues – the opera houses of La Scala (www.teatroallascala.org) in Milan or the Teatro Regio in Parma (www. teatroregioparma.org), the summer opera season in the Roman Arena in Verona (www.arena.it) – tickets are in high demand, so should be booked well ahead.

In Rome, the free *Museums of Rome* booklet and *Evento*, with a cultural programme for the month, can be picked up from all tourist offices. The English-language magazine *Wanted in Rome* is out every other Wednesday and has information about events throughout Italy (www.wantedinrome.com), and in Italian the weekly magazine Roma C'e has listings of all the city's entertainment.

Budgeting for your trip

Accommodation: A double room with breakfast in high season, tax included, should cost from under €100 in a simple hotel to around €150 in a mid-range hotel and anything over €300 in luxury hotels. Prices can be much lower out of season and in less fashionable areas.
Meals: Full meal at inexpensive restaurant €20–30, moderate €30–45, expensive €45–60 plus;

Festivals

The Italians' attachment to regional customs and religious festivals dwindled in the 20th century, but many continue. Here is a far from exhaustive list.

January: Piana degli Albanesi (near Palermo): a colourful Byzantine ritual for Epiphany.

February: Venice: historical Carnival, masked balls and processions in magnificent costumes. Viareggio: more contemporary Carnival with parade of floats. Agrigento: Almond Blossom Festival.

April: Rome: Pope's Easter Sunday blessing.

May: Assisi: Calendimaggio Christian and pagan festival. Naples: Miracle of San Gennaro (liquefaction of the saint's blood, first Sunday in May, also on 19 September and 16 December). Camogli (Riviera): Fish Festival, communal fish-fry in giant pan. Gubbio: wooden candle race, crossbow competition. Orvieto: Pentecost feast of the Palombella (Holy Ghost). Florence: Maggio Musicale (May–June), musical performances in various venues throughout the city.

June: Pisa: San Ranieri, jousting and torch-lit regatta on River Arno. Florence: medieval football game in costume. Spoleto: Festival dei Due Mondi (June–July), international theatre, prose, music and dance performances by leading artists from Europe and the Americas.

July: Siena: First Palio (2 July). Sardinia: "Sa Ardia" – more dangerous than Il Palio (6–7 July). Palermo: festival of patron Santa Rosalia. Venice: Redentore regatta. Rimini: Festival of the Sea. Rome: Noantri street festival in Trastevere. Perugia and other Umbrian cities: Umbria Jazz, one of the most important jazz festivals in Europe.

August: Siena: Second Palio (16 August). Venice: (late August, early September) Venice International Film Festival.

September: Naples: Piedigrotta, Neapolitan music and cuisine and the 19 September feast day of San Gennaro. Venice: historical Regatta.

October: Assisi: Feast of St Francis. Perugia: Franciscan Mysteries.

December: Rome: Christmas food and toy market on Piazza Navona. Assisi and Naples: Nativity scenes in streets.

light lunch €10–20. Drinks might add on around €3–10.

Sightseeing: Admission varies widely, from €5–14 but there is free entry to many public museums for EU citizens aged under 18 or over 65.

Transport: Around €8–15 per person per day.

Special tourist passes are available in many cities that combine unlimited travel on local transport for a set period with free or reduced admission to many attractions and other discounts, which can be a great help in keeping costs down. Among the most useful are the Roma Pass (www.romapass.it), the Milano Card, which gives a whole range of benefits for 3 days for just €13 (www.milanocard.it) and the Venicecard (www.hellovenezia.com or www.veniceconnected.com).

Children

Italians love children and take them everywhere. They are welcomed in restaurants in the evening as well as lunchtime (but note many restaurants do not open until 7.30pm), and the vast majority of hotels are happy to accept them. An extra bed or cot in a guest room costs around 30 percent extra.

On trains and most public transport children under 4 ride free, 4–12-year-olds are half-price. Many museums and sites have free entrance for children under 6, and public museums and sites are free for all EU citizens aged under 18. There is also usually a reduced price for all other under-18s.

Climate

In the Alpine region, winters are long and cold, but often sunny, while summers are short and pleasantly cool. The northern lakes and Po Valley see cold and foggy winters and warm, sunny summers. The rest of the country, even the northern Ligurian coast, has mild weather in winter. Summers are dry and hot to scorching, depending on how far south you go, but sea breezes often compensate for the searing heat.

The best time for a visit to the coasts and islands is from May/June to September, avoiding August itself when they're most crowded. The best time to visit the cities of Italy is in spring or autumn between April and June and again in September and October.

Disabled travellers

Italy's older cities are not easily navigable by disabled travellers: cobblestones, narrow pavements and cramped lifts make getting around tricky. The national tourism website www.italia.it has information on some access schemes around the country (under "Turismo Accessibile"), and the Rome-based CO.IN organisation offers information on disabled facilities in restaurants, museums, shops and stations; tel: 800-271 027; www.coinsociale.it (website in Italian only).

Transport in Italy's larger cities is gradually becoming more accessible, with increasing numbers of buses and trams wheelchair-accessible, but overall the situation is still patchy. Facilities are better on trains: on the Trenitalia website, www.trenitalia.com, look under "Other Services" for information (in English) on the facilities available to enable access to all trains and how to book assistance if required.

Accessible Italy is a non-profit English-speaking organisation that organises accommodation and tours for people with disabilities; tel: 378-941 111; www.accessibleitaly.com.

Eating out

Italian **breakfast** (colazione) is usually a light affair, consisting of a cappuccino and brioche (pastry) or simply a caffè (black, strong espresso).

Lunch (pranzo) is traditionally the main meal of the day, but this is gradually changing. However, when Italians have the time to indulge, an ideal one might run as follows: after an antipasto (hors d'oeuvre), there follows a primo (pasta, rice or soup) and a secondo (meat or fish with a vegetable known as a contorno) or just a salad. The meal ends with a dolce (dessert). Italians usually drink an espresso (but never a cappuccino) after a meal and sometimes a liqueur, such as grappa, amaro or sambuca. Traditionally, dinner (cena) is similar to lunch, but lighter. However, where it has become more normal to eat less at lunchtime, dinner is the main meal of the day.

Every region in Italy has its own typical dishes: Piedmont specialises in pheasant, hare, truffles and zabaglione (a hot dessert made with whipped egg yolks, sugar and Marsala wine). Lombardy is known for risotto alla Milanese (with saffron, onions and beef marrow), minestrone, veal

Italian chic.

and *panettone* cake, Umbria is best for roast pork and black truffles, and Tuscany is good for wild boar, chestnuts, steak and game. Naples is the home of mozzarella cheese and pizza and is good for seafood, and Sicily is the place to enjoy delectable sweets.

Italy still claims the best ice cream in the world, as well as the Sicilian speciality *granita* (crushed ice with fruit juice or coffee).

Opening times are generally 12/12.30pm–2/3pm for lunch, 7.30/8–10pm for dinner, and except in big cities and resorts you will rarely find restaurants (as opposed to small pizzerias and some other snack options) open outside these times. Restaurant bills will often include a €1–4 bread and cover charge, per person. Vegetarian dishes are fairly scarce, and note that even vegetable-based pasta dishes may be made with a meat stock.

Gay and lesbian travellers

Gay life in Italy is becoming more mainstream, helped by festivals such as Rome's summer-long Gay Village. Attitudes are generally more tolerant in the north: Bologna is regarded as Italy's gay capital, and Milan, Turin and Rome all have lively gay scenes. The Arcigay network provides all kinds of information in Italian (tel: 051-095 7241; www.arcigay.it), while information in English is on www.gay friendlyitaly.com.

Health and medical care

Citizens of non-EU countries must have a travel and health insurance policy before travelling in Italy (see page 400). EU nationals are entitled to free basic healthcare at state clinics or hospitals with an EHIC card, but must pay for some medicines. Most hospitals (*ospedale*) have an emergency department *(pronto soccorso)*, which is the first place to turn to in a real medical emergency, but some state hospitals – especially in the south – can be grim, so it's best also to have travel insurance, allowing you to use private healthcare. Hotels should be able to suggest a reputable private doctor, and Consulates keep lists of English-speaking doctors.

For minor complaints, seek out a chemist (*farmacia*), identified by a green cross. Normal opening hours are 9am–1pm and 4–7pm, but outside these hours the address of the nearest *farmacia* on emergency duty will be posted in the window.

Nightlife

Rome and Milan are the hotspots, but other large cities, especially university ones, have plenty of nightlife, particularly on weekend nights. In Rome, the liveliest areas are Testaccio, Ostiense and – very popular with tourists – Trastevere. Out of the cities, most of the action takes place in midsummer in the open-air clubs of coastal resorts. Rimini is the liveliest, with a whole strong of open-air clubs and bars. Listings are available from tourist offices, newsstands and in local newspapers.

Opening hours

Banks are generally open Mon–Fri 8am–1.30pm and 2.30–4pm. Museums and galleries have varied openings, but most are closed on Mondays, so take this very much into account. From Tuesday to Sunday they are typically open from 9am or 9.30am–4pm, or later in the larger cities.

Shops are usually open Mon–Sat 8.30 or 9am–1pm and 3.30 or 4–7.30 or 8pm, with some variations in the north where the lunch break tends to be shorter or non-existent and shops therefore close earlier. In areas serving tourists, hours are usually longer. Shops often close on Monday (or Monday morning). An increasing number of stores in cities and main resorts are open all day on Sundays.

Postal services

Local post office hours open Mon–Fri 8am–1.30pm, but every town has a main post office that opens Mon–Fri until 7/8pm and 8am–1/1.30pm Sat.

Stamps (*francobolli*) can more easily be purchased from *tabacchi*, tobacco shops. Rome's main post office at Piazza San Silvestro, open Mon–Sat 8.25am–7pm, is in a splendid Renaissance palazzo.

The Vatican runs its own postal service, reputed to be faster than the Italian service. When visiting St Peter's, buy Vatican-issued stamps for your postcards and post them immediately: they are only valid in the Vatican City's blue post boxes.

Public holidays

January: 1 New Year's Day, 6 Epiphany; **March/April**: variable Easter Mon; **April**: 25 Liberation Day; **May**: 1 Labour Day; **May/June**: variable Corpus Christi; **June**: 2 Anniversary of the Republic; **August**: 15 Assumption Day; **November**: 1 All Saints' Day; **December**: 8 Immaculate Conception, 25 Christmas Day, 26 St Stephen's Day.

Emergency Numbers

In Italy the EU-wide emergency number 112 normally connects only to the Carabinieri, one of two main police forces.
Police: 113, or 112 for the Carabinieri
Ambulance: 118
Fire service: 115
Coastguard: 1530

Embassies and Consulates

Australia: Via Antonio Bosio 5, Rome, tel: 06-852 721; www.italy. embassy.gov.au.
Canada: Via Zara 30, Rome, tel: 06-697 9121; www.canada international.gc.ca/italy-italie.
Ireland: Piazza Campitelli 3, Rome, tel: 06-697 9121; www.embassy ofireland.it.

South Africa: Via Tanaro 14, Rome, tel: 06-852 541; http://lnx.sudafrica. it.
UK: Via XX Settembre 80a, Rome, tel: 06-4220 0001; http://ukinitaly. fco.gov.uk.
US: Via Vittorio Veneto 119A, Rome, tel: 06-46741; http://italy.us embassy.gov.

Italians drink their coffee on the run, standing up at the bar.

Shopping

The attractions of shopping in Italy are based in Italians' design sense and – in the best clothes, shoes, jewellery and accessories – their centuries-old traditions of workmanship.

There is an abundance of gourmet delicacies that make the perfect gift – cheeses, salamis, Parma ham, Ligurian olive oil and the small-production Chianti and Orvieto wines that you may not find back home. The flea markets and street stalls in Florence are a bargain-hunter's paradise, where particularly good buys on leather goods, scarves and clothes are available. Other major cities have similar markets.

Popular souvenirs include blown glass from Venice, decorative and beautifully produced paper from Florence, high fashion from Milan and shoes and handbags anywhere.

In Rome, Via del Corso, Piazza di Spagna and Via del Babuino mark the boundaries of the *Tridente*, the classic window-shopping area for smart fashion, while Via del Babuino, Via Margutta, Via Giulia, Via dei Coronari and Via del Pellegrino are the main streets for antiques, *objets d'art* and paintings. In the old centre, streets around Piazza Navona, the Pantheon and Campo de' Fiori offer unusual handcrafted goods and smaller boutiques, while Via del Governo Vecchio is one of the best streets for stylish second-hand clothes.

Telecommunications

Italian phone numbers vary in length, but in all numbers, the area code, which starts with a 0, must be used whether you are calling from within or outside the area, for example, if calling Rome dial the full city code (06). The area codes of the other main cities are: Milan (02), Florence (055), Pisa (050), Venice (041), Turin (011), Naples (081), Como (031), Palermo (091). The code for Italy is 39. For directory enquiries, tel: 12; international enquiries, tel: 176.

Most public telephones now only take phone cards (carta telefonica), available from tobacco shops, post offices or some newsstands. Some phones also accept credit cards. Calls made from hotels will be very expensive.

On using mobile/cellphones, see page 401. Charges can be high if you use your mobile, so if you're going to stay for more than a week or two, it makes sense to buy a local pay-as-you-go phone.

Tipping

Tipping is not taken for granted in Italy, and most Italians tip very little, though a bit extra will always be appreciated.

A service charge of 10–15 percent may be added to restaurant bills; if not, 10 percent is ample. Taxi drivers do not expect a tip, but will appreciate it if you round up the fare. Custodians of sights and museums do expect a tip, particularly if they have opened something especially for you.

Tourist information

The Italian national tourist office (ENIT) has a central website, www.italia.it, and also a special information and help service, Easy Italia (tel: 039-039 039, or toll-free within Italy 800-000 039; www. easyitaly.com), which promises to answer enquiries by phone or email in several languages seven days a week. Once you have decided where in Italy you most wish to visit, it will be better to look at the websites of individual regions and cities, links to which are on www.italia.it which will have much more detail, including accommodation listings. Below the regions, each province also has its own tourist office (APT). Confusingly, tourist offices in Italy, like other Italian official departments, often change their web addresses, so finding them online sometimes take a little ingenuity. In cities and towns look out for the local APT office, often marked with an "i" or *Turismo*.

Rome

The Rome tourist office can currently be found through tel: 06-0608; www.turismoroma.it, which provides a very wide range of information on the city, including event and accommodation listings. Enquiries can be made by phone or online and there are also 10 tourist information points called PITs throughout the centre and at the airports. They also sell Roma Cards (see above) and other tickets.

Tourist offices abroad

These offices can all be contacted through www.enit.it.
Australia: tel: 02-9262 1666.
Canada: tel: 416-925 4882.
UK: tel: 020-7408 1254.
US: tel: 212-245 5618.

THE NETHERLANDS

ESSENTIAL TRAVEL TIPS

FACT FILE

Area: 41,500 sq km (16,000 sq miles), of which 18.4 percent is water.
Area below sea level: one-fifth
Capital: Amsterdam
Seat of government: The Hague
Population: 16.7 million
Language: Dutch
Religion: Roman Catholic (27 percent), Protestant (16 percent), Muslim (6 percent), unaffiliated (51 percent).
Time zone: CET/CEST, see page 402.
Currency: the euro (€)
International dialling code: 31

TRANSPORT

Getting to the Netherlands

By air

Nearly all visitors to the Netherlands from outside Europe and not travelling overland within the continent fly into Amsterdam's Schiphol Airport (tel: 0900-0141; www.schiphol.nl), 14km (9 miles) southwest of the city and a major international air hub with links to over 100 countries. There are in fact few parts of the world from where you cannot get a flight to Schiphol. It is also the hub for the Dutch airline **KLM** (tel: Neth 020-474 7747; www.klm.com).

Schiphol has its own railway station below the arrivals hall, from where trains leave for Amsterdam around every 15 minutes from about 5.30am–midnight daily, the trip taking about 15 minutes. The fare is €3.80, with an OV-chipkaart payment card

Travel tickets: the OV-chipkaart

The Netherlands has a very rational common ticket system for all public transport, national or local, buses or trains, based on an electronic smart card, the same size and shape as a credit card, the *OV-chipkaart*. Only on a few inter-urban trains can you still buy individual paper tickets (and these are being phased out), so you should get an OV card when you arrive in the country. You can buy the cards at the airport, train and Metro stations, tourist offices, tobacco shops and many supermarkets. There are several variants of the card, with different prices. The main distinction is between yellow "personal" cards, registered to an individual, which are of most use to Netherlands' residents, and blue "anonymous" cards, which are not registered to any one person and can be shared by several people, and are of most interest to visitors. Anonymous cards also come in two kinds, "disposable" ones charged

with a fixed amount of credit that are thrown away once this is used up, and reusable cards that can be topped up with more credit, which will work out cheaper if you stay longer than about 1 day in the country.

A rechargeable anonymous card costs an initial €7.50, after which you must load the card with some credit to activate it. The easiest way to do this is with cash at any sales point, but you can also do it in machines at stations and, once you have registered your account, online through www.ov-chipkaart.nl. Then, every time you get on and off a bus or train you must touch the card in and then touch out on the special card readers, which will deduct the corresponding amount from your card. There are reduced rates for children and people aged over 65.

A special information app for all Netherlands public transport is available for smart phones: see http://9292.nl.

(see page 436), and further discounts are available. Direct trains also run from the airport station to other destinations throughout the country.

There are also much smaller airports at Rotterdam, Eindhoven, Groningen and Maastricht, which have short-haul flights from around Europe, particularly with low-cost airlines such as **Ryanair** (www.ryanair.com) and **Vueling** (www.vueling.com).

By rail

Thalys high-speed trains from Paris get to Amsterdam in 3hrs 19mins; there are several trains each day, and there are also fast connections from all

over Germany. Brussels–Amsterdam takes around 2–3hrs, depending on how many stops the train makes. From the UK, train travellers have a choice between a Eurostar to Brussels, then a change of trains to Amsterdam and other Dutch destinations, or the **Dutch Flyer** (tel: UK 08457-484 950; www.dutchflyer.co.uk), a ticket combining a train to Harwich in the UK, a Stena ferry crossing to Hoek van Holland and then a Dutch train to anywhere in the Netherlands, at very competitive prices.

By road

Buses: Eurolines (www.eurolines.com) international buses run to

Amsterdam and several other Dutch cities from different parts of Europe, and Megabus (www.megabus. com) offers bus services from Paris, Brussels and many places in the UK at ultra-low fares.

Cars: The Netherlands has an excellent road network, which combined with the flat terrain makes it very easy to drive there quickly from any of the neighbouring countries. Amsterdam is 370km (230 miles) from Calais, and the approximate driving time is 4 hours; to drive from Paris takes about 5hrs 30mins.

By sea

There are several car ferry routes from the UK. **Stena Line** (tel: UK 0844 770 7070; www.stenaline.co.uk) sails between Harwich and Hoek van Holland near Rotterdam, with two sailings daily, taking about 7 hours. "Dutch Flyer" train+boat tickets are available for foot passengers. **P&O Ferries** (tel: UK 0871-664 2121; www.poferries.com) sails overnight between Hull and Rotterdam (10–12hrs) and **DFDS Seaways** (tel: UK 0871-522 9955; www.dfdsseaways .co.uk) has ferries each night from Newcastle to Ijmuiden, near Amsterdam (15hrs).

Getting around the Netherlands

By bicycle

The Netherlands is perhaps Europe's most bicycle-friendly country, and cycling is the main means of transport used by a great many Dutch people, young and old. This is helped of course by the flatness of almost the whole country except for the still gentle hills around Maastricht in the southeast, making cycling very easy. There are over 20,000km (12,400 miles) of dedicated cycling paths, including "cycle highways" that allow you to travel freely for long distances, and even when you have to use ordinary roads drivers are generally much more cycle-aware than in most countries, so cycling is also pretty stress-free. Cyclists also enjoy greater legal protection than elsewhere relative to motor vehicles.

Extensive information on local cycling routes is available from all tourist offices, which can also point you towards local bike rental shops, which are plentiful. Bikes can also be rented at train stations, and many hotels also have them for guests' use. Bikes can also be carried on trains for a small charge.

Canal Cruises and Boat Rides in Amsterdam

Amsterdam's 165 canals are one of its unique features, and canal cruises are among the most popular ways to get to know the city. Several companies operate from the canal basin opposite Centraal Station and some other points around the centre, and offer candlelit dinner cruises as well as day trips. Among those offering a full range of cruises are Holland International (tel: 020-625-3035; www.hir.nl) and Reederij Kooij (tel: 020-623 3810; www.rederijkooij.nl). The tourist board website again has a full listing.

By boat

There are a few scheduled boat and hydrofoil services in and around major cities, and boat tours, excursions and trips operating on the various bodies of water in the Netherlands. Around the IJsselmeer and in the northern provinces of Groningen and Friesland, boat-rental agencies offer a variety of craft, some with living accommodation. For a variety of options, see www.yachtcharter- ijsselmeer.nl.

By rail

Nederlandse Spoorwegen (NS) (Netherlands Railways; tel: 0900-9292; www.ns.nl) has a very dense and efficient network of express and more frequently stopping trains linking every part of the country, which makes trains the most convenient means of travel for most visitors. During the day there are services at least every half-hour on most lines and 4–8 trains per hour on busier routes, and at night there are trains hourly between Utrecht, Amsterdam, Schiphol, The Hague and Rotterdam. It's not possible to book seats on domestic services, and reservations are only required for long-distance international trains.

For journeys between towns on NS trains you can buy a single or return ticket, a 1-day travel card (€47) or use an *OV-chipkaart*. The www.ns.nl website has full timetable and fare information in English and a journey planner.

By road

As a densely populated country, the Netherlands has an equally dense and modern toll-free road system. The smaller country roads are in excellent condition, and this combined with the flat landscape makes this a very easy

Visitors can also take the Canal Bus, boats that run on three set routes around the central canals and on which, with 1- or 2-day ticket (€22–34), you can hop on and hop off as many times as you like to visit sights and catch another boat later (tel: 020-623 9886; www.canal.nl). Another alternative on the canals is to hire a pedalo-style pedal boat to power yourself; they are available from the Canal Bus company, while Boaty (tel: 06-2714 9493; www. amsterdamrentaboat.com) offers electrically powered boats for rent, with space for 6 people.

country to drive around.

There are ferry services on secondary roads crossing rivers and canals, with low fares, and nominal fees are charged for crossing some tunnels, bridges and dams.

Motoring advice: It is not legally obligatory to carry a warning triangle and yellow reflective jacket in your car, but it is strongly advisable. Drivers are expected to give way to cyclists, and also to buses as they leave bus stops. On urban and minor roads, Dutch drivers tend to observe speed limits (50kph/31mph in most towns, 80kph/49mph on many country roads) fairly punctiliously, so anyone who does not becomes conspicuous.

Getting around Amsterdam

By bicycle

Cycling is one of the most popular ways of getting around the city. Many locals only own bikes, not cars, and, as drivers find, habitually cycle as if they have complete priority over motor vehicles. There are numerous bike rental shops, where bikes can be rented for about €8–9 for 3 hours, €12–15 a day or for longer periods, and many also offer cycle tours, and sometimes motor scooters. Two central ones are Damstraat **Rent-a-Bike**, Damstraat 20–22, tel: 020-625 5029; www.rentabike.nl, and **Mike's Bike Tours**, Kerkstraat 134, tel: 020-622 7970; www. mikesbiketoursamsterdam.com, and a full listing is on the tourist office website www.iamsterdam.com, which also has a very useful section on the rules of Amsterdam cycling.

By car

Driving, on the other hand, is rarely ever the best way to travel around

AUSTRIA · BELGIUM · FRANCE · GERMANY · GREECE · ITALY · NETHERLANDS · PORTUGAL · SPAIN · SWITZERLAND

central Amsterdam, and few visitors bother with it. Drivers have to be prepared for parking problems, narrow canal streets (often blocked by delivery vans), complex one-way systems, hordes of cyclists, and trams that always have right of way.

By public transport

Like the whole of the Netherlands Amsterdam has a transport system that amply covers all needs, administered by the GVB (tel: 0900-8011; www.gvb.nl), whose website provides comprehensive information. There are Metro lines, which mainly run outside the old centre and into the suburbs, buses, tramlines and ferry lines from the main city to north Amsterdam. The old centre is also compact enough to walk around, so most visitors do not make much use of the Metro or buses, but hopping on and off the blue-and-white trams is a very handy and relaxing way to shorten distances when legs are tired. Several tram lines fan out in all directions from Centraal Station, and other lines intersect with them and run around the ring of canals.

All tickets are variants on the *OV-chipkaart* smart card (see page 436), so you must remember to touch your card in and out on the card readers when you get on and off any transport. If you do not already have a national OV card with some credit, you can get a GVB day card, giving unlimited travel within the city for from 1 to 7 days (€7.50–31), or the I-Amsterdam tourist card, giving unlimited travel on city transport, free admission to many museums and a wide range of discounts for 1–3 days, for €40–60. Simple 1-day cards can be bought on board buses and trams, but the other cards must be bought from the machines at Metro or train stations, tourist offices or GVB information offices. The main GVB help centre is outside Centraal Station, and provides every kind of transport information, and maps, in English.

By taxi

Taxis are numerous but in the city centre, because of its traffic problems, they are not allowed to stop anywhere in the street. Instead, you need to look for them at an authorised taxi rank, indicated with a T sign. There are ranks outside Centraal Station, by Dam square, in most of the main city squares and other locations. You can also call for a taxi on tel: 020-777 7777.

THE NETHERLANDS A–Z

Accommodation

There is a full range of accommodation available across the Netherlands, from hotels of various categories to small guesthouses and bed-and-breakfasts – especially along the coast – and apartments and cottages for short-term rentals. For anyone on a tight budget, low-priced hostels with shared rooms are a Dutch institution, used by people of all ages, and there are also plenty of well-equipped campsites. In cities, especially Amsterdam, some more unusual options such as houseboat rentals are also on offer.

The national tourism site www. holland.com has extensive information and an efficient accommodation-finding service, and so do local sites such as www.iamsterdam.com. It's advisable to book ahead in summer in Amsterdam and, in North Holland, during the April–May bulb season, but at other times of year rooms are generally not too hard to find.

Arts and activities

While Amsterdam is the hub of the arts as well as of so much else in the Netherlands, there are also lively cultural scenes in Rotterdam, The Hague, Utrecht and many smaller cities. The national website www.holland.com has introductory information, and every city and regional tourist office produces local cultural guides.

Amsterdam

The city tourist office provides extensive information on what's on and upcoming cultural programmes in its offices and on www.iamsterdam. com. The monthly magazine in English Time Out Amsterdam is also a good source of information on events, restaurants and other things to do in the city. The **AUB** Ticketshop, Leidseplein 26 (Mon–Fri 10am–7pm, Sat 10am–6pm, Sun noon–6pm), sells tickets for theatre, operas, ballets, concerts, museums and even cinemas, as well as transport tickets.

The great star of the city's cultural scene is the **Concertgebouw** (tel: 020-671 8345; www.concertgebouw. nl), home of the renowned Royal Concertgebouw Orchestra and the venue for concerts by many other world-famous performers, mostly of classical music but also including jazz and other styles. There are several

different concert series through the year, and if you don't get tickets for a full performance try one of the free lunchtime concerts by orchestra soloists and small ensembles. Almost as prestigious is the **Muziektheater** (tel: 020-625 5455; www.het-muziektheater.nl), near Waterlooplein, for opera and ballet, and the **Muziekgebouw aan't Ij** (tel: 020-788-2000; www.muziekgebouw.nl), Amsterdam's "concert hall of the 21st century" on the north bank of the River Ij, is a futuristic music venue opened in 2005 specialising in new music.

English-language theatre companies and comedians often perform in Amsterdam, and most films are shown in the original language, with Dutch subtitles.

Budgeting for your trip

The Netherlands is not the most expensive European country: accommodation costs can be a drain on your budget, but this is often balanced by reasonably priced restaurants and great-value public transport. Prices vary widely around the country, and a stay entirely in Amsterdam will cost about 20 percent more than if you spend time outside the city. Overall around €70–100 per person per day is a realistic budget for two people travelling together.
Accommodation: The starting rate for a double room is €50; for a decent mid-range hotel in most cities, expect to pay €100–200; above €300 is de luxe territory.
Meals: A 2–3-course meal should cost around €10–25 per person at a modest restaurant, €25–60 for somewhere more sophisticated, and €100 and beyond for gourmet cuisine. A glass of beer can cost as little as €2.50 and a glass of house wine €5.
Sightseeing: Entry to museums and other attractions for adults varies from around €8–15, but is free for children under 12, and there are reduced prices for under-18s and other discounts.

Tourist discount cards are helpful in cutting costs. The I-Amsterdam card gives unlimited use of public transport, entry to most museums in the city, a canal cruise and many discounts for other attractions and services for 1, 2 or 3 days. It can be bought from tourist offices or in advance online through www.iamsterdam.com, for €20–60. The Muzeumkaart gives entry to virtually all museums in the Netherlands for one years, for €44.95 for adults, or €22.50 for under-18s. It can also be bought from tourist offices (the website, www. muzeumkaart.nl, is only in Dutch).

Children

Children are welcome in restaurants and cafés, many of which serve a *kindermenu* (children's menu). It is easy to hire bicycles fitted with children's seats for getting about town or for excursions into the country. Children aged under 4 travel for free on all public transport, and there are big reductions in fares for those aged 4–11. At museums and many attractions, tickets are half-price for under-18s, and free for those under 10 or sometimes under 12.

Many hotels have well-sized family rooms, and also the Dutch were among the originators of the family holiday park concept, with all sorts of activities and facilities for families with young children in one spot, for maximum convenience. Center Parcs (www.centerparcs.com) is the best known, with several lavishly equipped parks around the country.

Specific top children's attractions in the Netherlands include, in Amsterdam, the Artis Zoo, Plantage Kerklaan 38–40 (www.artis.nl), in Enkhuizen, the Zuiderzeemuseum, Wierdijk 12–22, (www.zuiderzeemuseum.nl), and in The Hague the Madurodam miniature town, George Maduroplein 1 (www.madurodam.nl).

Climate

The Netherlands has a mild, maritime climate, but is wet and cool in winter, and because of its flatness there are often chilly winds off the North Sea from about October to April. Summers are generally warm, but you can expect rain at any time of year. Spring is relatively dry, and the favourite time for bulb enthusiasts. The advantages of a visit in winter are the cut-price package deals and the fact that museums and galleries are uncrowded.

Disabled travellers

In general Dutch institutions are highly aware of the need to improve access and facilities for disabled people, and ongoing efforts are made to improve facilities. On NS national railways, most stations are accessible, and most trains (including Schiphol Airport trains) have accessible entrances and toilets. If required, "journey assistants" can be arranged in advance through tel: 030-235 7822. A full description of the services available is on the NS English website under "Service". In Amsterdam, all trams, buses and stops are due to be made accessible, but this is not yet complete: the whole of

the Metro and most trams have good access, but many bus stops do not, so this is indicated on transport maps. Full details are on www.gvb.nl.

Though older Dutch townhouses tend to have steep staircases and no lifts, many hotels now have adapted rooms, and many restaurants have also improved access. Information on facilities around the country, and specialist tours, are provided in English by Accessible Travel Netherlands (tel: 06-5386 9092; www.accessibletravelnl.com.

Eating out

Dutch national cuisine has a limited range of dishes, falling into the meat and potatoes and hearty stews and soups categories, yet eating out in Amsterdam can be one of the highlights of the trip. The many nationalities in the city have brought their own cuisines to its restaurants, resulting in a huge range of dining options.

To stay more Dutch, you can choose from the simplest fare in an *eetcafé* or a more costly top-level restaurant. *Eetcafés* are a kind of informal local eatery, offering a daily changing menu with a choice of fish, meat or vegetarian main course. They are popular because they're reasonably priced, and tend to close quite early. *Broodjes*, filled bread rolls with cheese, meat, fish or salads, are Dutch favourites for lunch, and there are plenty of *Broodje* shops in every town. Vegetarianism is quite common

Festivals

Carnival, Maastricht, four days preceding Ash Wednesday. In the "capital" of the Catholic south of the Netherlands, the pre-Lenten Carnival is a major spectacle.
Koninginnedag (Queen's Day), 30 April. Amsterdam is the best place to celebrate the queen's official birthday, with a staggering number of street parties and open markets.
Vlaggetjesdag, Scheveningen, Saturday in mid-June. Celebrations surround the return of the year's first barrel of herring at this North Sea fishing port.
North Sea Jazz Festival, Rotterdam, three days in mid-July. Holland's top jazz festival sets feet tapping at the Ahoy concert venue.
Grachten Festival, five days in mid-July, Amsterdam. A feast of classical music centred on the city's canals and ending with the Prinsengracht concert.

in Holland, and there are vegetarian restaurants in most towns, and vegetarian options on many menus.

Embassies and Consulates

Embassies in The Hague
Australia: Carnegielaan 4, 2517 KH Den Haag, tel: 070-310 8200; www.netherlands.embassy.gov.au
Canada: Sophialaan 7, 2514 JP Den Haag, tel: 070-311 1600; www.canadainternational.gc.ca/netherlands-pays_bas.
Ireland: Scheveningseweg 112, 2584 AE Den Haag, tel: 070-363 0993; www.irishembassy.nl.
South Africa: Wassenaarseweg 40, 2596 CJ Den Haag, tel: 070-392 4501; www.southafrica.nl.
UK: Lange Voorhout 10, 2514 ED Den Haag, tel: 070-427 0427; http://ukinnnl.fco.gov.uk.
US: Lange Voorhout 102, 2514 EJ Den Haag, tel: 070-310 2209; http://thehague.usembassy.gov.

Consulates in Amsterdam
UK: Koningslaan 44, tel: 020-676 4343.
US: Museumplein 19, tel: 020-575 5330; http://amsterdam.usconsulate.gov.

Gay and lesbian travellers

The Netherlands, and Amsterdam in particular, has plenty to offer gay and lesbian visitors. Gays have long been more prominent in, and integrated into, everyday life than virtually anywhere else in Europe, or possibly the world, although more recently there have been a few disturbing incidents of homophobic violence. Amsterdam rightly considers itself to be Europe's gay capital, boasting a whole infrastructure of clubs, bars, restaurants, hotels, festivals and events. The Amsterdam Gay Pride festival, on the first weekend in August, is a particularly good time to be in town.

Amsterdam has embraced its "gay capital" role and there is a special gay information section (under "For You") on www.iamsterdam.com. There are also many "Gay Amsterdam" websites, but www.gayamsterdam4u.com is one of the most comprehensive.

Health and medical care

The standard of medical and dental services in the Netherlands is extremely high. Citizens of non-EU countries should have a travel and health insurance policy (see page

AUSTRIA
BELGIUM
FRANCE
GERMANY
GREECE
ITALY
NETHERLANDS
PORTUGAL
SPAIN
SWITZERLAND

400) so they can use state health services on a paying basis, although many services will be free. EU citizens can use Dutch state health services with an EHIC card; many non-urgent treatments must be paid for, but you can then reclaim the cost following instructions given with your EHIC card. A hospital is a *ziekenhuis* (or AZ), and an emergency department is indicated by *spoedeisende hulp* or sometimes *EHBO*. Most Dutch doctors speak good English.

Pharmacies/chemists *(Apotheek)* are normally open Mon–Fri 9am–5.30pm or 6pm. Late-night and Sunday chemists operate a duty rota, posted in all pharmacy windows.

Nightlife

Of all the Dutch cities, Amsterdam is the king, or queen, of Holland's nightlife, with the largest number of options, including music, dance, theatre and cinema, along with numerous bars and clubs. But its position is by no means undisputed. The Hague poses the strongest challenge for the highbrow crown, Rotterdam for its high-energy scene, and Utrecht makes its own contribution. The great thing is that all these cities lie within easy reach of each other by public transport or car, so it's possible to mix and match.

In Amsterdam, entertainment after dark focuses on three main areas: Leidseplein, popular with tourists and locals for restaurants, lively dance clubs and nightclubs; Rembrandtsplein for clubs and cabarets pandering to slightly older tastes; and the Red Light District, now rather more subdued than it once was. Visitors should always try out one of the numerous brown cafés, a classic grand café with a reading table and more of a modern ambience, or one of the new-wave bars with cool, white-washed and mirrored walls and a long list of cocktails. Many cafés and bars have live music, often jazz or blues.

Opening hours

Normal shopping hours are Mon–Sat 8.30/9am–6/6.30pm. Late-night shopping is usually Thursday. Food stores close at 4pm on Saturday, and some shops in the cities open on Sunday. Many shops close for one half-day a week, often Monday morning. Most bank branches are open Mon–Fri 9am–5pm, though some larger branches are also open on Saturdays. Many museums are closed on Mondays, and open Tue–Sun 10am–5/6pm.

Postal services

Main post offices open Mon–Fri 8.30am–6pm, Sat 9am–noon. Stamps are available from post offices, tobacconists, newsstands and machines attached to the red-and-grey post boxes. In Amsterdam the main post office is at Singel 250.

Public holidays

January: 1 New Year's Day; **March/April**: variable Good Fri/Easter Sun/Mon; **April**: 30 Queen's Birthday; **May:** 1 Labour Day, 5 Liberation Day; **May/June**: variable Ascension Day, Whit Monday (Pentecost) Day, **December**: 25 Christmas Day. 26 St Stephen's Day.

Shopping

Tourist offices provide useful shopping guides and maps. In Amsterdam, bargains are a rarity but browsing is fun, particularly in the markets and the small specialist shops, such as those selling antiques and Delftware. For general shopping the main streets are Kalverstraat and Nieuwendijk, for exclusive boutiques try P.C. Hooftstraat, and for the more offbeat shops head to the Jordaan, northwest of the centre, the artists' quarter. Two unusual shopping centres are also worth a visit: Magna Plaza opposite the Royal Palace and Kalvertoren on Kalverstraat.

Telecommunications

Most Dutch telephone numbers have

Emergency Number

Police/fire/ambulance: 112

10 digits, with an area code beginning with 0; omit this initial 0 when calling from abroad. The international dialling code for the Netherlands is 31.

Public phone boxes are mainly green, but also come in more compact and contemporary styles, since they are operated by different companies. Most take phone cards, but a few still take coins. Cards can be bought from tobacco shops, newsstands and many outlets, but note that they commonly only work in the phones of specific companies (Telfort cards are perhaps the most useful to have). Because of the high-level of mobile phone ownership in the Netherlands the number of public phones has declined markedly in the last few years, but in cities you can still find them at railway stations, large stores and cafés.

On using mobile/cellphones, see page 401. Mobile phone charges in the Netherlands tend to be more reasonable than elsewhere in Europe.

Tipping

Service charges and value-added tax are included in restaurant and bar bills. An extra tip of 5–10 percent can be left for extra attention, but this is not compulsory. Taxi meters also include the service charge, though it is customary to give an extra tip. A lavatory attendant expects a small tip.

Tourist Information

The Netherlands national tourist office website www.holland.com is an essential first port of call with a wide range of information, including an introduction to the country's various regions, cities and provinces, each of which also has its own information service and website. Within the country, every main town or city has a tourist information office (indicated by an *i*-sign, or sometimes *VVV* for tourist office in Dutch), often located just outside the main railway station. Multilingual staff will answer all your questions, provide maps and brochures, handle accommodation bookings and reserve tickets. There are charges for several of these services.

In Amsterdam, the city tourist office has a comprehensive website (www.iamsterdam.com) with links to

many other services in the region. Reservations and card purchases can be made online or by phoning tel: 020-201 8800. The main tourist information office is at Stationsplein 10, outside Centraal Station (Mon–Sat 9am–5pm, Sun 10am–5pm, and usually open later July–mid-Sept) and there are information touch-screens at many points around the city. There is also a large tourist information office at Schiphol Airport (daily 7am–10pm). At the Stationsplein office you can also buy tickets, tours and many other products.

Tourist offices abroad

All offices and the Netherlands tourist authority can be contacted through www.nbtc.nl.
UK and Ireland: tel: 07795-572 035.
US and Canada: tel: 212-370 7360.

PORTUGAL

ESSENTIAL TRAVEL TIPS

FACT FILE

Area: 92,072 sq km (33,549 sq miles), including Madeira and the Azores
Capital: Lisbon
Population: 10.6 million
Language: Portuguese
Highest mountain: Serra da Estrela 1,993 metres (6,539ft)
Religion: Roman Catholic (94 percent)
Time zone: WET/WEST, see page 402.
Currency: the euro (€)
International dialling code: 351

TRANSPORT

Getting to Portugal

By air

Lisbon's Portela Airport (tel: 218-413 500; www.lisbon-airport.com), 7km (4 miles) north of the city, is Portugal's primary international gateway, with many long-distance flights – especially from North America, Brazil and Africa – and others from all over Europe. Portugal's own main airline **TAP** (tel: 707-205 700; www.flytap. com) is the airport's biggest user, but it also has many flights with Air France, British Airways, United and many other operators.

Since summer 2012 the Metro (red line) has linked the airport to central Lisbon, the journey taking about 20–30 minutes. For information on Metro fares, see page 442. The special Aerobus shuttle bus service

also runs between the airport and central Lisbon, approximately every 20 minutes, daily 7am–11pm; tickets cost around €3.50. It is better than the Metro if you have a lot of luggage, especially at busy times. Local buses also run from the airport to other parts of the city; some stop at train stations, which is convenient for getting trains to the north. Taxis from the airport should cost around €10–15, or you can book a transfer through the airport website for about €32.

Many European low-cost airlines also fly frequently to Portugal, with flights to its other airports – Porto in the north, and Faro for the Algarve and the south – as well as to Lisbon. **EasyJet** (www.easyjet.com) in particular has flights to Lisbon, Porto and Faro from the UK, France, Germany and Italy, while **Ryanair** (www.ryanair.com) offers flights from all around Europe to Porto and Faro.

By rail

A semi-direct train service still runs daily between Paris and Lisbon. The TGV-Atlantique leaves Paris (Montparnasse) at 8.25am each day, connects with the Sud-Express sleeper train (Trenhotel) at Irún on the Spanish border, arriving in Lisbon late morning the next day. There is also a nightly sleeper train to Lisbon from Madrid, leaving at 9.50pm and arriving at 7.30am Portuguese time, and cross-border local trains between Porto and Vigo. For more information and bookings see www.raileurope.com or the Spanish railways website (www.renfe.com).

By road

Buses: Eurolines (www.eurolines. com) has scheduled bus services to Lisbon from several other European

cities, and the Spanish bus company ALSA (www.alsa.es) runs regularly to Lisbon and other Portuguese destinations from Madrid.
Cars: Good roads link Portugal with Spain at numerous border points. The busiest routes are the A-5 from Madrid, European route E90, which becomes the A6 to Lisbon inside Portugal, and the Spanish A-49 west from Seville to the Algarve (European route E-01), which becomes the Portuguese A22 once across the border. To drive from Madrid to Lisbon takes a little over 6 hours.

Getting around Portugal

Portugal has excellent modern highways, and secondary roads are mostly of a high standard. Bus routes are comprehensive although operated by a baffling number of bus companies. Train travel is generally more expensive and slower.

By air

Unless they travel to the Atlantic islands of Madeira or the Azores, domestic flights are little used by visitors, given mainland Portugal's compact size. However, there are flights several times daily to the islands, mostly operated by TAP.

By rail

Portugal's railways are operated by **Comboios de Portugal**. The north–south route (Braga–Porto–Lisbon–Faro) is good and fast, but there are also slow, scenic rides, especially in the north. The main categories of train in Portugal are: Regional "R" (slow); Inter-Regional "IR" (fast); Intercidades (Intercity) "IC"; and Alfa Pendular or "AP" (faster again, though still not up to high-speed train level).

AUSTRIA
BELGIUM
FRANCE
GERMANY
GREECE
ITALY
NETHERLANDS
PORTUGAL
SPAIN
SWITZERLAND

Generally, the most efficient routes are the Lisbon–Coimbra–Porto and the Lisbon–Algarve lines. Lisbon has four railway stations: Santa Apolónia, Rossio, Cais do Sodre and Oriente, plus Barreiro on the south side of the River Tejo. Santa Apolónia is the main terminus for national travel, and trains from Spain.

Fares are reasonable, such as €30–42 for an AP train from Lisbon to Porto, so rail passes are of limited benefit. Full information on timetables and fares is provided by **Comboios de Portugal**, on tel: 808-208 208 or in English the website www.cp.pt, which has a useful and user-friendly fare calculator.

By road

Buses: There are numerous private bus lines which tend to specialise in particular routes or areas of the country. Many travel agencies can book bus tickets.
Algarve: Eva Transporte, tel: 289-899 740; wwww.eva-bus.net.
Lisbon: Carris; www.carris.pt/en/home.
TST Transportes Sul Do Tejo, www.tsuldotejo.pt.
Porto: STCP, tel: 808-200 166 or 22-507 1000; www.stcp.pt.
Cars: Car rental agencies are numerous at airports and in the main tourist areas. It is not obligatory to carry a red warning triangle and reflective jacket in all cars, but strongly recommended, so your rental agency should provide them. Drivers should also be sure to carry their vehicle papers in the car; you will be required to show them if you are stopped by the police. If you drive in Lisbon, give way to trams.
Motoring advice: Drivers who use any of Portugal's motorways

(*autoestradas*) need to be very careful of the system of toll payment, which has been recently introduced. There are no toll booths where you pay directly, as in most of Europe, but instead charges are levied electronically by camera recognition of number plates. If you drive your own car into Portugal, at special "welcome points" at border crossings you should either buy a toll card to the value of €5–40, which will be registered against your car number, or register your credit card so that any charges will be made automatically. Other options are also available. If you rent a car, **always** ask the rental company what provision they have for toll payment, and confirm there are no outstanding charges against the car, which could make you as the driver liable to be stopped and fined. Most agencies now add any charges to your final bill.

Further details of the system are in English on www.portugaltolls.pt and on www.visitportugal.com under "Electronic Tolls". If you do not want to pay these charges, you have to be very careful not to enter any roads marked as toll routes.

Getting around Lisbon

Lisbon is a relatively straightforward city to navigate. The compact centre is small enough for strolling, and the bus, tram and Metro services are efficient and frequent.

By public transport

Lisbon has a modern Metro system, but also still has a few trams running, including the scenic number 28 that runs from Praça da Figueira to the atmospheric narrow streets of the Alfama, and the *elevadores* to the

city's hills. There are also bus routes throughout the city and surrounding area. You can pick up excellent local transport maps at tourist offices.
Buses are mostly operated by Carris (information tel: 213-613 000; www.carris.pt), which provides a full guide to its 78 routes in English on its website. Fares can be bought singly from the drivers on board (€1.75), or you can buy prepaid travel cards and other combinations from the Carris kiosks around the city.
Ferries cross the Tejo (Tagus) from Belém, Cais do Sodré station and other Terreiro do Paço to various points on the south bank, as alternatives to taking the Vasco da Gama bridge. They are operated by Transtejo (tel: 808-203-050; www.transtejo.pt) and run a frequent service.
Trams and funiculars are also run by Carris; there are 5 tram lines and four funiculars or *elevadores*, which are an essential Lisbon experience. Official national monuments, these ancient trains give panoramic views from their hilltop stations. The *elevadores* of Gloria and Lavra are located on either side of Praça dos Restauradores, and the Elevador da Bica climbs up the hill from Rua de São Paulo (near Cais do Sodré station) to Bairro Alto. In contrast, several tram lines have been modernised in recent years, and move at surprising speed, except when they get bogged down in traffic in rush hours.
The **Metro** (tel: 213-500 115; www.metrolisboa.pt) has four lines (blue, green, yellow and red) that cover much of the city and connect with local and long-distance overground trains at all the main rail stations. Lines operate daily 6.30am–1am, and Metro-only tickets cost €1.25 for a single ticket, or €5 for an all day combined bus-and-Metro card, which should be validated in special machines the first time you use it. You can also get rechargeable cards. Tickets can be bought from machines or counters at all stations.

The various city transport systems are complemented by local rail services for trips out to the surrounding towns. The Rossio station serves such places as Queluz and Sintra, and from Cais do Sodré, on the waterfront, electric trains make the run to and from Cascais.

Most visitors use single tickets, separate for Metro and buses, or the €5 one-day card, valid on the Metro and Carris buses, trams and *elevadores*. Other travel tickets are mainly oriented to longer stays. More

Lisbon tour bus

useful though is the **Lisboa Card**, a tourist discount card that gives unlimited travel on all local transport, free or reduced-price entry to many local and other discounts for 1, 2 or 3 days, for €17–33.50. It can be bought from tourist offices, including those at the airport and rail stations, or through www.golisbon.com.

By taxi

Taxis are abundant in Lisbon, and not expensive, with most metered trips within the city around €10. You can call for a radio taxi on tel: 214-942 527.

Casa da Calçada

PORTUGAL A–Z

Accommodation

Portugal naturally has plenty of traditional city hotels, functional business and, in areas like the Algarve, big beach resort hotels, but it also has plenty of individual accommodation with distinctive charm. Deserving special mention are the Pousadas, a state-sponsored chain of special and generally luxurious hotels in historic buildings, such as the Cidadela or citadel in Cascais (tel: 218-442 001; www.pousadas.pt). The Spanish association Rusticae (www.rusticae. es) also represents several distinctive small hotels around Portugal. Bed and-breakfasts and other rural accommodation have been relatively late in developing here, but a decent selection can be found on www.bed andbreakfast.com/portugal. Extensive listings of places to stay of all kinds are also provided on the national tourism website, www.visitportugal. com, and for Lisbon and the surrounding region on www.visitlisboa. com. Note: cheaper hotels in Lisbon often do not have central heating, so if visiting in winter it is best to check before you book.

Arts and activities

Portugal has acquired global recognition for its melancholy *fado* music. A fashionable exponent of *fado* today is Mariza, with her bold, contemporary image. The best place to listen to authentic *fado* is in the Alfama district, although choose carefully, as some *fado* houses are unabashedly geared to tourists. One of the best is the Casa de Linhares, Beco dos Armazéns do Linho 2, tel: 218-865 088, and the Museu

do Fado at Largo do Chafariz do Dentro 1, also in the Alfama (www. museudofado.pt) gives fascinating background to the music's history.

Lisbon is also home to the Orquestra Gulbenkian (tel: 217-823 000; www.musica.gulbenkian. pt), a very high-standard symphony orchestra, with an associated choir and chamber ensembles, which when not touring performs regularly at the city's premier arts complex, the Calouste Gulbenkian Foundation. For upcoming events, see also tourist office sites and other local websites.

Budgeting for your trip

Portugal remains one of the cheapest countries in Western Europe, particularly if you travel out of season, when many hotels dramatically reduce their rates. Some very approximate costs are:
Accommodation: A double room will in general cost from as little as €35–40 in a budget hotel, to around €50–70 in a mid-range establishment to €80 and upwards in somewhere quite luxurious.
Meals: A 2–3-course meal in a restaurant, from about €10–15 in somewhere simple, or about €25 in a moderate one or €40–50 in a locally expensive restaurant.
Sightseeing: Admission to most museums and attractions is around €4–5, and free or half-price for under-18s or under-12s.
Transport: Around €5 per day.
In Lisbon costs can be reduced even further with the **LisboaCard** tourist discount card *(see above Getting Around Lisbon)*.

Children

The most popular destination for children is likely to be the beach. The

beaches of the Algarve, with long, sandy, gently shelving beaches for small children and small rocky coves ideal for older children to explore, are perfect for family holidays. Pay attention to the beach warning flags, however. Green means the sea is calm and a lifeguard is on duty; green plus a checked flag means that no lifeguard is on duty; yellow stipulates no swimming; red means danger and warns bathers to stay ashore.

The top attraction in Lisbon for children is the **Parque das Nações** with its splendid aquarium (Oceanário de Lisboa), playgrounds, fountains, paddleboats and aerial cable cars. **Portugal dos Pequeninos**, in Coimbra, is a theme park of miniatures of Portugal's famous buildings, while the Monumento Natural das Pegadas dos Dinossáurios near Fátima will thrill the children with its dinosaur footprints.

The Algarve has a number of theme parks, zoos and water parks, including **Aquashow** near Quarteira Semino, **Slide & Splash**, near Lagoa, and **Aqualand** near Alcantarilha, reputedly Europe's largest. Another attraction is **Zoomarine**, a theme park with performing dolphins and sea lions, a parrot show, fairground rides and swimming pools.

Children under 4 travel for free on most public transport and those aged 4–11 travel for half the adult fare. There are also substantial reductions on admission to most museums and attractions for children under 12 or sometimes older. Children aged over 10 or so may be asked to provide proof of their age to qualify for discounts.

Climate

Portugal's climate is kind, especially in the exceptionally sunny Algarve,

AUSTRIA BELGIUM FRANCE GERMANY GREECE ITALY NETHERLANDS PORTUGAL SPAIN SWITZERLAND

where summers are warm and winters mild. Lisbon and the Alentejo, in particular, can be uncomfortably hot in summer. Further north the weather can be cold in winter, especially in the mountains.

Disabled travellers

Portugal is not the best when it comes to facilities for the disabled, although noticeable efforts have been made lately to improve the situation. Airports and train stations have access ramps, though getting on and off trains may still require assistance. In Lisbon the Metro has an ongoing access programme that has provided full access at 31 of its 52 stations, and on Carris buses there is an assistance service for disabled people, though this currently functions in Portuguese only. Most museums that are not in historic buildings presenting special problems are now also accessible, and a growing number of hotels have adapted rooms. For more information on facilities of all kinds, and attractive specialised tours, consult Accessible Portugal (tel: 217-203 130; www. accessibleportugal.com).

Festivals

February–March: Funchal, Loulé, Nazaré, Ovar, Torres Vedras: they have the biggest carnivals (Mardi Gras), but there are processions and fireworks everywhere with superb flamboyant costumes.
Lisbon: Fado Festival at various sites at Carnival time.
March–April: Braga: Pilgrimage to Bom Jesus is the largest of many Holy Week processions.
May: Barcelos: Feast of the Crosses music concerts and a spectacular display of fireworks on the River Cávado (first weekend). Algarve: International Music Festival throughout month at various sites.
June–July: Lisbon: Festival of music, dance and theatre all month, with lots of live music and special arts activities. Fairs and festivities for the People's Saints, honouring St Anthony (13 June), St John (24 June) and St Peter (29 June). Vila do Conde: Festa do Corpo de Deus procession in the Old Town's streets strewn with flowers. Vila Franca de Xira: running of bulls in the streets (first two Sundays of July).
July–August: Estoril/Cascais: Estoril International Music Festival.

August: Guimarães: "Festas Gualterianas", three-day festival dating from the 15th century, with torchlight processions, bands, folk dance groups and colourful medieval parade (4–6 August).
Viana do Castelo: Festa da Nossa Senhora da Agonia (Our Lady of Agony Festivities), famous religious festival with traditional costumes (weekend nearest to the 20th).
September: Lamego: festivities honouring Nossa Senhora dos Remédios, annual pilgrimage to Baroque shrine, with torchlight procession, folklore festival, fairs and fireworks, ending with triumphal procession (6–9 September). Nazaré: Nossa Senhora da Nazaré (Our Lady of Nazaré): fishermen carry an image of the town's patron saint in processions; also bullfights, fairs, concerts, folk dancing and singing (second week September).
October: Fátima: last pilgrimage of year (12–13 October). Vila Franca de Xira: lively October Fair that includes bull-running and bullfights (first two weeks).
December: Lisbon: Bolsa de Natal Christmas markets throughout the city.

Lisbon's trams wind their way around the steep, narrow streets.

Eating out

Portuguese cuisine is true to its origins, the food of fishermen and farmers. Traditional dishes are found in both expensive restaurants and the simplest of cafés. But the Portuguese can also be very inventive; you're likely to sample combinations like clams and pork, sole and bananas, or pork and figs.

Emergency Numbers

All emergencies: 112
Other local emergency numbers can also be used, but it is easier to call 112.

Seafood fans are in luck in Portugal, with a surfeit of fresh fish and shellfish. The humble but noble Portuguese sardine is an inexpensive standard, especially down south, and with a hunk of local rustic bread and a bottle of house wine, you can feast well on a small budget. Note that it's not a good idea to order a seafood or fish dish on a Monday as, traditionally, Portuguese fishing fleets have a day off on Sundays.

Portions in Portuguese restaurants tend to be rather large. You can also ask for a half-portion (*uma meia dose*) which is usually charged at around two-thirds of the full price.

Some of the best dishes are regional stews – the *ensopadas* of the Alentejo, *caldeiradas* of the Algarve and *açordas* of Estremadura. Also don't miss the sweet treats – in particular, the delicious custard tarts (*pastéis de nata*).

Many restaurants and cafés offer an *ementa turística* – tourist menu. The term does not, however, imply a poor-grade international tourist meal, but rather an economically priced three-course set meal. Another inexpensive option is the *prato do dia* (dish of the day). Be wary of the *couvert* (cover); this is brought to the table at the beginning of a meal and usually comprises cream cheese, fish paste, olives and bread. It is not free, and you can send it back if you like.

Embassies and consulates

Australia: Avenida da Liberdade 200, 2nd Floor, Lisbon, tel: 213-101 500; www.portugal.embassy.gov.au.
Canada: Avenida da Liberdade 198–200, 3rd Floor, Lisbon, tel: 213-164 600; www.canadainternational. gc.ca/portugal.
Ireland: Avenida da Liberdade 200, 4th Floor, Lisbon, tel: 213-308 200; www.embassyofireland.pt.
South Africa: Avenida Luis Bivar 10, Lisbon, tel: 213-192 200; www. embaixada-africadosul.pt.
UK: Rua de São Bernardo, 33, Lisbon, tel: 808-203 573; http://ukinportugal. fco.gov.uk.
US: Avenida das Forças Armadas, 16, Lisbon, tel: 217-702 122; http:// portugal.usembassy.gov.

Gay and lesbian travellers

In a country heavily influenced by the Catholic Church, attitudes towards gays are not as tolerant as elsewhere in Europe. Lisbon is the most important city in Portugal's gay scene and offers a number of bars and clubs catering to a gay crowd. In certain enclaves of the Algarve, such as "the Strip" in Albufeira, gay visitors will find accommodating bars and restaurants. The website www.portugalgay.pt, contains a travel guide for gays and lesbians, with information in English and other languages.

Health and medical care

Citizens of non-EU countries should have a travel and health insurance policy before travelling in Portugal (see page 400). EU nationals are entitled to free basic healthcare at state clinics or hospitals with an EHIC card, but a few treatments must be paid for, and the cost reclaimed later. Main hospitals (hospital) have an emergency department (urgências). Hotels should be able to suggest a reputable private doctor, and consulates keep lists of English-speaking doctors. State hospitals are often overcrowded: in Lisbon the British Hospital, Rua Tomás de Fonseca Edificios B & F, tel: 217-213 400; http://bhlxxi.galileisaude. pt, is a private clinic that also offers dental care.

Pharmacies

In Lisbon, a rota of emergency, night service and Sunday schedules are posted on the door of all pharmacies. If you can't find one, dial 118 for the Farmácias de serviço.

Nightlife

Nightlife in Portugal means different things to different people. While listening to fado in one of the bars or restaurants of Lisbon's Alfama may be the typical way to spend an evening out, the city also has a very buzzy modern club scene, with big dance venues concentrated particularly towards the river in the Belém district, around Avenida 24 de Julio, and other venues in the east towards Santa Apolonia station, or in the Bairro Alto. Follow the crowds to find the best spots. For music and other live events, the official Agenda Cultural site (www.agendalx.pt) is a good introduction.

Opening hours

Most shops open for business Mon–Fri 9am–1pm and about 3–7pm. Some shops and particularly bigger city stores are also open Sat 9am–1pm, but closed Sun and holidays. Most bank branches open Mon–Fri 8.30am–3pm and are closed Sat, Sun and holidays.

Postal services

Most post offices (called CCT) are open Mon–Fri 9am–6pm; smaller branches close for lunch 12.30–2.30pm. In larger cities, the main branch may be open at weekends. In Lisbon the central post office at Praça dos Restauradores is open Mon–Fri 8am–10pm, and Sat, Sun 9am–6pm, and offers the best service to tourists.

Public holidays

January. 1 New Year's Day, **February/March**: variable Mardi Gras; **March/April**: variable Good Friday/Easter Sun/Mon; **April**: 25 Freedom Day; **May**: 1 Labour Day; **May/June**: variable Corpus Christi; **June**: 10 Portugal Day, 24 St John's Day; **August**: 15 Assumption Day; **October**: 5 Republic Day; **November**: 1 All Saints' Day; **December**: 1 Restoration Day, 8 Immaculate Conception, 25 Christmas Day, 26 St Stephen's Day.

Shopping

Portuguese handicrafts range from wicker furniture to blankets and rugs to hand-carved toothpicks. The most famous Portuguese handicrafts include ceramic tiles (azulejos) and pottery, Arraiolos rugs and embroidery and lacework. In Lisbon, the Baixa quarter is good for shopping and, of course, the Vila Nova de Gaia just outside of Porto is the place to visit for the port wine lodges, where you can taste the port and pick up a bottle. Fado music is also a good buy here, and easy to find in most music shops.

Telecommunications

To call Portugal from abroad, tel: 351, followed by 21 for Lisbon. Inside Portugal, Lisbon's code is 021. Though mobile phones now far outnumber landlines in Portugal it's still possible to find public phones. Some still accept coins too, but in general to use them you will need a phone card, available from Portugal Telecom shops, post offices and many newsstands. You can also make calls – international and local – from post offices, which may be cheaper, and there are also private phone offices in many cities offering low-rate international calls. To reach an English-speaking international operator, tel: 098 (international service) or 099 (European service).

On using mobile/cellphones, see page 401. Mobile phone charges are relatively low, but if you stay for more than a week or two you might still want to take advantage of the many budget offers presented by the main service providers Vodafone, TMN and Optimus.

Tipping

A tip of between 5–10 percent is normal for service in restaurants and for taxi drivers.

Tourist information

A broad range of information, including accommodation links, is provided by the national tourist office's site visitportugal.com, and different regions and cities also have their own services. Tourist offices are easy to find in towns throughout the country.

For Lisbon, the city visitors' bureau (tel: 210-312 700; www. visitlisboa.com) also provides all kinds of detailed information on the city on its site, and produces a monthly magazine guide, Follow Me Lisboa. It also has a second site, www.askmelisboa.com, for sales of the Lisboa Card, other discount cards and tickets for all sorts of local attractions. A very handy addition to these official sites as an introduction to the city is the private www.golisbon. com, which can pick up on things the other sites miss.

The main tourist information office, the Lisboa Welcome Centre, is in Praça do Comercio (tel: 210-312 810), and open daily 9am–8pm. Other information desks are at the airport, Santa Apolónia train station, and in the Palacio Foz, and there is a special "Y Lisboa" office oriented to youth tourism at Rua Jardim do Regedor 50, near Restauradores, open daily 10am–7pm.

Tourist offices abroad

Canada: tel: 416-921 7376; www. insideportugaltravel.com.
US: tel: 212-764 6137; www.inside portugaltravel.com.

AUSTRIA
BELGIUM
FRANCE
GERMANY
GREECE
ITALY
NETHERLANDS
PORTUGAL
SPAIN
SWITZERLAND

SPAIN

ESSENTIAL TRAVEL TIPS

FACT FILE

Area: 505,955 sq km (194,885 sq miles)
Capital: Madrid
Population: 47 million
Languages: Spanish (Castilian), and Catalan, Basque and Galician all enjoy equal status in different regions.
Highest mountain: Mulhacén in the Sierra Nevada 3,478 metres (11,413 ft)
Religion: Roman Catholic (71 percent) but only 14–22 percent attend church regularly.
Time zone: CET/CEST, see page 402.
Currency: the euro (€)
International dialling code: 34

TRANSPORT

Getting to Spain

By air

For travellers from outside Europe the principal entry point into Spain is Madrid's Barajas Airport (tel: 902 404 704; www.aena-aeropuertos.es), which has flights from many parts of the world and especially Latin America. From Barajas new arrivals can get ongoing connections to any part of Spain. Some long-haul flights also arrive at Barcelona's El Prat Airport (tel: 902-404 704; www.aena-aeropuertos.es), including several from the USA, Canada, and Asia.

Madrid-Barajas is the main base for Spain's principal airline **Iberia** (tel: 902 400 500; www.iberia.com), but

is also used by a great many other airlines.

From within Europe there is a far wider choice of airports allowing direct travel to every Spanish region, with a huge number of flights that reflects Spain's position as one of Europe's foremost holiday destinations. After Madrid and Barcelona the Spanish airports with the next-largest numbers of flights are Palma on Mallorca, Málaga, Alicante and Seville, but there are also busy airports in every corner of Spain, such as at Girona, Valencia, Bilbao, Santiago de Compostela, Asturias, Menorca and Ibiza. The low-cost airlines such as **Ryanair** (www.ryanair.com), **easyJet** (www.easyjet.com) and Spanish-based **Vueling** (www.vueling.com) are the main users of the smaller airports, but the main carrier airlines have also been obliged to compete, and fares to Spain are often very low.

Transport from the airports

Barajas Airport is 13km (8 miles) east of Madrid. The quickest route into the city is with the suburban rail (*Cercanías*) line C1, which runs from Terminal T4 (where most international flights arrive) direct to Recoletos and Atocha in central Madrid, daily 6am–midnight, and taking about 20 minutes. Single tickets cost €2.40, but if you are staying in Madrid it may be worth getting a multi-journey ticket at the airport. Alternatively, Metro line 8 runs from all the airport terminals to Nuevos Ministerios station, where it connects with the rest of the city Metro network; this route will take longer to get to the city centre, from 30 minutes to an hour at peak times. There is also an express bus service to Atocha station (about 40 minutes, single ticket €5) and local buses,

which are the cheapest but also the slowest means of transport. On a weekday taxis from Barajas to central Madrid should cost around €25–30, depending on traffic and with a €5.50 supplement for airport trips, but fares are higher at night and at weekends.

El Prat Airport is 12km (7 miles) southwest of Barcelona. A local train line (*Rodalies* in Catalan) runs from the airport through the city centre, daily approximately 5.40am–11.30pm, and takes about 25 minutes, continuing onto the coast line north of the city. A single ticket costs €2.20, and is separate from Barcelona city transport tickets (see page 448). Alternatively Aerobus buses run from outside the airport terminals every 5–10 minutes during the day to the city centre, Plaça Catalunya, taking around 35 minutes (€5.95), and there are also local bus routes. Taxis from the airport will cost around €25–35, depending on traffic, and including a supplement for airport trips and baggage, with higher rates at night and at weekends.

At smaller airports there are usually low-priced and frequent bus services, often timed to coincide with flights, and taxis are always available.

By rail

High-speed trains, combining the Spanish AVE and French TGV lines, now run daily between Paris and Barcelona, making the journey in about 7hrs 40mins. There are also nightly sleeper train services from Paris to Spain: the "Francisco de Goya" train leaves Gare d'Austerlitz in Paris every night at 6.53pm, arriving in Madrid-Chamartin at 9.10am, and the "Joan Miró" train leaves Austerlitz at 8.23pm, arriving in Barcelona's Estació de França at 8.05am. In addition, the "Pau Casals" trains run three days a week to Barcelona from Zürich, and "Salvador Dalí" three times a week to Barcelona from Milan. With adjustable wheels, these are the only trains that currently cross the border: rail lines in Spain (and Portugal) were built to a broader gauge than the rest of the European rail network, so with other services you must take a train to Hendaye (on the Atlantic side) or Cerbère (on the Mediterranean) on the border, and then cross over to get a Spanish train on the other side. For information and bookings see www.raileurope.com, and the Spanish railways website (www. rcnfe.com).

By road

Buses: Eurolines (www.eurolines. com) buses run to Barcelona, Madrid and other Spanish cities from most parts of Europe. Fares are very low, but travelling times are very long. **Cars**: Spain is naturally entirely connected to the European motorway network, but the geography of its border with France, with the high Pyrenees mountains in the middle, means that traffic tends to get concentrated into just two routes: European route E70 along the Basque coast (A63 in France, AP-8 in Spain) and route E15, the Mediterranean motorway (A9 in France, AP-7 in Spain) near the east coast. These consequently can get very congested in summer, especially the A9/AP-7. If you have time, it's much more enjoyable to take one of the slower routes through the high Pyrenean passes.

Driving hard, it's possible to get from Paris to Barcelona by motorway in around 10–12hrs, and to Madrid in about 15–20hrs, but with stops – which are essential for safety – each journey would take a good deal longer.

By sea

On the north coast, **Brittany Ferries** (tel: UK 0871-244 0744; www. brittanyferries.com) has regular car ferry sailings from Britain, from Portsmouth to Santander and Bilbao, and from Plymouth to Santander. These are large "cruise ferries", each crossing taking about 20–24hrs. **LD Lines** (tel: France 0825-304 304; www.ldlines.fr) also sails between St-Nazaire and Gijón.

In southern Spain, there are frequent ferries between Algeciras, Málaga, Motril, Almería and Alicante and the two Spanish enclaves on the Moroccan coast, and Tangier, Oran and Algiers. **Acciona**

The beautifully renovated Estació de França in Barcelona.

Trasmediterranea (tel: Spain 902-454 645; www.trasmediterranea.es) has the largest number of services.

Getting around Spain

By air

Due to its size Spain has an extensive domestic flight network, linking all the main cities. Many services are provided by Iberia, but other airlines such as **Vueling** (www.vueling.com) and **Air Europa** (www.aireuropa.com) are very competitive on price, and non-Spanish airlines such as Ryanair also now offer Spanish internal flights. Flights are naturally particularly popular for getting to the Balearic Islands, and unless you wish to take a car are generally more convenient than ferries.

By rail

Unless you are in a hurry, travelling by train is a much more attractive way of getting around Spain than flying. Most trains are operated by the national railway company **RENFE** (tel: 902-320 320; www.renfe.com). The stars of its network are the high-speed AVE trains, ultra-fast and very modern trains that run from Madrid to Barcelona, Seville, Huesca, Valladolid (via Segovia), Valencia and some other cities. Since you do not have to waste time at airport check-in and bag collection, travelling by AVE, especially Madrid–Barcelona, can often be quicker than flying, and prices are also competitive. However, there are gaps in the network that have not been upgraded to AVE standard, such as the Mediterranean coast line between Barcelona and Valencia and most lines in Asturias and Galicia, where trains, while still comfortable, are noticeably slower.

In Madrid long-distance lines converge on two main stations, Chamartín for lines from Catalonia,

the north and Galicia, and Atocha for trains from Valencia, Andalucía and the southeast, including Portugal. Many trains also stop at both stations.

The RENFE also has many regional routes (called *Media Distancia*), which stop at most or all stations and so are very much slower, and local networks (*Cercanías*, or *Rodalies* in Catalonia), around all the main cities. Details are on the RENFE website. Tickets for AVE and long-distance trains must be booked ahead, which is most easily done online, though you can also buy tickets at all stations. Regional tickets can also be booked online, though this is not essential, while *Cercanías* tickets are normally bought from machines at stations. Holders of Eurail and other rail passes are often required to pay supplements to use AVE trains, so once again unless you use trains a great deal they may not give you big savings in Spain.

As well as the RENFE's lines there are also separate rail services in some parts of Spain. In Catalonia the Catalan government's **Ferrocarrils de la Generalitat de Catalunya** or **FGC** (tel: 012; www.fgc.cat) operates several suburban lines around Barcelona and from Barcelona to Montserrat, Manresa and Igualada. Services are coordinated with the local RENFE *Rodalies* lines. In the Basque Country the **Euskotren** (tel: 902-543 210; www.euskotren.es), run by the Basque government, has lines between Bilbao and San Sebastián along the coast and to towns inland such as Guernica, and connects with the Bilbao Metro. Lastly, the **FEVE** (tel: 985-982 381; www.feve.es) is a line that runs all the way along the north coast through innumerable stations from Bilbao to El Ferrol in Galicia, a slow but charming way to see some of Spain's most attractive regions. However, this line is also used by the **Transcántabrico** luxury trains, which run between

San Sebastián and Santiago de Compostela, with gourmet cuisine and various excursions en route (tel: 902-555 902; www.eltranscantabrico. granlujo.com).

By road

Buses: Spain has an excellent bus network, slower but cheaper and often more frequent than trains. They are particularly useful in areas not well served by railways, such as the north coast between Asturias and Santander (given the slow speed of the FEVE). On major routes and at holiday times it is advisable to book your ticket in advance.

Bus routes are operated by different companies in different parts of the country. In Madrid many routes converge on the **Estación Sur de Autobuses** at Calle Méndez Alvaro 83 (Metro Méndez Alvaro), the city's central bus station. It has a website (www.estacionautobusesmadrid.com), but for information it's often better to locate individual companies.

Cars: Many major highways have been built or upgraded in the last 20–30 years, so are in impressively good condition. Full motorways are called *Autopistas* and have tolls (*peaje*, or *peatge* in Catalan), and are identified as AP-3, AP-6, etc. To pay tolls, you normally collect a ticket at one of many toll stations, and then hand it in when you leave the motorway, and will be charged according to how far you have travelled. Tolls are quite high, but there are also many motorway-standard multi-lane highways that are toll-free, especially in the north and west. These are called *Autovias* and identified as A-2, A-30, and so on.

Minor roads are in good condition and rarely congested, except near the coast in peak holiday seasons. **Motoring advice**: Drivers must carry a red warning triangle, a yellow reflective jacket and the car's papers in their car. Fines can be levied on the spot. A feature of Spanish roads, especially in small towns and villages, is a type of traffic light operated by electronic sensors. If you drive towards it at more than the local speed limit, it will turn red; slow down, and it will go back to flashing yellow, allowing you to pass.

By sea

Ferries run daily from Barcelona, Valencia and Dénia to the three Balearic Islands of Mallorca, Menorca and Ibiza, and there are also inter-island ferries. There's often a choice of slow or slightly more expensive fast ferries. **Acciona Trasmediterranea** (tel: 902-454 645; www. trasmediterranea.es) and **Balèaria** (tel: 902-160 180; www.balearia.com) compete on most routes, so it's worth comparing schedules and prices.

Getting around Barcelona

By public transport

Barcelona has a similarly impressive integrated transport network, coordinated by the **TMB** (tel: 012; www.tmb.cat), which publishes all information in English as well as Catalan and Spanish.

For most visitors, the **Metro** is the most convenient way of getting around the city, with eight lines that operate Mon–Thur 5am–midnight, Fri 5am–2am, and then continuously

from 5am on Saturdays to midnight on Sundays. The Metro lines are supplemented by the urban lines of **Catalan railways** (FGC), which run to Tibidabo and Pedralbes, and modern tramlines in the Olympic Village area and on Avinguda Diagonal.

While most visitors tend only to use the Metro and FGC, Barcelona's **bus** routes, which mostly run daily from about 5.30am–11pm or later, are particularly handy for filling in holes in the Metro network, and seeing more of the city en route. Details of routes are indicated at bus stops. At night several night bus routes operate from Plaça Catalunya. For trips to suburban towns, the airport and nearby beach towns such as Sitges, the *Rodalies* or local rail lines operated by the **RENFE** are coordinated with those run by the FGC. Barcelona-Sants is the city's main rail station, and most local overground lines also run through it. **Tickets and passes**: The same tickets are valid for the Metro, buses and local trains within the city, which can be bought from TMB information centres and machines at all Metro stations. Prices vary by zone, but since the whole of central Barcelona is in Zone 1 most visitors only need that. Single tickets for Metro or bus cost €2, but as in Madrid it's much better to get a multi-journey card, called in Barcelona a *targeta*. Many different ones are available, but of most use to visitors are the T-Dia, which gives unlimited travel for 1 day for €7, and the T-10, which gives 10 journeys for €9.45. With a ticket or one unit from a *targeta*, you can change between trains or buses as many times as you need within the same 75 minutes without being

The Boqueria market in Barcelona.

charged again. Each time you enter the Metro or board a bus you must put your *targeta* into the platform gates or bus machines. Travel cards are also available for 2, 3, 4 or 5 days (€13–28.50), and Barcelona too offers a tourist pass, the Barcelona Card, which gives unlimited local travel, reduced admission to many museums and attractions and other discounts for 2, 3, 4 or 5 days, for €29–47. It is available from tourist offices, with further price reductions if you order it online.

The TMB has five information offices, at Diagonal, Sagrada Família, La Sagrera and Universitat Metro stations and Sants railway station, where you can buy all tickets and get other information.

By taxi

Painted black and yellow, Barcelona's taxis are another symbol of the city, and easy to find except on very busy weekend nights. Fares are higher than in Madrid, and higher after 10pm and on Sundays. Phone for a cab through **Radio Taxi** 033, tel: 933-033 033; www.radiotaxi033.com.

Getting around Madrid

By public transport

Like other Spanish cities Madrid and its region has an excellent public transport system in which the Metro, city buses and local suburban trains and buses are integrated together, coordinated by the **CTM** (tel: 012; www.ctm-madrid.es), which provides a good deal of information in English, in leaflets, on its website and on station platforms. Specific Metro information is also on www.metromadrid.es. For most visitors the **Metro** is the most convenient way of getting around the city, with 12 lines and 4 suburban tramlines that all run daily 6am–1.30am. With a Metro map, available free at all stations, it's easy to work out how to get to any part of the city.

Madrid also has over 150 **bus** routes, which run daily from about 6am–11pm or later, with variations on each route. Details of routes are indicated at bus stops. For visitors, buses are generally most useful for filling in some gaps in the Metro network, and are easier to use for people with mobility problems. At night several night bus routes operate, nearly all of which pass through Plaza de Cibeles on the Paseo del Prado. The 10 *Cercanías* or suburban rail lines, which mostly

What's on in Barcelona

The most readily available place to find listings of what's on in the main cities, including film programmes, are the weekly *Guía del Ocio* magazines, with entirely separate editions in Madrid (www. guiadelocio.com/madrid), Barcelona (www.guiadelociobcn.com) and several other cities, on sale at all newsstands. Tourist offices also run outwards from Atocha station, are useful for getting to towns around Madrid such as El Escorial, and to the airport.

Tickets and passes: The same tickets are used for Metro, buses and *Cercanías* trains within the city, which can be bought from machines at all Metro stations. Single tickets (which can also be bought on board buses) cost €1.50, but it's much better to get a Metrobús card, which gives 10 journeys for €12.20, and can be shared by more than one person. Each time you enter the Metro or board a bus you must put your Metrobús into the platform gates or bus machines, which will cancel one unit each time. Monthly travel cards are available, and there is also a Madrid Tourist Travel Pass, available from tourist offices and giving unlimited travel for from 1 to 7 days for €8–33.40. For details see www. madrid.touristtravelpass.com.

By taxi

Madrid taxis are white, with a red stripe on the front doors, and at most times are easy to hail on main streets. Fares are moderate, but are higher after 10pm and on Sundays. To call for a cab phone Radio Teléfono Taxi, tel: 902 478 200; www.radiotelefono-taxi.com.

SPAIN A–Z

Accommodation

Hotels in Spain are officially classified in five categories marked by stars, but this tells you more about the amount of facilities an establishment has than its quality, atmosphere or charm. *Hostales* (one to three stars) and *pensiones* (one to two stars) have traditionally been less comfortable and cheaper than hotels, but there are now many exceptions to the rule.

provide attractive event guides, and in Barcelona you can also take a look at the free English-language monthly *Metropolitan* (www. barcelona-metropolitan.com) and *Time Out Barcelona* (in Catalan, www.timeout.cat). Barcelona also has a cultural information centre at the Palau de la Virreina (La Rambla 99), which sells tickets for many events.

Hotels in Spain once tended to be pretty conventional – big resort hotels on the coast, functional business hotels in cities – but there has been something of a revolution in the last 20 years. There is now a much bigger choice of very stylish boutique accommodation and charming small hotels, in cities – especially Barcelona – but still more so in the countryside. The main wine regions in particular boast some stunning hotels. There has also been a growth of bed-and-breakfast type countryside guesthouses or *casas rurales*, often combined with self-catering cottages for rent.

In a class of their own are the *Paradores*, a state-run chain of luxurious hotels occupying historic buildings like converted castles and monasteries, or in spectacular locations (tel: 902 547 979; www. parador.es). Special deals out of season can make them surprisingly affordable.

The best places to look for introductory listings of places to stay in Spain are the regional and city tourism websites, not any Spain-wide authority. Many attractive small hotels across Spain are represented by the private **Rusticae** association (tel: 902-103 982; www.rusticae. es); they are all of a consistently high standard. For country guesthouses, try www.guiarural. com or www.toprural.com. Spain's many campsites are listed on www. campingfecc.com.

Arts and activities

Information on cultural activities can be obtained at national, local and city tourist offices. Main seasons tend to be from September to May; during summer, cultural activity mainly moves into festivals and open-air concerts.

Barcelona

Barcelona also has a full agenda of cultural activities, which also includes events such as the multi-arts Festival del Grec in July.

The opera house, **Gran Teatre del Liceu** (tel: 934-859 913/00; www.liceubarcelona.cat.) is fully on a par with the best European opera houses, and offers productions including recitals, ballet and opera for children.

The two key venues for classical music are **L'Auditori**, which offers a broad programme including family concerts (Plaça de les Arts; tel: 932-479 300; www.auditori.cat) and the magnificent *Modernist* **Palau de la Música Catalana** (tel: 932-957 200; www.palaumusica.org). Most theatre in Barcelona is in Catalan, but the Mercat de les Flors (tel: 932-562 600; www.mercatflors.org) is a vibrant centre for dance, movement and other performance arts. Barcelona also has a very varied music scene that takes influences from around the world.

Madrid

Madrid's main venues are the **Teatro Real** (tel: 91-516 0660; www.teatro-real.com) for opera and ballet, the **Auditorio Nacional de Música** (tel: 91-337 0100; www.auditorionacional.mcu.es) for orchestral music and the **Teatro de la Zarzuela** (tel: 91-524 5400; www.teatrodelazarzuela.mcu.es) for a variety of other concerts including Spanish light opera, *zarzuela*.

Madrid is also a great place to hear the best flamenco live, in intimate venues. **Casa Patas at Calle Cañizares** 10 (tel: 913-690 496; www.casapatas.com) is one of the most respected.

Eating Out

The Spanish take their food very seriously, and you will rarely be disappointed by the variety and flavour of the hearty portions served in local *restaurantes*. Each region has its culinary strengths, from the seafood creations of the north to the rice platters of the east, from the roasts of the central area to the succulent hams and fried fish of the south. And for every dish, there is usually a locally grown wine to match.

Venta, posada, mesón, casa de comidas and *fonda* are all synonyms for restaurant. Many bars also double as restaurants, serving both tapas and full meals. The menu will be displayed outside or at the door, giving an idea of what you can expect to pay.

Most restaurants offer a good-value *menú del día* (set menu). This is normally a three-course meal, including house wine, at a reasonable set price, although it may only be available at lunchtime. Meals chosen from the full carta will be more expensive.

Buying tickets

Throughout Spain, tickets can be bought from the venues themselves, in person or online, or through various agencies. The **Fnac** book and music stores (tel: 902-100 632; www.fnac.es) handle bookings for all kinds of events through their website (under "Entradas") and have ticket desks in their main stores; in Madrid, the most central is at Calle Preciados 28; in Barcelona, in the Triangle centre, just off Plaça Catalunya. Other

The prices on the menu often include a service charge, but it is customary to leave a tip of 5–10 percent if you have been served efficiently. In bars, additional small tips of a few coins are customary. Prices are lower if you stand or sit at the bar rather than occupy a table.

Two things to note: tapas are ordered and priced individually, and their cost can mount up, so a meal entirely of tapas can easily be more than a set restaurant menu; also, check how much your meal will cost when ordering fish or seafood that is priced by the 100g weight. The price is based on the uncooked weight and can be more than you expected.

One essential thing for visitors to adapt to is Spanish mealtimes. Lunch generally begins around 1.30–2pm, dinner at 8.30–9pm, or later on hot summer nights and at weekends. In tourist areas or big cities you can get food at most times of the day, but if you insist on eating earlier you will miss out on the best Spanish food.

services are **Telentrada** (tel: 902-101 212; www.telentradas.com) and Ticketmaster (tel: 902-533 353; www.ticketmaster.es), which also sell tickets for football matches and other sports. All are easy to use in English.

Budgeting for your trip

Accommodation: From around €50–70 per night for a double room in a rural guesthouse, to €80–100 in a pleasant small boutique hotel

Tapas originated in the south but are now popular in bars all over Spain.

to anything over €150 in upscale city hotels. Anywhere near the coast prices are always higher in July and August, and cities are more expensive during special events.

Meals: A lunchtime set menu in a mid-range restaurant can be €10–15, but a meal from the full menu will be more like €20, going up to €30–60 in more sophisticated restaurants.

Sightseeing: Admission to museums and sights costs from around €5 in small centres to €12–15 in major museums, with major reductions for anyone aged under 18 or over 65. The tourist discount cards offered in many cities are very useful in cutting admission costs.

Transport: One of Spain's bargains, and can be as little as €10 per person per day.

Children

Children under age 4 travel free on nearly all public transport in Spain, but above that age the full fare may be charged on local transport unless they have one of several cards, generally available only to residents. On RENFE trains children aged 4–13 travel for 40 percent of the adult fare. There are bigger concessions at public museums: admission is free to all those under 18, or sometimes under 16.

Long, sunny days and soft, safe, sandy beaches mean that coastal Spain is a favourite family destination. Many hotels have special features for kids, and when the sea and the sandcastles start to wear thin, try some of the following:

Eating out: The Spanish take their children out at night, so why not do likewise? There are no restrictions on children accompanying adults into bars, restaurants or cafés, as long as they are well behaved.

Fiestas: Older children will love the firework displays and music, while the younger ones watch wide-eyed as dancers and giant papier-mâché figures perform. Larger fiestas often have special entertainment for children.

Funfairs: Most big cities or resorts have a *parque de atracciones* where the rides range from the old-fashioned carousel and big wheel to

Emergency Numbers

Ambulance, fire service and other emergency services: 112
National Police: 091
Municipal Police: 092

Festivals

The best way to experience Spanish customs is to watch a small-town *fiesta* (festival), offering locals the chance to dress up in costume, dance through the night, let off firecrackers or run with bulls. Every community, whatever its size, has its own fiesta – with the larger towns and cities often celebrating more than one. Check with the tourist office for details of local celebrations during your stay. Here's a selection of the very best from around the country:

February/March: Carnival before the beginning of Lent. Processions in Santa Cruz de Tenerife, Cádiz, Sitges and many other places.

March/April: Las Fallas Festival in Valencia, with the setting alight of hundreds of papier-mâché figures. Semana Santa (Holy Week). Processions of hooded penitents in all major cities from Palm Sunday until Easter Sunday, with the most famous in Seville.

April: Seville's famous Feria (Spring Fair) with colourful parades, plenty of *sevillana* music and bullfights. In

high tech thrills. Barcelona's funfair at Tibidabo, accessible by funicular railway, deserves a special mention for its old-fashioned rides and tremendous views.

Go-karting: Go-kart tracks are common along the Costas and in the islands.

Theme parks: There are giant fun parks at **Port Aventura** (tel: 977-779 090; www.portaventura. cat) near Tarragona on the Costa Daurada, **Terra Mítica** (tel: 902-020 220; www.terramiticapark.com) near Benidorm, **Isla Mágica** (tel: 902-161 716; www.islamagica.es) in Seville and the movie-based **Parque**

Alcoi on the Costa Blanca people stage mock battles between "Moors and Christians".

May: Festival of the Patios in Córdoba and International Horse Fair in Jerez de la Frontera.

May/June: Fiesta de San Isidro: bullfighting, concerts and funfairs in Madrid. Corpus Christi: festivities everywhere, especially in Granada, Toledo, Sitges and the Canary Islands. El Rocío pilgrimage in Andalucía.

July: Fiesta de San Fermín: bull runs, bullfights and festivities in Pamplona. Festival of the Virgen del Carmen, patroness of fishermen. Festival of St James, Santiago de Compostela, with firework displays and bonfires.

August: Assumption: national holiday on 15 August with numerous towns holding festivals.

September: Logroño Wine Harvest: wine festival in Jerez de la Frontera. Mercè Festival: music and "fire running" in Barcelona.

October: Pilar Festival: processions, bullfights and folklore in Zaragoza.

Warner (tel: 918-211 234; www. parquewarner.com) outside Madrid, but there are also smaller parks along the coasts.

Water parks: A highly popular alternative to the beach. While kids shoot down waterslides and ride the machine-made waves, parents can top off their tans in landscaped gardens. Additional attractions often include bowling and mini-golf.

Climate

As a general rule, late spring to early summer and late summer to early autumn are the best times for visiting

Spanish nightlife usually starts in a bar before it's time for a late dinner.

Innovative footwear.

most parts of Spain. This avoids the most oppressive heat, not to mention the crowds and high-season hotel rates. In winter, temperatures plummet in the mountains and high central plains.

Summer temperatures in the north are ideal for swimming and sunbathing, but expect rain any time in the northwest. For winter sun, the south coast, the Balearics and parts of the central and southeastern coast are pleasantly mild all year, and in Andalucía and Ibiza swimming is even an option in winter. Of course, winter is the season for skiing in the Pyrenees and Andalucía's Sierra Nevada.

Disabled travellers

Facilities for the disabled have improved greatly in the last 20 years. On RENFE trains, all AVEs, many other trains and many stations are accessible, and free assistance is available to anyone who needs it, under the ATENDO programme (under "Atendo" on the RENFE

website, though in Spanish only). It also gives a list of accessible stations. On local transport, all recently built Metro stations in Madrid, Barcelona and other cities are fully accessible, and access is gradually being extended to other stations. Most city buses are now accessible, so it's worth exploring bus routes as alternatives to the Metro. All taxis are required to take wheelchairs for no extra charge, but you can also call for an adapted larger taxi, in Madrid from **Eurotaxi** (tel: 912-667 478), in Barcelona from **Taxi Amic** (tel: 934-208 088) and from other companies in most cities; tourist offices will have details.

Major museums and sights are now accessible, except where their layout makes this very difficult. Adapted rooms have been getting more common in hotels, and most regional tourism websites have some details on facilities. For Catalonia the tourist authority has a dedicated site, www. turismeperatothom.com, on facilities and accommodation.

Embassies and consulates

Australia: Torre Espacio, Paseo de la Castellana 259D, Madrid, tel: 913-536 600; www.spain.embassy. gov.au.
Canada: Núñez de Balboa 35, Madrid, tel: 913-828 400; www. canadainternational.gc.ca/spain-espagne.
Ireland: Paseo de la Castellana 46, tel: 914-364 093; www. embassyofireland.es.
South Africa: Claudio Coello 91, tel: 914-363 780; www.dirco.gov.za/ madrid.
UK: Torre Espacio, Paseo de la Castellana 259D, tel: 902-109 356; http://ukinspain.fco.gov.uk.
US: Calle Serrano 75, tel: 915-872 240; http://madrid.usembassy.gov.

Gay and lesbian travellers

Attitudes to gay people in much of Spain have become pretty relaxed. There are plenty of gay- and lesbian-friendly hotels, clubs and bars, as well as resorts, throughout the country. In Madrid the Chueca district is the city's "gay village", with a whole clutch of gay venues; Barcelona too has a vibrant, but more diffuse, gay scene, and the beach town of Sitges just to the south has long been a gay mecca. There are many gay websites on different parts of Spain in English, but some that provide a good introduction are www.gayiberia.com and www.pridebarcelona.org, which has plenty of links.

Health and medical care

Public health services are generally of a high standard. Citizens of non-EU countries must have a travel and health insurance policy before travelling in Spain (see page 400). EU nationals are entitled to free basic healthcare at state clinics or hospitals with an EHIC card, and most treatments are entirely free. Most hospitals (*hospitales*) have an emergency department (*urgencias*, or *urgències* in Catalan), and there are also smaller health centres (*centro sanitario, centro de asistencia primaria, CAP* or similar) in many towns and districts that can provide immediate assistance. There are also many private clinics and doctors, which hotels will be able to recommend, and consulates keep lists of English-speaking doctors.

For minor complaints, look for a *farmacia* (pharmacy) identified by a big sign with flashing green cross. They are open Mon–Fri 9.30am–1.30pm and 5–8pm, Sat 9am–1.30pm, and outside these hours local duty rotas operate. Lists of current duty pharmacies or *farmacias de guardia* are posted in all pharmacy windows, local newspapers, and, often, in tourist offices.

Nightlife

Spaniards are enormously social, and there is some sort of nightlife even in smallish cities. Big cities such as Barcelona, Madrid or Valencia are bywords for late-night partying, there are nightclubs in all beach resorts, and of course Ibiza is one of the clubbing capitals of the world, so it's impossible to sum up what is on offer in just a few sentences.

Language

Castilian Spanish (*Castellano*), is spoken throughout the country, but other languages enjoy equal status, or are sometimes the primary language, in different regions, and their prominence has greatly increased thanks to administrative decentralisation. These languages are Catalan, in Catalonia itself, the Balearics and the Valencian region; Basque (*Euskera*) in the Basque Country and northern Navarra; and Galician (*Galego*) in Galicia.

In Catalonia, including Barcelona, Catalan is the primary language used on most street and road signs, with Spanish in second place, and this is also the case with *Galego* in much of Galicia. Basque is often less visible to outsiders except in rural areas. Any recognition of local languages will always be appreciated, and visitors in Catalonia will find it handy to recognise a few words such as *Sortida* (exit, instead of Spanish *Salida*).

Since Spaniards eat late, they rarely begin to "go out" until after 11pm, beginning in a bar and then only heading on to clubs after midnight–2am, although in some cities (notably Madrid) there have been attempts to limit bar and club hours in the last few years.

Opening hours

Most smaller **shops** open 9.30/10am–1.30/2pm and then reopen again in the afternoon from 4.30/5pm–8pm, or a little later in summer. Most are closed on Saturday afternoons and all day Sunday. However, big stores and malls are generally open without interruption six days a week 10am–9pm, and frequently on Sunday. Rules on Sunday opening vary by region, but in general have been getting looser.

Neighbourhood food shops open earlier, from about 8/8.30am, and nearly always close for lunch. Traditional food markets begin work early, around 7/8am, and are often closing by 1/2pm, except for the biggest city markets, and even these are quieter in the afternoons.

Bank opening hours vary slightly, but most open Mon–Fri 8.30/9am–2pm and Sat 9am–12.30/1pm. All are closed Sunday and holidays. Several banks have at least one major branch in each city open until 6pm.

Postal services

The few remaining district post offices are only open Mon–Fri 9am–2pm, Sat 9am–1pm and are closed Sunday. Principal post offices are open 9am–2pm and 4–7pm for general services. Post boxes are painted yellow and in two parts – one marked *ciudad* (for local mail) and the other marked *provincias y extranjero* (for the rest of the country and abroad). Stamps are sold at post offices and at the *estancos*, or tobacconist shops. For more information see the Spanish postal service website, www.correos.es.

Public holidays

January: 1 New Year's Day, 6 Epiphany; **March**: 19 St Joseph's Day (San José); **March/April**: variable Maundy Thursday/Good Friday; **May**: 1 Labour Day; **May/June**: variable Corpus Christi; **July**: 25 St James's Day (San Diego); **August**: 15 Assumption Day; **October**: 12 National Day; **November**: 1 All Saints'

Day; **December**: 8 Immaculate Conception, 25 Christmas Day. These are the main national holidays, but the list varies each year, and each autonomous region also has its own particular holidays.

Shopping

Well-known Spanish souvenirs include *damasquino* jewellery, knives and swords from Toledo; ceramics from Toledo, Valencia, Granada and Seville; filigree silver from Córdoba; *botas* (wineskins), castanets, Spanish dolls and bullfighting posters.

Madrid

Madrid offers visitors every shopping possibility from all the regions of Spain. For craftwork, leather goods, footware and furniture, try **Artespaña** shop (Hermosilla 14) and the craft and ceramic shops around Calle Mayor. Department stores and tourist shops are in the centre between Puerta del Sol and Plaza Callao, and along the Gran Vía. Upscale fashion boutiques line Calle Serrano and its adjoining streets in the Salamanca area.

Telecommunications

To call Spain from abroad, tel: 34. Spanish landline numbers all have 9 digits; the area code (91 for Madrid, 93 for Barcelona) is an integral part of each number, so you must dial it even for a local call. Numbers beginning 900 are toll-free; 902 numbers are information lines at rates slightly higher than normal. All mobile numbers begin with a 6.

Phone booths (*cabinas*) are still quite easy to find, particularly at train stations. Most work with phone cards, which you can buy for various values at *estancos* (tobacco shops), newsstands and other outlets. At major train stations there are also phone shops (*locutorios*) that can be more convenient and cheaper for making long-distance calls.

On using mobile/cellphones, see page 401. Charges for using Spanish networks with foreign phones have been high, but are coming down.

Tourist information

The Spain-wide tourist office website www.spain.info provides an extensive range of information, and accommodation listings, but hugely greater detail is available on the tourism websites of each of Spain's autonomous regions. Nearly all cities

also have impressive information services, such as www.esmadrid.com or www.barcelonaturisme.com. Tourist offices are well signposted and easy to find in cities and nearly every town along the coast, often in the main square. As well as giving information tourist offices also sell local discount tourist cards, which are always worth enquiring about.

Barcelona

The Barcelona tourist board (tel: 932-853 834; www.barcelonaturisme.com) has a huge and prominently signposted information centre beneath the Plaça Catalunya in the centre of the city (open daily 8.30am–8.30pm), and smaller information points in Plaça Sant Jaume (in the city hall), at the airport, Sants railway station, the cruise terminal and on the Rambla, supplemented by temporary kiosks open during summer. As well as information Barcelona Turisme offers a wide range of products at its centres, including walking tours, Barcelona Cards (see above Getting around Barcelona) and the Articket, which gives admission to 7 leading museums for €28.50.

Madrid

Madrid's tourist office (tel: 917-012 210; www.esmadrid.es) has information centres in the Plaza Mayor and a larger one in the underpass beneath Plaza Colón (both open daily 9.30am–8.30pm) and other information points at Barajas Airport, Chamartín station, Plaza de Callao, Plaza Cibeles and near the Prado Museum. In addition, during the Easter, Christmas and summer seasons there are also temporary booths in many points around central Madrid. Offices provide maps, a free magazine (*esMadrid*) and plenty of other material.

Tourist offices abroad

All offices can be contacted through www.spain.info.
Canada: tel: 416-961 4079.
UK: tel: 020-7317 2010.
US: tel: 212-265 8822.

Tipping

As a guideline, tipping is frequent in bars, *cafeterías* and restaurants (8–10 percent), taxis (5 percent), for cinema and theatre ushers, and bellboys (according to services rendered).

SWITZERLAND

ESSENTIAL TRAVEL TIPS

FACT FILE

Area: 41,285 sq km (15,935 sq miles)
Capital: Bern (pop. 126,000)
Population: 7.9 million (with 21 percent foreigners)
Languages: Swiss-German (62.7 percent), French (20.4 percent), Italian (6.5 percent), Romansch (0.5 percent), other languages (9 percent)
Highest mountain: Not the Matterhorn 4,478 metres (14,692ft) but the Dufourspitze/Monte Rosa 4,634 metres (15,202 ft)
Religion: Catholic (42 percent), Protestant (35 percent), Muslim (4 percent)
Time zone: CET/CEST, see page 402.
Currency: Swiss franc (SFr)
International dialling code: 41

TRANSPORT

Getting to Switzerland

By air

Switzerland's best-served airports are at Zürich and Geneva, but there also international airports at Bern, Lugano and Basel (called the **Basel-Mulhouse-Freiburg EuroAirport**, tel: 03-89 90 31 11; www.euroairport.com, because it is actually in French territory, and shared by three countries). **Geneva** (tel: 0900 571 500; www.gva.ch) and **Zürich** (tel: 0900-300 313; www.zurich-airport.com) airports both have direct intercontinental flights from virtually every part of the world, and

a big choice of European flights. Zürich-based **Swiss** (tel: 848-700 700; www.swiss.com) is the country's largest airline, but many foreign carriers also fly to Zürich, Geneva and Basel. Of the low-cost airlines, **easyJet** (www.easyjet.com), as well as flying Swiss routes from the UK, has a separate Swiss subsidiary, **easyJet Switzerland** (www.easyjet.com/ch), which has routes to every part of Europe and some destinations in the Middle East, mainly from Geneva and Basel.

Travel from the airports: Zürich and Geneva airports both have their own train stations which are part of the national fast-train network; frequent trains each hour run between them and the main railway stations in their cities and other destinations, and at Geneva you can pick up a Unireso ticket that allows you to travel free on city public transport for the first 80 minutes of your stay. Many Swiss hotels also provide free shuttle buses from airports if you have a booking. Taxis from the airports will cost around SFr 30–35 in each city. From Basel-Mulhouse-Freiburg Airport, which is in

France, there are buses to the Swiss train station at Basel sbb that take about 25 minutes.

By rail

Swiss rail lines are closely connected with those in surrounding countries, and several high-speed TGV Lyria trains run each day from the Gare de Lyon in Paris to several Swiss destinations (Geneva, Neuchâtel, Bern, Lausanne, Basel and Zürich). Journey times are around 3–4 hours. Fast trains also run between Zürich and Cologne, and also to Milan and Vienna, and there is an overnight sleeper service between Geneva and Barcelona. For information and bookings see www.raileurope.com.

By road

Buses: Eurolines (www.eurolines.com) buses run to the main Swiss cities from other parts of Europe, but given the speed and comfort of rail travel most people prefer the train.
Cars: Routes into northern Switzerland are mostly fairly level, so driving is easy and fast; Alpine routes to Italy and Austria are much more

Fly-Rail Services

With the "Fly-Rail Baggage" service, train passengers don't have to lug their baggage around the airport any more. Instead, it is unloaded from planes arriving at Zürich and Geneva and forwarded by train directly to its destination point. The same service applies for the return trip: you can send your baggage – up to 24 hours in advance – directly through to your destination airport from the town where you've been staying.

Travellers may also check in at over 50 train stations (including Basel, Berne, Geneva, Lausanne, Lugano, Lucerne, Neuchâtel, St Gallen and Zürich) and obtain a boarding pass up to 24 hours prior to departure.

The service is offered from any airport around the world, no matter which airline you fly. Further information from www.sbb.ch, under "Station & services/Baggage".

Crossing the border

Although not a member of the EU, Switzerland is part of the Schengen area, so travellers can enter Switzerland by car, train and plane from all neighbouring countries without the formality of border controls. Travellers on flights directly from outside Europe, though, and from the UK and Ireland must pass through Swiss immigration.

spectacular, and slower. To drive to Zürich takes about 6hrs 30 mins, from Cologne about 5–6hrs.

Getting around Switzerland

Given the size of the country, internal flights are little used in Switzerland, but it has excellent public transport, represented internationally by the Swiss Travel System (www. swisstravelsystem.ch) that is one of the country's major attractions by itself, offering many wonderfully scenic train and boat rides.

By boat

Regularly scheduled boats cruise all the big Swiss lakes. There are steam-driven paddle steamers to put you in a nostalgic mood on Lake Geneva, Lake Zürich, Lake Brienz and Lake Lucerne. It's also possible to take a trip along the Rhine, Rhône, Aare and Doubs rivers. For timetables and other information, the best sources are local tourist offices.

By rail

More than 5,780km (3,400 miles) of electrified railways open up the remotest sections of the country with trains every hour on most lines and every half-hour on the busiest. More than 100 trains call at Zürich Airport each day.

Swiss Federal Railways (tel: 0900 300 300; www.sbb.ch) is referred to by its initials, which vary between the official languages: sbb (German), CFF (French) and FFS (Italian). Through their website, in English, you can get comprehensive information on all services and buy tickets. As well as the various national tourist travel passes, a big choice of more specific travel cards and tickets is available, such as a 1-day travelpass, giving unlimited travel on all transport for a day (SFr 68), and various youth cards, and cheap upgrades to first class. Over

100 trains have dining or bistro cars, and all long-distance trains have buffets or trolley refreshments.

While the SBB operates all the main lines in Switzerland, another essential part of the Swiss rail networks are its narrow-gauge mountain railways, which are semi-independent. Most famous is the Rhaetian Railway (tel: 081-288 6565; www.rhb.ch), a Unesco World Heritage site, from Chur to Davos, St Moritz and Italy, but also celebrated is the Matterhorn-St Gotthard line (tel: 027-927 7000; www.matterhorngotthardbahn.ch) from Disentis, near Chur, to Zermatt. The two jointly operate the Glacier Express (tel: 027-927 7000; www. glacierexpress.ch) between St Moritz and Zermatt, one of the world's most famous, and most glorious, train rides. Other beautiful but shorter lines include the Golden Pass line from Montreux to Lucerne (tel: 021-989 8190; www.goldenpass.ch), the Berner Oberland line from Interlaken, or the Zentralbahn (tel: 058-668 8000; www.zentralbahn.ch) between Interlaken and Luzern.

All these and other railways are coordinated and in some cases run by the SBB, but each often has its own travel passes, and there are also travel cards for individual districts, creating a complex range of ticket options (many are listed on the SBB website) that can only be understood if you have a fair knowledge of Swiss geography. For visitors it's generally easier just to get single tickets or one of the SBB all-Switzerland travel cards.

By road

Buses: The **Alpine** PostBus (phone local offices, details on website; www. postauto.ch) network takes travellers over the principal mountain roads and covers 9,800km (6,090 miles), reaching any points that do not have a train service. The buses are all modern and comfortable. Bus tours are also available, listed on the website.

Cars: Twenty-five major roads running through Alpine tunnels or over the passes form one of the main attractions for visitors; depending on the snow, they are open from May or June to late autumn. Special rail facilities are provided for motorists wishing to transport their cars through the tunnels. In less mountainous areas travel is much quicker.

Motoring advice: Drivers must have a red warning triangle in the car; yellow jackets are not obligatory,

but recommended. Snow chains are compulsory in mountain areas in winter. In many towns, parking is allowed only for cars displaying a blue disc, which can be bought from petrol stations, newsstands and many restaurants. Pedestrians expect to have right of way on many minor roads in Switzerland, so be very careful when driving; police are also strict in enforcing speed limits. Swiss motorways carry tolls, but you do not have to stop at toll stations to pay. Instead, all normal-sized vehicles are required to have a sticker on the windscreen called a *vignette*, which costs SFr 40 and can be bought at border crossings and from post offices, petrol stations, tourist offices and some other outlets in Switzerland. It will be valid for 14 months, from 1 December to 31 January, not from the date you buy it. Rental cars should all come with a *vignette*; if you tow a caravan or other trailer you will need an extra one. Once you have one, the roads you are allowed to drive on include the Gotthard and Bernardino tunnels. There are precise rules for how the sticker must be placed on the windscreen, so make you do this correctly.

Tickets and passes: A range of passes are on offer: the most popular is the Swiss Pass, which gives unlimited travel on most trains, buses and lake ferries and discounts on mountain railways for 4, 8, 15, 22 or 30 days for SFr 266–590, together with free admission to many museums and other benefits. The Swiss Flexi Pass allows you to space out your travelling over non-consecutive days for a slightly higher price, and with a Swiss Family Card, children under 16 travel free with their parents is they have their own ticket. Details of all passes are on the website, where they can be bought online.

City transport

All the main Swiss cities – Zürich, Geneva, Bern – have regularly modernised tram networks that provide the most convenient transport in city centres, as well as trolleybuses and buses. All have easy-to-use integrated ticket systems: with Geneva's *Unireso* system some tickets are valid in neighbouring areas in France, while in Zürich you can get a ZürichCard, which gives unrestricted travel on most transport in the city and region for 24 or 72 hours (SFr 20–40). City tramlines are supplemented by suburban rail lines,

AUSTRIA BELGIUM FRANCE GERMANY GREECE ITALY NETHERLANDS PORTUGAL SPAIN SWITZERLAND

called *S-Bahn* in German-speaking areas and *RER* in French-speaking ones. Tickets are usually valid for all networks. From Geneva, the SBB's regional RER lines run all the way along Lac Léman (Lake Geneva) to Lausanne.

SWITZERLAND A–Z

Accommodation

There are around 5,000 hotels, motels, pensions, youth hostels, mountain sanatoria and health resorts in Switzerland. Design hotels, holiday chalets and apartments and bed-and-breakfast-type places have also all grown in popularity in the last few years, together with farmhouse stays. World-famous Alpine resorts such as Davos specialise in ultra-luxurious accommodation, but there are also plenty of more modest but still charming options. Extensive information, including a dedicated page on farmhouse holidays, is provided on the national website www.myswitzerland.com. For more conventional and city hotels, the Swiss Hotel Guide (www.swisshotels. com) is also a useful source.

Arts and activities

There is a rich musical life in Switzerland, with quite small places hosting internationally renowned soloists. Switzerland Tourism publishes regular information on all kinds of events, including details

Swiss Museum Pass

The Swiss Museum Pass (adults SFr 155) gives admission to more than 470 museums throughout Switzerland. The pass is valid for a year, and is obtainable from participating museums. Note that unfortunately some of the main galleries (for example in Zürich and Basel) are not included in the pass. The museum pass is included in some of the national tourist cards, such as the Swiss Pass (see page 455); full information is available from tourist offices.

Concerts

All larger cities maintain at least one theatre and a symphony orchestra, and even the smaller outlying communities put on

of music festivals, art exhibitions, sightseeing, as well as a listing of more than 100 museums and art collections open to the public. More events and programmes can be found on regional websites.

Budgeting for your trip

It is a myth that Switzerland is expensive. Of course there are plenty of expensive hotels, restaurants and shops, but it is easy to find ways of saving money.

Accommodation: Except in the most celebrated mountain towns, attractive double rooms can generally be found from about SFr 70, up to SFr 500 or more in luxury locations.

Meals: A full meal in an inexpensive restaurant should cost around SFr 30–50, one in a more elaborate venue about SFr 80 per person or more.

Sightseeing: Admission to most large museums costs around SFr 10–15, but they are usually free for children under 16, and costs can be further reduced with a tourist pass (see above).

Transport: from about SFr 40 per day, but less if you make full use of travel passes.

Children

Switzerland is well geared up for young visitors, from family-friendly hotels and accommodation (www. reka.ch) to special experiences, such as sleeping on straw in an Alpine cowshed (see www.myswitzerland. com), an igloo (www.iglu-dorf.com) or a yurt (www.goldenpass.ch and click

dramatic and musical events. In the concert scene, the leading venue is Lucerne's spectacular **Kultur- und Kongress-zentrum** (KKL; tel: 041-226 7777; www.kkl-luzern.ch) designed by Jean Nouvel, which presents wide ranging programme. **Zürich's Opera** (tel: 044-268 6400; www.opernhaus.ch) has an international reputation, and is also home to the Zürich Ballet. In general, the theatre and concert season begins in September and ends in June. In summer, there are several highly acclaimed festivals featuring world-class performers, the best known at Lausanne, Zürich, Thun, Braunwald, Sion, Gstaad, Interlaken, Lucerne, Ascona and Vevey.

on "Rochers-de-Naye"). There are adventure playgrounds for all ages, railed toboggan runs (the longest in the world is at Churwalden, www. pradaschier.ch), scooters and monster bikes on which to freewheel down mountains on traffic-free paths, and major zoos at Basel, Bern, Langnau and Zürich.

Up to eight children aged under 6 can travel for free per one paying adult on all SBB trains, and those aged 6–16 travel for half the adult fare. Special children's travel cards are available, and similar concessions are given on other public transport. Admission to most museums is free to anyone under 16, or sometimes under 18.

Climate

In the centre of Europe, the Swiss climate is influenced by maritime and continental air masses. Summers are mostly warm at lower altitudes, although they can be quite wet with frequent thunderstorms. Winters are generally cold with plenty of cloud, snow and fog.

The high mountains mean great differences can occur within just a short distance – one valley can be sunny and dry while the next is shrouded in mist. The Ticino area bordering the Italian lakes is markedly warmer and sunnier than the rest of the country throughout the year.

Bring a warm fleece, raincoat, waterproof boots and an umbrella, even in the height of summer, and likewise, sunglasses and sunscreen even in the depths of winter.

Disabled travellers

Access facilities in general are of a high standard. Many SBB trains and stations are accessible, and there is a dedicated call centre for enquiries and booking assistance if required (tel: 0800-007 102). Full details are under "Stations and Services/ Passengers with a Handicap" on www.sbb.ch. In cities, trams are being adapted to be made accessible (in Zürich, most have been) and nearly all buses have low boarding platforms. Mountain railways are more of a problem, though the Glacier Express is fully accessible and has adapted toilets. Virtually all museums are easy to get into and around.

Many hotels throughout the country also now have adapted rooms, and the **Ski2Freedom** organisation (www.ski2freedom.com) is an essential source of orientation on disabled-friendly winter sports centres and possibilities.

Eating out

The French, German and Italian influences make for great variety in cuisine in the three areas. Though the origins of the country's staple dishes are rustic, there is nothing basic about Swiss cuisine at its best, but really good food needs seeking out, as there are plenty of restaurants that serve sustaining rather than refined dishes.

Best-known dishes include *fondue*, made with melted cheese and wine, into which speared bread is dipped; *rösti* – grated fried potatoes; *raclette* – hot cheese dribbled over potatoes and served with gherkins and pickled onions; in Ticino, saffron risotto and polenta made of cornmeal; and the now universal breakfast, muesli.

Lunch is served from 11.30am and dinner from 6–9pm, though in the larger cities there are restaurants taking orders into the small hours.

Embassies and consulates

Australia: Chemin de Fins 2, 1211 Geneva 19, tel: 022-799 9100; www.geneva.mission.gov.au.
Canada: Kirchenfeldstrasse 88, 3005 Berne 6, tel: 031-357 3200; www.canadainternational.gc.ca/switzerland-suisse.
UK: Thunstrasse 50, 3005 Bern, tel: 031-359 7700; http://ukinswitzerland.fco.gov.uk.
US: Embassy, Sulgeneckstrasse 19, CH-3007 Bern, tel: 031-357 7011; http://bern.usembassy.gov.

Gay and lesbian travellers

Attitudes among the Swiss towards homosexuality are open-minded and progressive. All cities have gay communities and areas where there are gay bars and entertainment venues; the age of consent for gay sex is 16, the same as for heterosexuals. A law recognising same-sex unions came into effect in 2007. Switzerland's de facto gay capital is

Emergency Numbers

All emergencies: 112, though in Switzerland most people still use the local numbers.
Ambulance: 144
Police: 117
Fire service: 118
Breakdown service: 140

Festivals

There are numerous festivals throughout the year. For information and tickets contact Switzerland Tourism, tel: 00800-100 200 29 (from Switzerland or abroad) or visit www.myswitzerland.com. Another good website (in German) is www.events.ch.

Jazz and folk music festivals are held in Basel, Bern, Lugano, Nyon, Montreux, Willisau and Zürich, which has a Gay Pride parade every July. There's a similar annual event in Geneva.

Health and medical care

Health services are of very high quality. Citizens of non-EU countries should have a travel and health insurance policy (see page 400), though despite Switzerland not being part of the EU, EU nationals are still entitled to free basic healthcare from the Swiss public insurance system with an EHIC card. However, you will still have to pay for most treatments, and then claim back the cost (which can be high) following the instructions given you with your EHIC card. You should also check that any doctor you are referred to is registered with the Swiss health service and is treating you on those terms; doctors in Switzerland are nearly all private, but are then contracted by the health service, so you can be treated privately or not. Dental treatment is not covered by the EHIC.

In an emergency, call for an ambulance or go to the emergency department of the nearest hospital. All hospitals have emergency wards with doctors on 24-hour duty, and every city and larger villages have a number for an emergency doctor. This can be found in local newspapers or on the general information number 111.

Pharmacies are usually open Mon–Fri 8am–noon and 1.30–6.30pm and Sat 8am–noon, with local variations. All have duty rota lists on their doors showing lists of local pharmacies open outside normal hours, which can also be obtained from tel: 111.

Language

Switzerland has four national languages. German is spoken in central and eastern Switzerland; French in the west; Italian in the southern part of the country; and just 0.5 percent of the population speaks Romansch in southeastern Switzerland. The Swiss, though, are oddly poor at speaking each others' languages, and so make increasing use of English.

Money

Switzerland is of course the only country in this book that does not use the euro but still has its own currency, the Swiss franc (SFr, CHF or SF), the value of which is usually around €1 = SFr 1. In many areas near the Swiss borders, such as Geneva, many businesses accept euros as well as Swiss francs, but as you go further into the country you will only be able to use francs. Changing money in Switzerland is very easy: there are change desks near all border crossings and, especially, at main railway stations (which generally give the best rates). Bank branches, too, will nearly always exchange euros and other currencies. Try not to have many Swiss francs left over when you leave the country, as you will lose if you change them back into euros.

Nightlife

Disregard the rumour that nightlife in Switzerland is pretty provincial; in larger cities you'll find a wide variety of stylish bars and nightclubs.

Opening hours

Offices are open Mon–Fri 8am–noon and 2–6pm. Shops of all kinds are usually open Mon–Sat 8am–12.30pm and 1.30–4pm, but in larger cities they also open during lunchtime. Many shops are also closed on Monday mornings, but have one day a week when they open late until 9pm, usually Wednesday or Thursday. There are also local and regional differences.

In cities, banks and bureaux

Zürich. There are also regular rendezvous points for film and TV industries: the competition for the Rose d'Or in Lucerne, international film festivals in Locarno, Nyon and Les Diablerets, and film and literature days in Solothurn. Among the biggest traditional festivals is Fasnacht in Basel, a 3-day Carnival that starts on the Monday after Ash Wednesday.

Tipping

Officially in Switzerland all services are included in the price, but it is widespread practice to acknowledge good service by tipping. In restaurants, the bill is normally rounded up for snacks, and 2 or 3 francs extra are usually added to the bill for a meal.

de change open Mon–Fri 8.30am–4.30pm, but in the countryside these hours are usually Mon–Fri 8.30am–noon and 2–4.30/5.30pm. Very few bank branches are open at weekends, but exchange offices are frequently open. Museums are always closed one day a week, usually Mondays.

Postal services

Post offices are generally open Mon–Fri 7.30am–noon and 1.45–6.30pm, Sat until 11am. Stamps can be purchased at post offices, postcard kiosks and stamp machines. Post boxes are yellow and are often set into walls.

Public holidays

January: 1 New Year's Day, 2 Berchtold's Day; **March/April**: variable Good Friday/Easter Monday; **May/June**: variable Ascension, Whit Monday; **August**: 1 National Day; **December**: 25 Christmas Day, 26 Boxing Day.

Shopping

If you're searching for something typical and of good quality, try one of the Schweizer Heimatwerk (Swiss Handicraft) shops, located in Zürich, Basel and Geneva.

Cheese: Swiss cheeses are best known for their use in cooking, especially Gruyère and Emmental, but there are hundreds of small mountain producers making a variety of cheeses and charcuterie. Visits to them can often be arranged by local tourist offices.

Chocolates: Synonymous with Switzerland, made here since the early 19th century, and the first factory opened in 1819.

Sausages: The sausage known as the *cervelat* is the most common, combining beef and pork, and smoked and boiled.

Wines: Swiss wines are little known outside the country because production levels barely meet domestic demand, but some fine wines come from the Valais, Vaud and Ticino, some from the highest vineyards in Europe. Fruit schnapps are drunk as a *digestif*.

Telecommunications

To call Switzerland from abroad, tel: 41. Phone numbers consist of a 2- or 3-digit area code (Bern, 031, Basel, 061, Geneva, 022, Zürich, 01) followed by a 7-digit number; area codes always begin with a 0, which you must dial within Switzerland, but omit if calling from abroad. Numbers beginning 0800 are toll-free; 0900 numbers are information lines at rates slightly higher than normal. For directory assistance, dial 113; international calls 114 or 191; information (in English) 111.

Public phone booths can be most easily found at rail stations, airports and post offices, but there are still a few in most towns. Most can only be used with phone cards, which can be bought for Sfr 5, 10, 20 or 50 from train stations, post offices, newspaper shops and phone shops.

On using mobile/cellphones, see page 401. Local rates for using foreign phones are fairly reasonable.

Tourist information

The national tourism agency Switzerland Tourism maintains an excellent website, www.myswitzerland. com, with suggestions that include walking, cycling and canoeing routes, and has a very efficient information service through the international phone line, tel: 00800-100 200 29. There is also a special "Switzerland Mobility" site with ideas for hiking, mountainbiking, cycling and canoeing, at www.schweizmobil.ch.

In addition, each Canton and city has its own tourism promotion service, such as www.valais.ch or www. graubunden.ch, for more detailed information. They also operate the local information offices in nearly all towns, which are never hard to find.

Tourist offices abroad

All these offices can be contacted through www.myswitzerland.com or the phone line tel: 00800-100 200 29/30 (US and Canada 011800-100 200 29/30).

Australia: tel: 02-9262 1377.

UK: 30 Bedford Street, London WC2E 9ED, tel: 020-7420 4934.

US: Swiss Center, 608 Fifth Avenue, New York, tel: international toll-free 011800-100-200-29/30, or US only 1-877-794 8037.

Swiss francs; Switzerland is the only country in this guide not to use euros.

CREDITS

Photo Credits

AISA 82BL
akg-images 138BL
Alamy 35, 76, 138/139T, 331BL, 375BL
Andrea Pistolesi 347T
Ann Frank Stichting 166T
Annabel Elston/Apa Publications 148, 152T, 248T
Apa 300B
AWL Images 84/85, 86/87, 210/211, 214, 246, 326
Bigstock 28T, 194, 222B, 227, 247, 361, 364, 369, 371BL, 374/375T
Bildarchiv Preussischer Kulturbesitz 51
Bill Wassman/Apa Publications 222T, 225T, 228, 316
Britta Jaschinski/Apa Publications 7MR, 8MR, 9BR, 9TL, 18/19, 74, 230/231, 232/233, 234, 235, 241, 242, 243B, 244, 245T, 245B, 248B, 249, 250, 251, 253, 254, 255, 283, 298T, 320, 321, 323, 327T, 327B, 328T, 328B, 329T, 329B, 375TR, 398, 404, 407, 425, 432, 435
Corbis 9ML, 12BL, 55, 56, 81, 256/257T, 257ML
Dreamstime 10M, 58/59T, 82BR
Elma Okic/Rex Features 256BL
FLPA 330BL, 331TR
FMGB Guggenheim Bilbao Museoa 139ML
Fotolia 29T, 120B, 125, 240, 372, 374BL
fotoLibra 6BL, 59BR
Futuroscope 122T
Getty Images 50, 54, 66, 75, 256BR, 257BR, 358, 375BR
Glyn Genin/Apa Publications 6MR, 7ML, 7MR, 24, 32, 139BR, 142, 143, 151, 152B, 153, 174/175, 176/177, 178, 185, 186, 187, 192B, 193, 195, 198, 200T, 200B, 201, 202T, 202B, 204, 205, 206, 207, 291, 310, 418/419, 420T, 421, 424
Greg Gladman/Apa Publications 2/3, 7TR, 20, 67, 72, 73, 154/155, 156/157, 158, 159, 162, 163, 165,

166B, 167, 171B, 172T, 262, 300T, 301B, 301T, 302T, 305B, 305T, 332/333, 334/335, 337, 355, 357, 373, 401
Gregory Wrona/Apa Publications 353
Ilpo Musto/Apa Publications 6BR, 10BL, 65, 58BL, 412, 414
Images of Holland 172B
iStockphoto 6M, 7BR, 8ML, 9MR, 12T, 28B, 29B, 31B, 58BR, 59ML, 59BL, 140/141, 149, 169, 170, 190, 196B, 196T, 197, 199, 203, 209ML, 212/213, 215, 218, 219, 220, 221T, 221B, 229, 243T, 257BL, 260/261, 284, 285, 287, 288B, 288T, 289, 294, 295, 296, 298B, 303T, 322B, 336, 342, 343, 344, 345, 346, 347B, 348, 350, 351, 356, 359, 360, 362, 363T, 363B, 365, 366/367, 367, 368, 371T, 374BR
Jerry Dennis/Apa Publications 150
Jochen Tack/Images of Holland 171T
Jon Santa Cruz/Apa Publications 64, 139TR, 179, 182, 183, 188, 189, 191, 420B, 423
Jon Spall/Apa Publications 252
Julian Love/Apa Publications 70, 146, 147, 396, 408
Jurjen Drenth/Images of Holland 173
Kevin Cummins/Apa Publications 59TR, 69, 79, 106B, 107T, 110T, 111T, 139BL, 308/309, 311, 324T, 324B, 325T, 325B, 427
Keystone/Photopress 208BR
Library of Congress 49, 53
Lydia Evans/Apa Publications 8MR, 11T, 22, 88, 376/377, 378/379, 380, 381, 384, 385, 386, 387, 388, 389, 390T, 390B, 391, 392, 393T, 393B, 394, 395
Mark Read/Apa Publications 192T
Ming Tang-Evans/Apa Publications 45, 97, 102, 103, 104, 105, 106T, 107B, 108, 109T, 109B, 110B, 111B
Museu Nacional de Arte Atiga 40

Neil Buchan-Grant/Apa Publications 10BR, 13B, 23, 62/63, 68, 89R, 208/209T, 258/259, 263, 290, 293, 302B, 304, 430, 434
Nikos Daniilidis/Acropolis Museum 317
NPL 331BR
Orient Express 83BL
Pictures Colour Library 8BL
RhB 82/83T, 83ML
Rijksmuseum 138BR
Scala Archives 34, 41, 44, 47, 208BL, 209BR
Steve McDonald/Apa Publications 8TL, 13T, 16/17, 77, 257TR, 278, 279, 297, 299
Still Pictures 330/331T, 330BR, 331ML
SuperStock 7TL, 168
Susan Smart/Apa Publications 268, 269, 270, 271T, 271B, 272B, 272T, 273T, 273B, 274, 275T, 275B, 276T, 276B, 277
Swissimage 223, 224, 225B, 226
Sylvaine Poitau/Apa Publications 1, 4/5, 11B, 12BR, 14/15, 21, 26/27, 30T, 31T, 38, 57, 60/61, 71, 78, 80, 89L, 92/93, 94/95, 96, 112, 113, 114, 115, 116T, 116B, 117T, 117B, 118, 119, 120T, 121B, 121T, 122B, 123B, 123T, 124, 126, 127B, 127T, 128T, 129T, 132T, 132B, 133B, 134T, 134B, 135T, 135B, 136, 137T, 137B, 303B, 374MR, 413, 418
Team Nowitz/Apa Publications 306/307, 314, 315, 318B, 318T, 319T, 319B, 322T, 403
The Art Archive 33, 36, 37
TIPS 83BR
Tom Smyth 282
Topfoto 39L, 39R
VFE 83TR
Volkswagen AG 209BL
Wadey James/Apa Publications 9TR, 128B, 129B, 131T, 131B, 133T
Out of copyright 30B, 42, 43, 46, 48, 52, 209TR, 349

Insight Guide Credits

Distribution

UK
Dorling Kindersley Ltd
A Penguin Group company
80 Strand, London, WC2R 0RL
customerservice@dk.com

United States
Ingram Publisher Services
1 Ingram Boulevard, PO Box 3006,
La Vergne, TN 37086-1986
customer.service@
ingrampublisherservices.com

Australia
Universal Publishers
PO Box 307
St Leonards NSW 1590
sales@universalpublishers.com.au

New Zealand
Brown Knows Publications
11 Artesia Close, Shamrock Park
Auckland, New Zealand 2016
sales@brownknows.co.nz

Worldwide
Apa Publications GmbH & Co.
Verlag KG (Singapore branch)
7030 Ang Mo Kio Avenue 5
08-65 Northstar @ AMK
Singapore 569880
apasin@singnet.com.sg

Printing
CTPS-China

© 2013 Apa Publications (UK) Ltd
All Rights Reserved

First Edition 1984
Seventh Edition 2013

www.insightguides.com

Project Editors
Siân Lezard and Carine Tracanelli

Series Manager
Carine Tracanelli

Art Editor
Shahid Mahmood

Map Production
Apa Cartography Department

Production
Tynan Dean and Rebeka Ellam

INDEX